I0818101

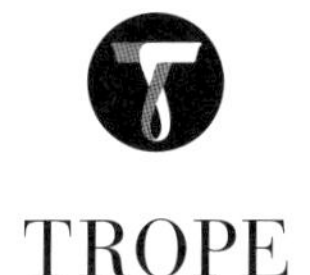

TROPE

MEXICO CITY DREAMING

TROPE PUBLISHING Co.

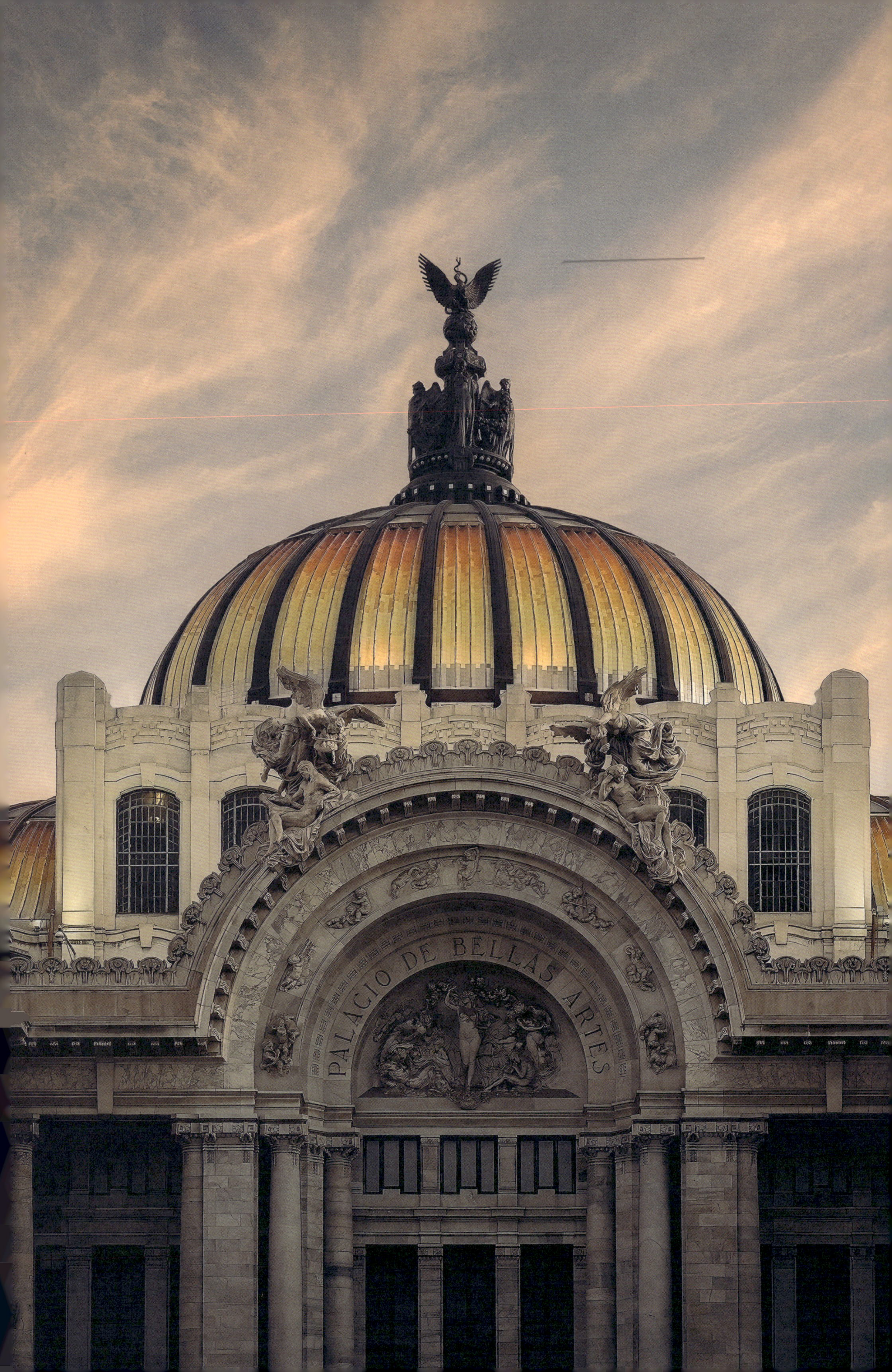
PALACIO DE BELLAS ARTES

FOTOGRAFÍAS DE PHOTOGRAPHS BY

JAIR HERNÁNDEZ

ISAAC JERO

ROBERTO LOZANO

OSCAR REYGO

VIDAL RIVERA

PRÓLOGO DE FOREWORD BY

CARLOS GÓMEZ

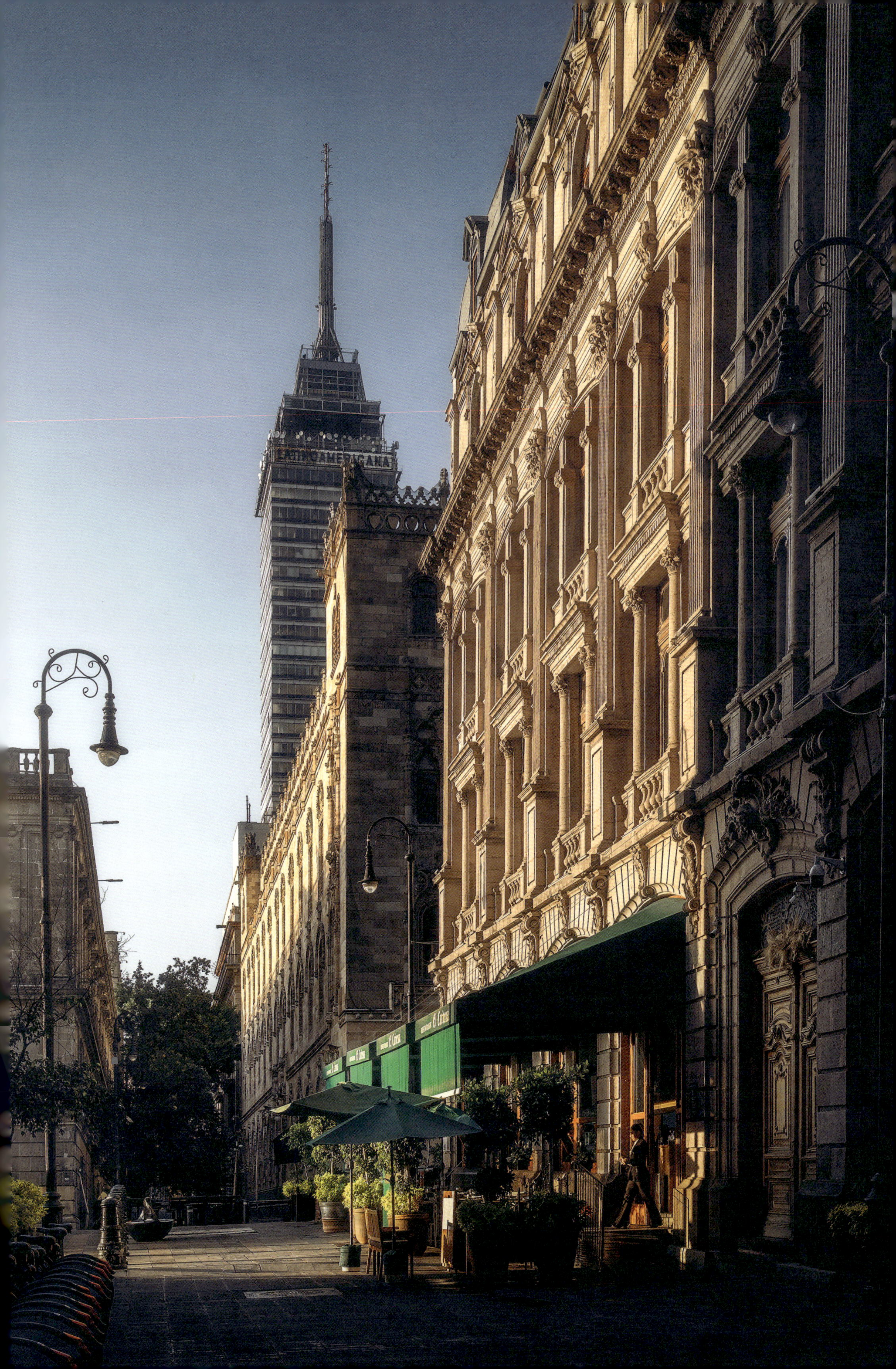
LATINOAMERICANA

La Ciudad de México es considerada uno de los destinos culturales más importantes del mundo. Para entender porqué es tan destacable esta ciudad, se necesita comprender el complejo tejido histórico que hay detrás de esta urbe latinoamericana. Alrededor del año 250 d. Centró en erupción el volcán Xitle, que se encuentra ubicado en la sierra que limita los actuales territorios del sur de la Ciudad de México, destruyendo casi por completo el asentamiento prehispánico de Cuicuilco. Este lugar fue predecesor de grandes ciudades como Teotihuacán en el periodo clásico; México-Tenochtitlán, Texcoco, Azcapotzalco, Iztapalapa y Chalco, en el periodo posclásico.

Hoy en día es común visitar los barrios del pedregal de San Ángel, el barrio de Coyoacán y Ciudad Universitaria, todos ellos levantados sobre piedra volcánica. Suele olvidarse que esta arquitectura volcánica fue clave para el desarrollo del estilo arquitectónico y sobre todo durante el tiempo de la gran México-Tenochtitlán. Esta ciudad se formó sobre un islote en el lago de Texcoco en 1325, se conectó con el resto de tierra mediante un sistema artificial de cultivo llamado chinampas, sistema que sigue vigente en la zona de Xochimilco al sur de la ciudad. Los habitantes de esta gran urbe, llamados mexicas, supieron aprovechar los recursos que se encontraban a su alrededor, llegaron a hacer uso de la piedra volcánica (basalto, tezontle y diorita) para la construcción de sus templos y palacios.

Cuando llegaron los castellanos encabezados por Hernán Cortes, se quedaron maravillados por el estilo arquitectónico de la ciudad, sus canales y la infraestructura con la que contaba la capital Mexica. Llegaron a compararla con diversas ciudades europeas, resaltando el apodo de "la Venecia del Nuevo Mundo." Lamentablemente esto no los detuvo para conquistar la ciudad, proceso que culminó con la caída de la gran México-Tenochtitlán el 13 de agosto de 1521.

Una vez consumada la conquista española, México-Tenochtitlán pasó a conocerse de manera oficial en 1535 como Ciudad de México, capital de la Nueva España. Los castellanos deciden retomar ciertos materiales usados durante el tiempo mexica, como la piedra volcánica, en particular del tezontle y la cantera, para la construcción de ciertos templos religiosos incluida la Catedral Metropolitana de la Ciudad de México. Para esta construcción se usaron restos del antiguo Templo Mayor.

Durante los tres siglos que duró el dominio castellano, en el territorio que denominamos México, el estilo arquitectónico que predominó en esta ciudad capital fue el barroco. Este estilo arquitectónico inició en la Nueva España alrededor del año 1630 y se desarrolló entre el siglo XVII y principios del siglo XIX. Las obras arquitectónicas de este tipo de corriente se caracterizan por tener una ornamentación excesiva y recargada, donde se representa de diferentes maneras la luz, la sombra y la intensidad de la obra. Las edificaciones del estilo barroco mexicano se distinguen principalmente por su gran tamaño, sus patios centrales y las columnas con efectos teatrales. El objetivo principal de estas edificaciones era dar a conocer la riqueza y el poder de la Iglesia católica en ese momento.

A la caída del régimen castellano en 1821, la nueva nación llamada México fue cambiando paulatinamente, con el objetivo de crear su propia identidad. Pasó de un intento fallido de Imperio entre 1821 y 1823, a la creación de la primera República Federal en 1824. Fue entonces, con el nacimiento de la República que se decidió hacer un cambio en el nombre de la capital conocida como la Ciudad de México y pasó a llamarse Distrito Federal a partir del 18 de noviembre de 1824. Este fue uno de los muchos cambios por los que pasó el país en sus años formativos. A causa de la transformación política y social, el paisaje urbano también se vió afectado.

Los gobiernos liberales del siglo XIX buscaban mostrar modernización y progreso en el paisaje de la ciudad, así que se inspiraron en los modelos arquitectónicos de las grandes ciudades europeas: por ello se promovió la apertura de amplias avenidas, la creación de parques y edificios públicos, que simbolizaron la entrada del joven país en una época de modernidad. Sin embargo, el precio del progreso fue la destrucción total de algunos edificios coloniales en el centro del Distrito Federal; se demolieron parcialmente conventos e iglesias, cambiando así el paisaje de la vieja metrópoli.

No fue hasta el periodo denominado como el Porfiriato (1876-1911) que se realizaron cambios más profundos en el diseño del paisaje urbano, siendo el estilo Ecléctico el que predominó en las nuevas construcciones como: el Palacio de Bellas Artes, el Palacio Postal, el Edificio Boker, el Monumento a la Independencia. Además surgieron colonias elegantes como: la Roma y Juárez en donde se podían ver mansiones de estilo francés. Todos estos cambios buscaban reflejar el nuevo aire cosmopolita de la élite Porfiriana. Sin embargo, esta modernización también hizo visible las desigualdades urbanas; mientras el centro de la ciudad y las nuevas colonias mostraban lujo y orden, las periferias carecían de cualquier servicio básico y de oportunidades, estos problemas terminarían desencadenando la Revolución Mexicana de 1910.

Tras la Revolución Mexicana el arte y la arquitectura se transformaron en instrumentos para la creación de una unidad nacional, adoptando así el Movimiento Moderno que buscaba el reordenamiento de la ciudad y la creación de una imagen de progreso en la capital mexicana. Algunos de los arquitectos más relevantes durante este periodo fueron: Luis Barragán "el arquitecto por excelencia en conjugar una nueva arquitectura con la cultura mexicana," Mario Pani con su plan de desarrollo de vivienda, Enrique del Moral, José Villagrán y Juan O'Gorman, todos ellos estuvieron a cargo de la construcción de diversos edificios en el Distrito Federal, buscaban modernizar el paisaje urbano. Estos personajes trabajaron de la mano de grandes muralistas mexicanos como: Diego Rivera, José Clemente Orozco y David Alfaro Siqueiros, quienes a traves de su arte buscaron la conciliacion nacional y la creacion de un sentimiento nacionalista en el pais.

Hoy en día, la Ciudad de México acoge a casi 22 millones de personas. Es posible encontrar en esta metrópoli, algunos edificios galardonados con el Premio Pritzker como son: la Torres Reforma, de Richard Meier & Partners; las oficinas Bacardí, a cargo de Mies Van der Roheen y la Torre BBVA, de Rogers Stirk Harbour Partners, por mencionar algunos. Es así, que la Ciudad de México contiene un *collage* de estilos, de historias y de paisajes entre que en conjunto recrean escenarios de vida. Estos lugares conjugan diferentes capítulos de la basta historia de la capital mexicana la cual abre sus brazos para recibir a los visitantes extranjeros, haciéndolos partícipes de las tradiciones de la ciudad.

CARLOS GÓMEZ

Historiador y guía turístico certificado de la Ciudad de México

Mexico City is considered one of the world's most important cultural destinations. To understand what makes this city so remarkable, it's essential to grasp the complex historical layers behind this Latin American metropolis. Around the year 250 AD, the Xitle volcano—located in the mountains bordering what is now southern Mexico City—erupted, almost entirely destroying the pre-Hispanic settlement of Cuicuilco. This settlement was a predecessor to major cities such as Teotihuacán in the Classic period, and Mexico-Tenochtitlan, Texcoco, Azcapotzalco, Iztapalapa, and Chalco in the Postclassic period.

Today, it's common to visit neighborhoods like the Pedregal de San Ángel, Coyoacán, and the University City campus, all built on volcanic rock. It is often forgotten that this volcanic landscape was crucial to the development of the region's architecture, especially during the era of great Mexico-Tenochtitlan. Founded on an island in Lake Texcoco in 1325, the city was connected to the mainland through an artificial agricultural system called chinampas—a technique still used in Xochimilco in the southern part of the city. The inhabitants of this metropolis, known as the Mexica, made use of the natural resources around them, including volcanic stone (basalt, tezontle, and diorite) for building temples and palaces.

When the Spaniards led by Hernán Cortés arrived, they were astonished by the city's architecture, its canals, and the sophisticated infrastructure of the Mexica capital. They compared it to several European cities and even called it "the Venice of the New World." Unfortunately, this admiration did not prevent them from conquering the city, a process that ended with the fall of Mexico-Tenochtitlan on August 13, 1521.

After the Spanish conquest, Mexico-Tenochtitlan officially became known as Mexico City in 1535, capital of New Spain. The Spaniards reused certain materials from the Mexica era—especially volcanic stones like tezontle and cantera—for the construction of religious buildings, including Mexico City's Metropolitan Cathedral. Materials from the former Templo Mayor were incorporated into its construction.

During the three centuries of Spanish rule in the territory now known as Mexico, the dominant architectural style in the capital was Baroque. This style emerged in New Spain around 1630 and developed throughout the 17th and early 19th centuries. Baroque architecture is marked by lavish, elaborate ornamentation and dramatic contrasts of light and shadow. Mexican Baroque buildings are notable for their grand scale, central courtyards, and theatrical columns. Their main purpose was to express the wealth and power of the Catholic Church.

After the fall of Spanish rule in 1821, the new nation—now called Mexico—began changing gradually to create its own identity. After a short-lived attempt at empire from 1821 to 1823, the First Federal Republic was established in 1824. With the birth of the Republic came a name change for the capital: Mexico City officially became the Federal District on November 18, 1824. This was one of many transformations the country underwent in its formative years. As political and social changes unfolded, the urban landscape shifted as well.

Liberal governments of the 19th century sought to reflect modernization and progress in the city's landscape, drawing inspiration from major European capitals. They created wide avenues, parks, and public buildings to symbolize the young nation's entry into an age of modernity. But this progress came at the cost of destroying parts of the colonial city center. Convents and churches were partially demolished, altering the appearance of the old metropolis.

More profound changes arrived during the Porfiriato (1876-1911), when the Eclectic architectural style dominated new projects such as the Palace of Fine Arts, the Postal Palace, the Boker Building, and the Angel of Independence. Elegant neighborhoods like Roma and Juárez emerged, filled with French-style mansions. These developments reflected the Porfirian elite's cosmopolitan aspirations. However, modernization also exposed deep urban inequalities: while the city center and new neighborhoods displayed wealth and order, the outskirts lacked basic services and opportunities—conditions that contributed to the outbreak of the Mexican Revolution in 1910.

After the Revolution, art and architecture became tools for building national unity, giving rise to the Modern Movement, which aimed to reorganize the city and project an image of progress. Key architects of this era included Luis Barragán, Mario Pani, Enrique del Moral, José Villagrán, and Juan O'Gorman. They were responsible for major buildings in the Federal District and sought to modernize the city's urban landscape. They worked alongside great Mexican muralists like Diego Rivera, José Clemente Orozco, and David Alfaro Siqueiros, whose art aimed to foster national reconciliation and a collective sense of identity.

Today, Mexico City is home to nearly 22 million people. Across the metropolis, one can find buildings recognized with the Pritzker Prize, such as Torre Reforma by Richard Meier & Partners, the Bacardí offices by Mies van der Rohe, and the BBVA Tower by Rogers Stirk Harbour + Partners, among others. Mexico City is a collage of styles, stories, and landscapes that together form vivid urban scenes. These places weave together different chapters of the capital's vast history, welcoming visitors and inviting them to take part in the city's traditions.

CARLOS GÓMEZ

Historian and certified tour guide of Mexico City

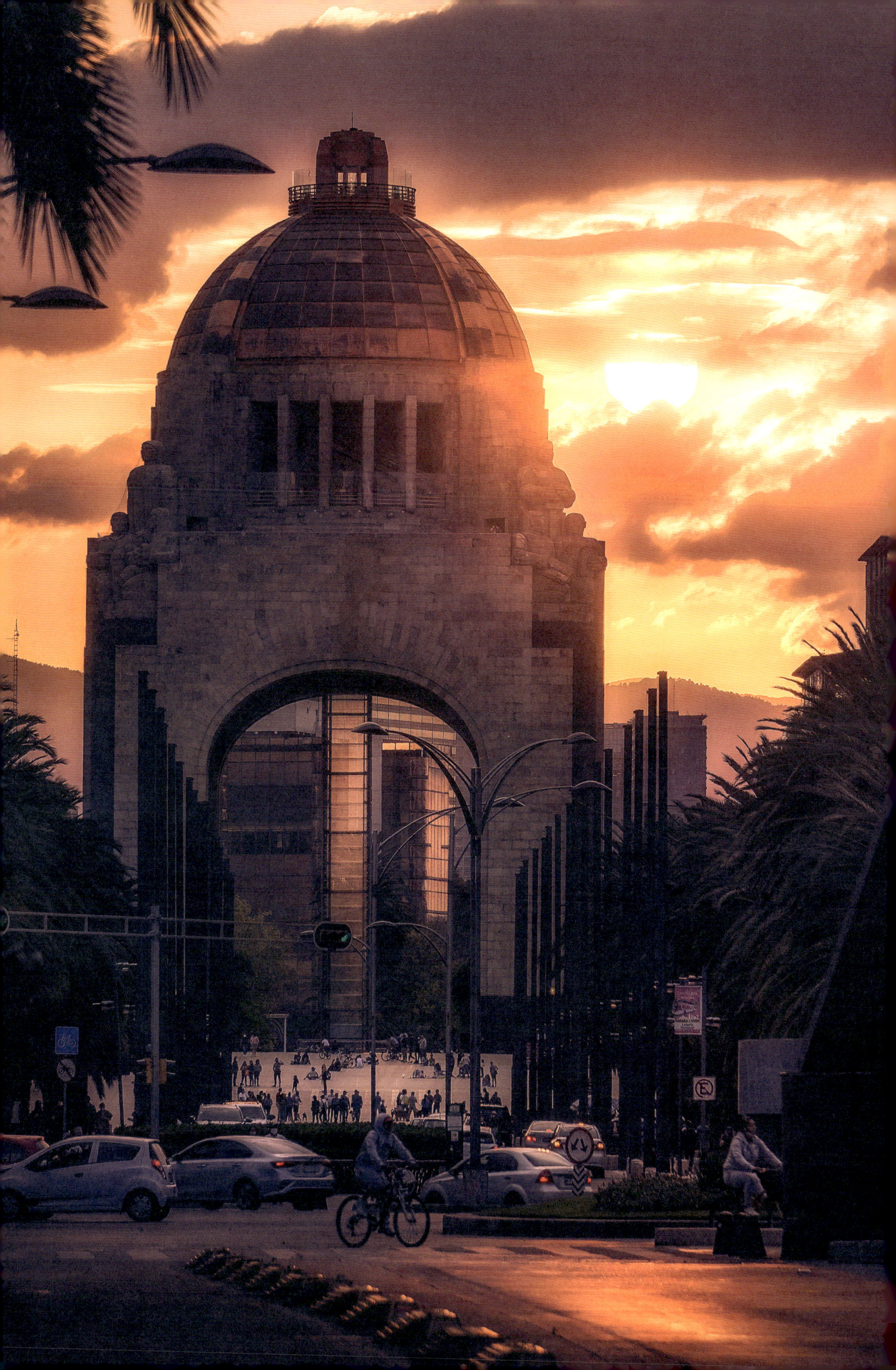

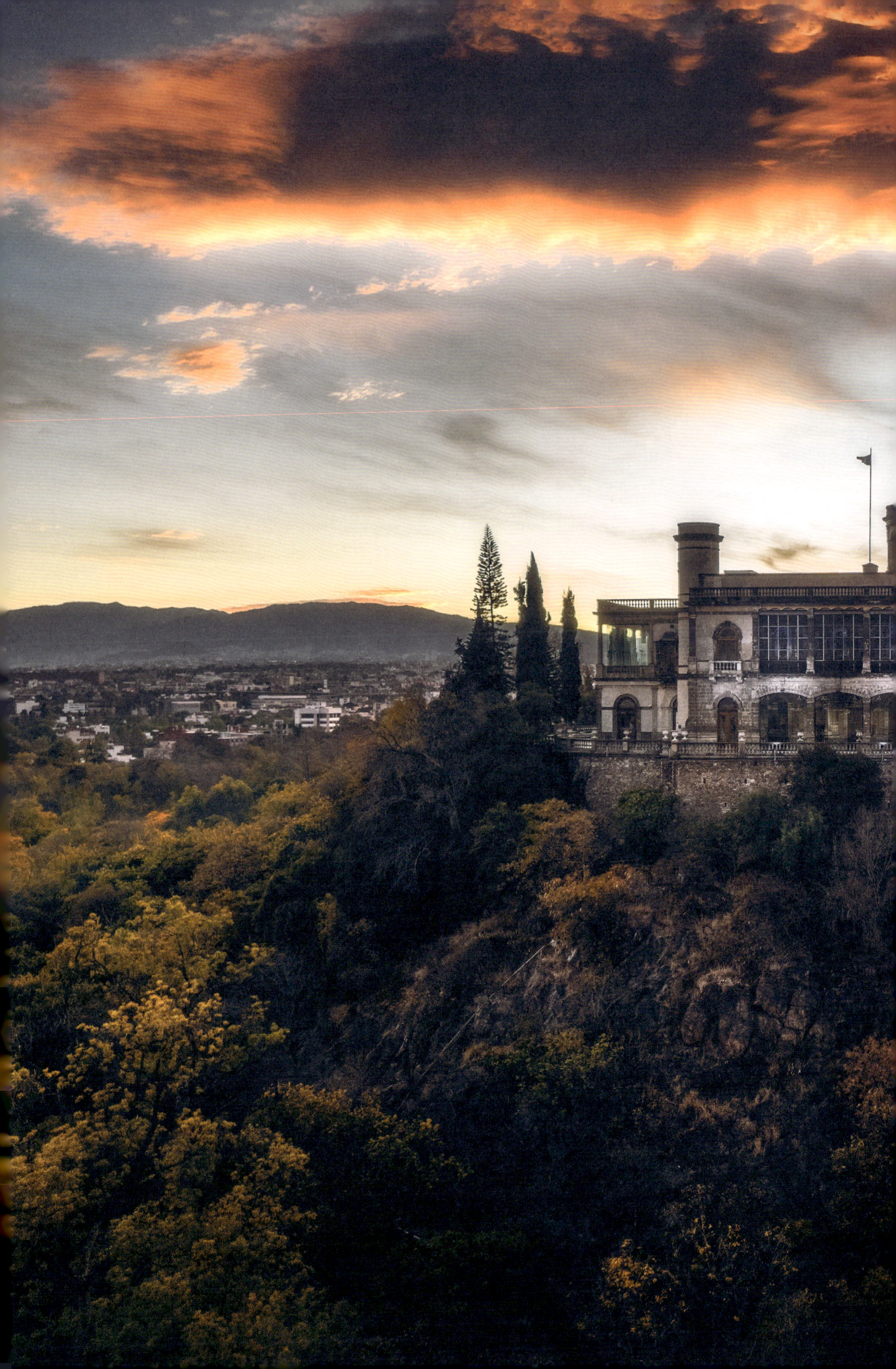

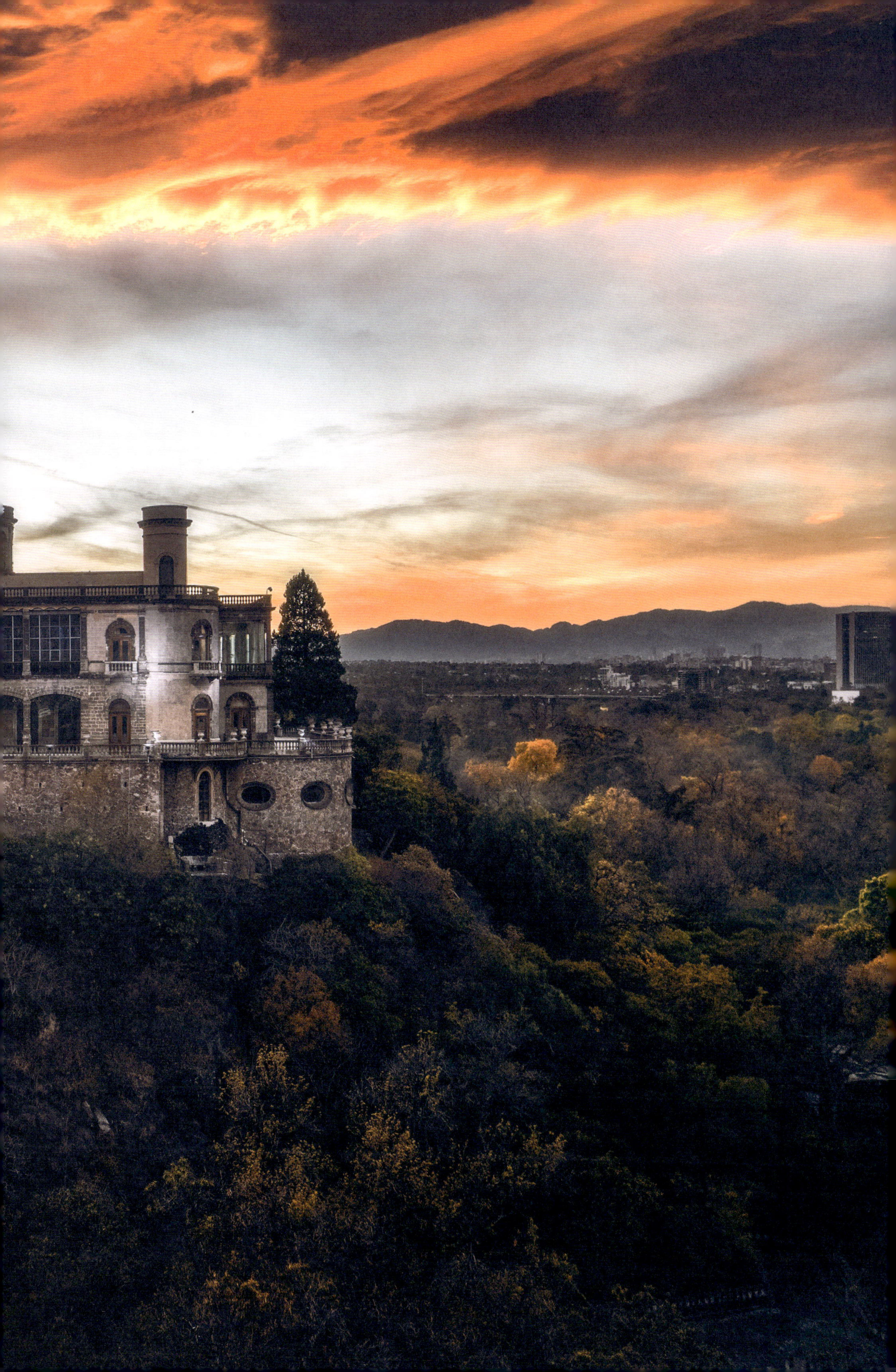

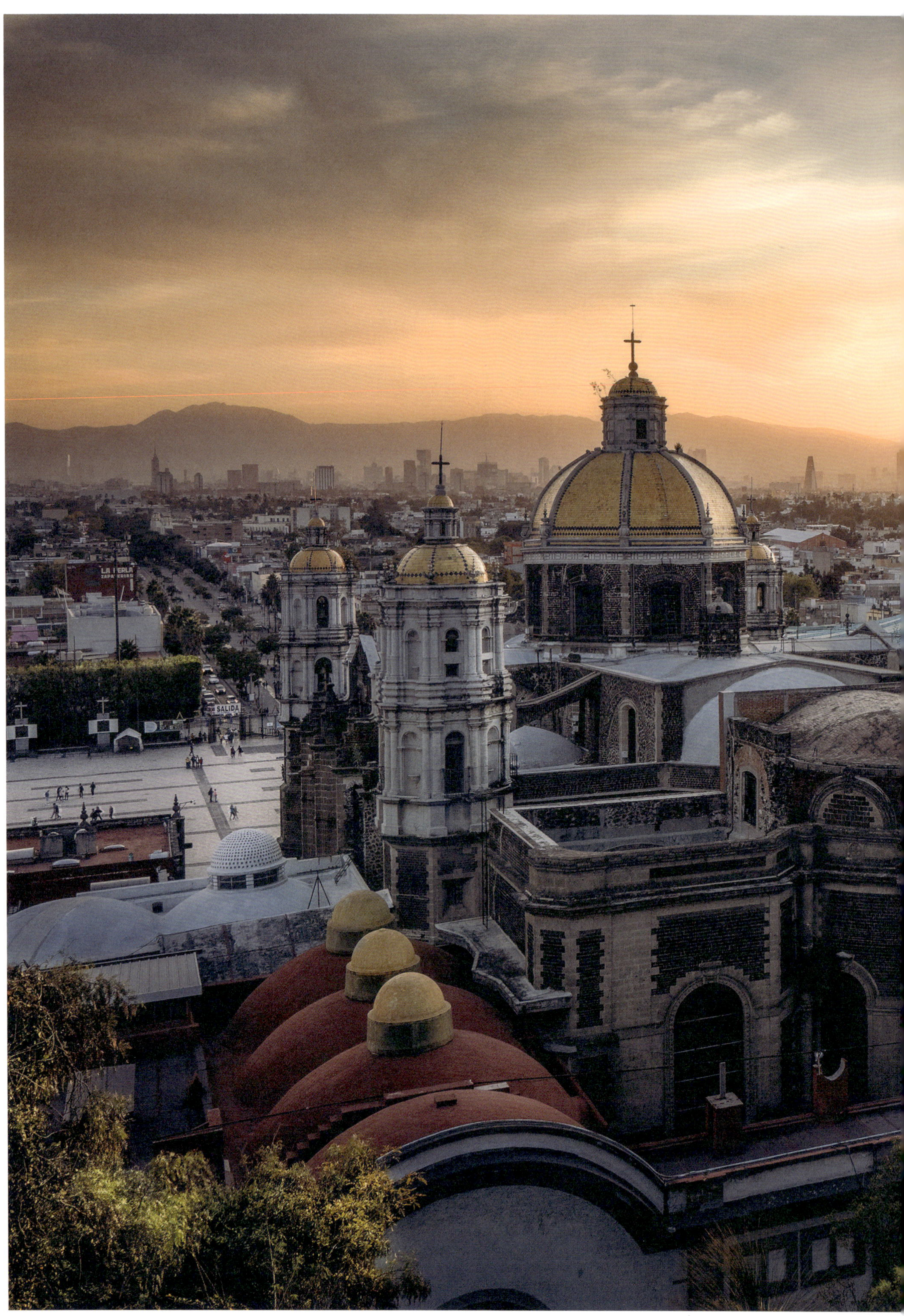
SALIDA

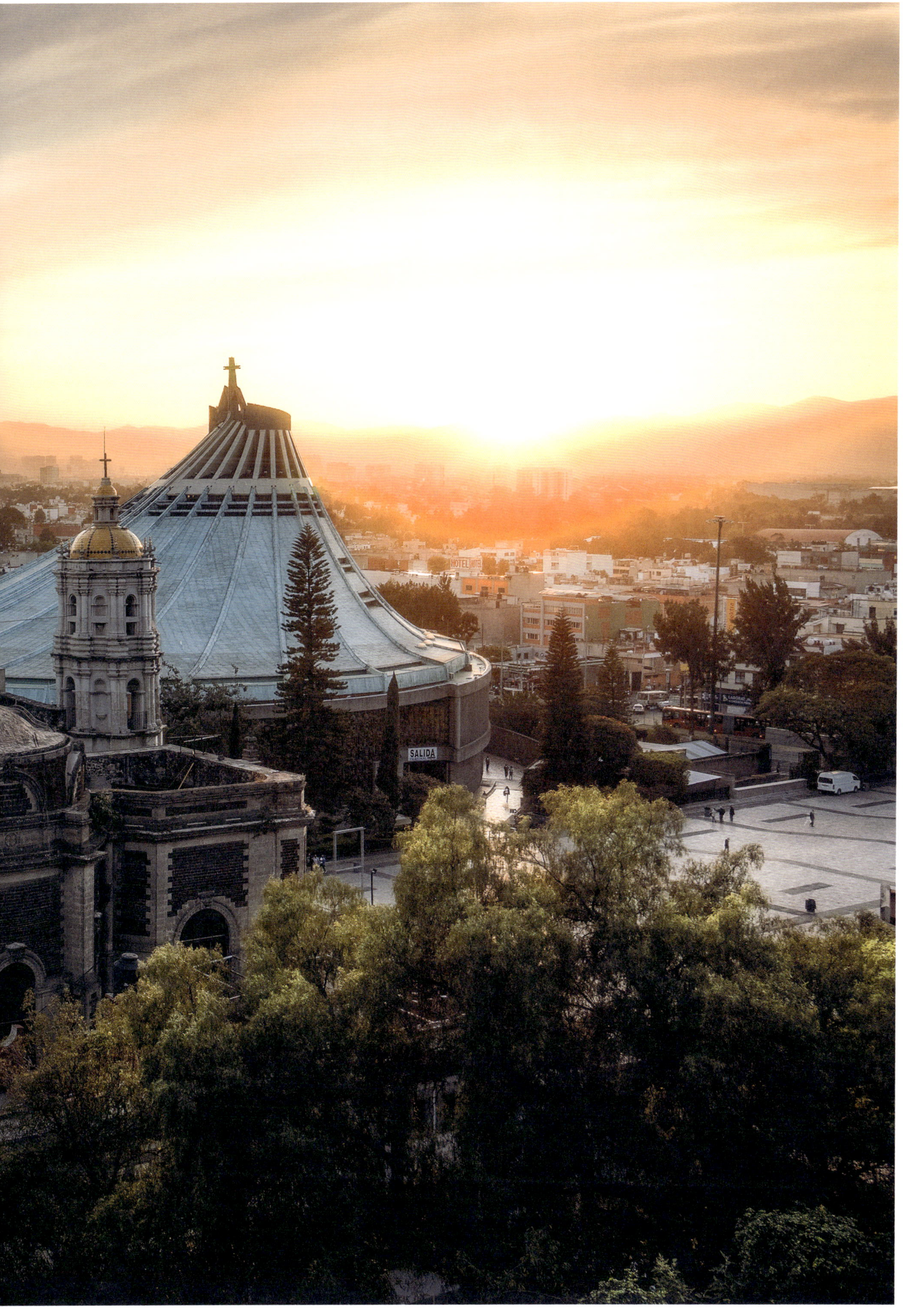
HOTEL
SALIDA

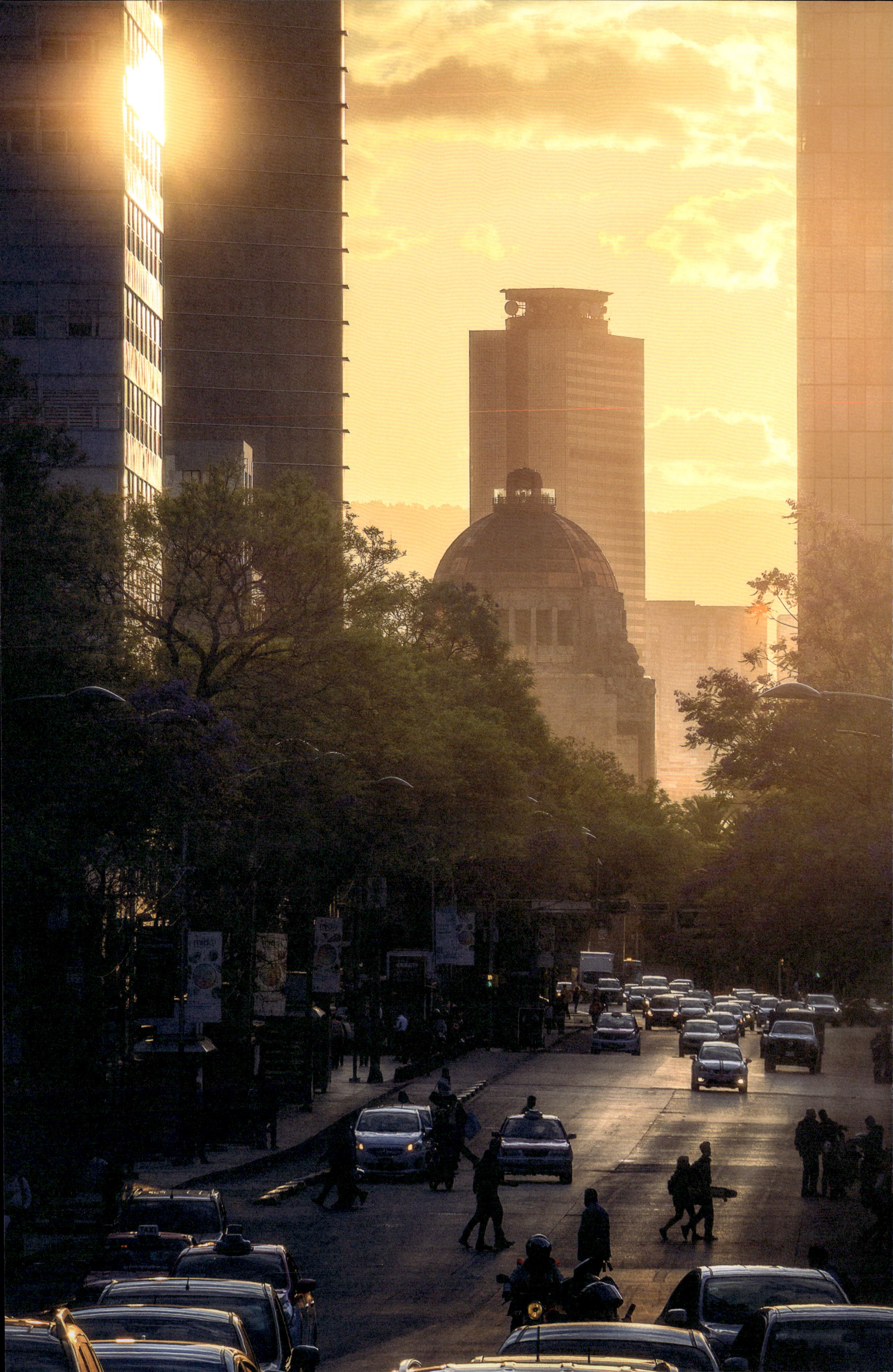

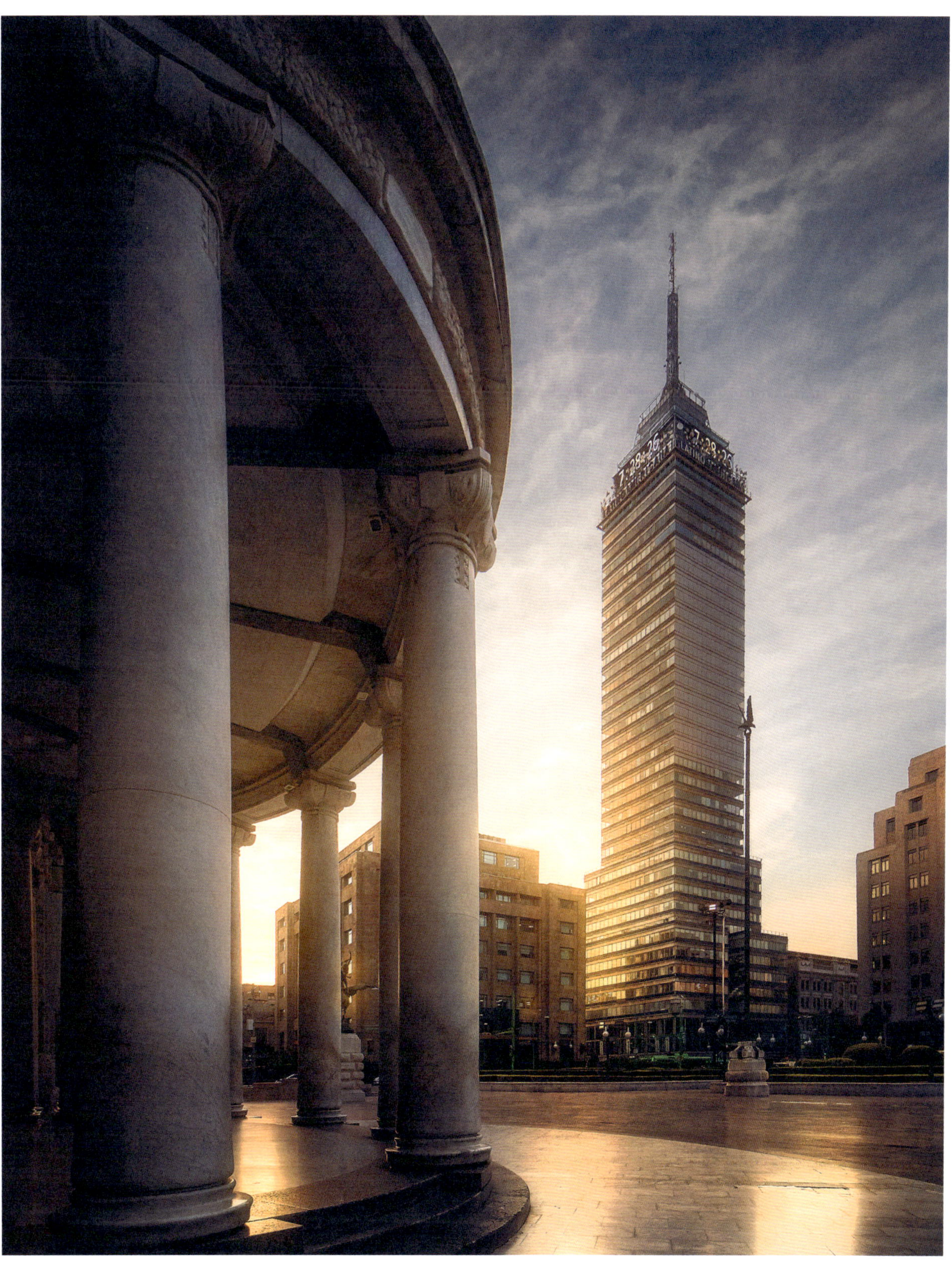

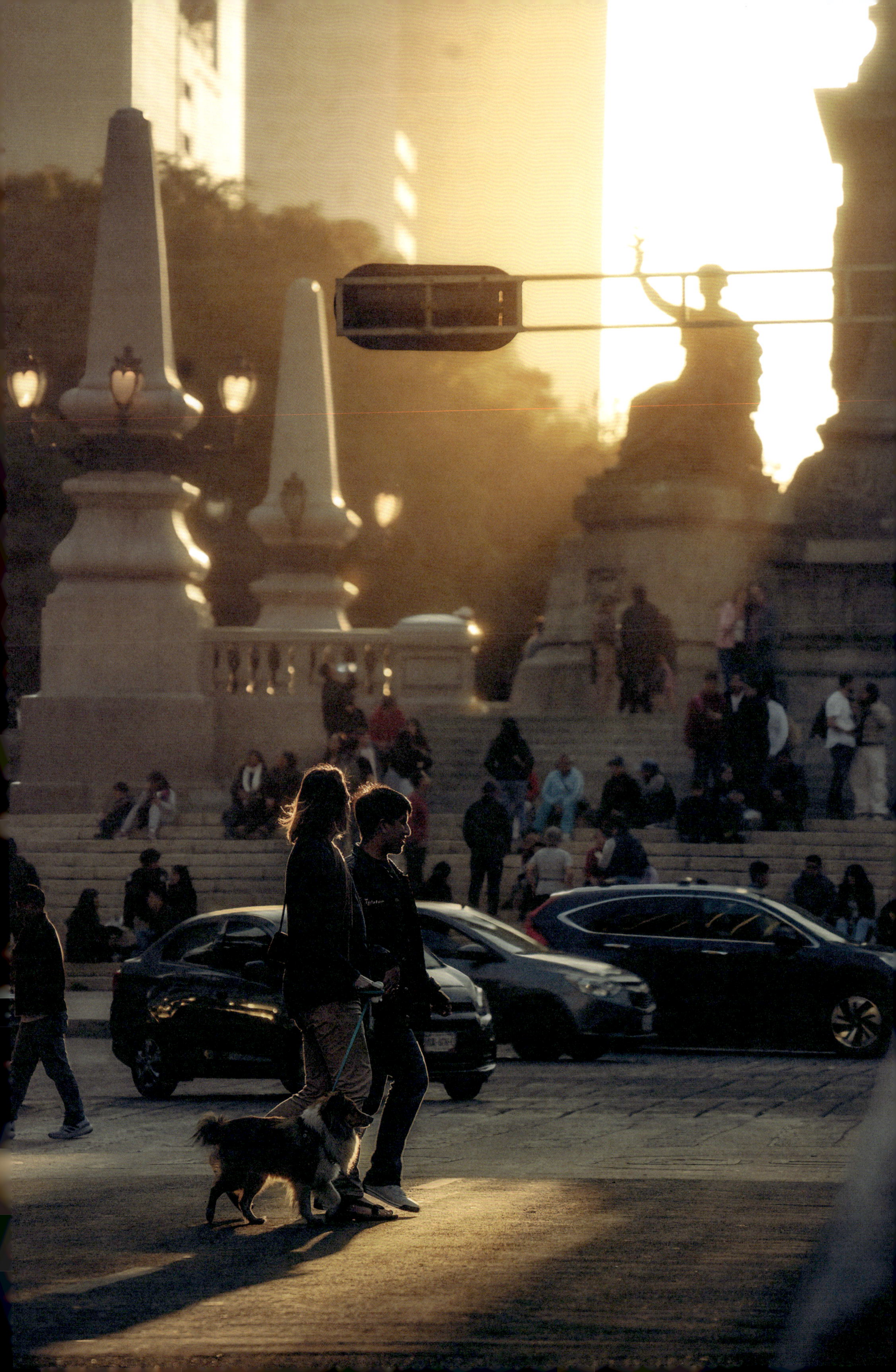

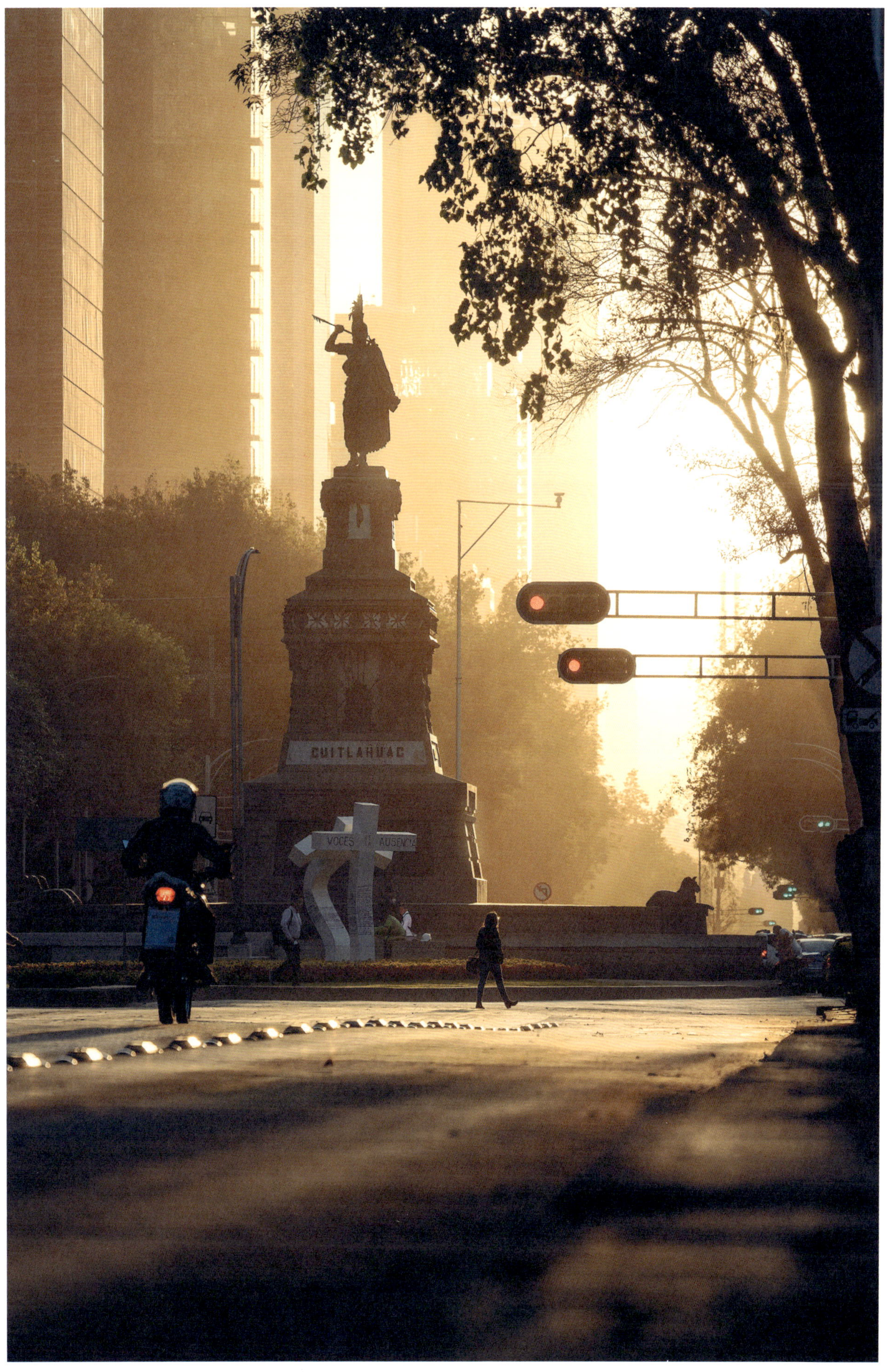
CUITLAHUAC
VOCES
AUSENCIA

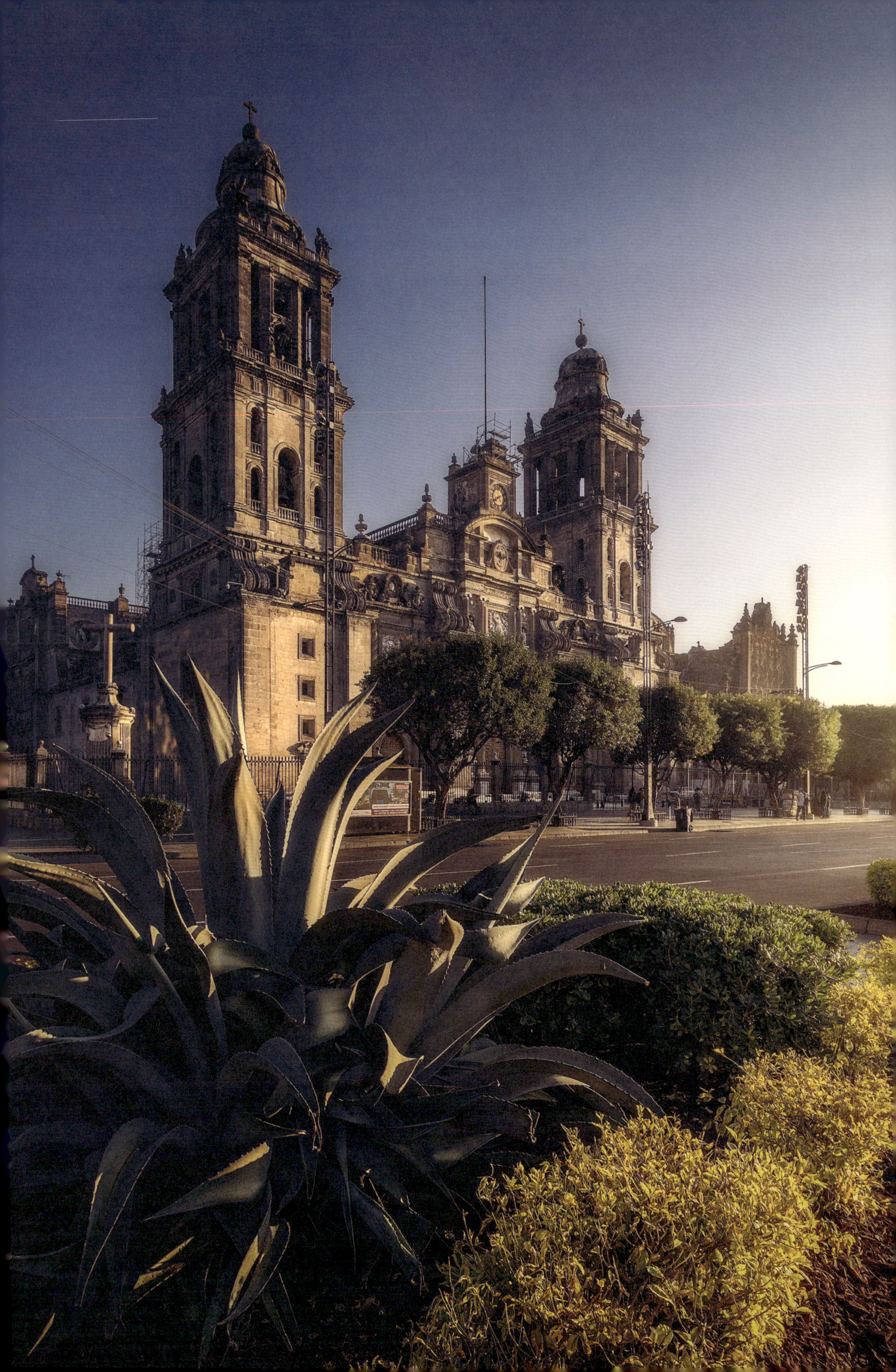

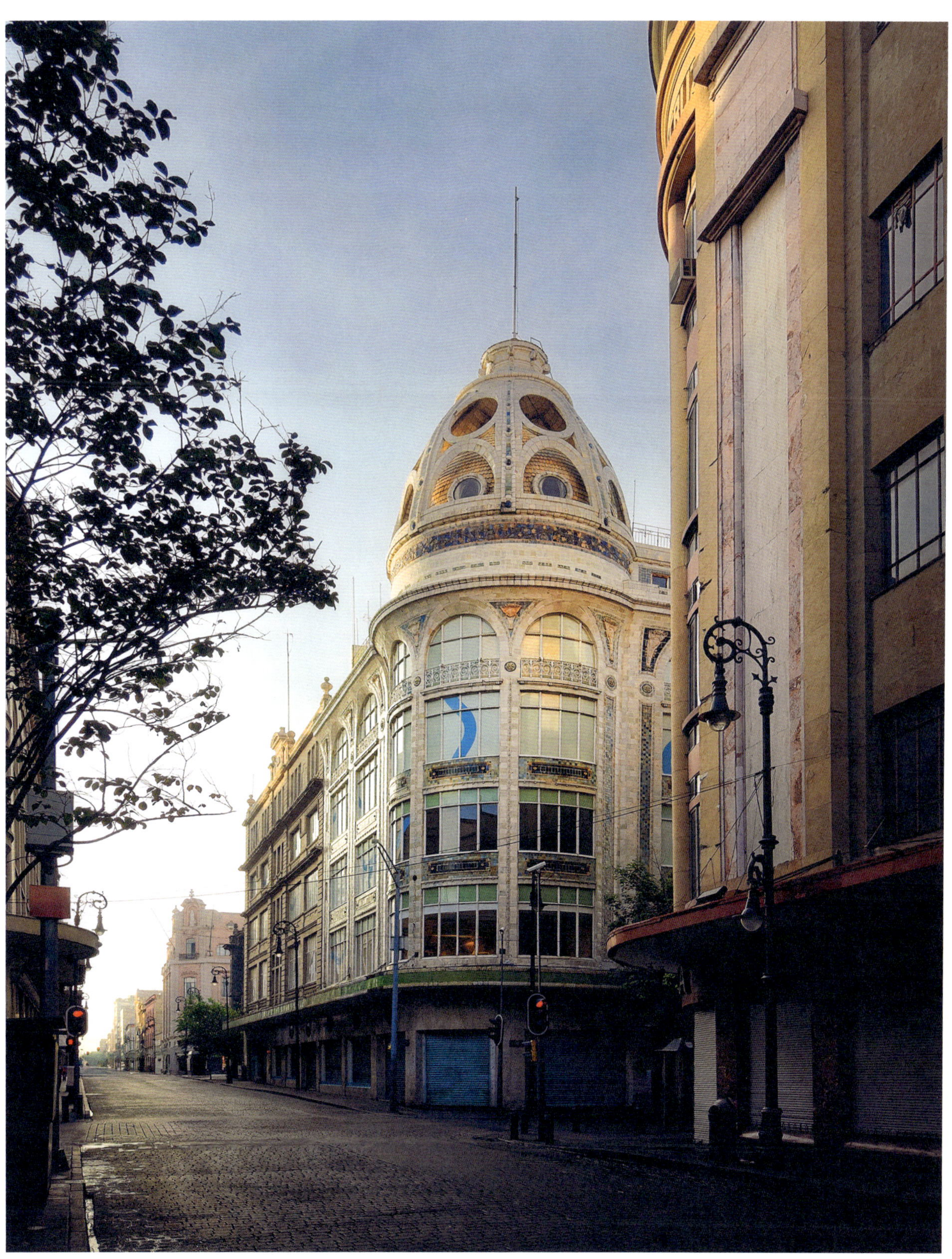

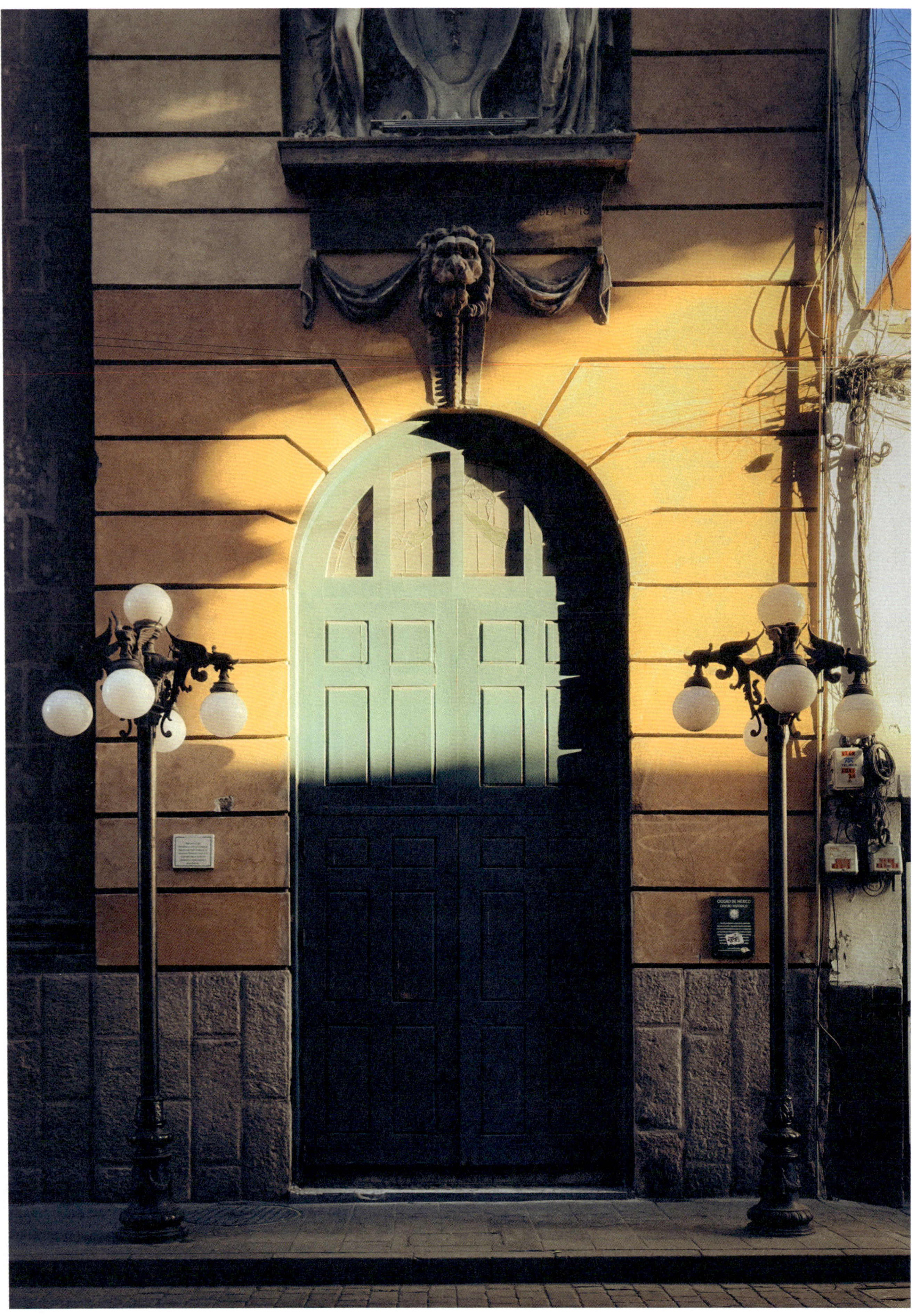

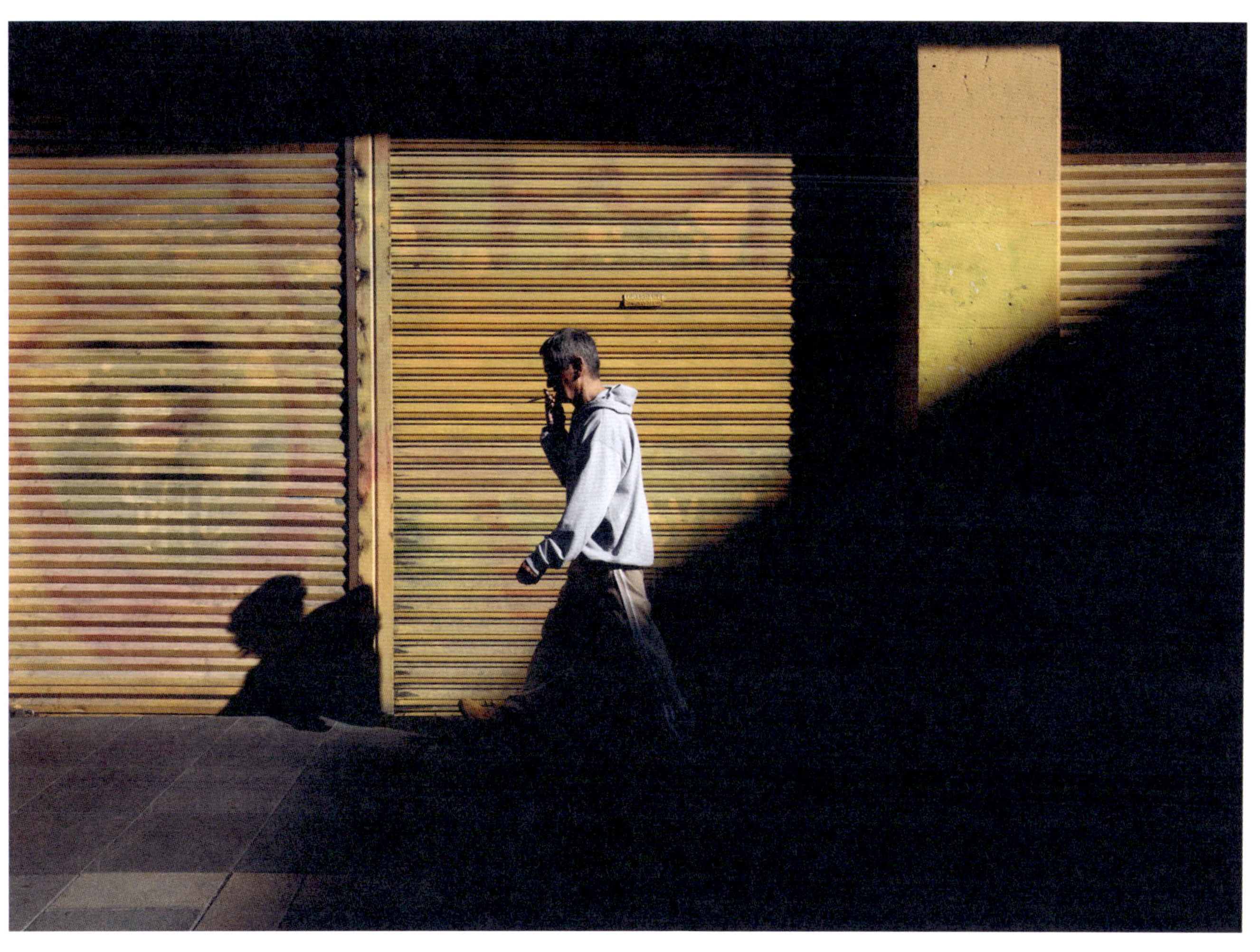

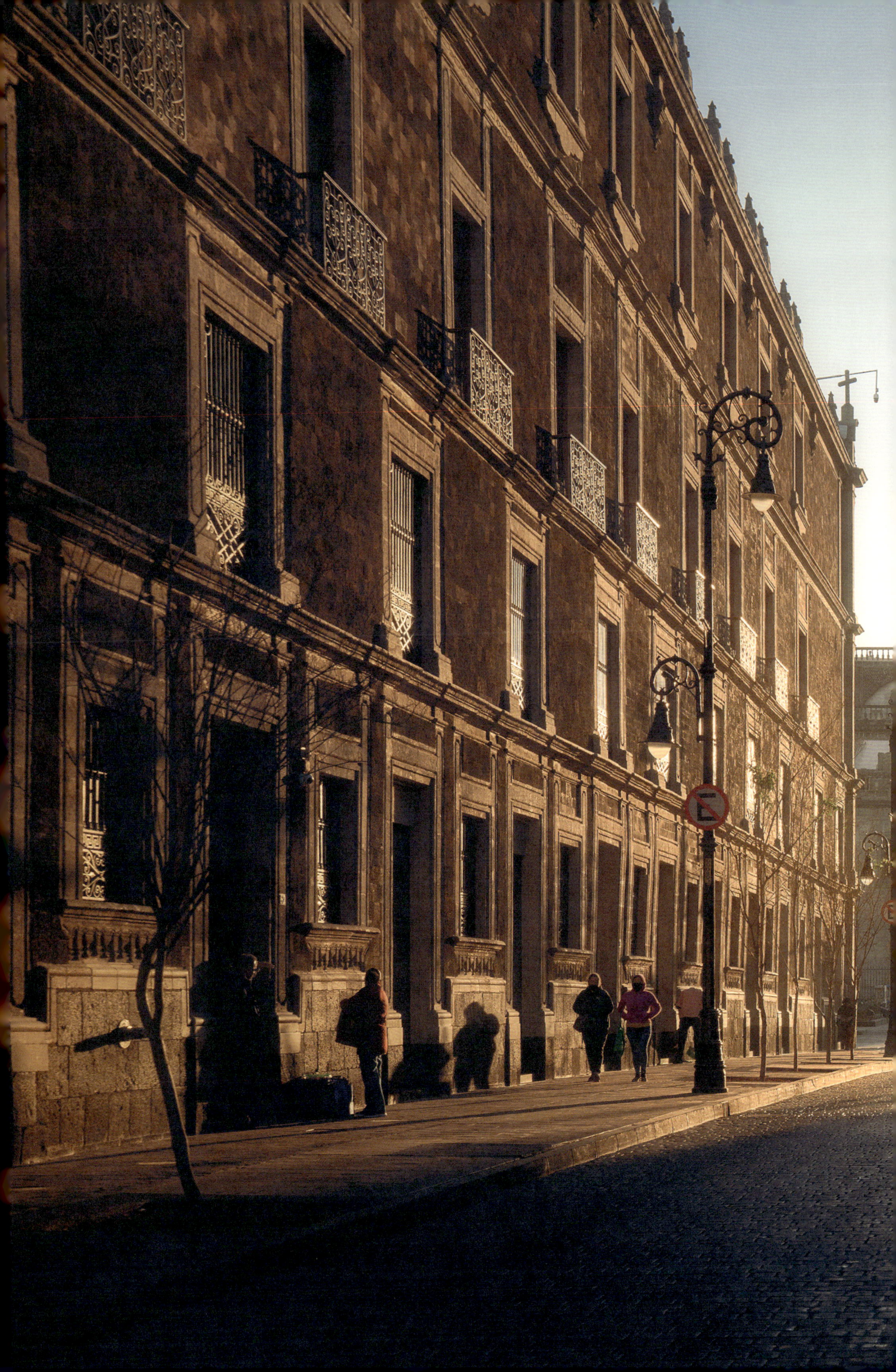

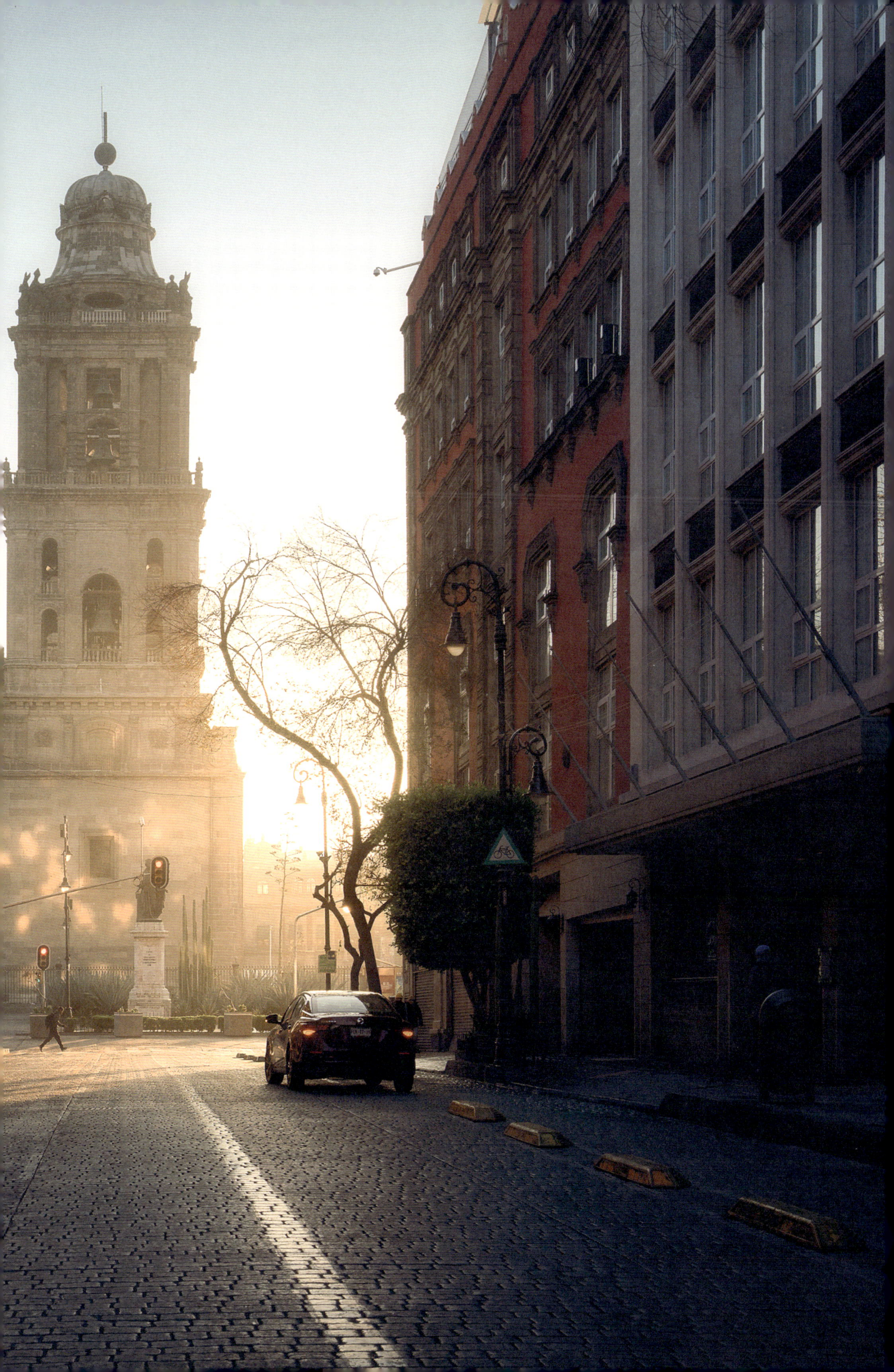

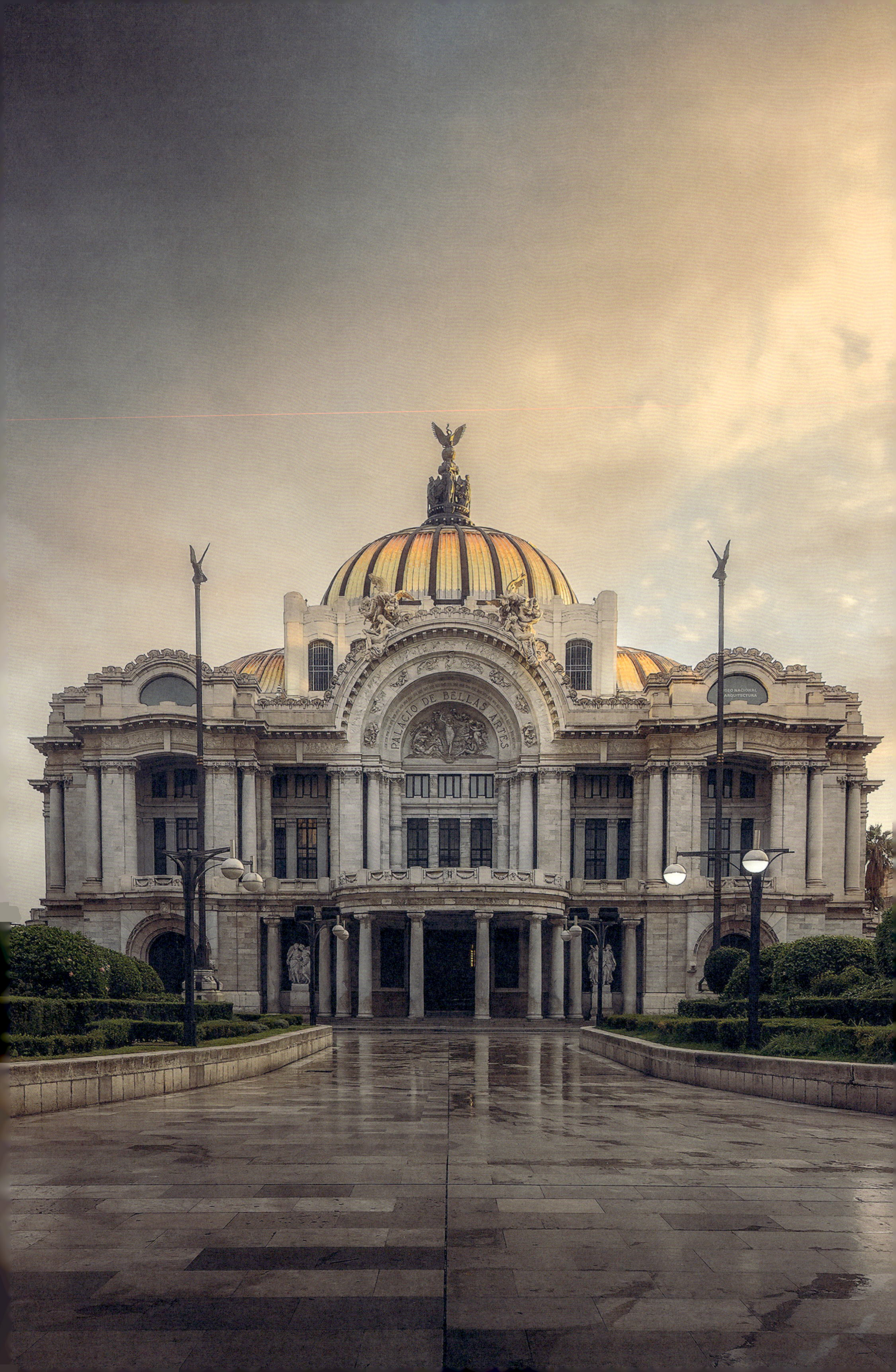
PALACIO DE BELLAS ARTES

Mexico City [is] one of my favorite cities in the world because the people there are kind and generous and loving.

ANDREW ZIMMERN

American Chef and Restaurateur

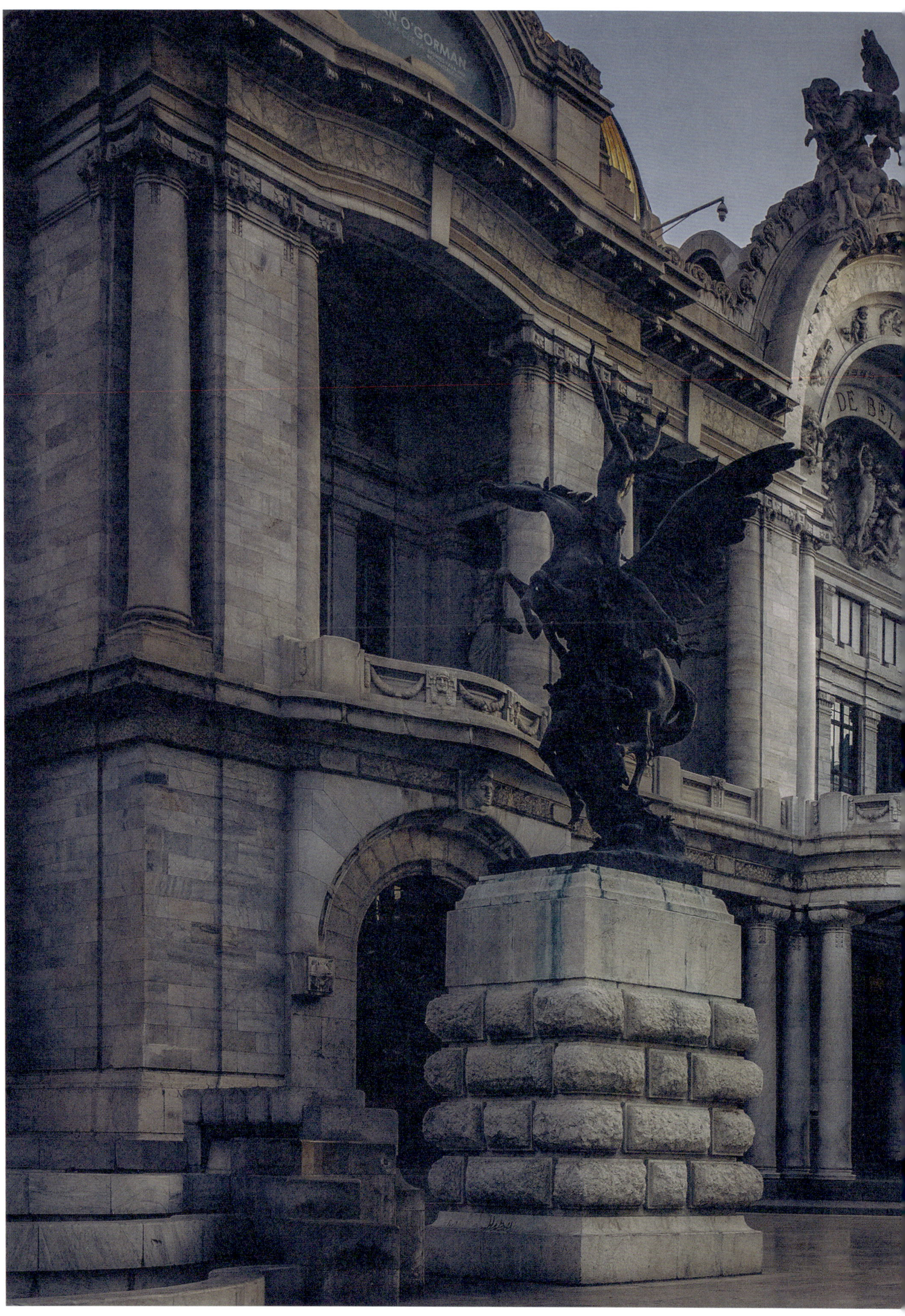

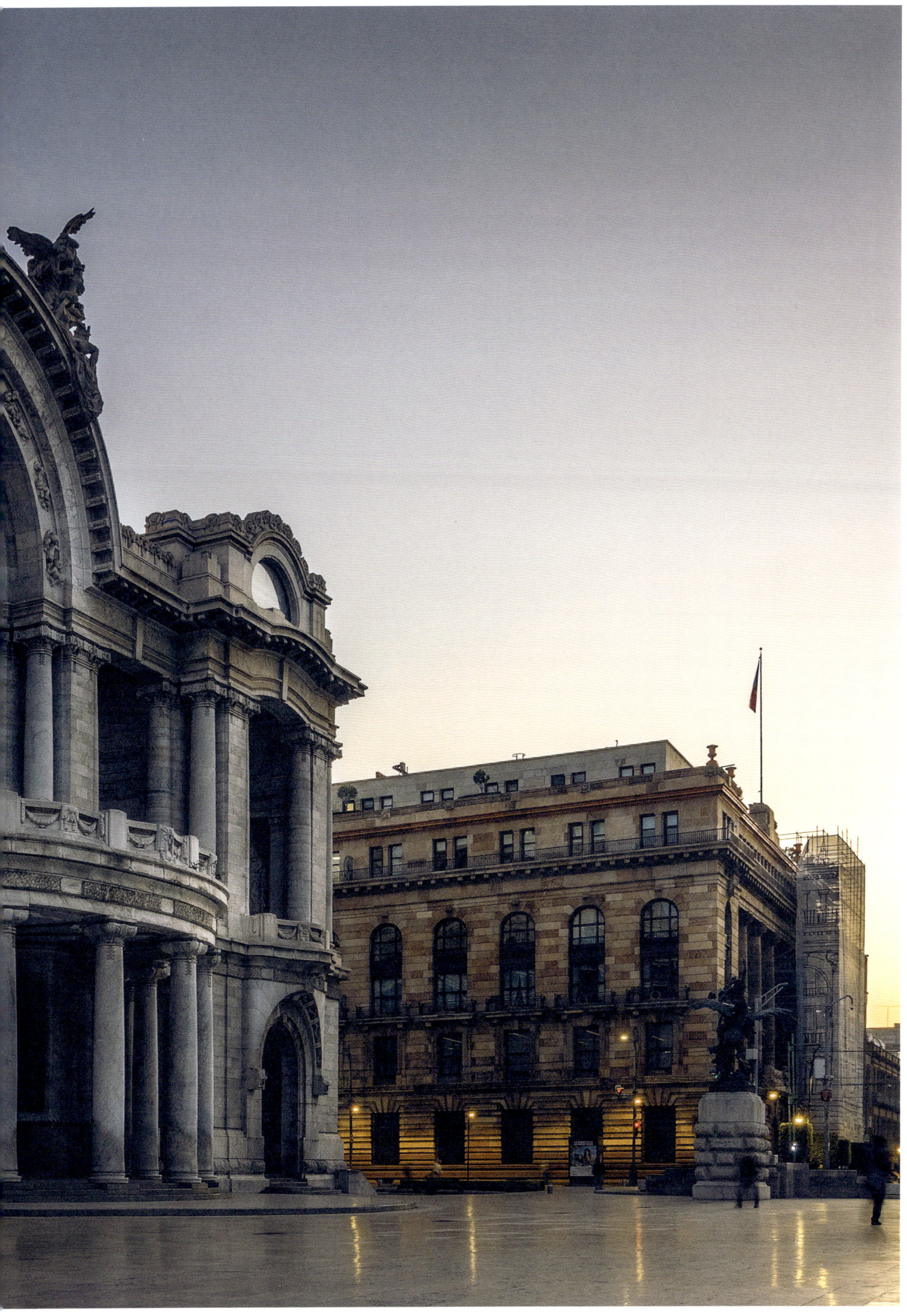

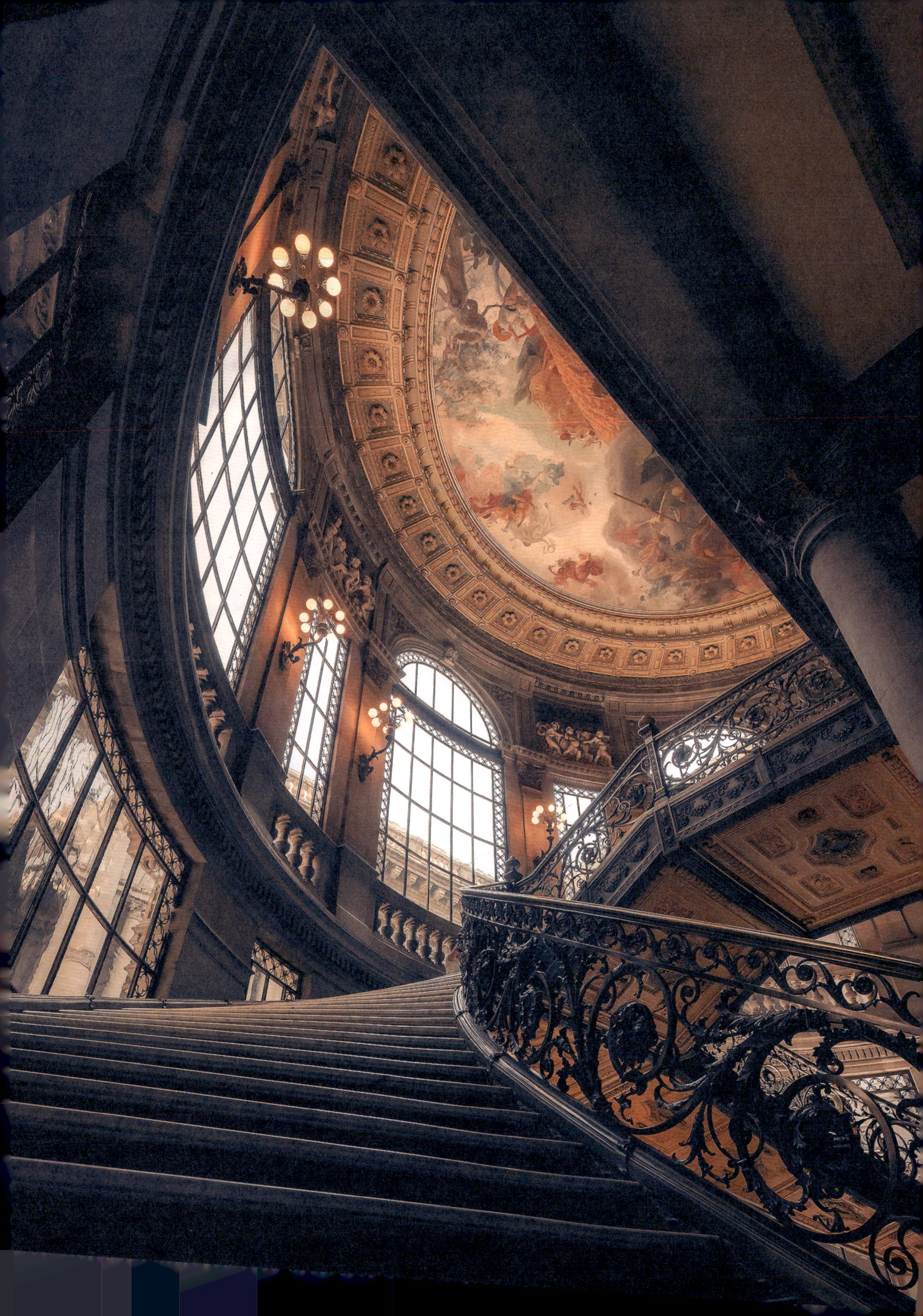

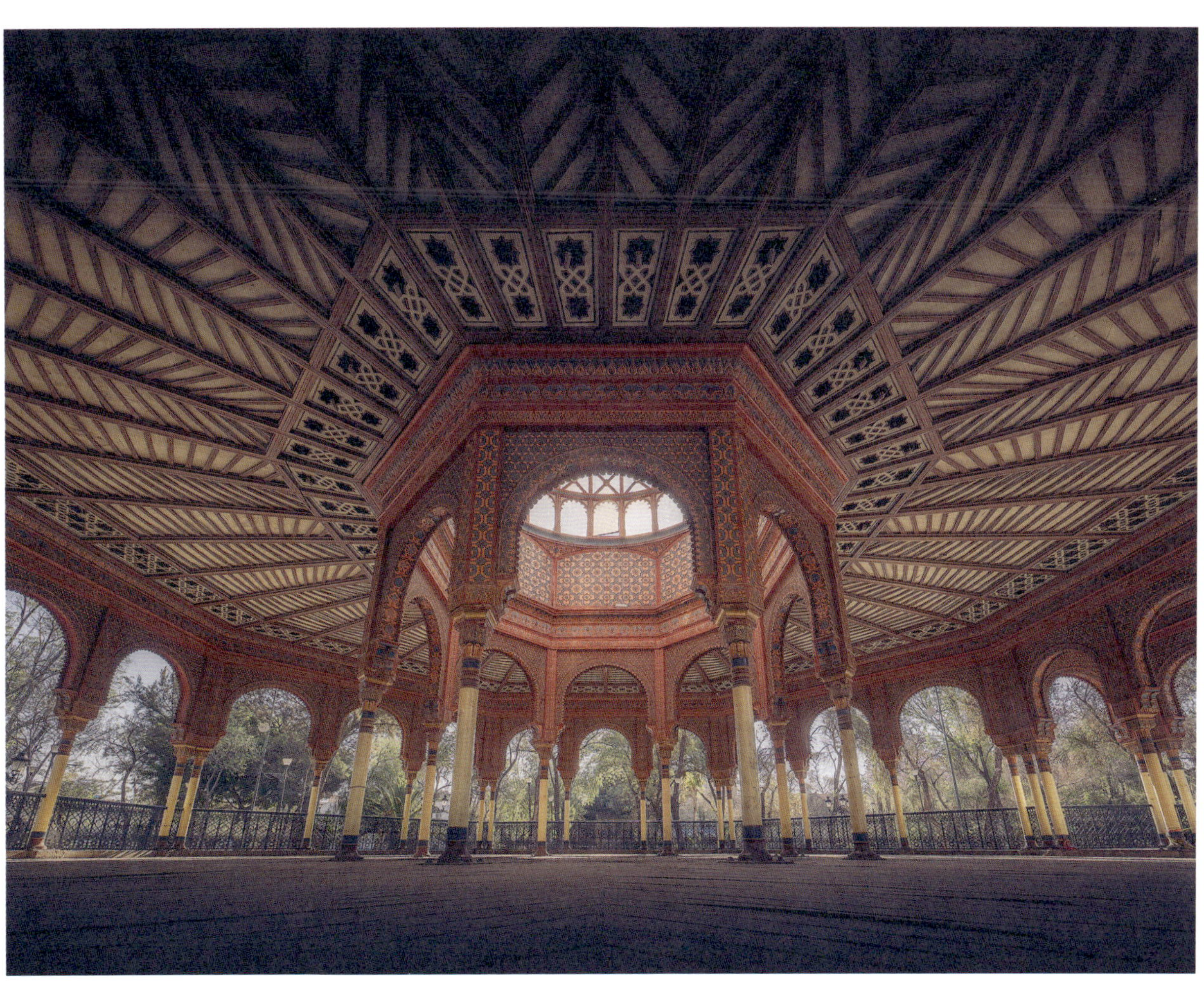

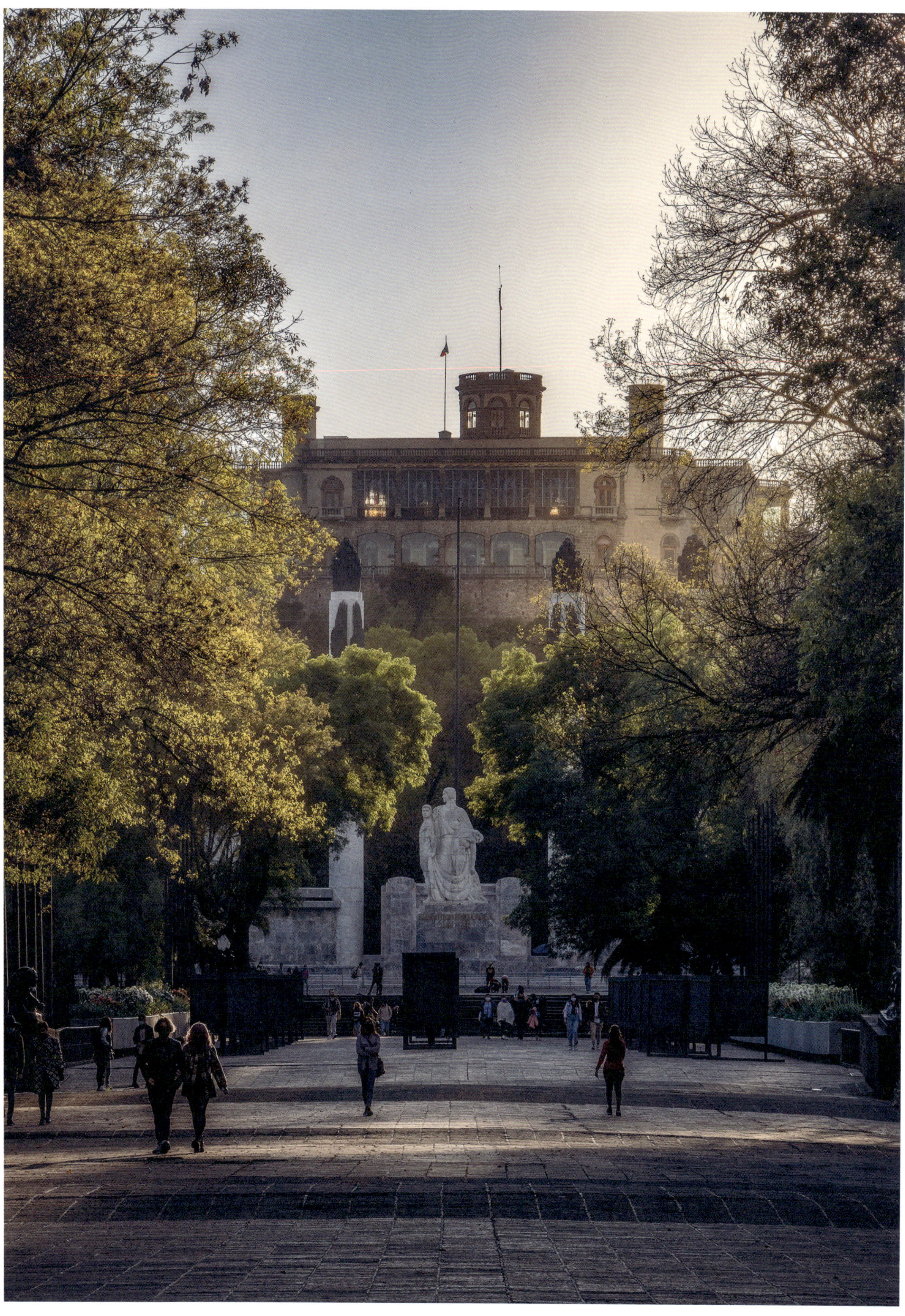

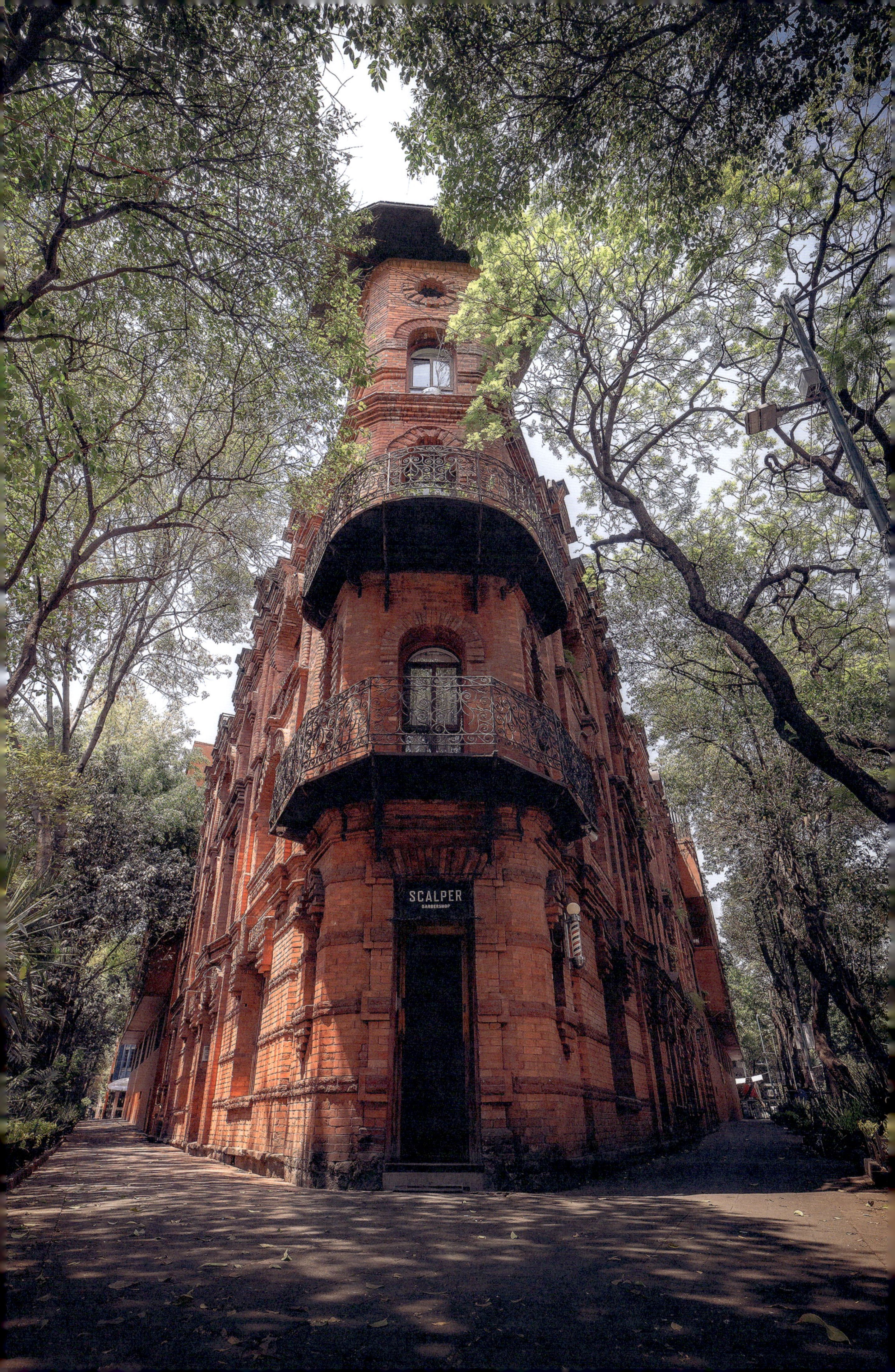
SCALPER
BARBERSHOP

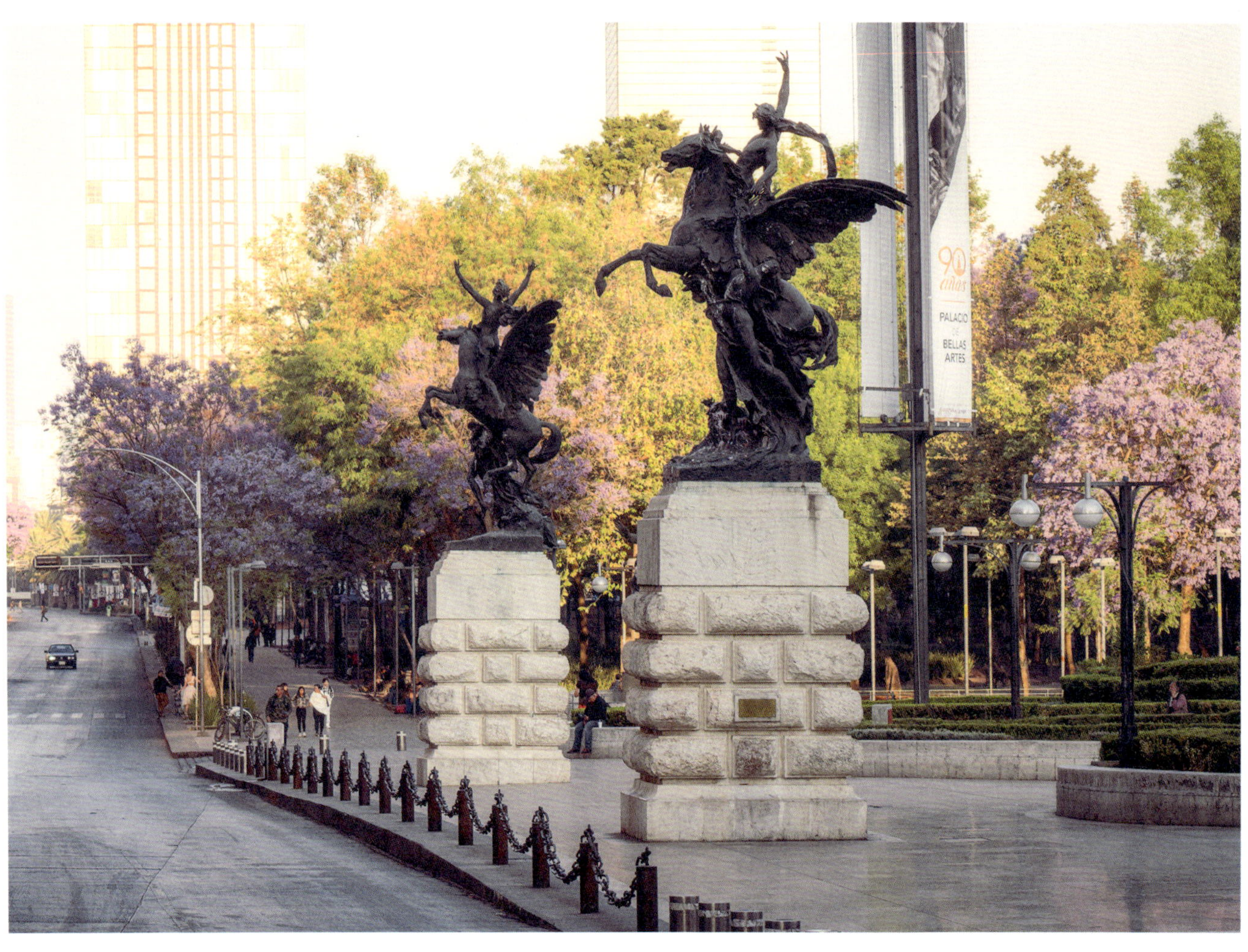
90
años
PALACIO
DE
BELLAS
ARTES

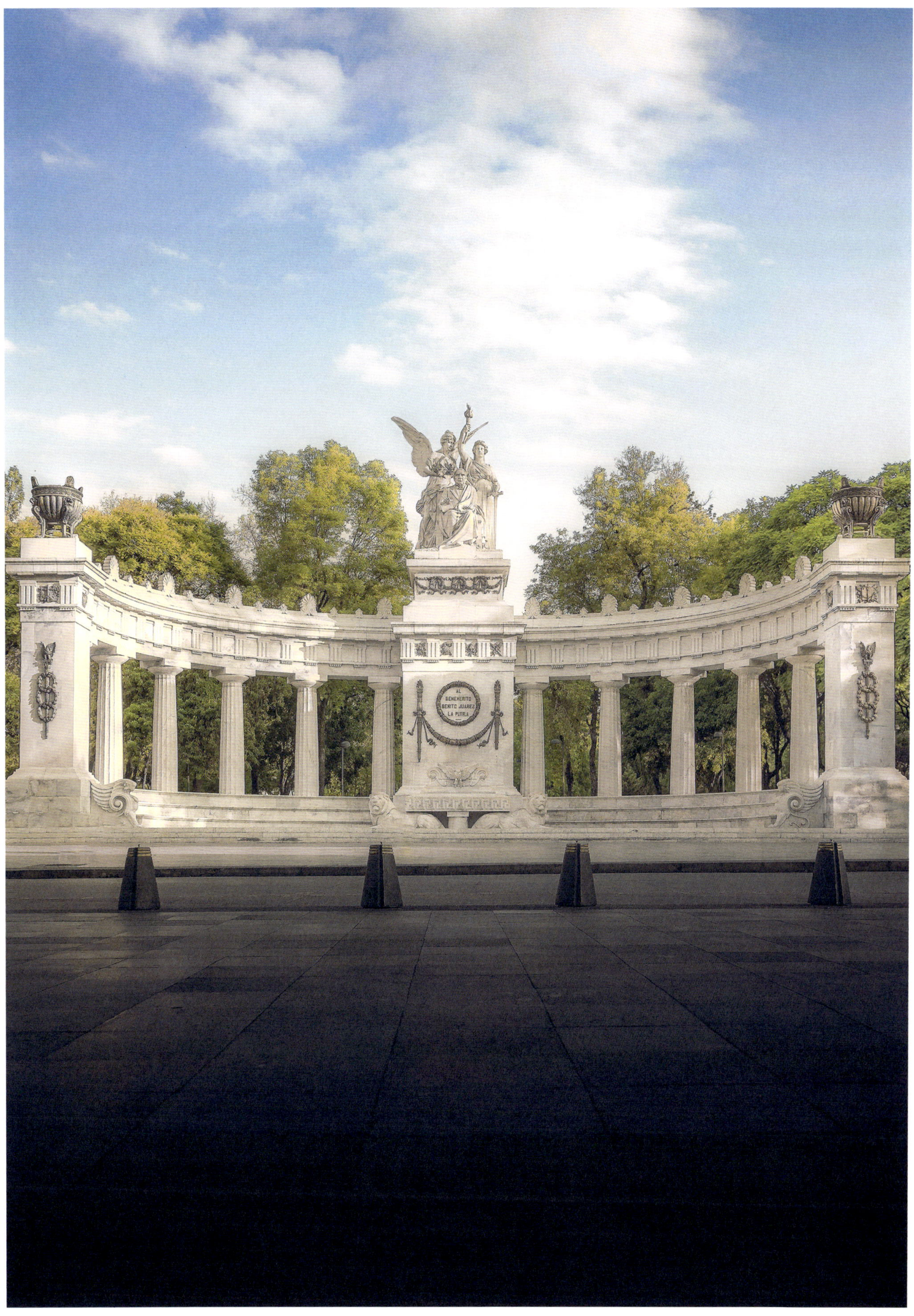
AL
BENEMERITO
BENITO JUAREZ
LA PATRIA

Life in Mexico is a rich and rewarding experience, a place where you can truly immerse yourself in the culture and learn to appreciate the beauty of simplicity.

PICO IYER

Essayist and Novelist

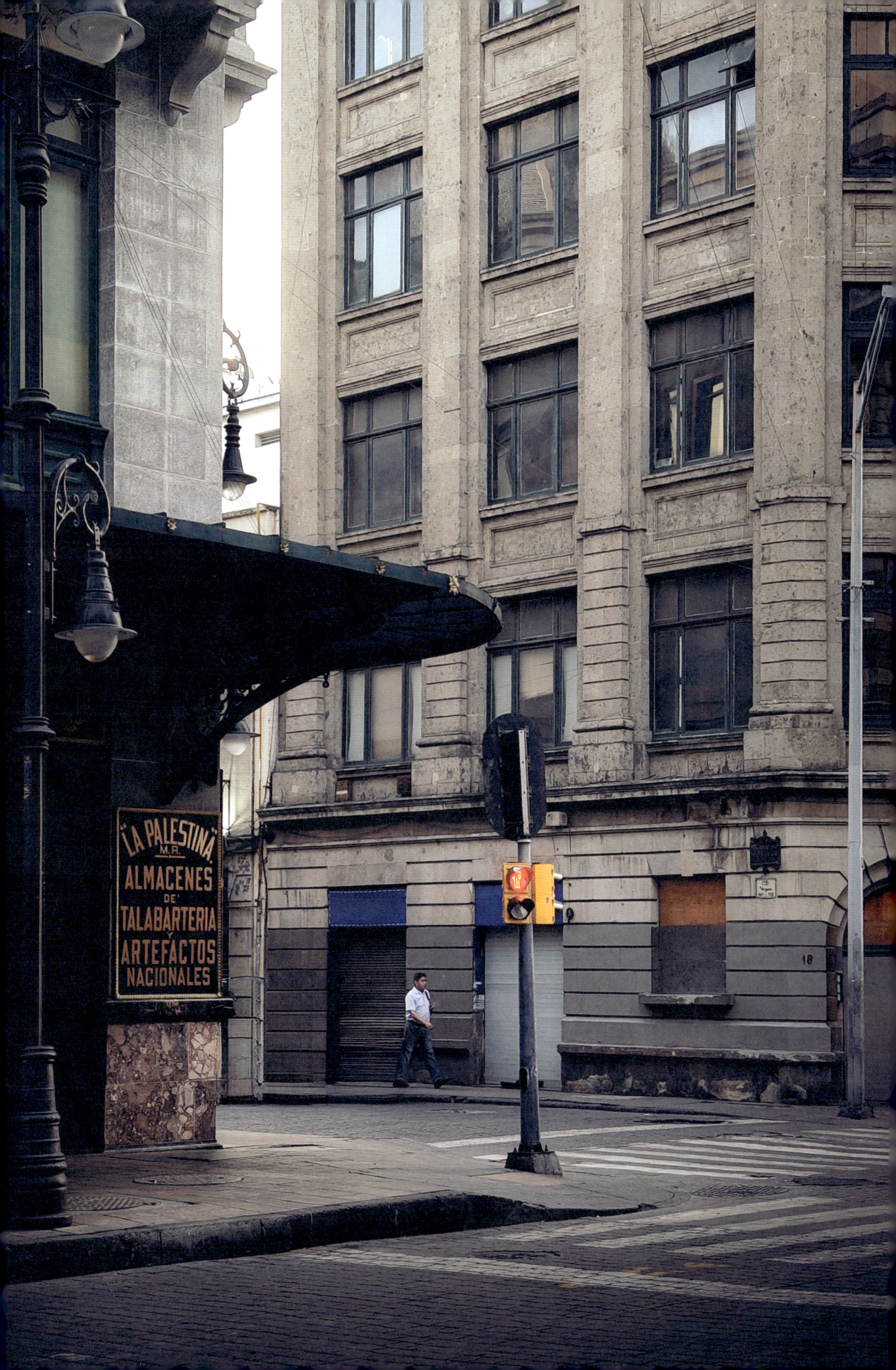
"LA PALESTINA"
M.R.
ALMACENES
DE
TALABARTERIA
Y
ARTEFACTOS
NACIONALES

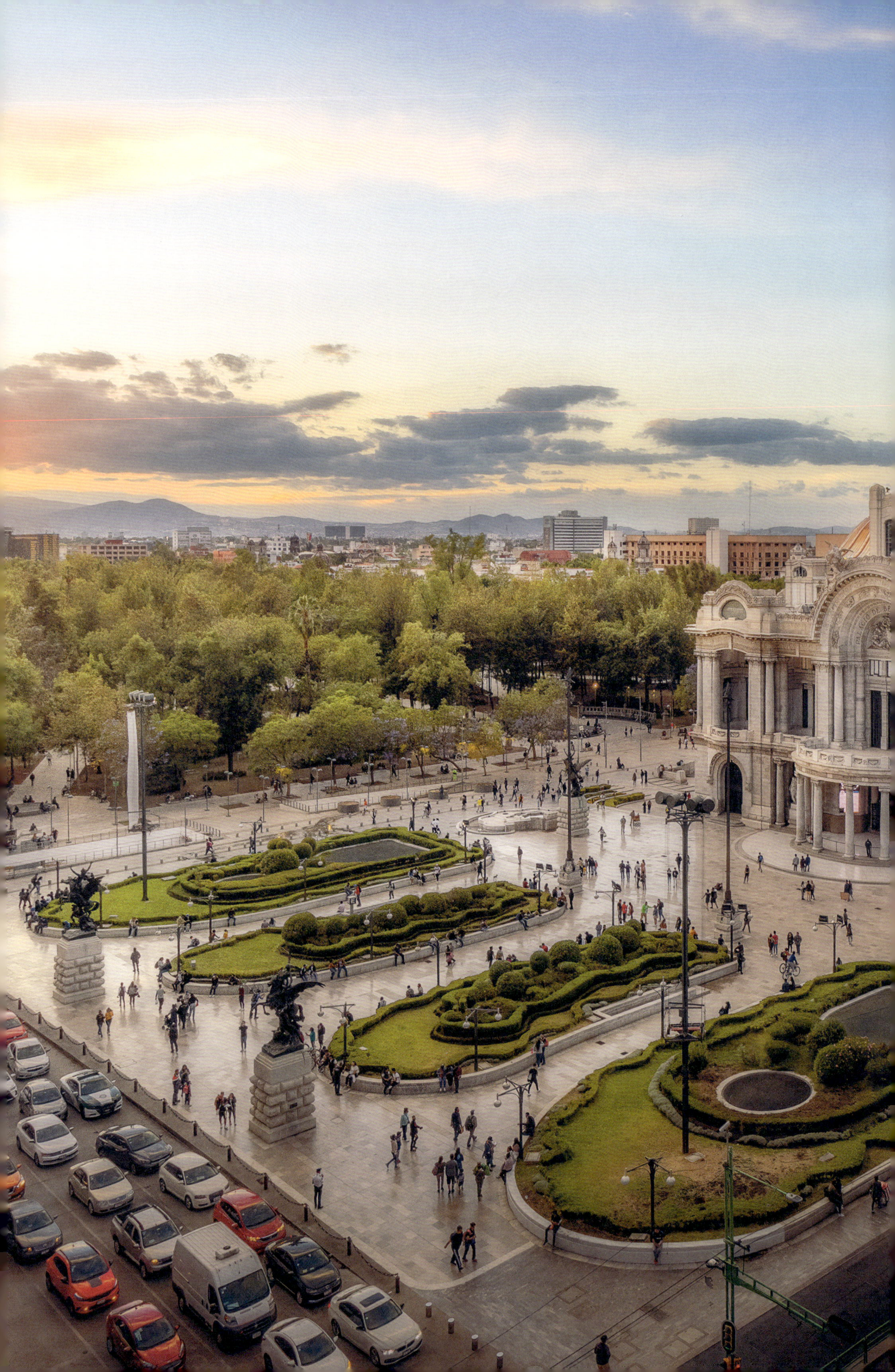

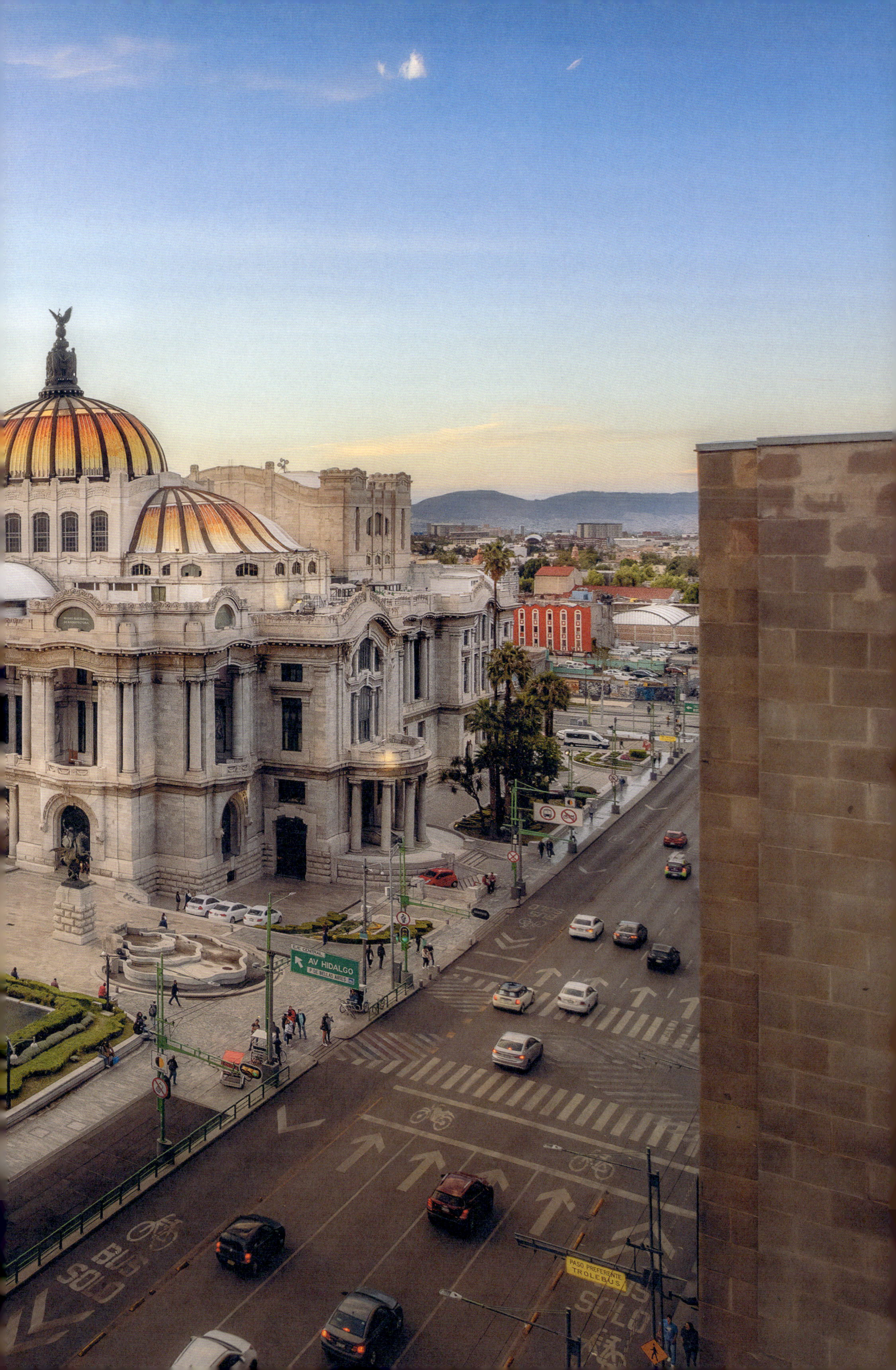
EJE CENTRAL
AV HIDALGO
P. DE BELLAS ARTES
PASO PREFERENTE
TROLEBUS
SOLO BUS

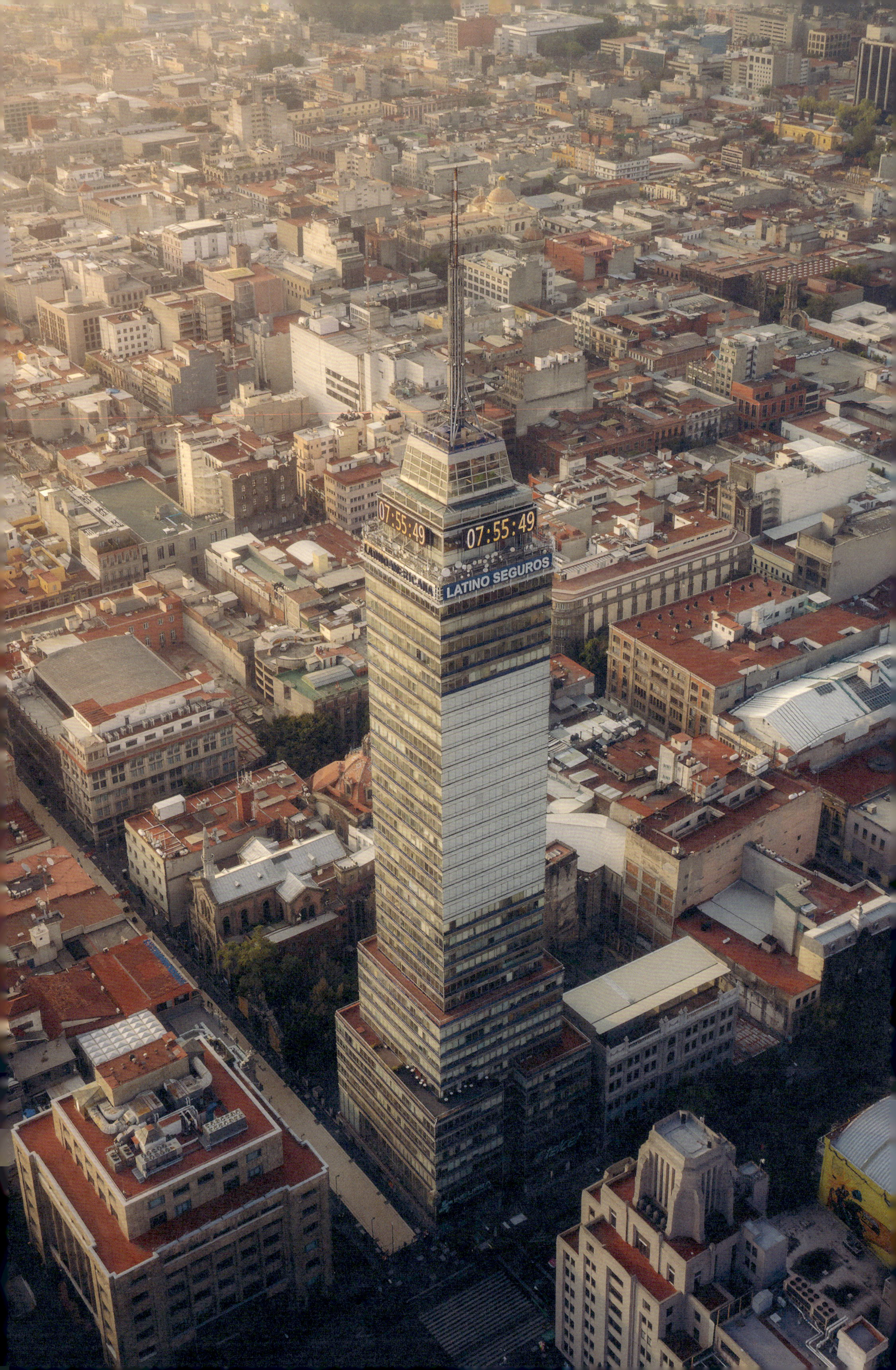
07:55:49
07:55:49
LATINO SEGUROS

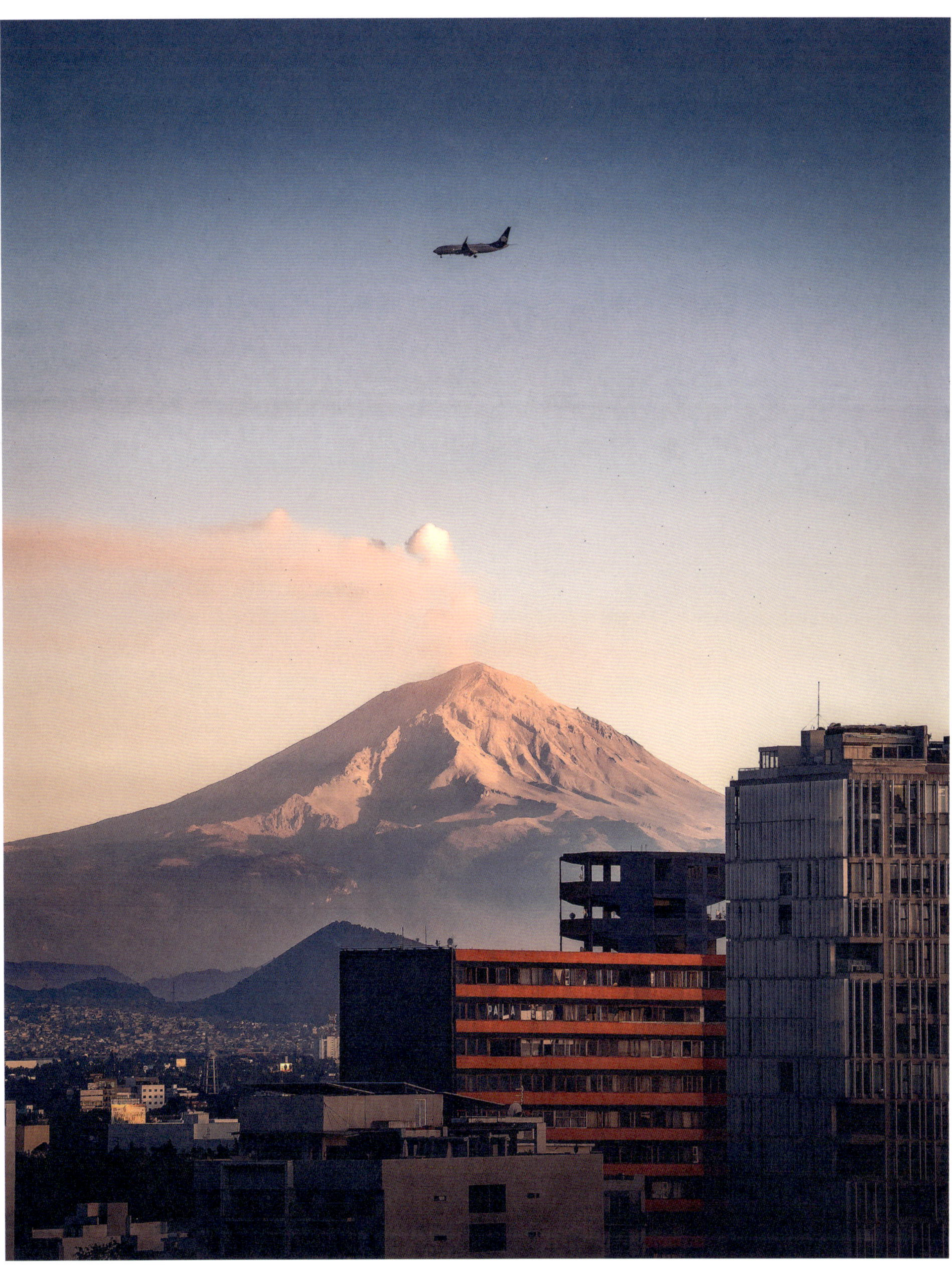

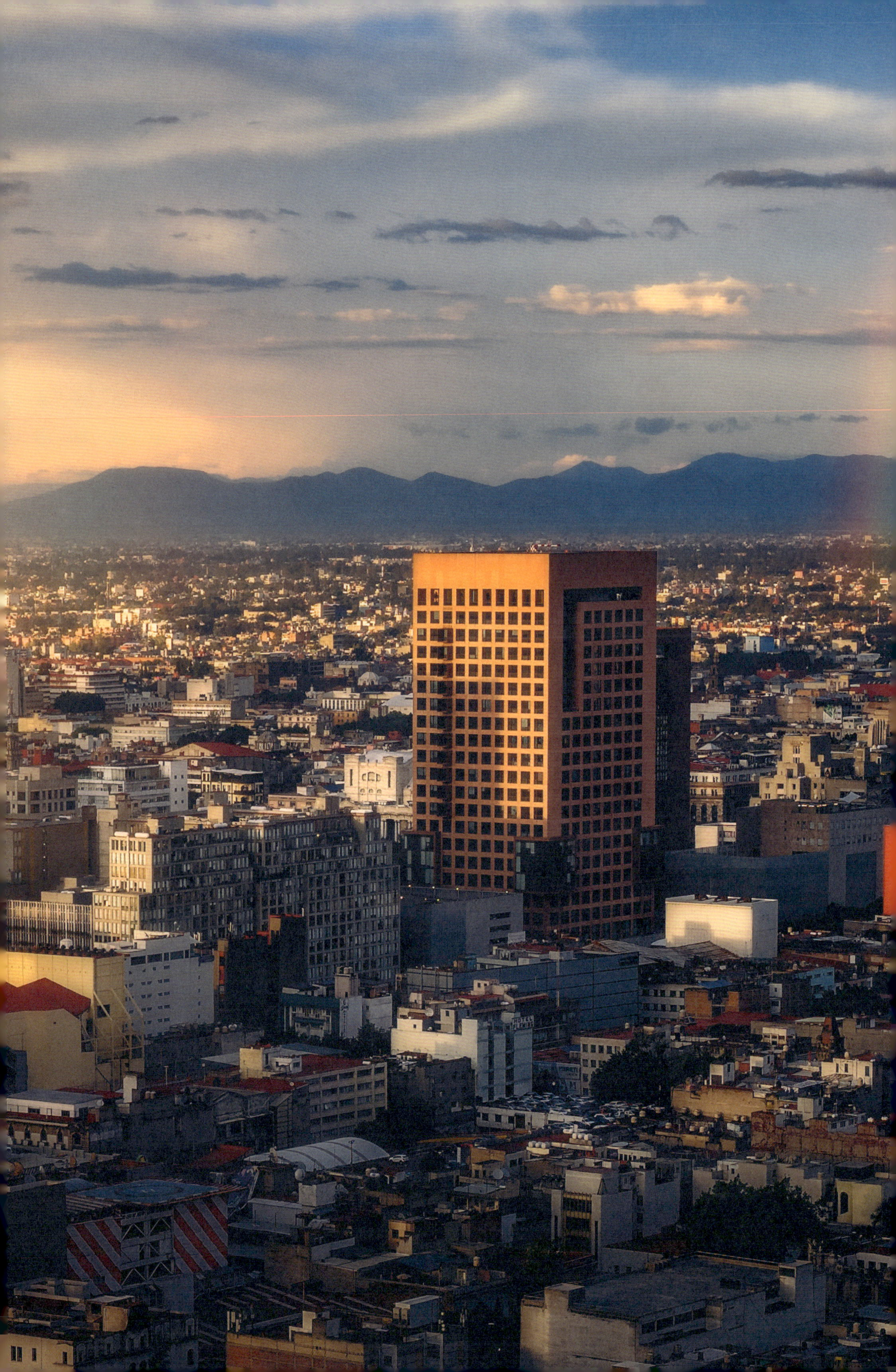

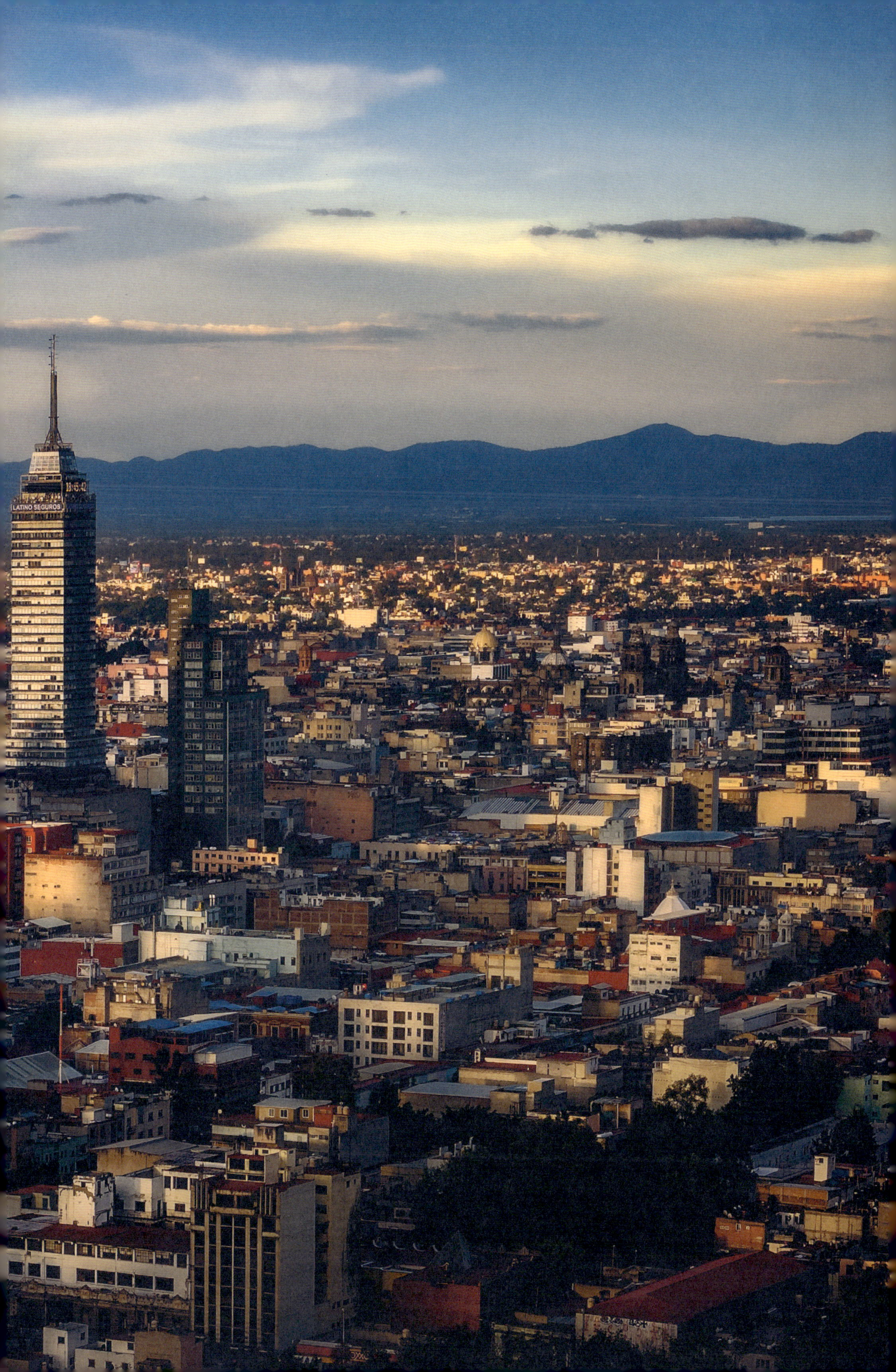
LATINO SEGUROS

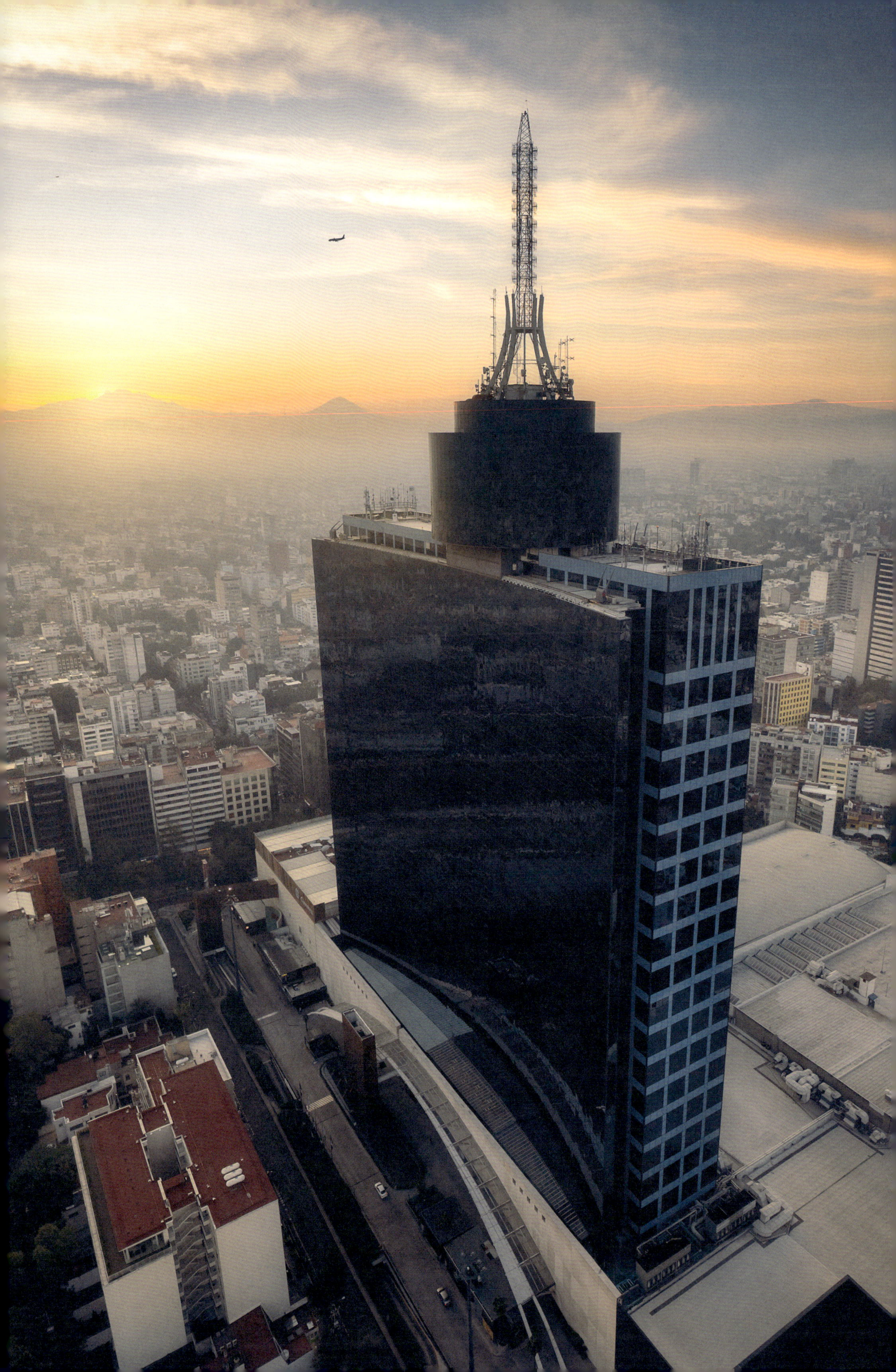

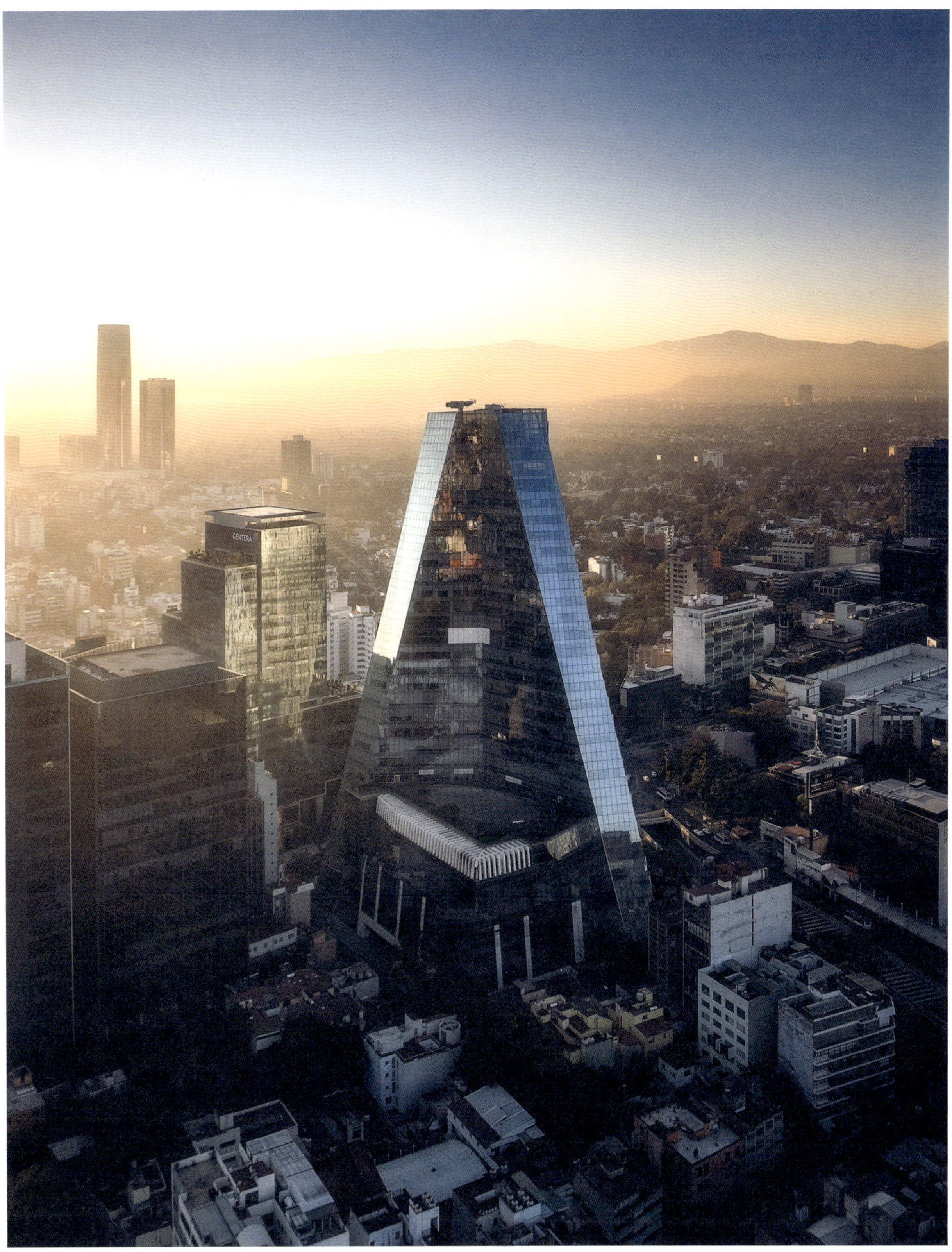
GENTERA

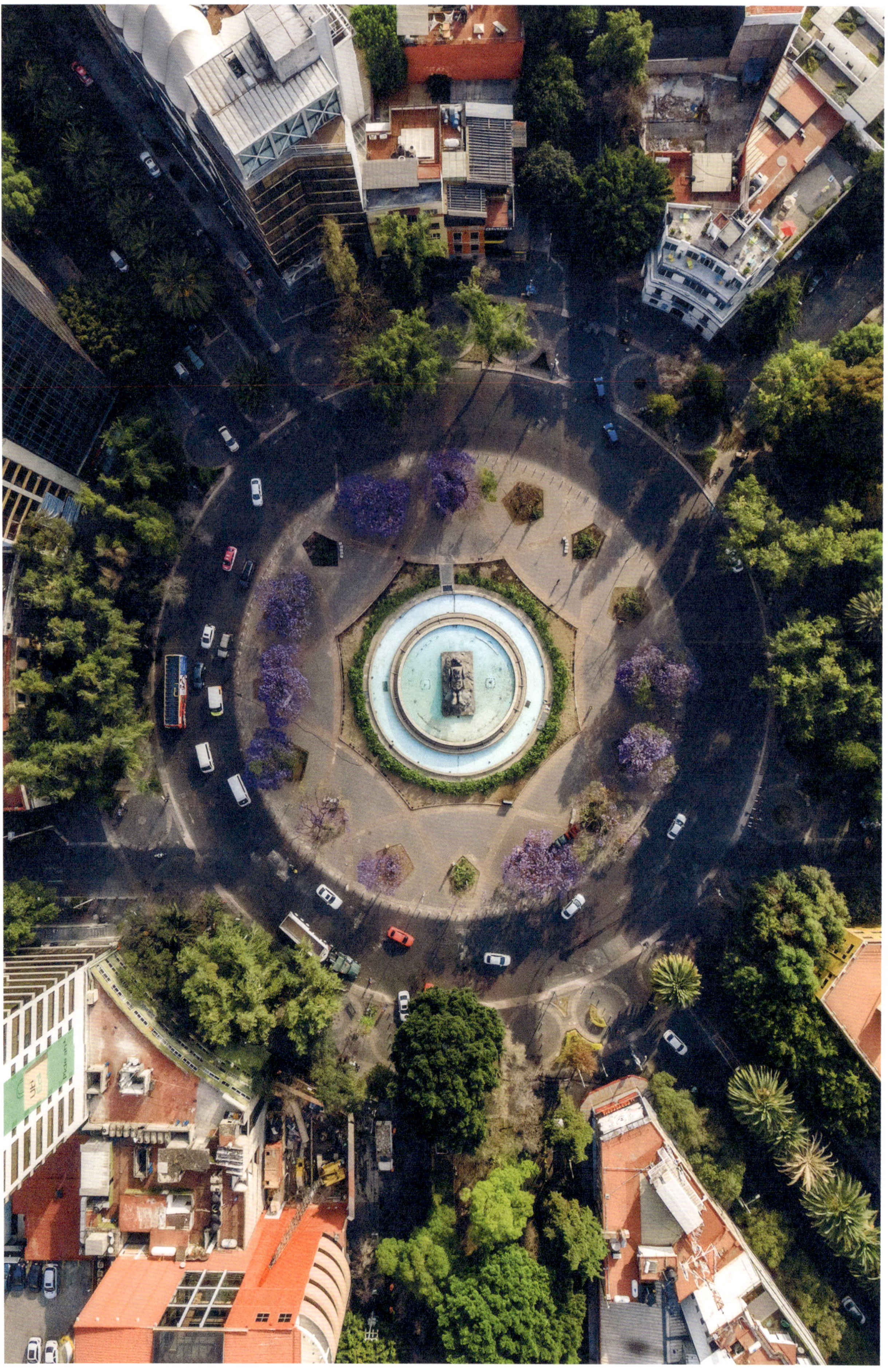

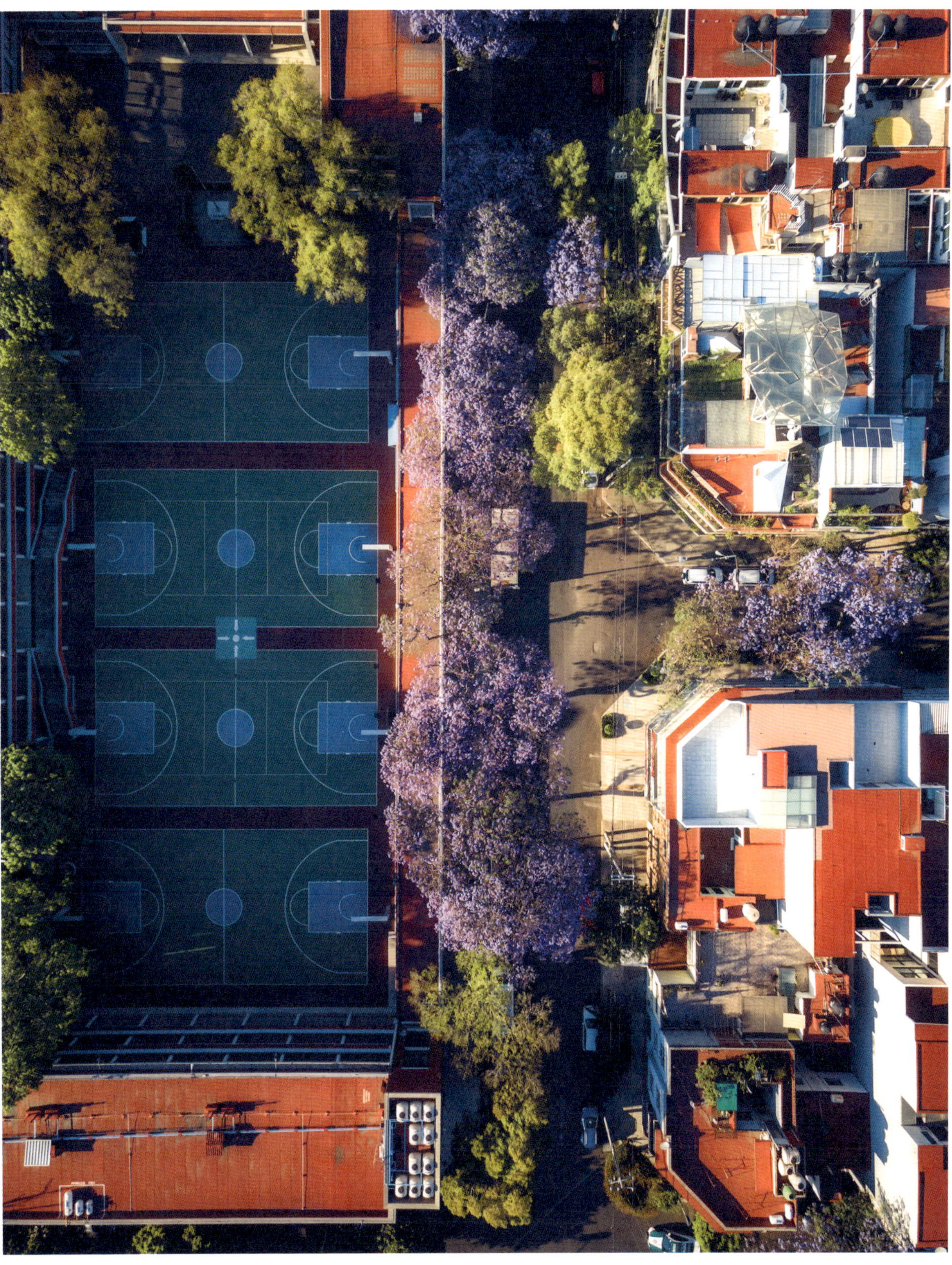

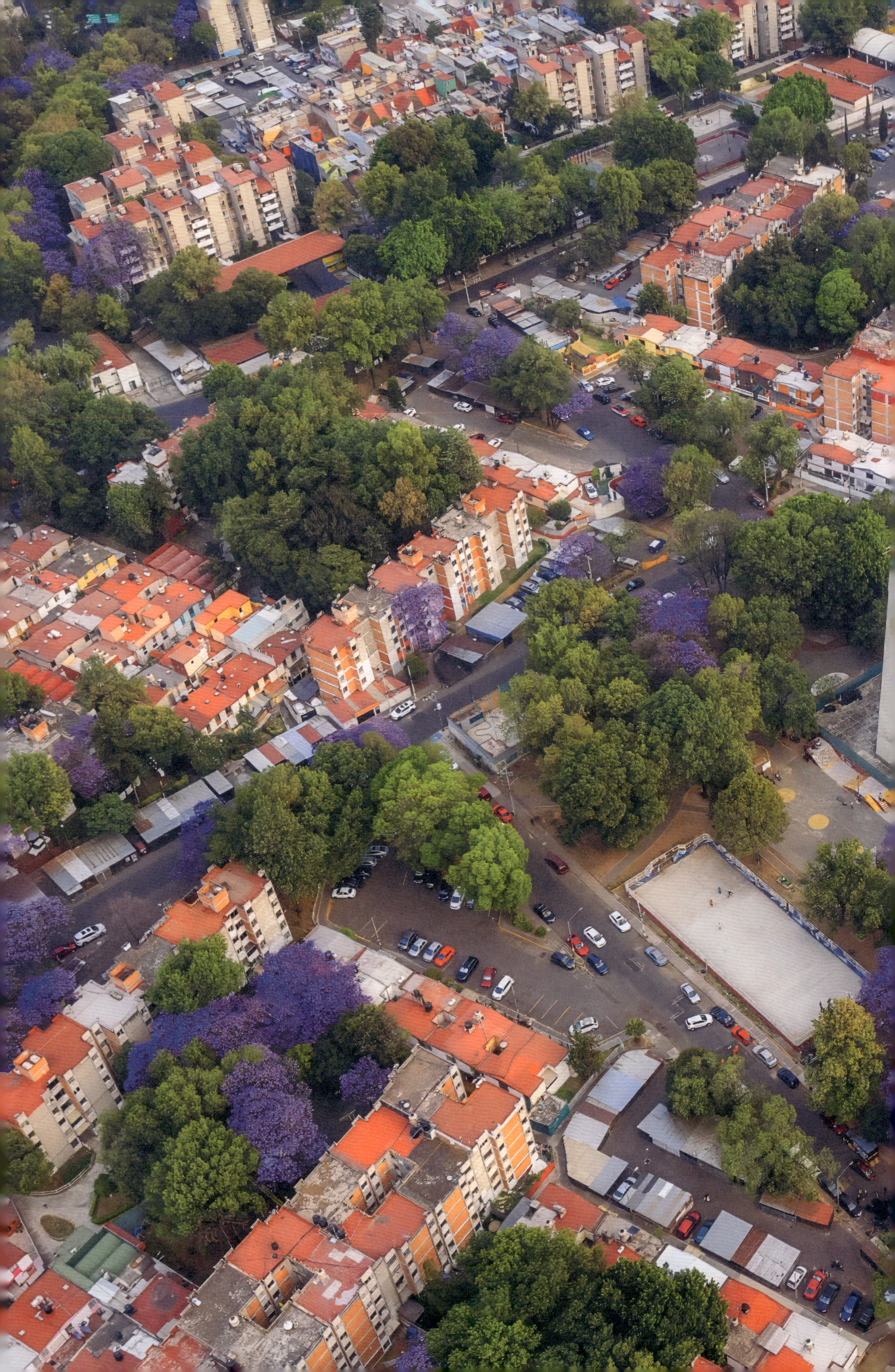

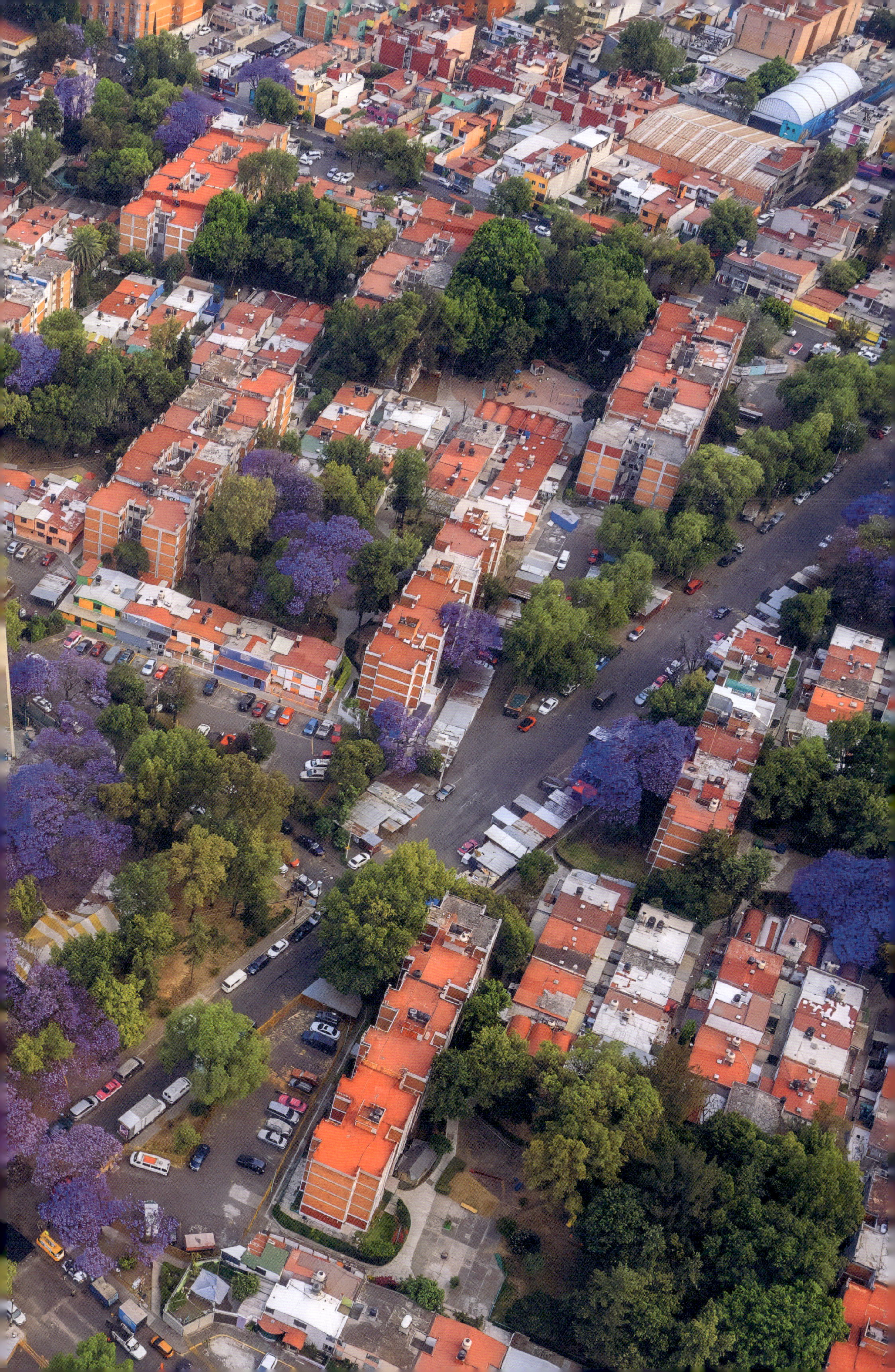

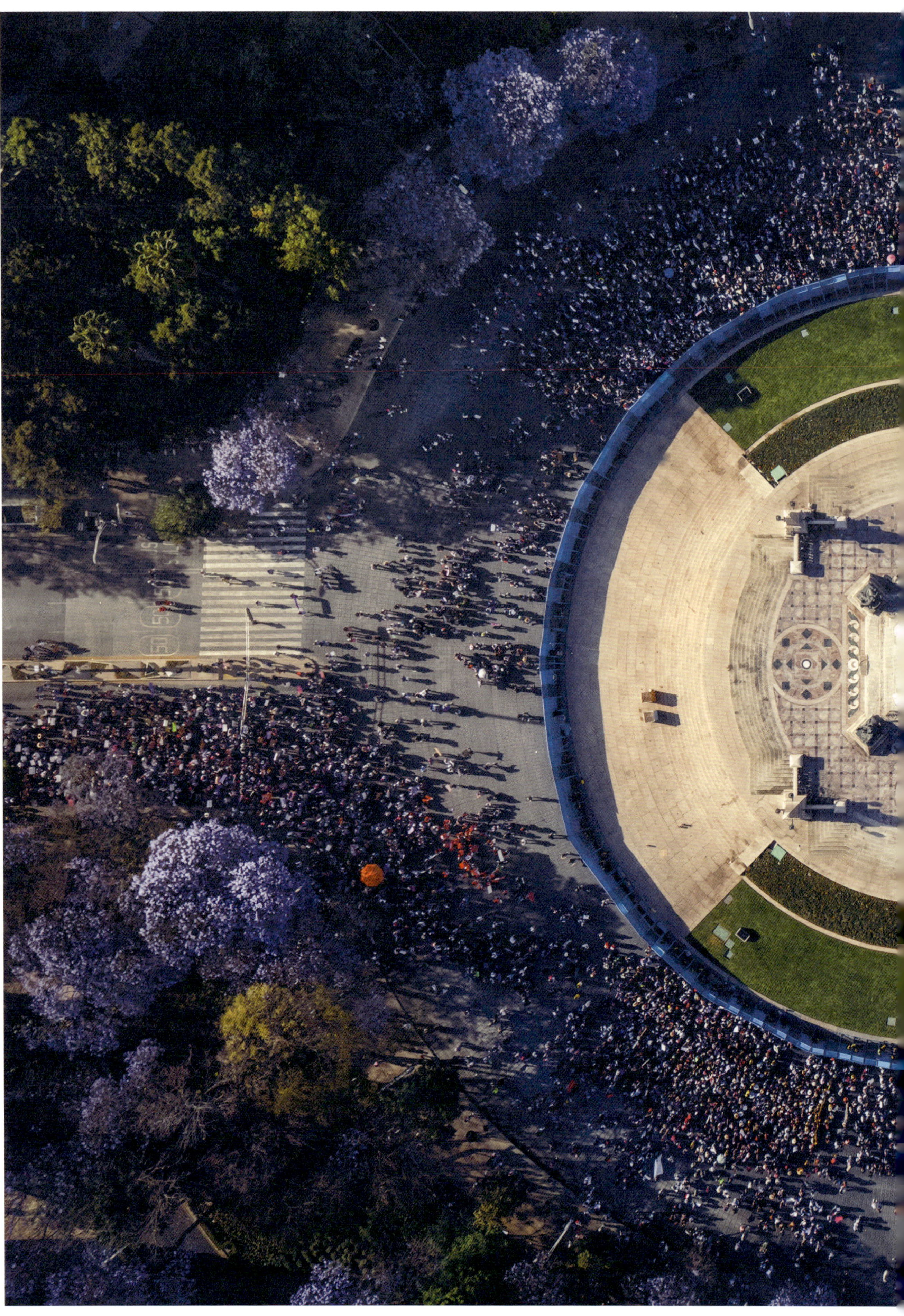

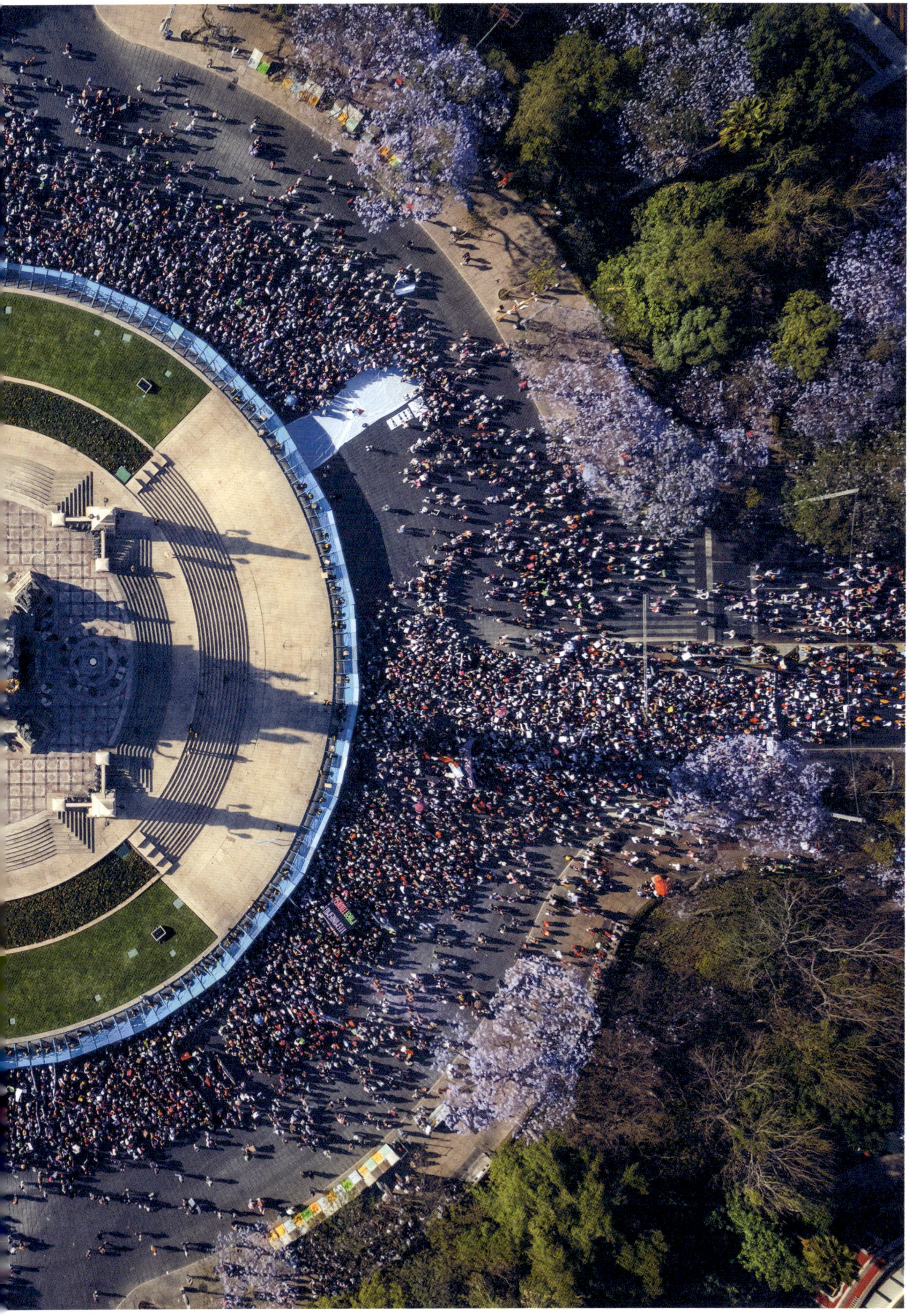

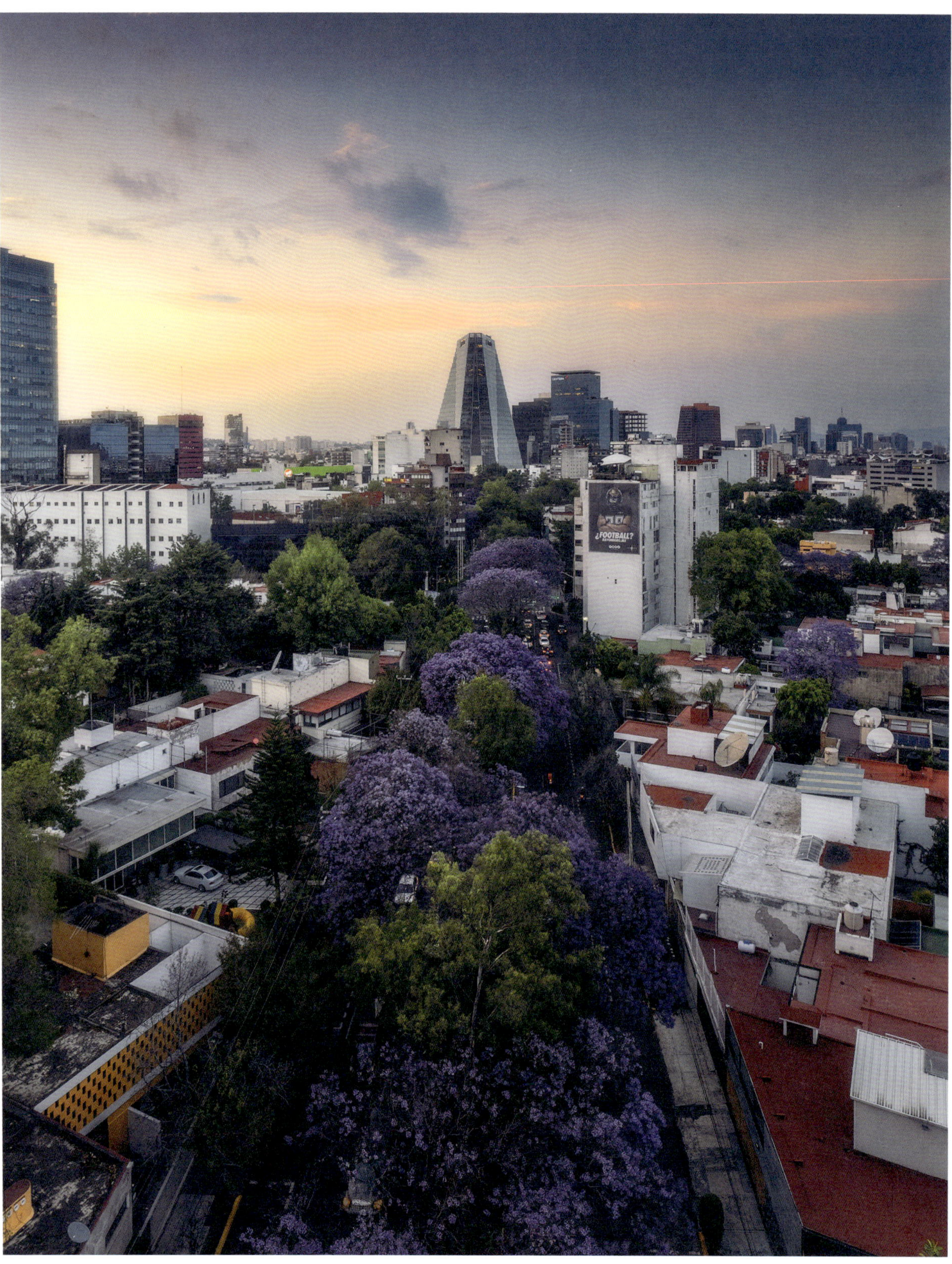
¿FOOTBALL?

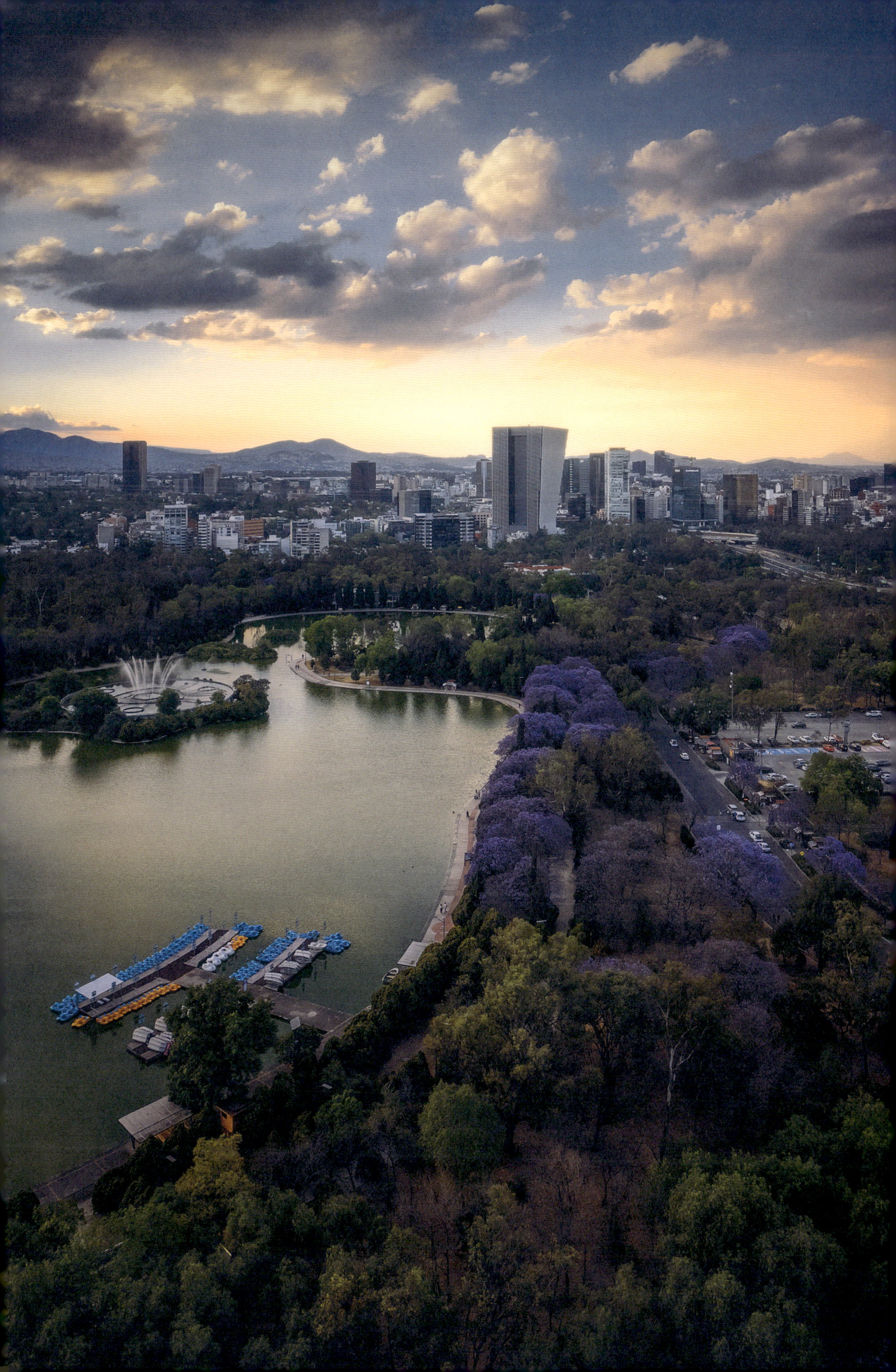

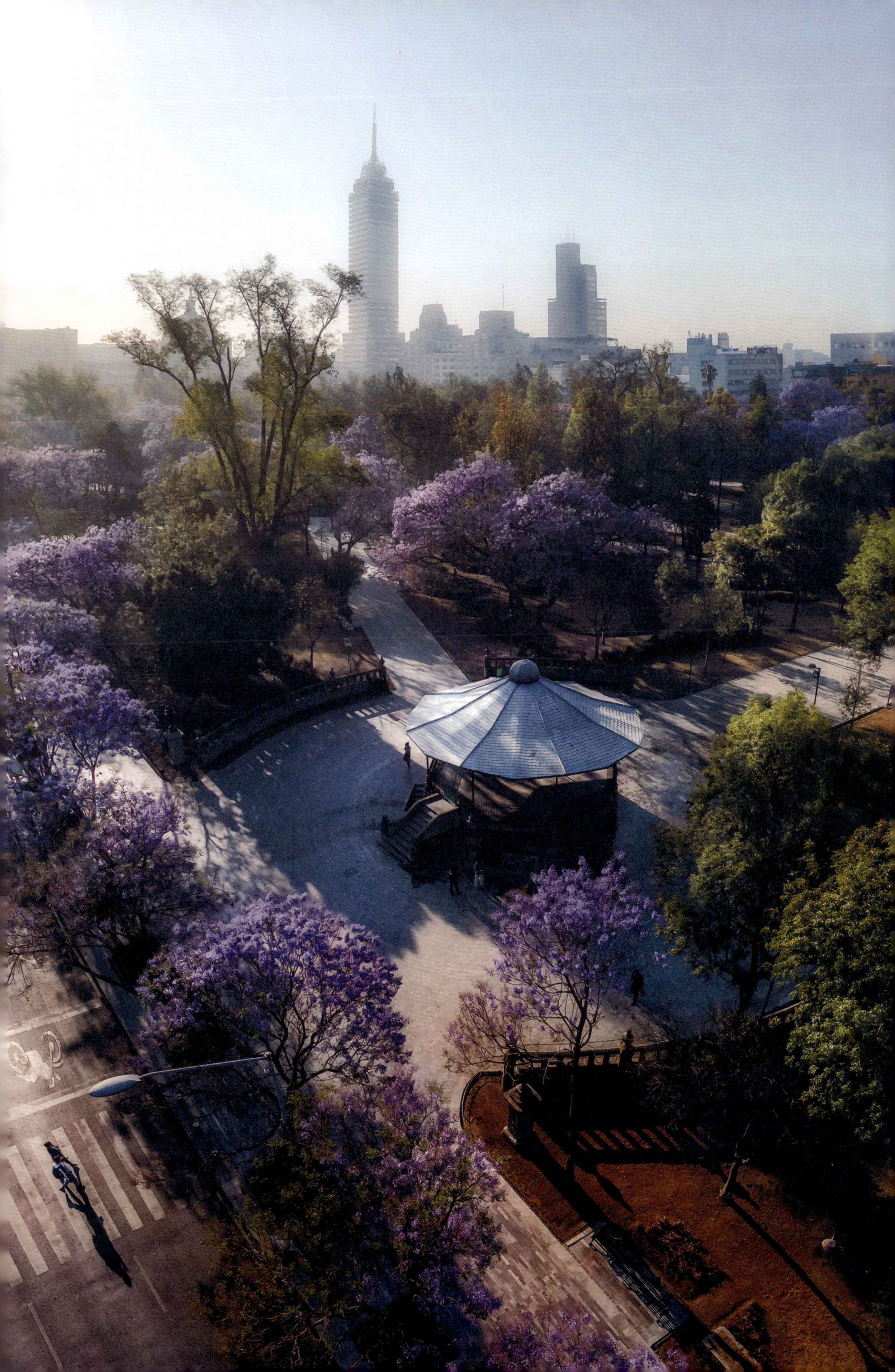

Mexico City is the most vibrant and exciting city in Latin America.

ANTHONY BOURDAIN

Chef and Author

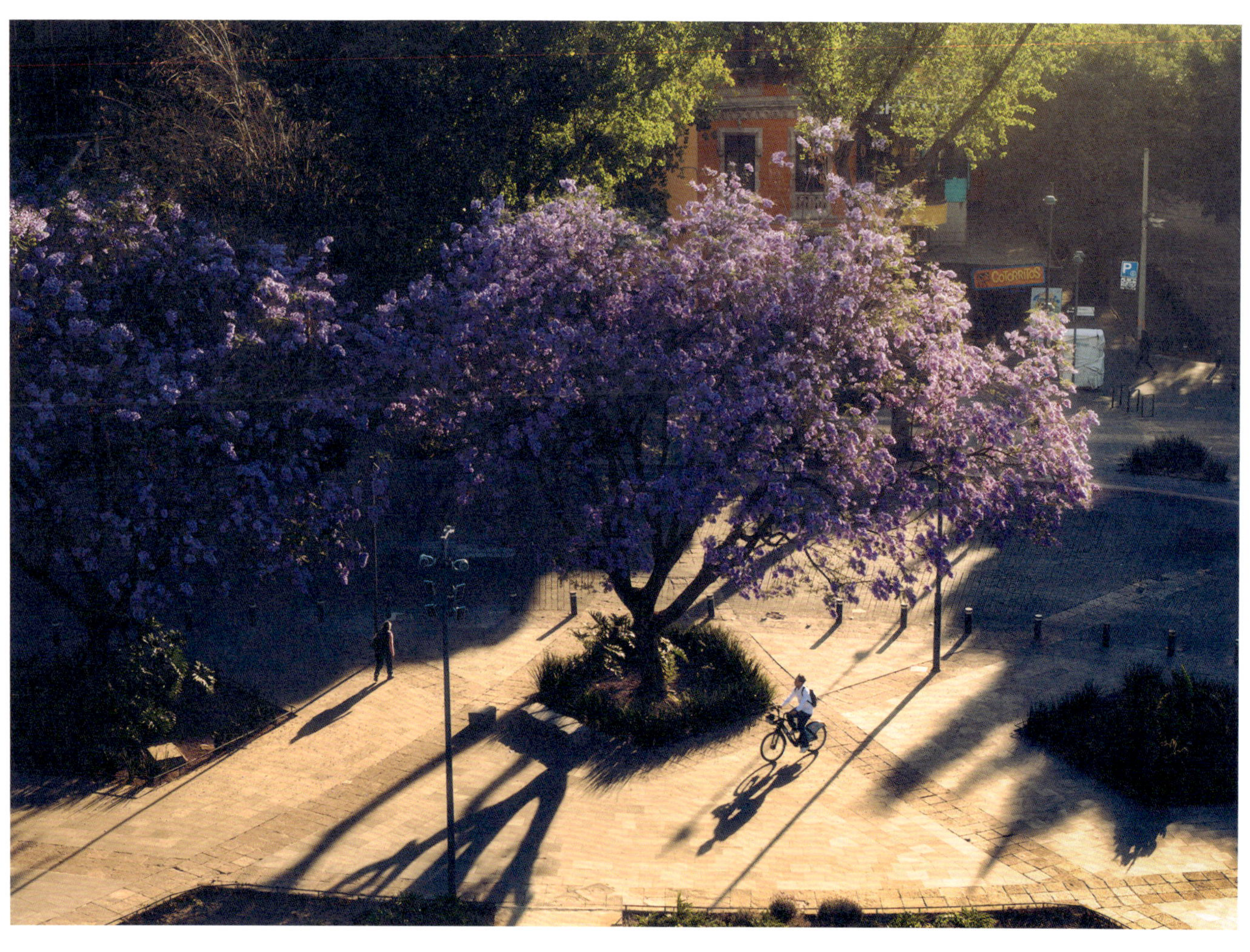
COTORRITOS
P

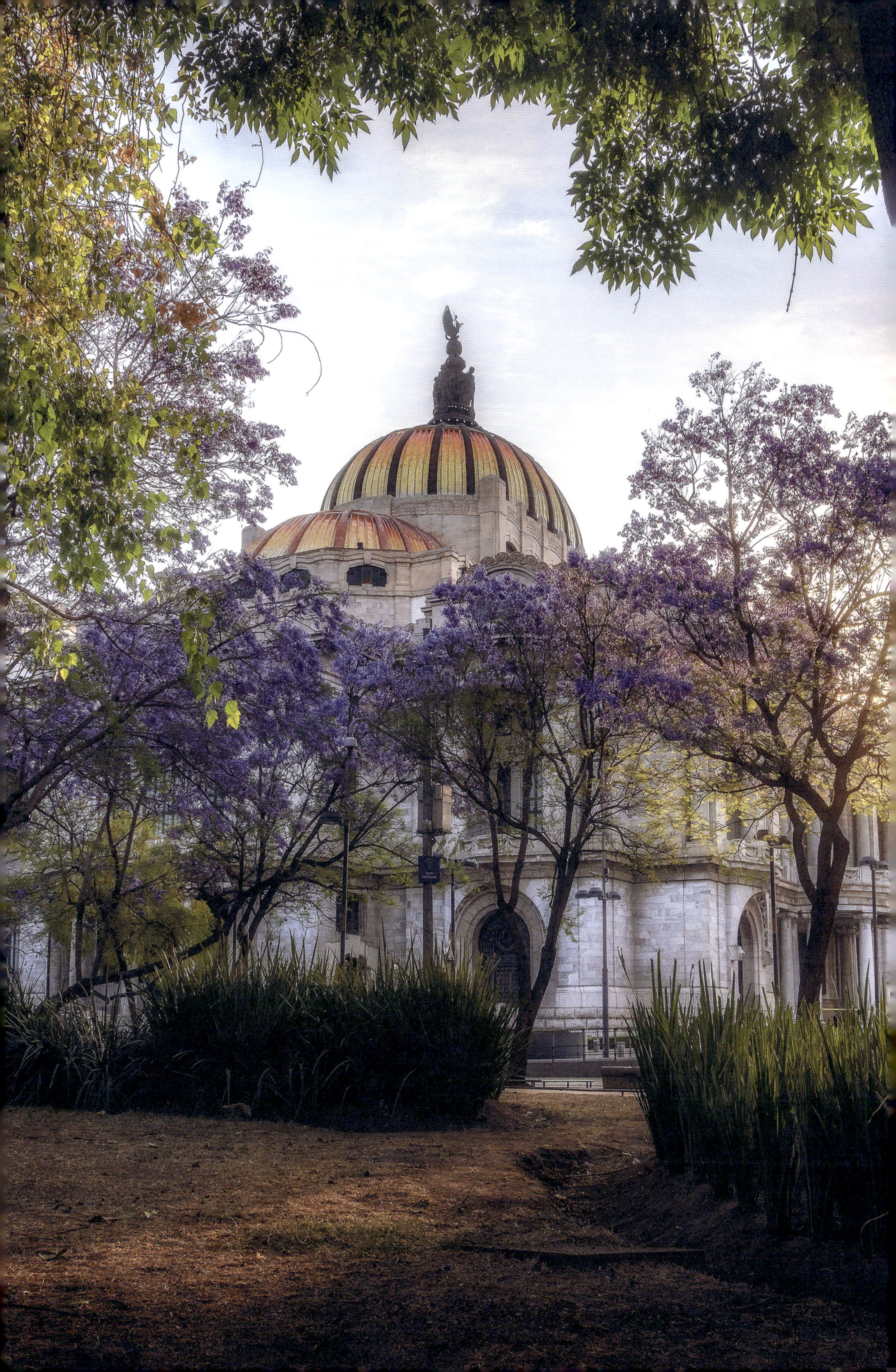

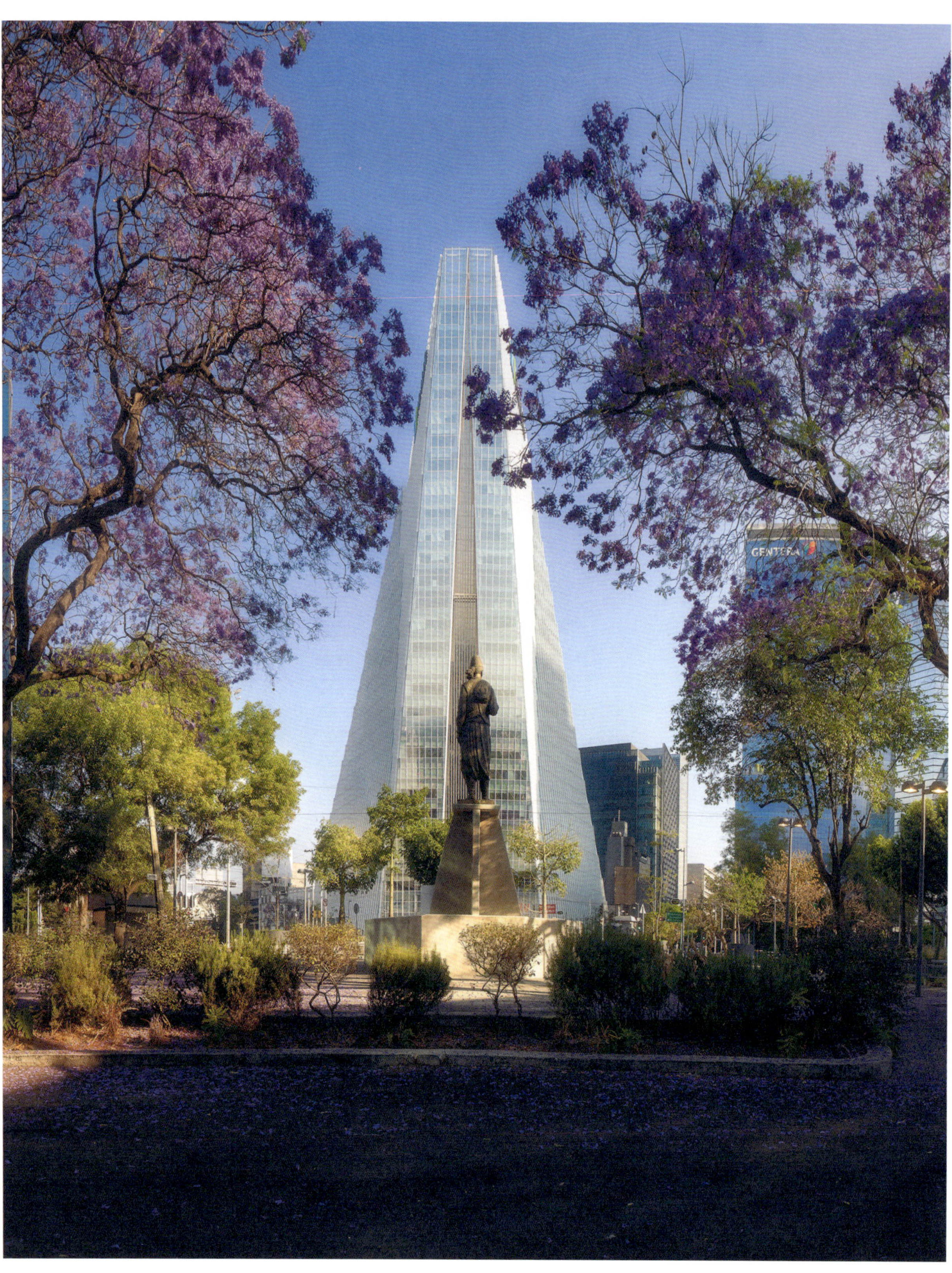
GENTERA

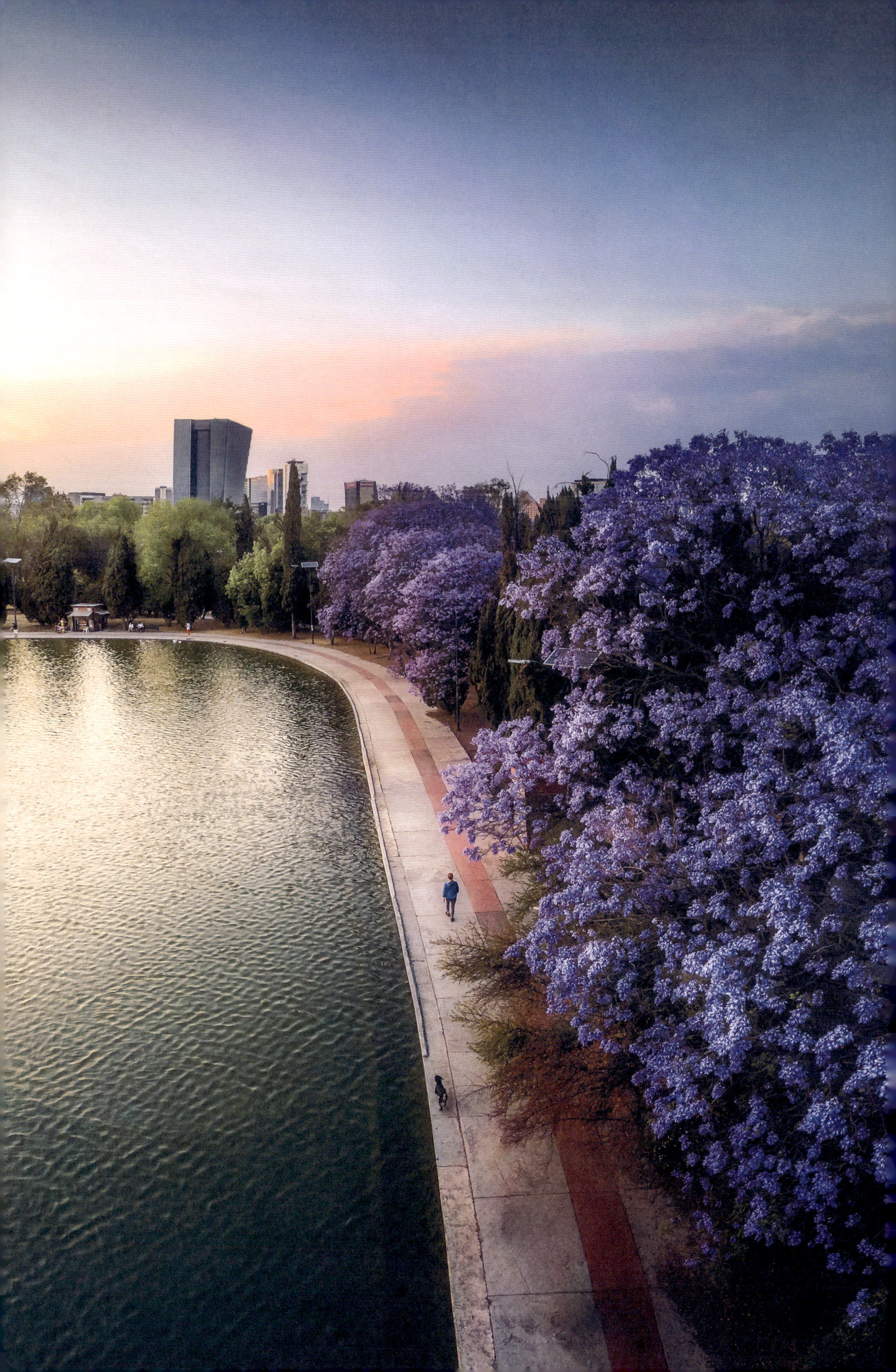

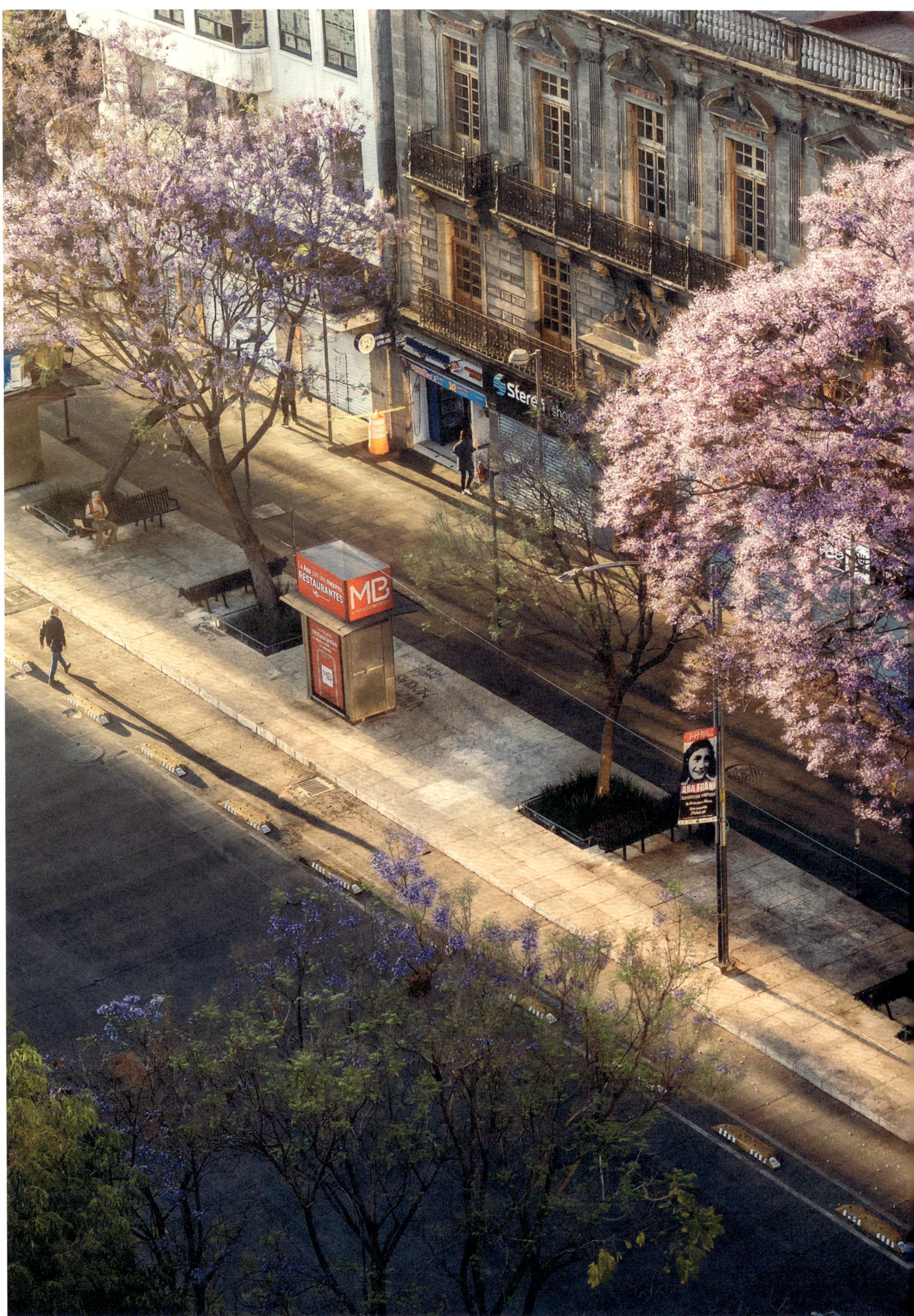
RESTAURANTES
MB

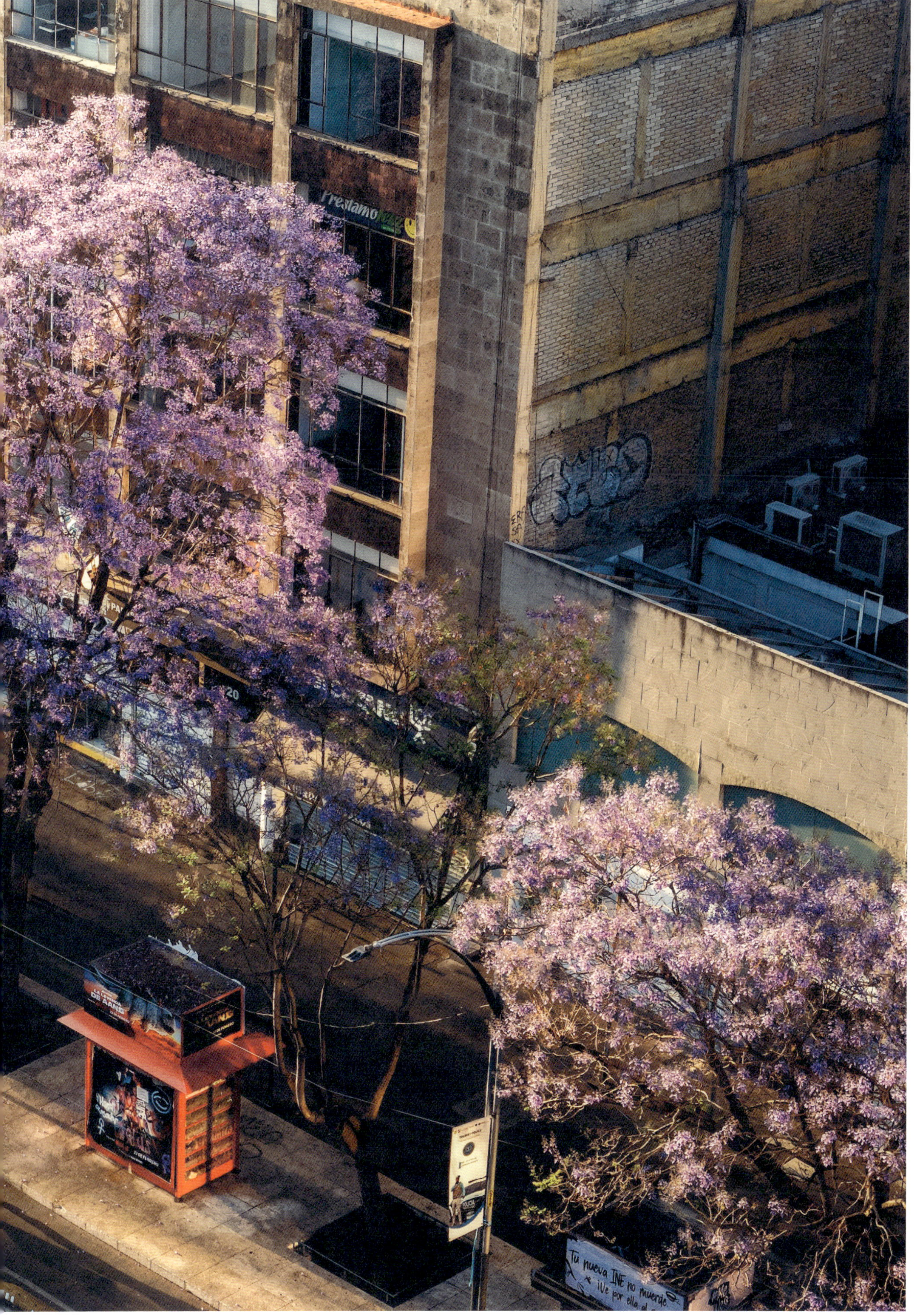
Prestamo
Tu nueva INE no muerde
¡Ve por ella al

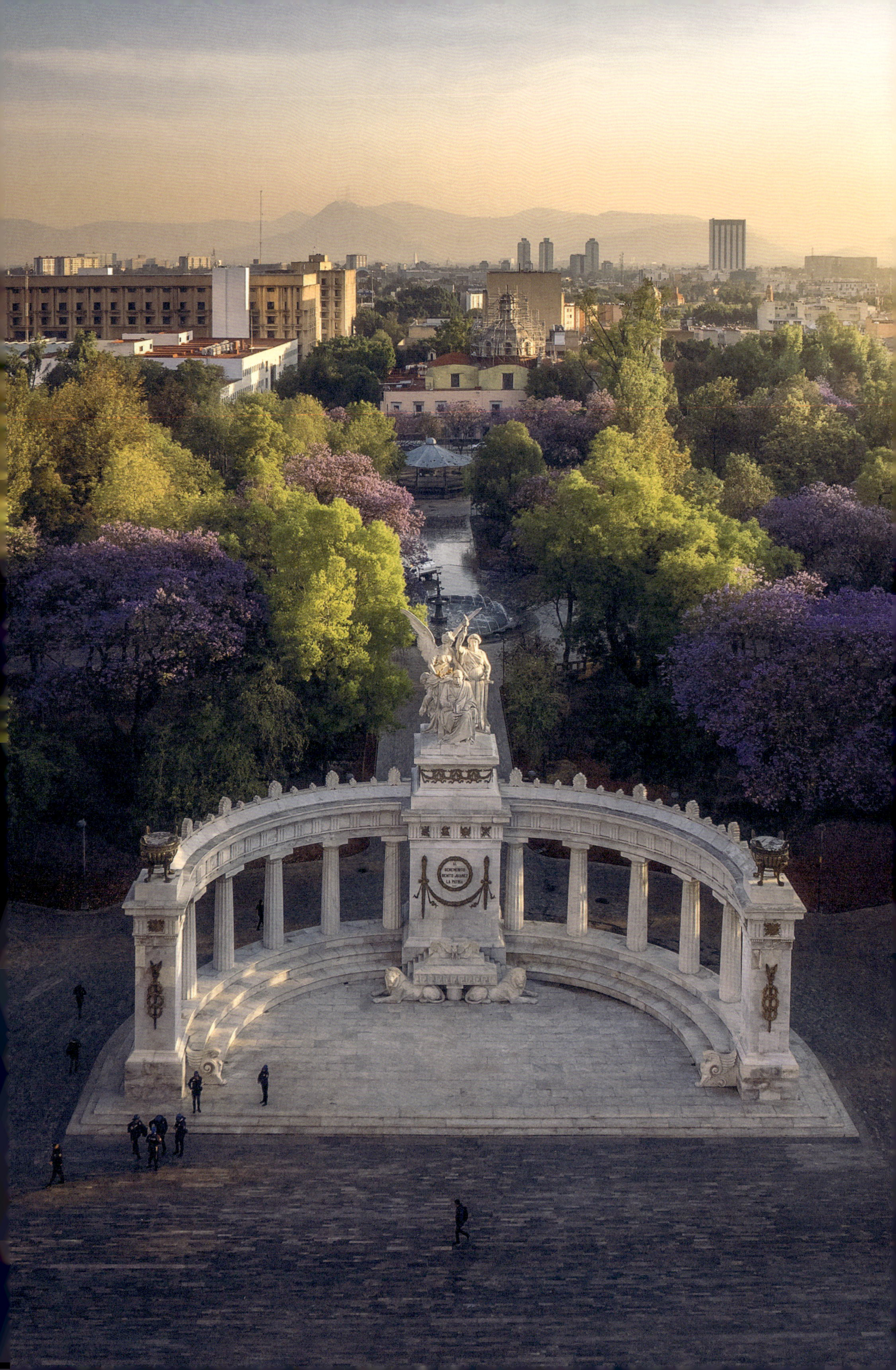

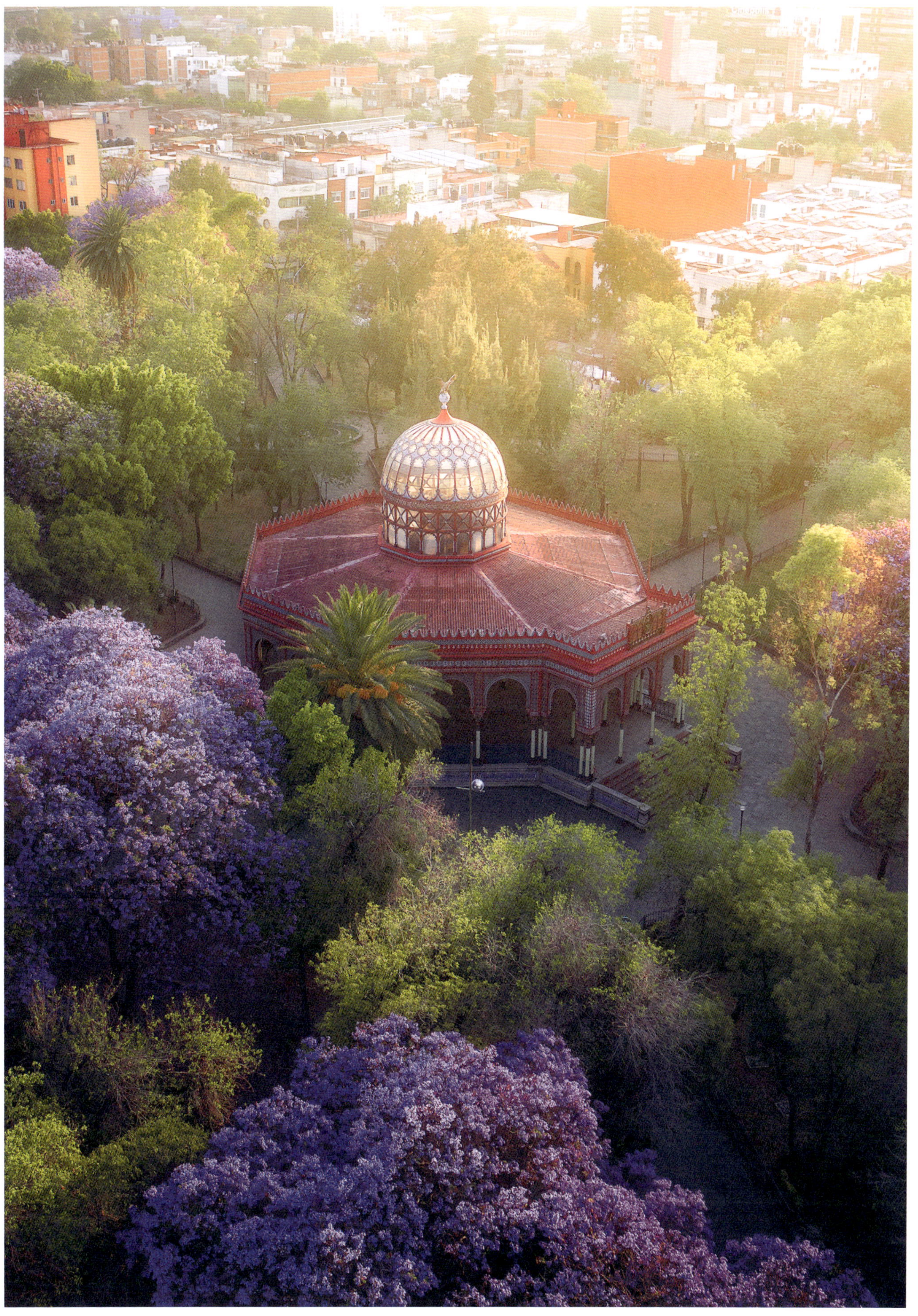

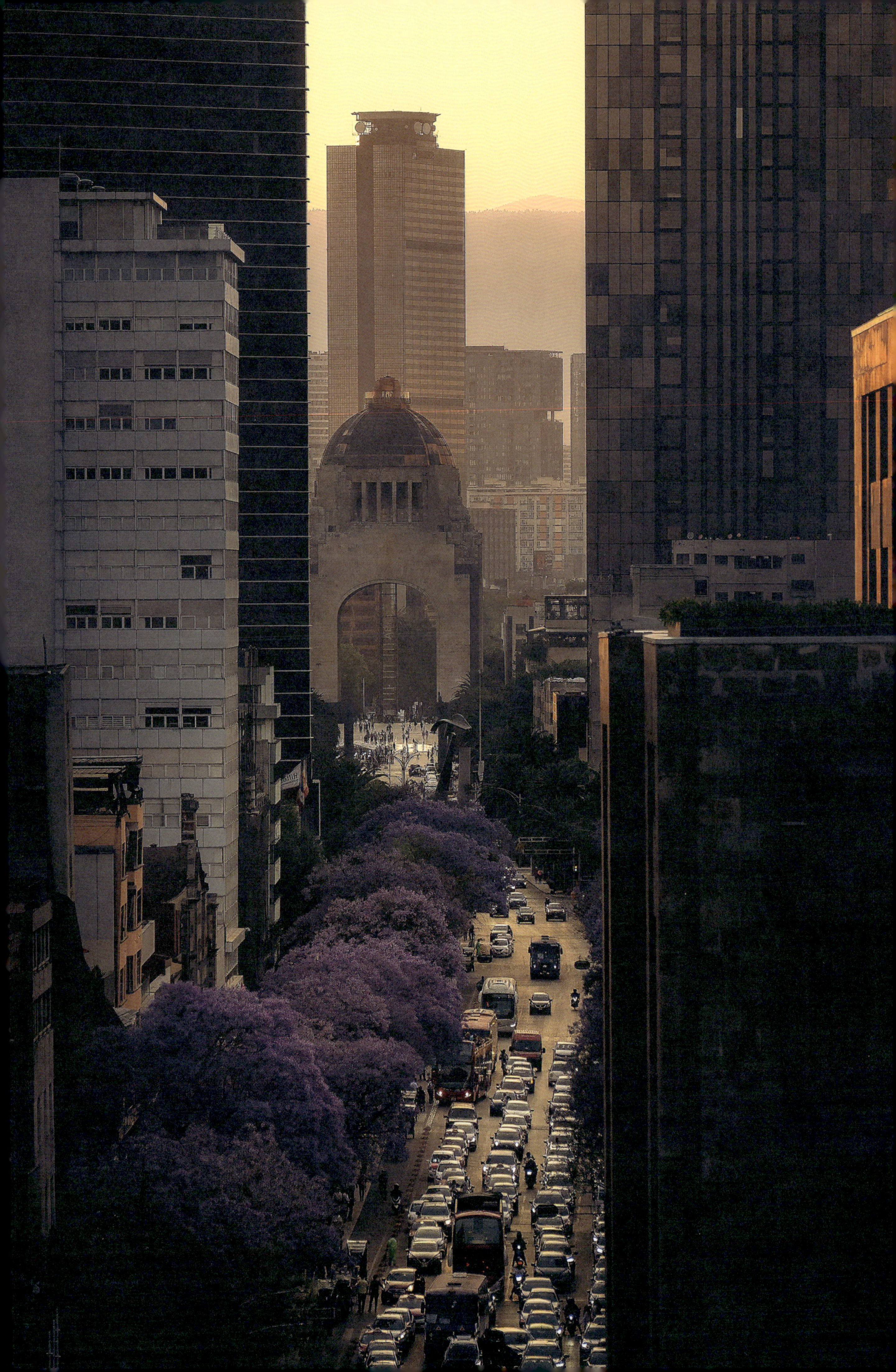

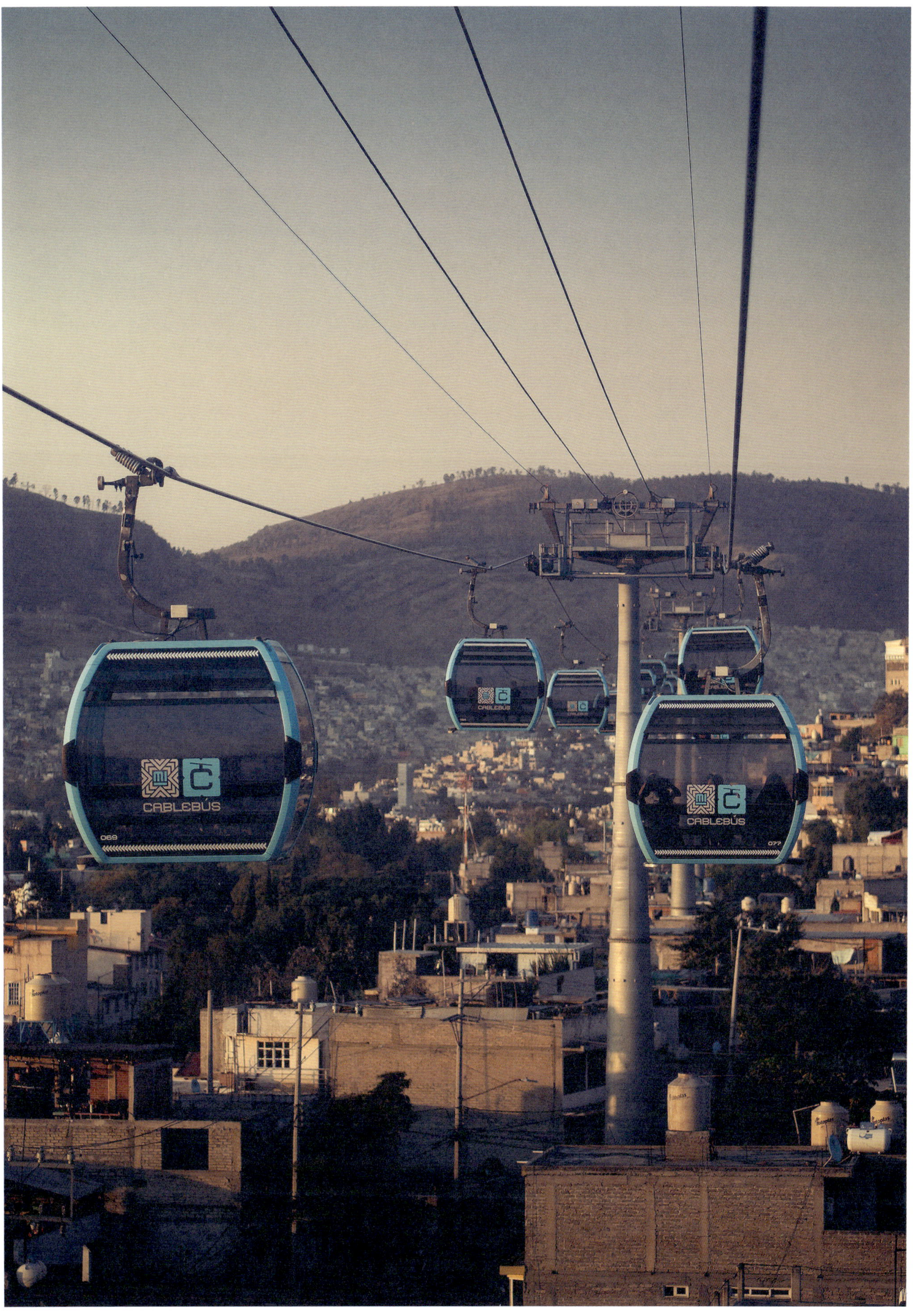
CABLEBÚS
CABLEBÚS
CABLEBÚS

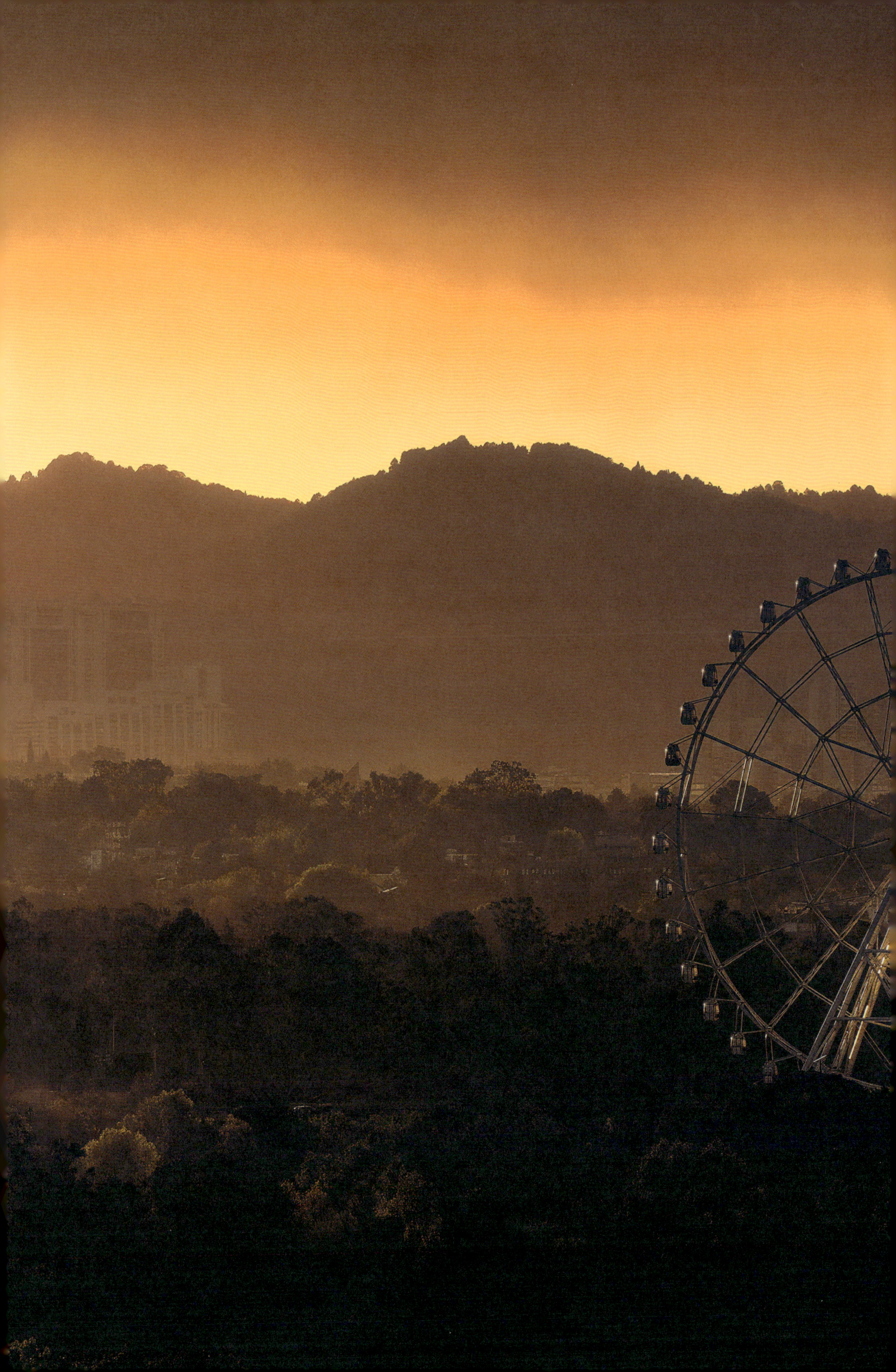

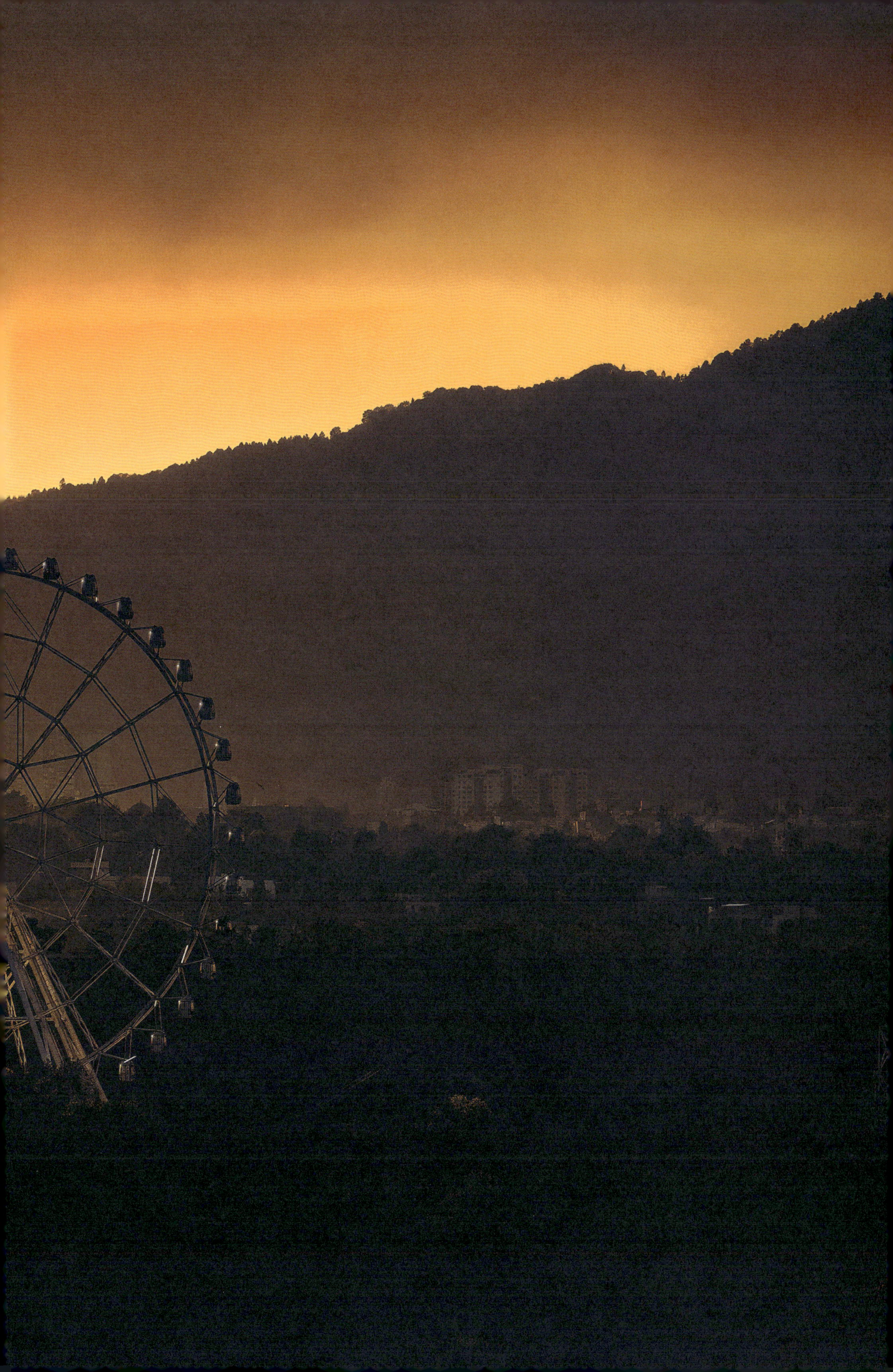

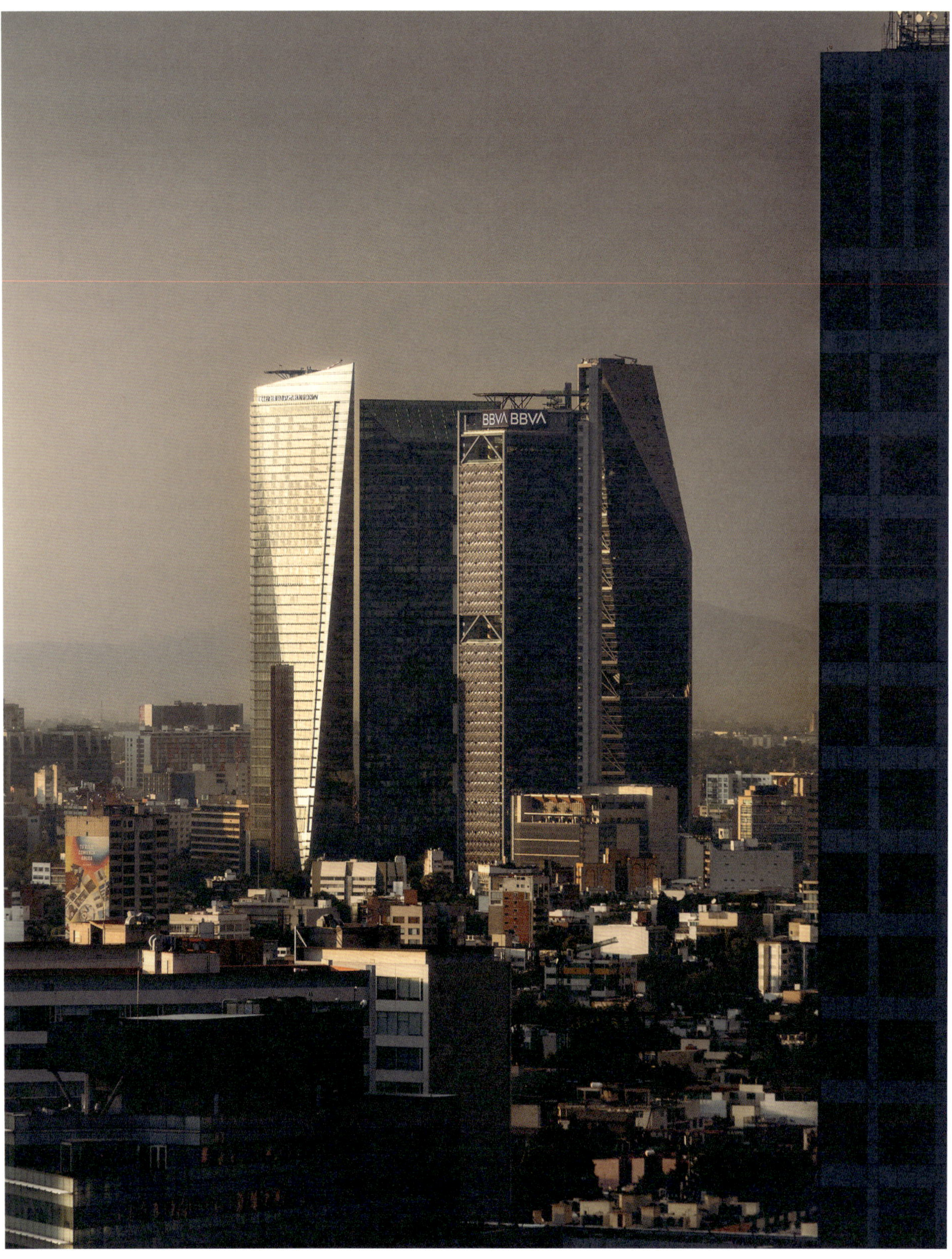
BBVA BBVA

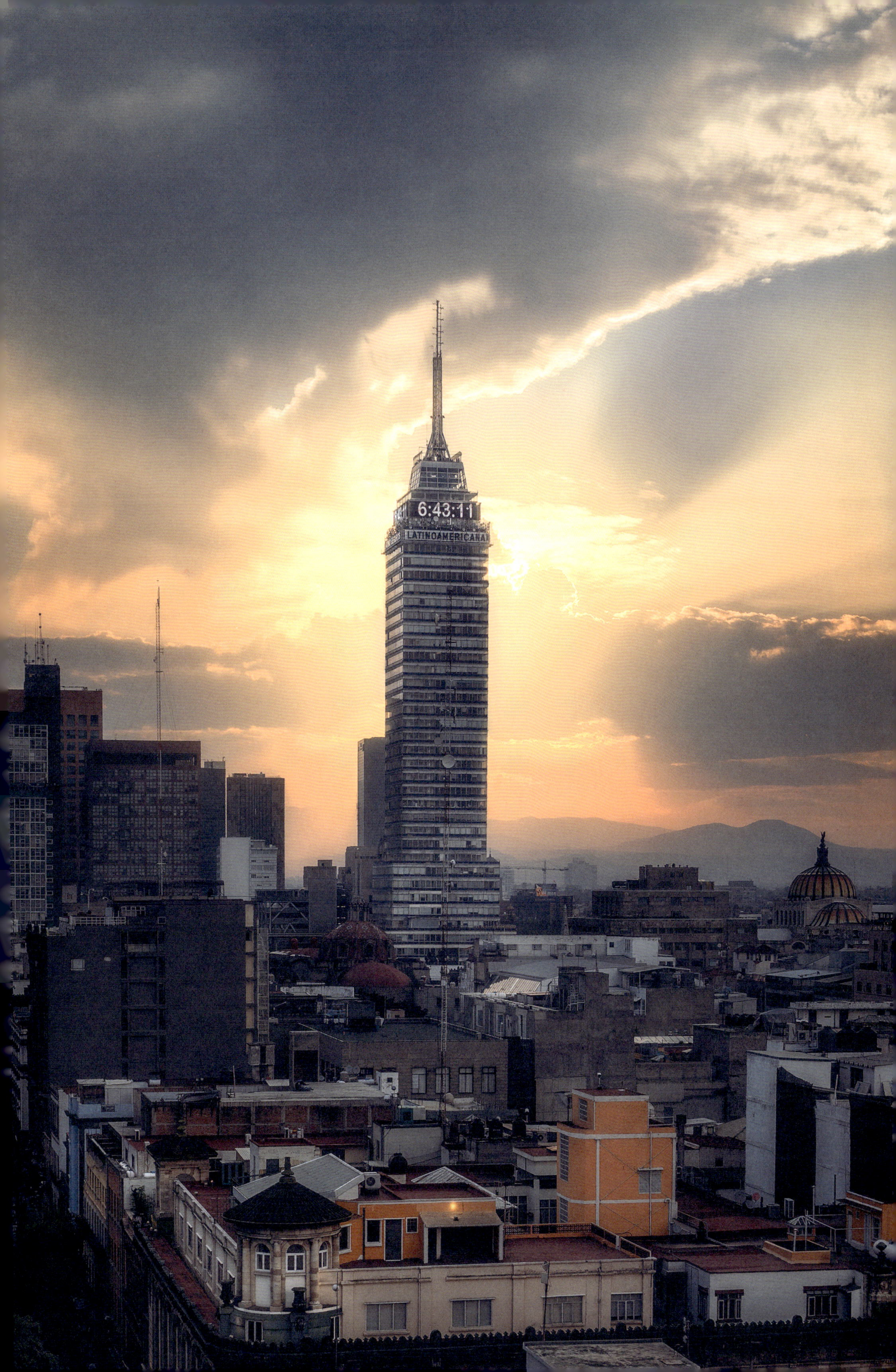
6:43:11
LATINOAMERICANA

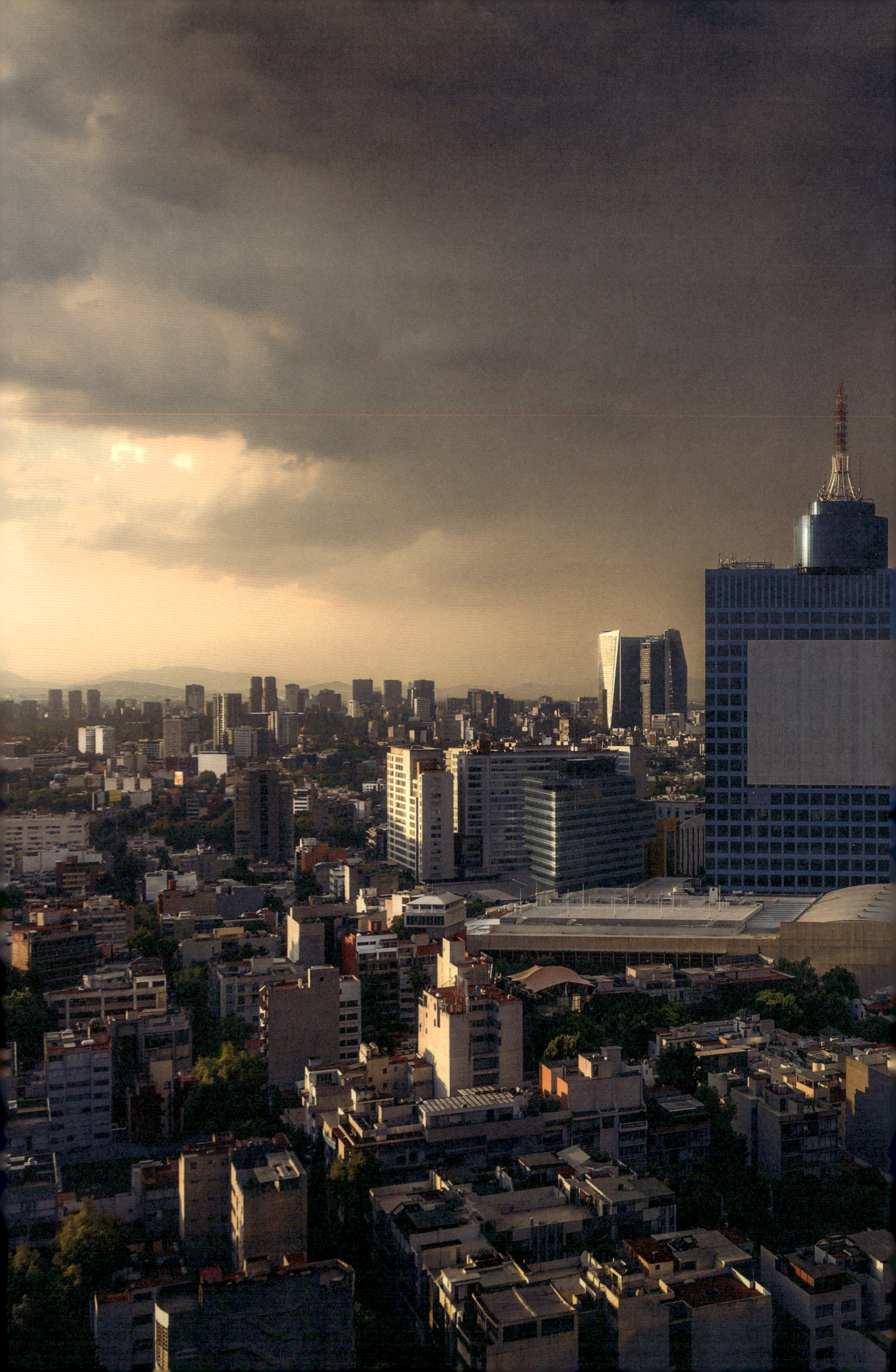

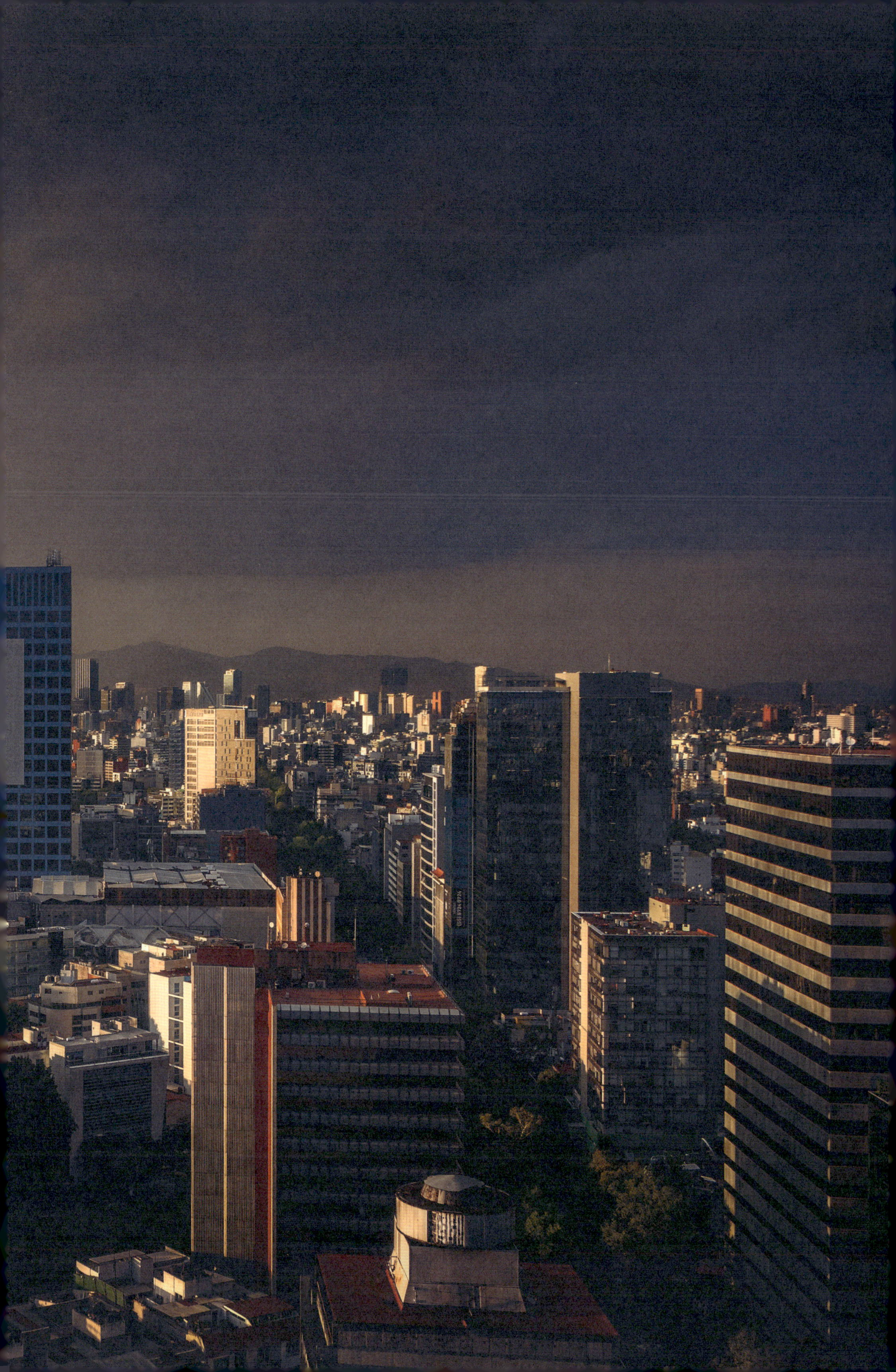

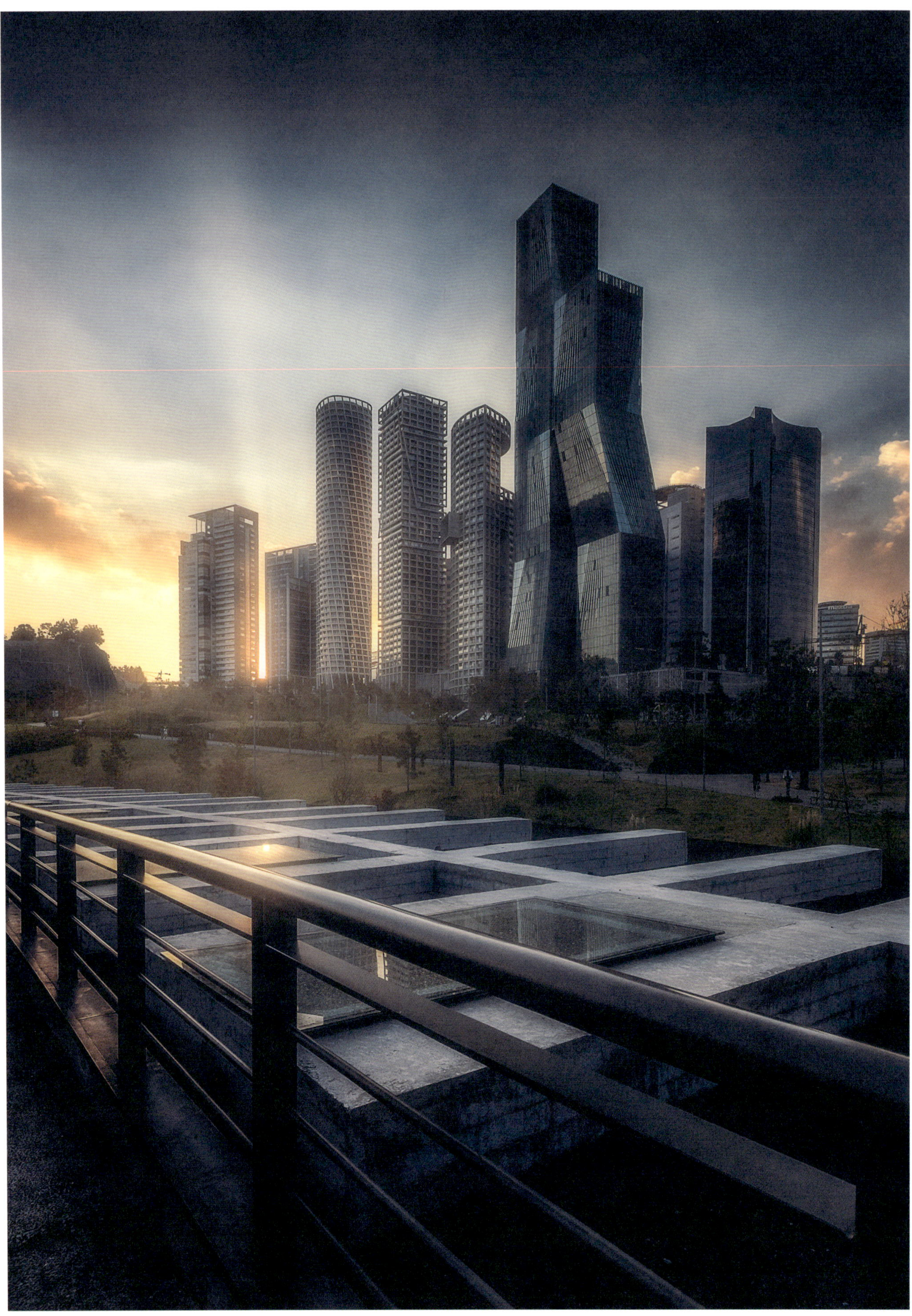

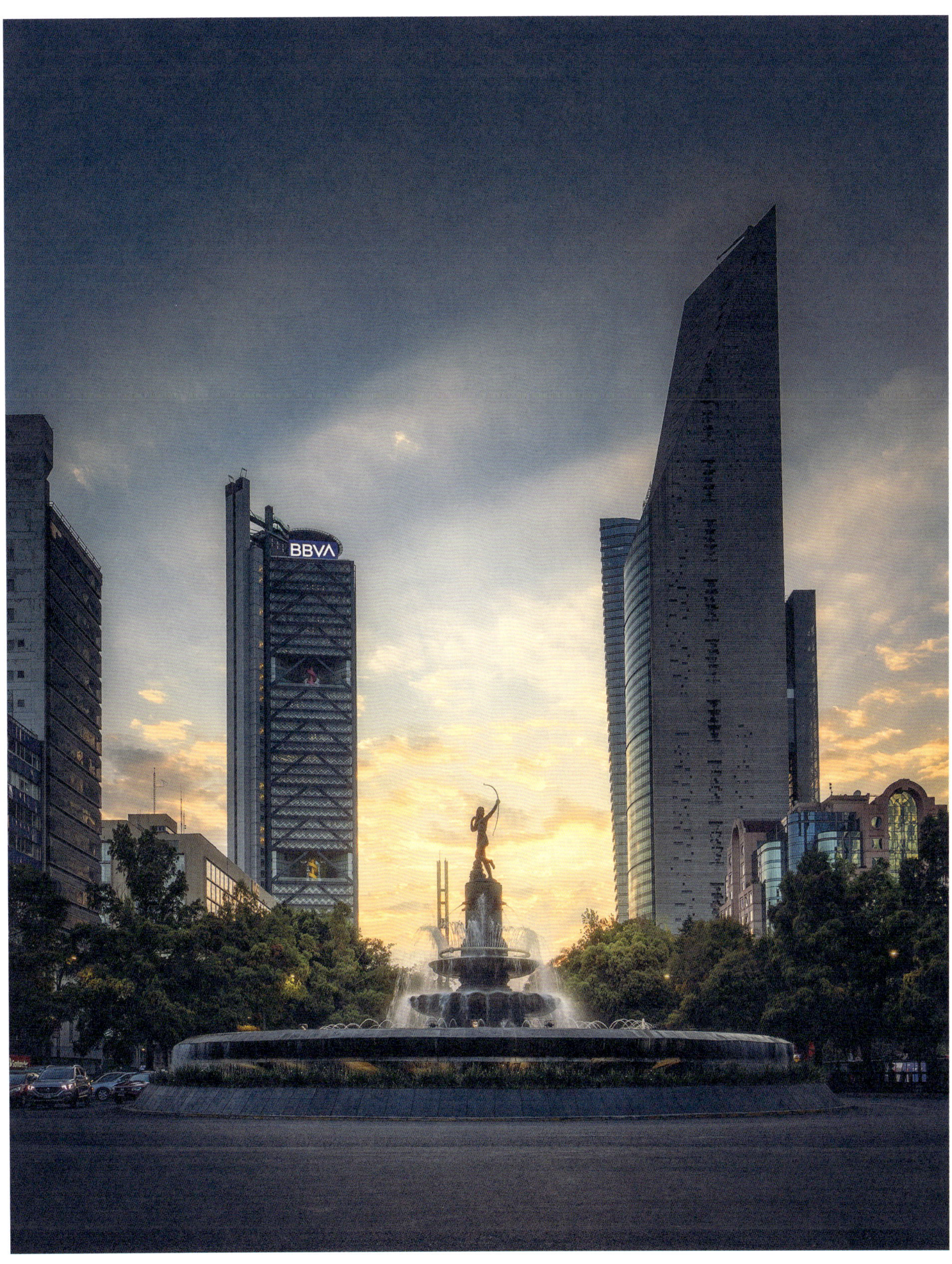
BBVA

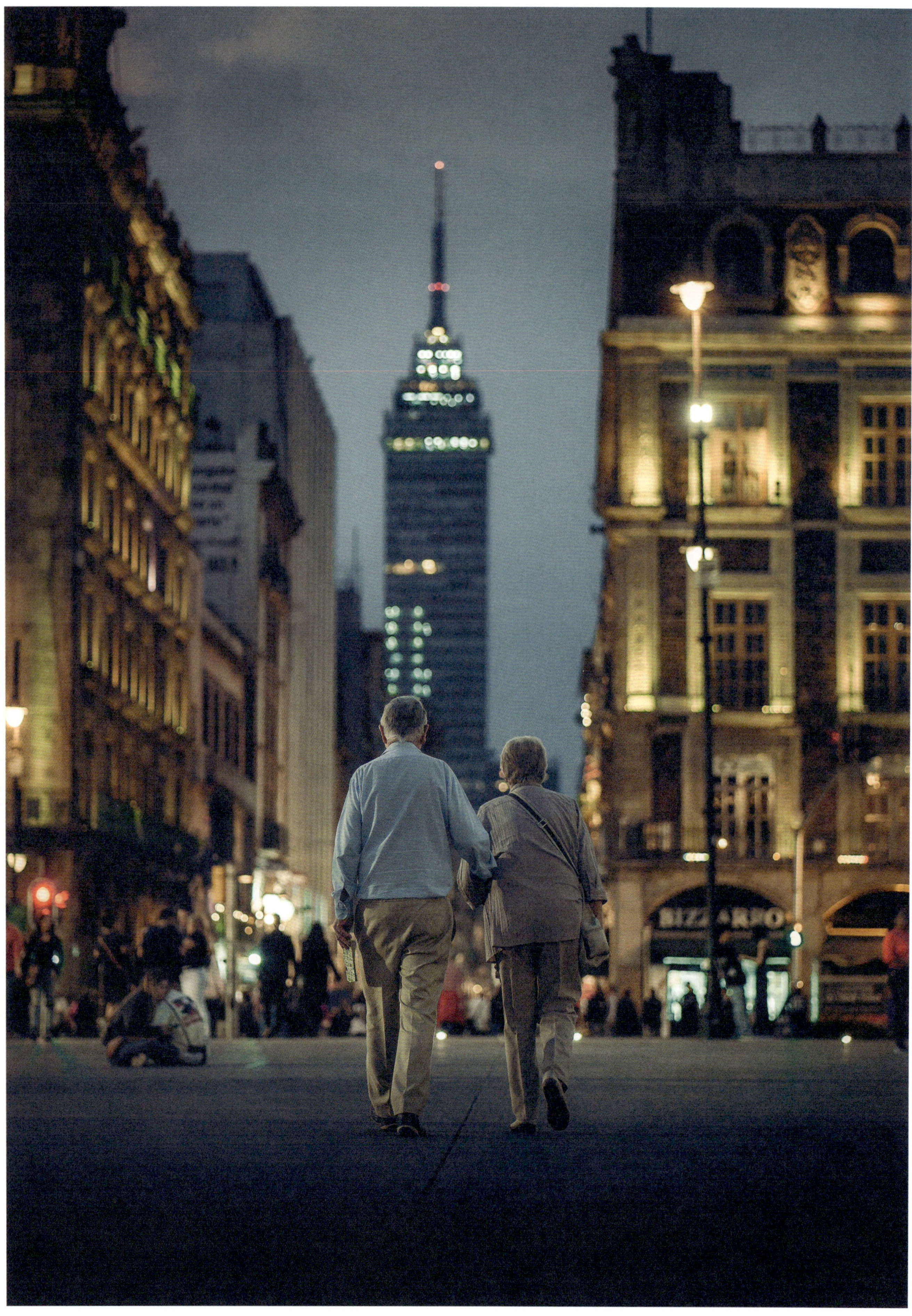

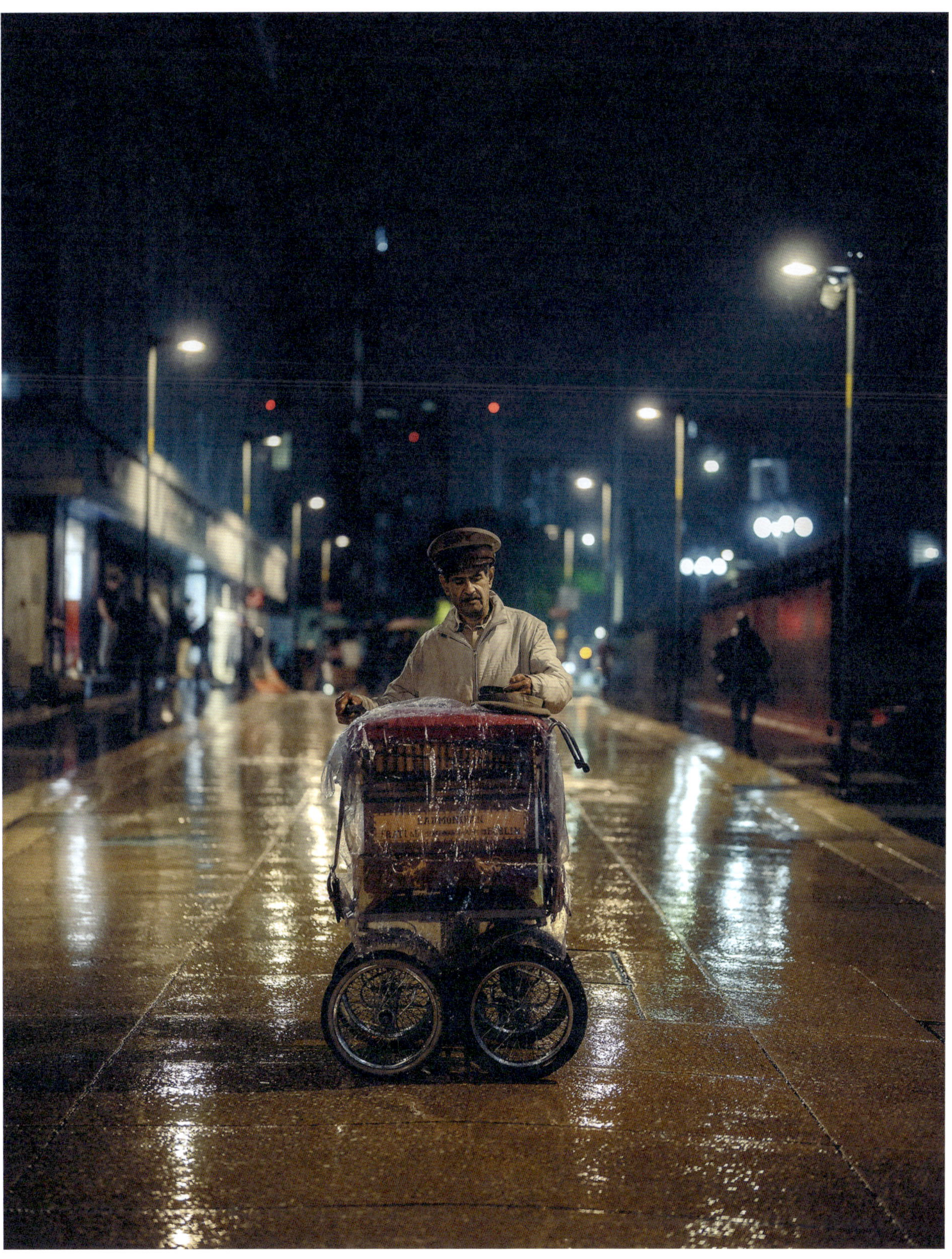

As a city, it is always compelling.
But every day in Mexico City,
I give thanks that I am alive.

ALEJANDRO GONZÁLEZ IÑÁRRITU

Mexican Filmmaker

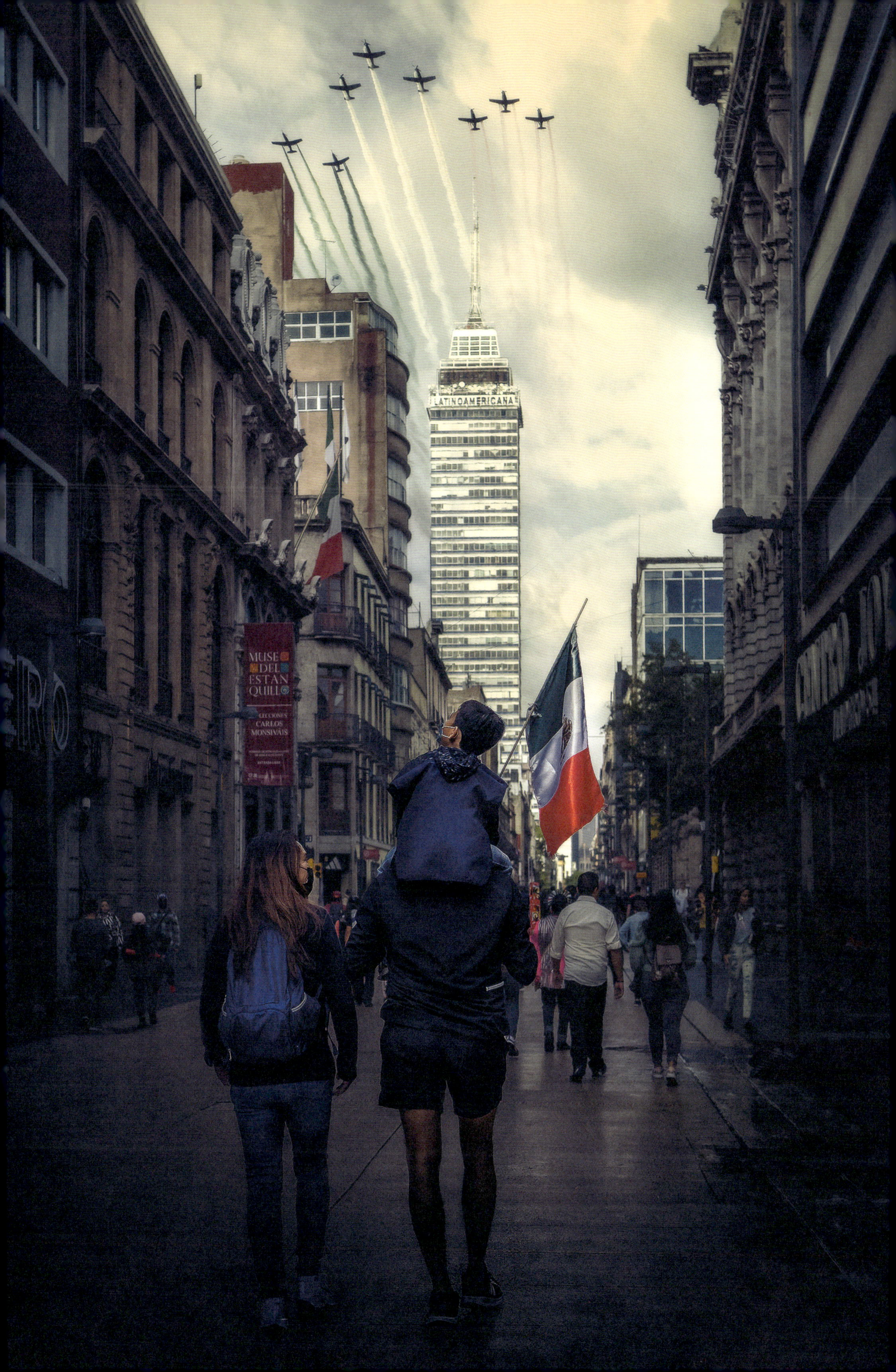
LATINOAMERICANA
MUSE DEL ESTAN QUILL
CARLOS
MONSIVÁIS

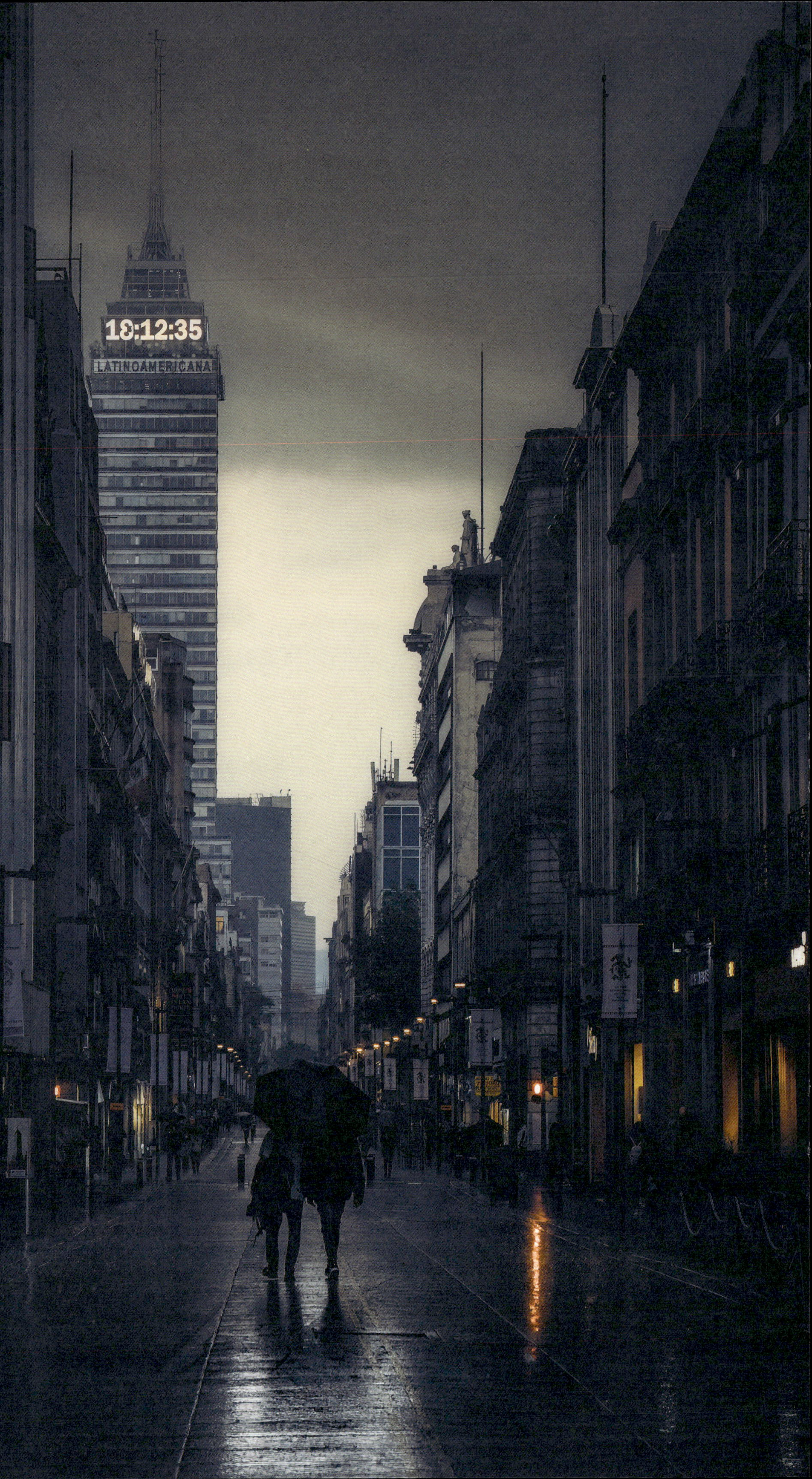
18:12:35
LATINOAMERICANA

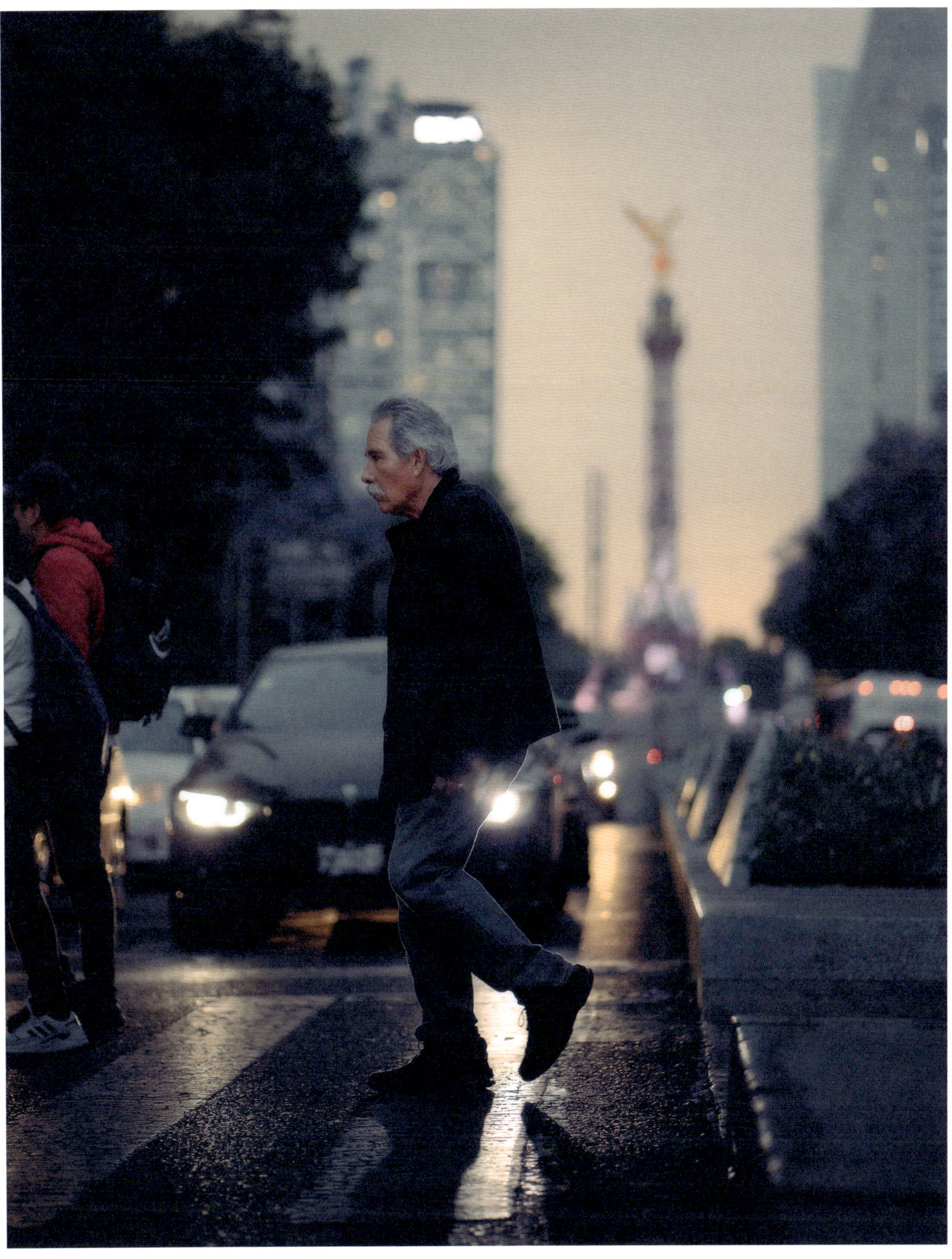

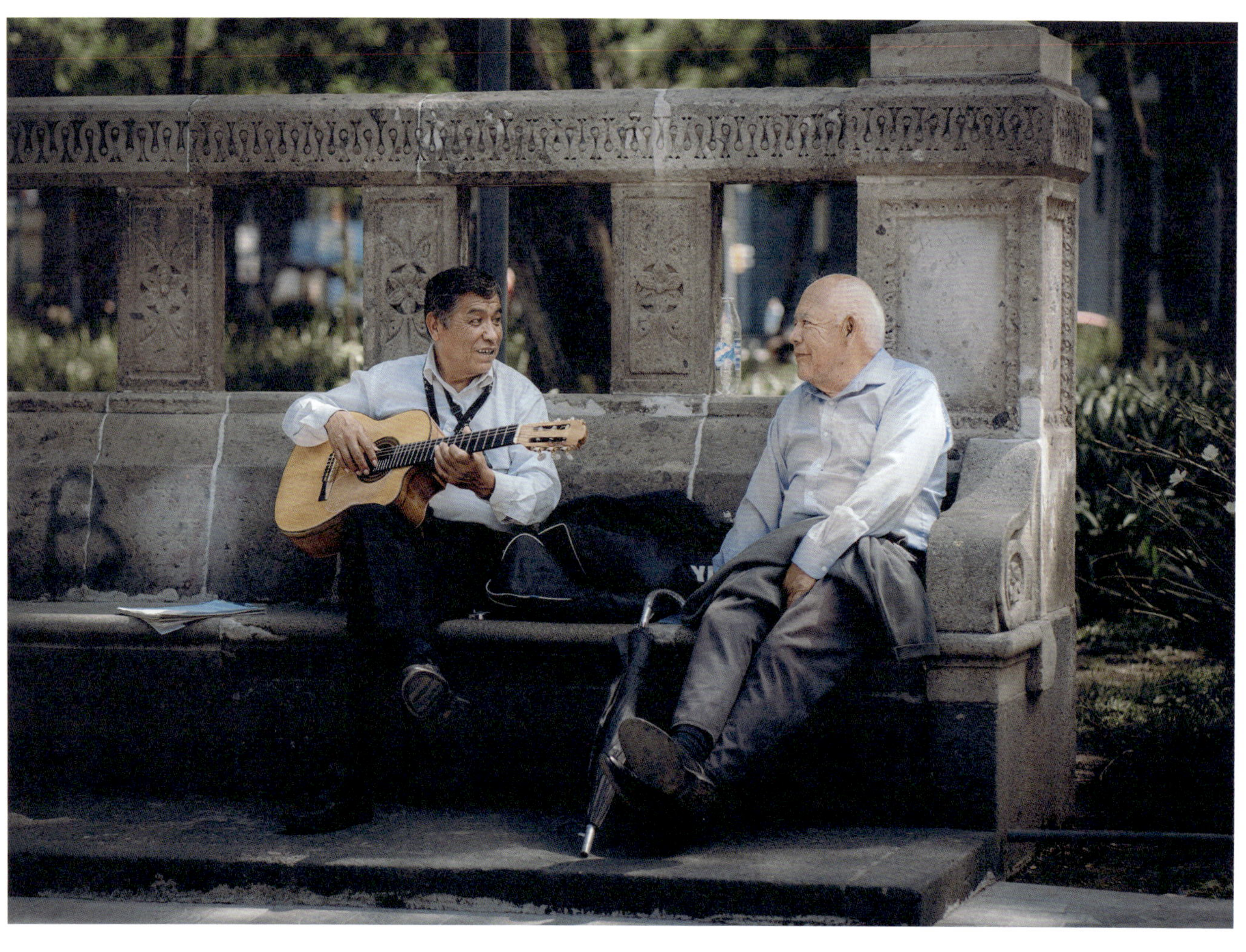

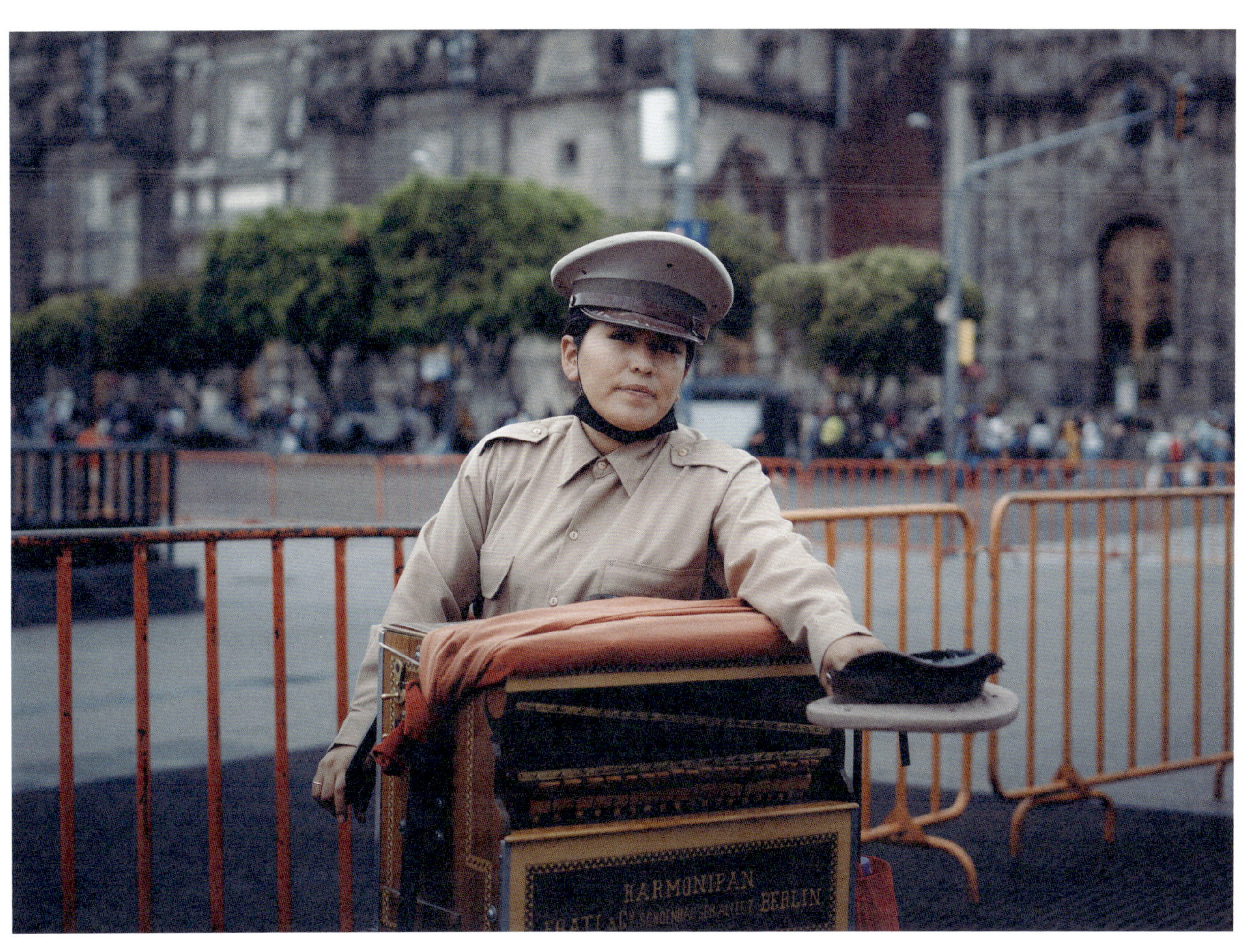
HARMONIPAN
BERLIN

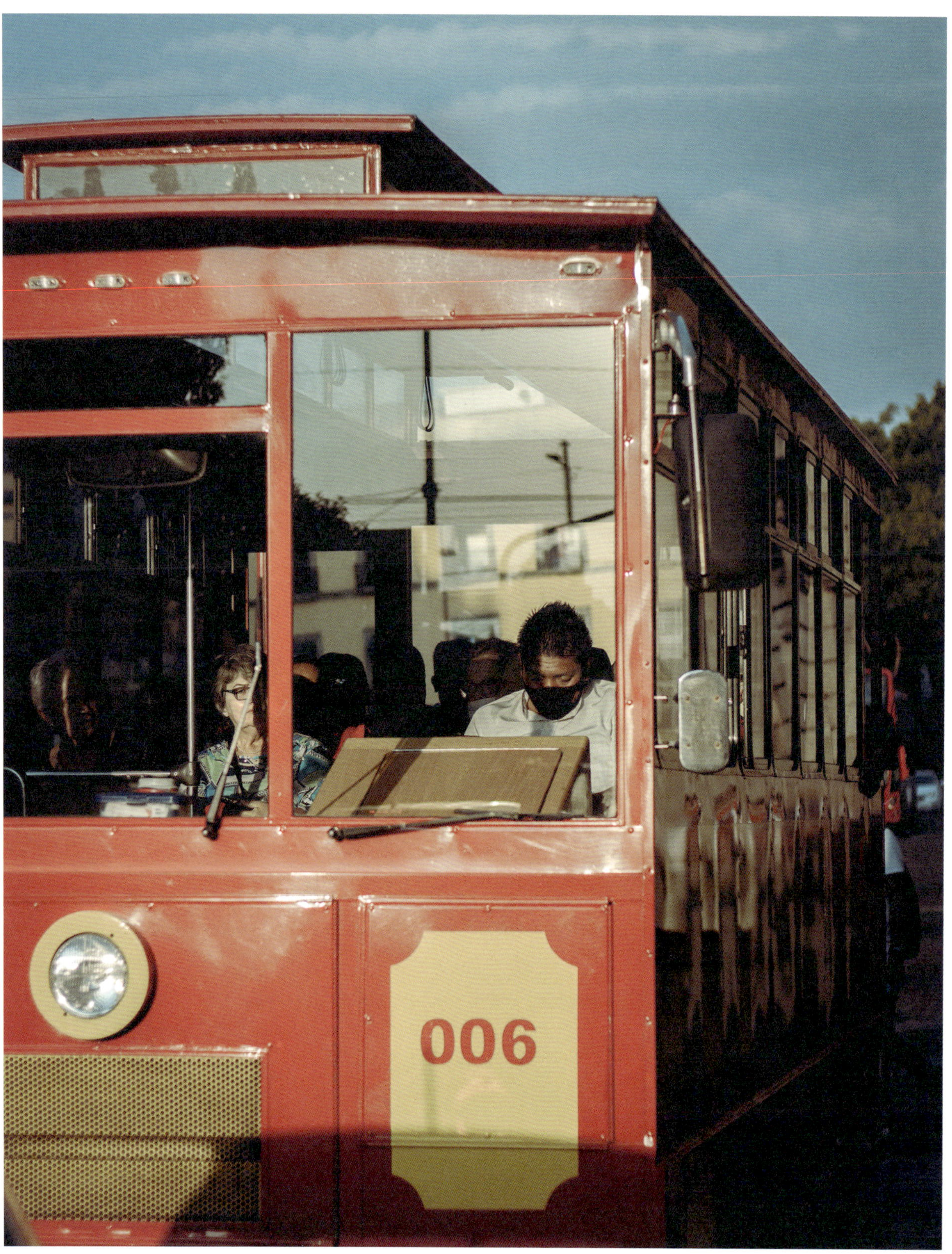
006

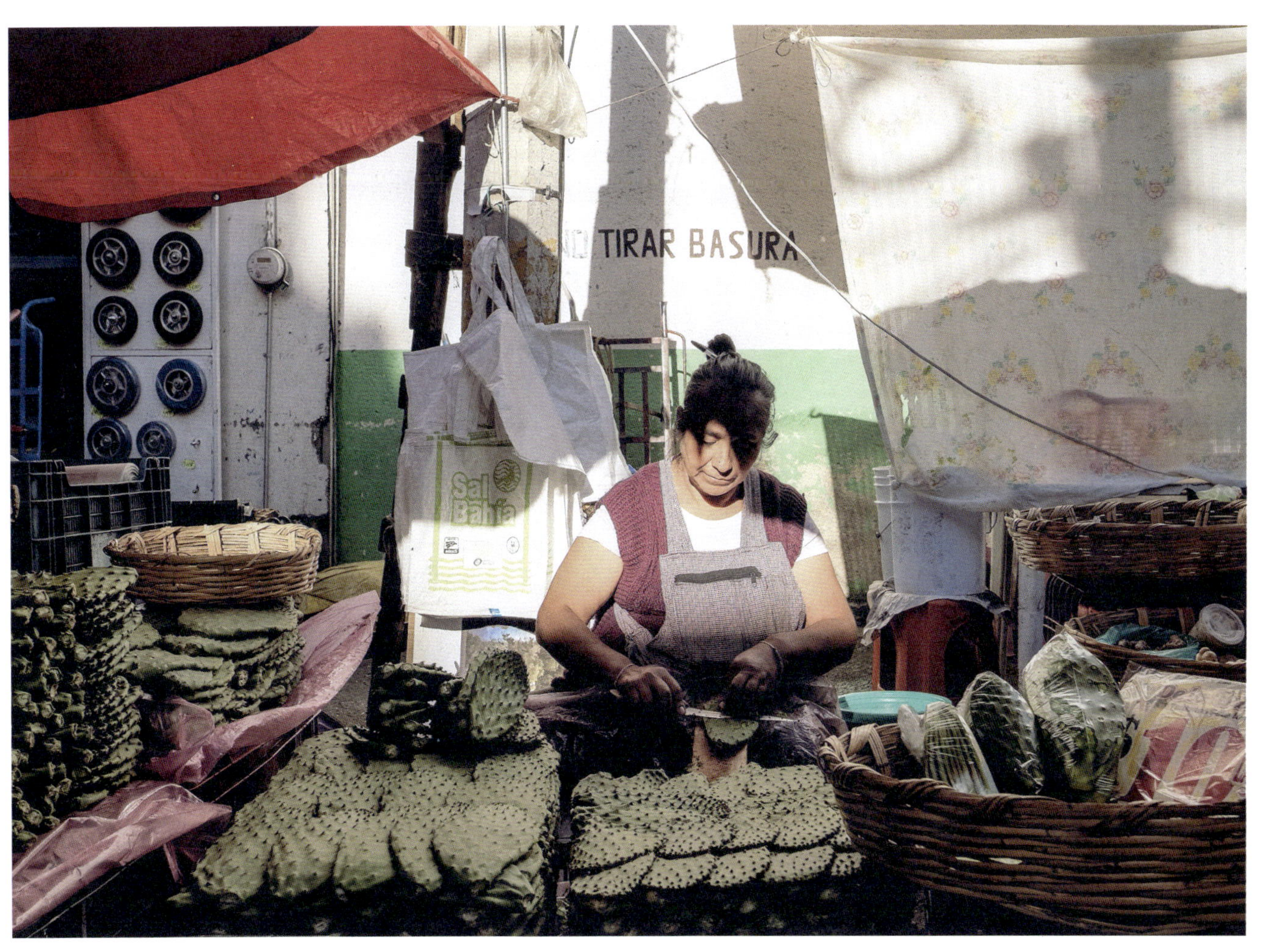
TIRAR BASURA
Sal Bahía

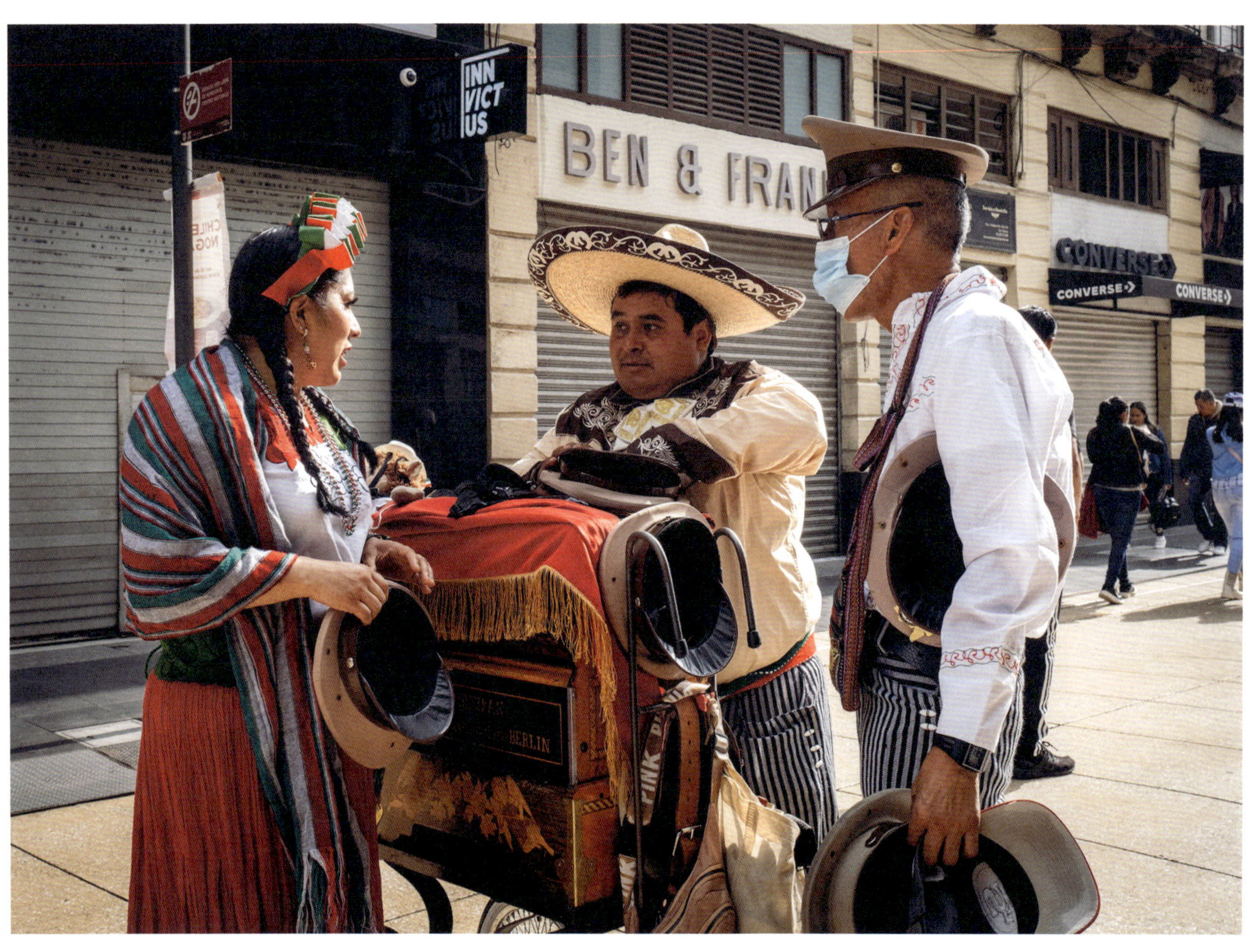
INN
VICT
US
BEN & FRAN
CONVERSE
CONVERSE
CONVERSE
BERLIN

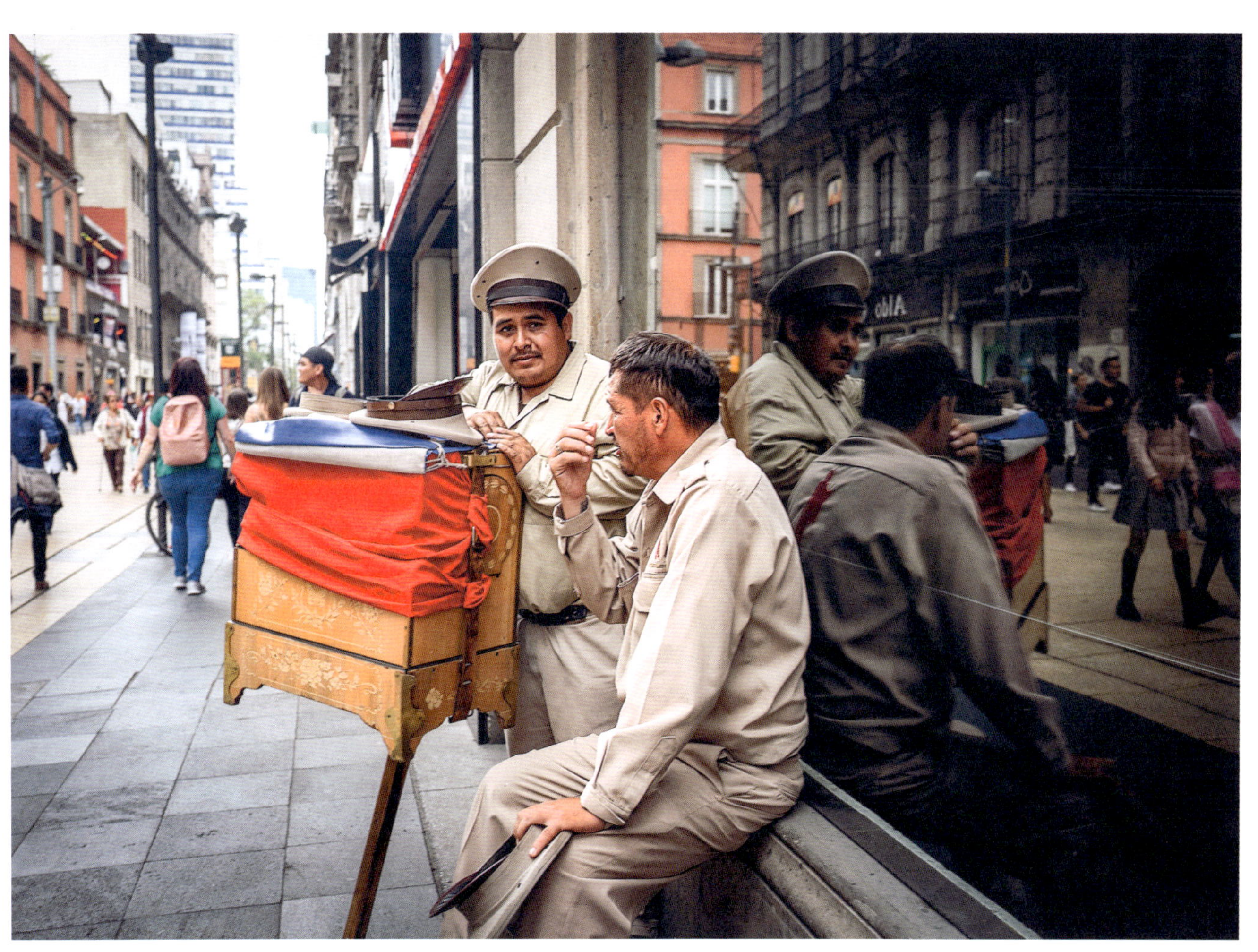

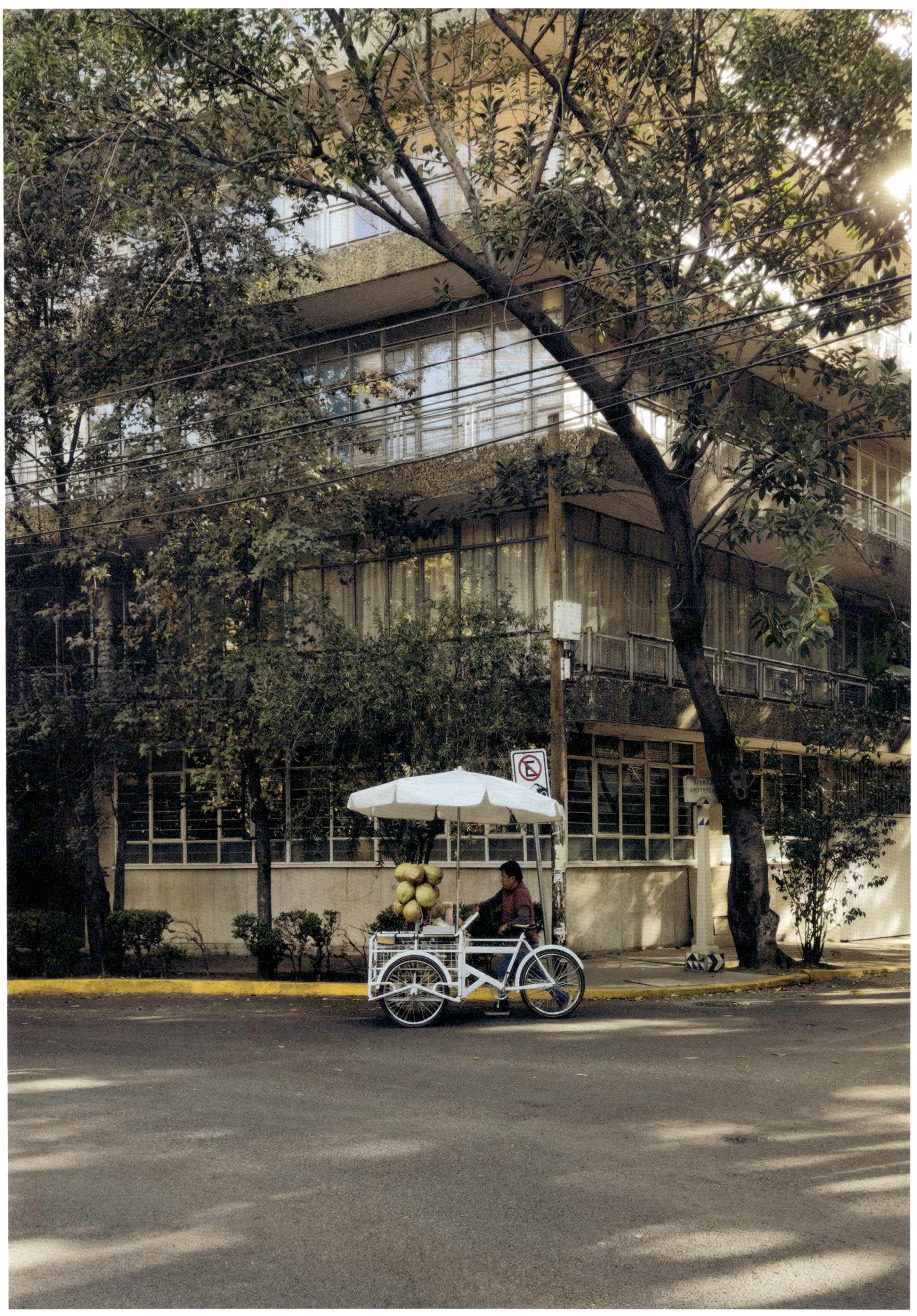

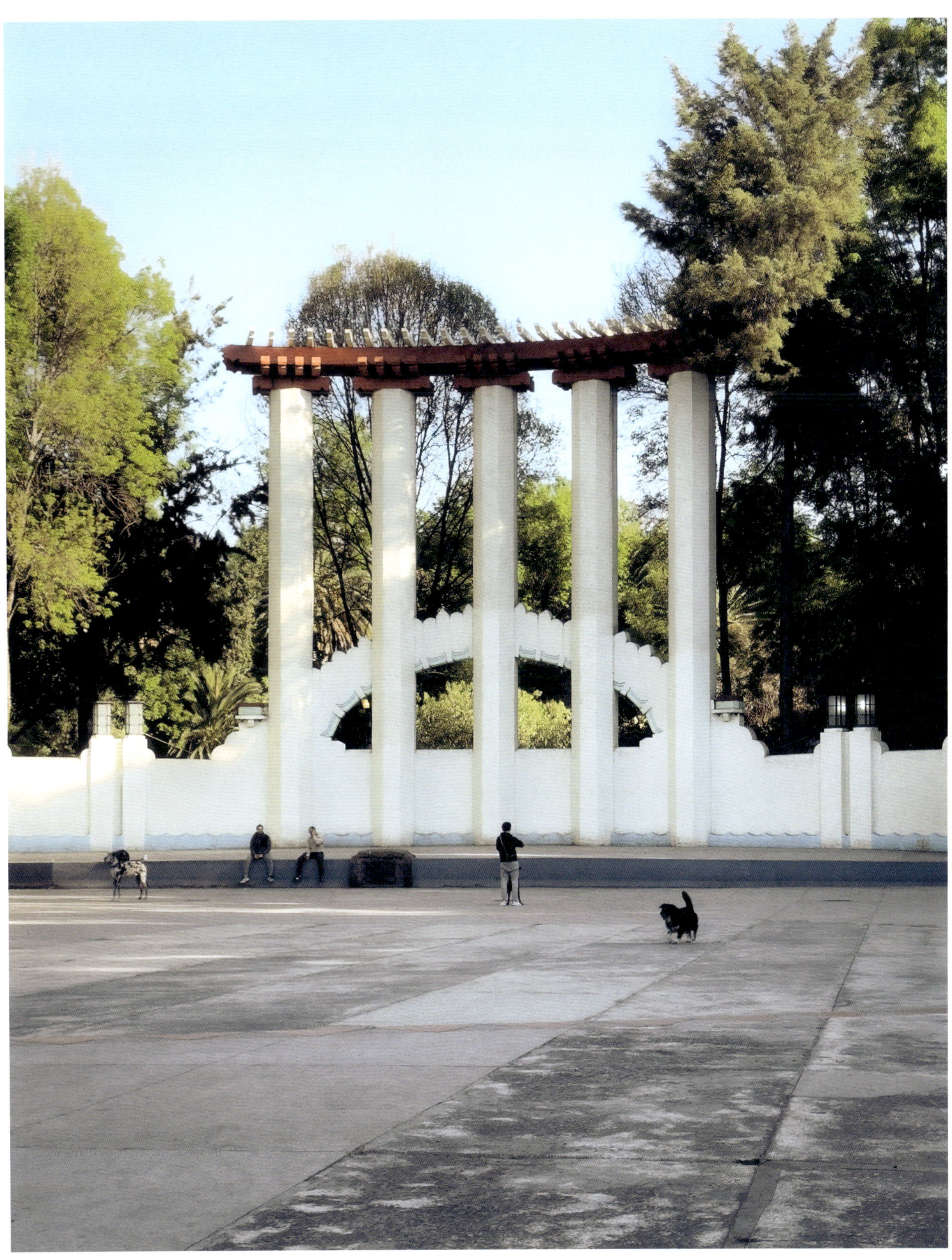

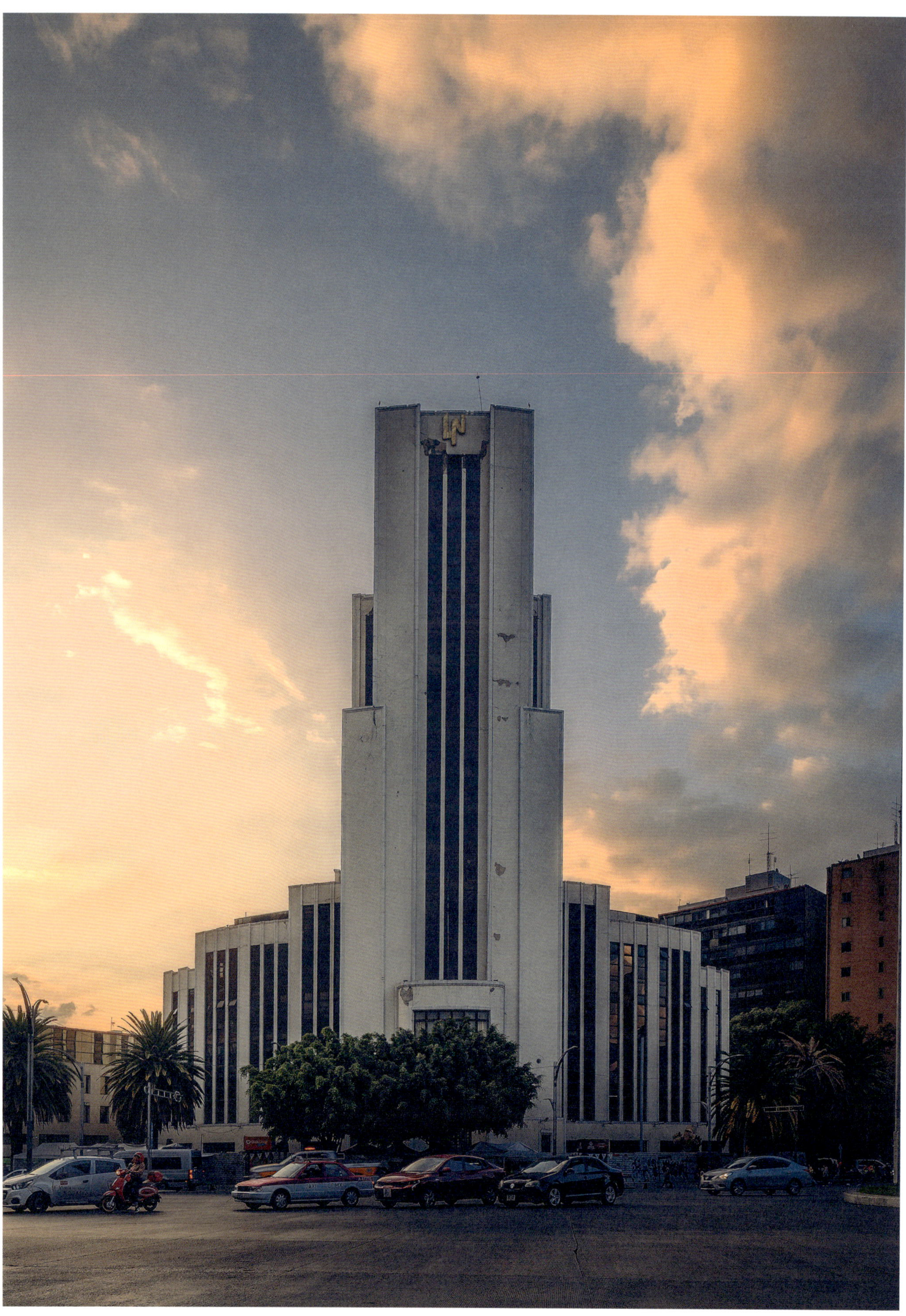

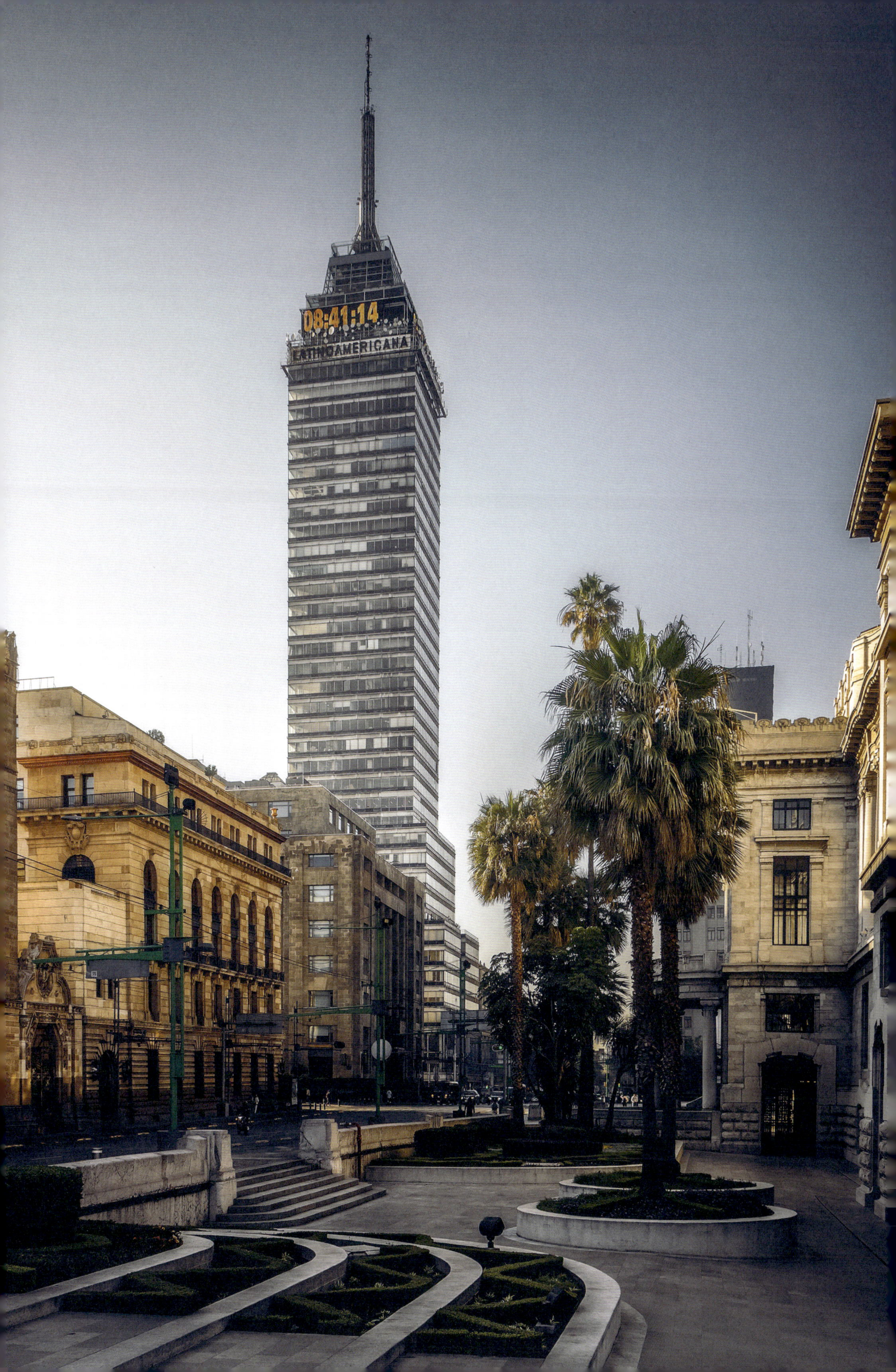
08:41:14
LATINOAMERICANA

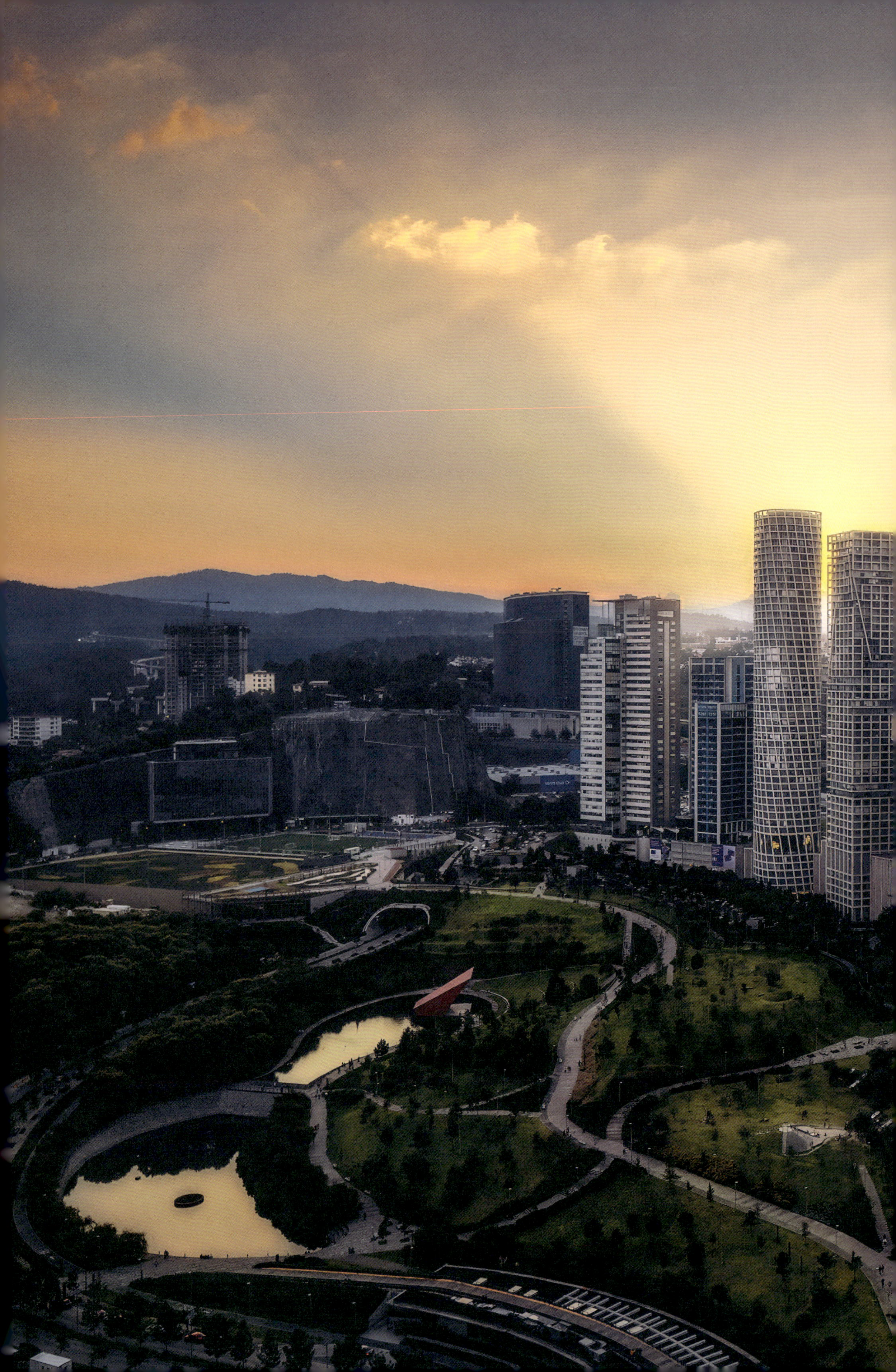

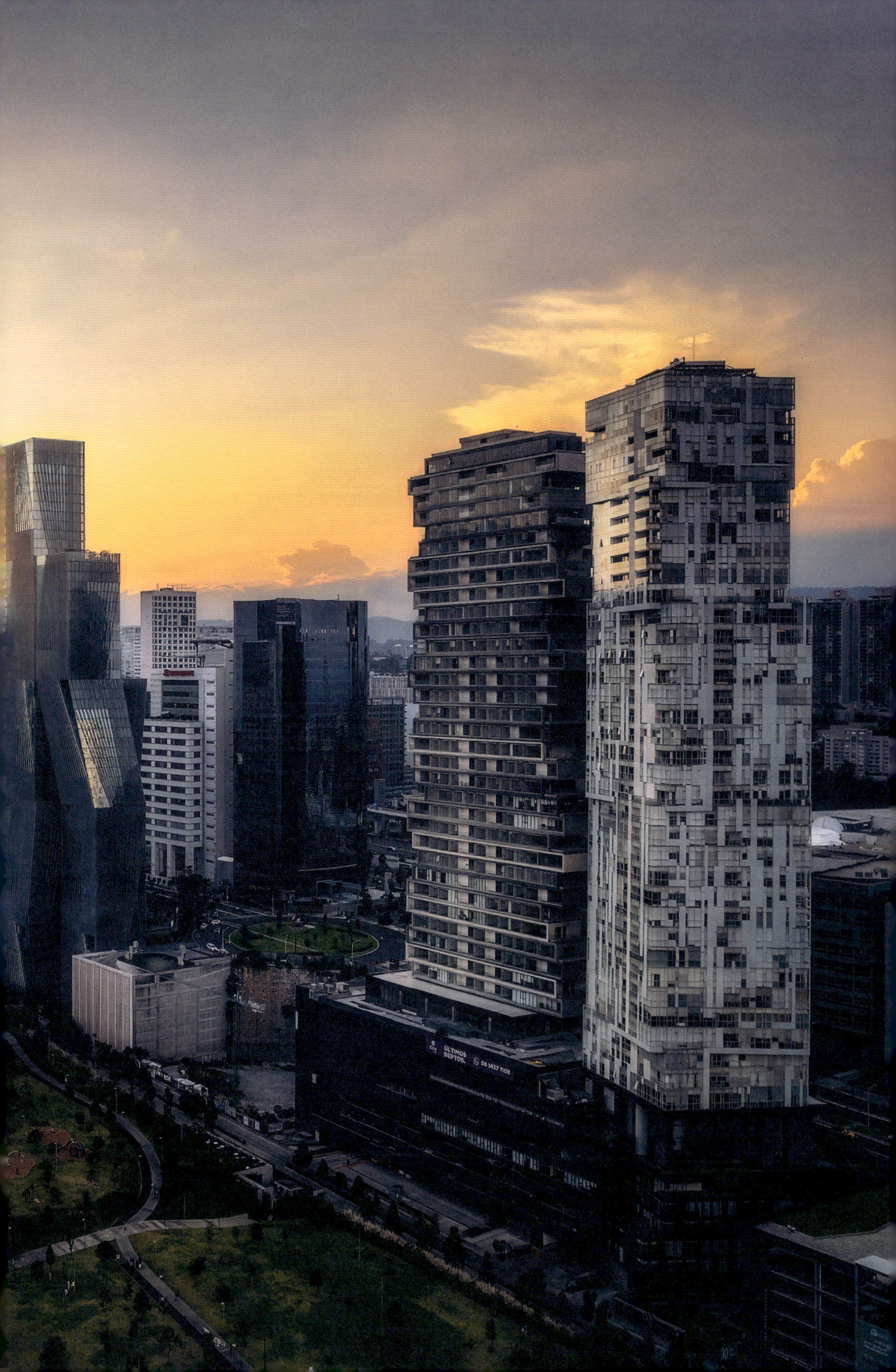
ÚLTIMOS
DEPTOS.

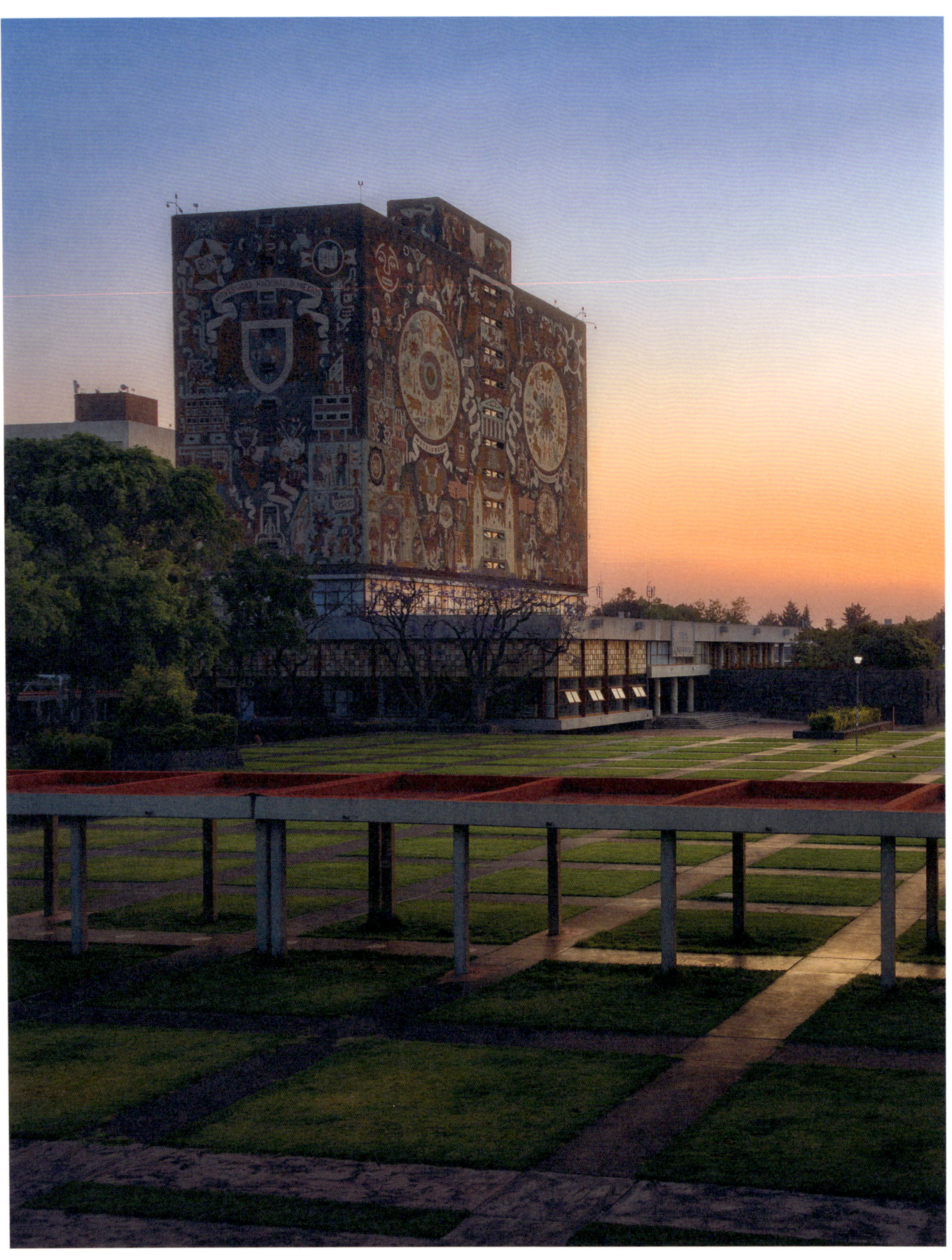

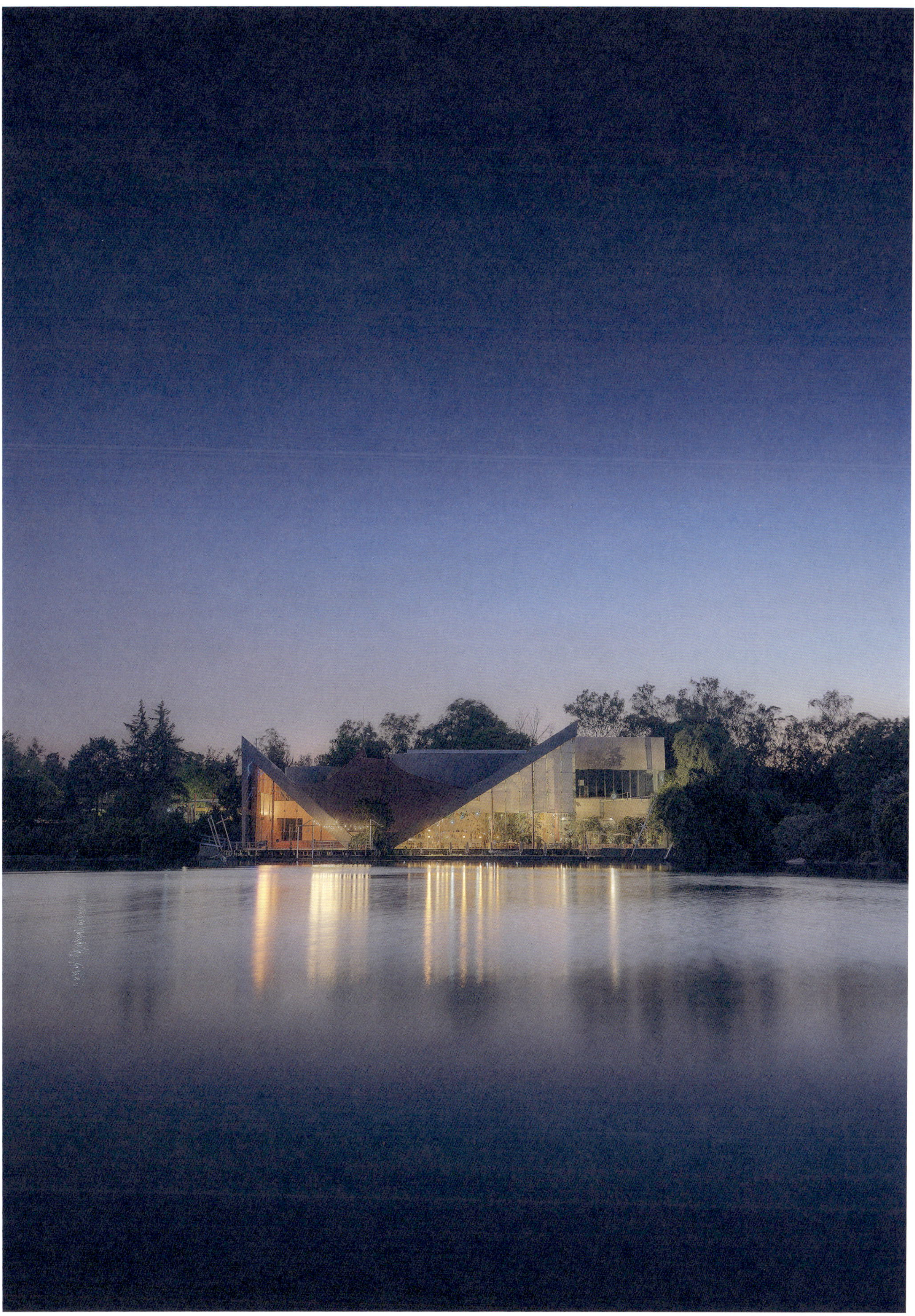

At almost 8,000 feet, Mexico City feels like an elaborate altar laid under the sky.

GUY TREBAY

American Reporter and Critic

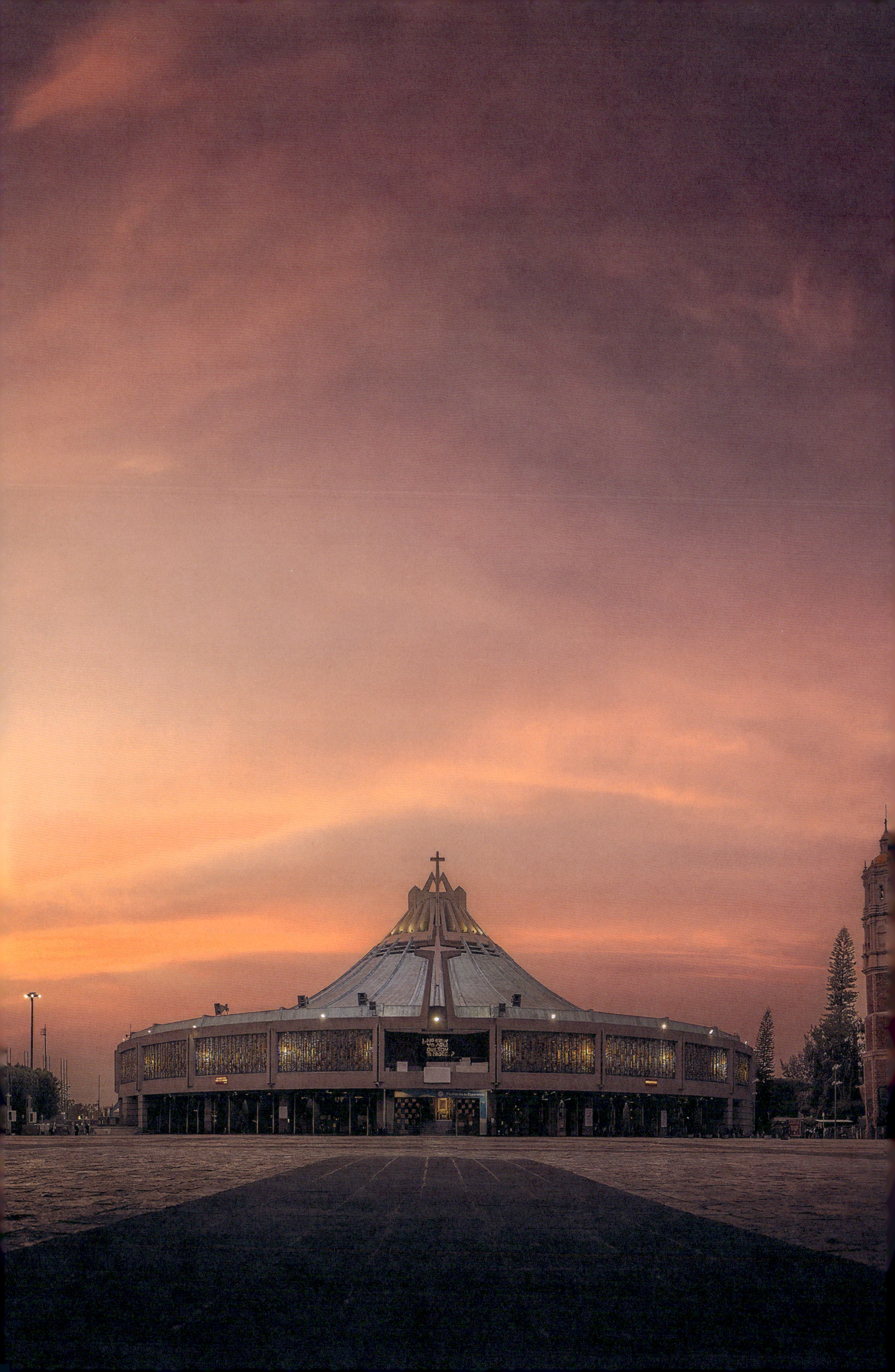

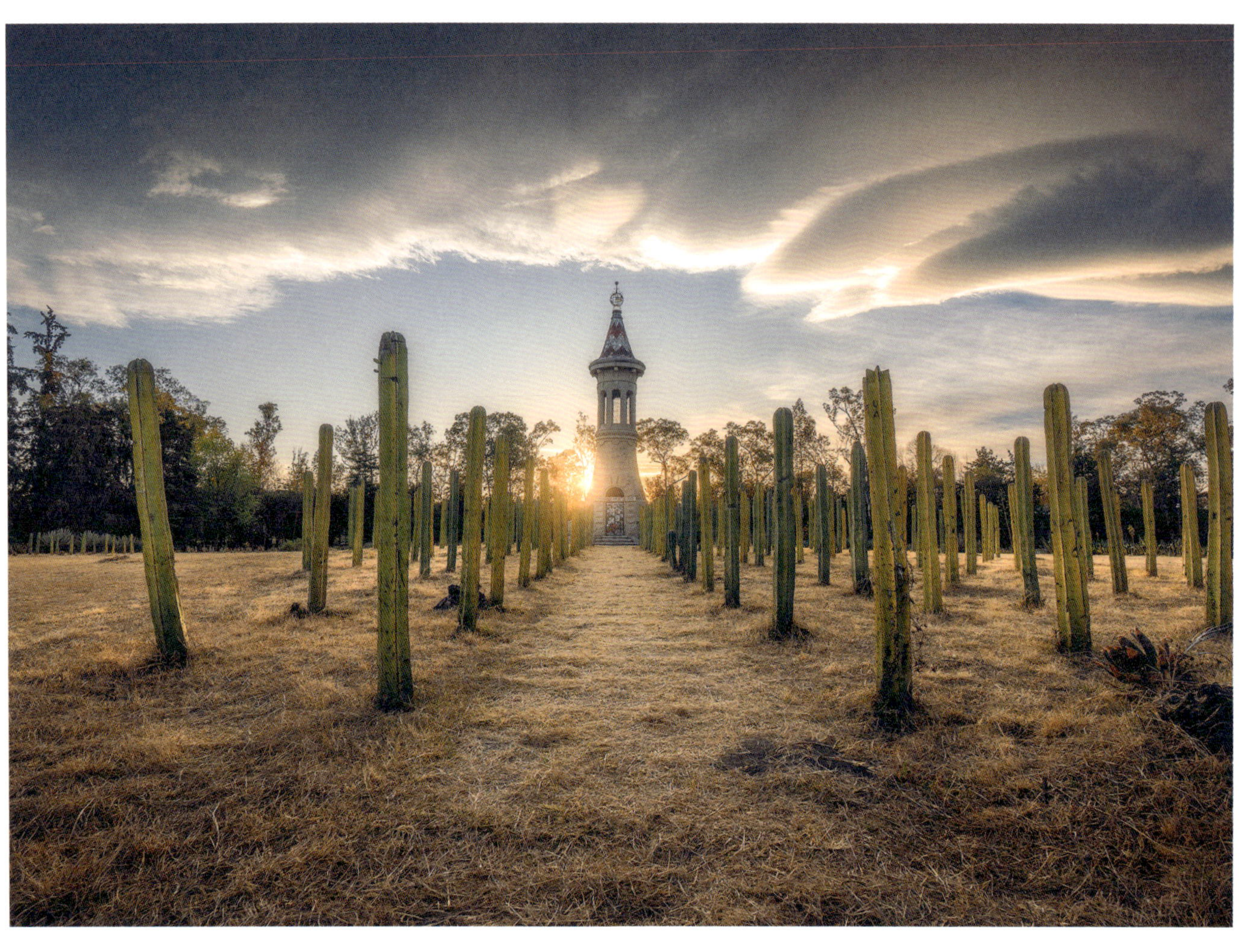

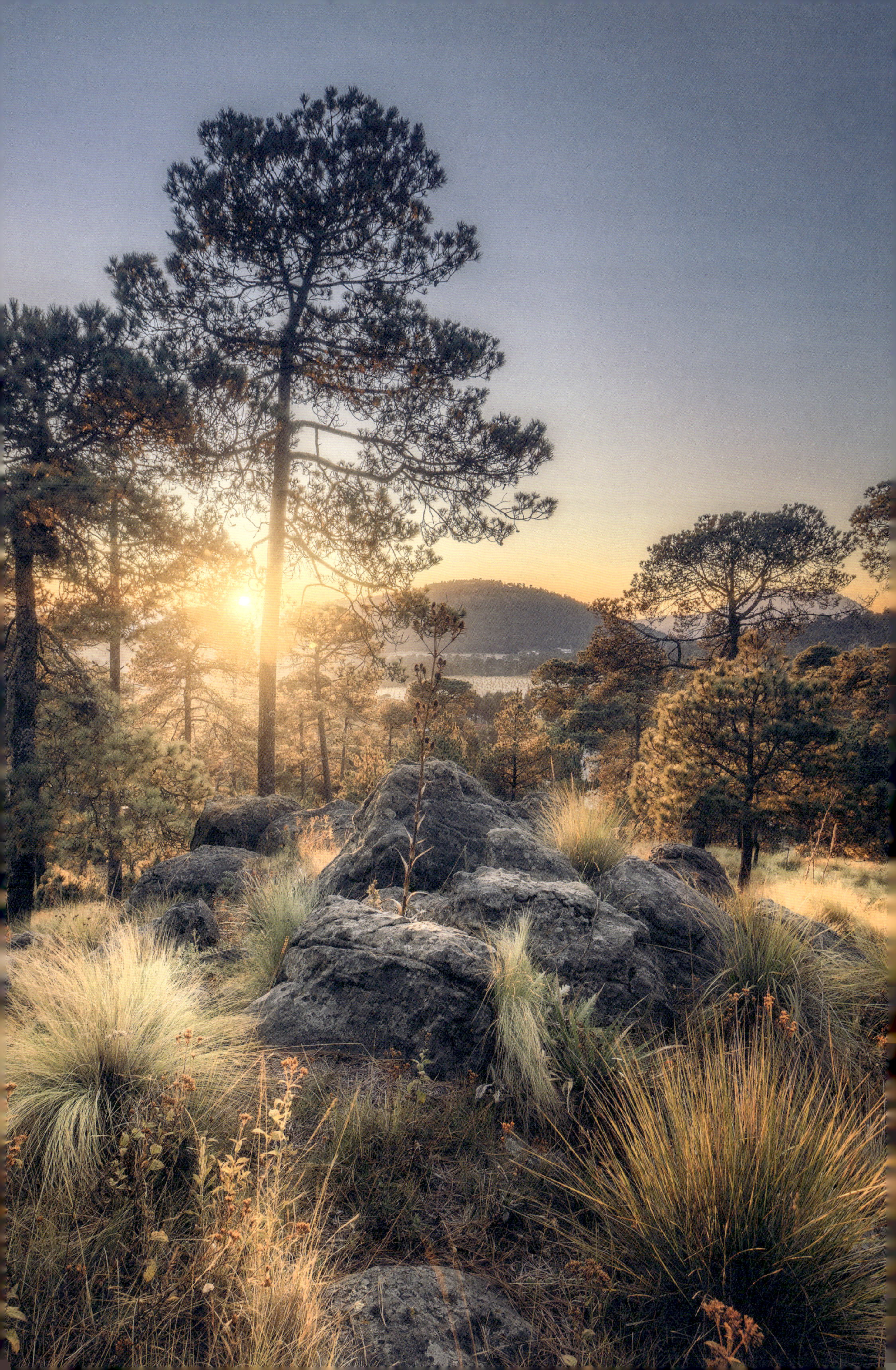

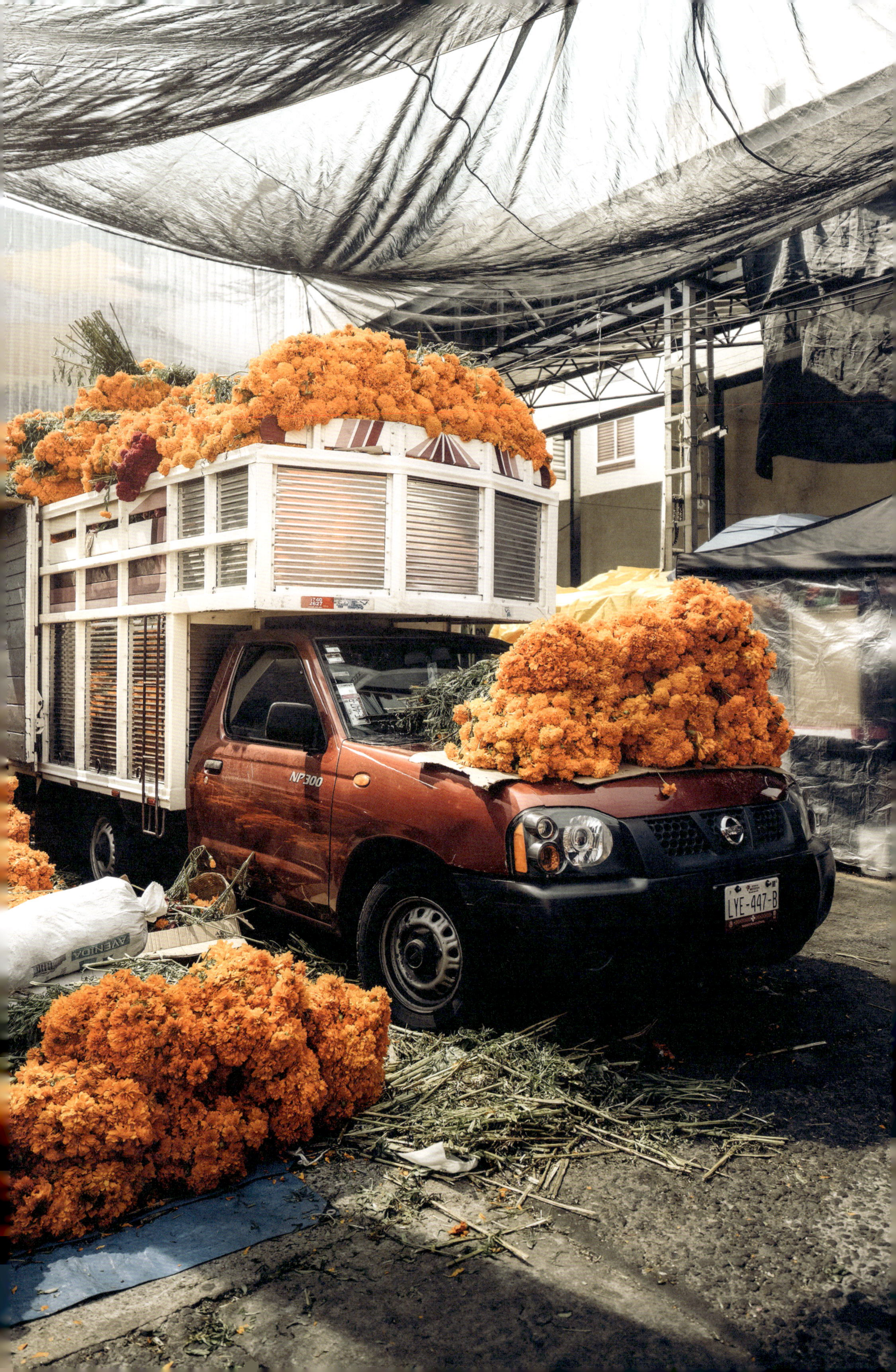
NP300
LYE-447-B

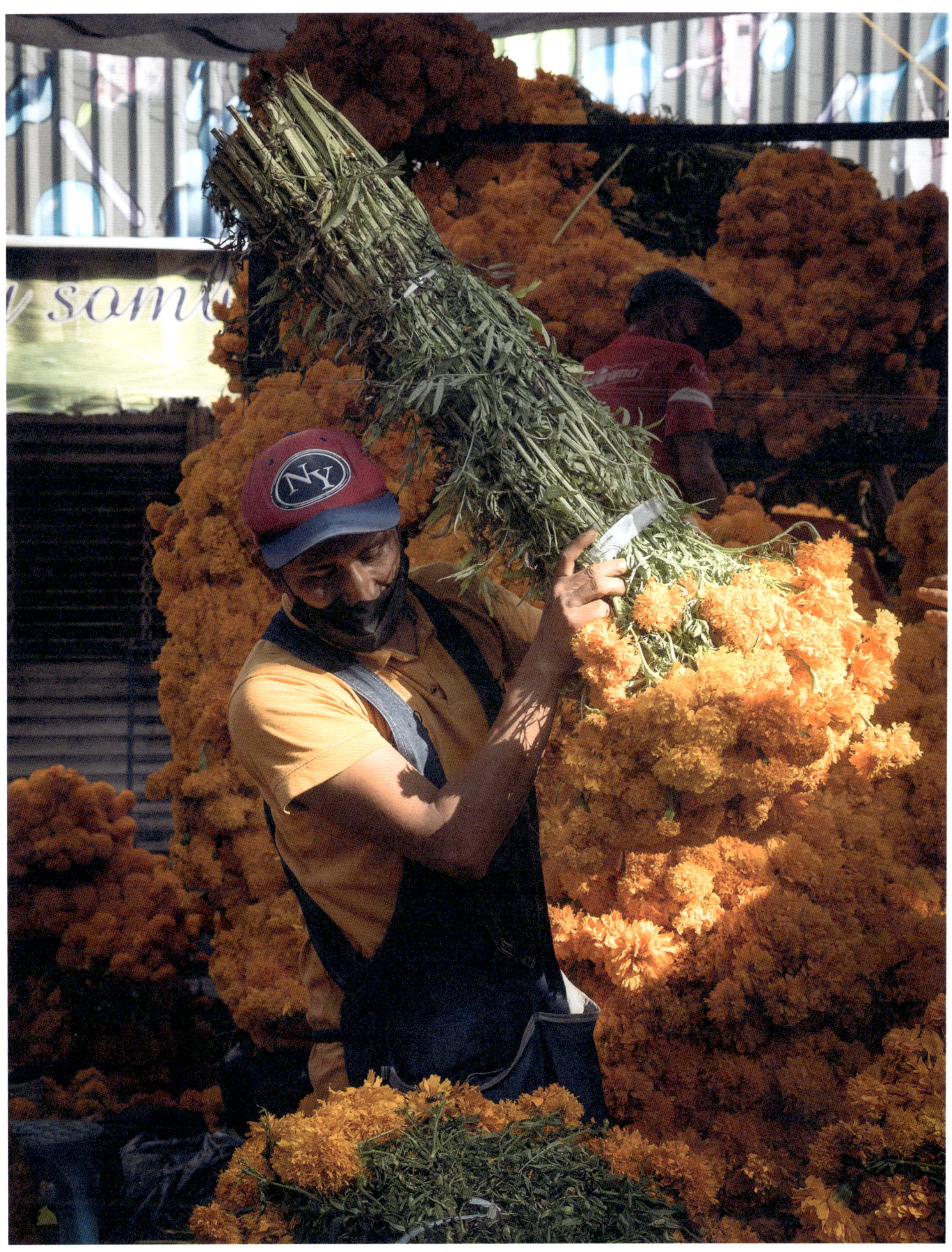
NY

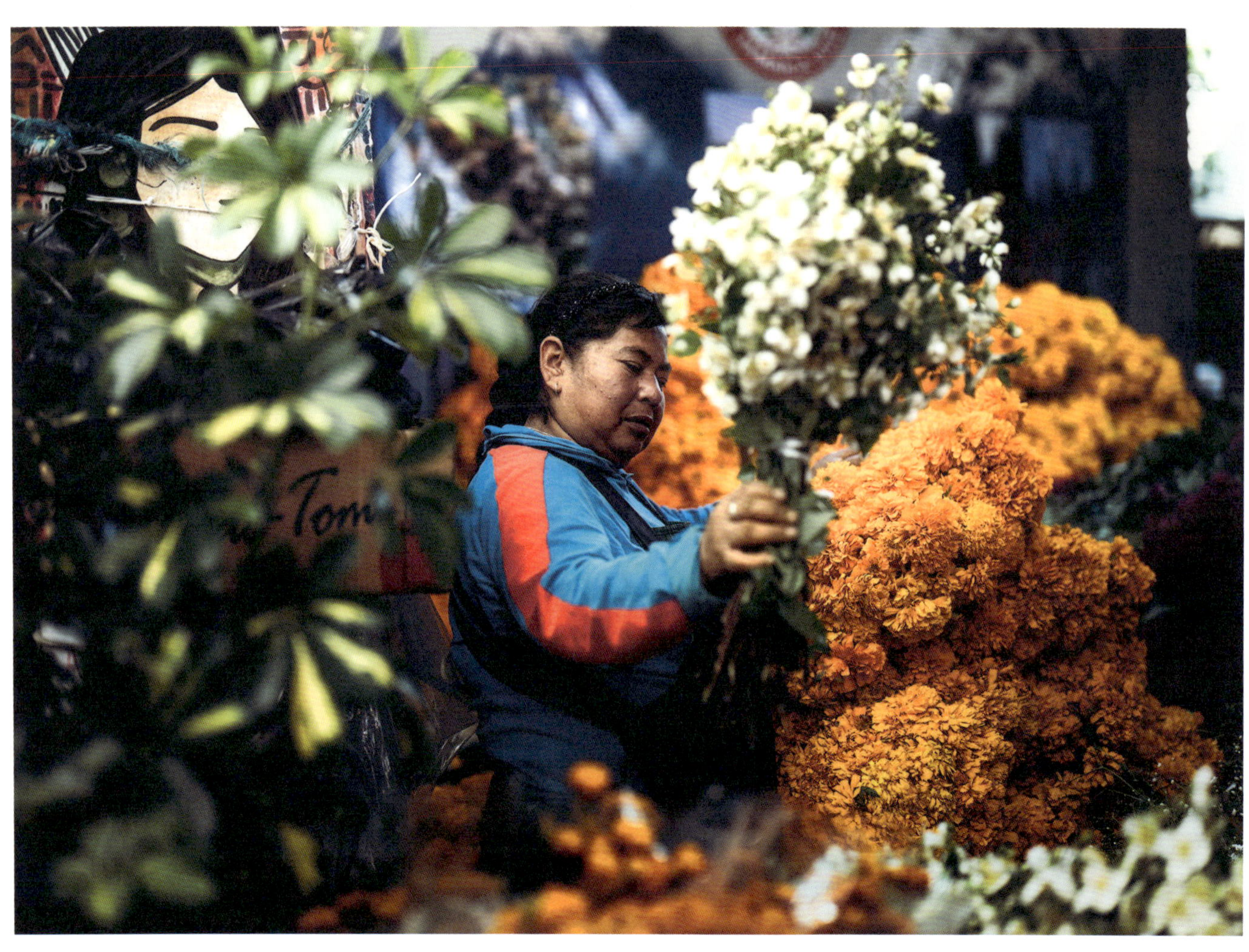

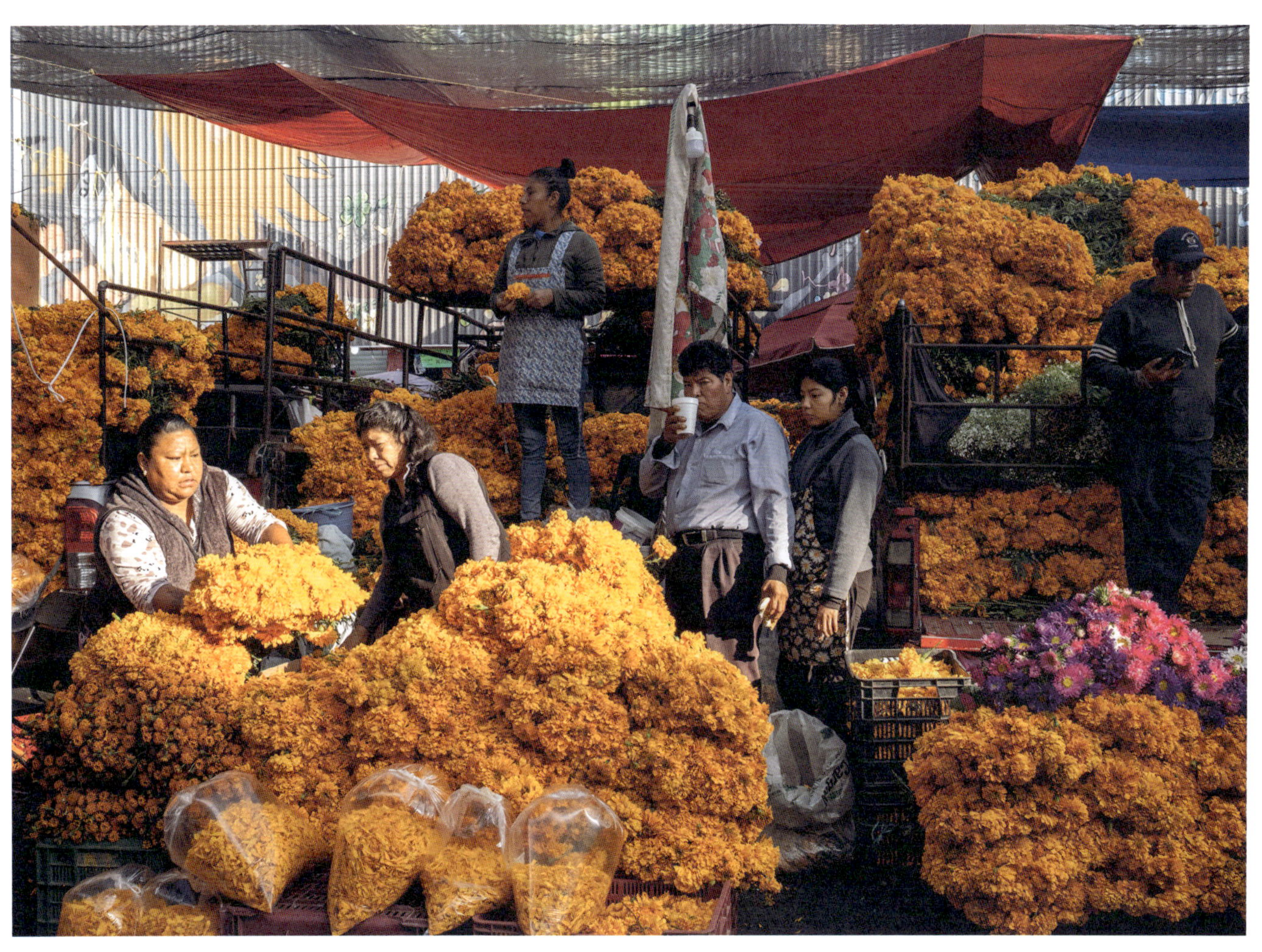

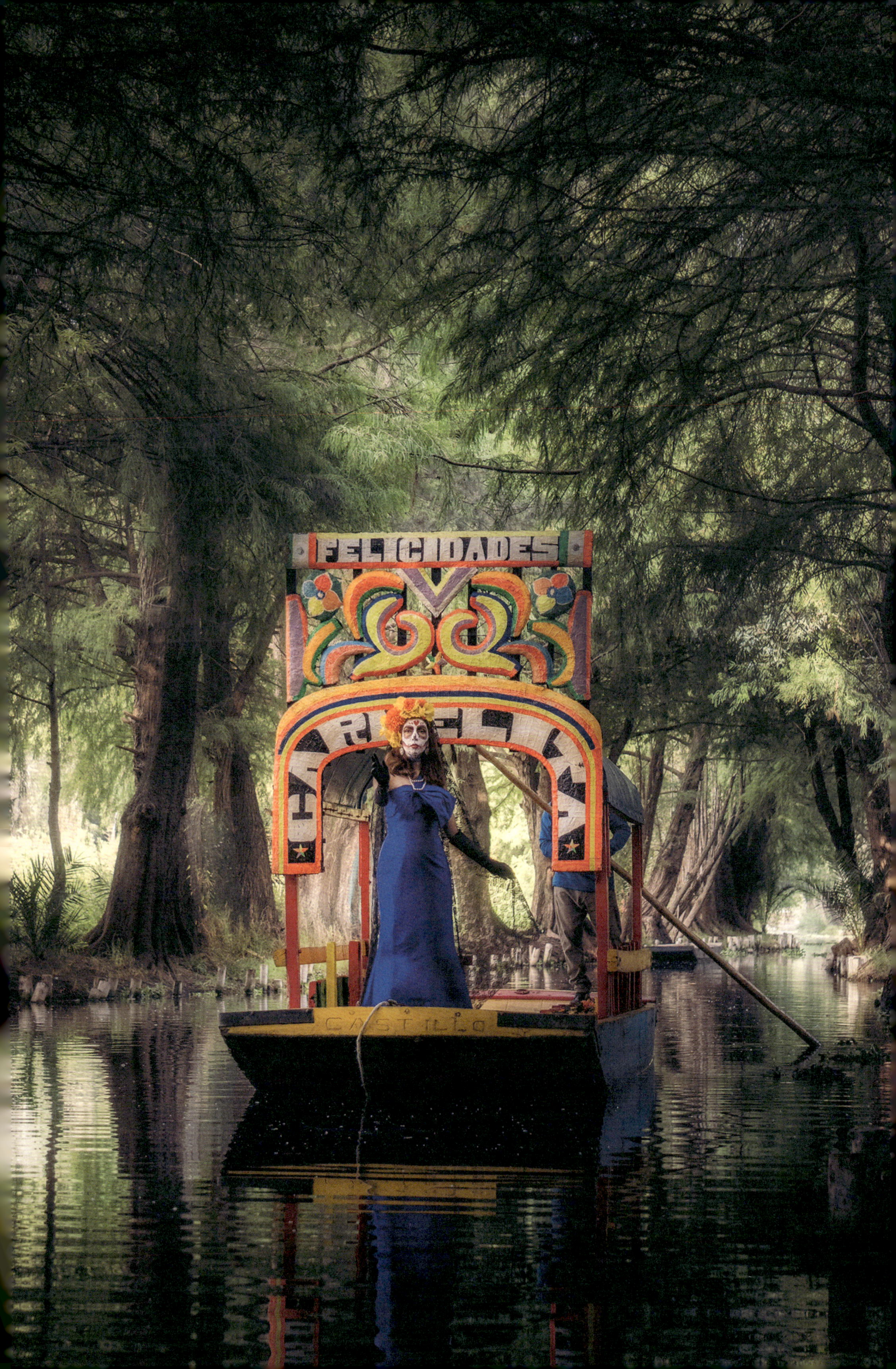
FELICIDADES
CASTILLO

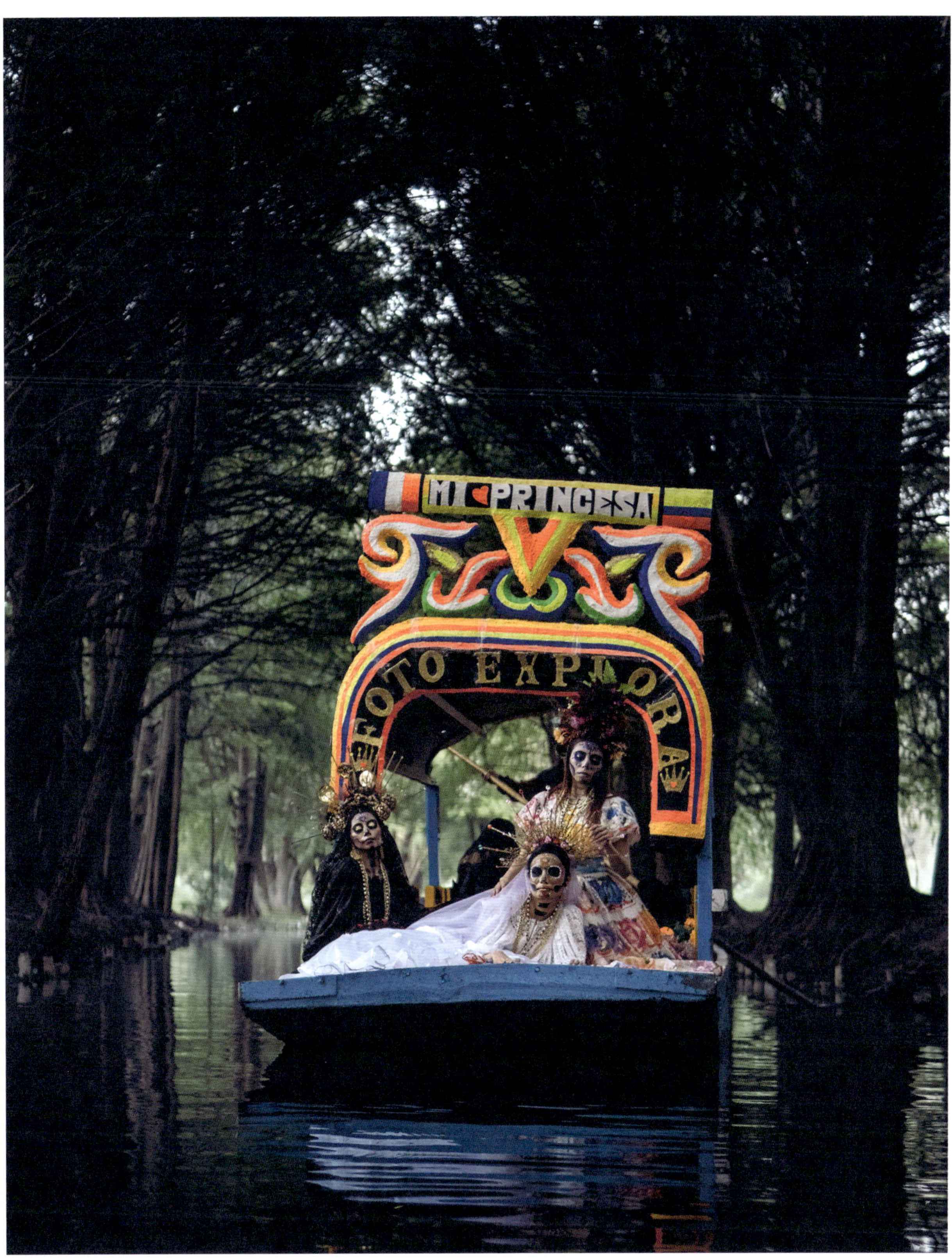
MI PRINCESA

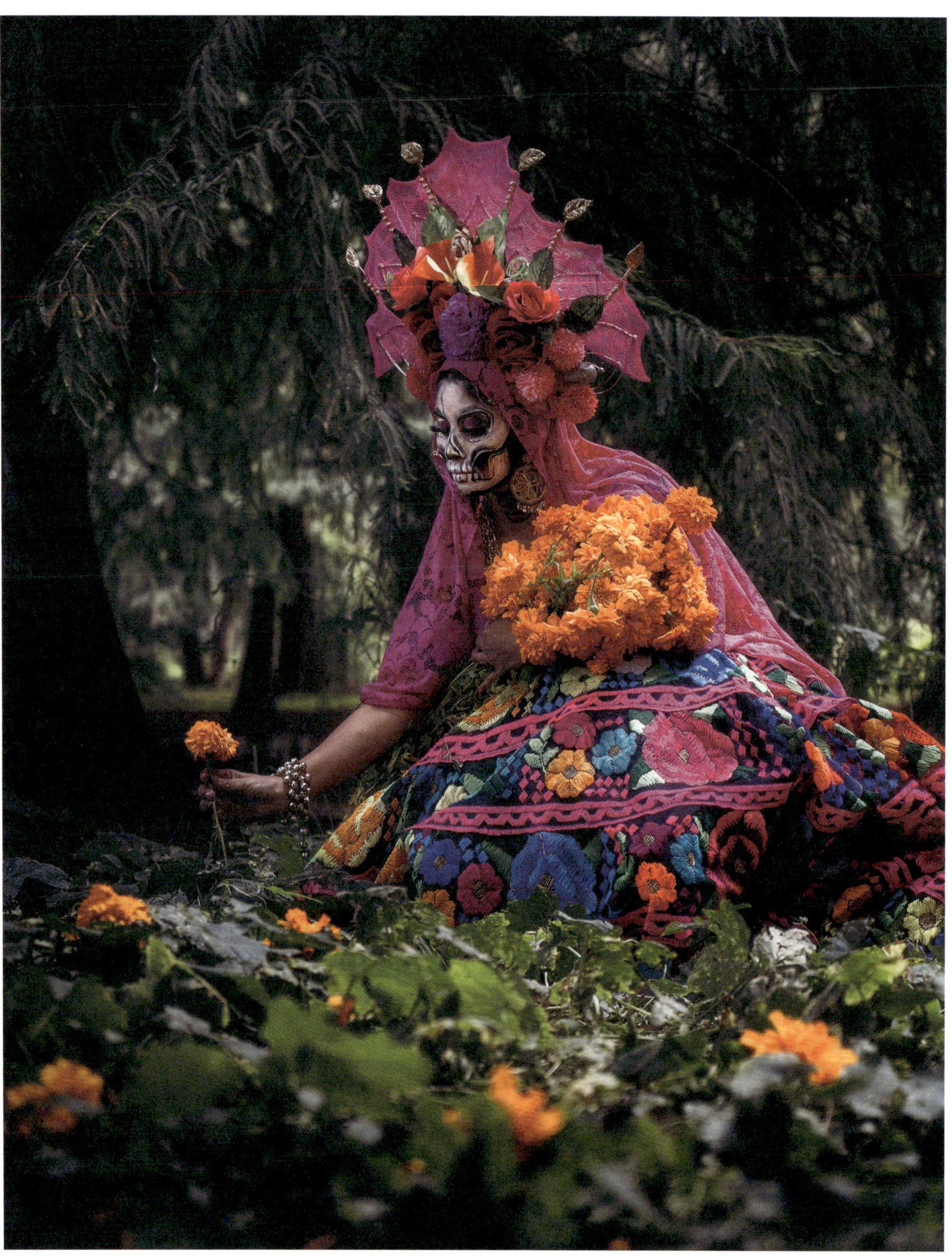

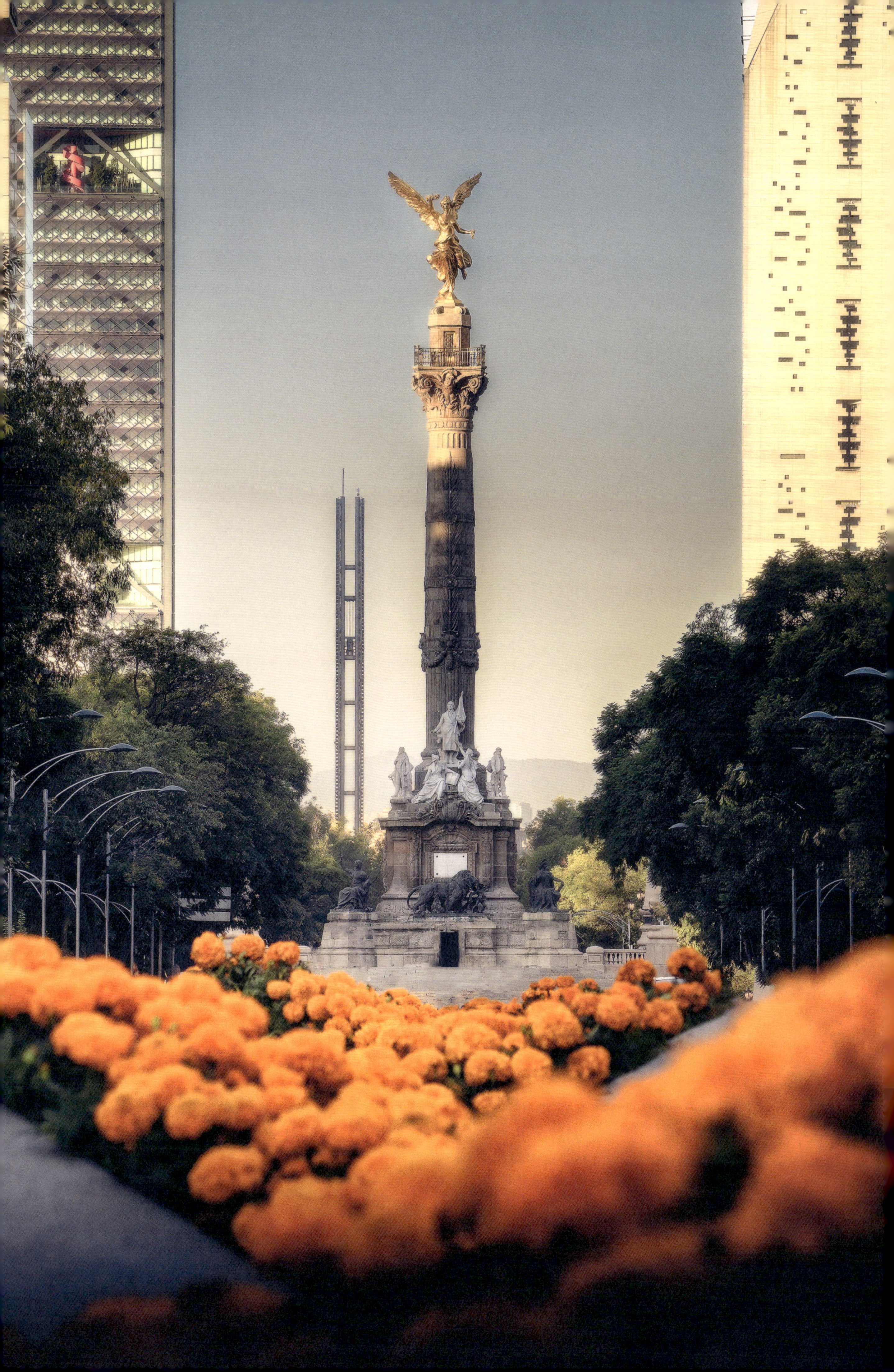

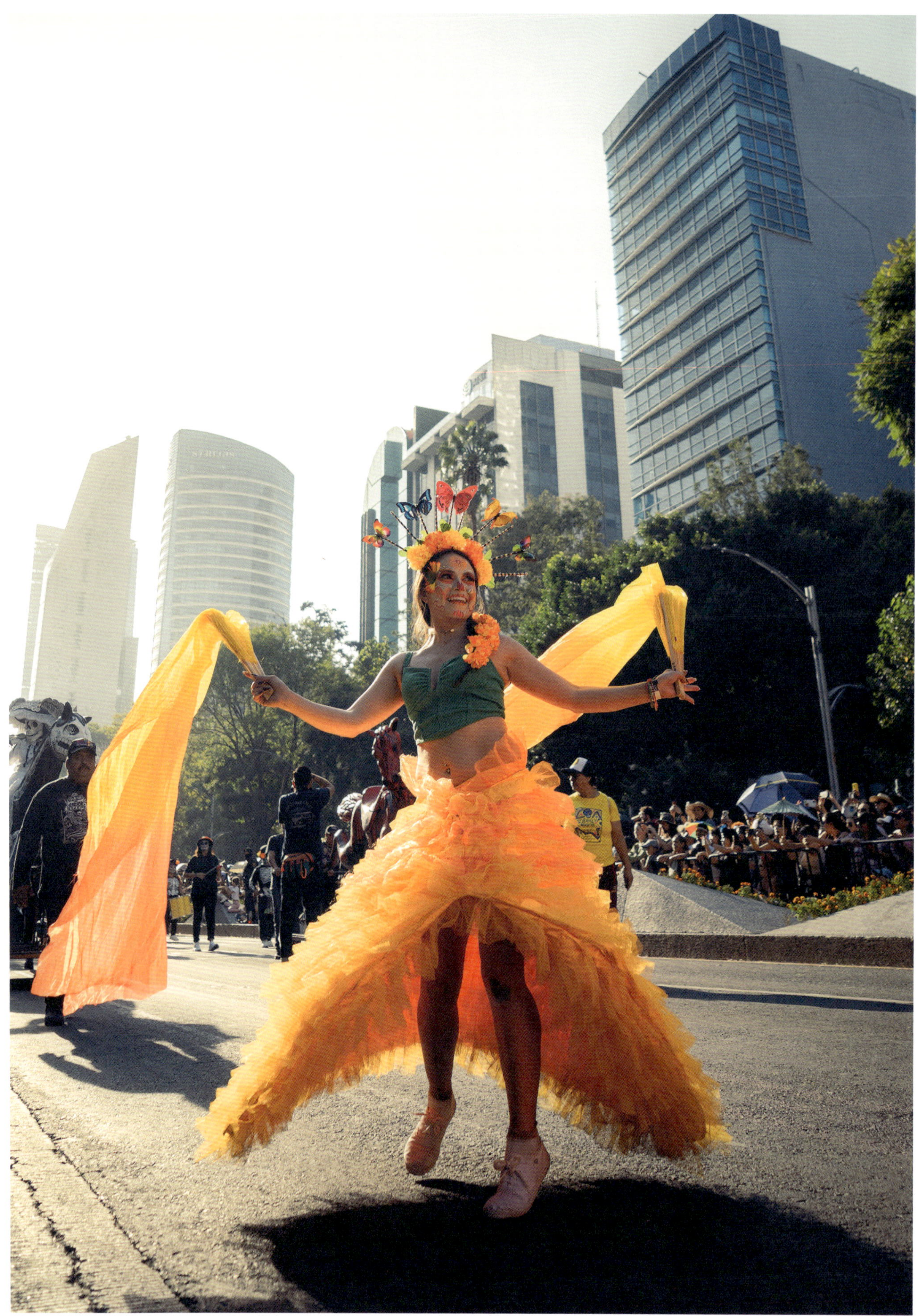

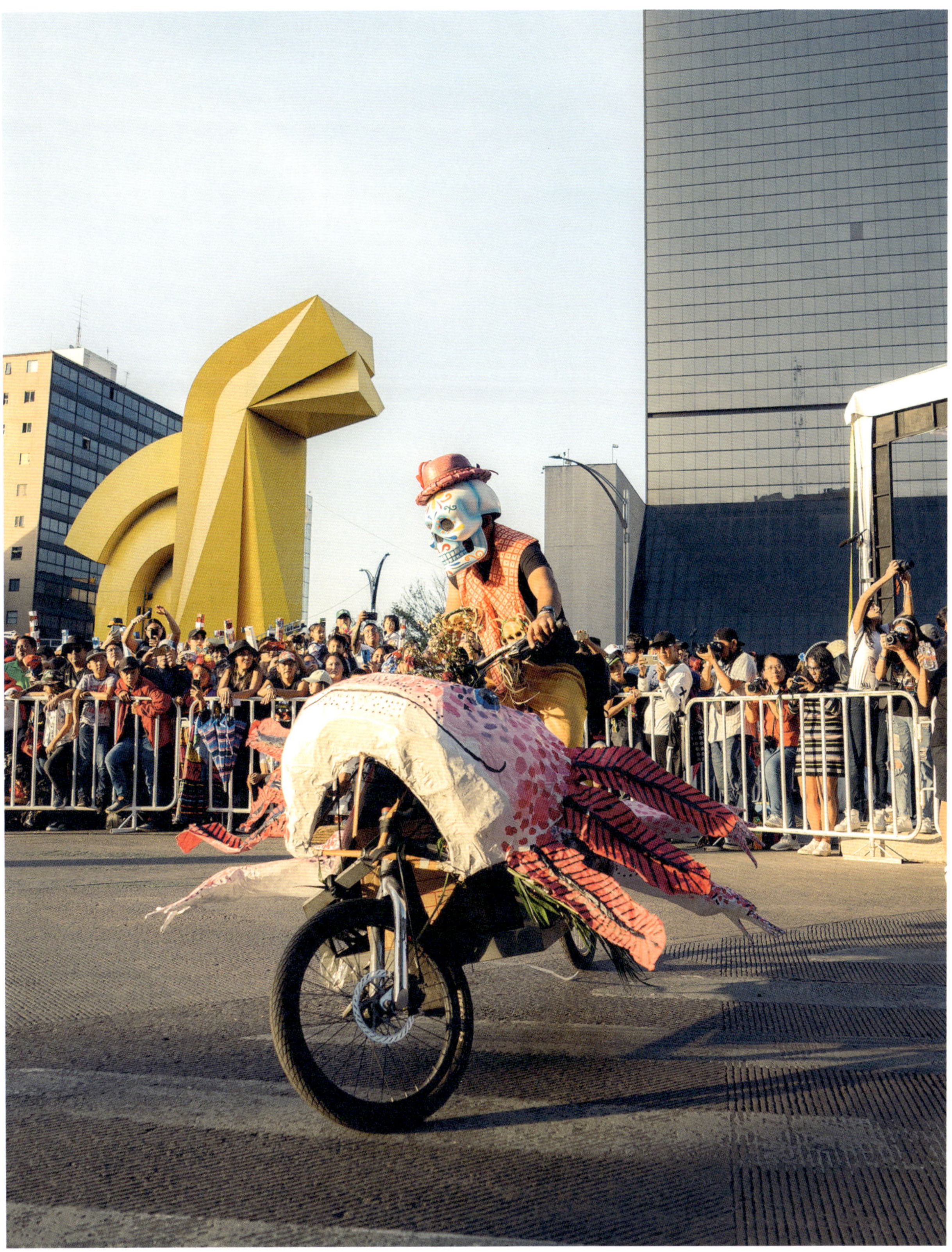

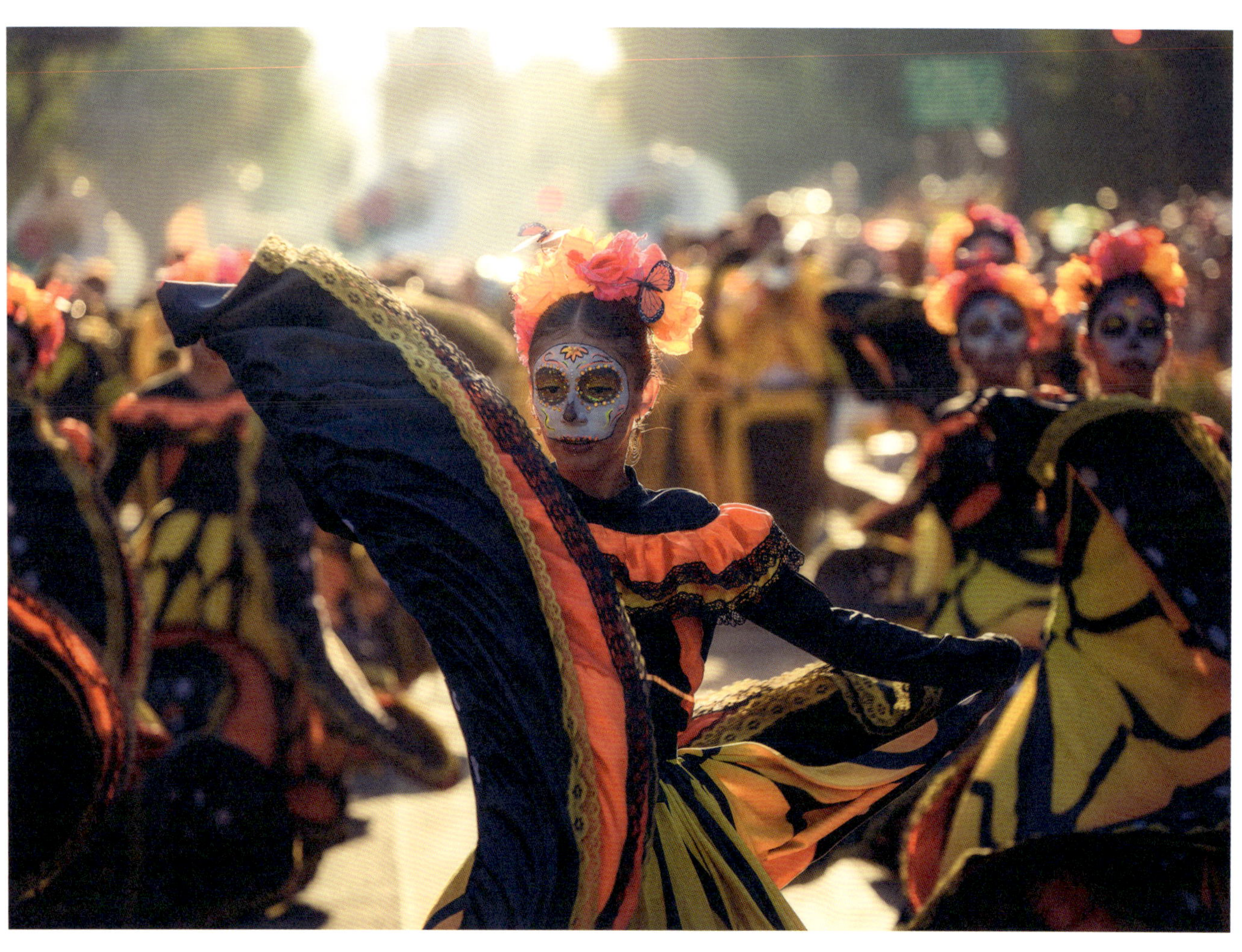

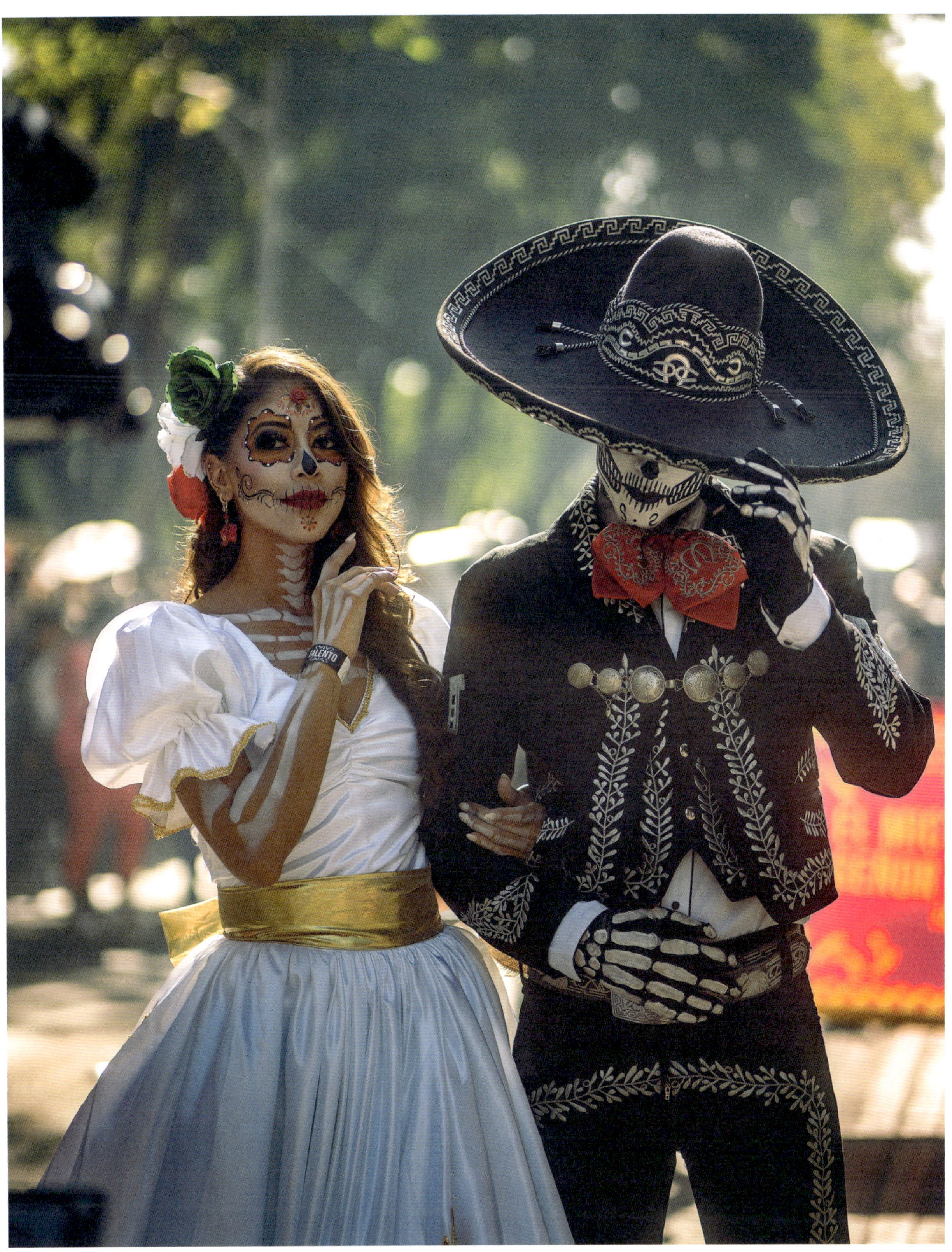
TALENTO

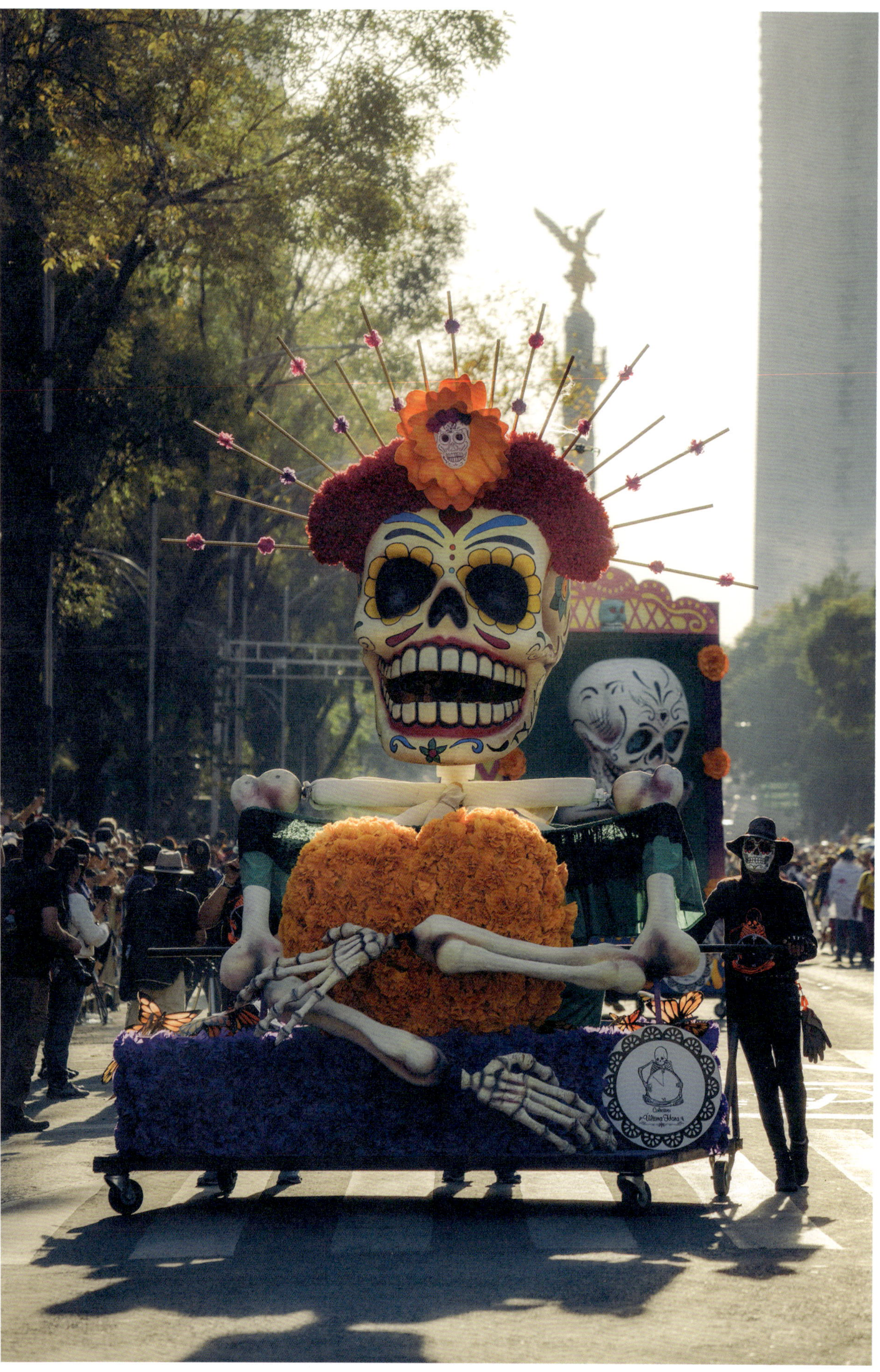

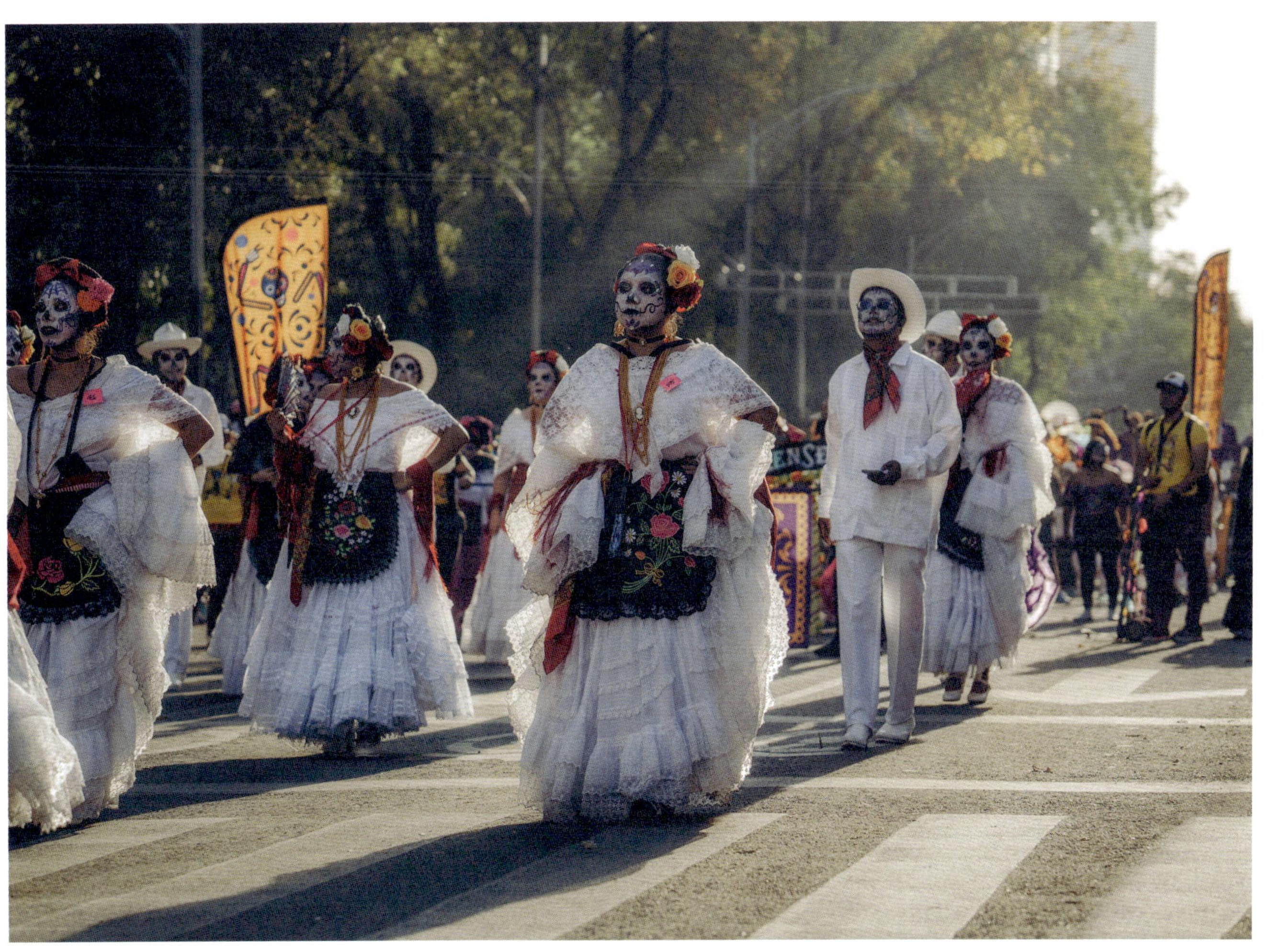

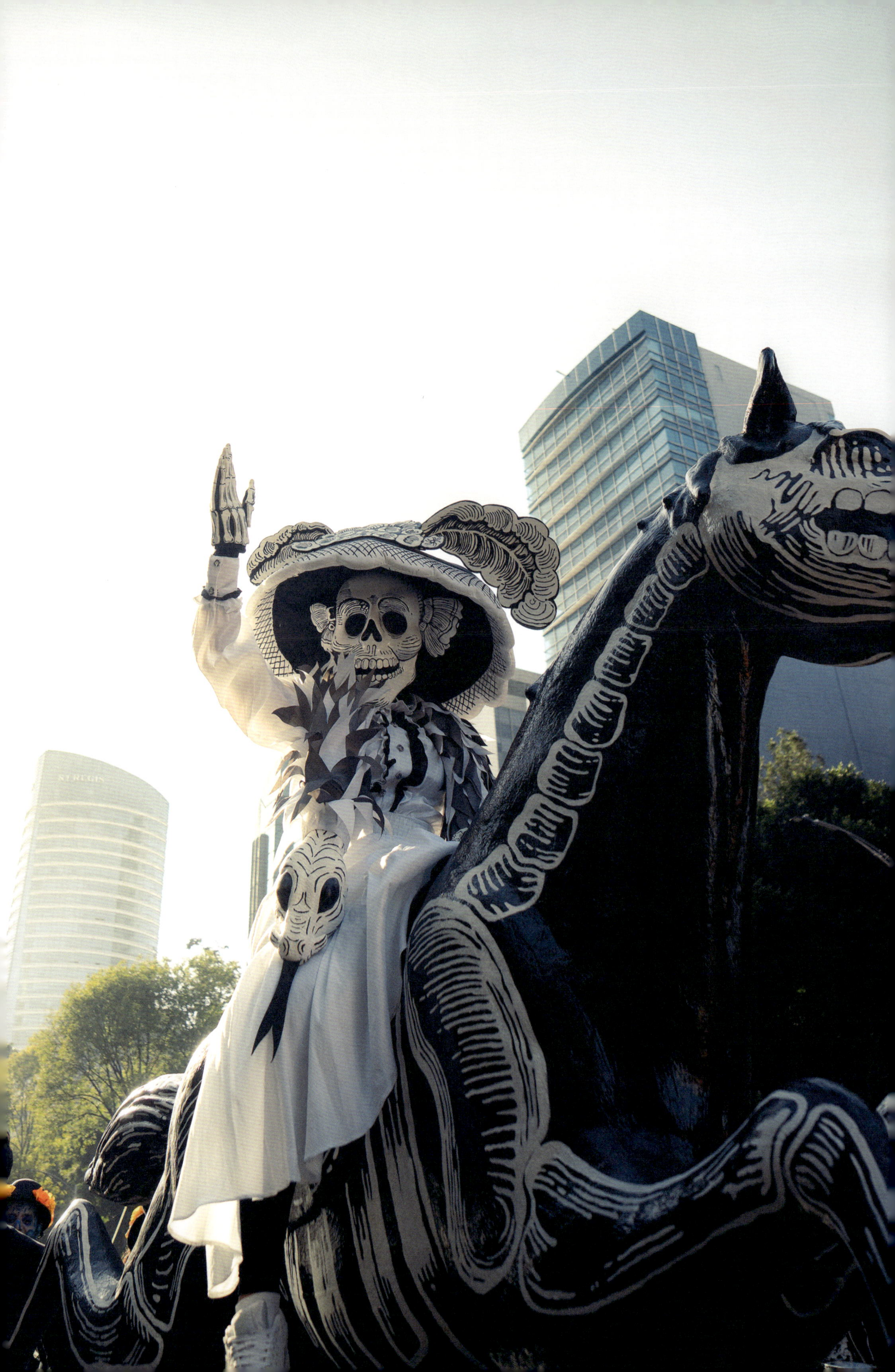

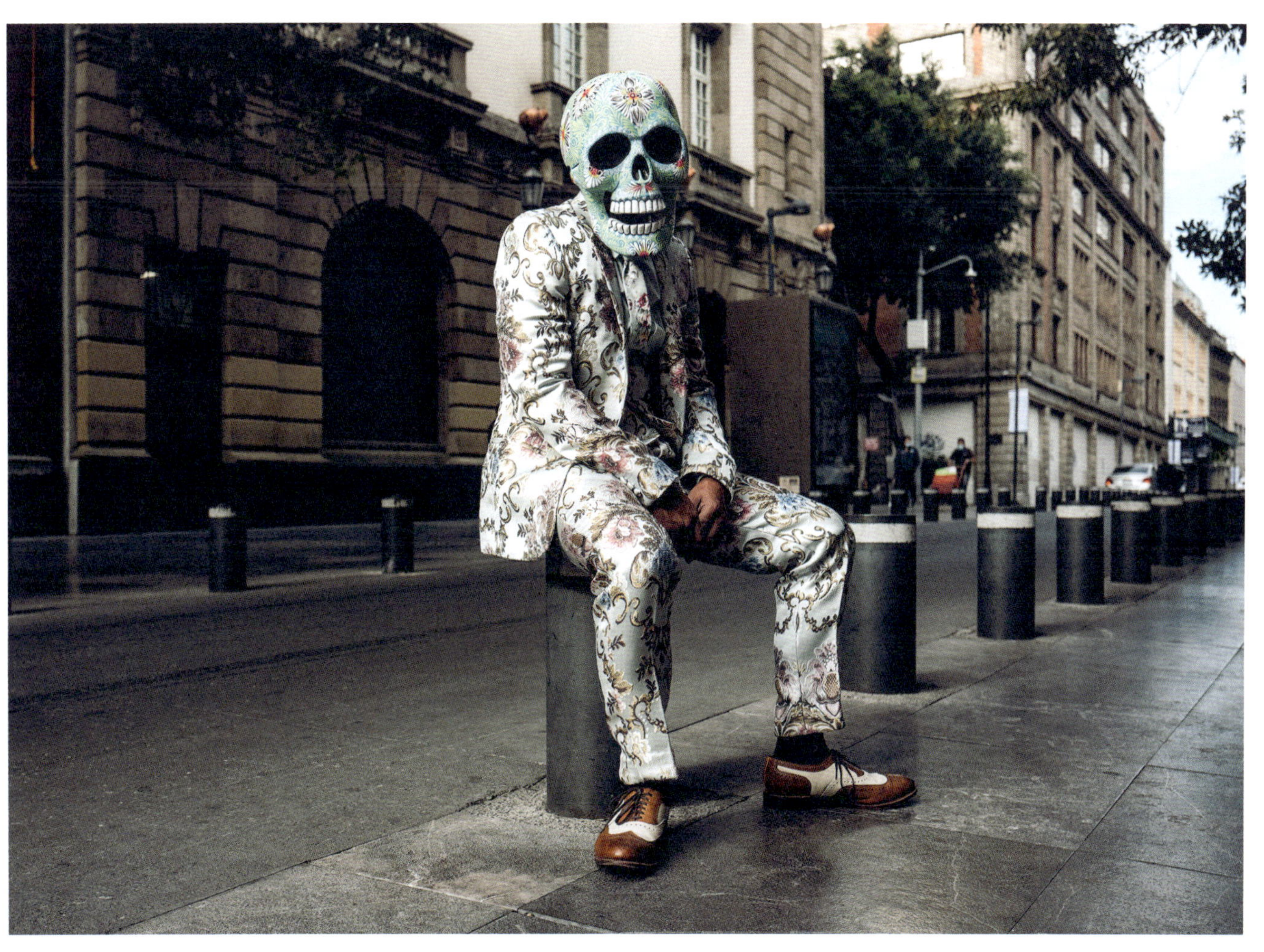

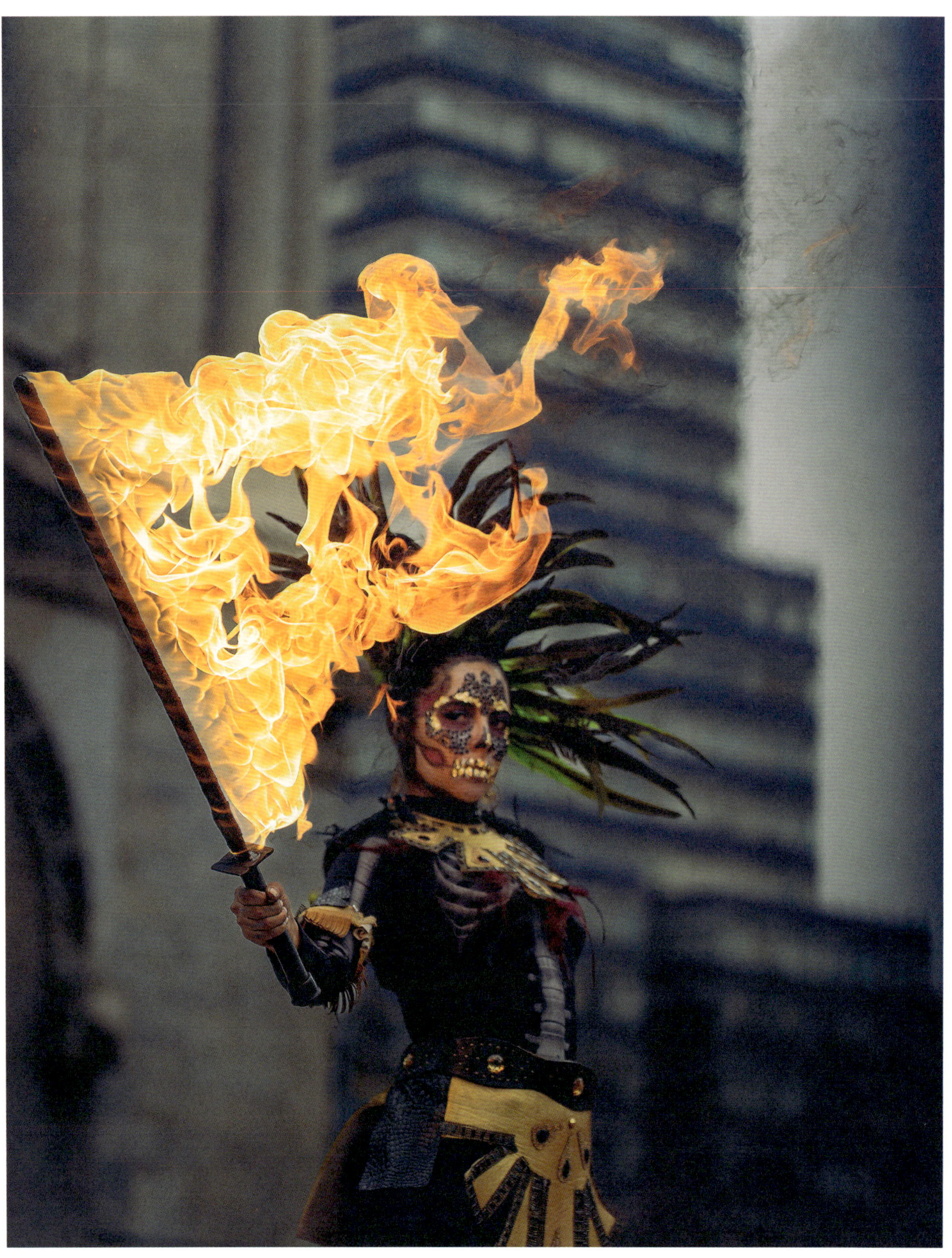

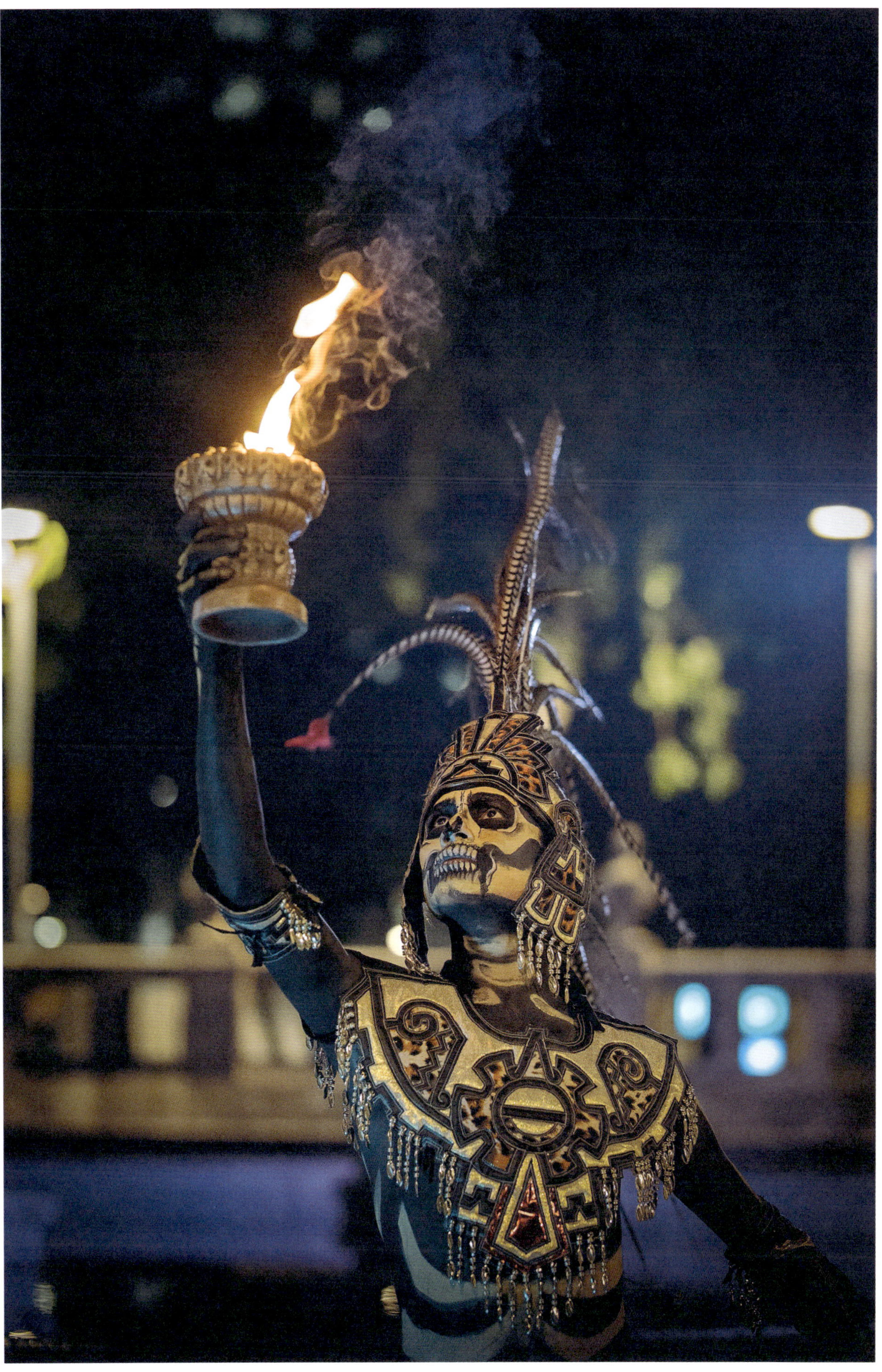

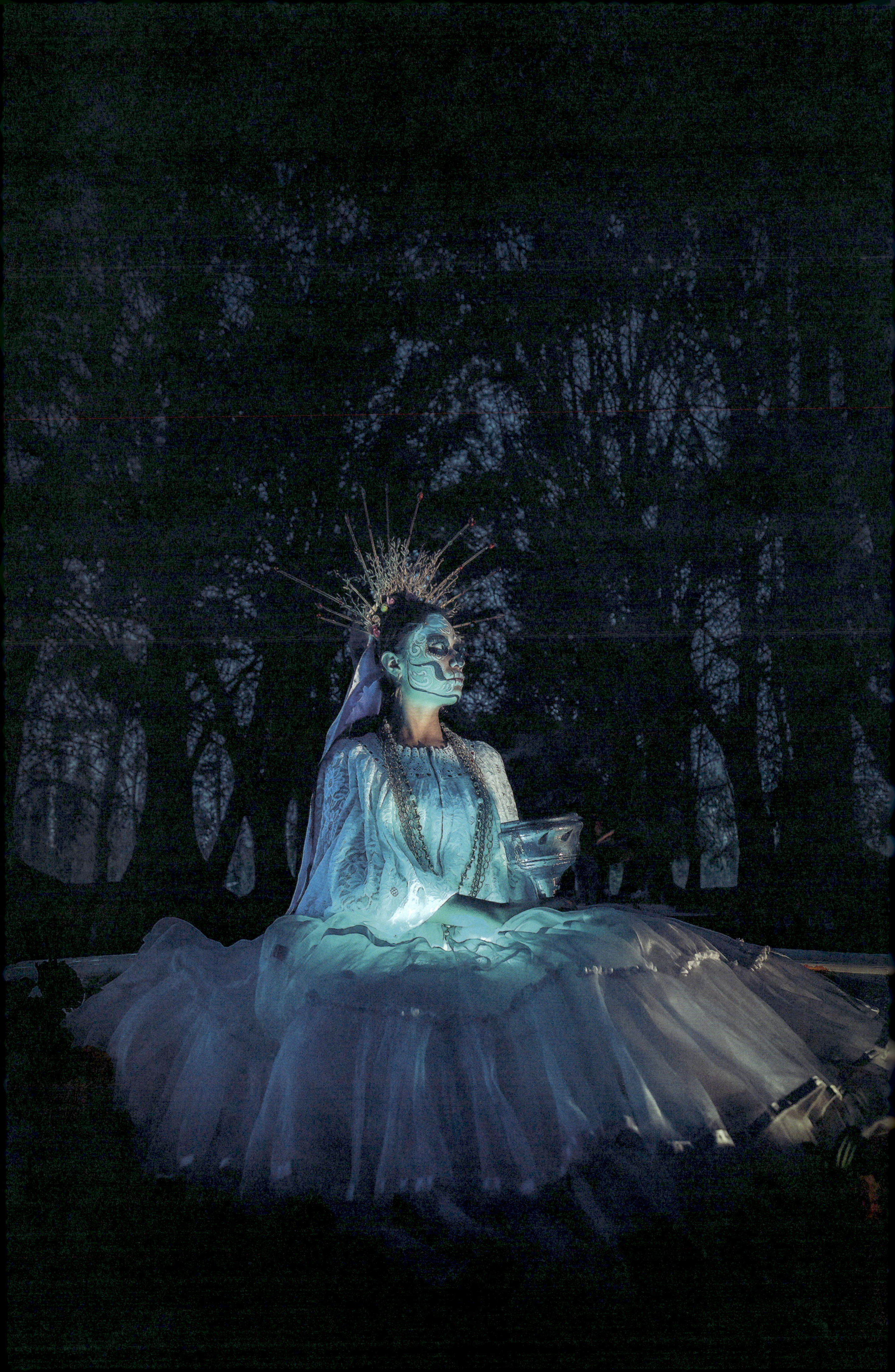

Nothing is absolute. Everything changes, everything moves, everything revolves, everything flies and goes away.

FRIDA KAHLO

Mexican Painter

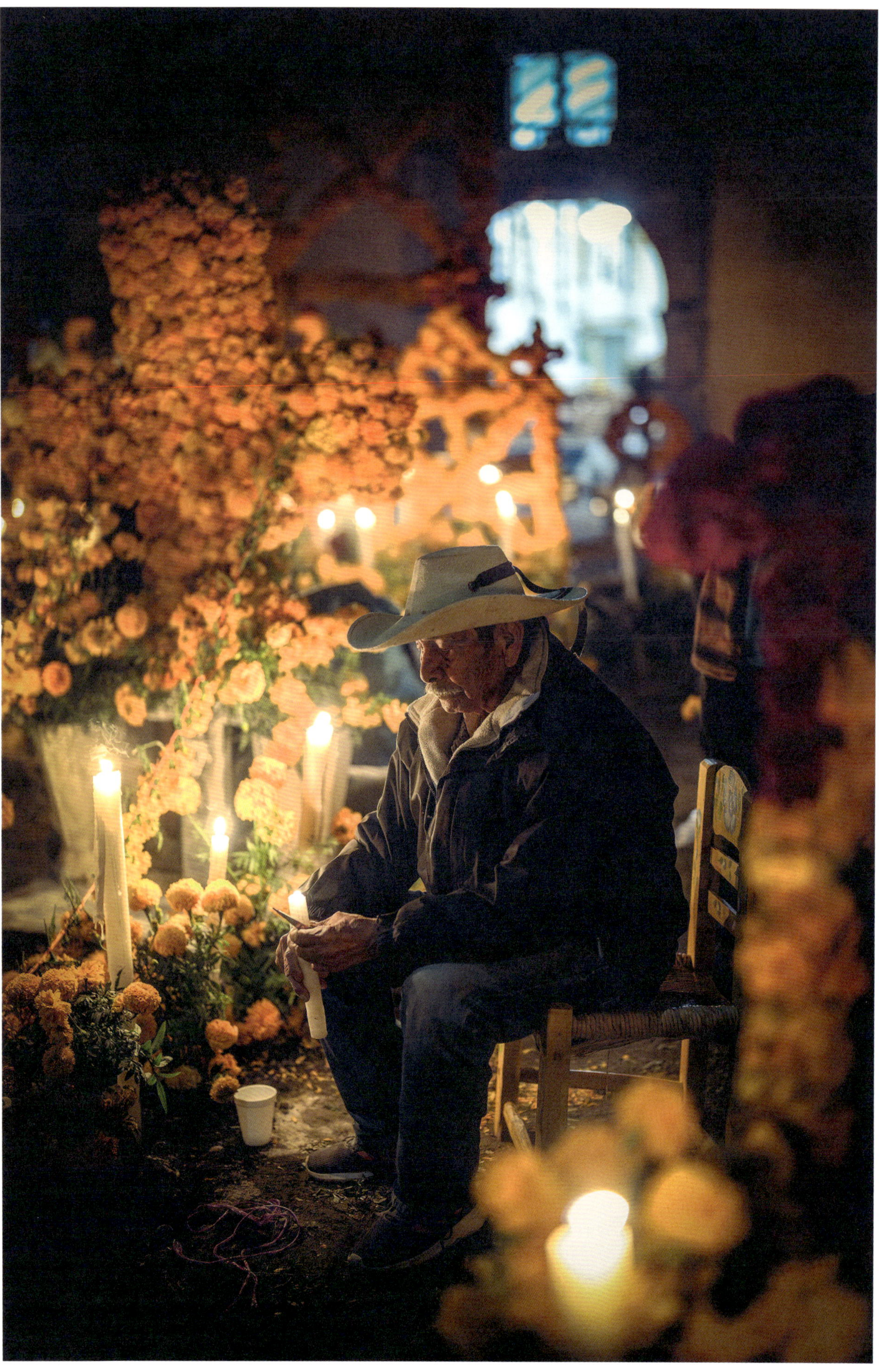

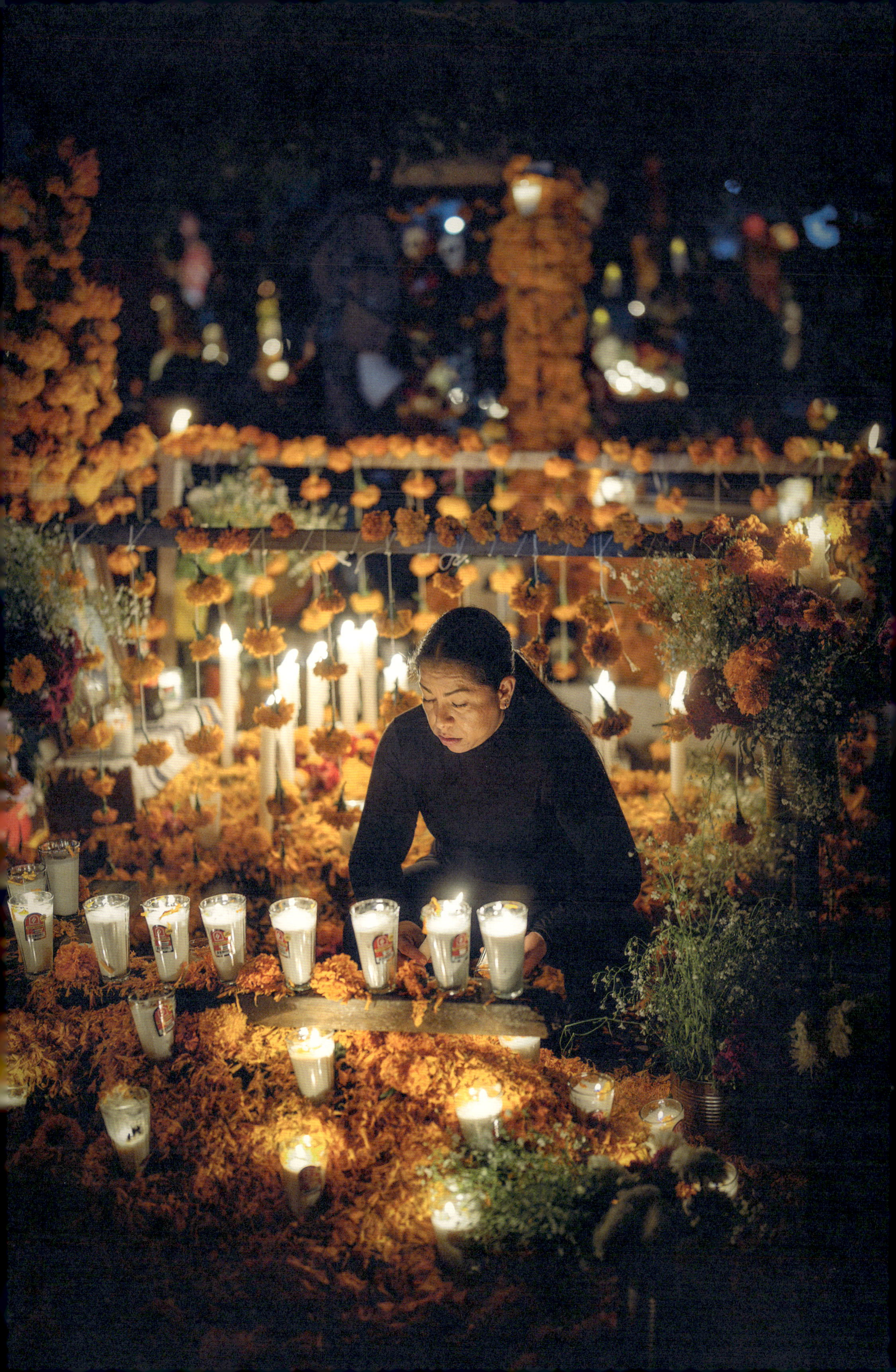

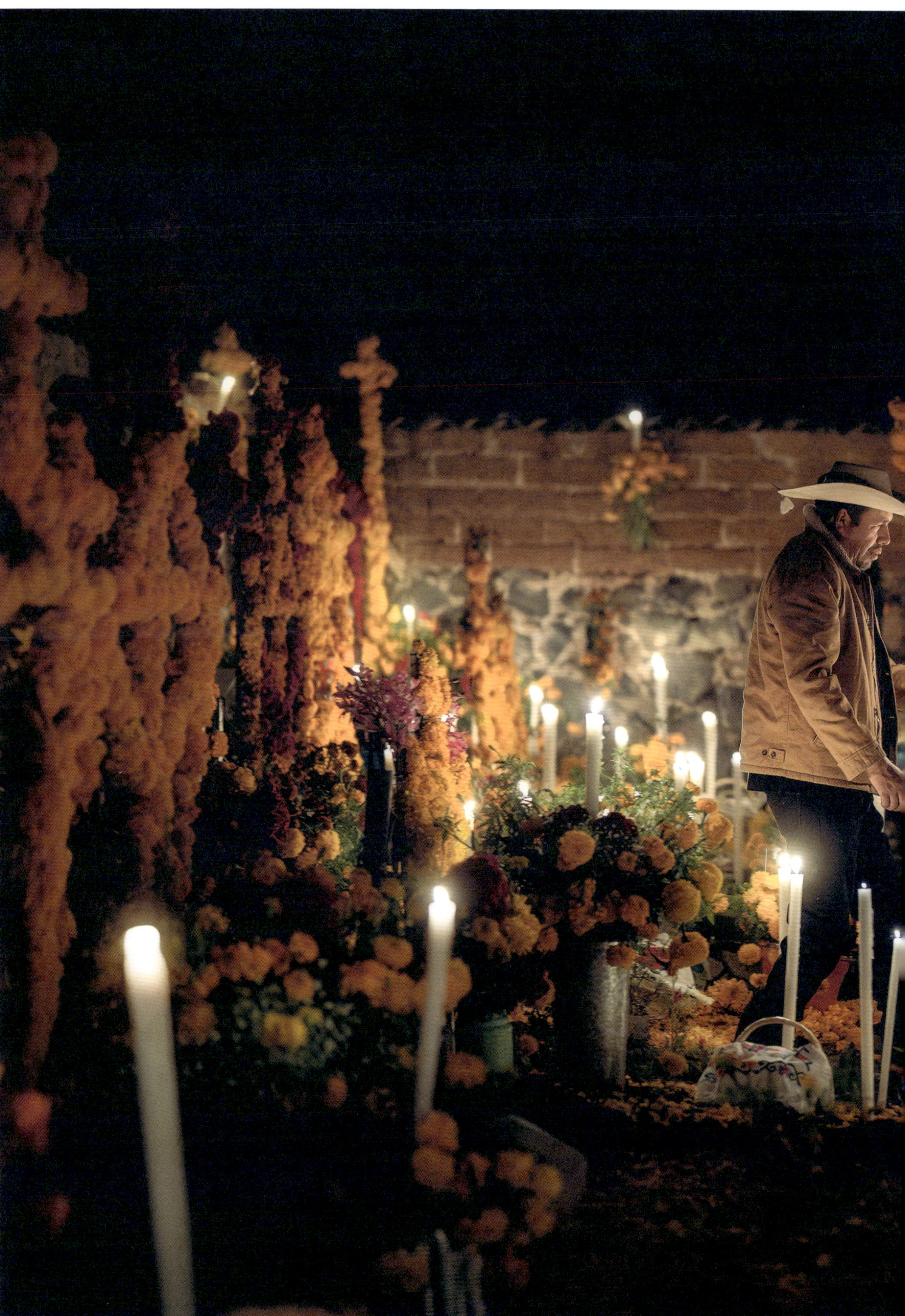

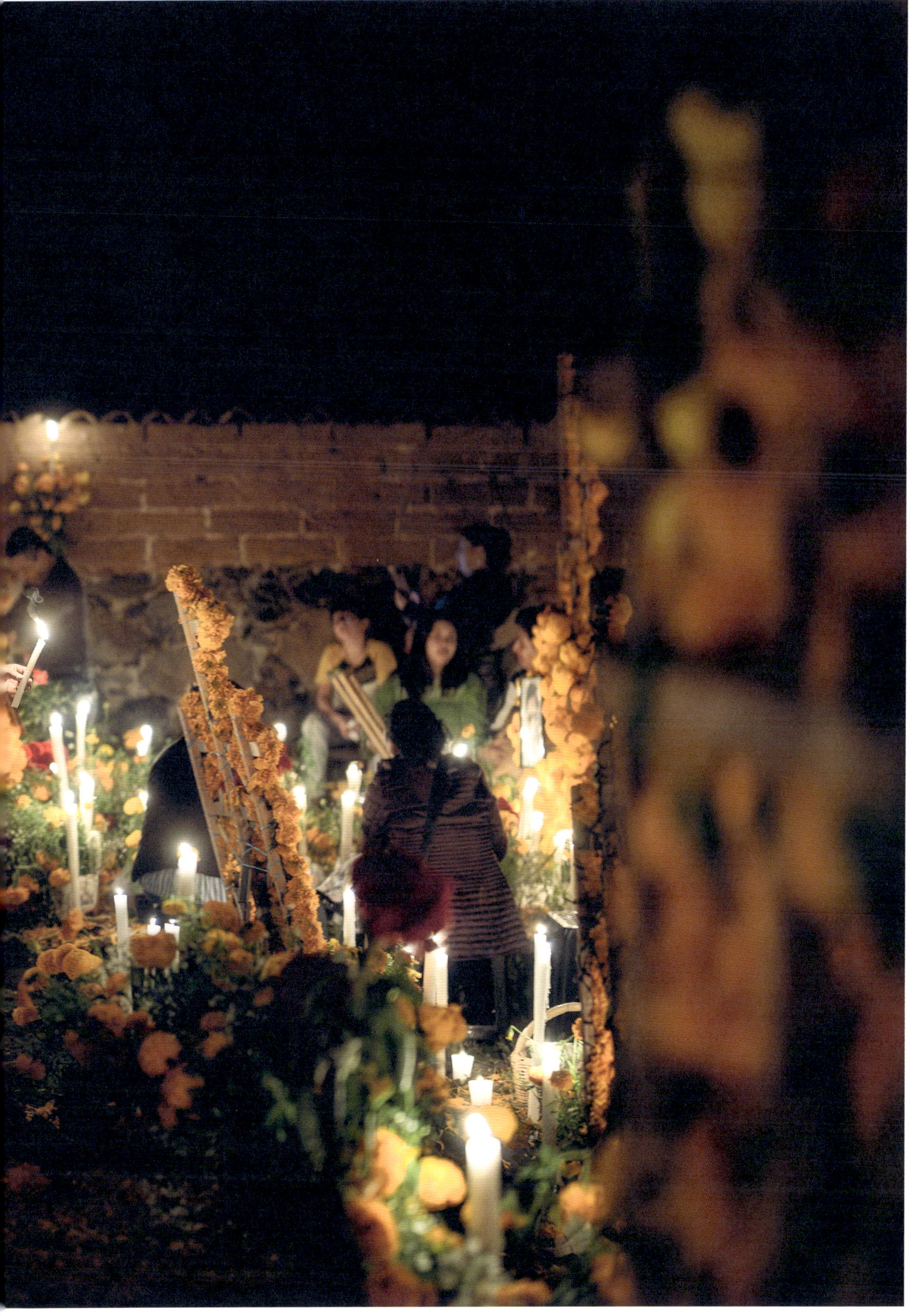

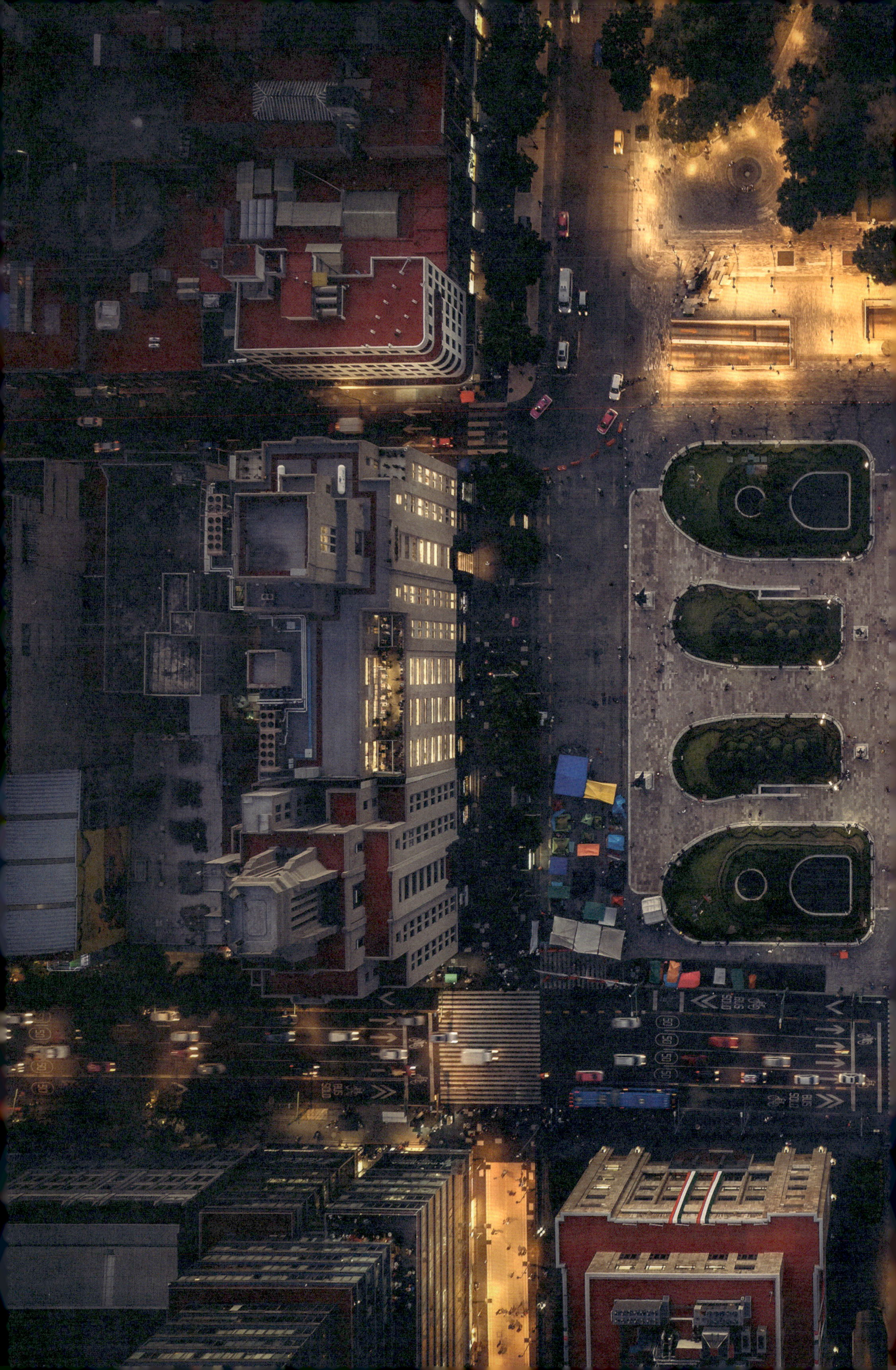

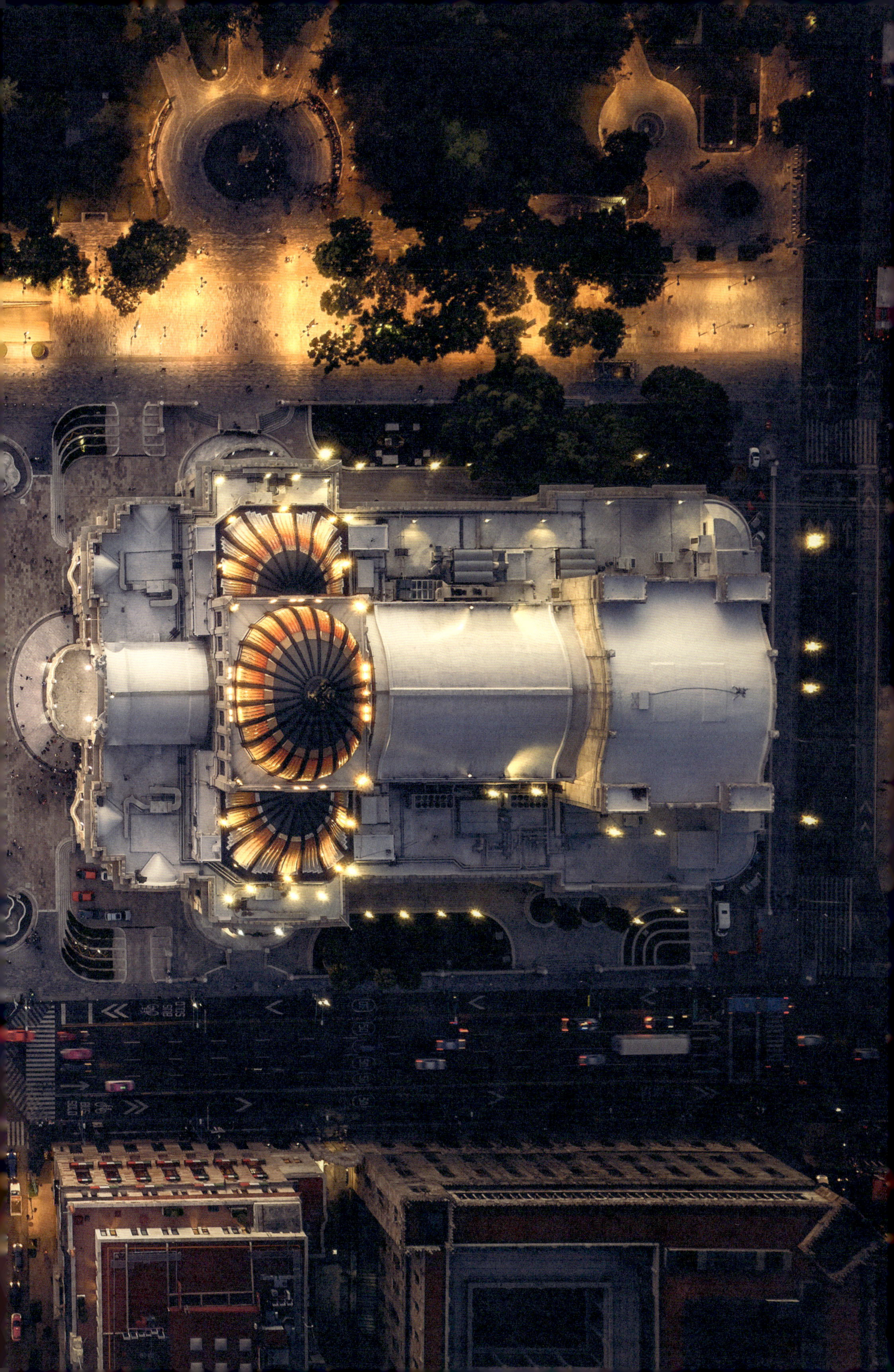

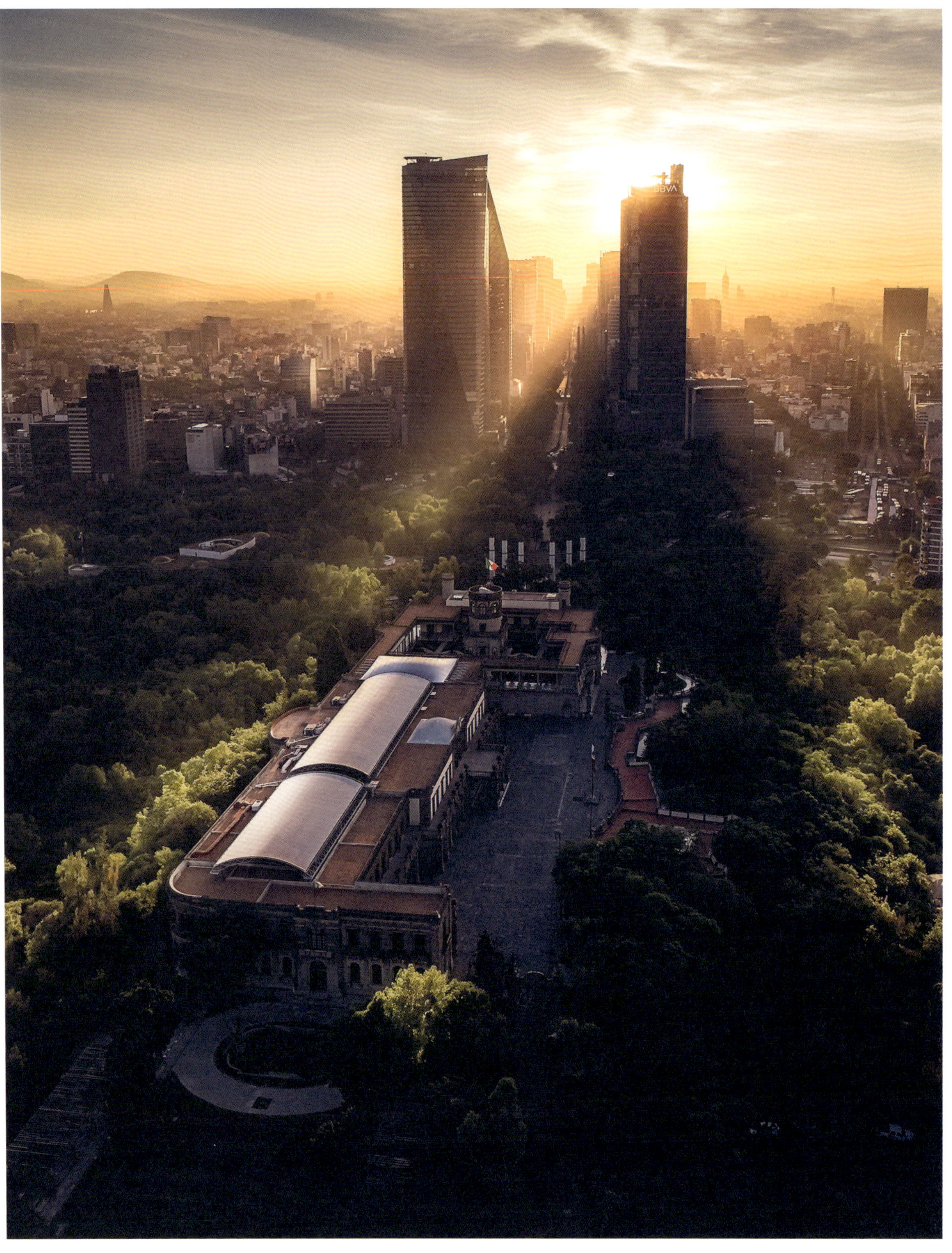

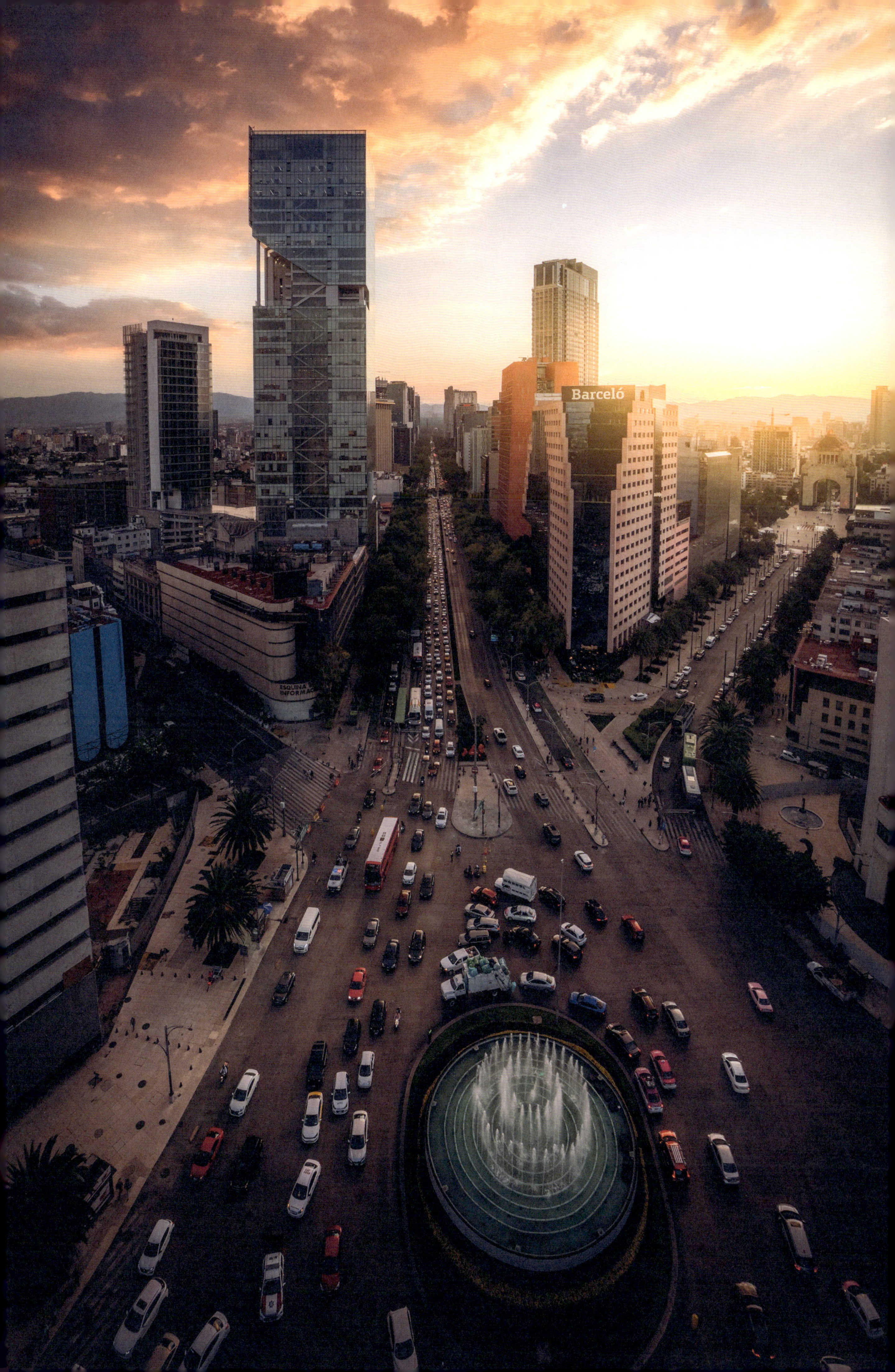
Barceló

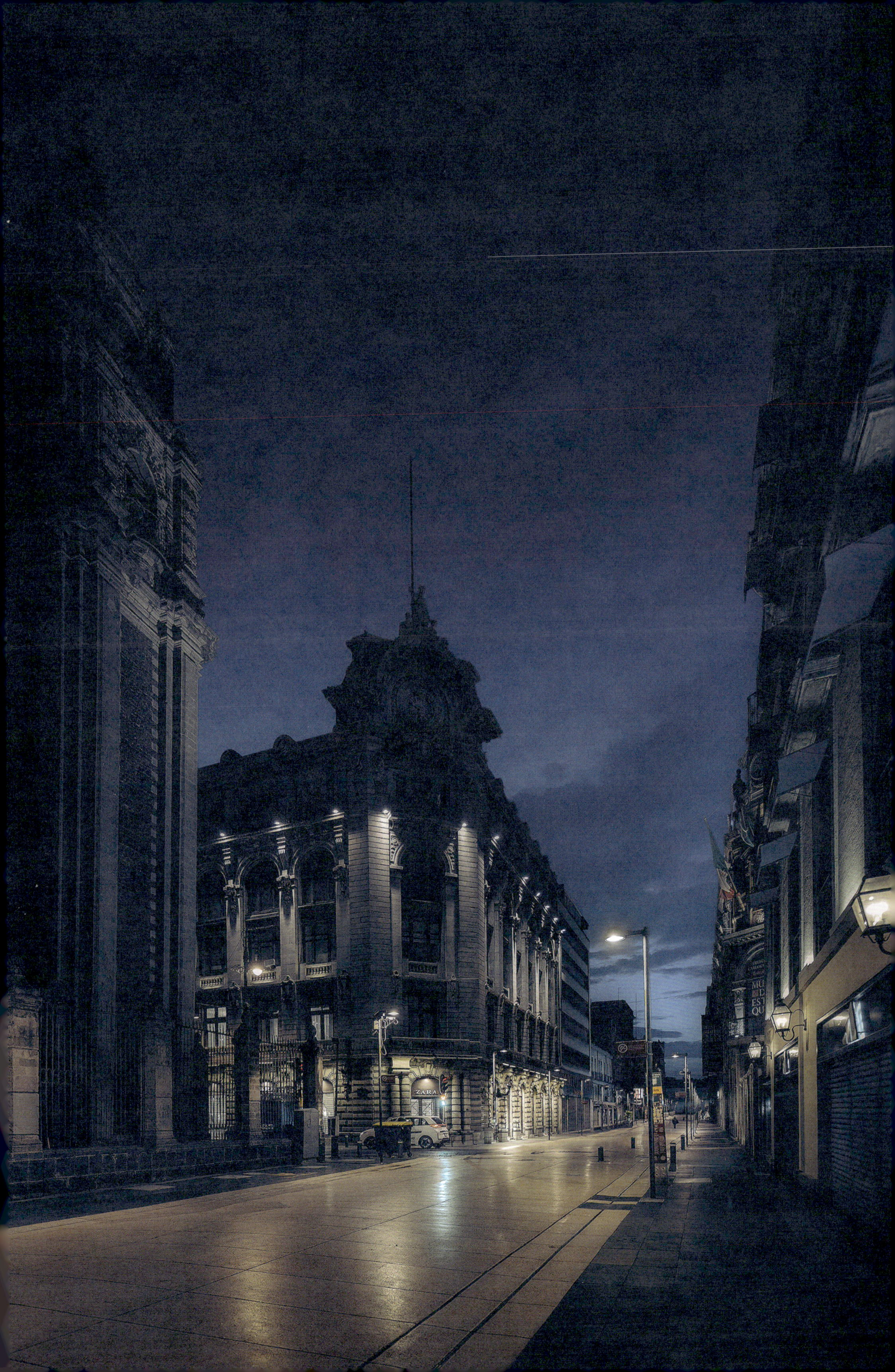
ZARA

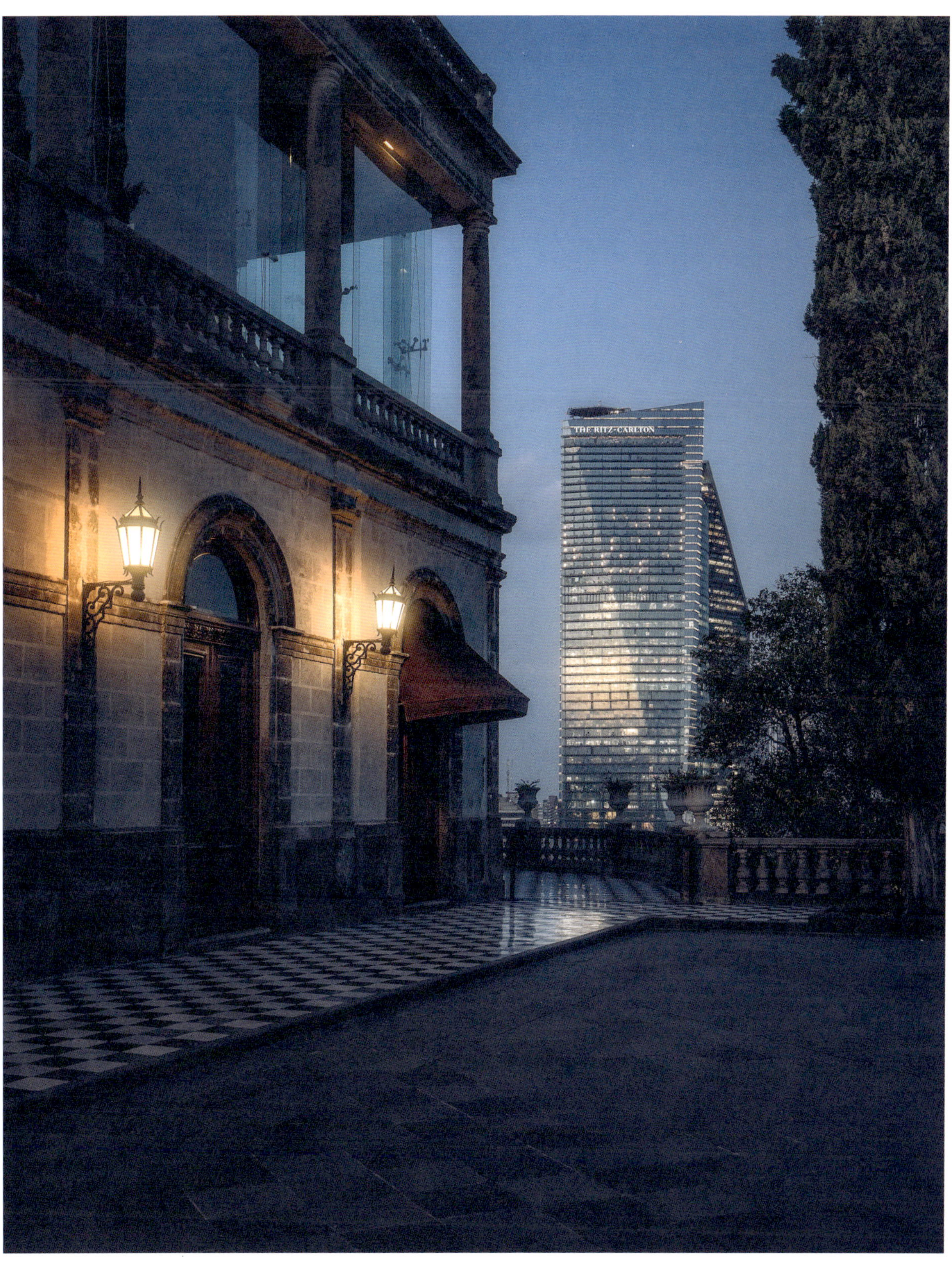
THE RITZ-CARLTON

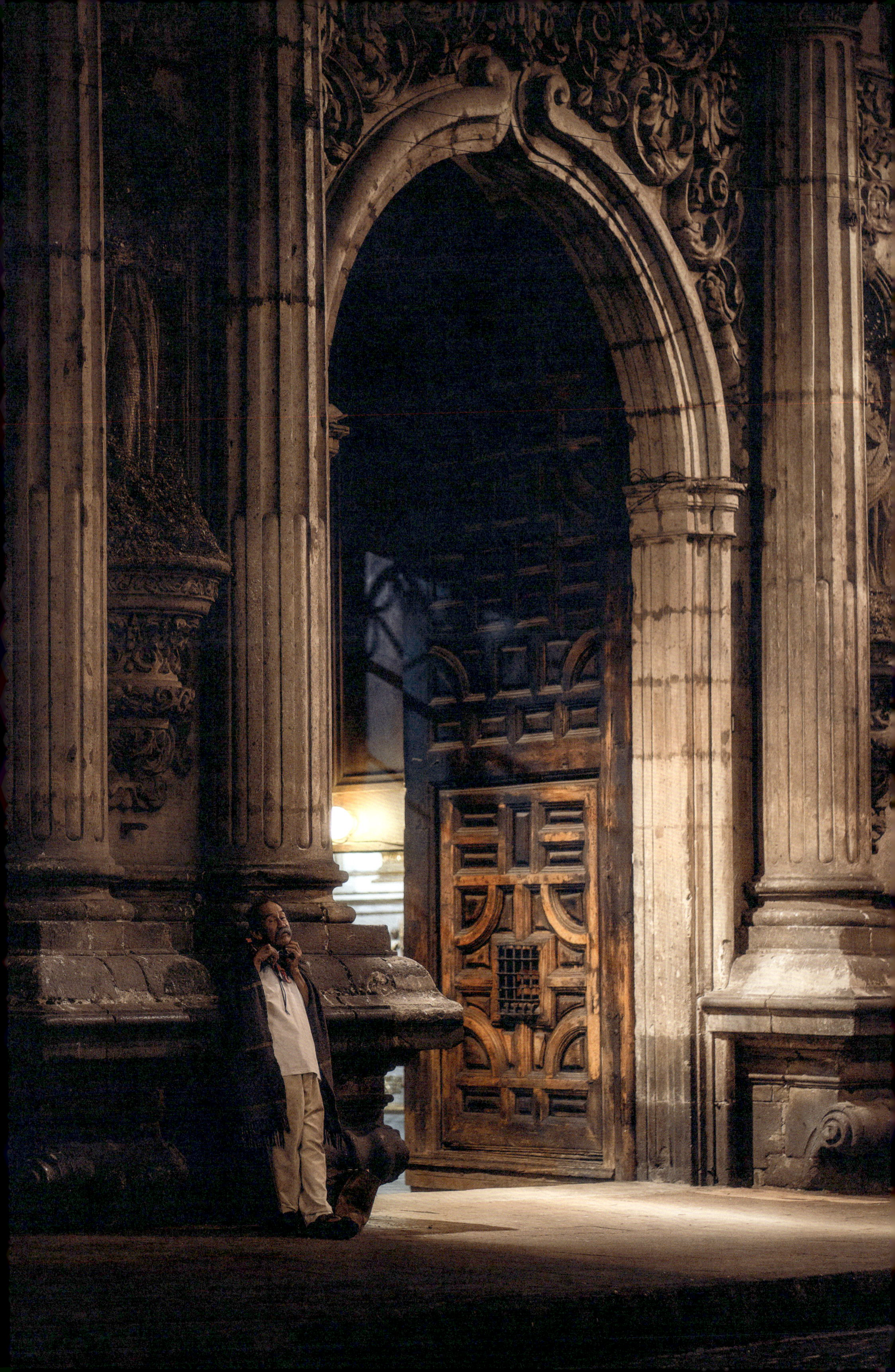

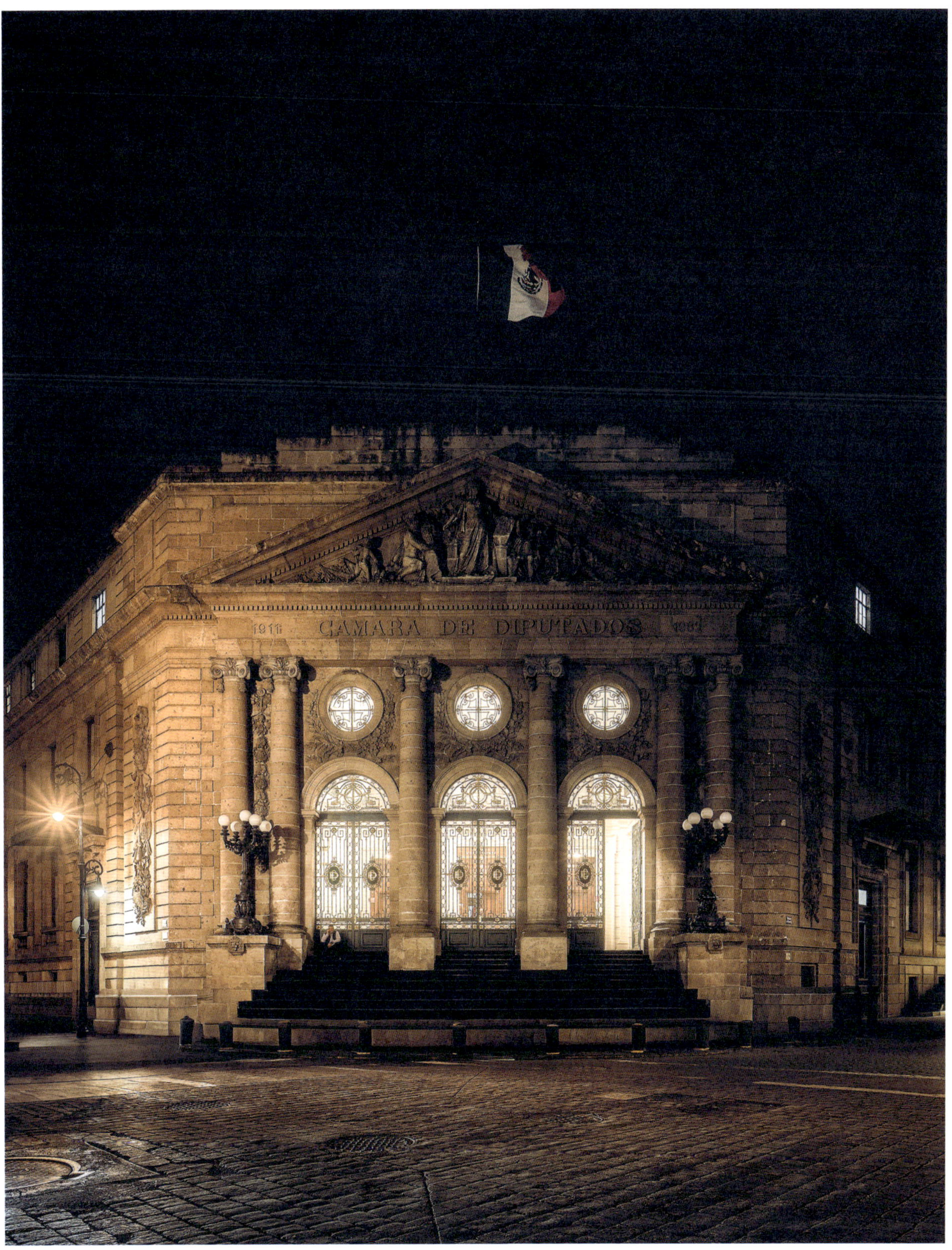
1911
CAMARA DE DIPUTADOS

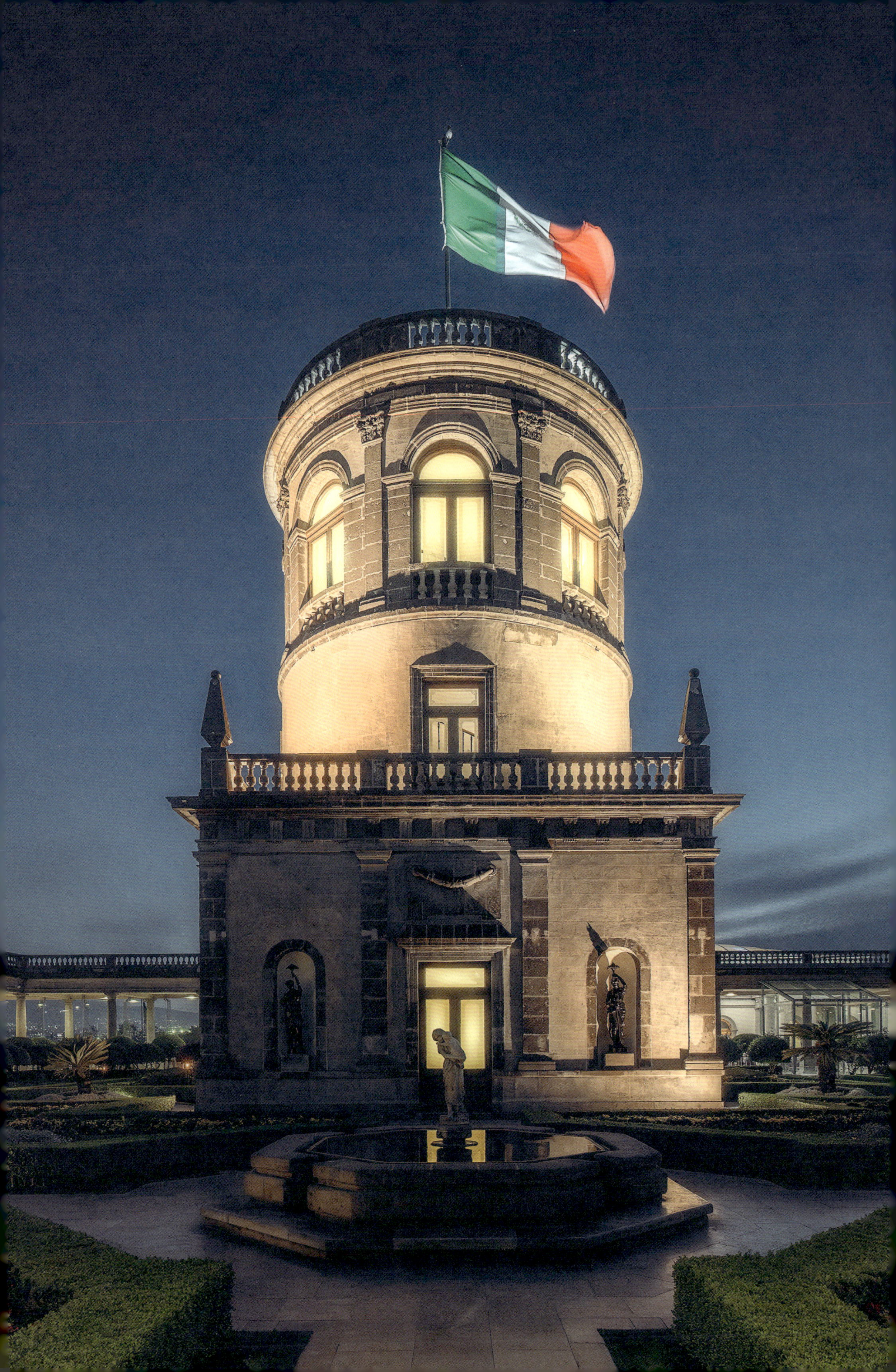

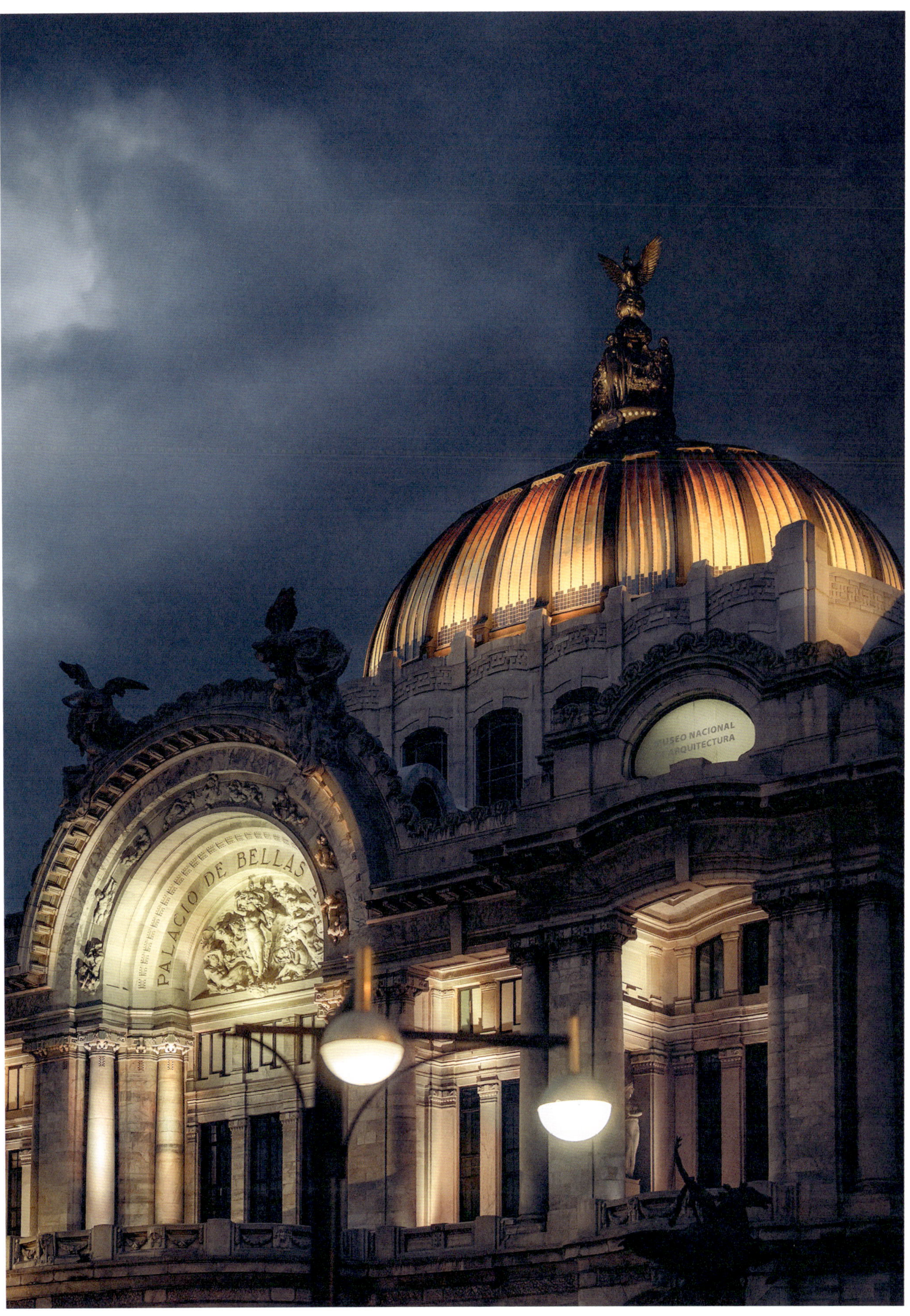
PALACIO DE BELLAS
NACIONAL
ARQUITECTURA

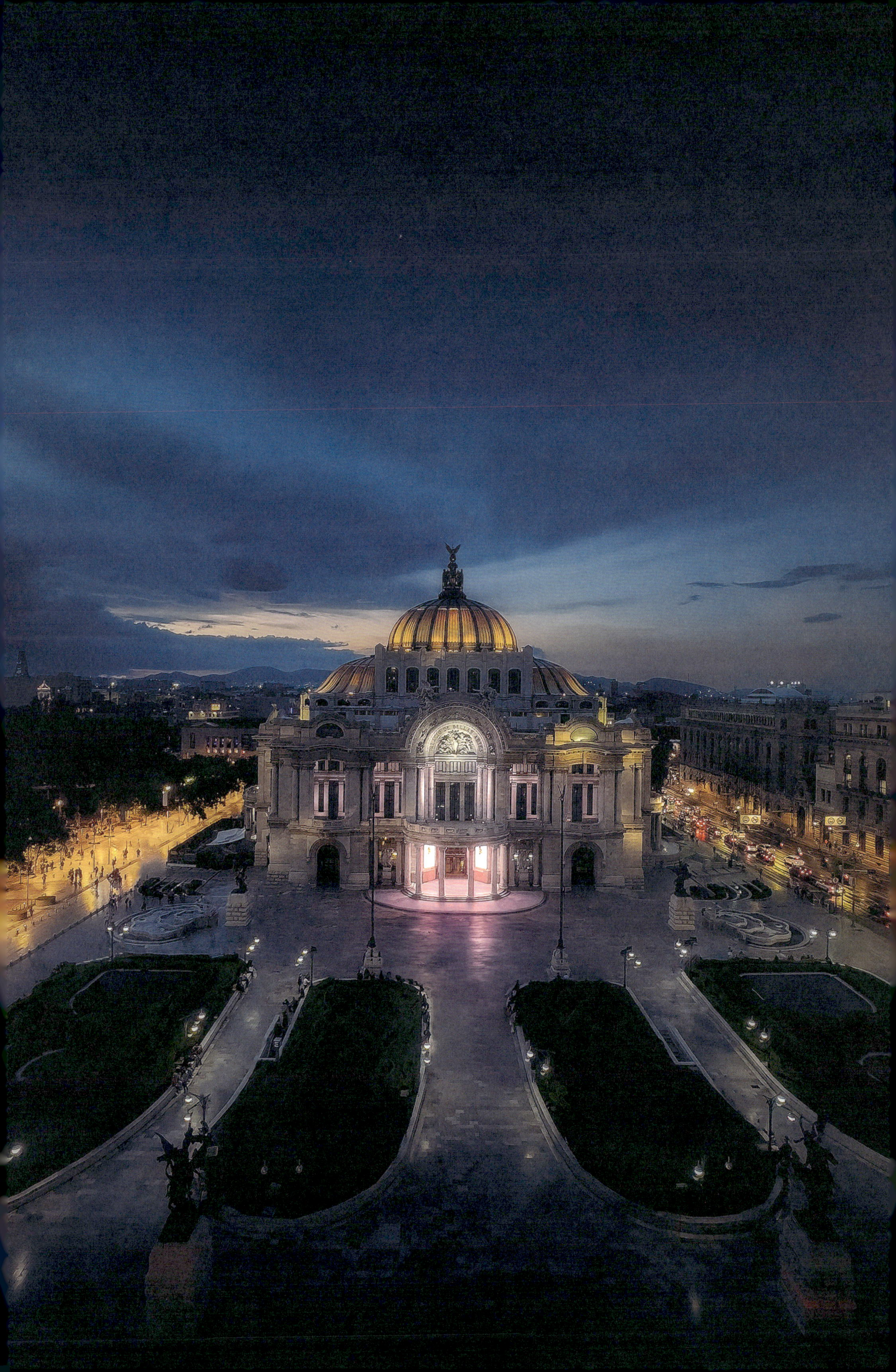

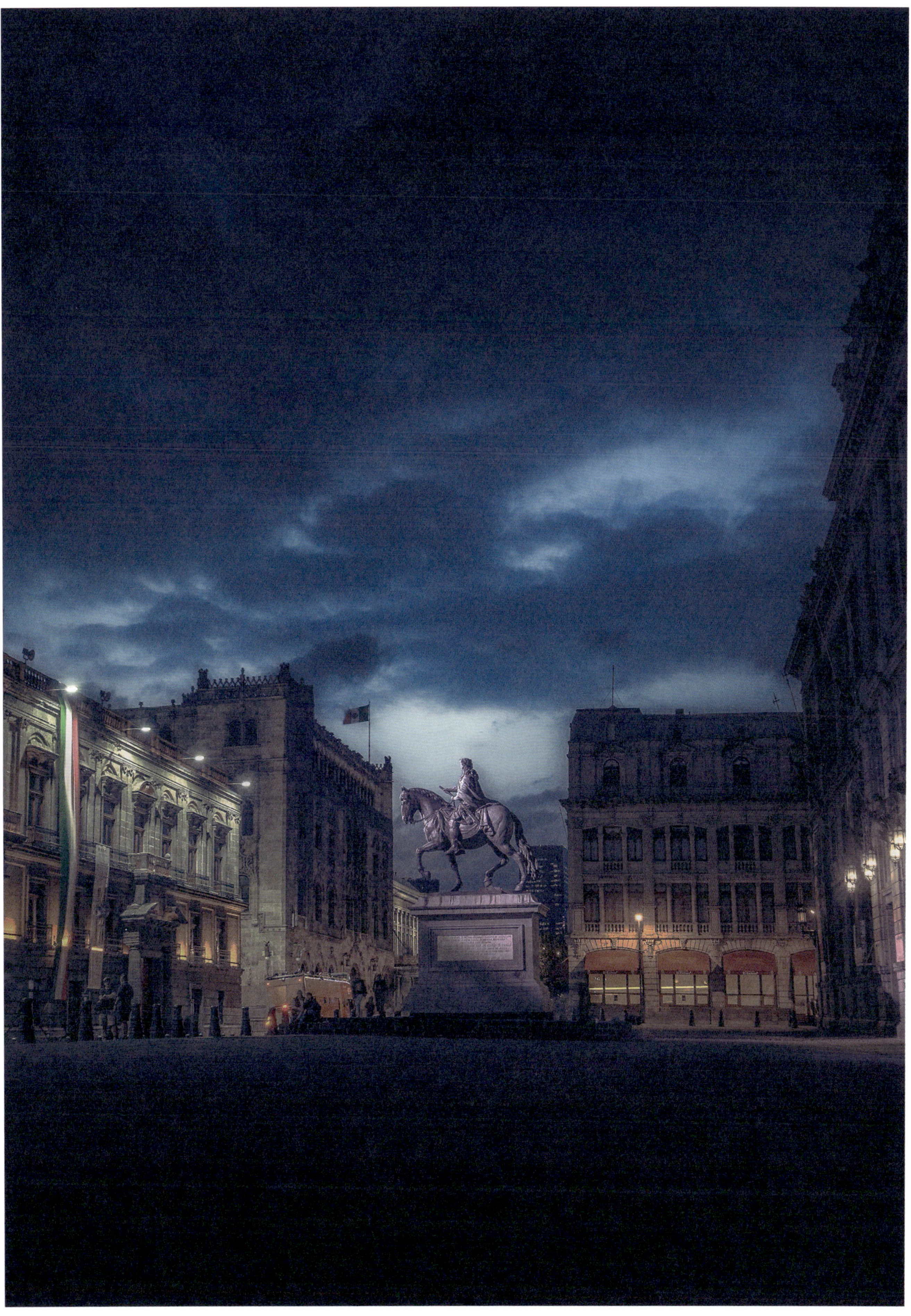

Mexico is not a country of the past but of the infinite future.

OCTAVIO PAZ
Mexican Poet and Diplomat

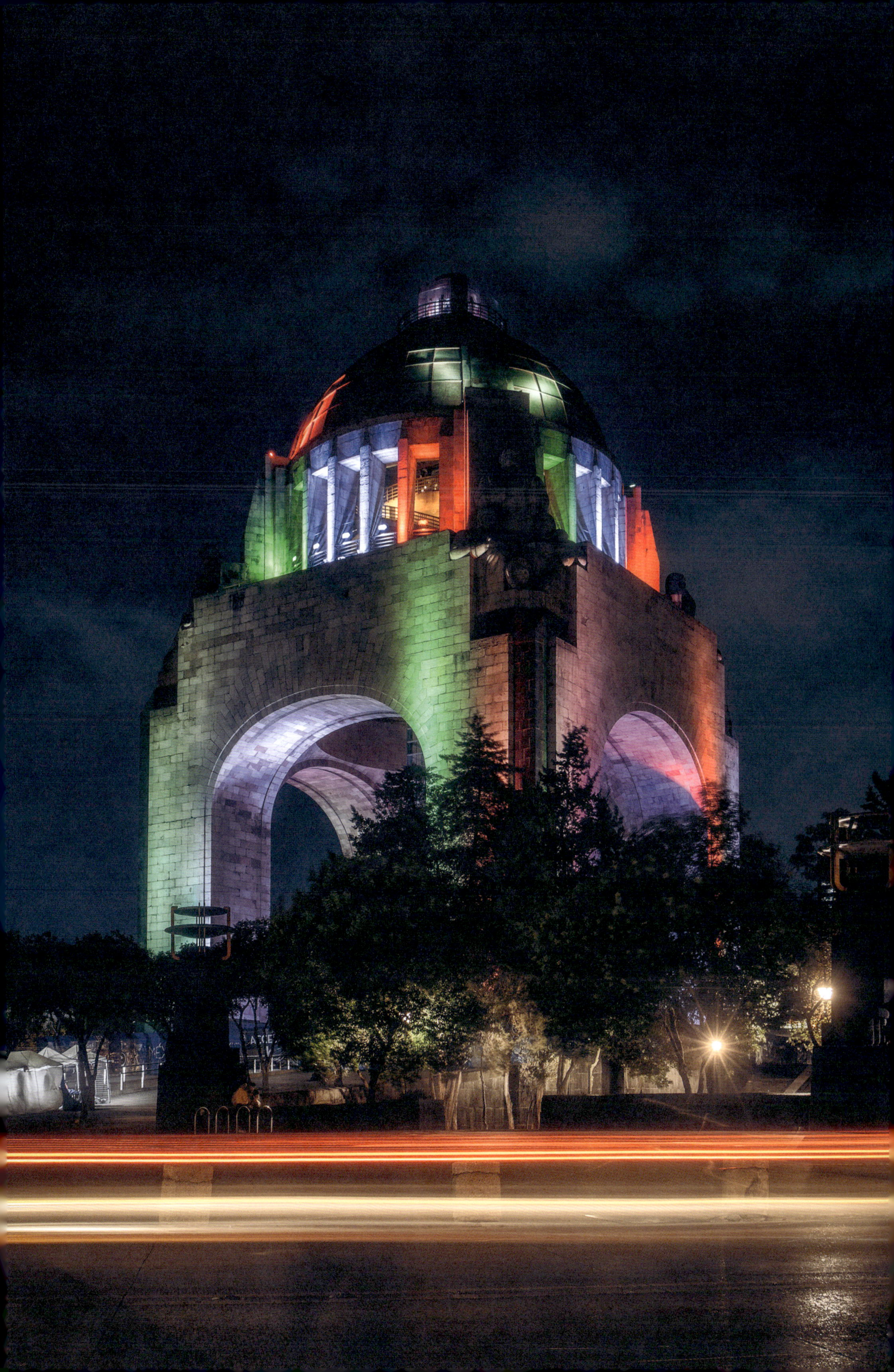

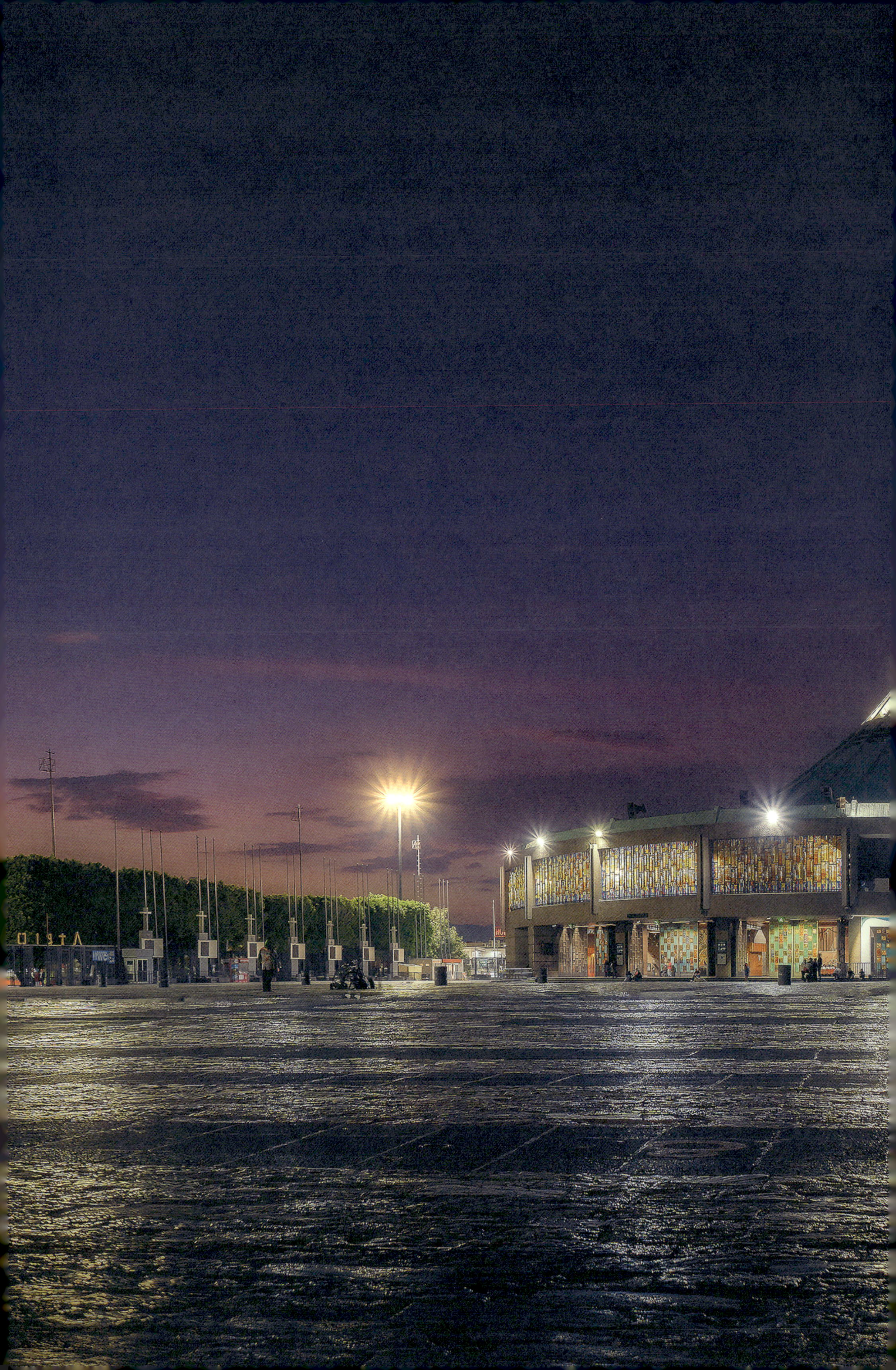

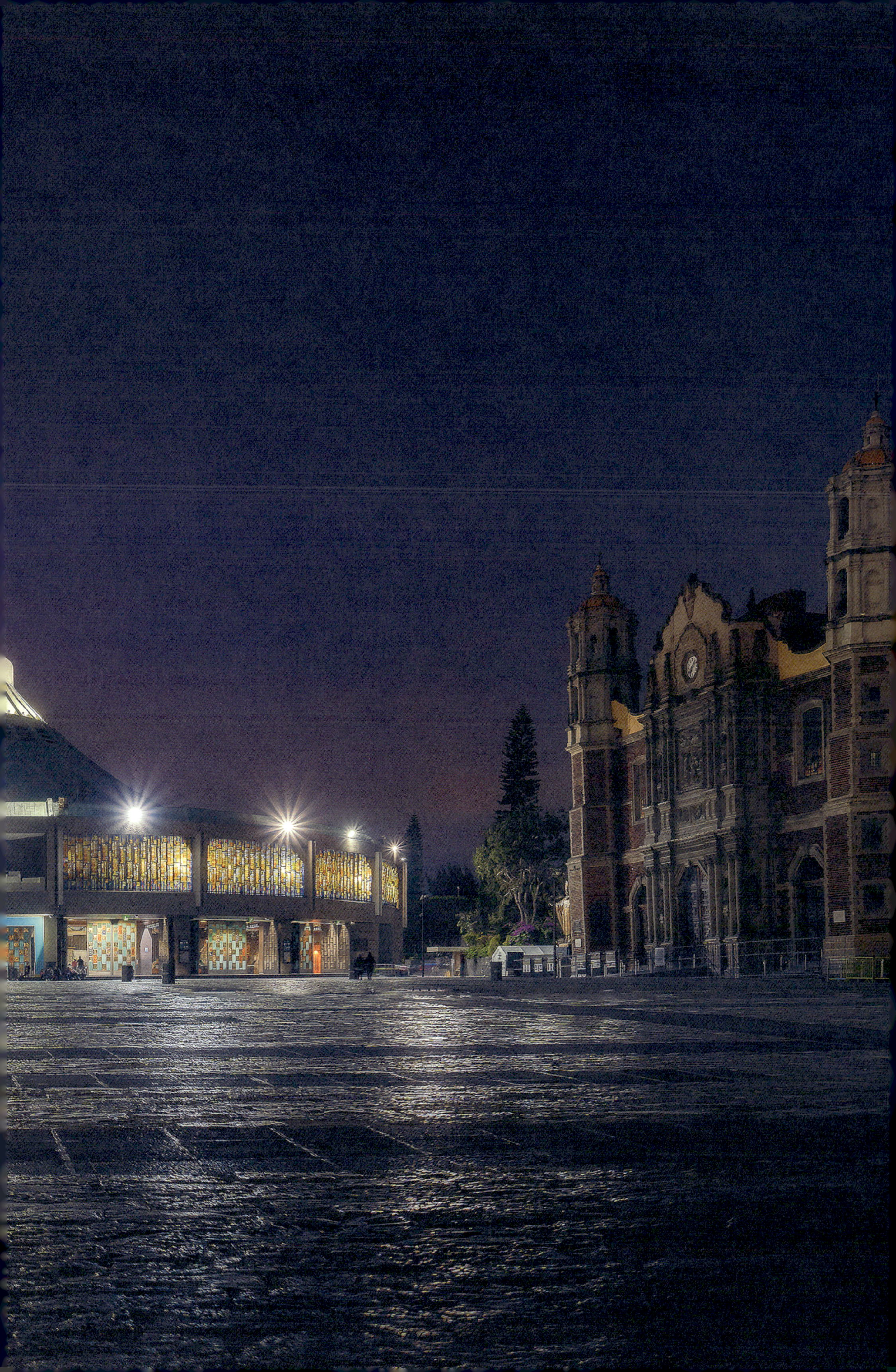

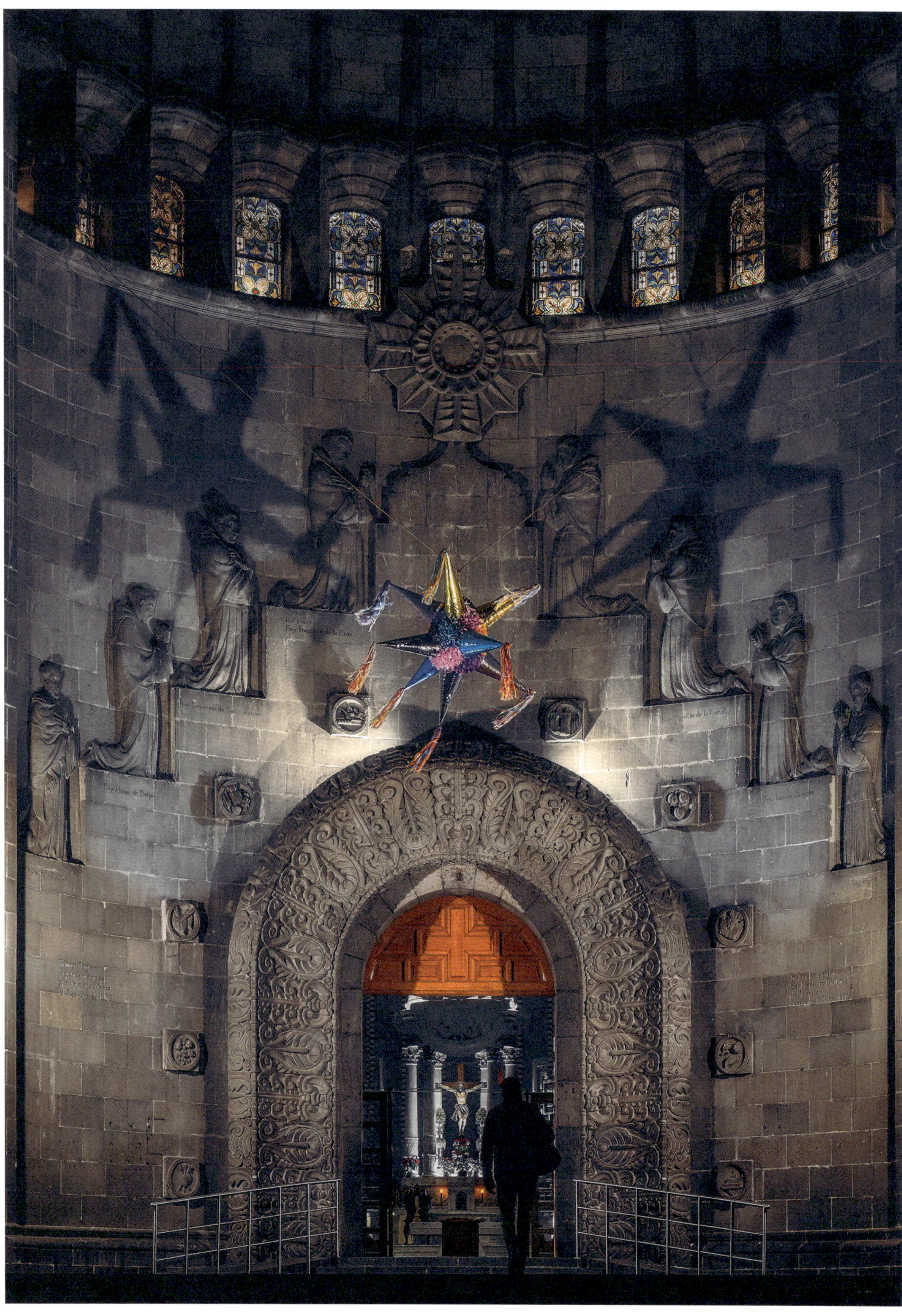

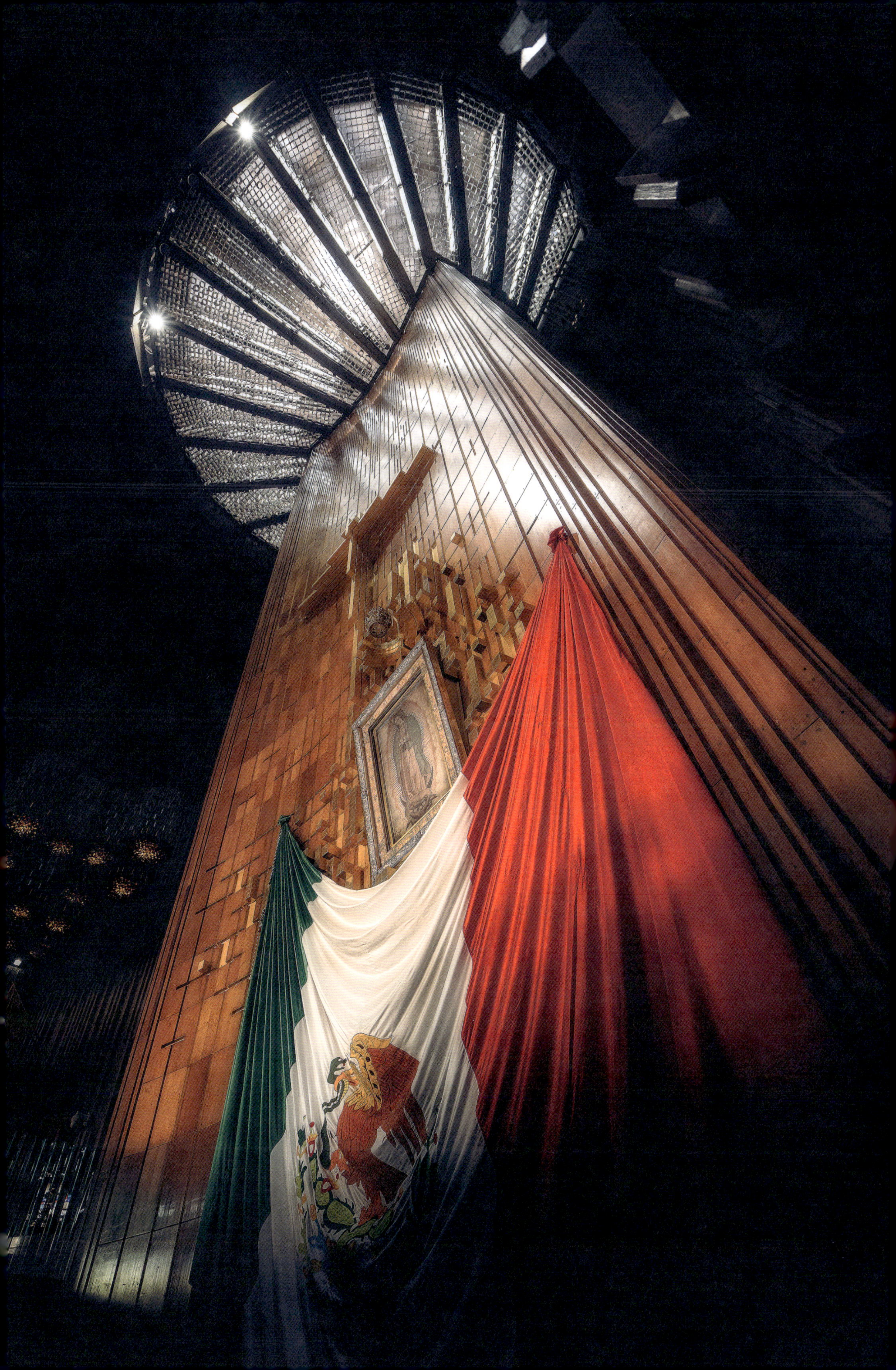

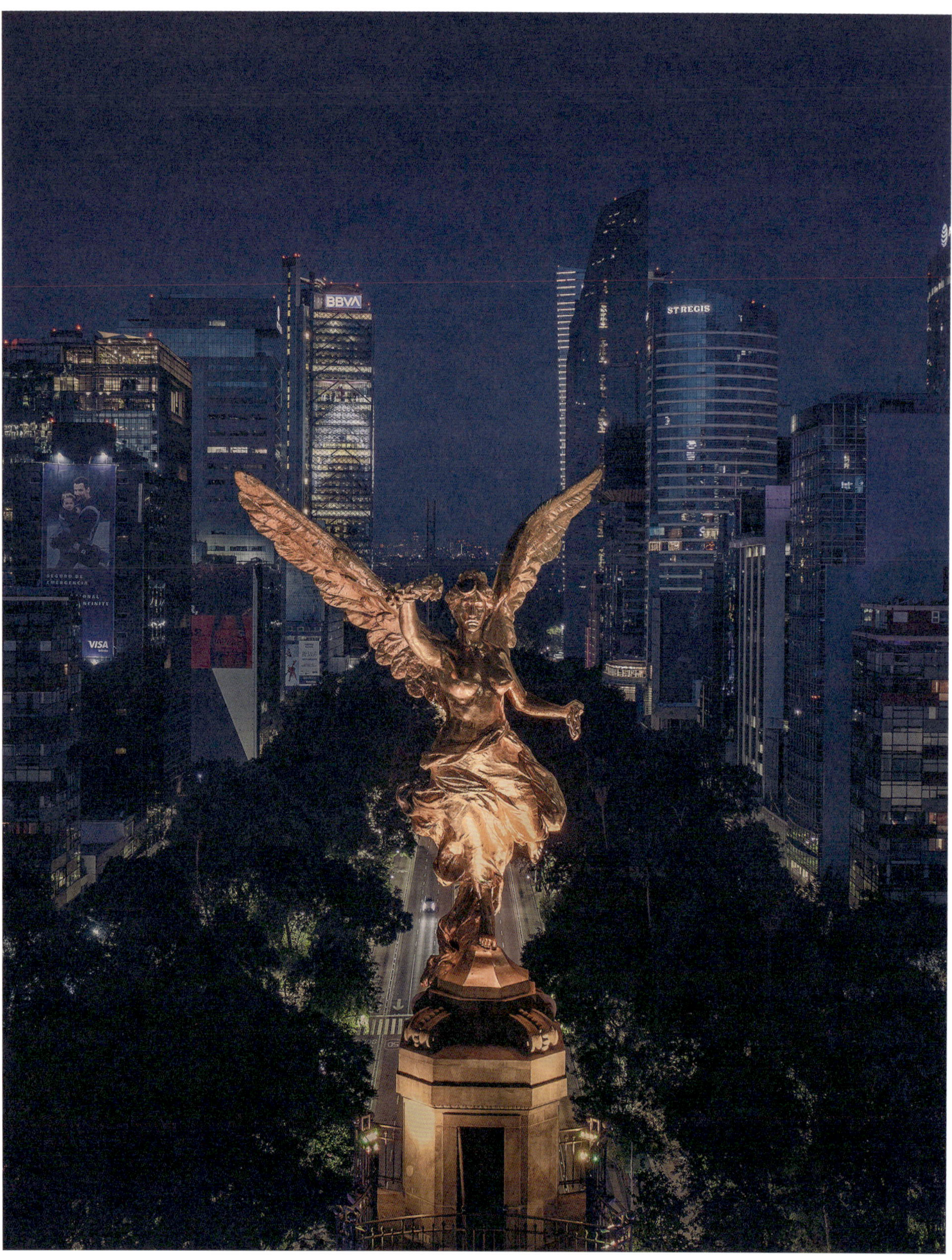
BBVA
ST REGIS
VISA

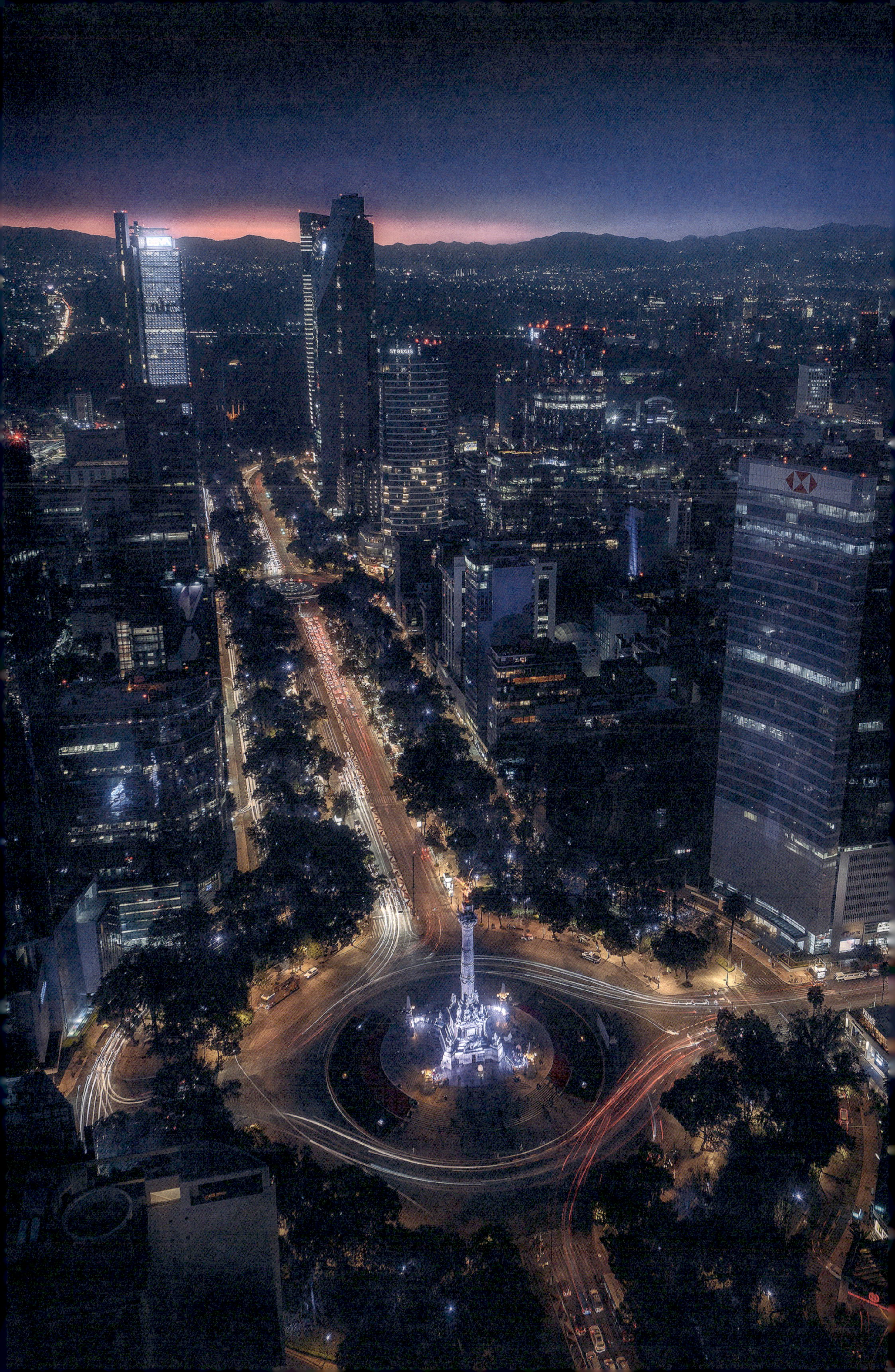

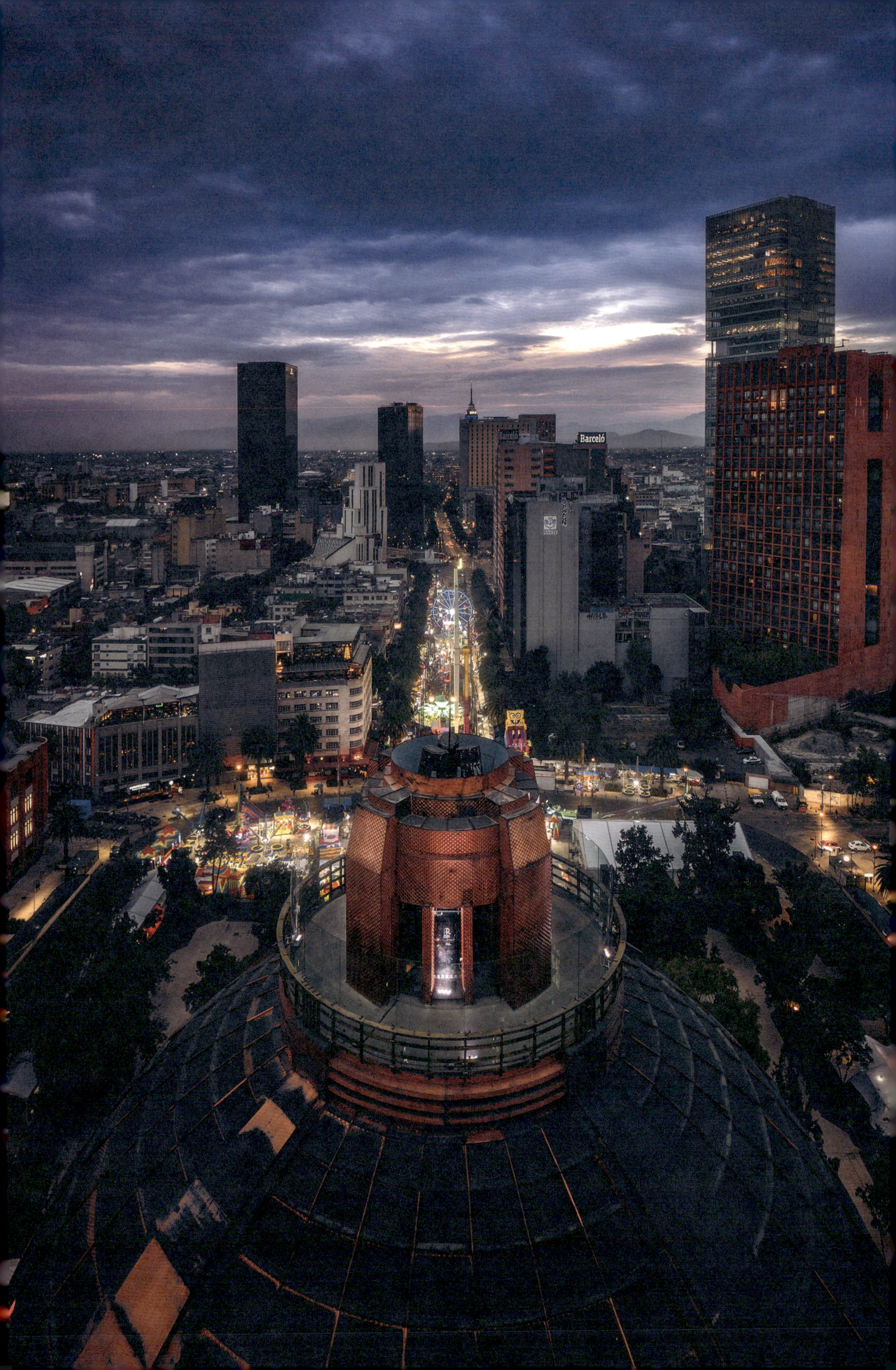
Barceló
Barceló

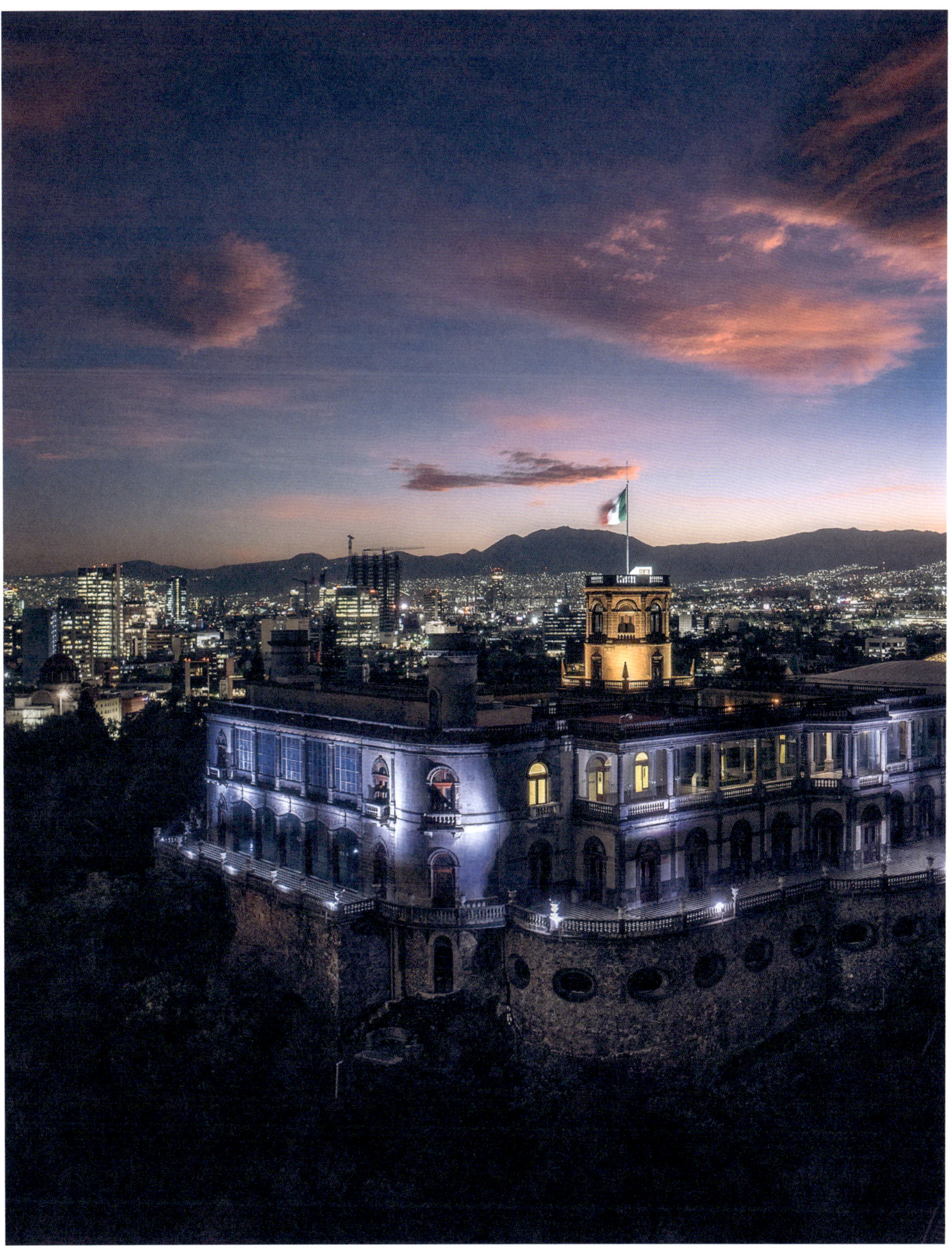

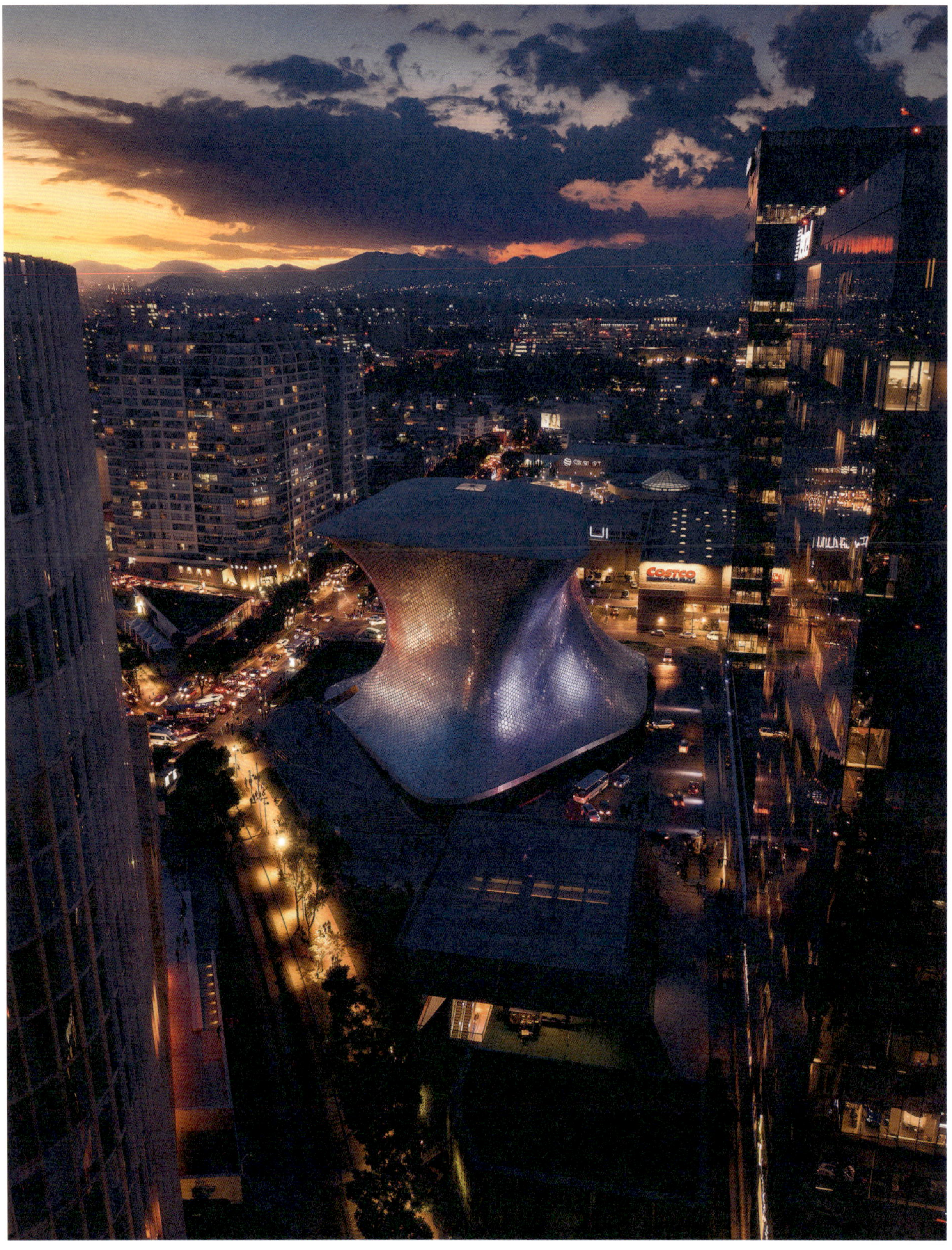
COSTCO

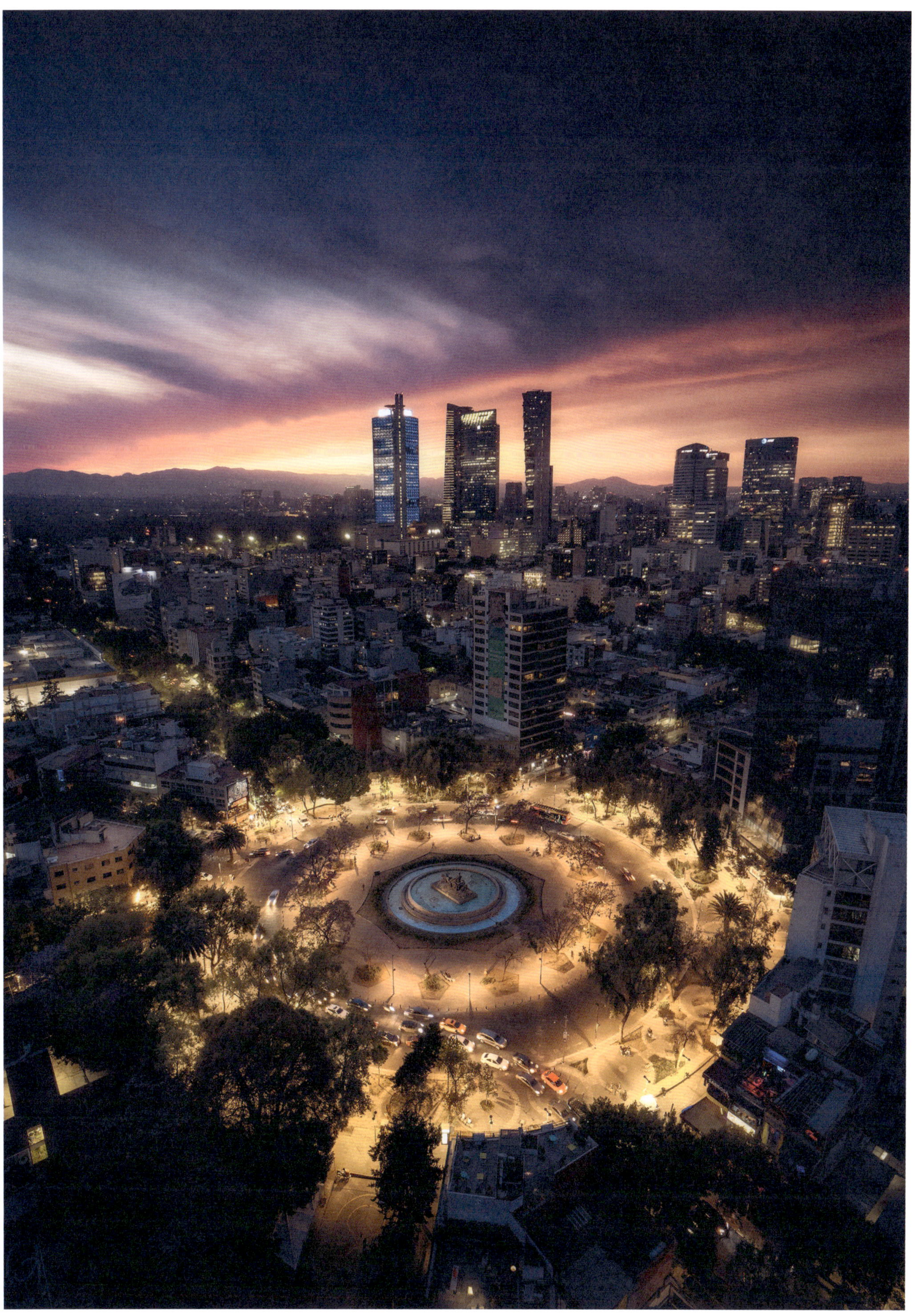

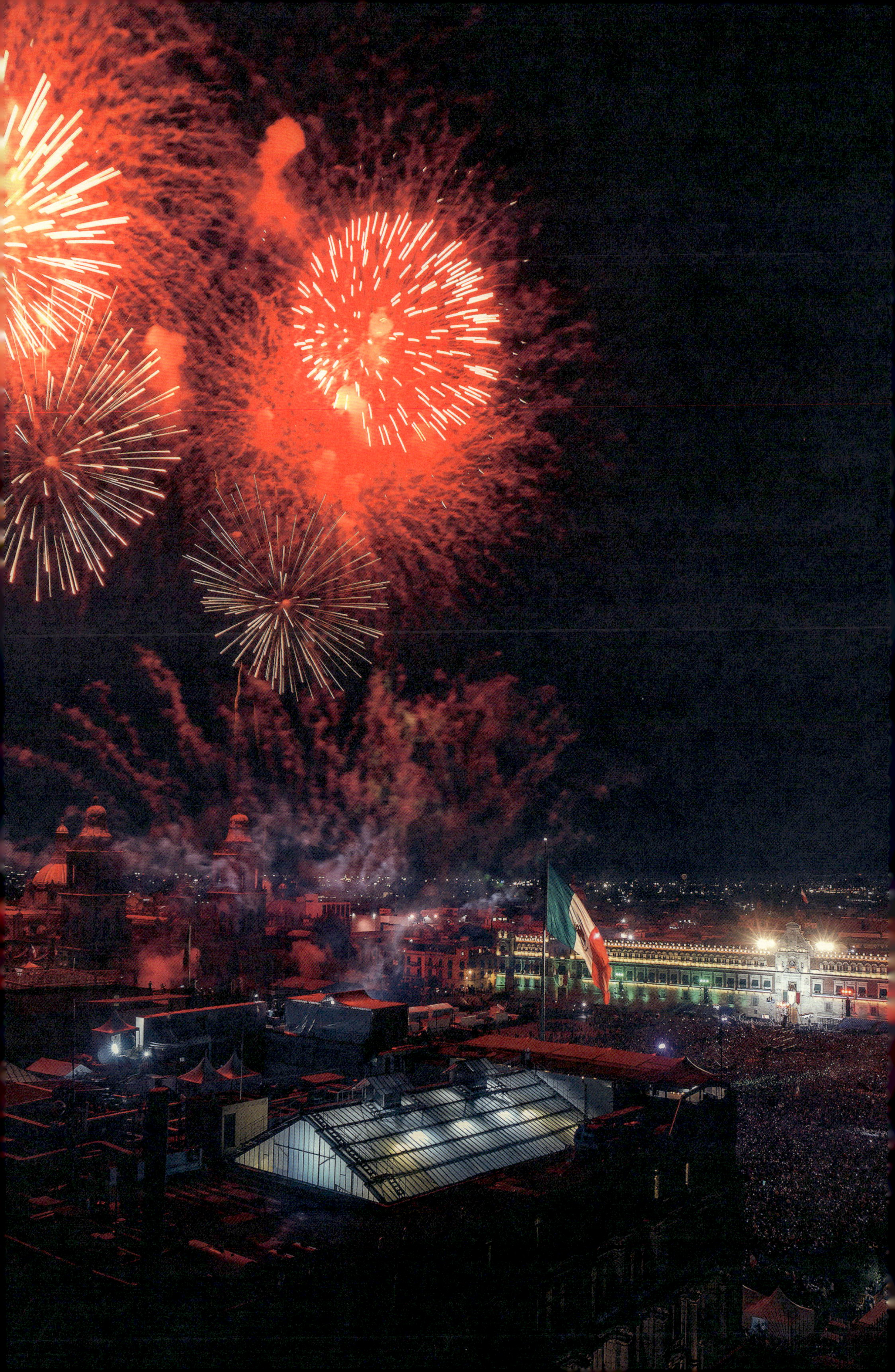

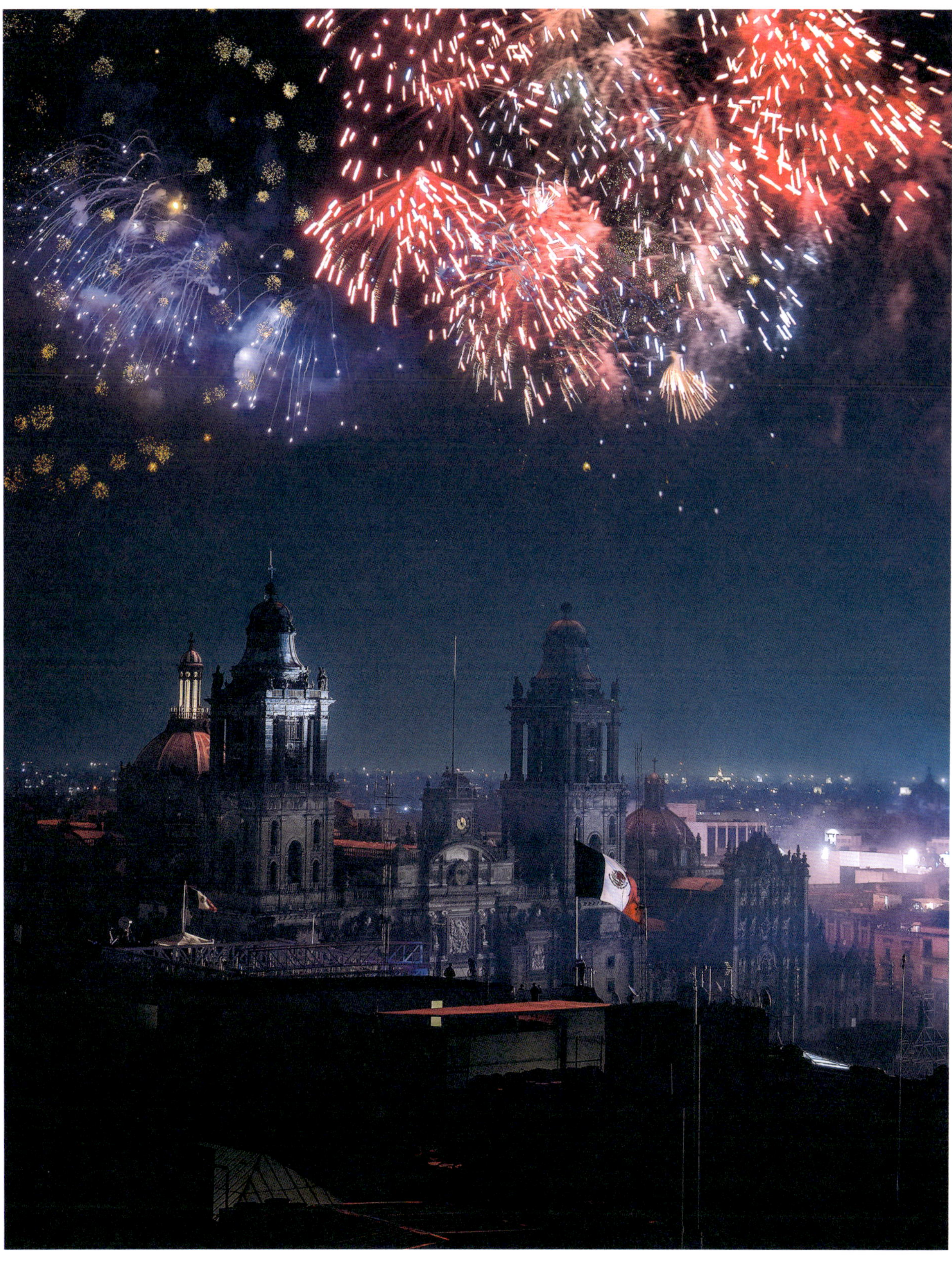

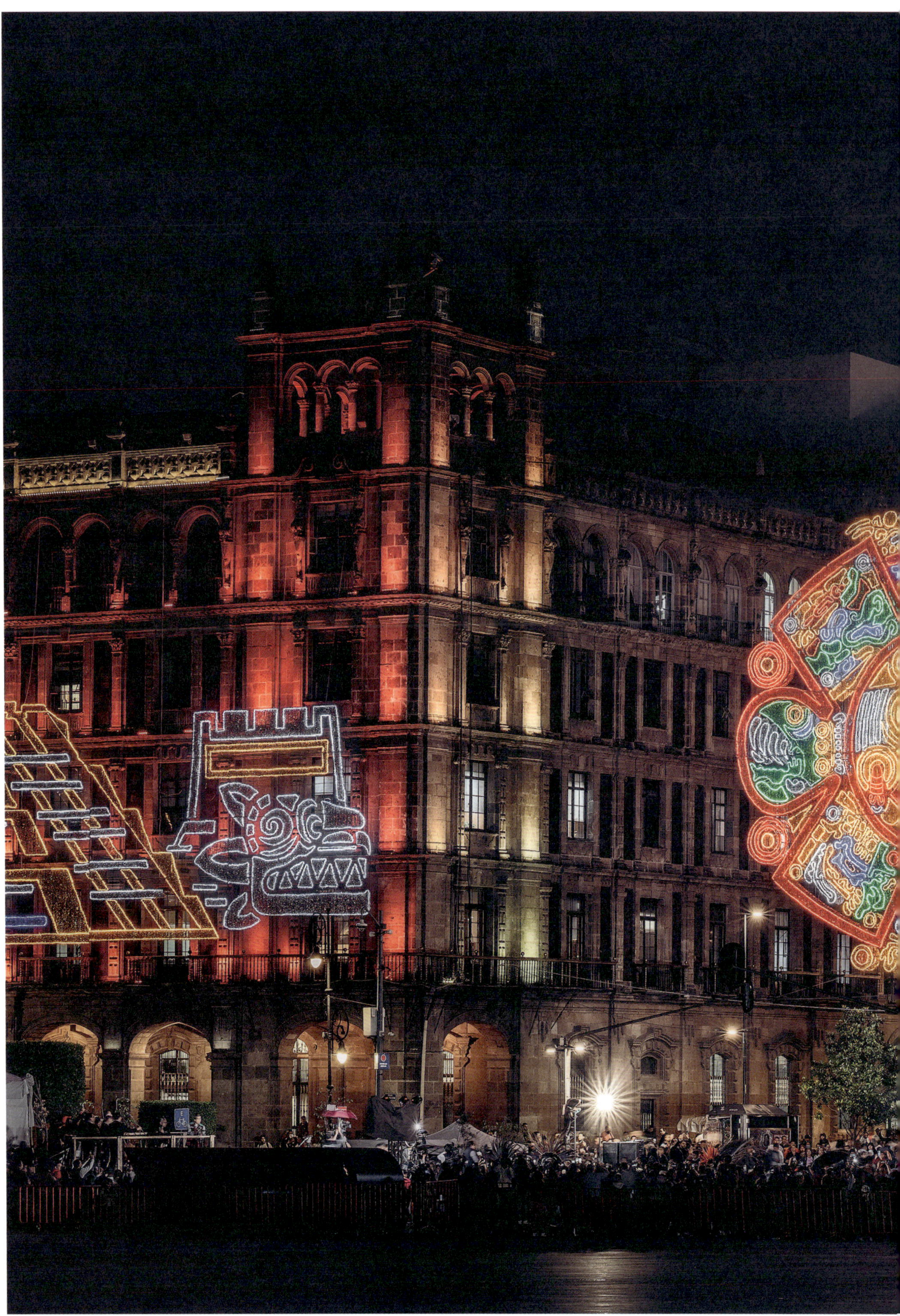

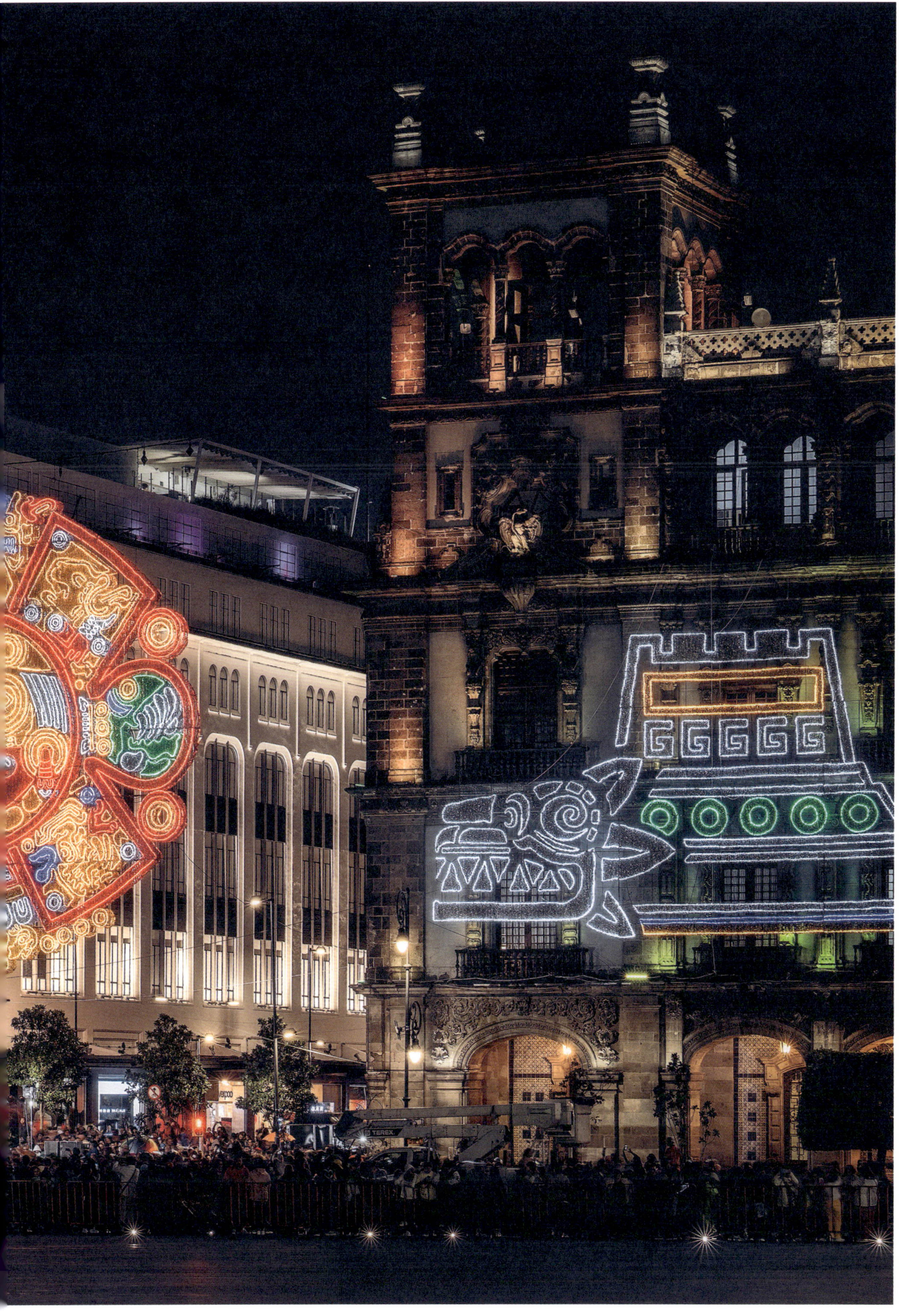

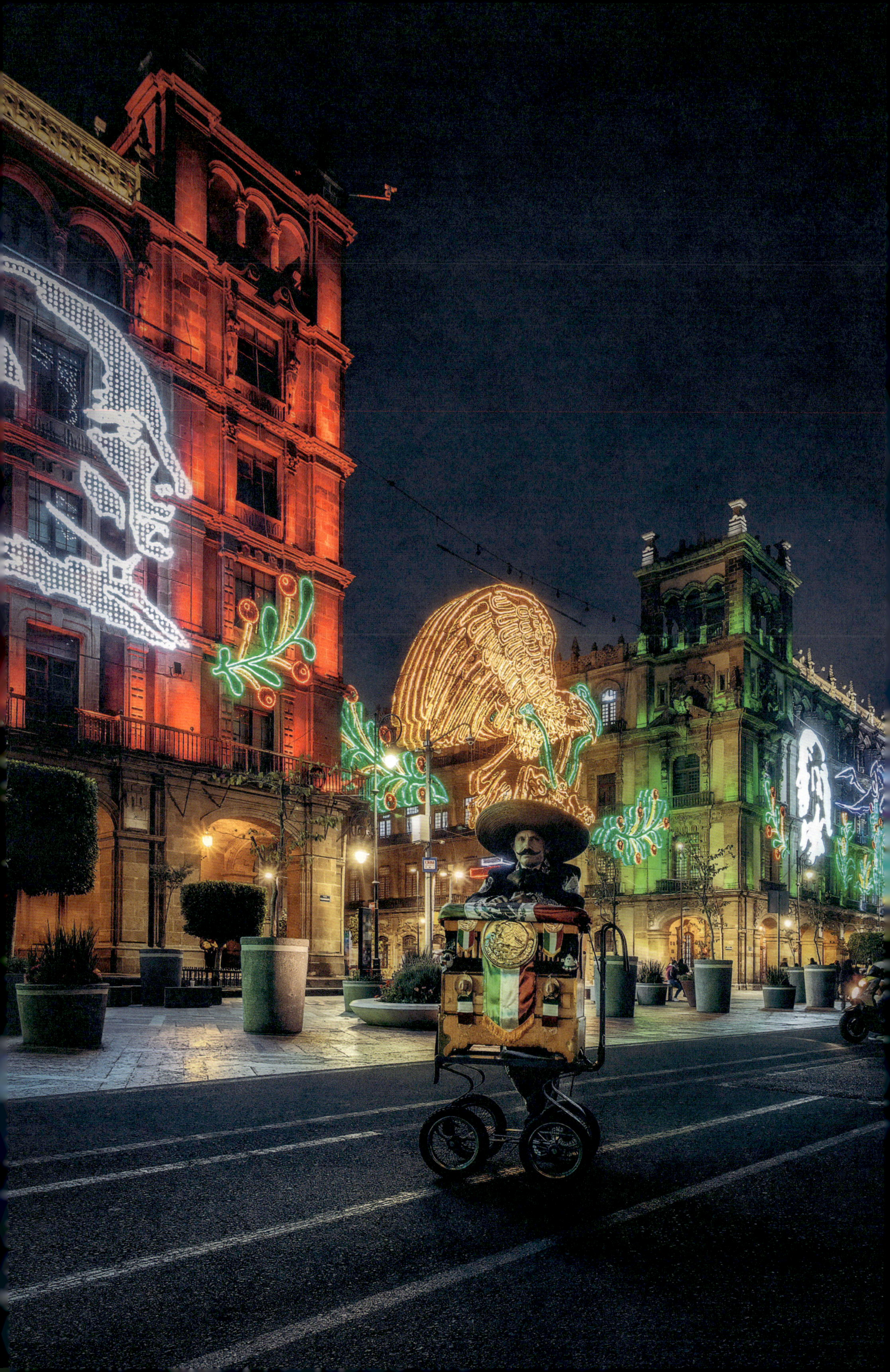

Spend a day in Centro Histórico and you're guaranteed to walk away with a deeper, richer, more robust understanding of and appreciation for our incredible culture.

AARÓN SÁNCHEZ

Mexican-American Chef and Restaurateur

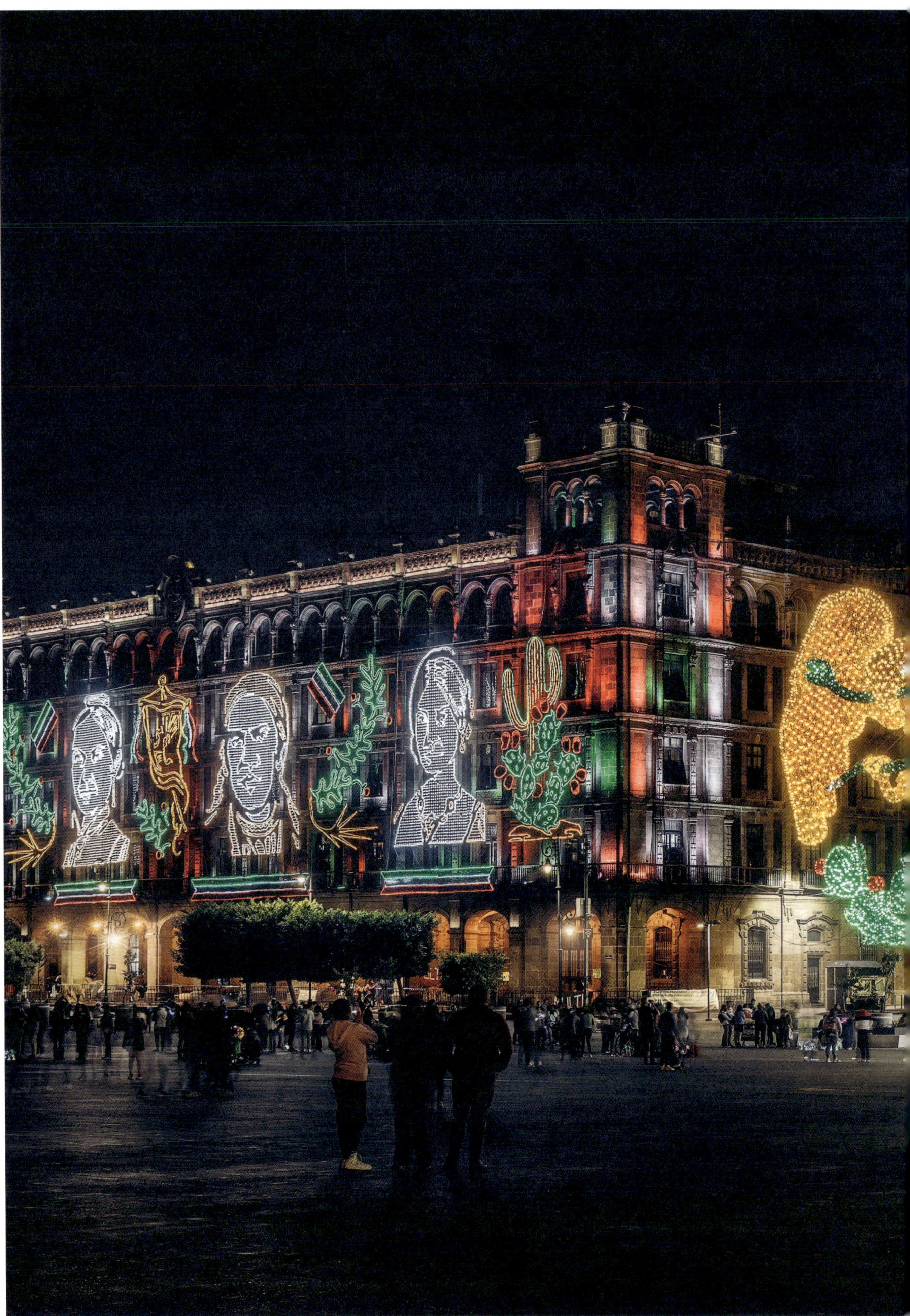

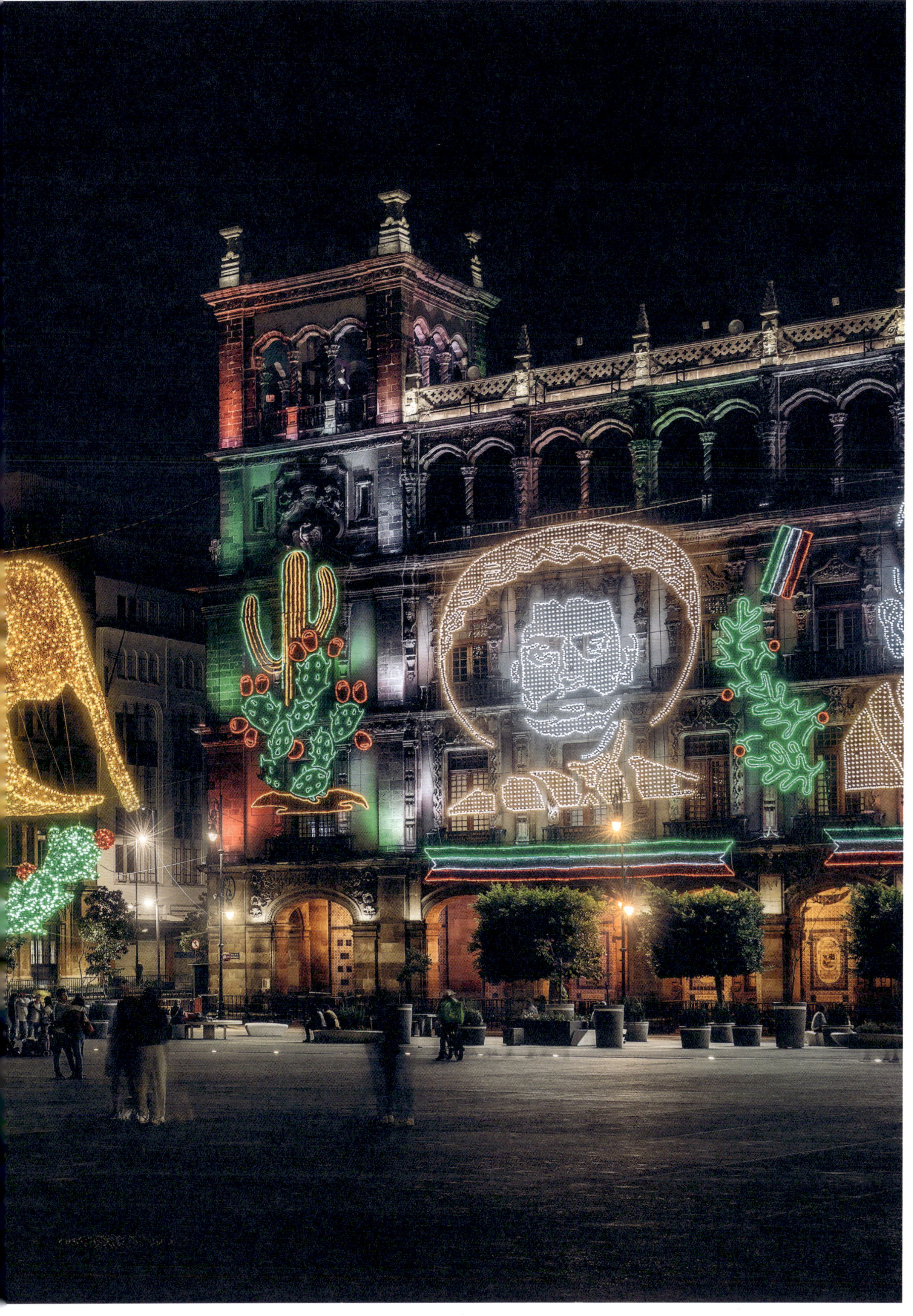

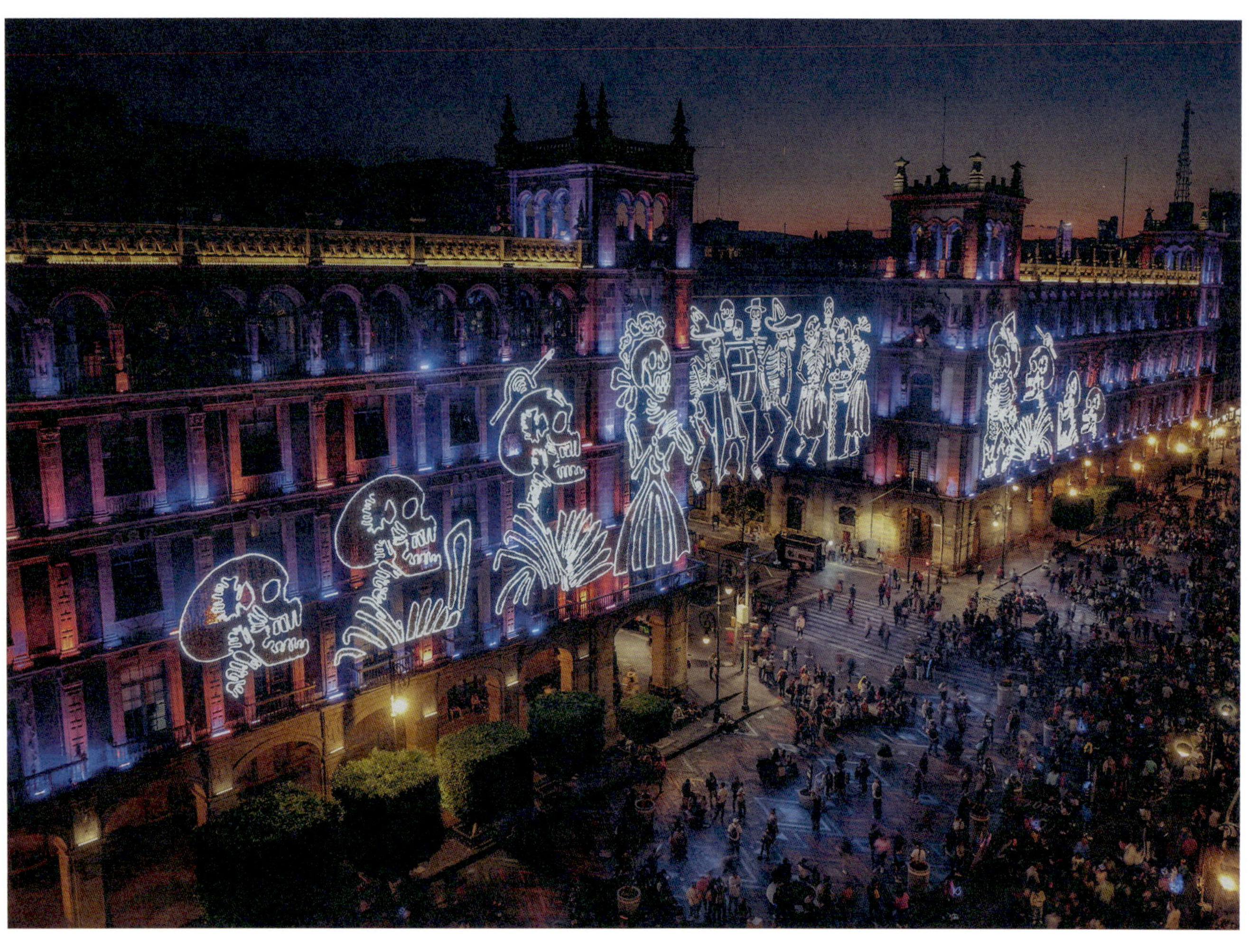

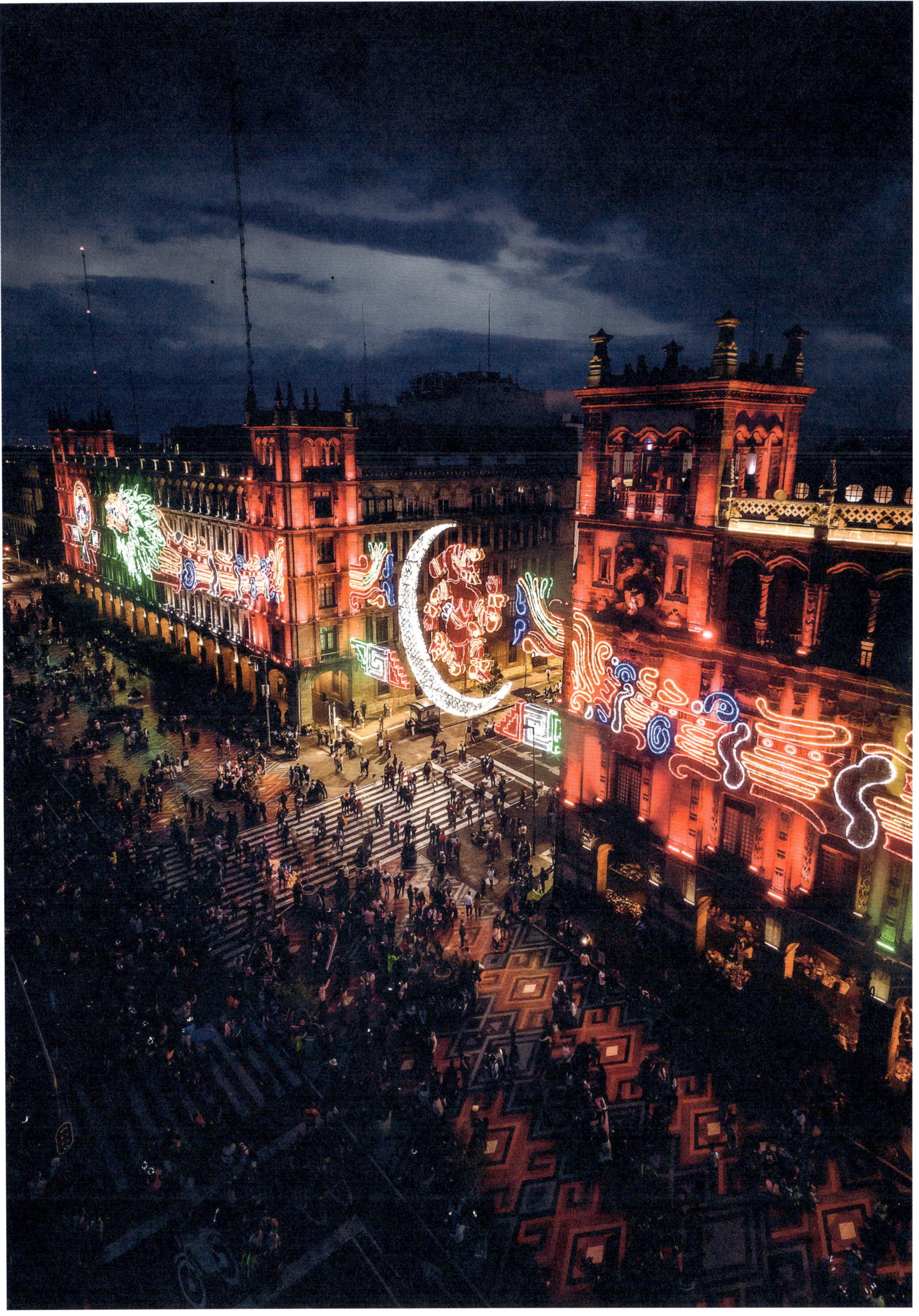

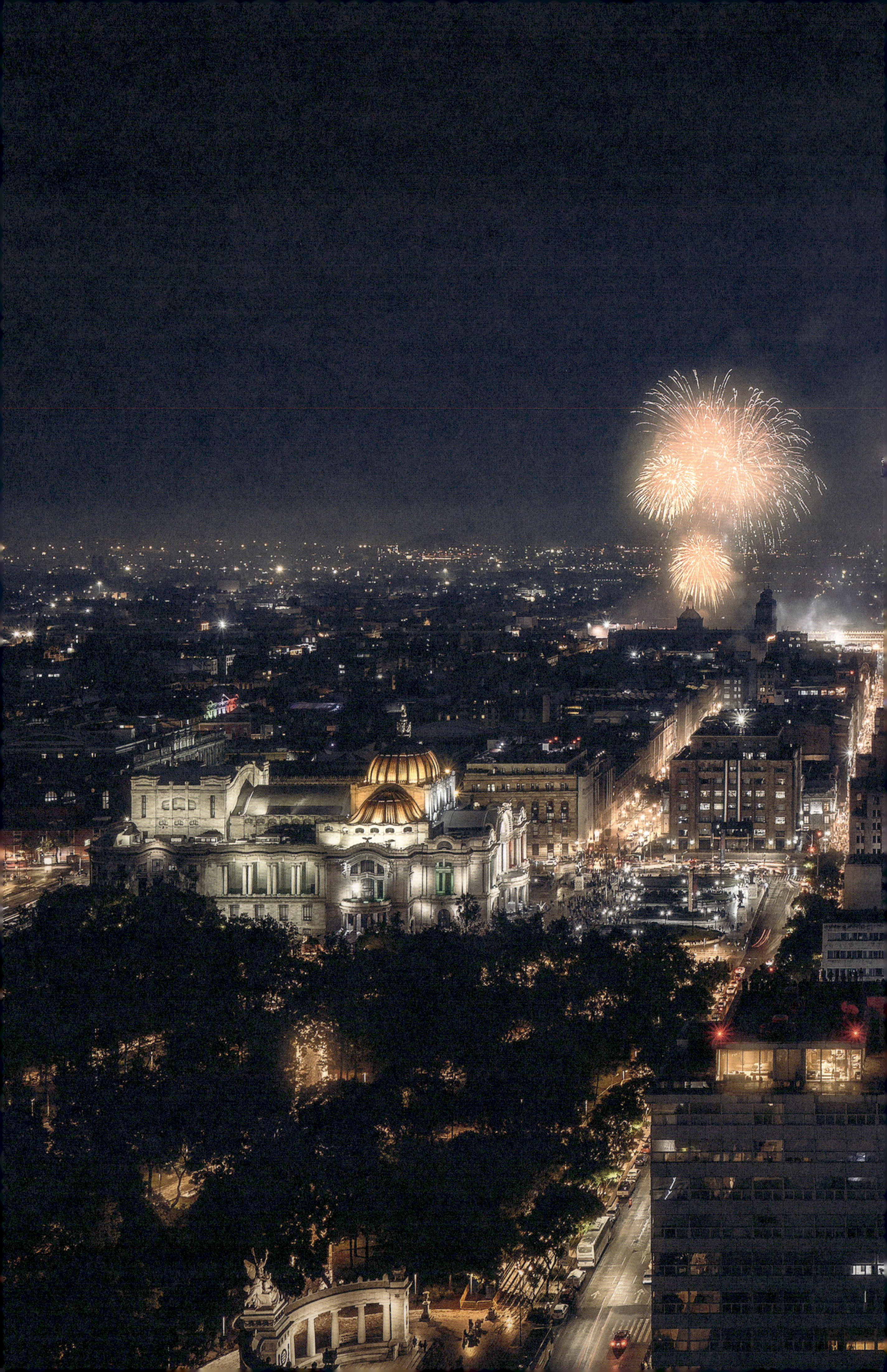

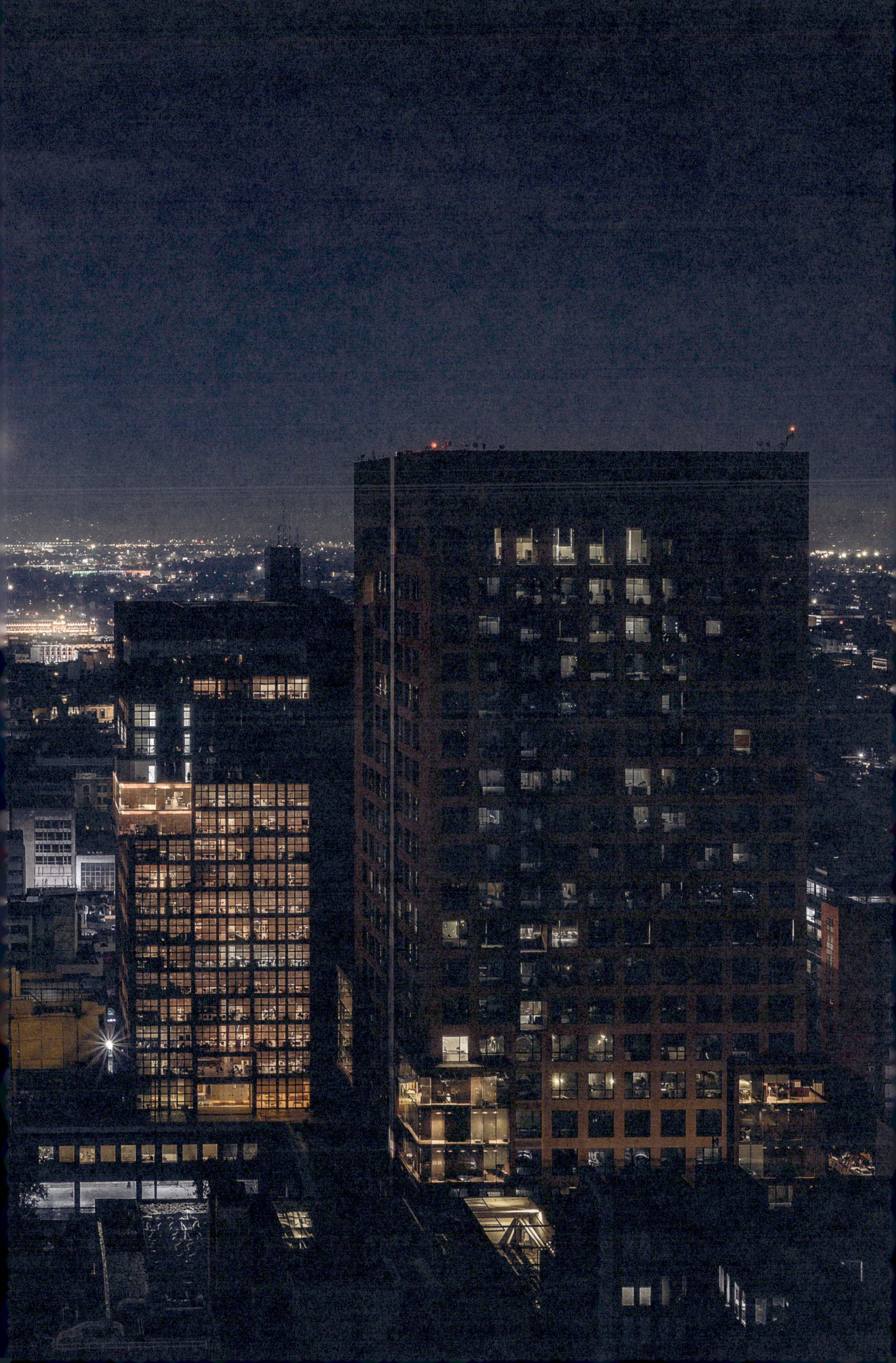

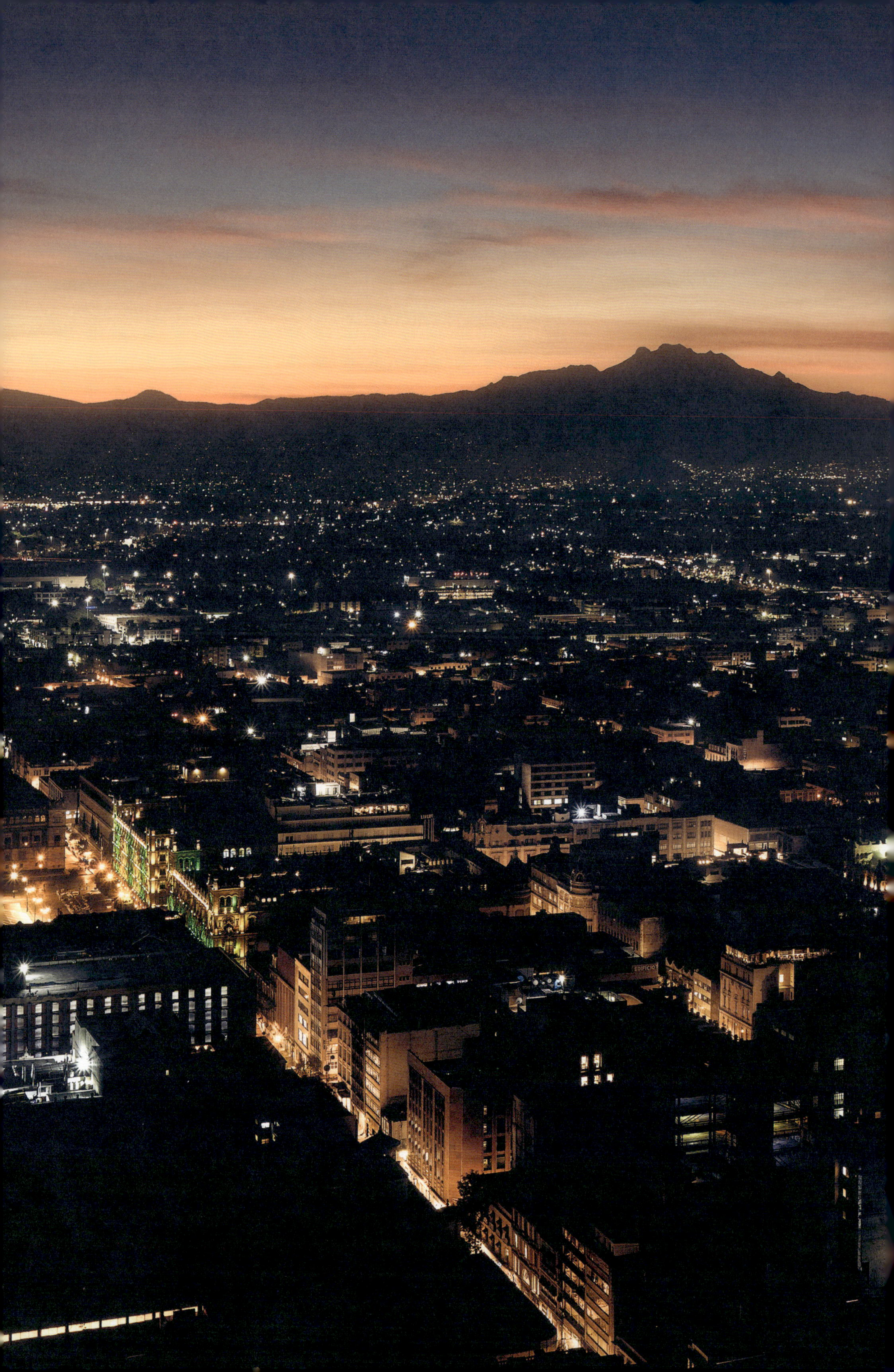

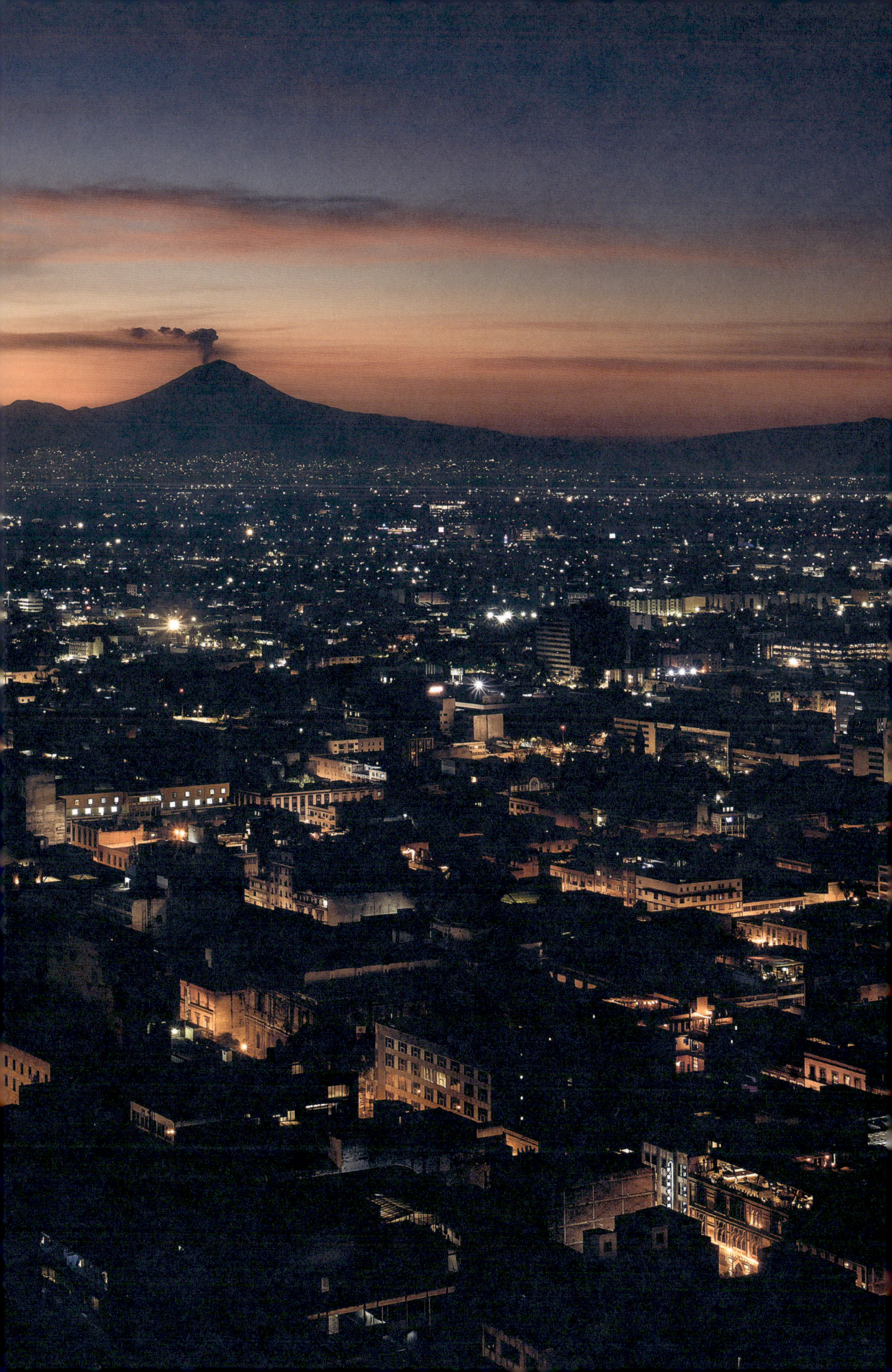

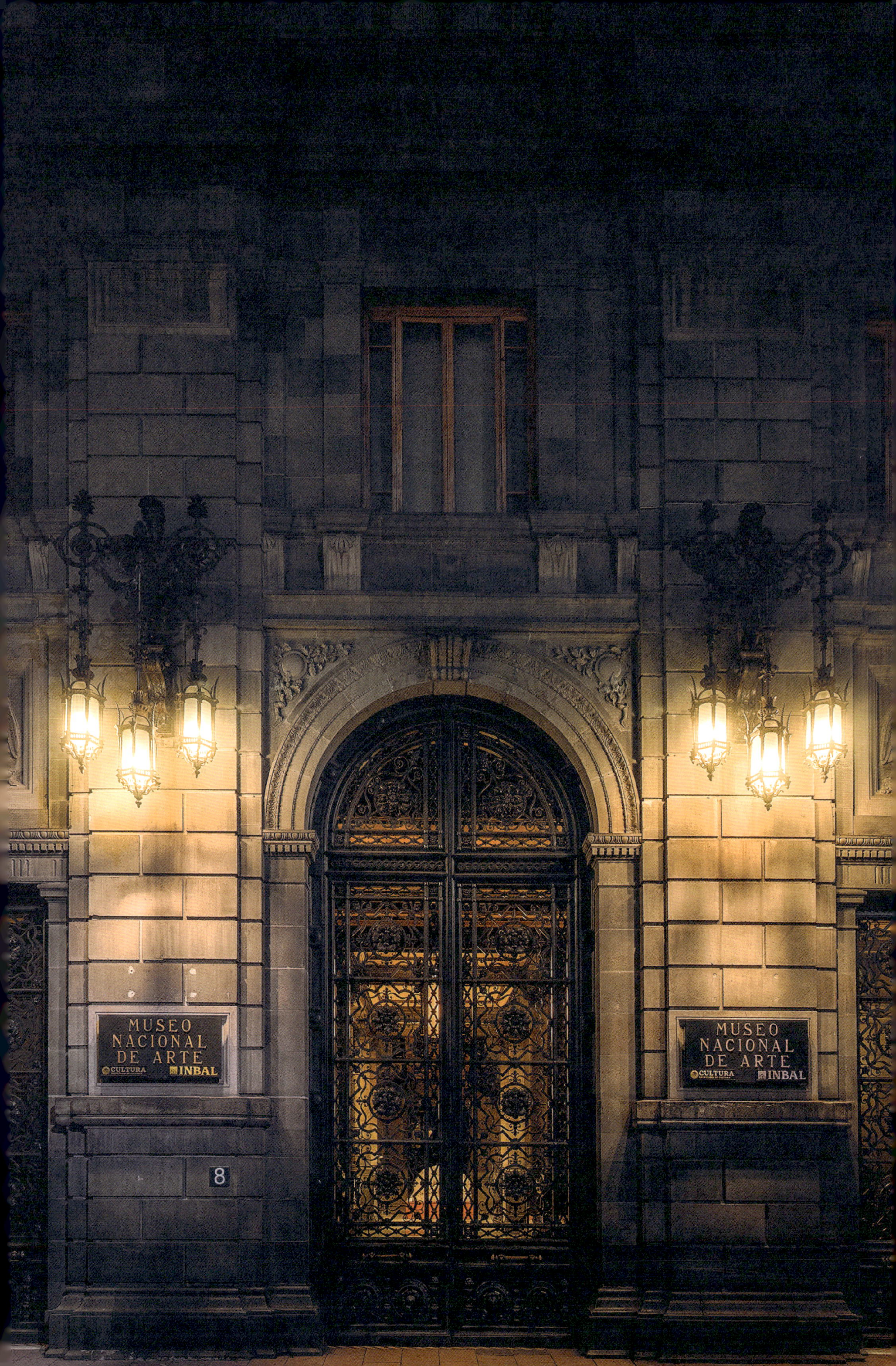
MUSEO
NACIONAL
DE ARTE
CULTURA
INBAL
8
MUSEO
NACIONAL
DE ARTE
CULTURA
INBAL

COLABORADORES CONTRIBUTORS

CARLOS GÓMEZ *@viajando_con_carlos*

Carlos Gómez es el ejemplo vivo del "Chilango", un título que lleva con orgullo y que se traduce en un profundo amor y conocimiento por la caótica Ciudad de México. Es en esta capital, cuna de civilizaciones antiguas y crisol de la memoria, donde su pasión por la historia, el arte y la vida colectiva echó raíces.

Desde una época temprana, Carlos se sintió intensamente atraído por las capas del tiempo que definen a México, una fascinación que ha moldeado una vida dedicada a revelar y desentrañar su historia. Su sólida base académica comenzó con una Licenciatura en Historia por la Universidad Nacional Autónoma de México (UNAM), complementada con diversos diplomados en Historia del Arte, Arqueología y Antropología.

Esta sed de conocimiento no se quedó en las aulas. Carlos es, además, un Guía de Turistas certificado por el gobierno de la Ciudad de México, una labor que le ha permitido convertirse en un narrador natural e inmersivo. Durante más de seis años, ha desvelado la riqueza de los epicentros culturales mexicanos a viajeros de más de 50 países, llevando la historia de los textos a la experiencia vívida de las calles.

Carlos Gómez is the living embodiment of the "Chilango," a title he wears with pride and which translates into a deep love for and knowledge of the chaotic city of Mexico City. It is in this capital, the cradle of ancient civilizations and a melting pot of history, that his passion for history, art, and collective life takes root.

From an early age, Carlos felt intensely drawn to the layers of time that define Mexico, a fascination that has shaped a life dedicated to revealing and unraveling its history. His solid academic foundation began with a Bachelor's degree in History from the National Autonomous University of Mexico (UNAM), complemented by various diplomas in Art History, Archaeology, and Anthropology.

This wealth of knowledge didn't remain confined to the classroom. Carlos is also a certified tour guide by the Mexico City government, a profession that has allowed him to become a natural and engaging storyteller. For more than six years, he has unveiled the richness of Mexican cultural epicenters to travelers from more than 50 countries, bringing history from the pages of books to the vivid experience of the streets.

JAIR HERNÁNDEZ *@torobravophotography*

Jair es un fotógrafo mexicano apasionado por la fotografía callejera y documental. Tras pasar una década en Panamá, Jair encontró en la fotografía una forma de meditación, una manera de sumergirse en el presente y descubrir la belleza artística en las escenas cotidianas y espontáneas.

Su lente se siente atraído por el encanto de la vida urbana, capturando retratos cautivadores de las personas que encuentra en las calles. Adoptando los colores vibrantes que caracterizan a su natal Ciudad de México, ha pasado de la fotografía en blanco y negro a la fotografía a color.

Su visión creativa no ha pasado desapercibida, y ha recibido importantes premios y reconocimientos, entre ellos: Finalista en el concurso de Livorno, Italia (2024), Mención Honorífica en el concurso Pispa de París (2024) y Ganador de México En Una Imagen (2022).

Jair is a Mexican photographer with a passion for street and documentary photography. Having spent a decade in Panama, Jair found in photography a form of meditation, a way to immerse himself in the present moment and uncover the artistry in everyday candid scenes.

Jair's lens is often drawn to the allure of street life, capturing compelling portraits of strangers he encounters on the streets. Embracing the vibrant colors that define his native Mexico City, he has transitioned from black and white to color photography.

His creative vision has not gone unnoticed, with notable awards and achievements including: Finalist at Livorno-Italy contest (2024), Honorable Mention at Pispa-Paris contest (2024), and Winner of Mexico En Una Imagen (2022).

ISAAC JERO *@isaac_jero*

Isaac Jero es un fotógrafo afincado en la Ciudad de México cuyo trabajo gira en torno a la exploración de la luz, el territorio y la narrativa visual. Durante más de ocho años, ha cultivado una práctica que fusiona la precisión técnica con una refinada sensibilidad estética, trabajando en géneros como el paisaje, la fotografía urbana, nocturna—con una particular fascinación por la Vía Láctea—y la fotografía documental. Sus imágenes invitan a reflexionar sobre la relación entre la presencia humana y el entorno, revelando la sutil belleza que surge en los espacios que se encuentran entre lo natural y lo construido.

A través de composiciones equilibradas y una meticulosa atención al detalle, Isaac transforma escenas aparentemente ordinarias en fragmentos visuales de tiempo y emoción. Su obra trasciende la mera documentación, situando la fotografía como una extensión de la percepción, un medio a través del cual la quietud y el asombro se traducen en imágenes perdurables.

Isaac Jero is a Mexico City-based photographer whose work revolves around the exploration of light, territory, and visual narrative. For more than eight years, he has cultivated a practice that merges technical precision with a refined aesthetic sensibility, working across genres such as landscape, urban, night—with a particular fascination for the Milky Way—and documentary photography. His images invite reflection on the relationship between human presence and the surrounding environment, revealing the subtle beauty that arises in the spaces between the natural and the constructed.

Through balanced compositions and meticulous attention to detail, Isaac transforms seemingly ordinary scenes into visual fragments of time and emotion. His work transcends mere documentation, situating photography as an extension of perception—a medium through which stillness and wonder are translated into enduring images.

ROBERTO LOZANO *@_roberttz*

Nacido en la Ciudad de México, Roberto Lozano es diseñador y fotógrafo. Descubrió el poder de la fotografía a través de un proyecto de cortometraje universitario. Tras ganar un concurso de diseño, pudo comprar su primera cámara, lo que marcó el inicio de una pasión que hoy abarca la fotografía de paisajes, retratos, fotografía callejera y fotografía con drones. Además de crear, Roberto disfruta compartiendo sus conocimientos impartiendo cursos de fotografía y edición, motivado por inspirar a otros a desarrollar su propia visión.

Born in Mexico City, Roberto Lozano is a designer and photographer who discovered the power of photography from a university short film project. After winning a design competition, he was able to buy his first camera, marking the beginning of a passion that today encompasses landscape, portrait, street and drone photography. In addition to creating, Roberto enjoys sharing his knowledge by teaching photography and editing courses, motivated by inspiring others to develop their own vision.

OSCAR REYGO *@reygolens*

Oscar Reygo es un fotógrafo autodidacta radicado en la Ciudad de México. Su temprana fascinación por los paisajes urbanos y la arquitectura lo llevó a dedicarse a la fotografía a los quince años. A lo largo de los años, ha explorado diversos géneros, pero la fotografía de paisajes urbanos sigue siendo su trabajo más personal y reconocido.

A través de su lente, Oscar captura la esencia de las ciudades que visita, especialmente la Ciudad de México, su ciudad natal, utilizando una luz que resulta a la vez dramática y sutil. Su trabajo lo ha llevado a colaborar con marcas de renombre internacional y a impartir diversos talleres de fotografía en México.

Oscar Reygo is a self-taught photographer based in Mexico City. His early fascination with cityscapes and architecture led him to pursue photography at the age of fifteen. Over the years, he has explored various genres, yet cityscape photography remains his most personal and recognized work.

Through his lens, Oscar captures the essence of the cities he visits, especially his hometown Mexico City, using light that feels both dramatic and soft. His work has led him to collaborate with globally recognized brands and to teach several photography workshops across Mexico.

VIDAL RIVERA *@vidal.riv*

Vidal Rivera es un fotógrafo afincado en Ciudad de México. Cuando comenzó a fotografiar, lo impulsaba principalmente la curiosidad y la espontaneidad, capturando lo que veía sin pensar demasiado en un marco conceptual. Con el tiempo, se dio cuenta de que la cámara no era solo una herramienta para registrar la realidad, sino un espacio donde la experiencia podía ralentizarse para crear nuevas perspectivas. Para él, la documentación es una forma de situarse en el mundo, de relacionarse con lo que nos rodea y de permitir que la dimensión emocional emerja a través del encuentro. Su trabajo está guiado por una carga afectiva y por la confianza en la imagen como un espacio donde la percepción y la memoria mantienen vivas nuestras historias.

Vidal Rivera is a photographer based in Mexico City. When he first began photographing, he was driven mostly by curiosity and immediacy, photographing what he saw, without thinking too much about a framework. Along the way, he realized that the camera was not a tool to record reality, but a space where experience could slow down to create new perspectives. For him, the documentation is a way of placing oneself in the world, of relating to what surrounds us, and allowing the emotional dimension to emerge through the encounter. His work is guided by an affective charge and trusting the image as a space where perception and memory keep our stories alive.

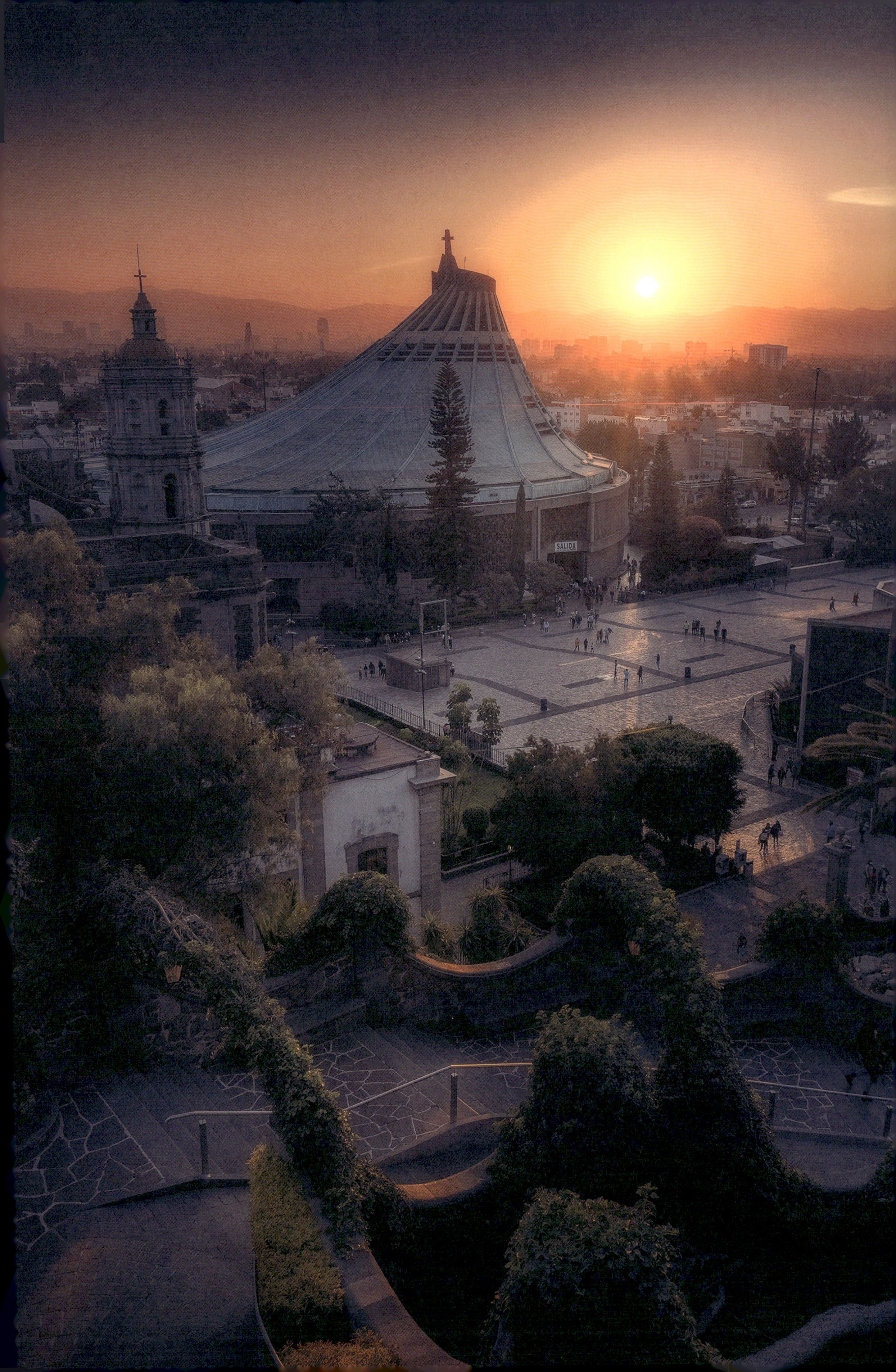
SALIDA

MEXICO CITY DREAMING

The Trope Dreaming series is a curated collection of contemporary images that present some of the world's most photogenic cities through a particularly romantic and ethereal lens. The fifth edition in the Dreaming series, *Mexico City Dreaming* brings together the work of five Mexico City-based photographers—Jair Hernández, Isaac Jero, Roberto Lozano, Oscar Reygo, and Vidal Rivera—to present a modern view of one of the world's most exciting capitals.

The images in this collection expertly capture the warmth and elegance of Mexico City. Built on the ruins of the Aztec capital Tenochtitlan and surrounded by mountains and volcanoes, Mexico City blends ancient heritage with Spanish colonial architecture and modern development. Its historic center, anchored by the Zócalo and the Metropolitan Cathedral, reflects centuries of political and religious influence, while Chapultepec Park, one of the largest urban parks in the Americas, spanning more than 1,600 acres, serves as both a historic and cultural centerpiece of Mexico City with its forest, lakes, gardens, and museums.

Whether you're familiar with Mexico City or experiencing the city's historic charm for the first time, this collection provides a magical portrait of the city, taking you beyond the landmarks to the soul of Mexico City.

Michelle Fitzgerald

Editor

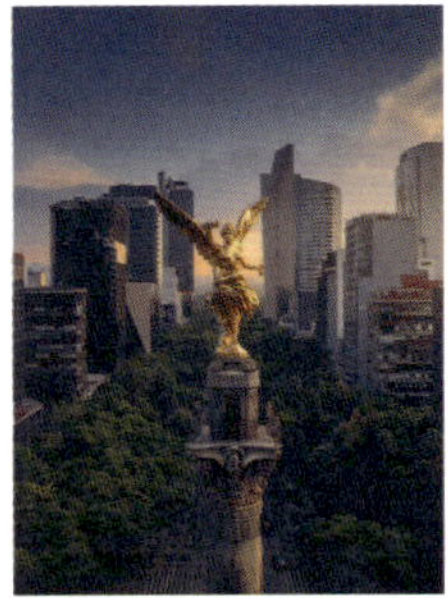
Cover Oscar Reygo
Ángel de la Independencia

The Angel of Independence

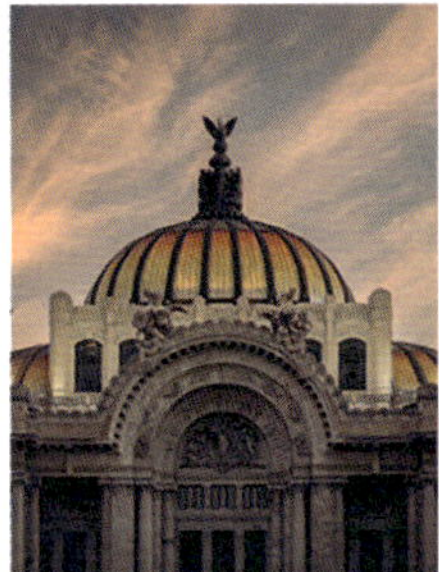
2 Vidal Rivera
Palacio de Bellas Artes

The Palace of Fine Arts

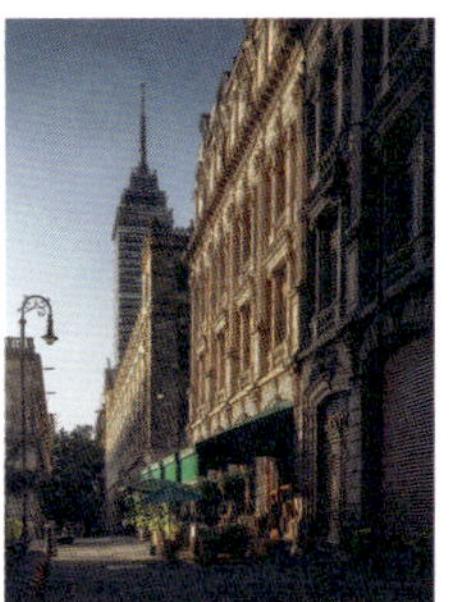
4 Oscar Reygo
Torre Latinoamericana

Latinoamericana Tower

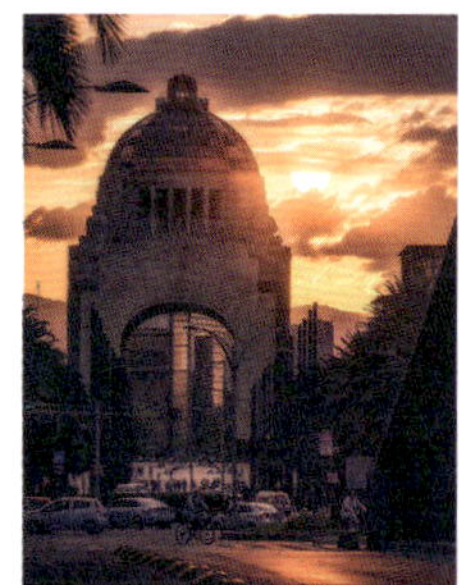
9 Roberto Lozano
El Monumento a la Revolución

The Monument to the Revolution

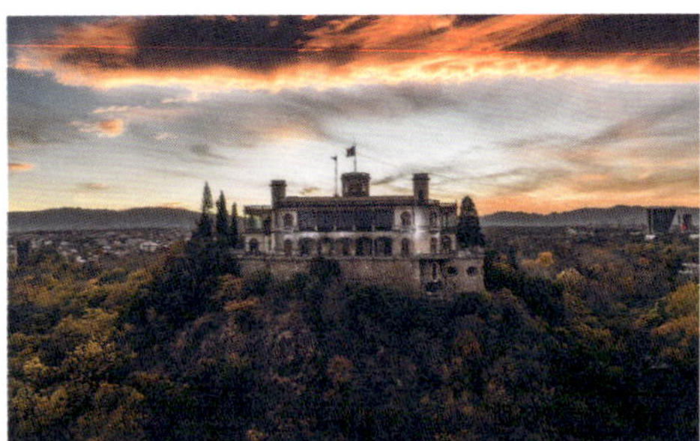
10-11 Oscar Reygo
Castillo de Chapultepec

Chapultepec Castle

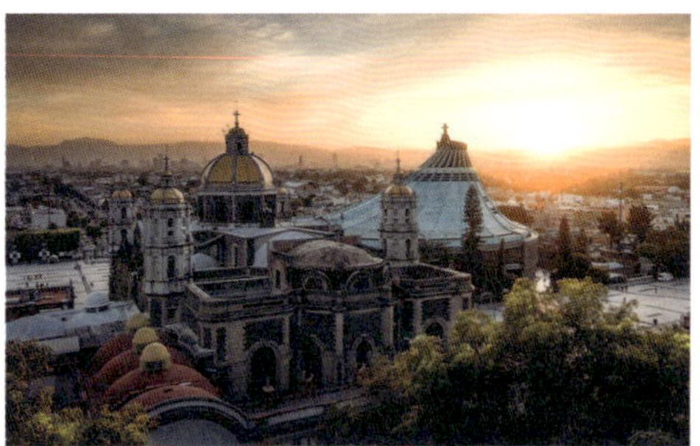
12-13 Oscar Reygo
Basílica de Santa María de Guadalupe

Basilica of Our Lady of Guadalupe

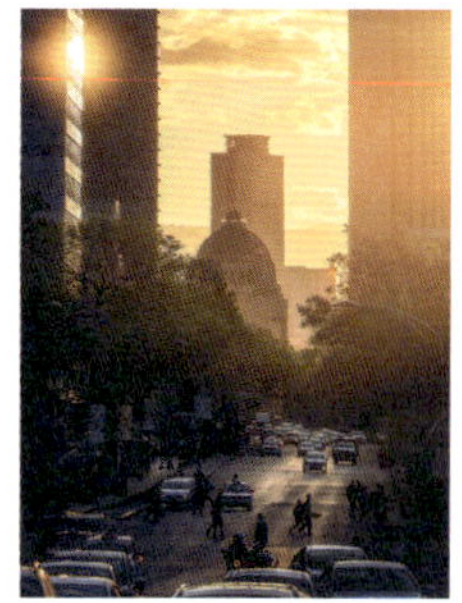
14 Oscar Reygo
El Monumento a la Revolución

The Monument to the Revolution

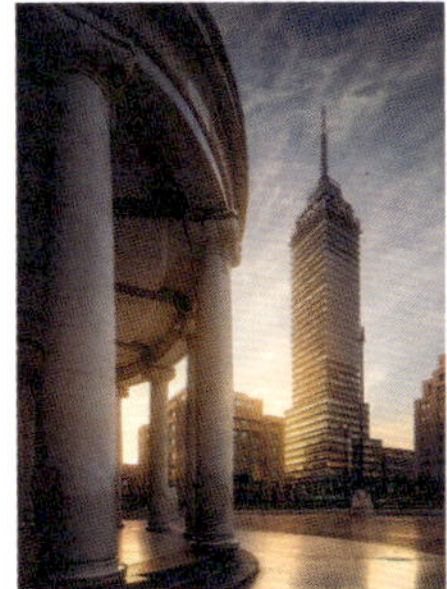
15 Vidal Rivera
Torre Latinoamericana

Latinoamericana Tower

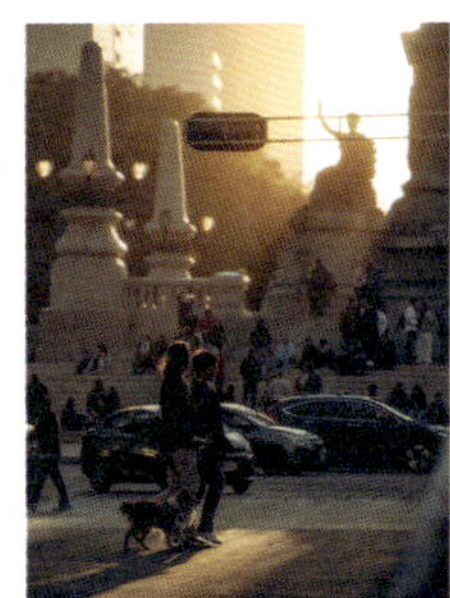
16 Isaac Jero
Paseo de la Reforma

Paseo de la Reforma

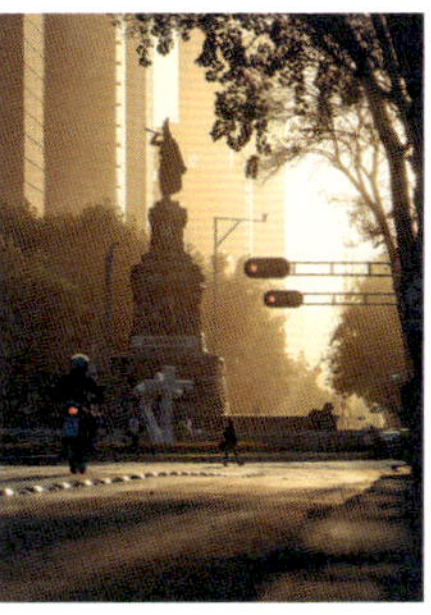
17 Isaac Jero
El Monumento a Cuauhtémoc

Monument to Cuauhtémoc

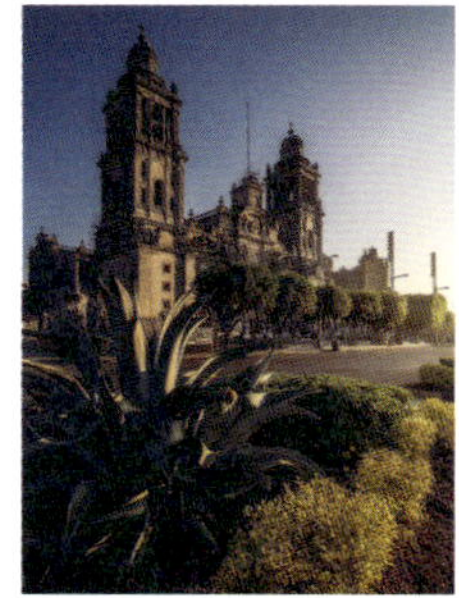
18 Oscar Reygo
Catedral Metropolitana

Mexico City Metropolitan Cathedral

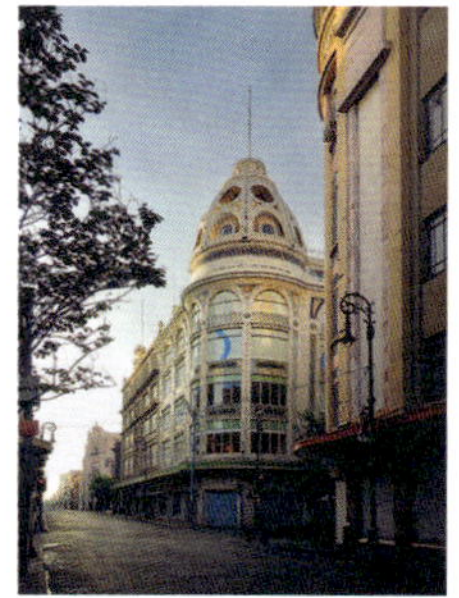
19 Roberto Lozano
Centro Histórico

Historic Center

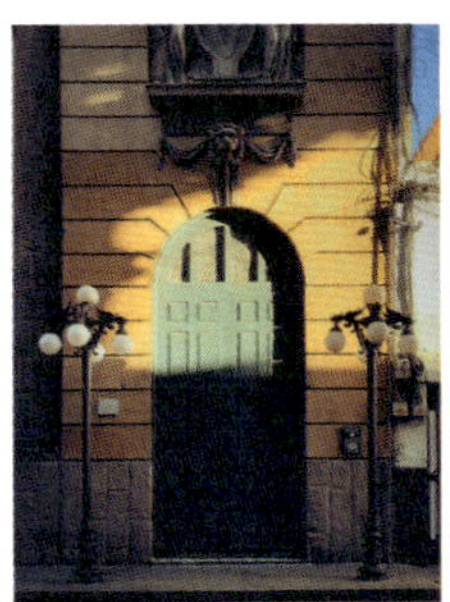
20 Oscar Reygo
Centro Histórico

Historic Center

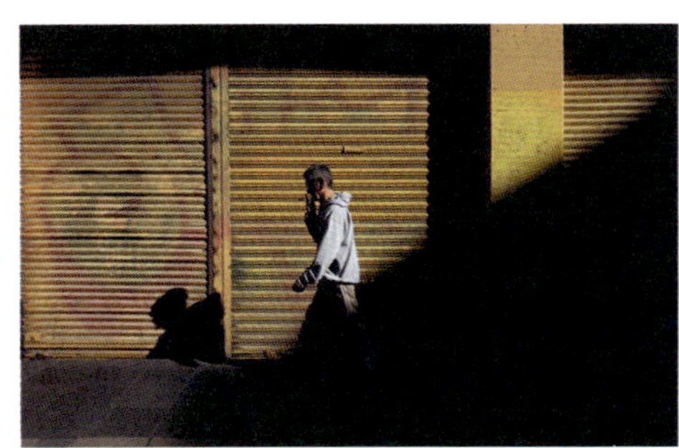
21 Jair Hernández
Centro Histórico

Historic Center

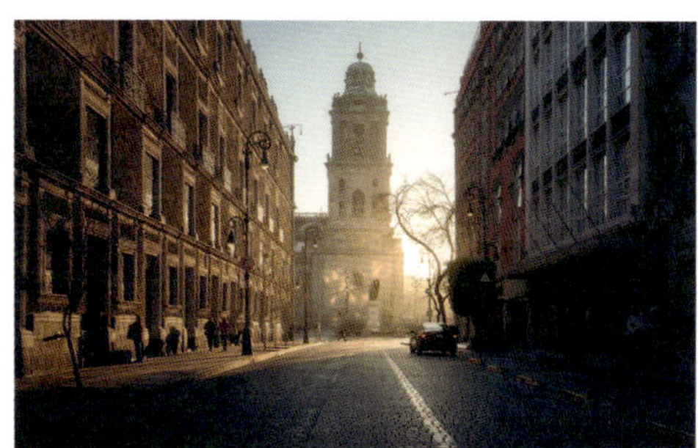
22-23 Vidal Rivera
Catedral Metropolitana

Mexico City Metropolitan Cathedral

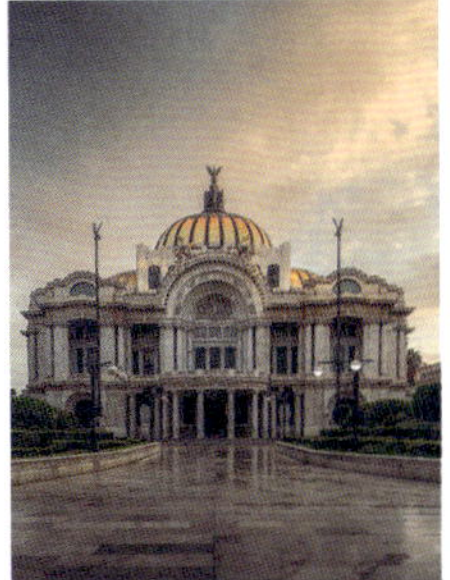

24 Roberto Lozano
Palacio de Bellas Artes

The Palace of Fine Arts

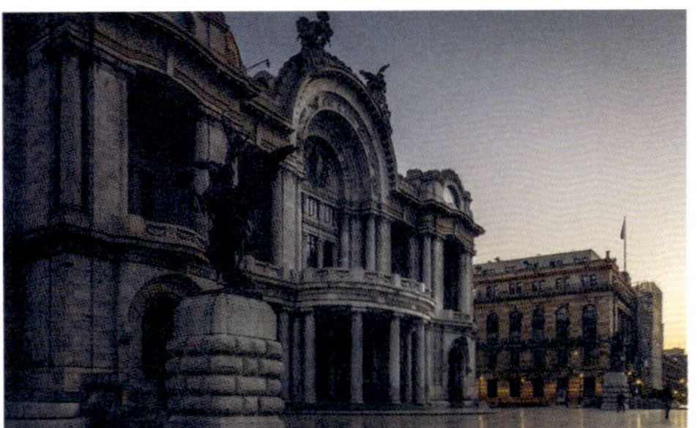

26-27 Oscar Reygo
Palacio de Bellas Artes

The Palace of Fine Arts

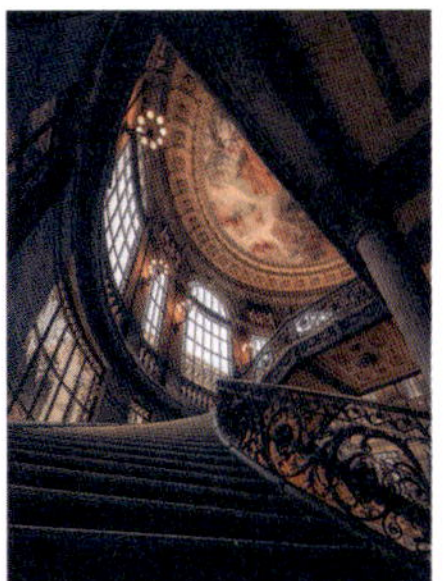

28 Roberto Lozano
Museo Nacional de Arte

National Art Museum

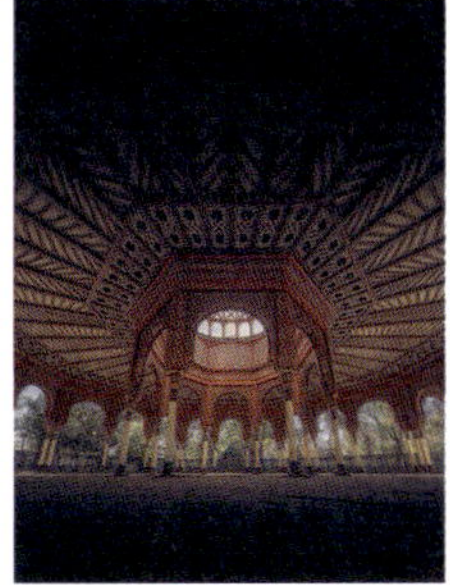

29 Roberto Lozano
Kiosco Morisco

Morisco Kiosk

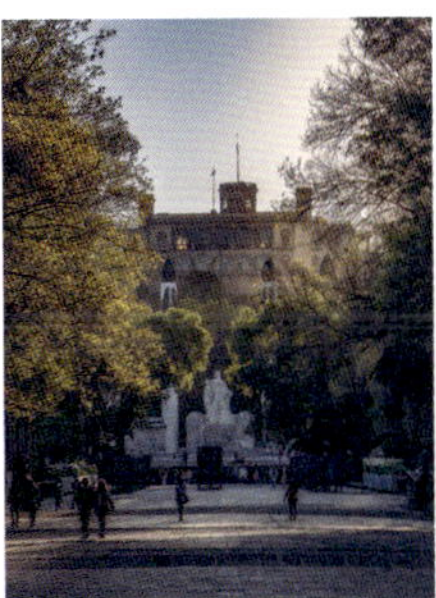

30 Oscar Reygo
Bosque de Chapultepec

Chapultepec Park

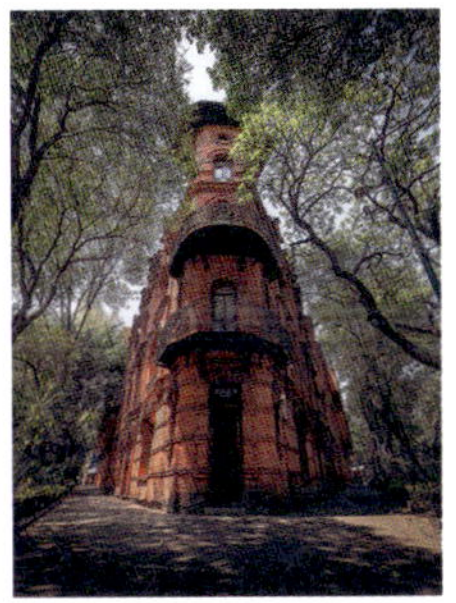

31 Roberto Lozano
Colonia Juárez

Colonia Juárez

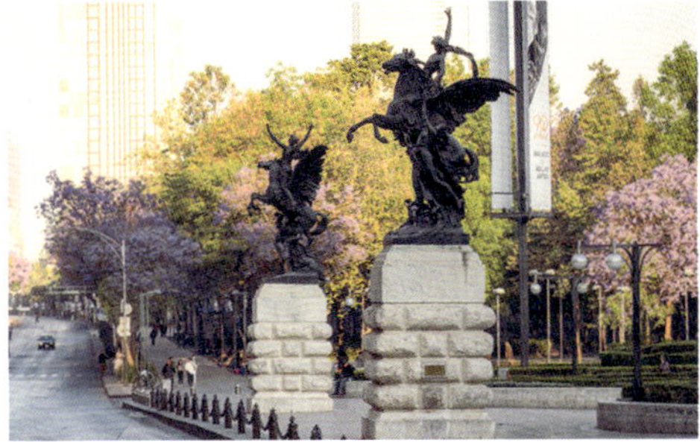

32 Oscar Reygo
Alameda Central

Alameda Central

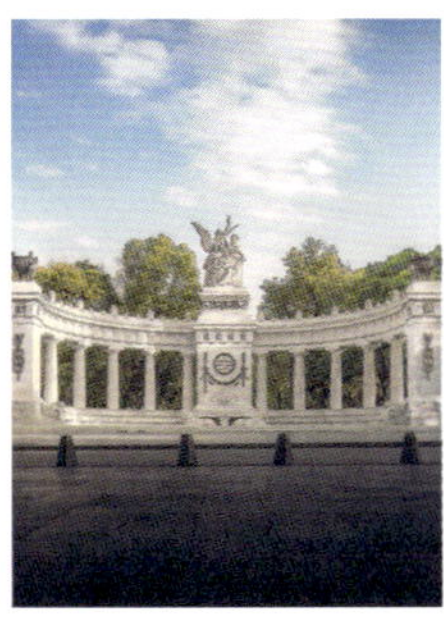

33 Roberto Lozano
Hemiciclo a Juárez

Benito Juárez Hemicycle

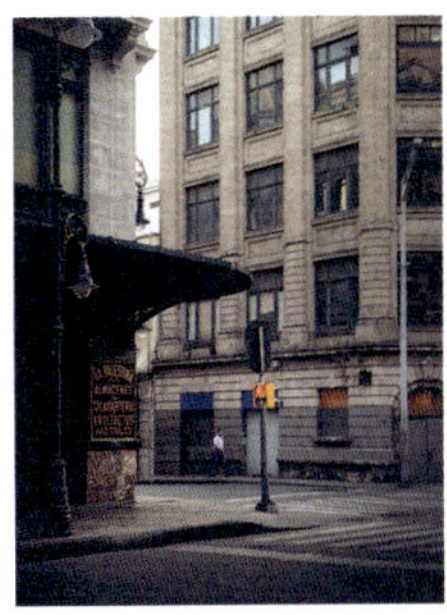

35 Roberto Lozano
Centro Histórico

Historic Center

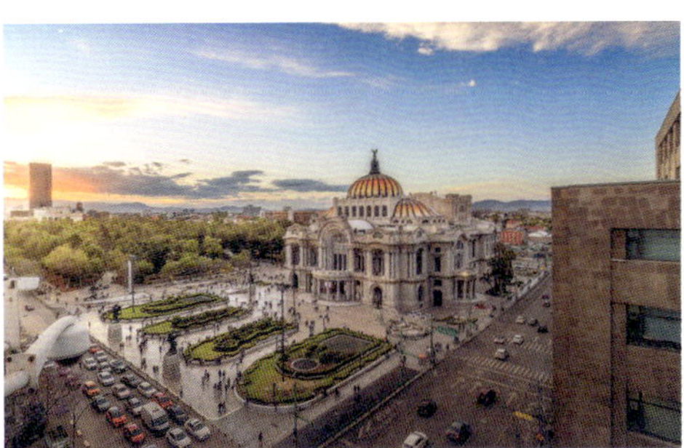

36-37 Oscar Reygo
Palacio de Bellas Artes

The Palace of Fine Arts

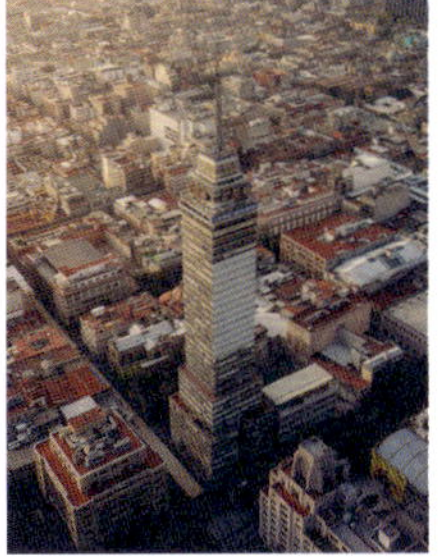

38 Roberto Lozano
Torre Latinoamericana

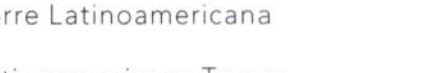

Latinoamericana Tower

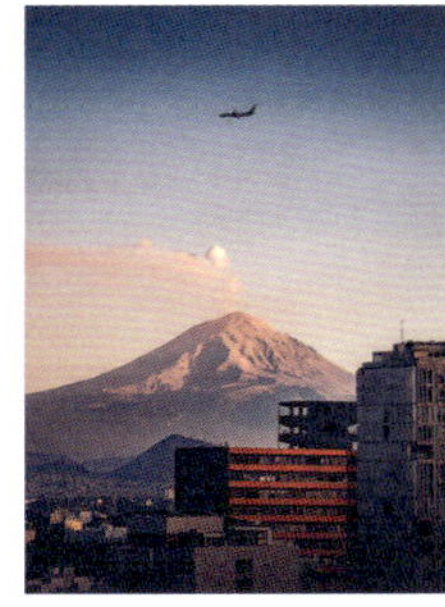

39 Roberto Lozano
Popocatépetl

Popocatépetl Volcano

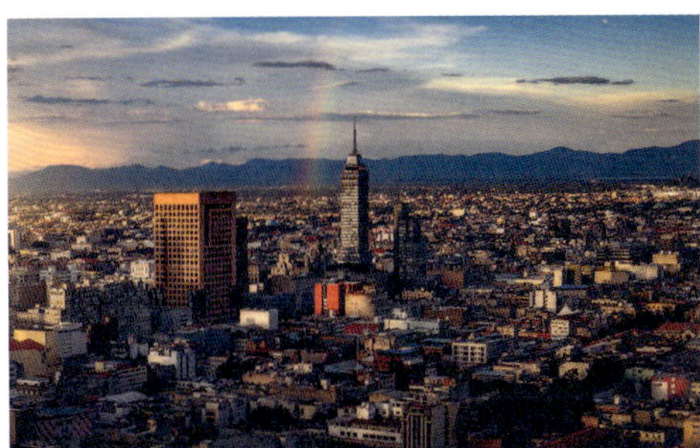

40-41 Oscar Reygo
Centro de la Ciudad de México

Downtown Mexico City

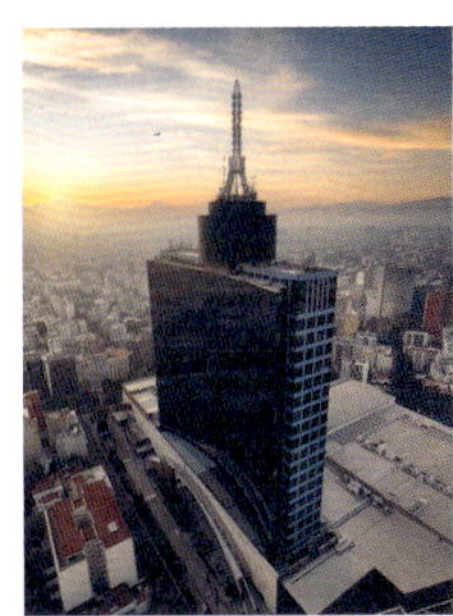

42 Vidal Rivera
World Trade Center Ciudad de México

Mexico City World Trade Center

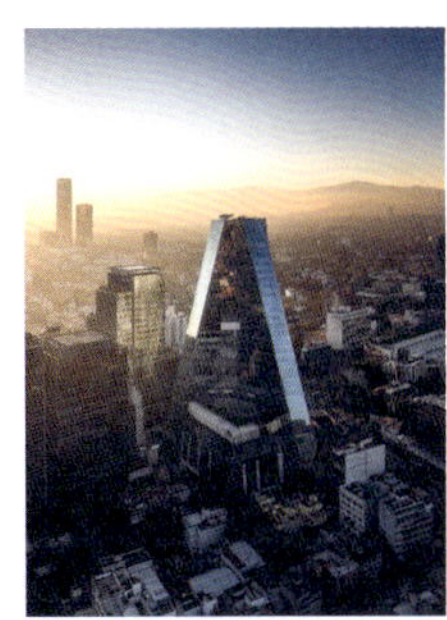

43 Oscar Reygo
Torre Manacar

Manacar Tower

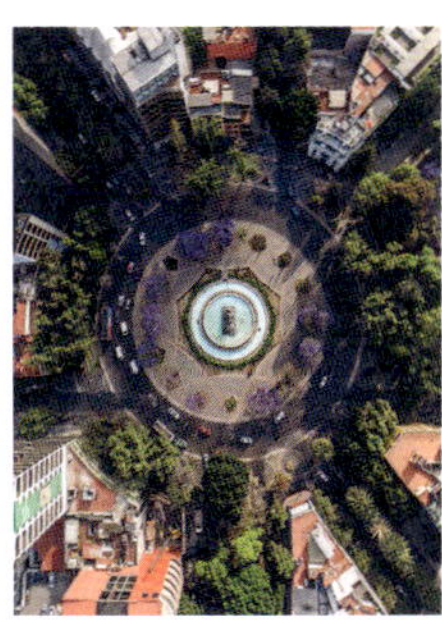

44 Oscar Reygo
Fuente de Cibeles

The Fountain of Cybele

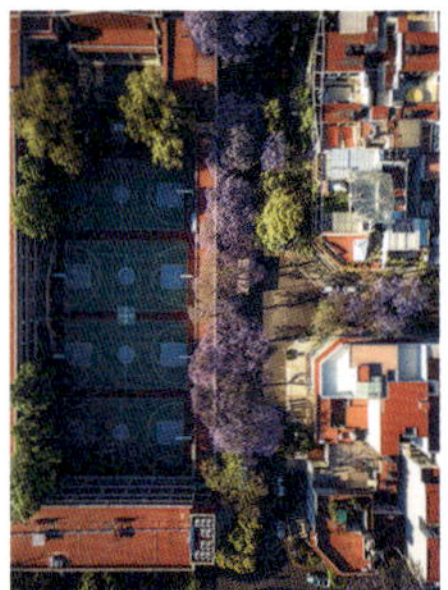

45 Isaac Jero
Jacarandas cenital

Above jacaranda trees

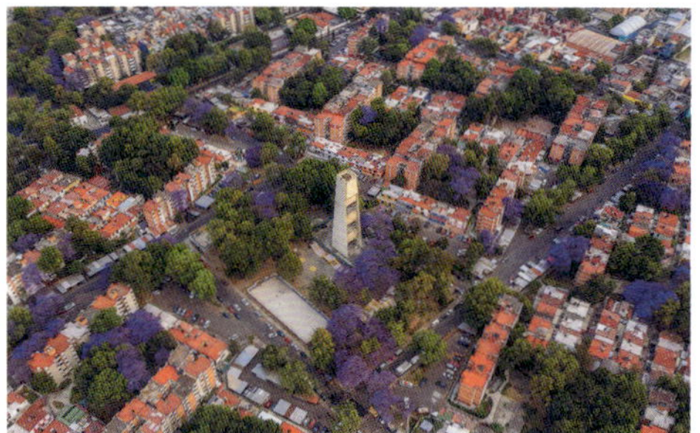

46-47 Oscar Reygo
Azcapotzalco

Azcapotzalco

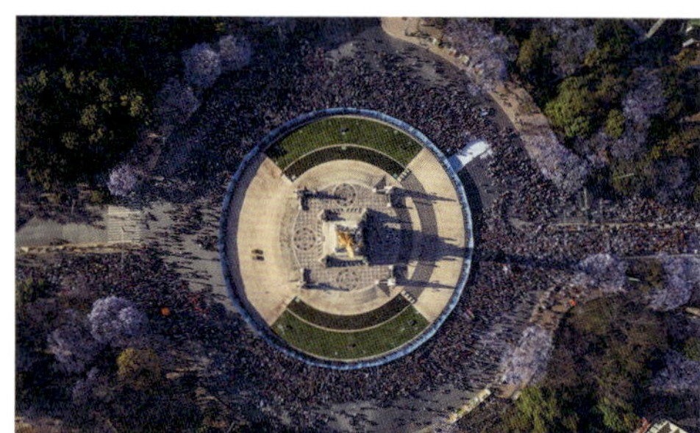

48-49 Isaac Jero
Ángel de la Independencia

The Angel of Independence

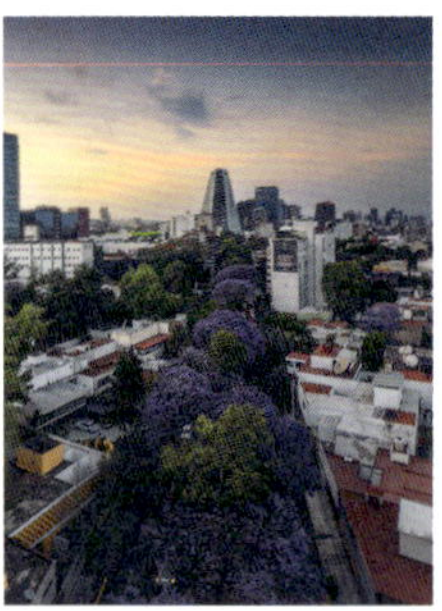

50 Oscar Reygo
Torre Manacar

Manacar Tower

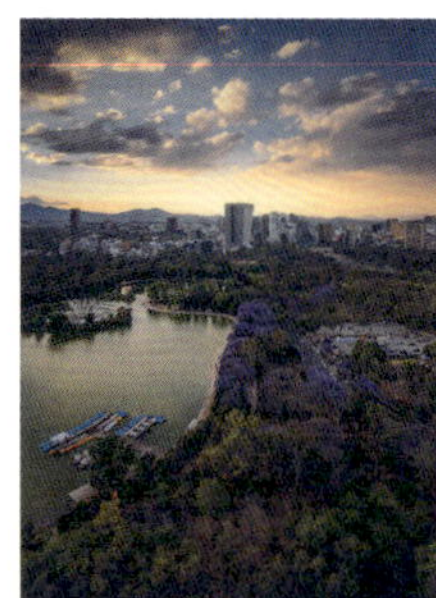

51 Oscar Reygo
Bosque de Chapultepec

Chapultepec Park

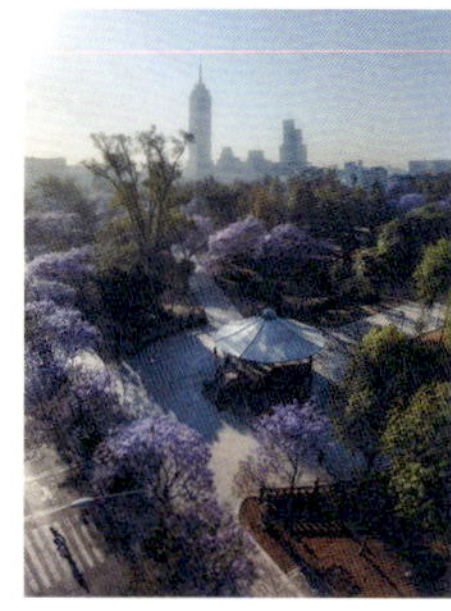

52 Isaac Jero
Alameda Central

Alameda Central

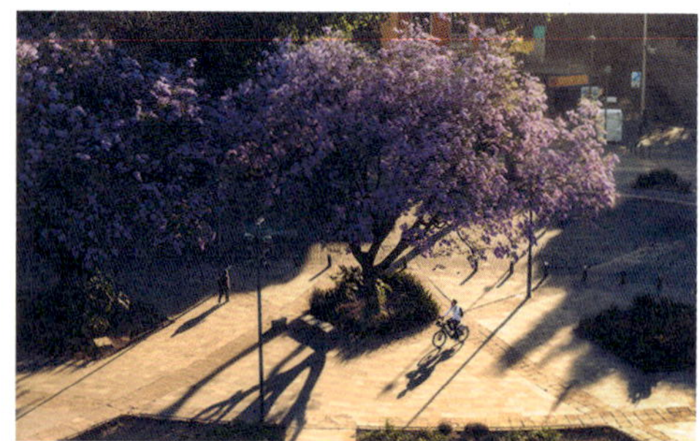

54 Isaac Jero
Fuente de Cibeles

The Fountain of Cybele

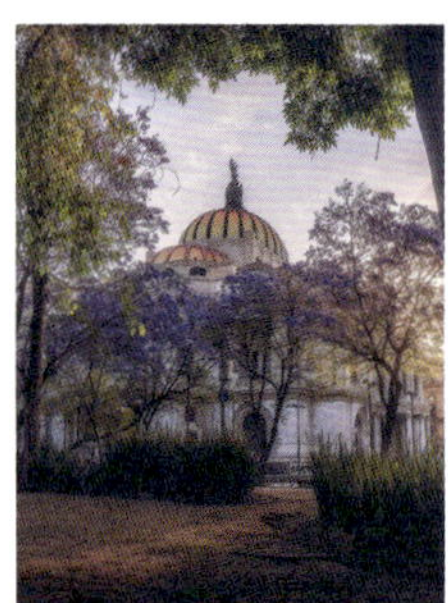

55 Roberto Lozano
Palacio de Bellas Artes

The Palace of Fine Arts

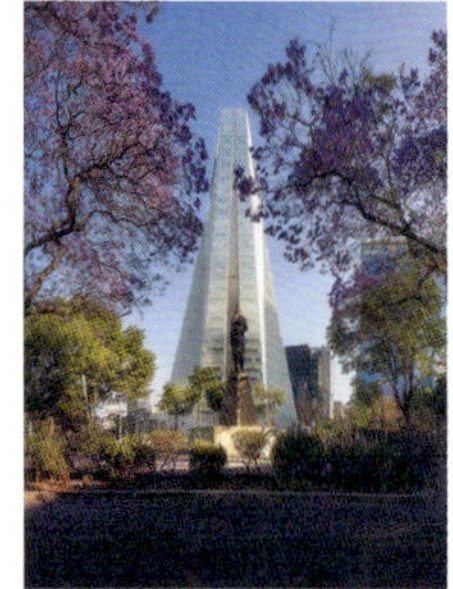

56 Vidal Rivera
Torre Manacar

Manacar Tower

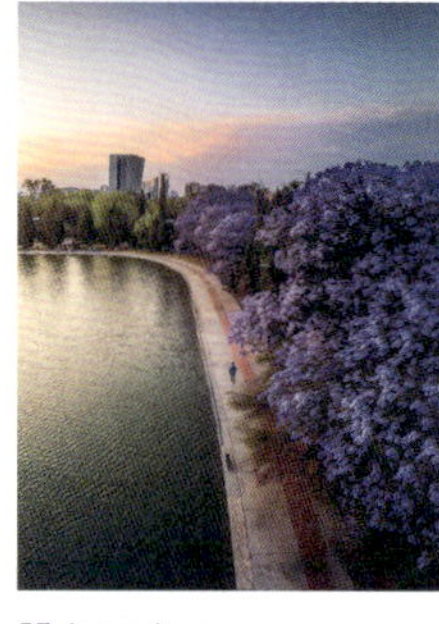

57 Isaac Jero
Lago Mayor de Chapultepec

Chapultepec Main Lake

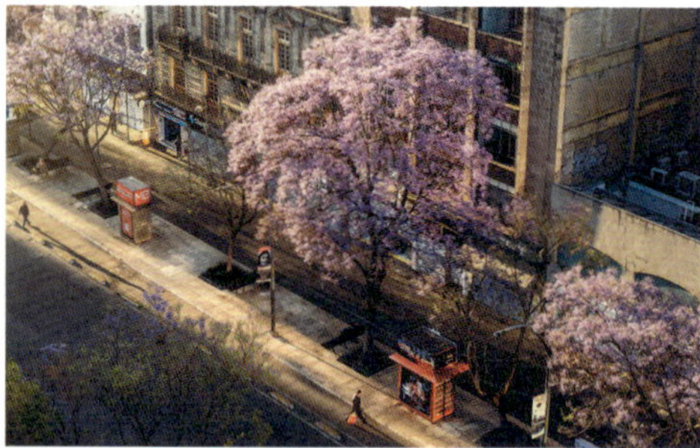

58-59 Isaac Jero
Alameda Central

Alameda Central

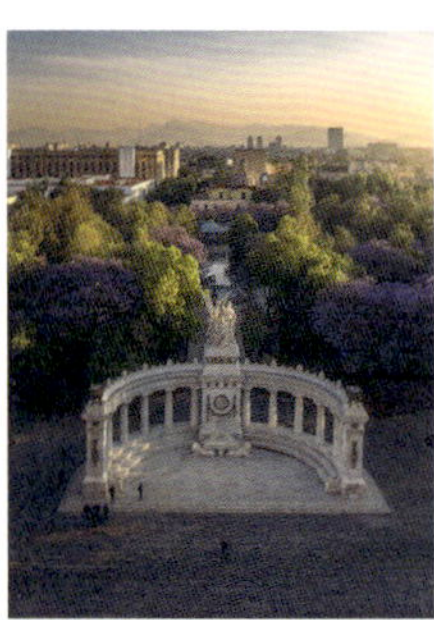

60 Oscar Reygo
Hemiciclo a Juárez

Benito Juárez Hemicycle

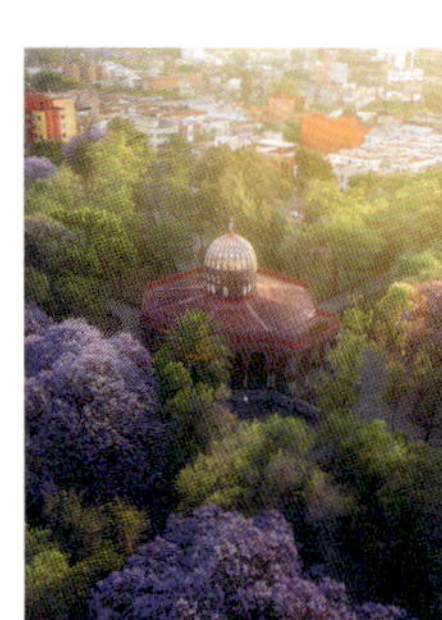

61 Vidal Rivera
Kiosco Morisco

Morisco Kiosk

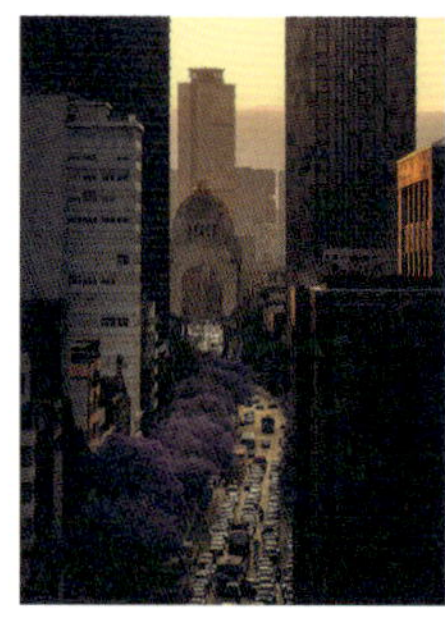

62 Roberto Lozano
El Monumento a la Revolución

The Monument to the Revolution

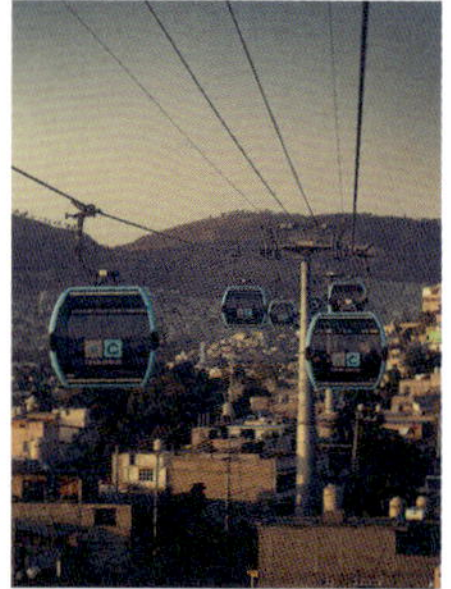

63 Roberto Lozano
Cablebús

Cable car

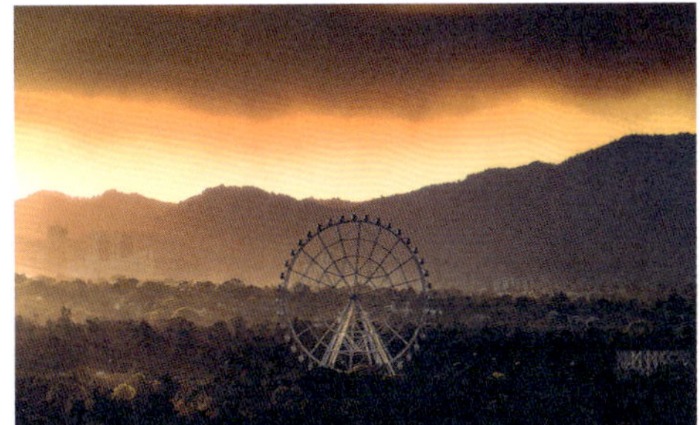

64-65 Oscar Reygo
Parque Urbano Aztlán

Aztlán Urban Park

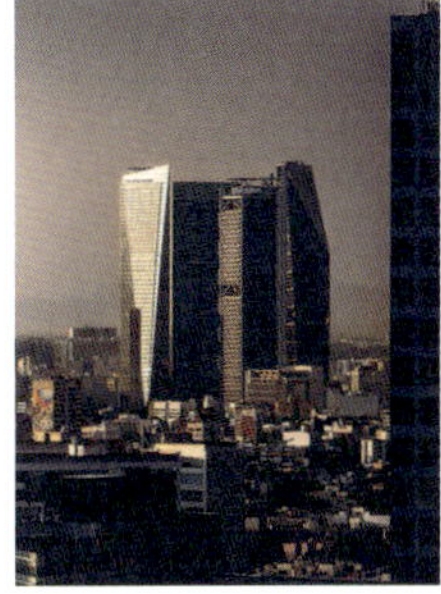

66 Oscar Reygo
Torres en el Paseo de la Reforma

Towers on Paseo de la Reforma

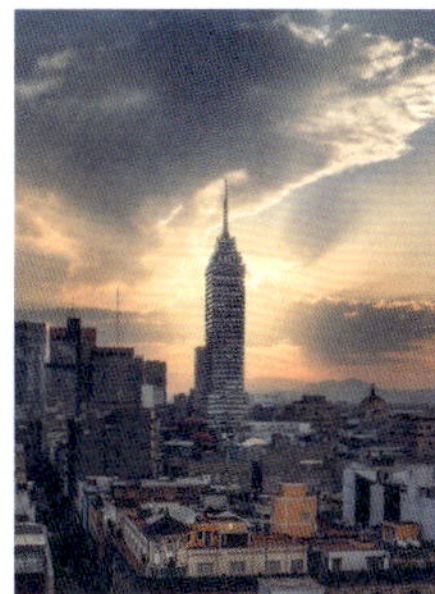

67 Oscar Reygo
Torre Latinoamericana

Latinoamericana Tower

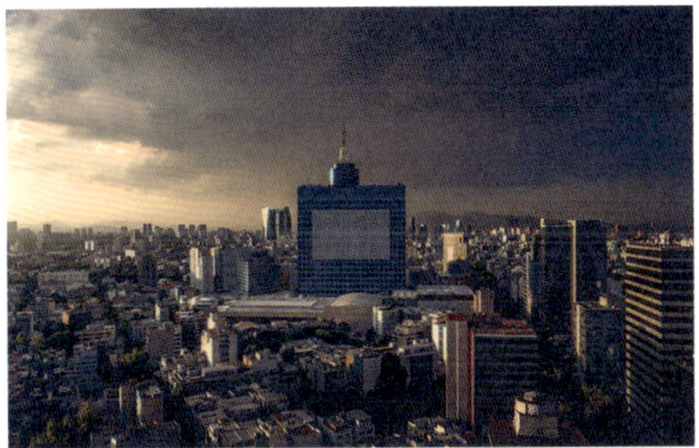

68-69 Oscar Reygo
World Trade Center Ciudad de México

Mexico City World Trade Center

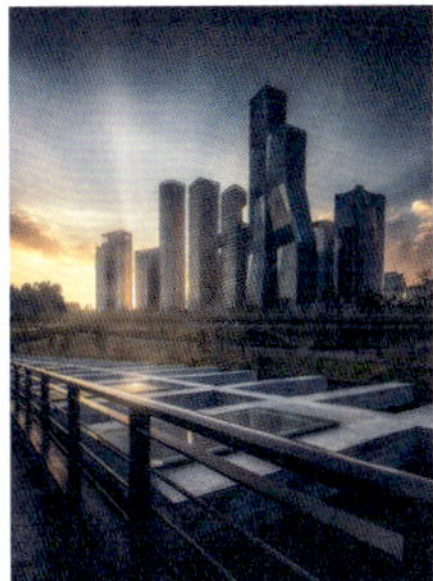

70 Oscar Reygo
Santa Fe

Santa Fe

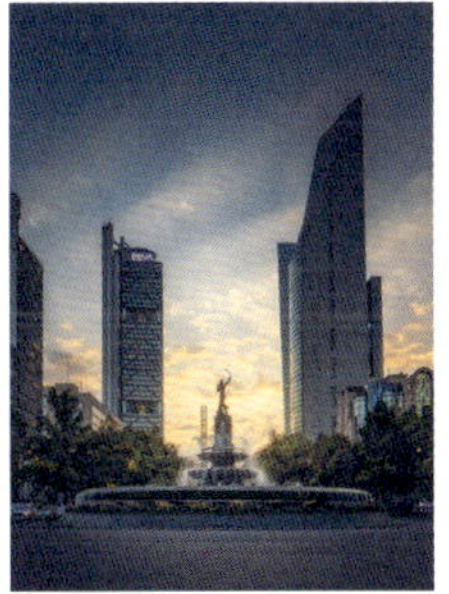

71 Oscar Reygo
Fuente de la Diana Cazadora

Diana the Huntress Fountain

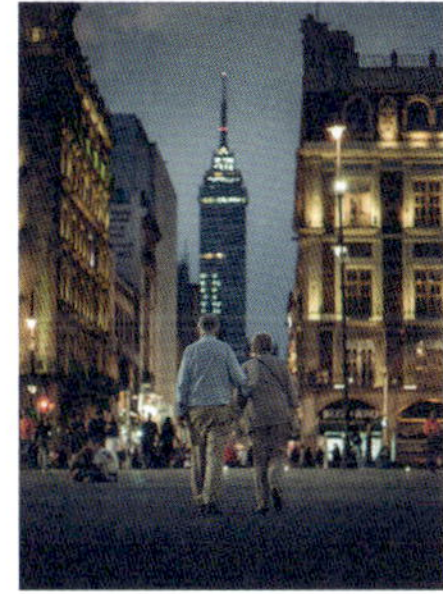

72 Roberto Lozano
Zócalo

Zócalo

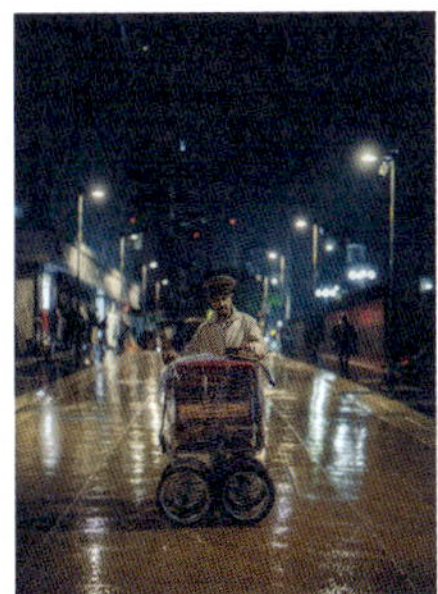

73 Isaac Jero
Organillero

Barrel organ player

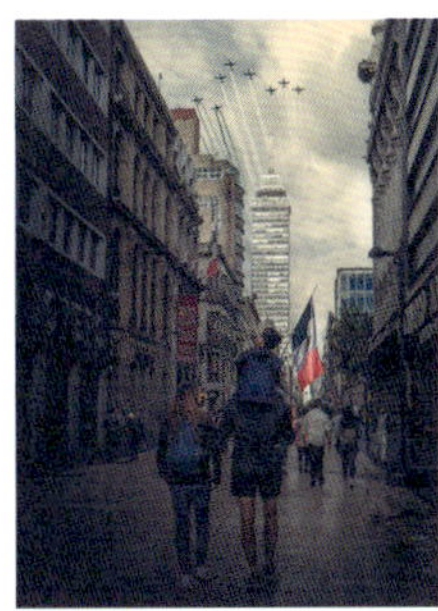

75 Roberto Lozano
Torre Latinoamericana

Latinoamericana Tower

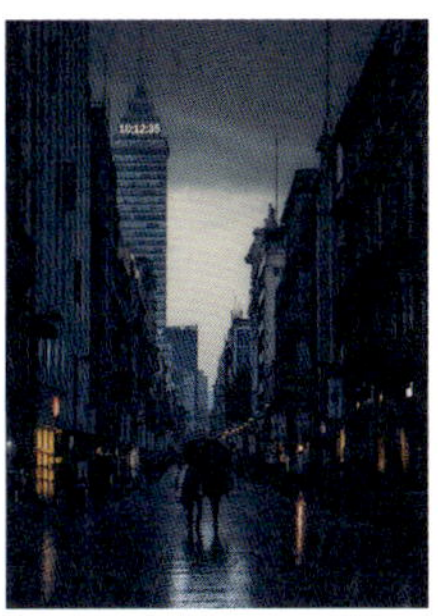

76 Isaac Jero
Torre Latinoamericana

Latinoamericana Tower

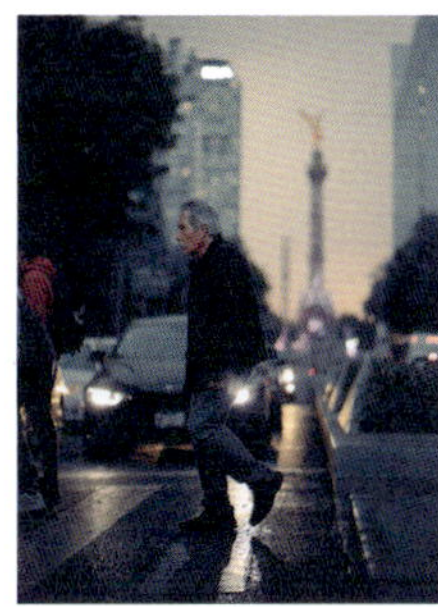

77 Roberto Lozano
Paseo de la Reforma

Paseo de la Reforma

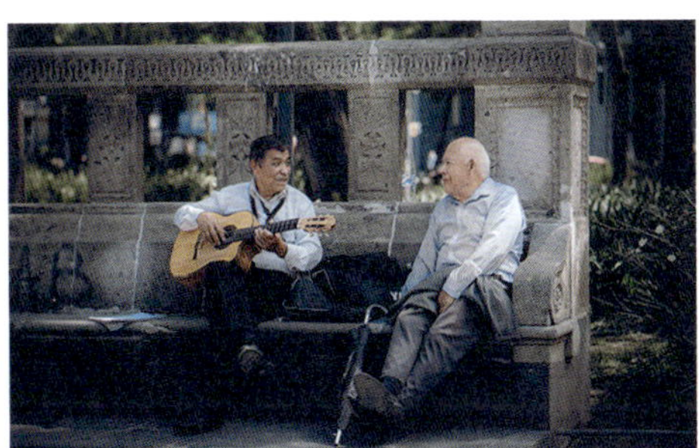

78 Vidal Rivera
Alameda Central

Alameda Central

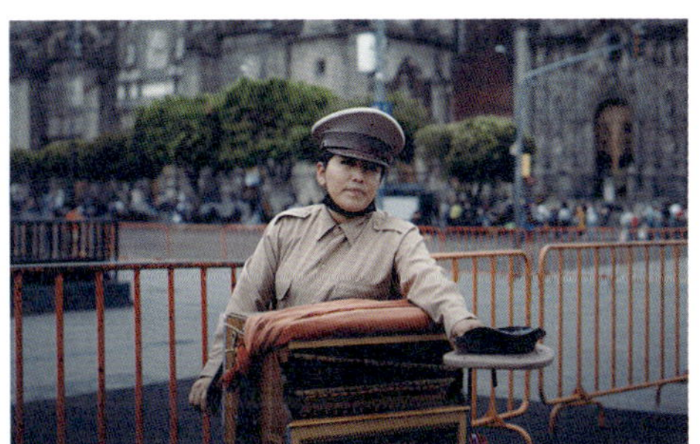

79 Vidal Rivera
Zócalo

Zócalo

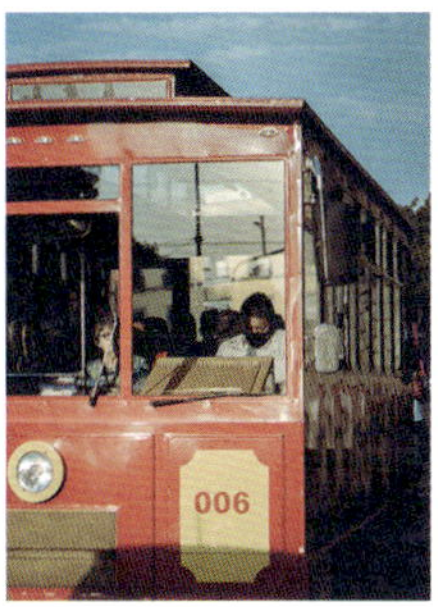

80 Oscar Reygo
Tranvía Turístico

Tourist tram

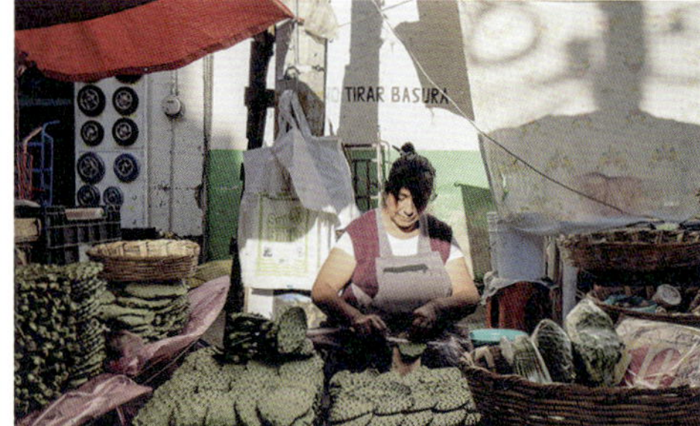

81 Jair Hernández
Mercado de la Merced

La Merced Market

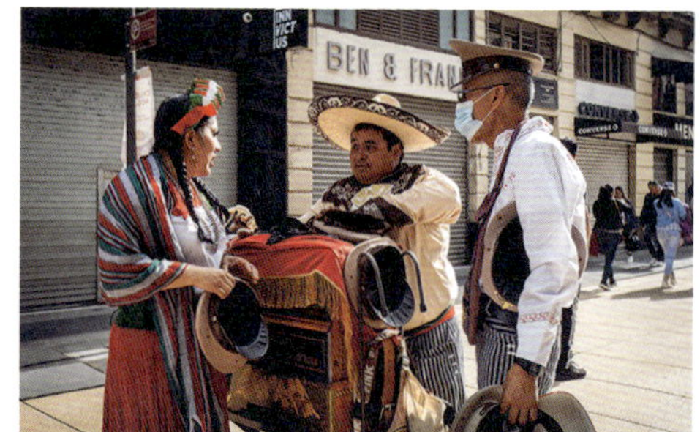

82 Jair Hernández
Organillero en el Centro Histórico

Barrel organ player in the Historic Center

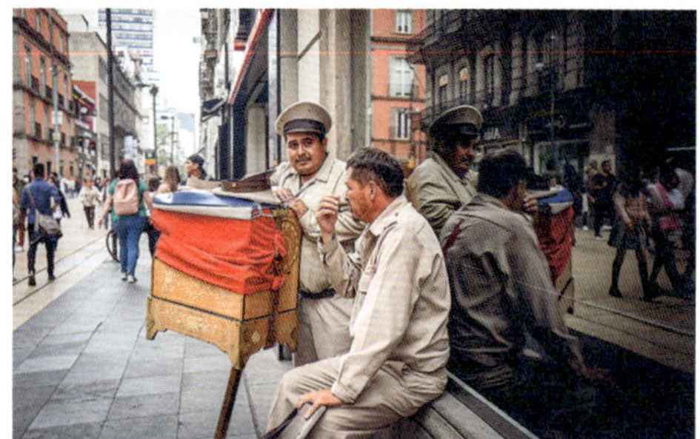

83 Jair Hernández
Organillero en el Centro Histórico

Barrel organ player in the Historic Center

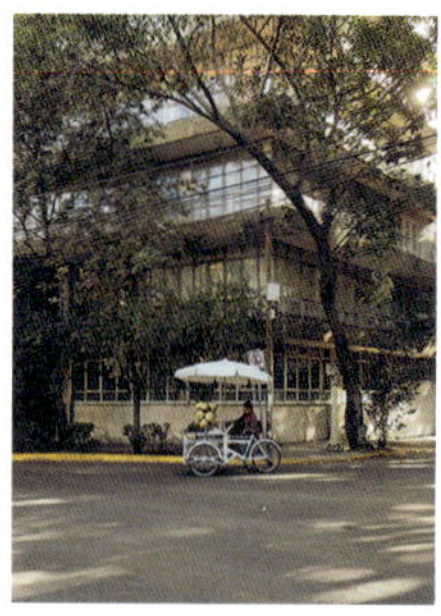

84 Oscar Reygo
Frutero en La Condesa

Fruit vendor in La Condesa

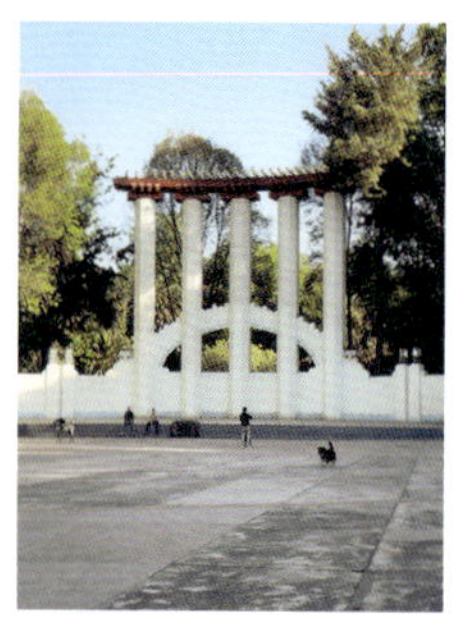

85 Oscar Reygo
Foro Lindbergh en Parque México

Lindbergh Forum in Parque México

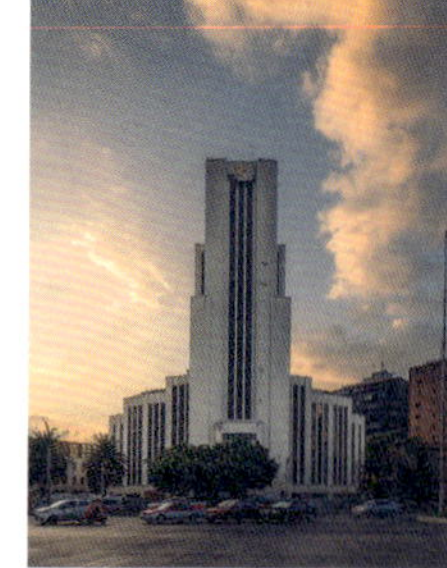

86 Oscar Reygo
Edificio El Moro

The Moro Building

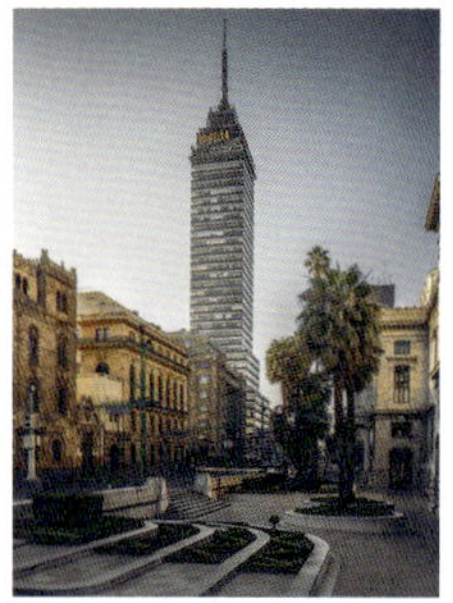

87 Oscar Reygo
Torre Latinoamericana

Latinoamericana Tower

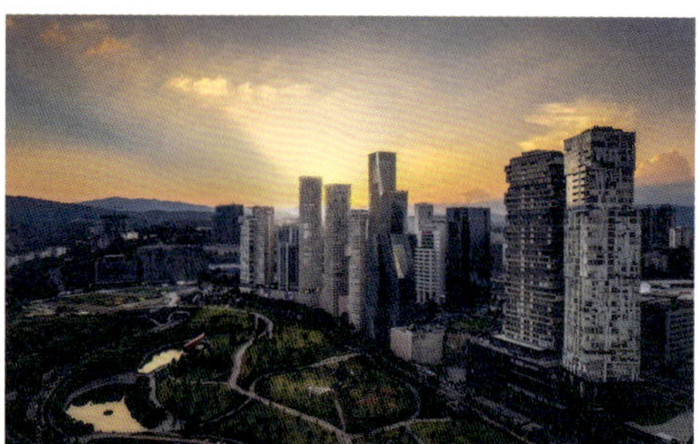

88-89 Oscar Reygo
Santa Fe

Santa Fe

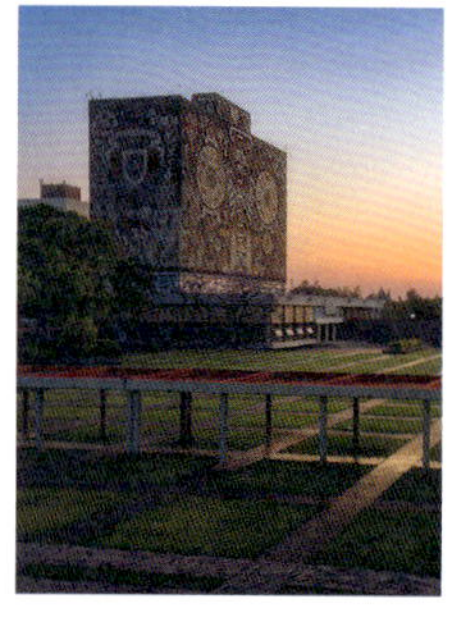

90 Vidal Rivera
Biblioteca Central, UNAM

Central Library, UNAM

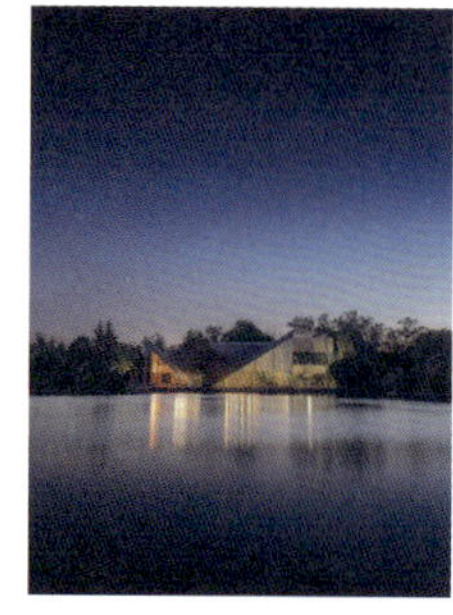

91 Roberto Lozano
Restaurante en el Lago Mayor de Chapultepec

Restaurant on Chapultepec Main Lake

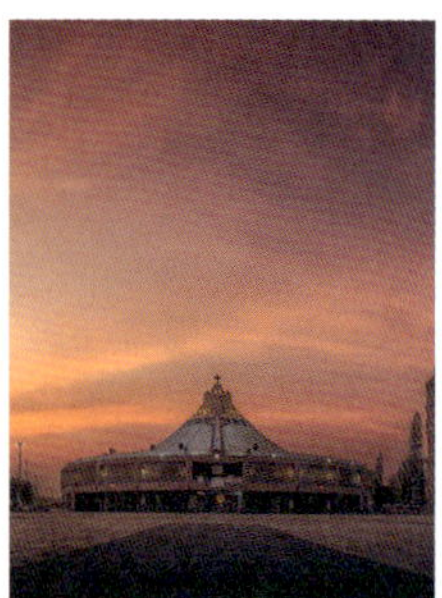

93 Roberto Lozano
Basílica de Santa María de Guadalupe

Basilica of Our Lady of Guadalupe

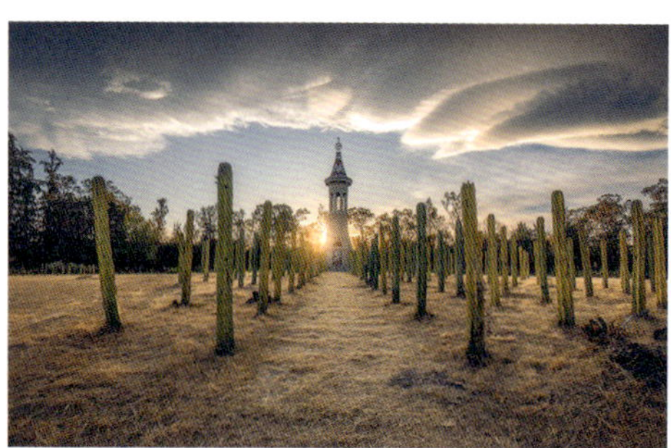

94 Oscar Reygo
Bosque de Chapultepec

Chapultepec Park

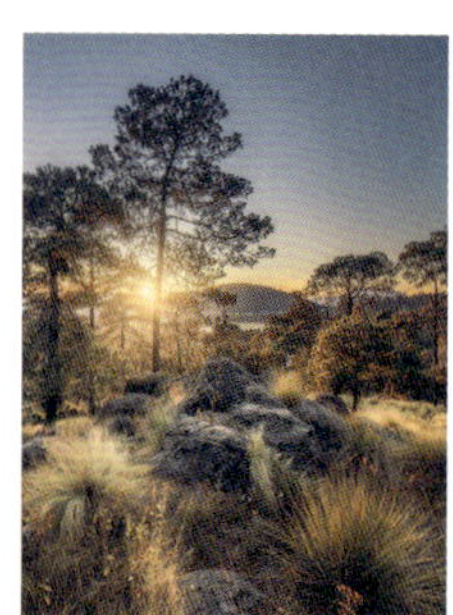

95 Oscar Reygo
Parque Nacional Cumbres del Ajusco

Cumbres del Ajusco National Park

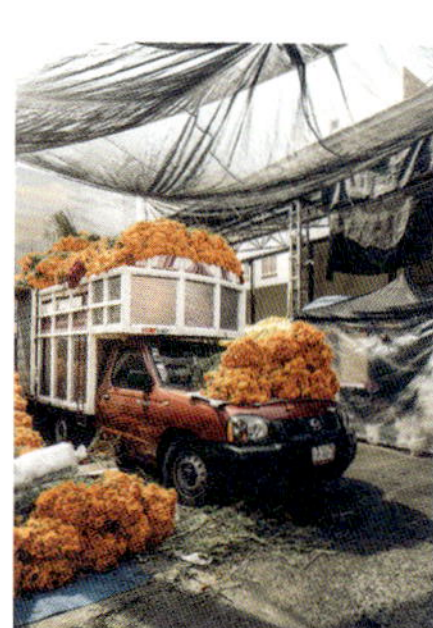

96 Isaac Jero
Mercado Jamaica

Jamaica flower market

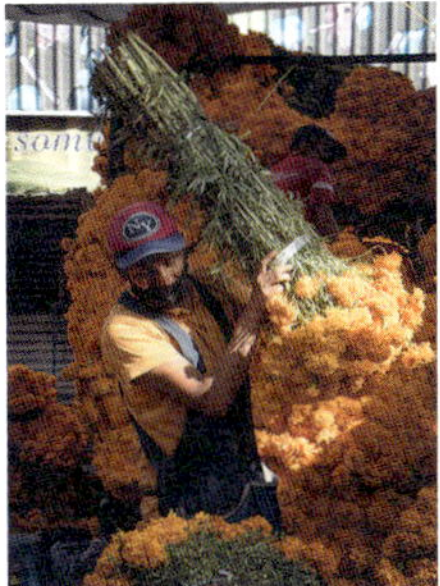

97 Isaac Jero
Mercado Jamaica

Jamaica flower market

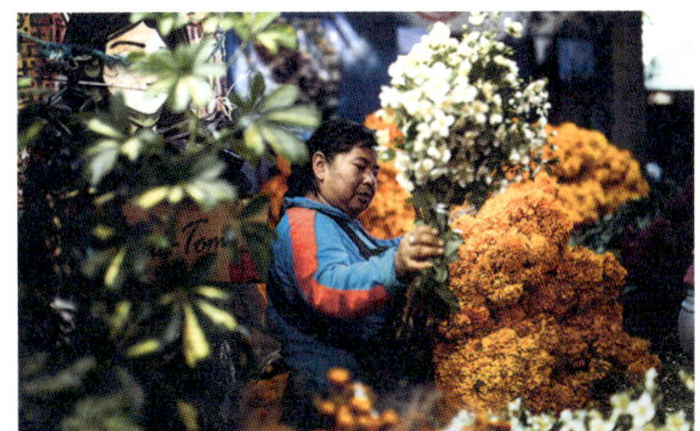

98 Isaac Jero
Mercado Jamaica

Jamaica flower market

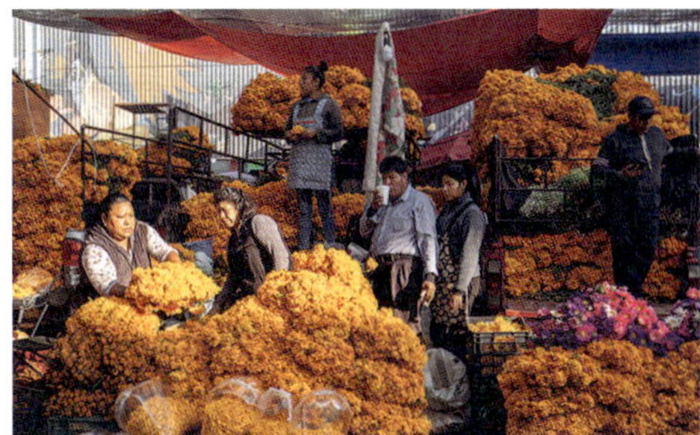

99 Jair Hernández
Mercado Jamaica

Jamaica flower market

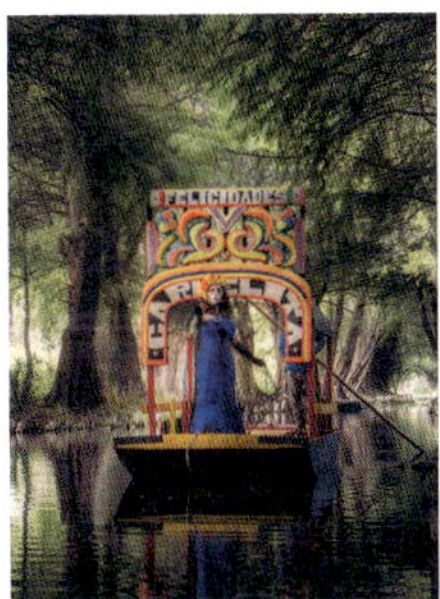

100 Roberto Lozano
Trajinera de Xochimilco

Trajinera boat on Xochimilco canal

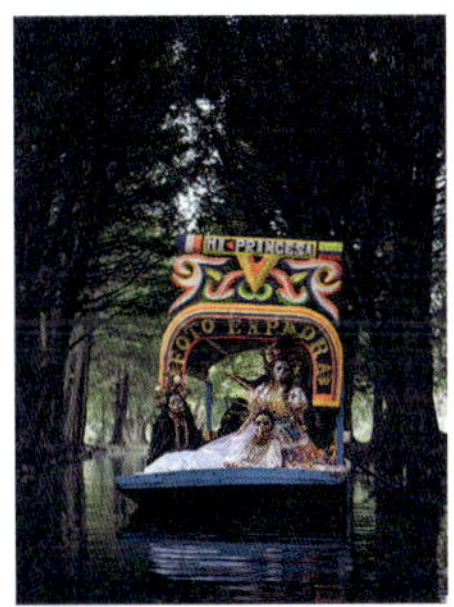

101 Roberto Lozano
Trajinera de Xochimilco

Trajinera boat on Xochimilco canal

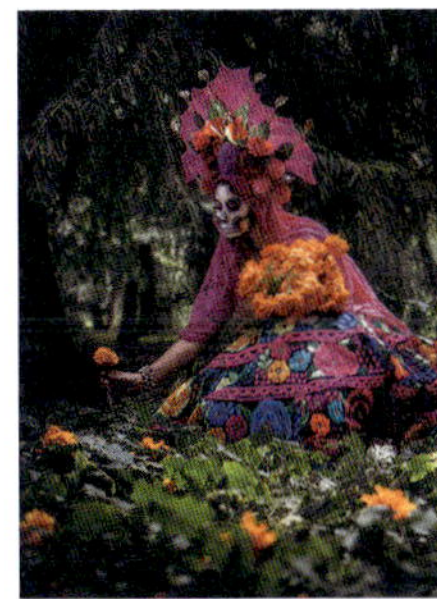

102 Oscar Reygo
Xochimilco

Xochimilco

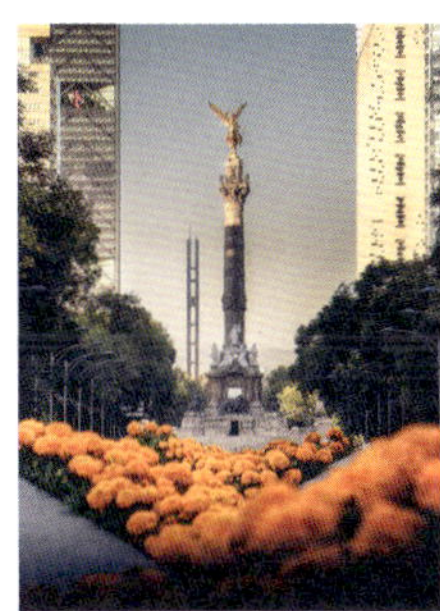

103 Roberto Lozano
Ángel de la Independencia

The Angel of Independence

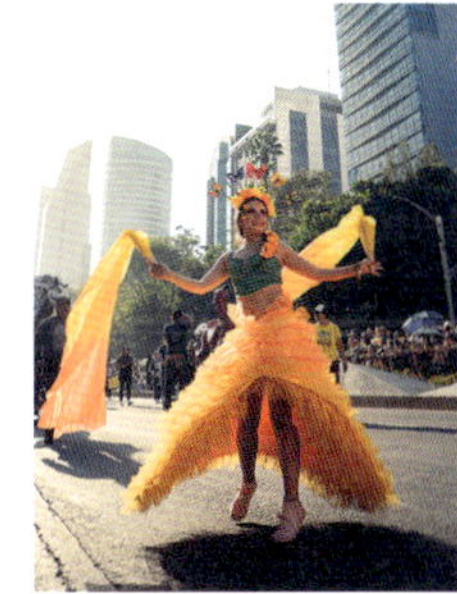

104 Oscar Reygo
Desfile de Día de los Muertos

Day of the Dead Parade

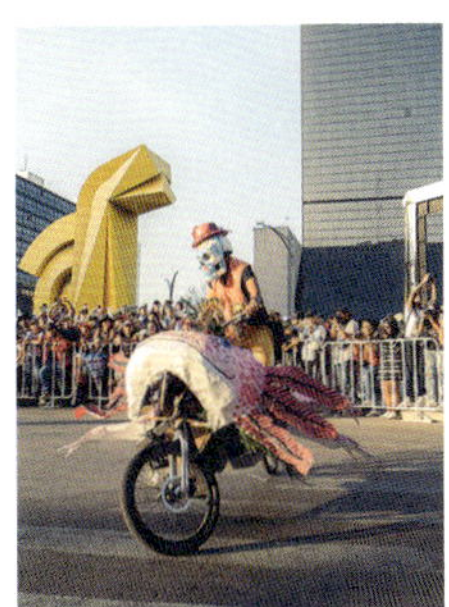

105 Oscar Reygo
Desfile de Día de los Muertos

Day of the Dead Parade

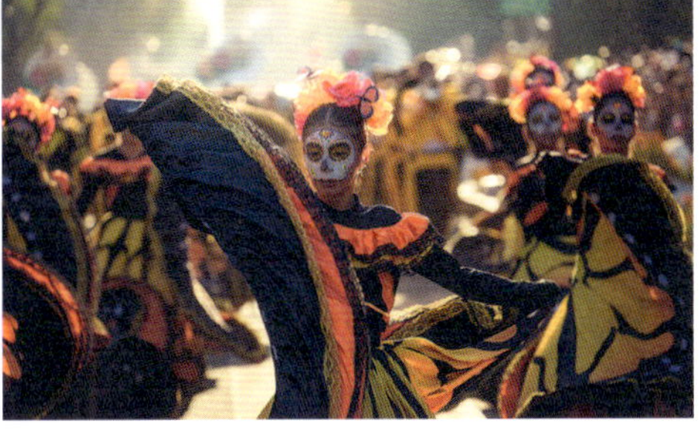

106 Isaac Jero
Desfile de Día de los Muertos

Day of the Dead Parade

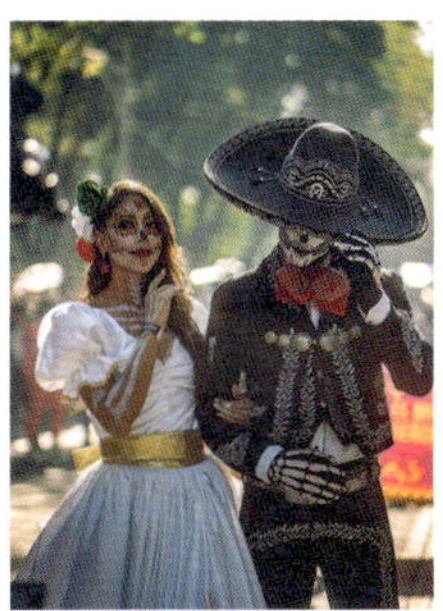

107 Roberto Lozano
Desfile de Día de los Muertos

Day of the Dead Parade

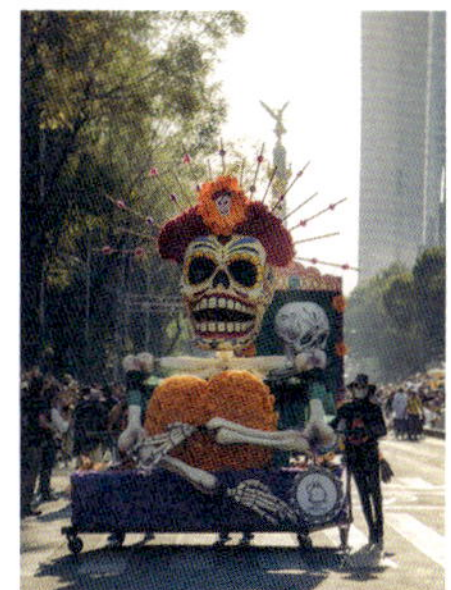

108 Isaac Jero
Desfile de Día de los Muertos

Day of the Dead Parade

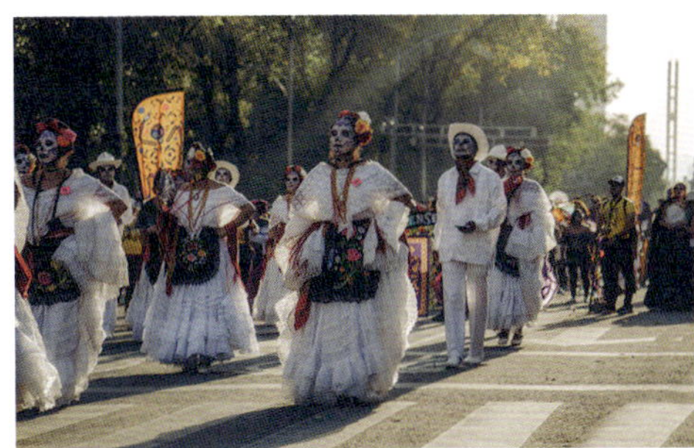

109 Isaac Jero
Desfile de Día de los Muertos

Day of the Dead Parade

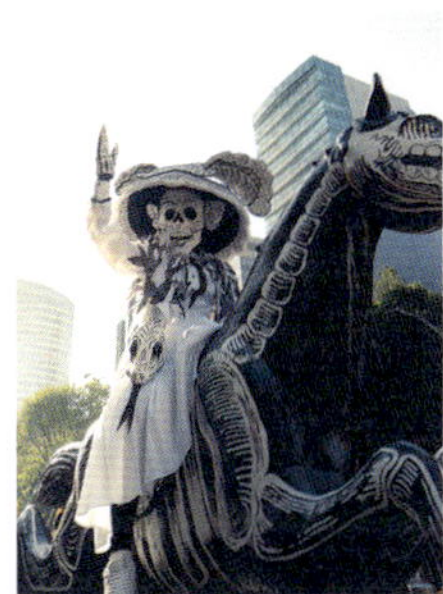

110 Oscar Reygo
Desfile de Día de los Muertos

Day of the Dead Parade

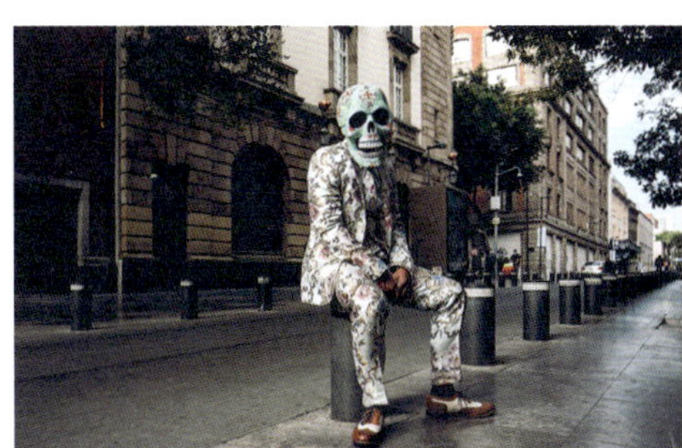

111 Jair Hernández
Centro Histórico

Historic Center

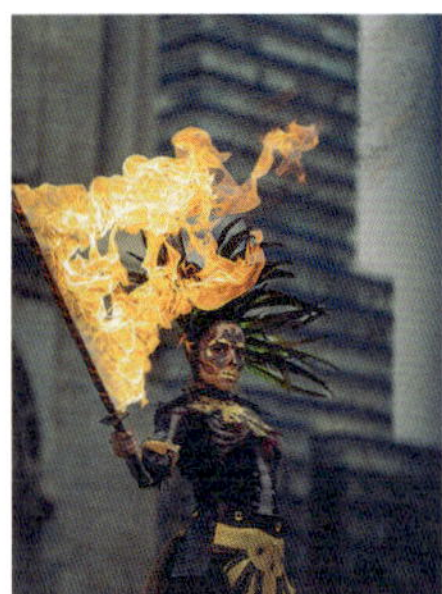

112 Roberto Lozano
Centro Histórico

Historic Center

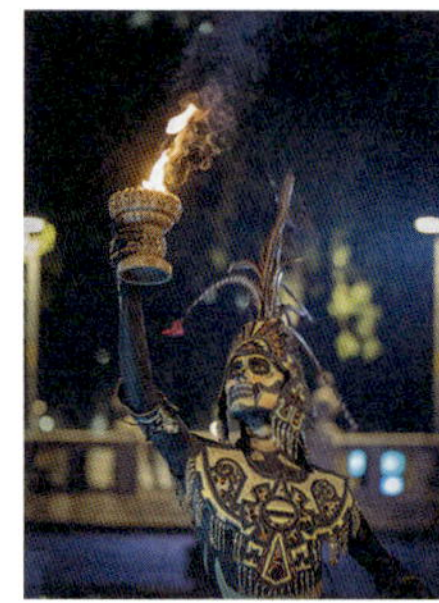

113 Roberto Lozano
Alameda Central

Alameda Central

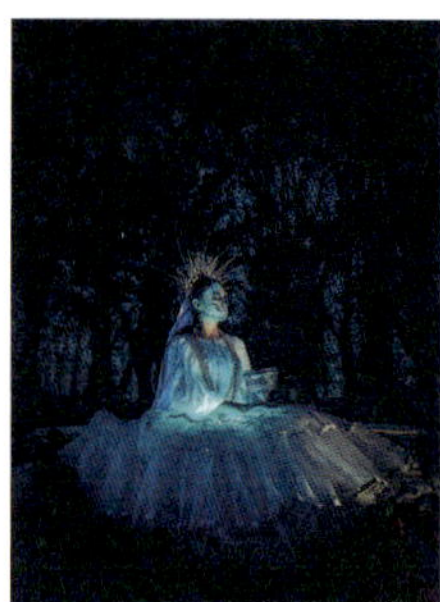

114 Roberto Lozano
Xochimilco

Xochimilco

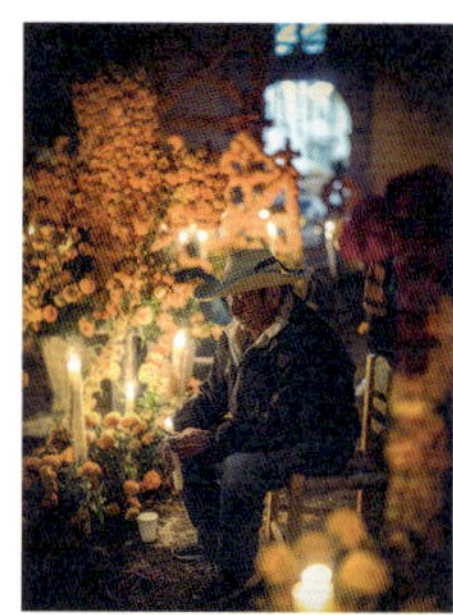

116 Isaac Jero
Día de los Muertos

Day of the Dead

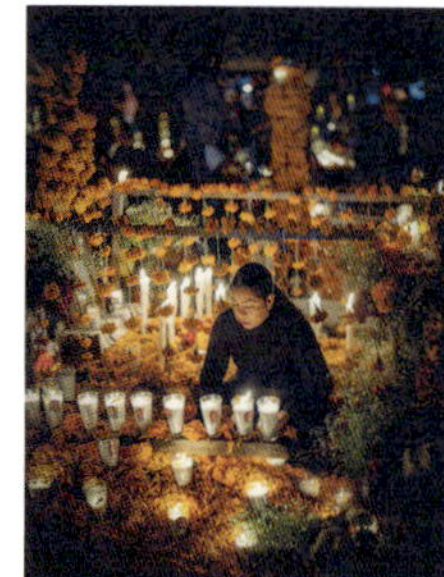

117 Isaac Jero
Día de los Muertos

Day of the Dead

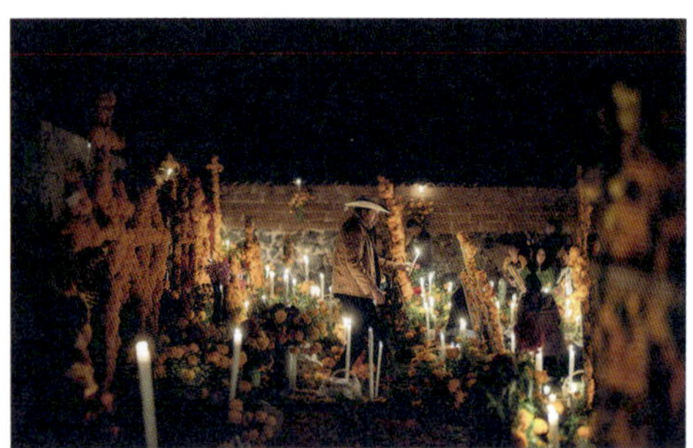

118-119 Isaac Jero
Día de los Muertos

Day of the Dead

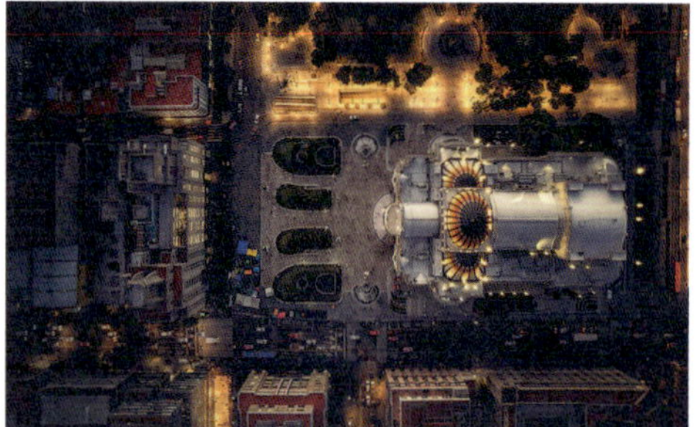

120-121 Isaac Jero
Palacio de Bellas Artes

The Palace of Fine Arts

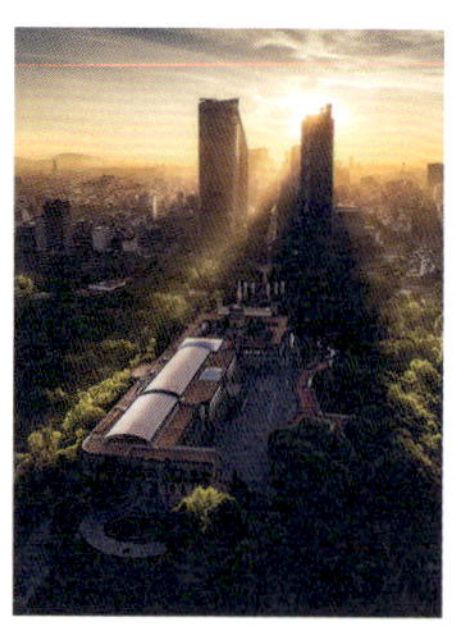

122 Isaac Jero
Castillo de Chapultepec

Chapultepec Castle

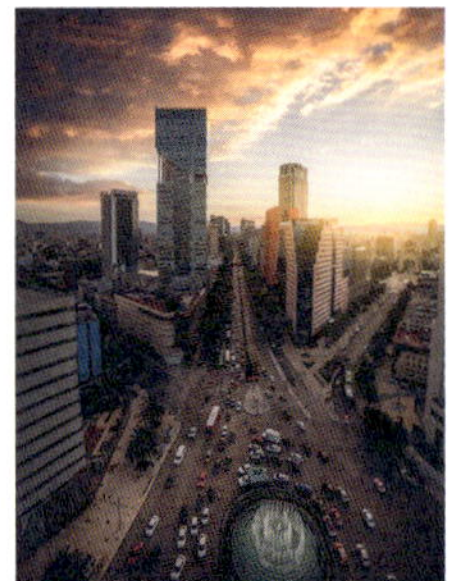

123 Isaac Jero
Paseo de la Reforma

Paseo de la Reforma

124 Roberto Lozano
Edificio La Mexicana de Centro Histórico

Edificio La Mexicana in the Historic Center

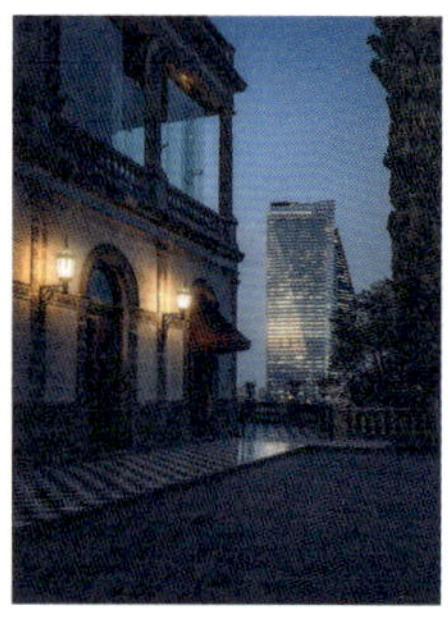

125 Oscar Reygo
Castillo de Chapultepec

Chapultepec Castle

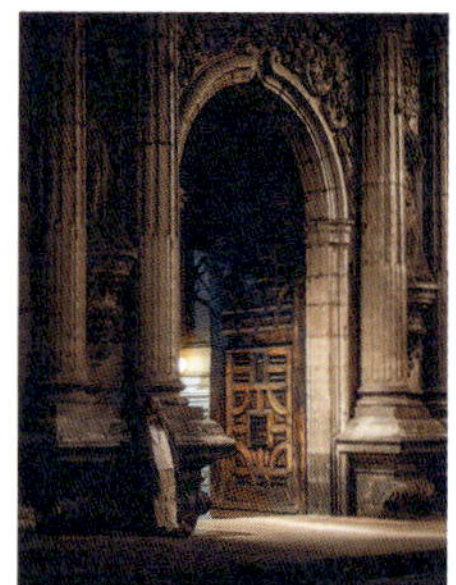

126 Oscar Reygo
Templo de San Felipe Neri

Church of San Felipe Neri

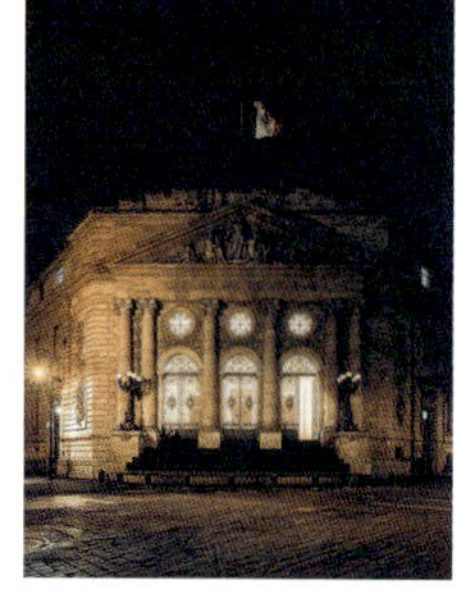

127 Oscar Reygo
Palacio Legislativo de Donceles

Donceles Legislative Palace

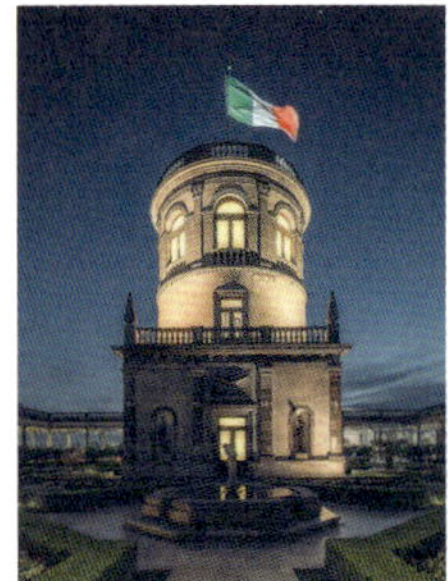

128 Oscar Reygo
Castillo de Chapultepec

Chapultepec Castle

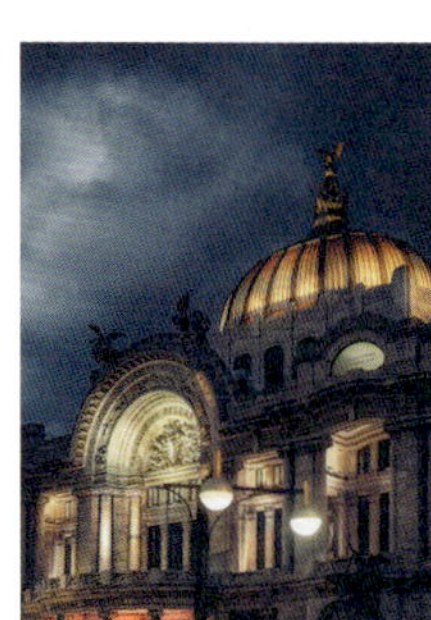

129 Isaac Jero
Palacio de Bellas Artes

The Palace of Fine Arts

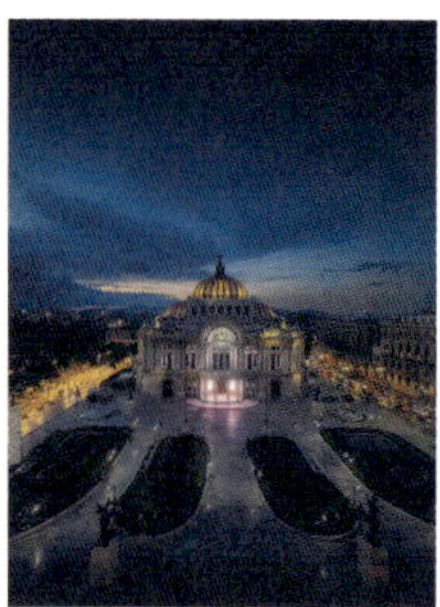

130 Roberto Lozano
Palacio de Bellas Artes

The Palace of Fine Arts

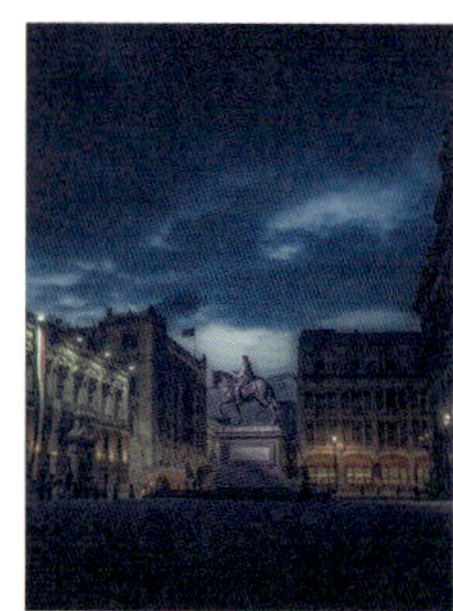

131 Roberto Lozano
El Caballito

Equestrian statue of Charles IV of Spain

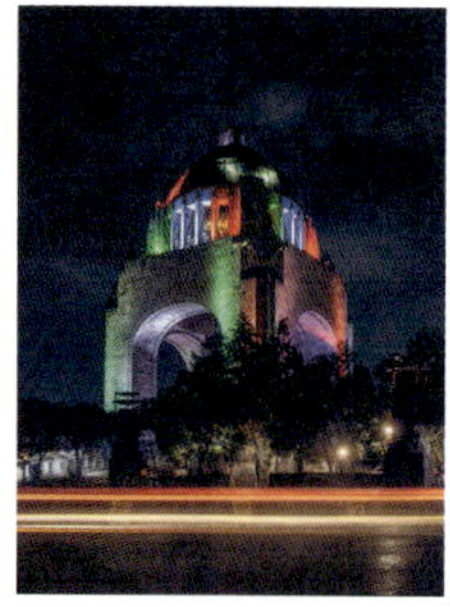

133 Oscar Reygo
El Monumento a la Revolución

The Monument to the Revolution

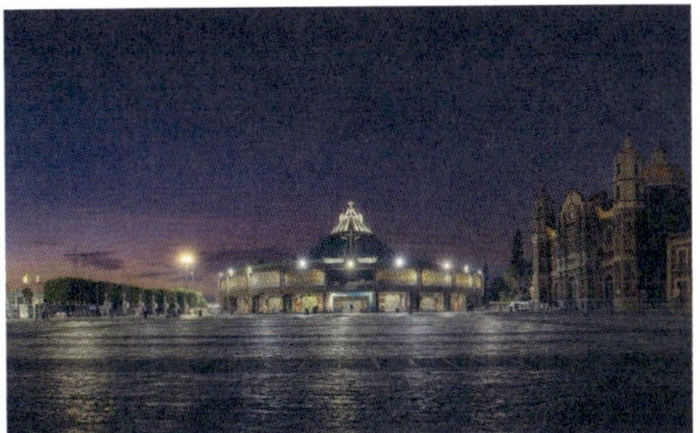

134-135 Roberto Lozano
Basílica de Santa María de Guadalupe

Basilica of Our Lady of Guadalupe

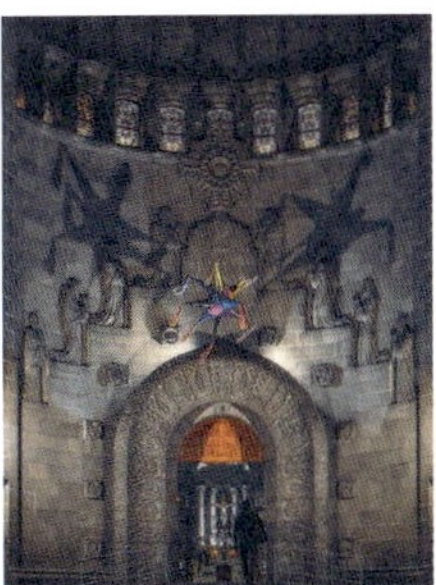

136 Oscar Reygo
Parroquia de San Agustín de Polanco

St. Augustine Parish in Polanco

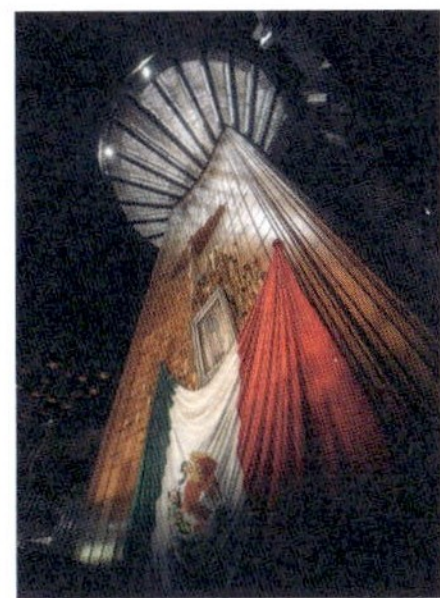

137 Roberto Lozano
Basílica de Santa María de Guadalupe

Basilica of Our Lady of Guadalupe

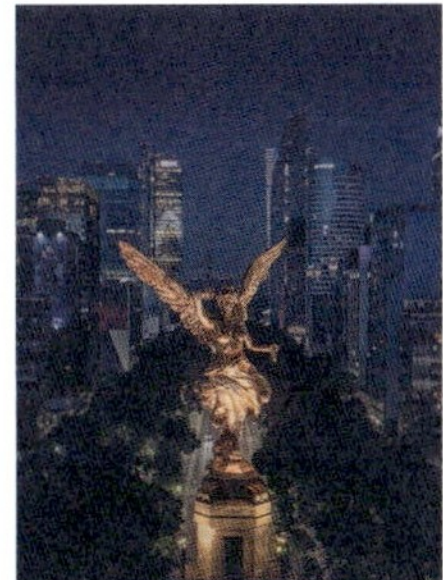

138 Roberto Lozano
Ángel de la Independencia

The Angel of Independence

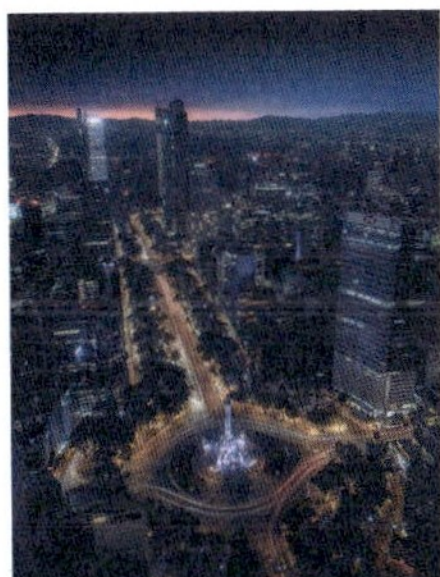

139 Roberto Lozano
Paseo de la Reforma

Paseo de la Reforma

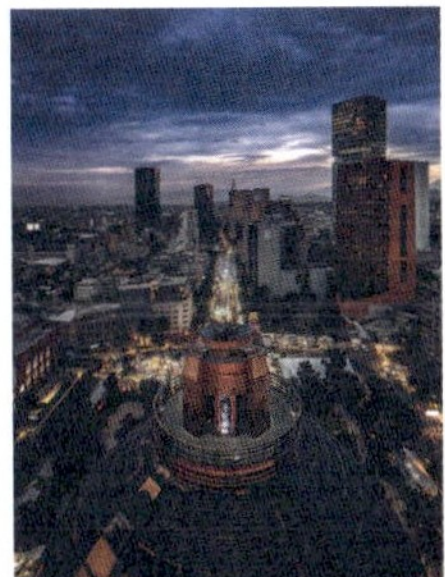

140 Oscar Reygo
El Monumento a la Revolución

The Monument to the Revolution

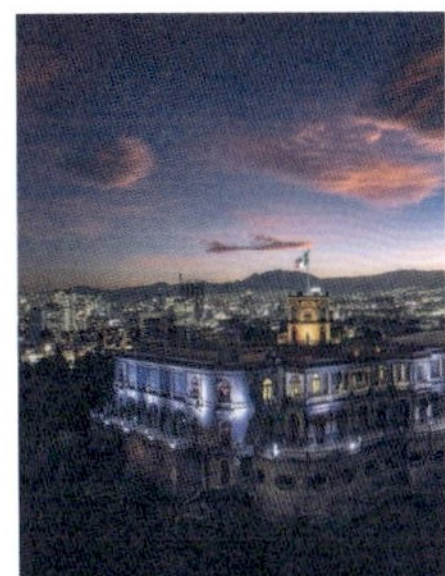

141 Oscar Reygo
Castillo de Chapultepec

Chapultepec Castle

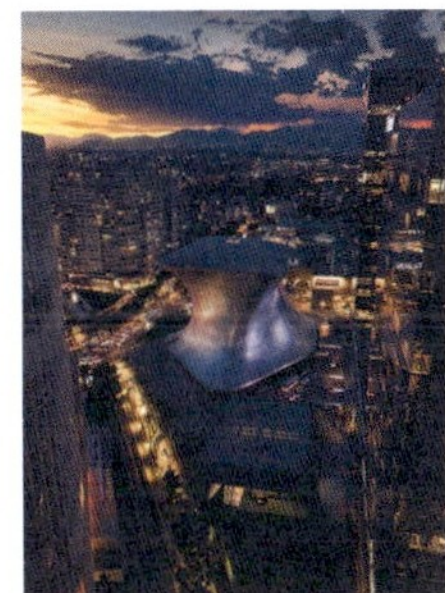

142 Vidal Rivera
Museo Soumaya

Soumaya Museum

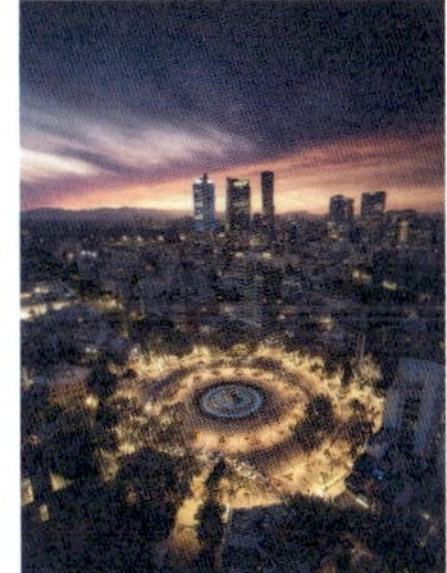

143 Isaac Jero
Fuente de Cibeles

The Fountain of Cybele

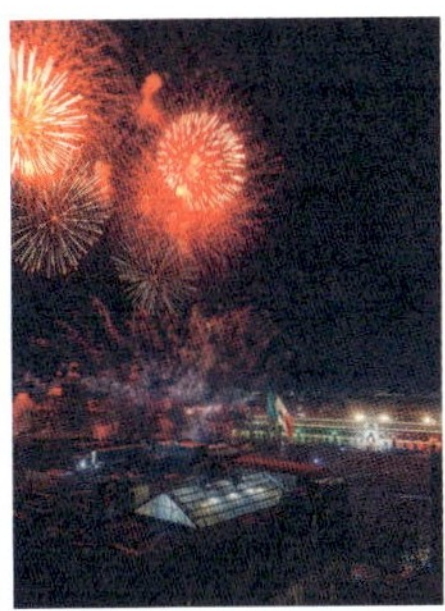

144 Roberto Lozano
Fuegos Artificiales en el Zócalo

Fireworks in the Zócalo

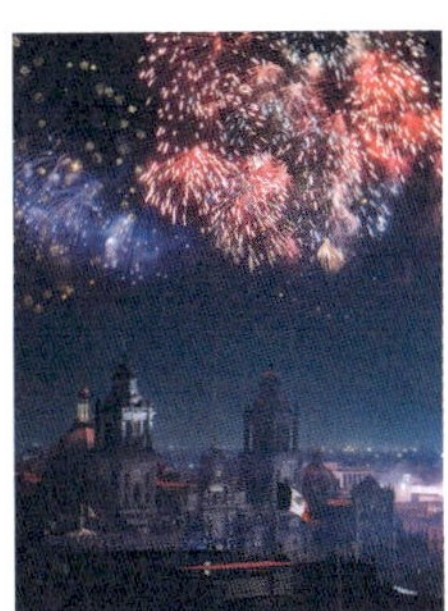

145 Roberto Lozano
Fuegos Artificiales en el Zócalo

Fireworks in the Zócalo

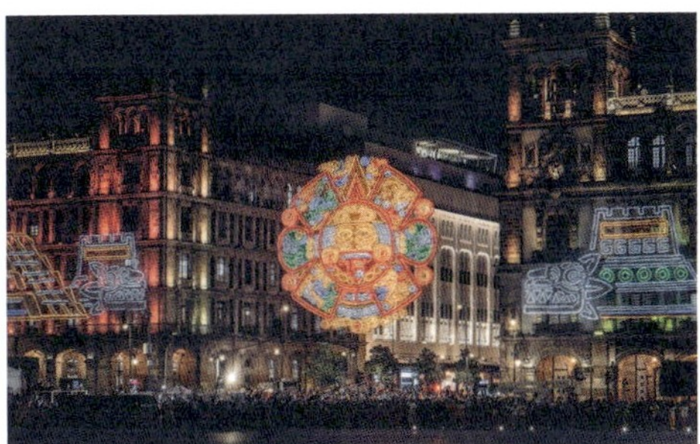

146-147 Oscar Reygo
Zócalo

Zócalo

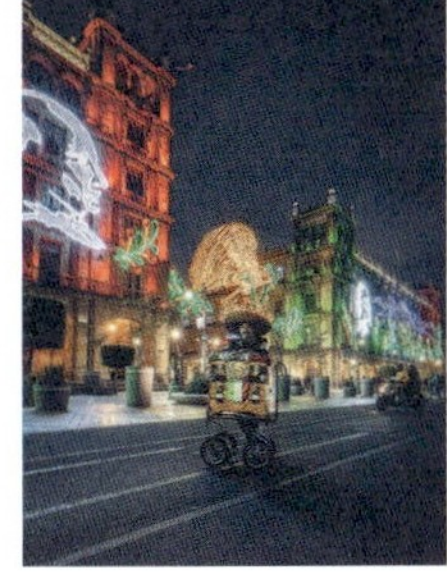

148 Oscar Reygo
Zócalo

Zócalo

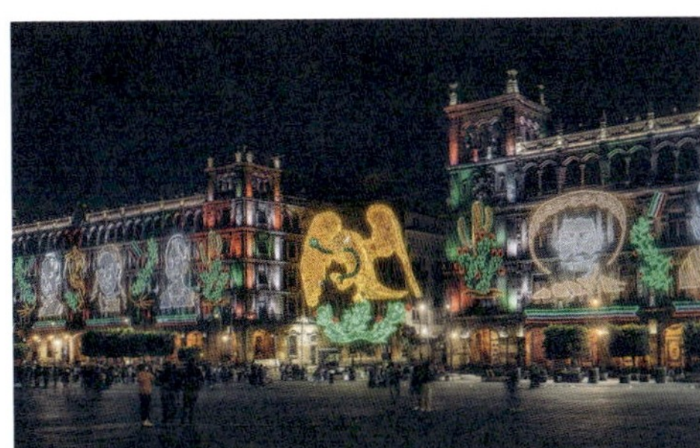

150-151 Oscar Reygo
Zócalo

Zócalo

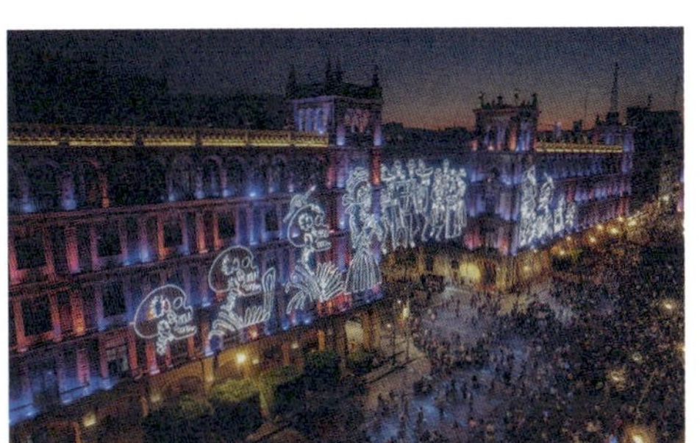

152 Isaac Jero
Día de los Muertos en el Zócalo

Day of the Dead in the Zócalo

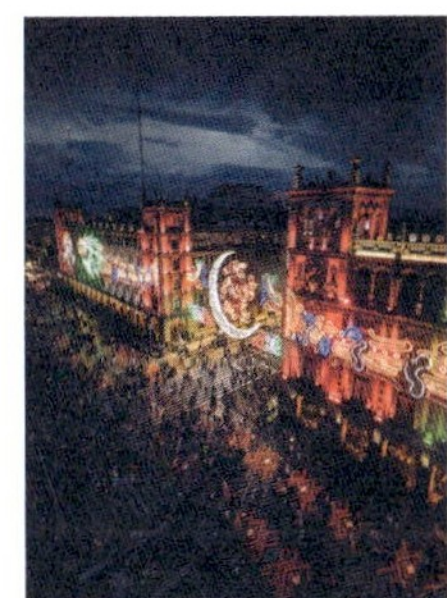

153 Oscar Reygo
Zócalo

Zócalo

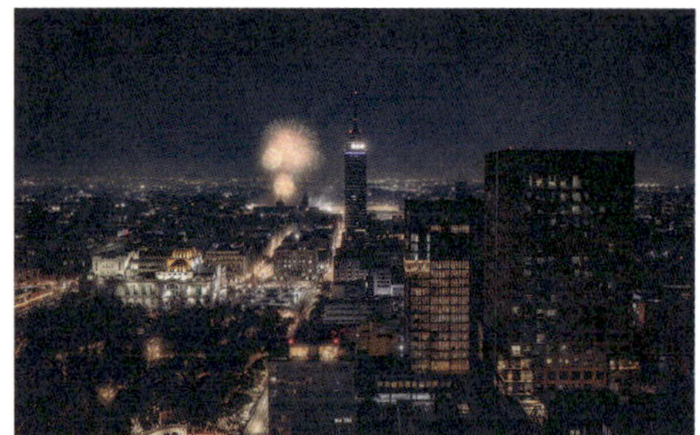

154-155 Oscar Reygo
Centro Histórico

Historic Center

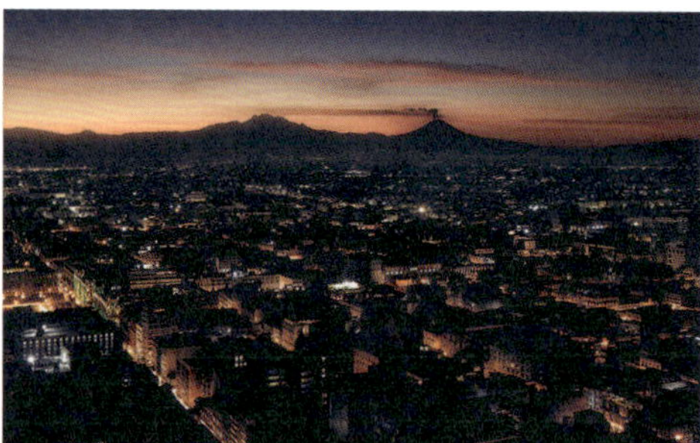

156-157 Oscar Reygo
Encima de la Ciudad de México

Above Mexico City

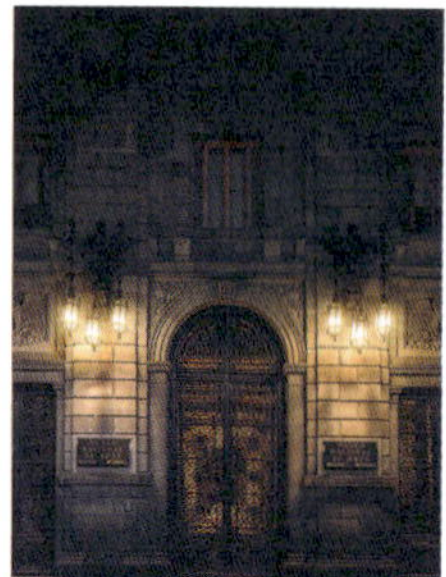

158 Oscar Reygo
Museo Nacional de Arte

National Museum of Art

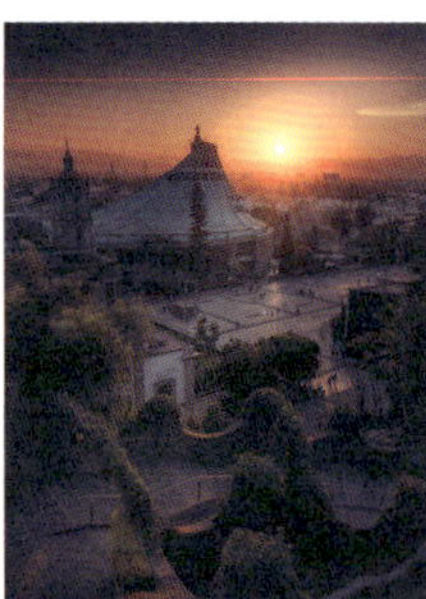

162 Roberto Lozano
Basílica de Santa María de Guadalupe

Basilica of Our Lady of Guadalupe

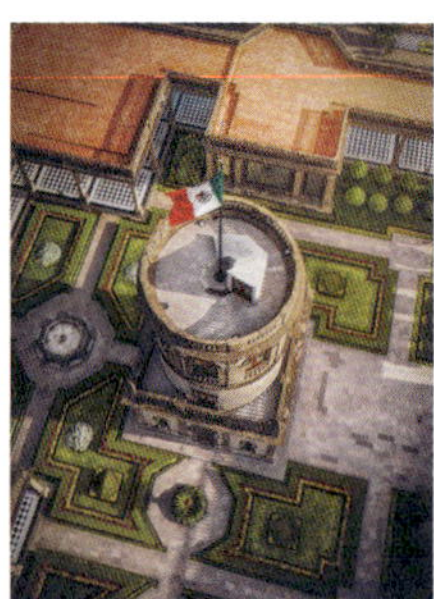

173 Vidal Rivera
Castillo de Chapultepec

Chapultepec Castle

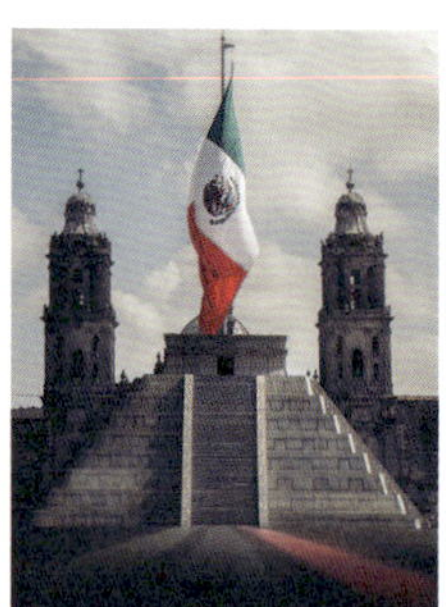

175 Roberto Lozano
Zócalo

Zócalo

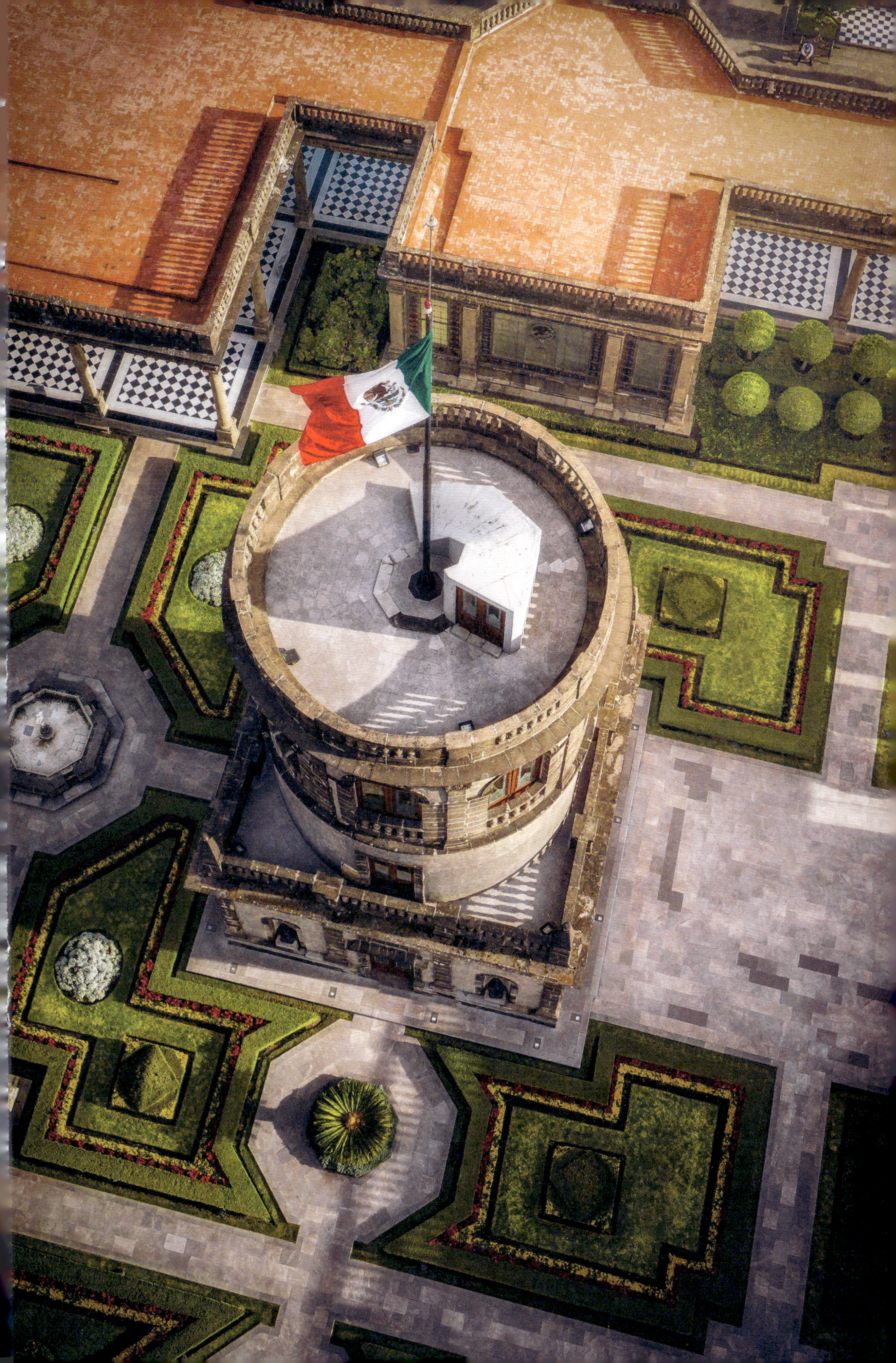

Special thanks to Oscar Reygo and Carlos Gómez

LCCN: 2026932866
ISBN: 978-1-951963-60-6

Printed and bound in China
First printing, 2026

Trope Publishing Co.
Chicago, Illinois, USA

Photographs are available for purchase.
For inquires, go to trope.com
or email the gallery at info@trope.com

+ INFORMATION:
For additional information
on our books and prints,
visit trope.com

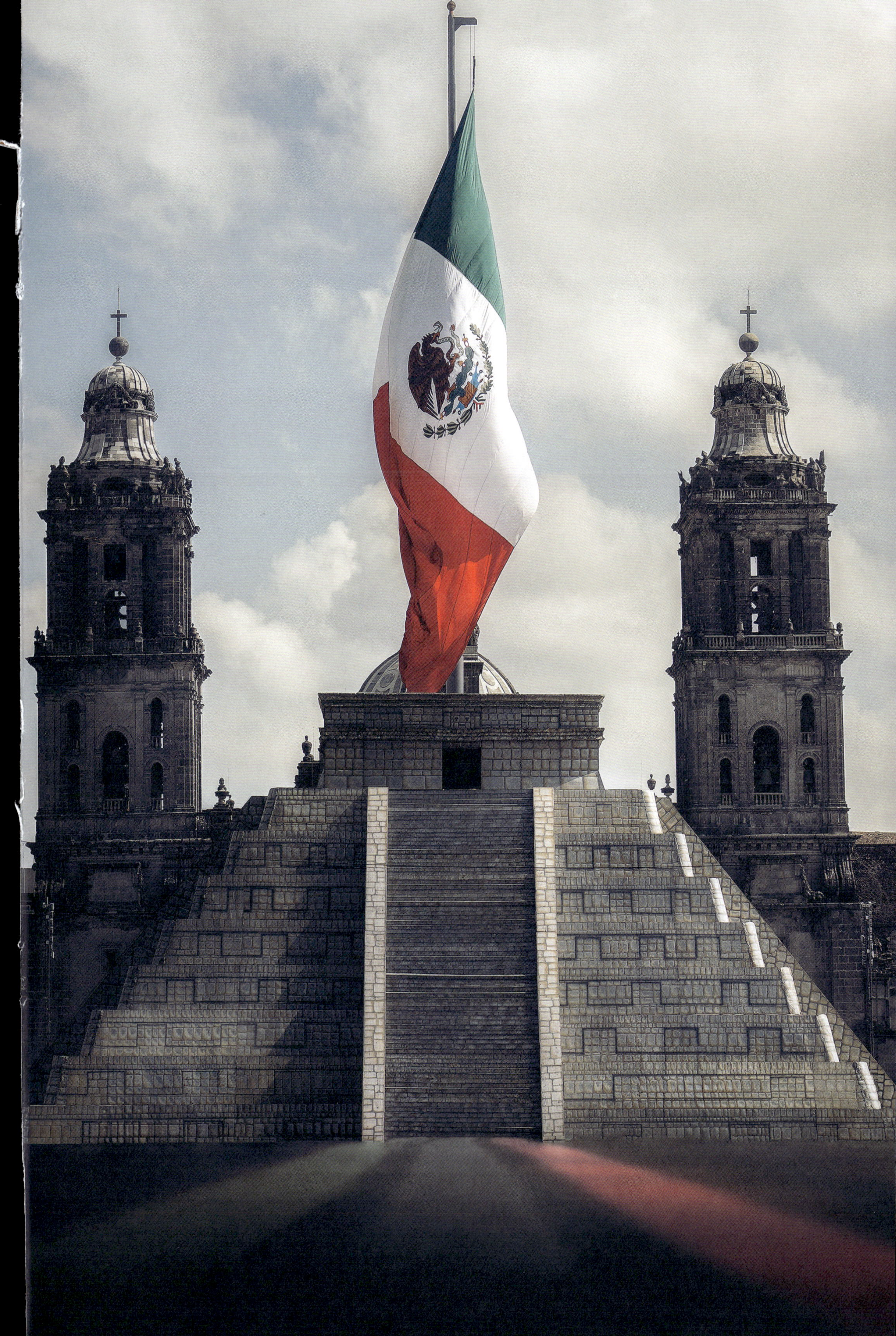

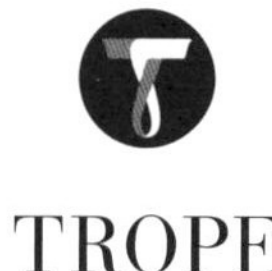

TROPE PUBLISHING Co.

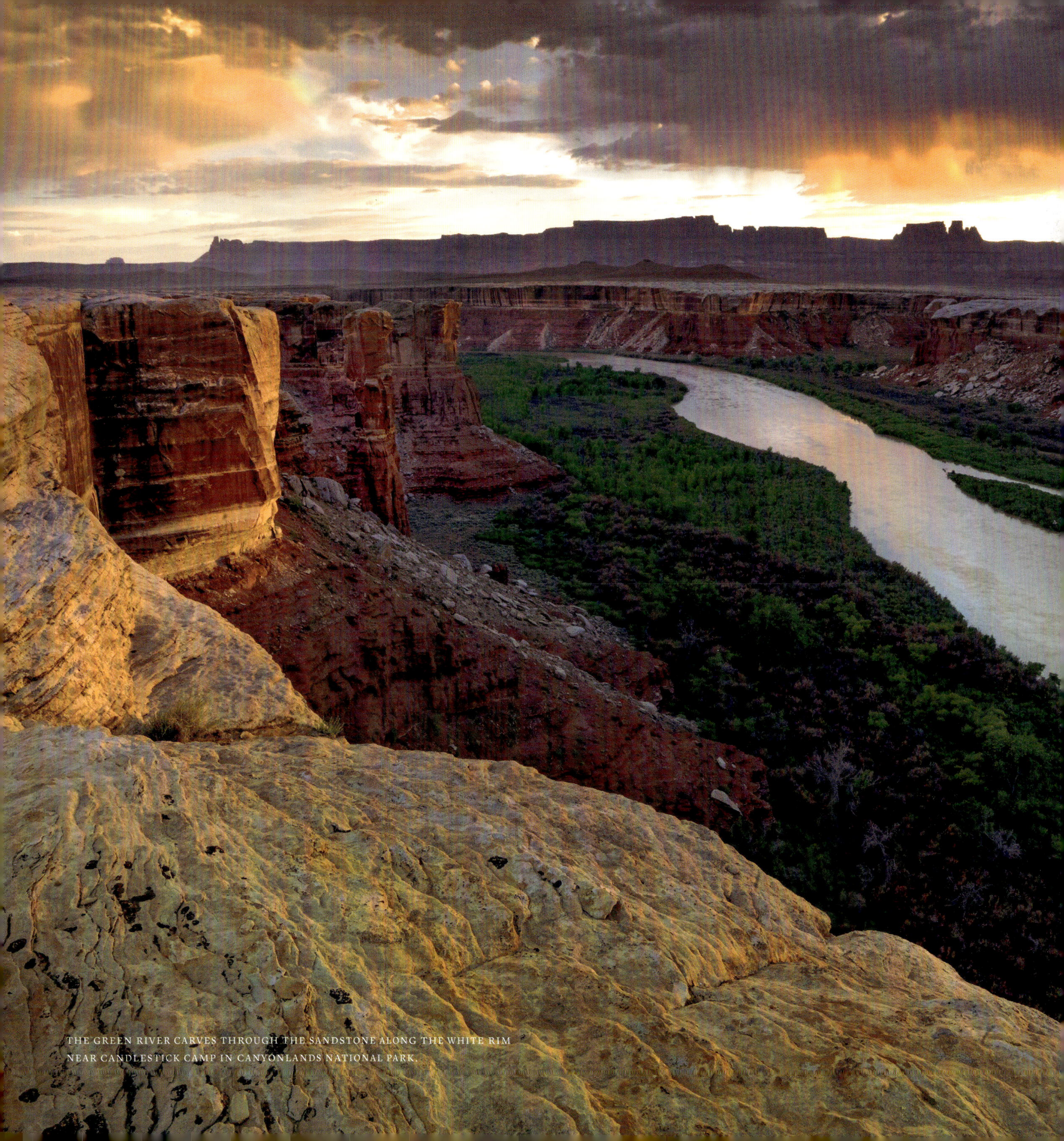

THE GREEN RIVER CARVES THROUGH THE SANDSTONE ALONG THE WHITE RIM NEAR CANDLESTICK CAMP IN CANYONLANDS NATIONAL PARK.

UTAH

DISCOVER THE BEEHIVE STATE

PHOTOGRAPHS BY MARK LISK

Published by Familius LLC, www.familius.com
PO Box 1249, Reedley, CA 93654

Familius books are available at special discounts for bulk purchases, whether for sales promotions or for family or corporate use. For more information, contact Familius Sales at orders@familius.com.

Library of Congress Control Number: 2025951485

Print ISBN 9798893961379
Ebook ISBN 9798893961607

Printed in China

Edited by Sarah Echard and Gretchen Picklesimer Kinney
Cover design by Brooke Jorden
Book design by Derek George

10 9 8 7 6 5 4 3 2 1

First Edition

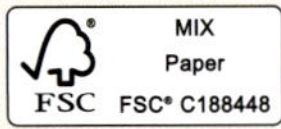

CONTENTS

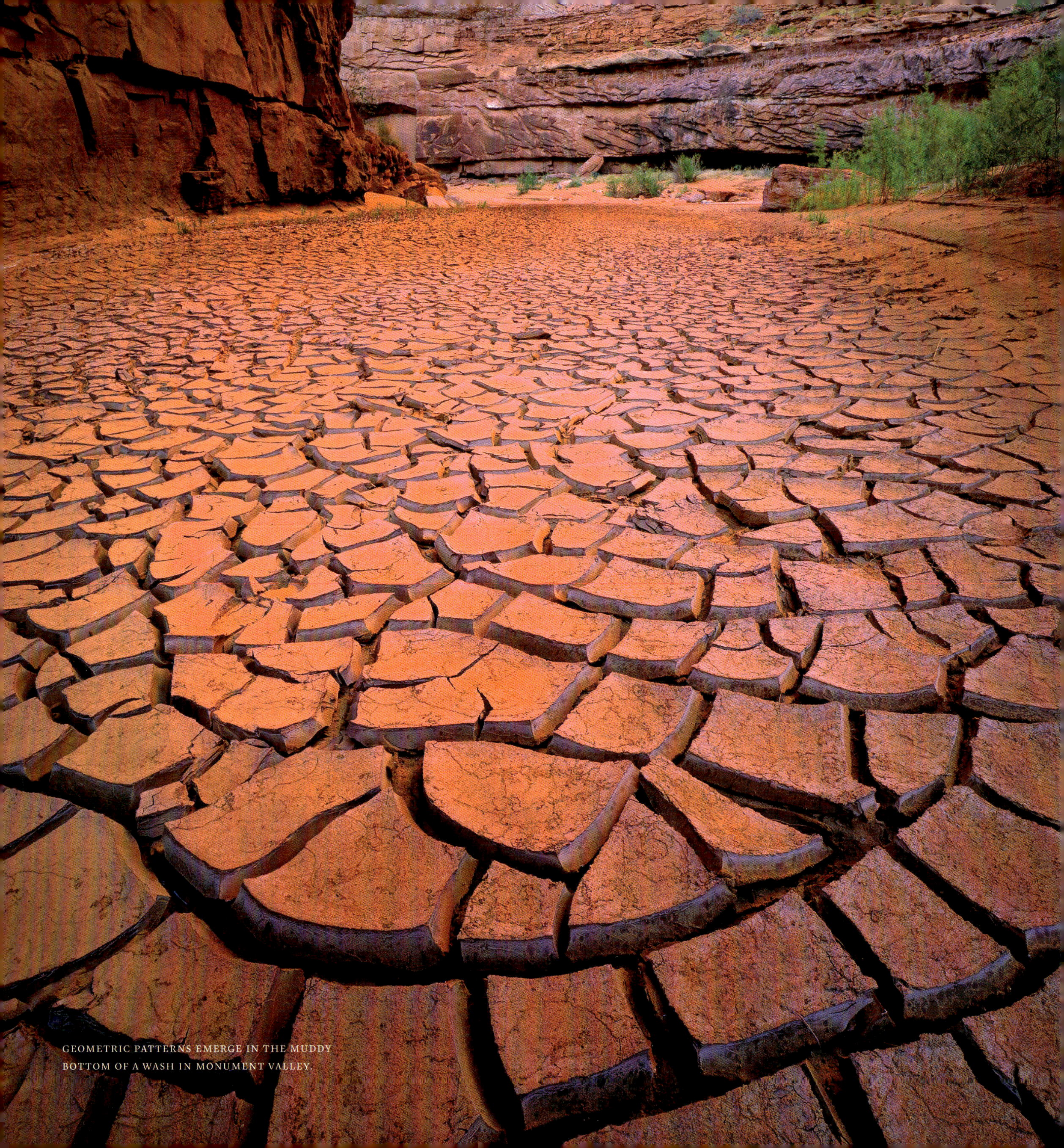

GEOMETRIC PATTERNS EMERGE IN THE MUDDY BOTTOM OF A WASH IN MONUMENT VALLEY.

WELCOME TO UTAH

MARK LISK

FROM CAMP, MY EYES TRACK ACROSS MILES OF sandstone towers that extend endlessly into the Maze. At this high desert perch, I can see into two deep river canyons, the Colorado River and the Green River. This is the heart of the Colorado Plateau, taking up the majority of the Utah landscape. These two mighty rivers merge and cut through some of the most beautiful and wild country in all of America.

Water, the most serious instrument of change within the plateau, has shaped seven monuments and all five of Utah's national parks: Arches, Bryce Canyon, Canyonlands, Capitol Reef, and Zion. Nowhere in America is this redesign more evident, and nowhere is this transformation more alluring.

> "The landscape everywhere, away from the river, is of rock—cliffs of rock; plateaus of rock; terraces of rock; crags of rock—ten thousand strangely carved forms."
>
> —JOHN WESLEY POWELL

The Green River flows south from its headwaters in Wyoming's Wind River Range and cuts through the highest regions of the plateau in Northern Utah. In Utah's northern tier, the Uinta Mountains and the Wasatch Mountains form the Colorado Plateau's northern boundary. The Uinta Mountains are one of the few ranges in the Rocky Mountains that run east-west, with its highest peak, Kings Peak, climbing to 13,528 feet. The Wasatch Mountains follow a traditional north-south axis from the neighboring Idaho border to Mount Nebo (11,877 feet) near Nephi. Snowfall from these two high ranges feeds rivers and streams like the Strawberry River, Currant Creek, Rock Creek, and Lake Fork River. All flow into the Duchesne River, contributing to the powerful Green River, and then into the Colorado River just above Cataract Canyon.

This is the core of the Colorado Plateau. It is here, overlooking the Maze District in Canyonlands National Park, I get an awareness of the indigenous people that have stood here before me and an appreciation for what Major Powell must have felt in his expeditions into this unsettled landscape.

> "An unknown distance yet to run, an unknown river to explore."
>
> —JOHN WESLEY POWELL

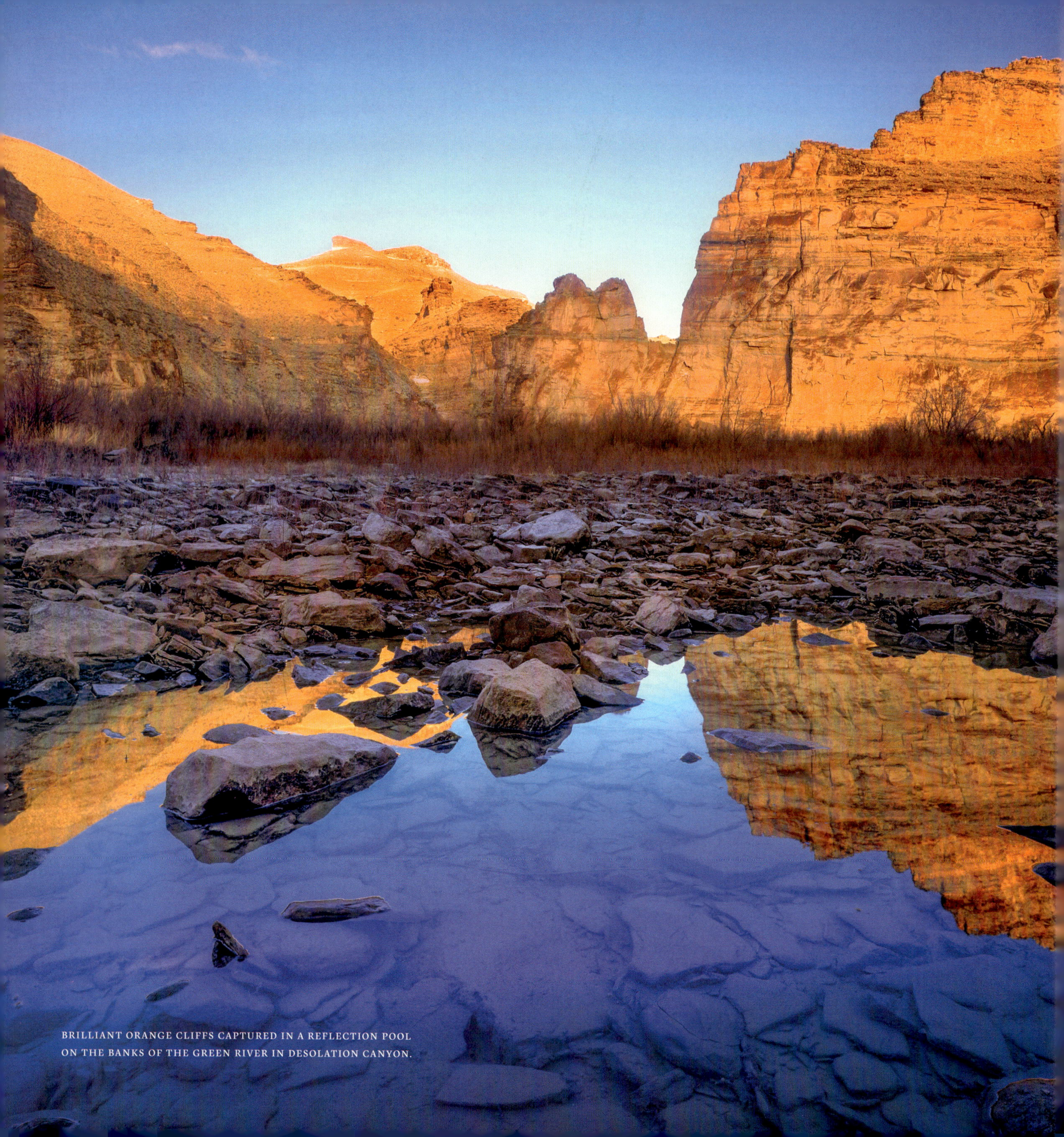

BRILLIANT ORANGE CLIFFS CAPTURED IN A REFLECTION POOL ON THE BANKS OF THE GREEN RIVER IN DESOLATION CANYON.

NORTH MOUNTAINS–UPPER GREEN

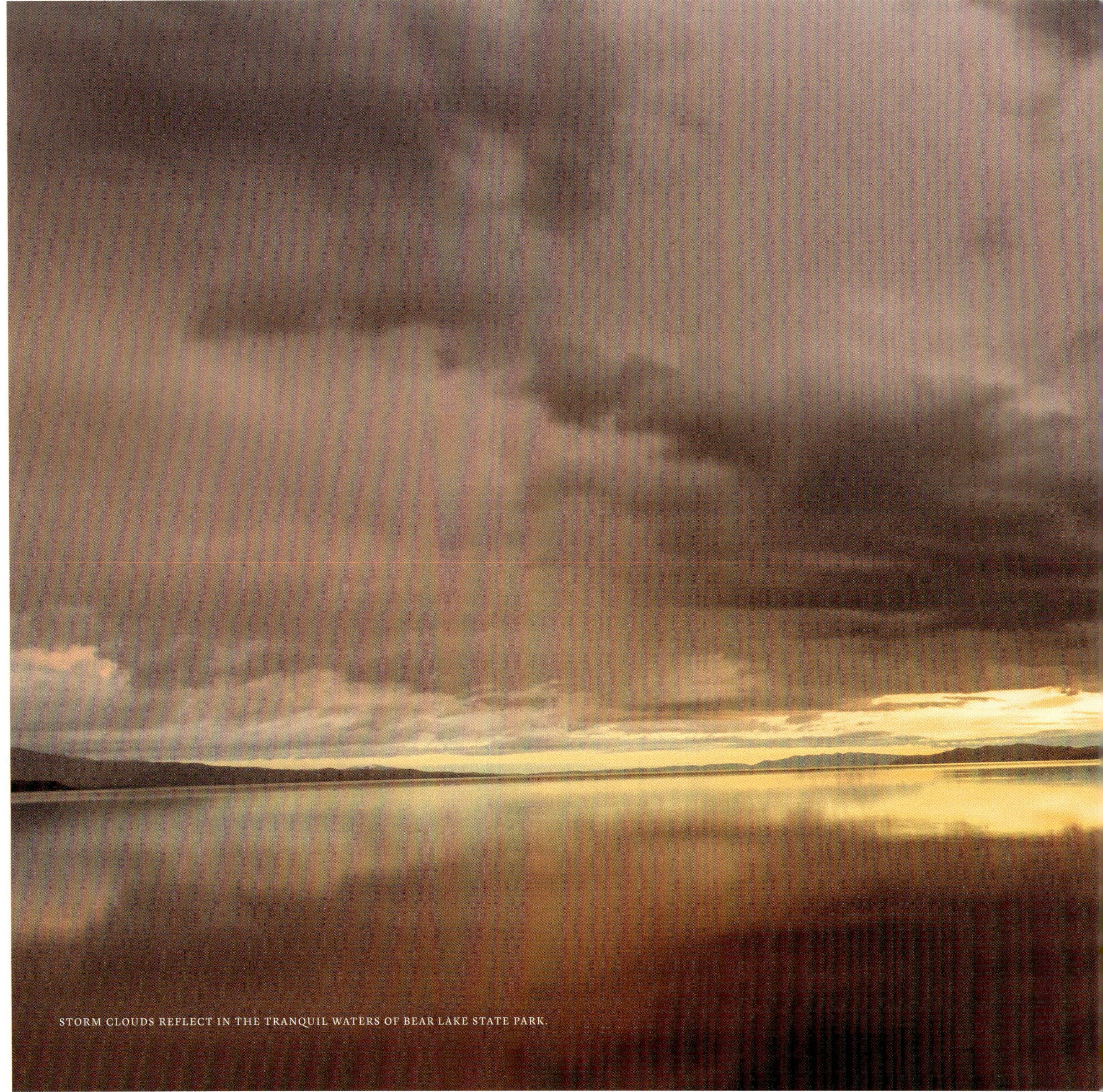

STORM CLOUDS REFLECT IN THE TRANQUIL WATERS OF BEAR LAKE STATE PARK.

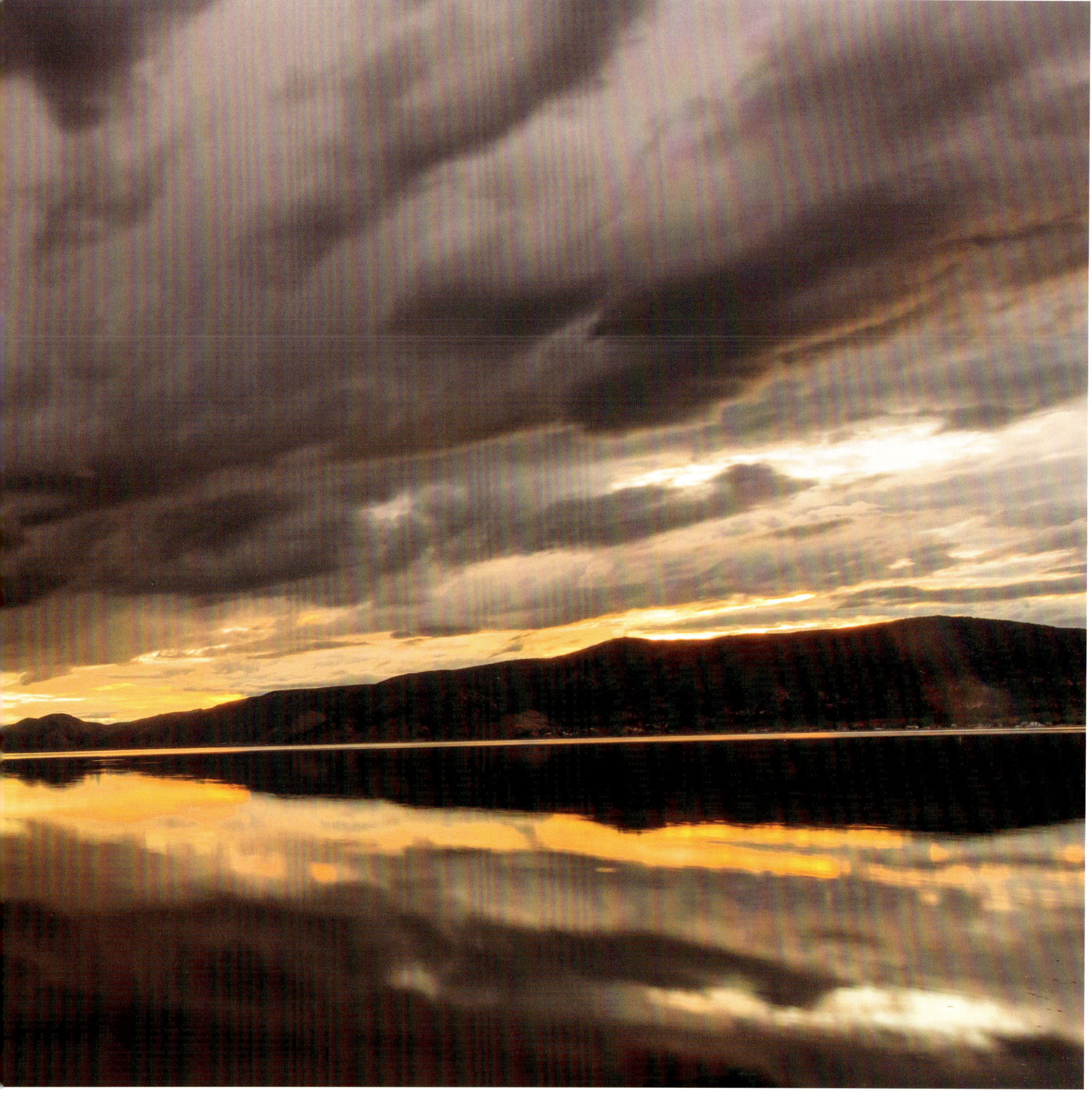

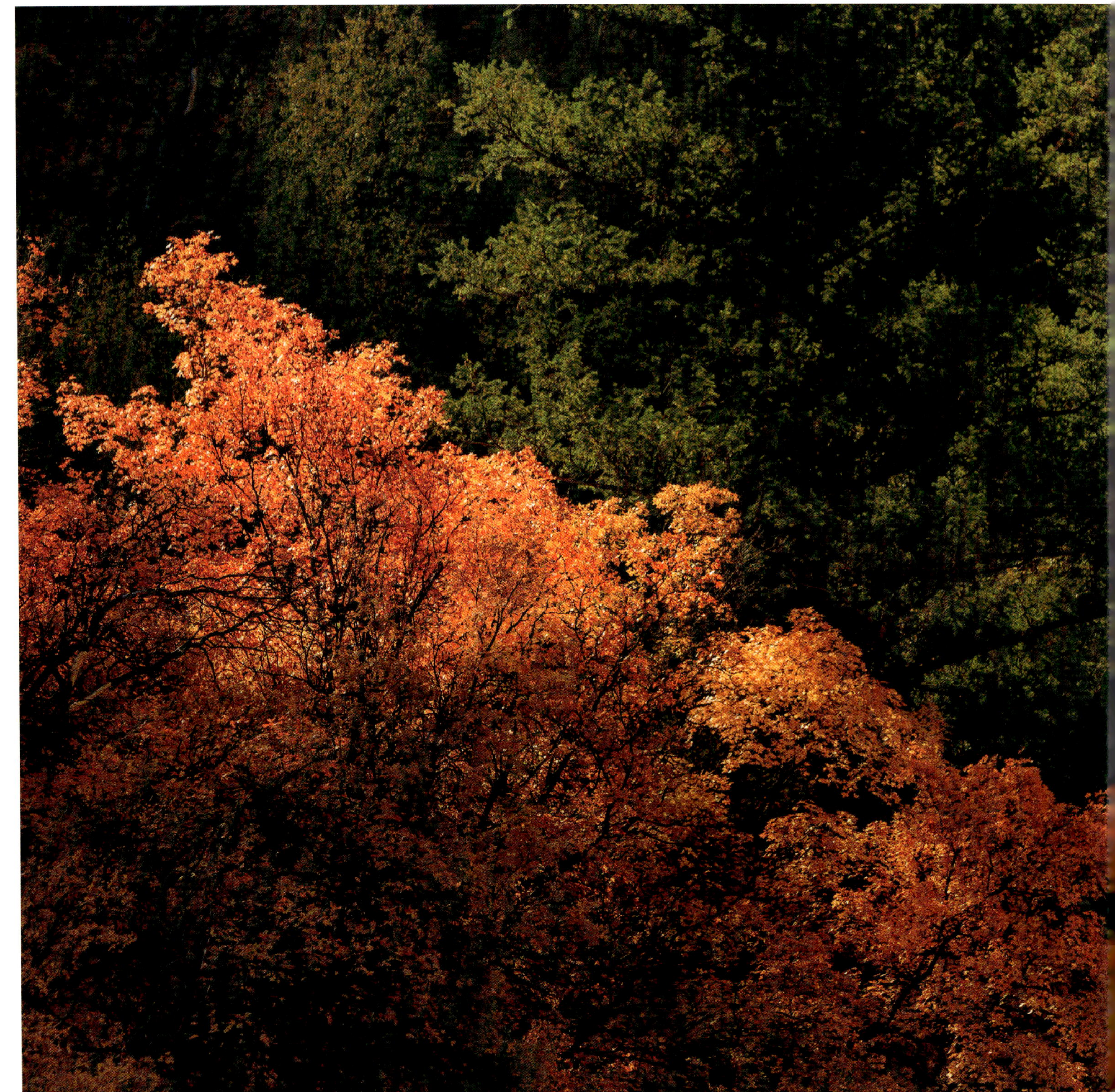

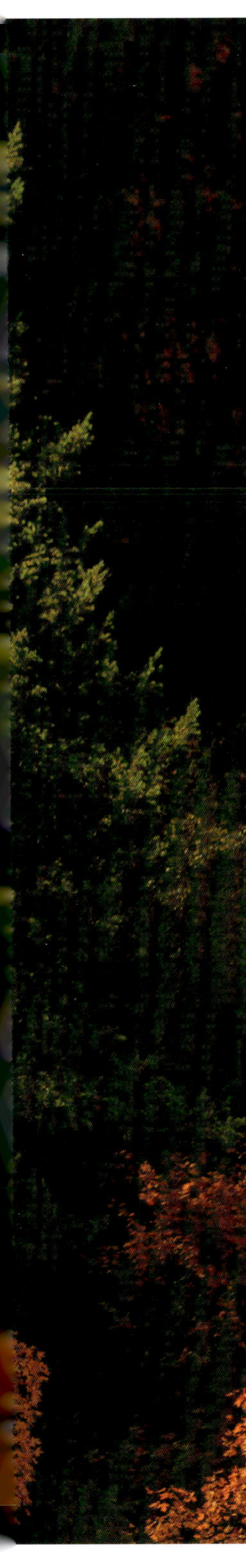

◀

MAPLES SHOW OFF THEIR COLORS IN THE SHADOWS OF LOGAN CANYON.

▶

DETAIL OF A BIGTOOTH MAPLE IN LOGAN CANYON.

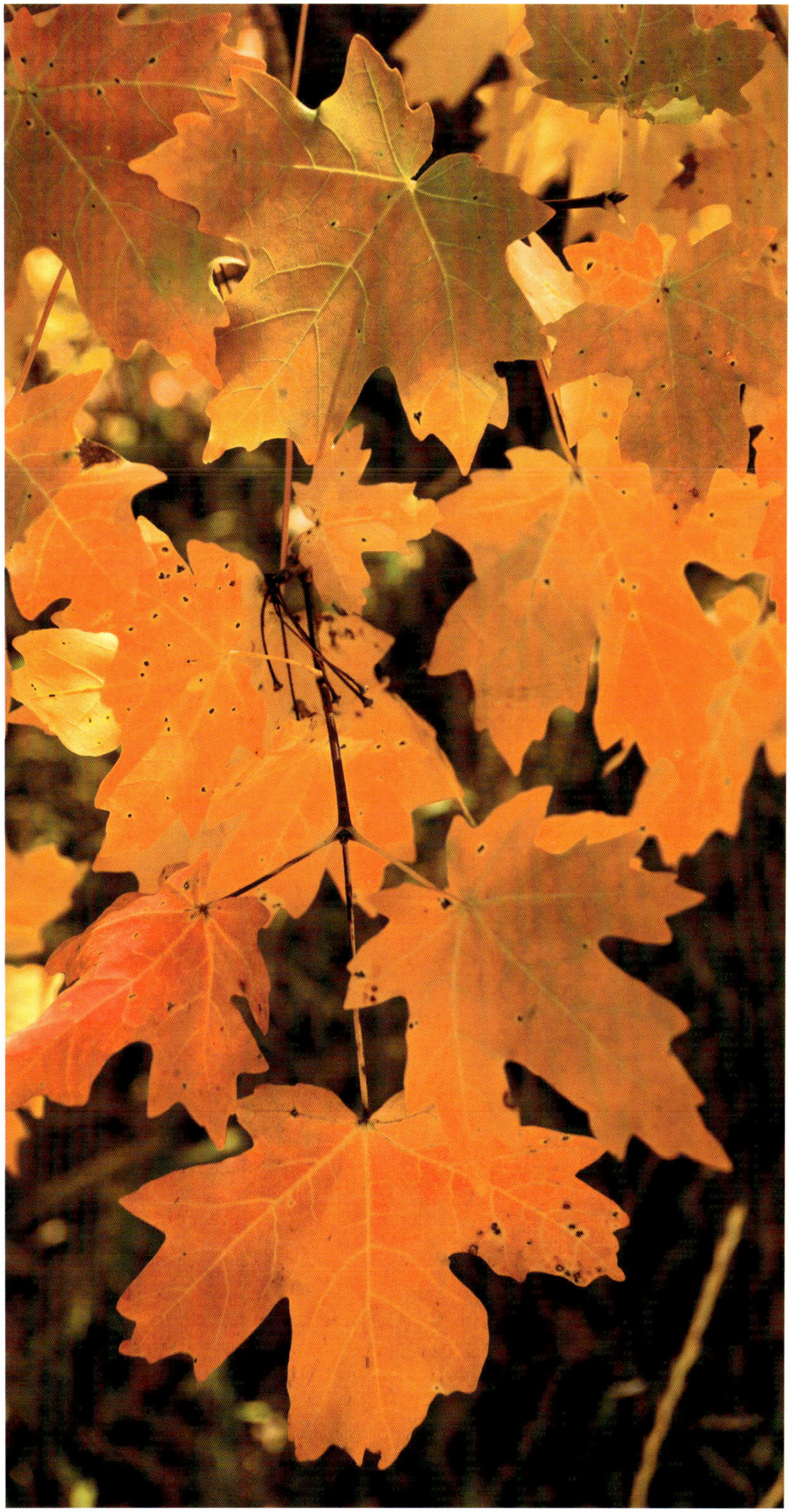

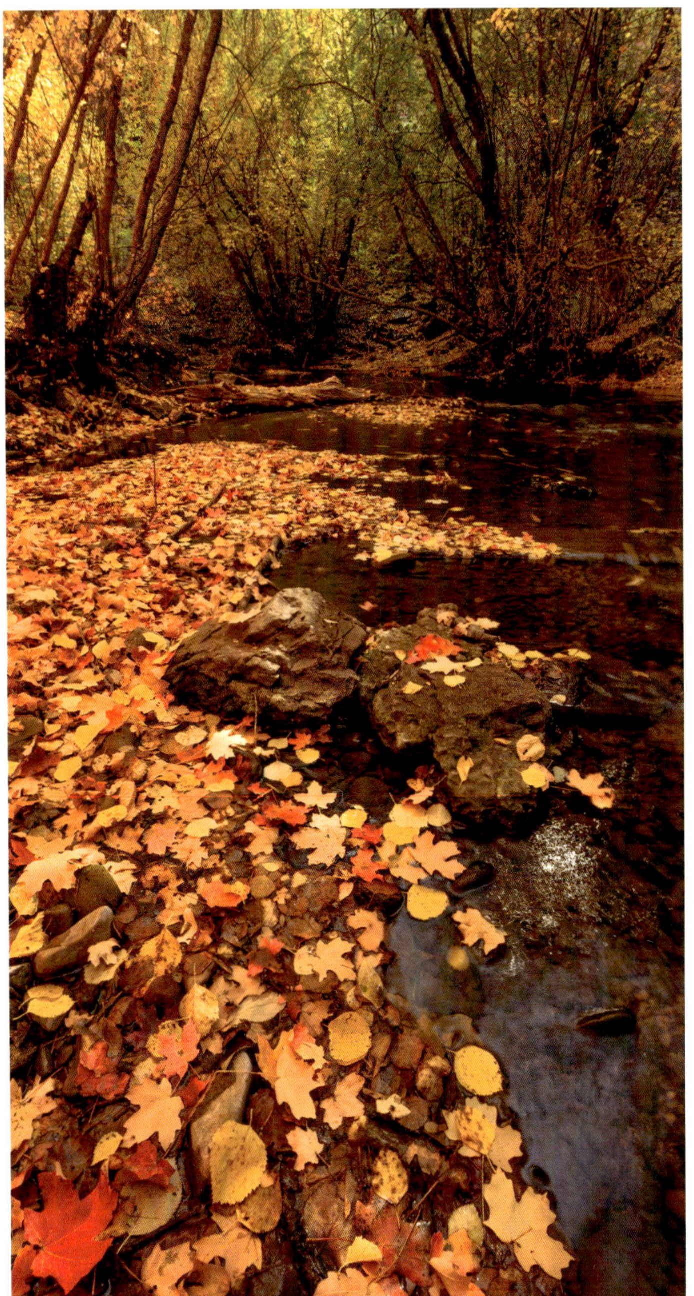

A DENSE CANOPY OF LEAVES BLANKETS THE BANKS OF THE RIGHT-HAND FORK OF THE LOGAN RIVER IN LOGAN CANYON.

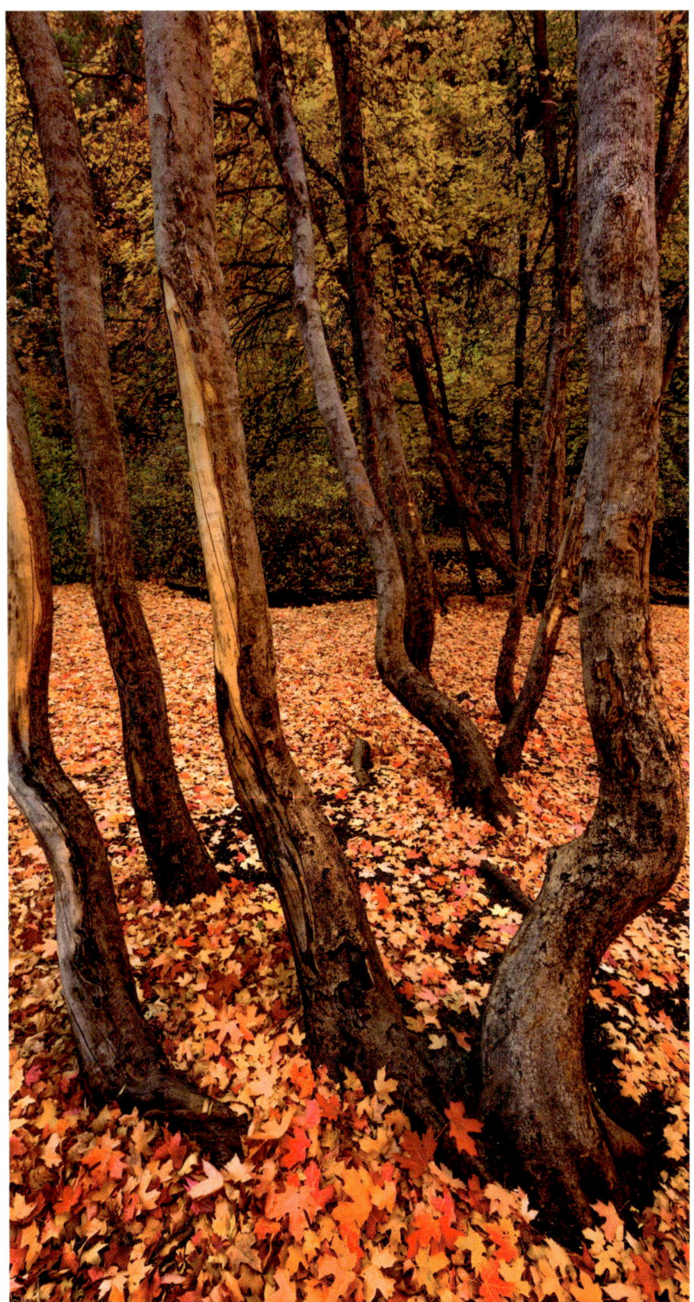

TWISTED MAPLE TRUNKS DEEP IN THE WASATCH NATIONAL FOREST.

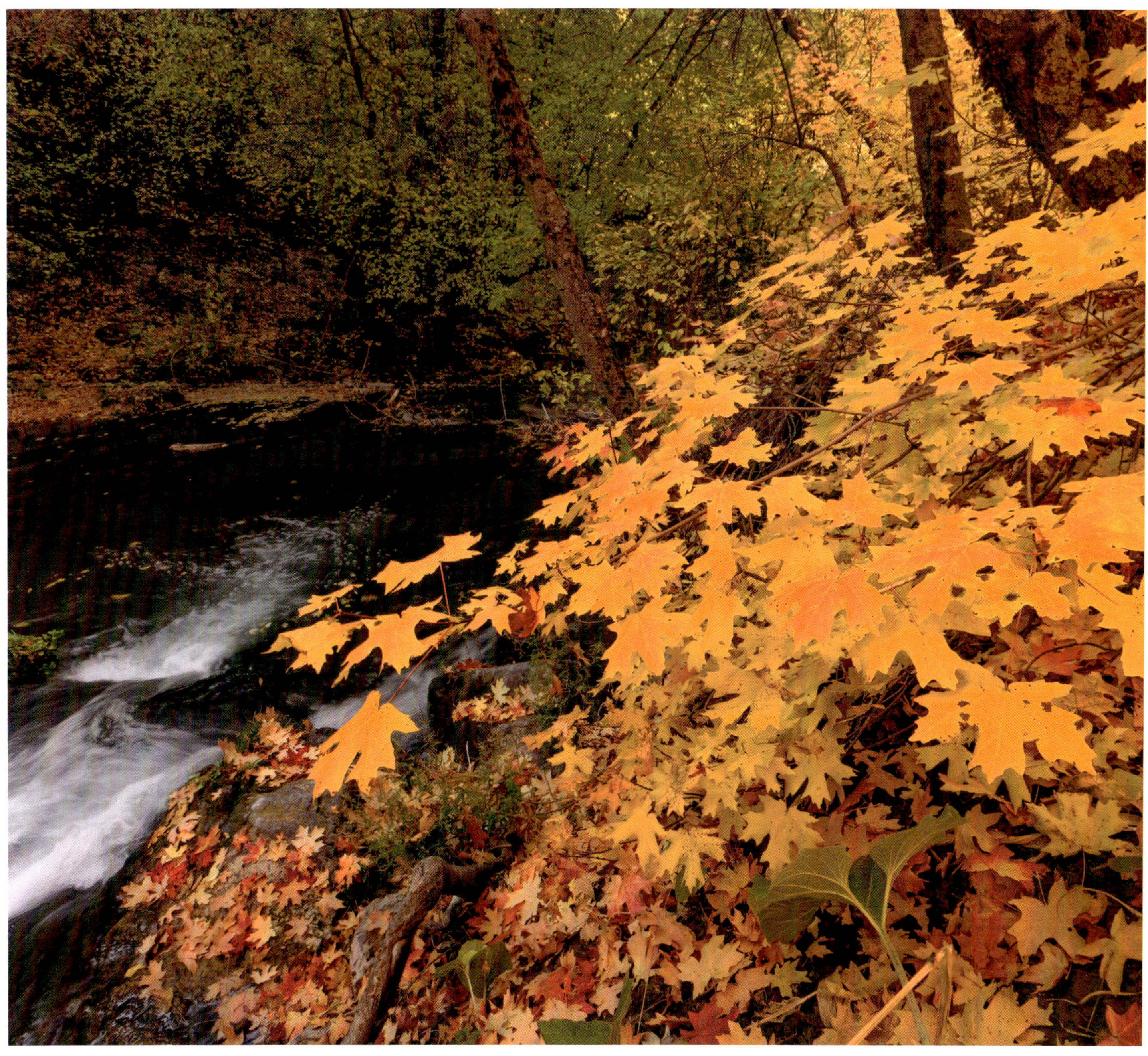

THE RIGHT HAND FORK OF THE LOGAN RIVER GLIDES PAST THE FALL FOLIAGE OF BIGTOOTH MAPLES IN LOGAN CANYON.

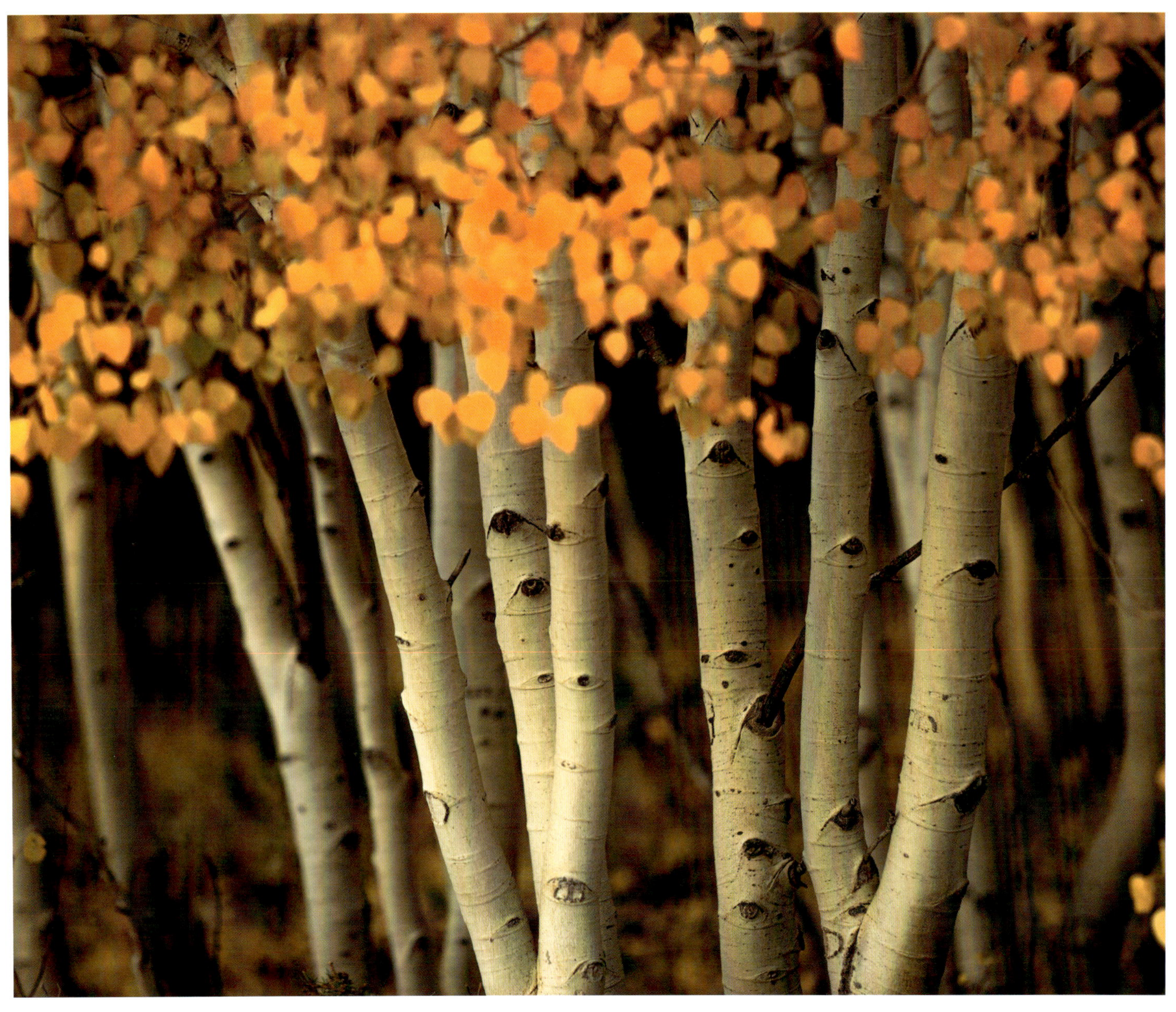

▲
QUAKING ASPENS GLOW IN THE TWILIGHT OF THE WASATCH MOUNTAINS.

▶
THE LATE MORNING SUN BURSTS THROUGH A CANOPY OF ELMS IN THE WASATCH NATIONAL FOREST.

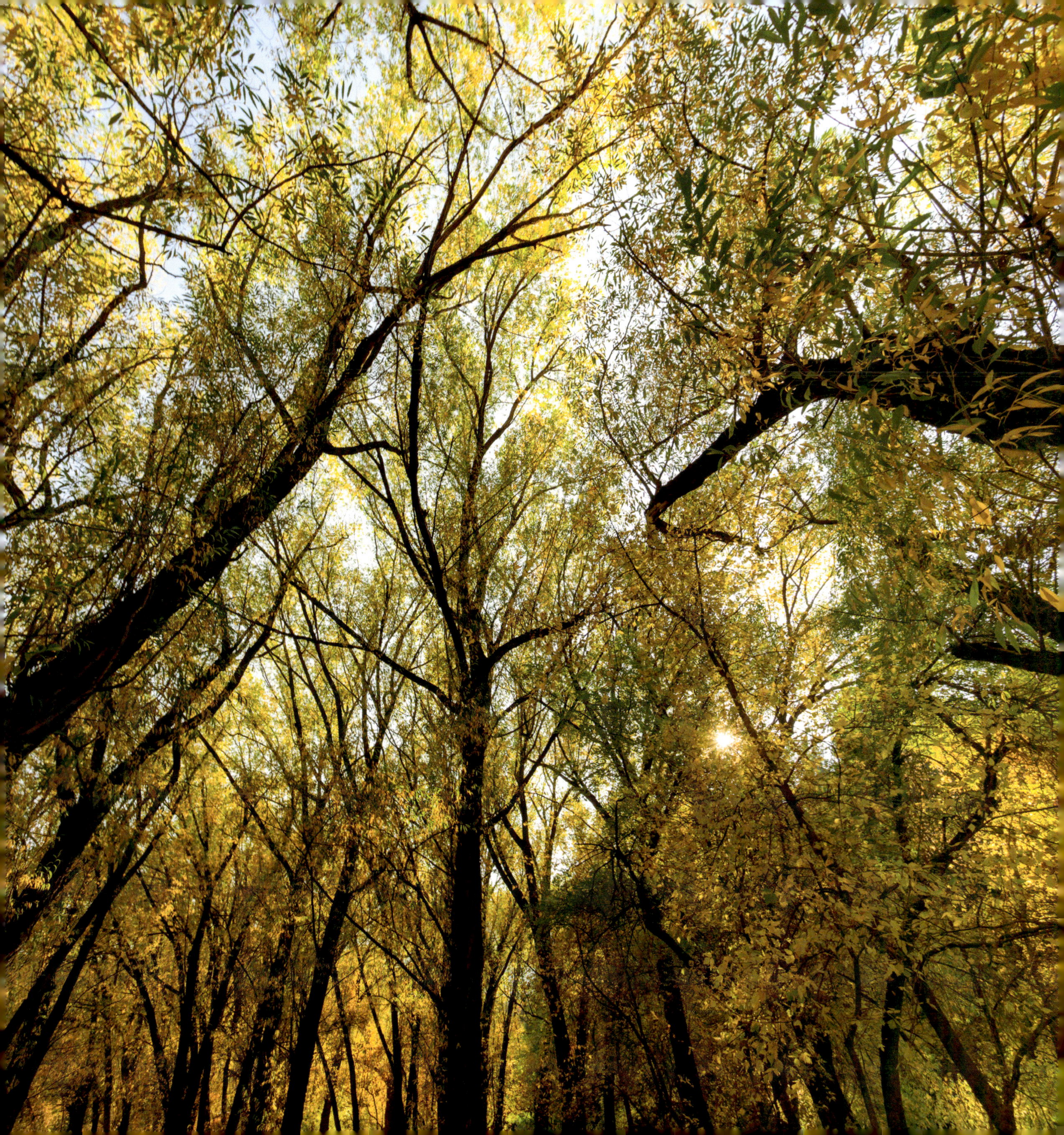

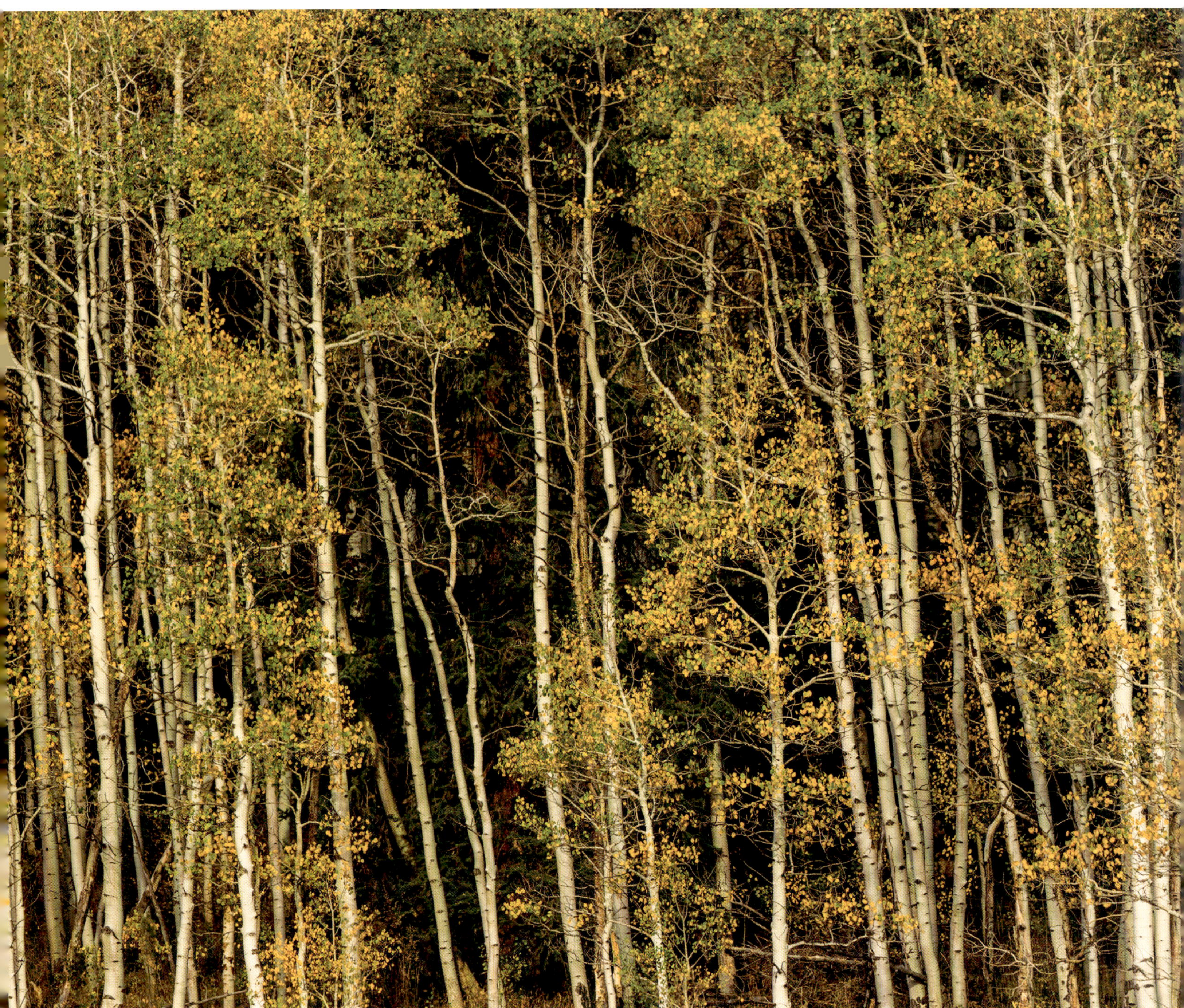

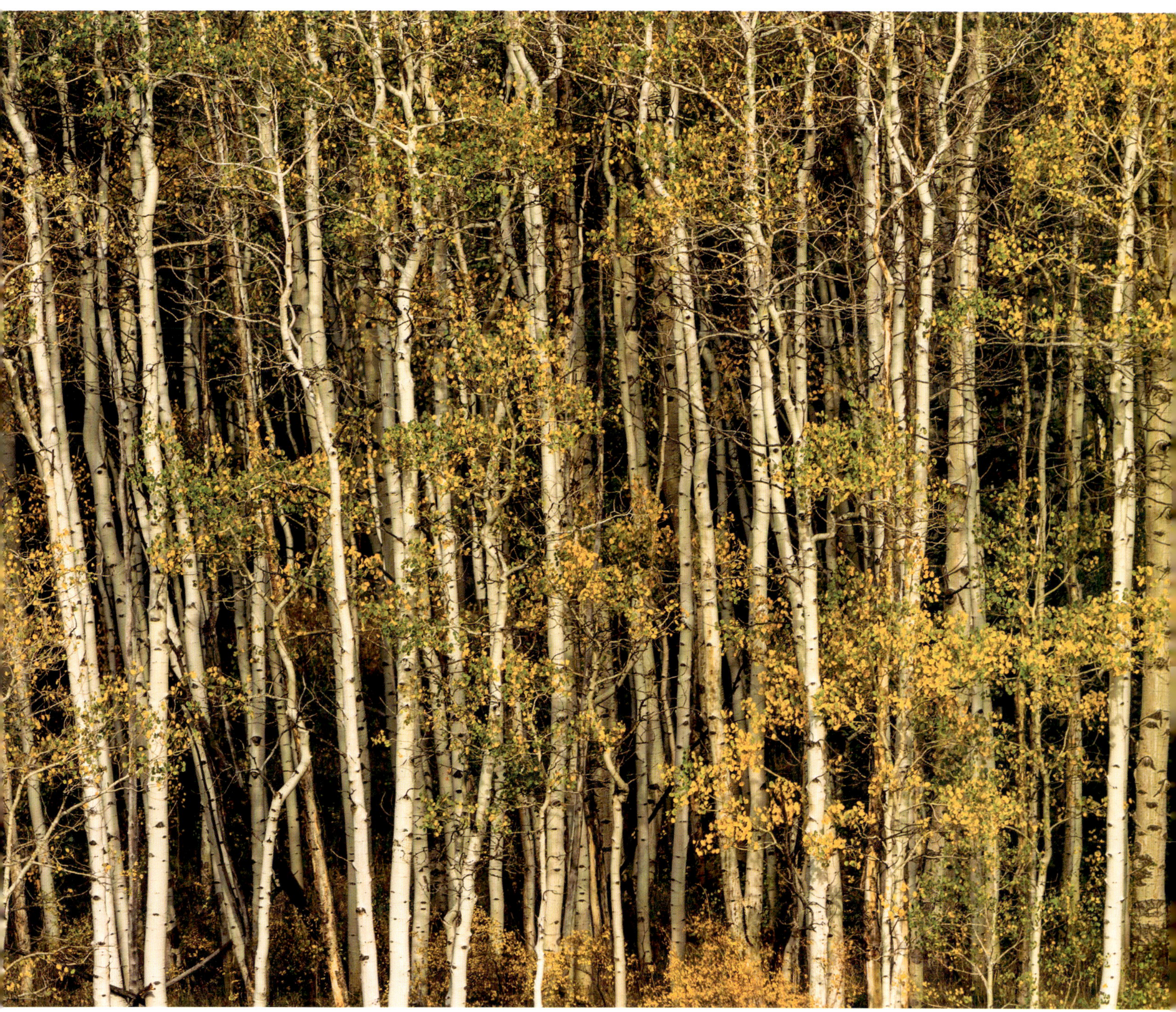

SLIM ASPEN TRUNKS AND FALL LEAVES CREATE GEOMETRIC PATTERNS IN THE WASATCH MOUNTAINS.

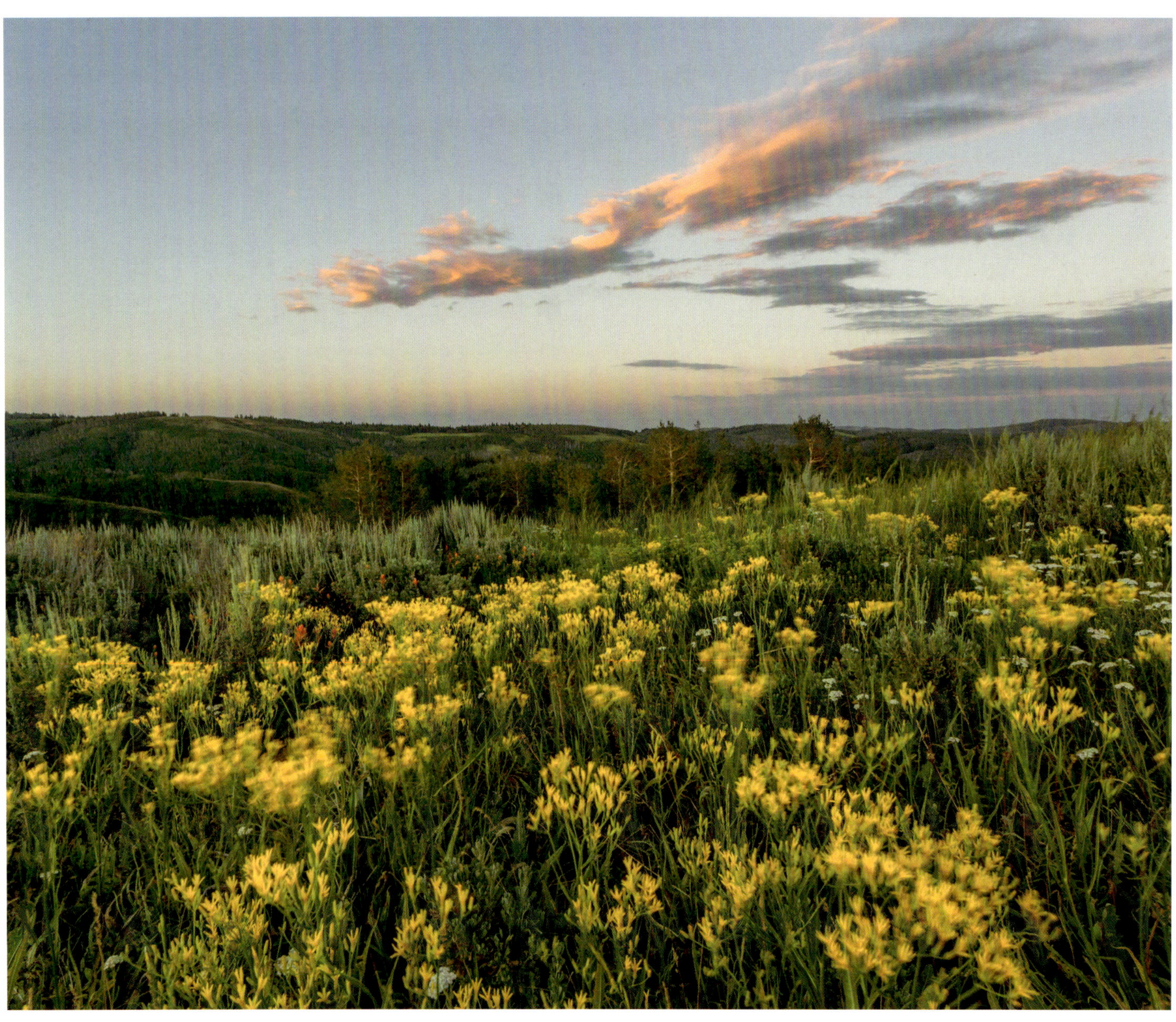

WILDFLOWERS EXPLODE ALONG A RIDGELINE ABOVE DRY CREEK IN THE WASATCH RANGE.

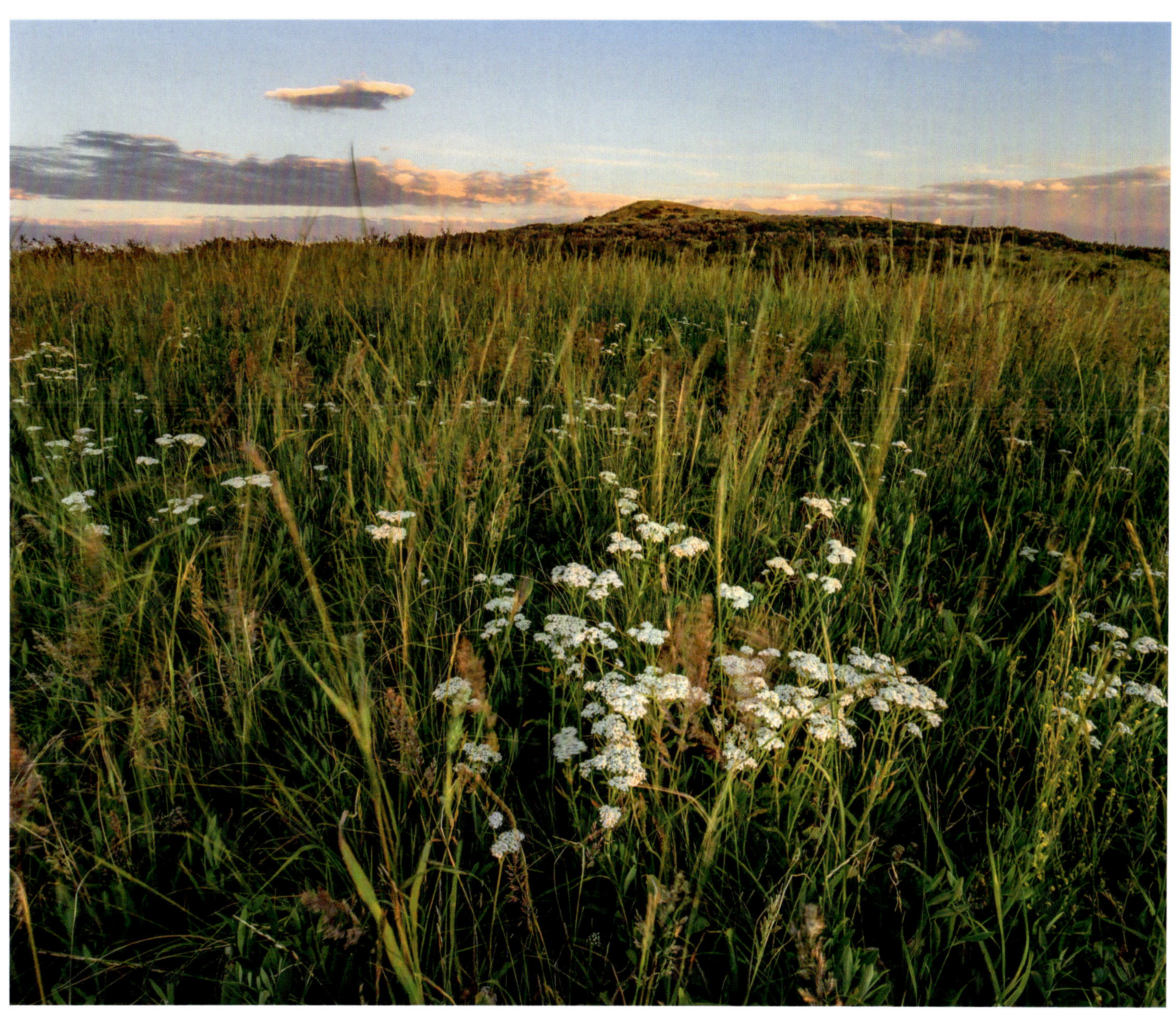

LONG GRASSES COVER A RIDGE NEAR MONTE CRISTO PEAK IN THE WASATCH RANGE.

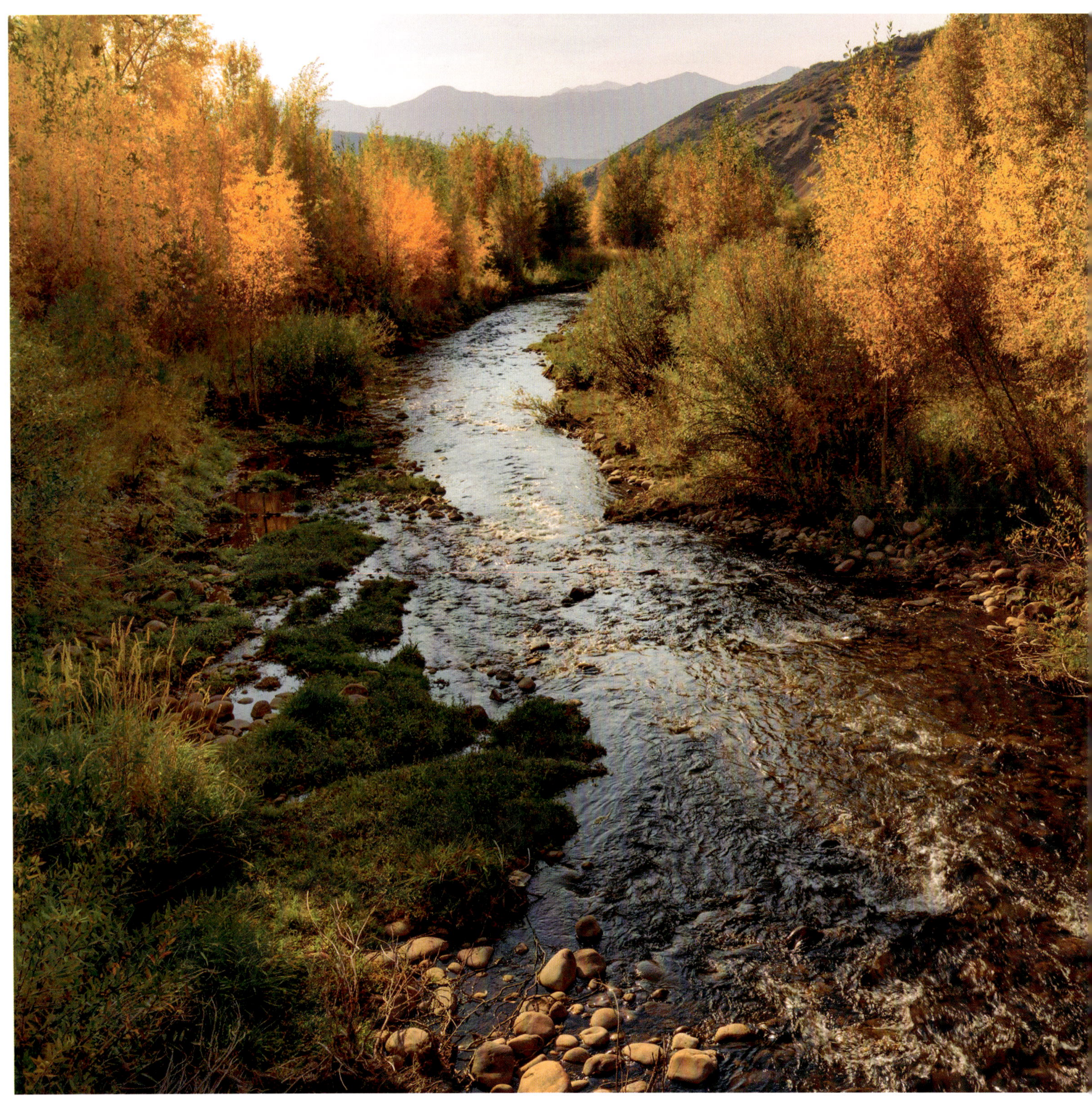

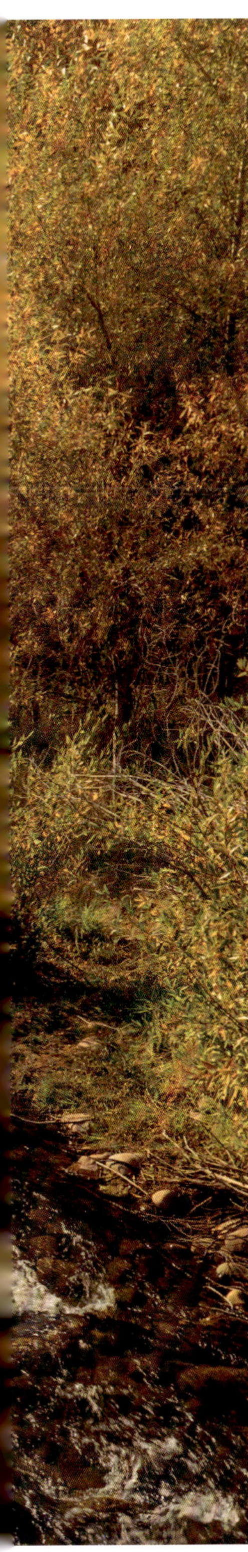

◀

GOLDEN TREES LINE THE BANKS OF THE PROVO RIVER IN JORDANELLE STATE PARK.

▶

WATER TRICKLES OVER SLATE BENCHES AT LOW WATER ALONG THE PROVO RIVER.

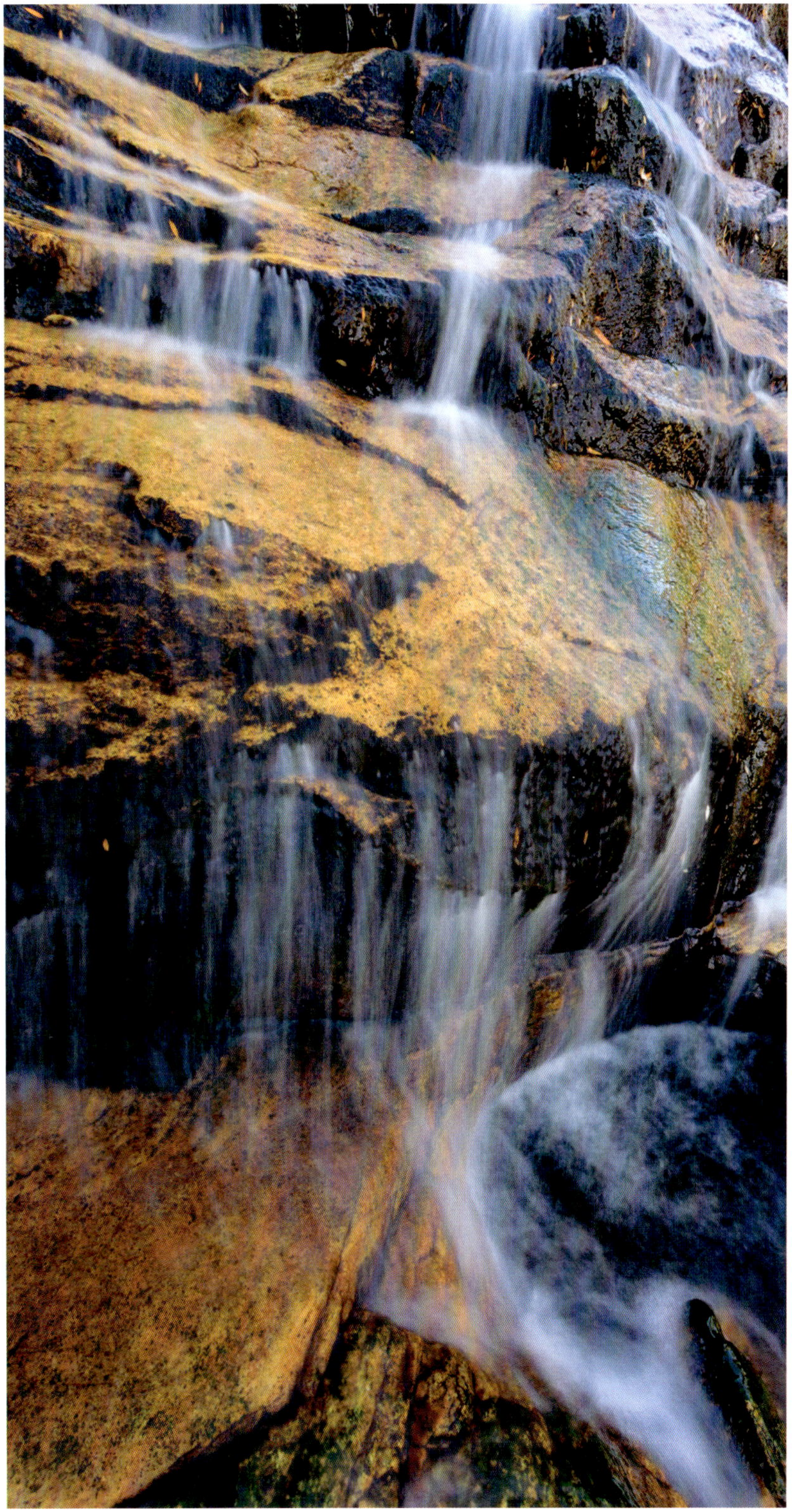

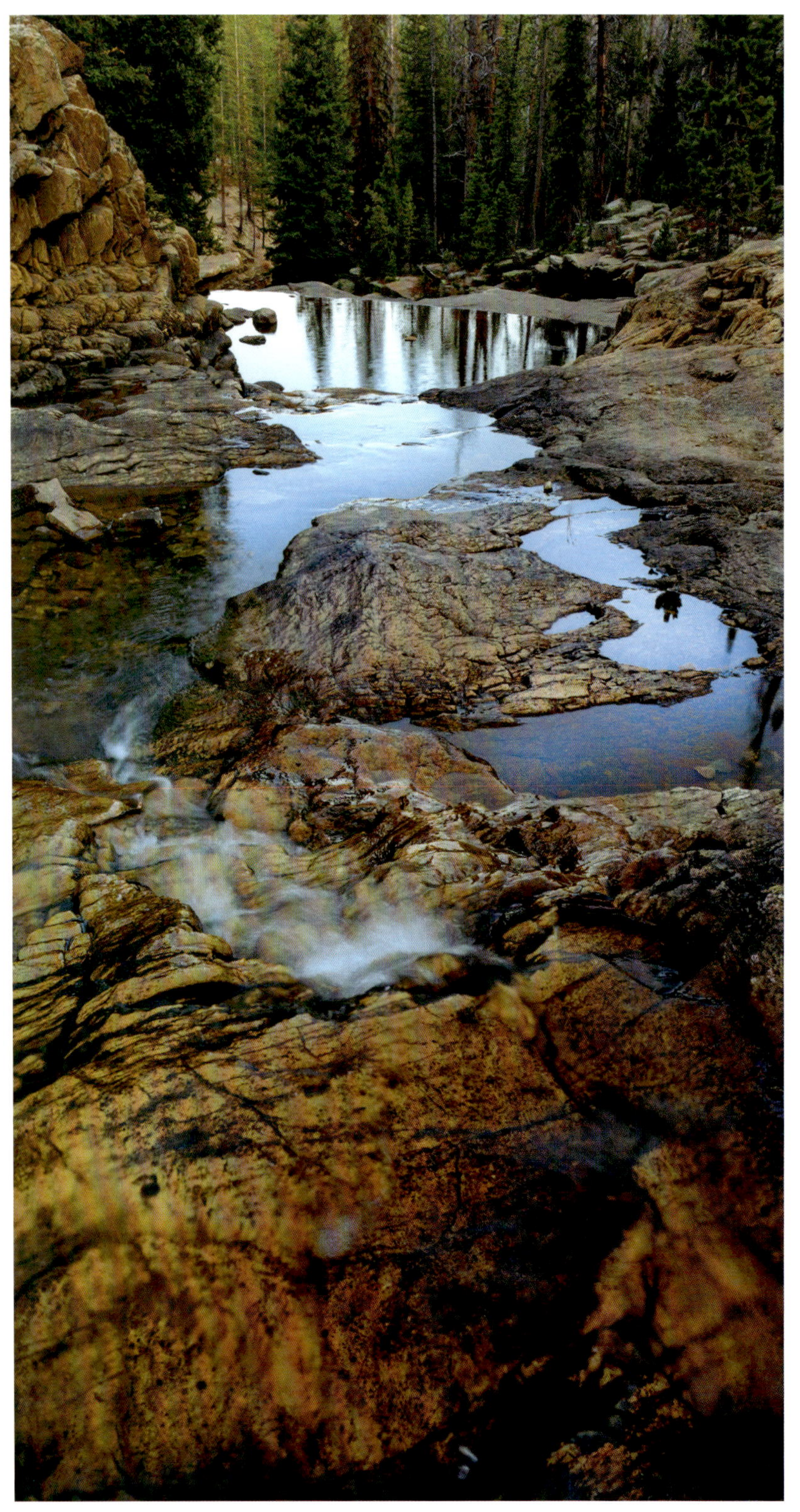

◀

LOW WATER AT PROVO RIVER FALLS IN THE UINTA MOUNTAINS.

▶

CALM POOLS FORM ON THE PROVO RIVER IN SLATE GORGE, HIGH IN THE UINTA RANGE.

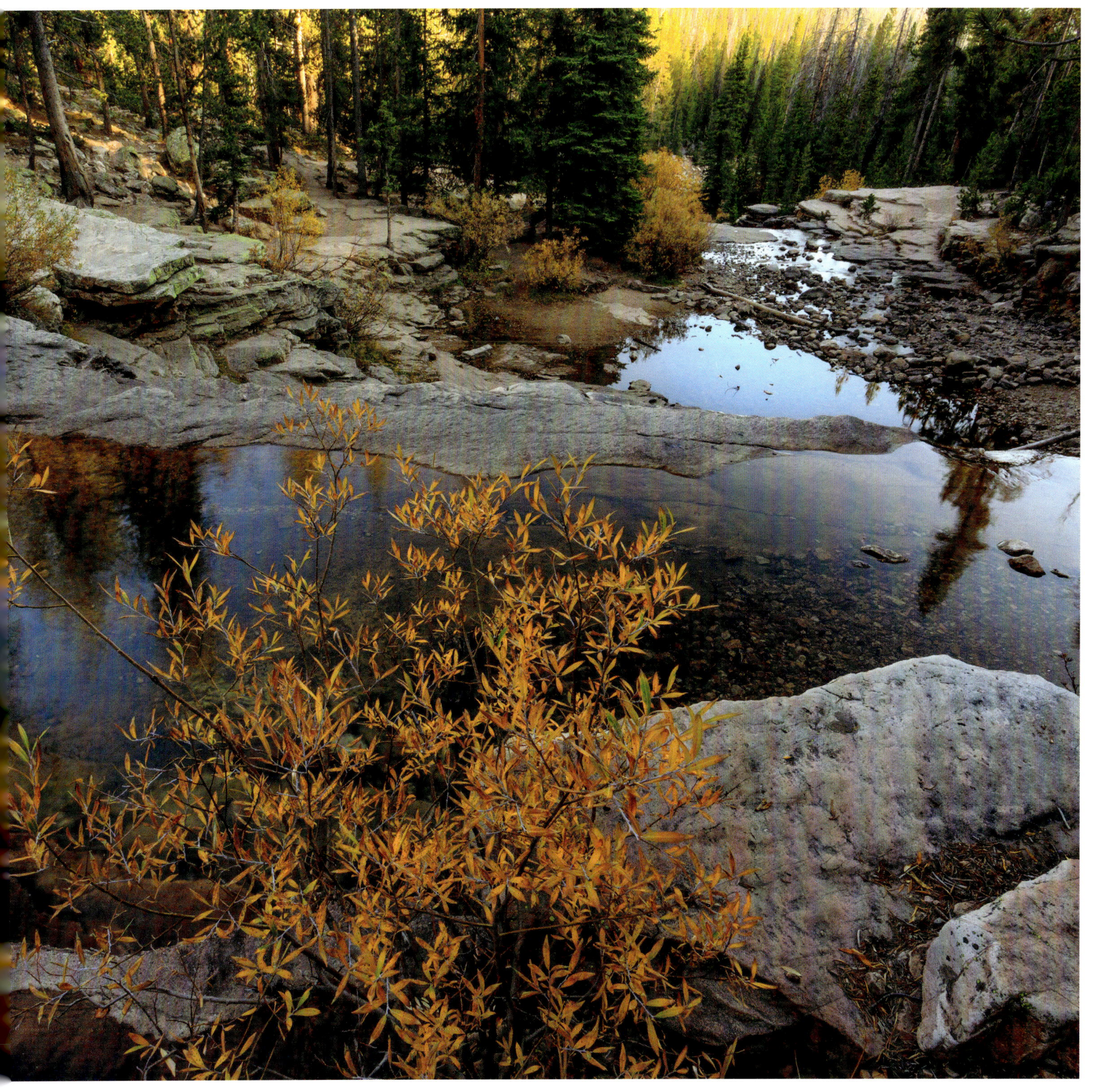

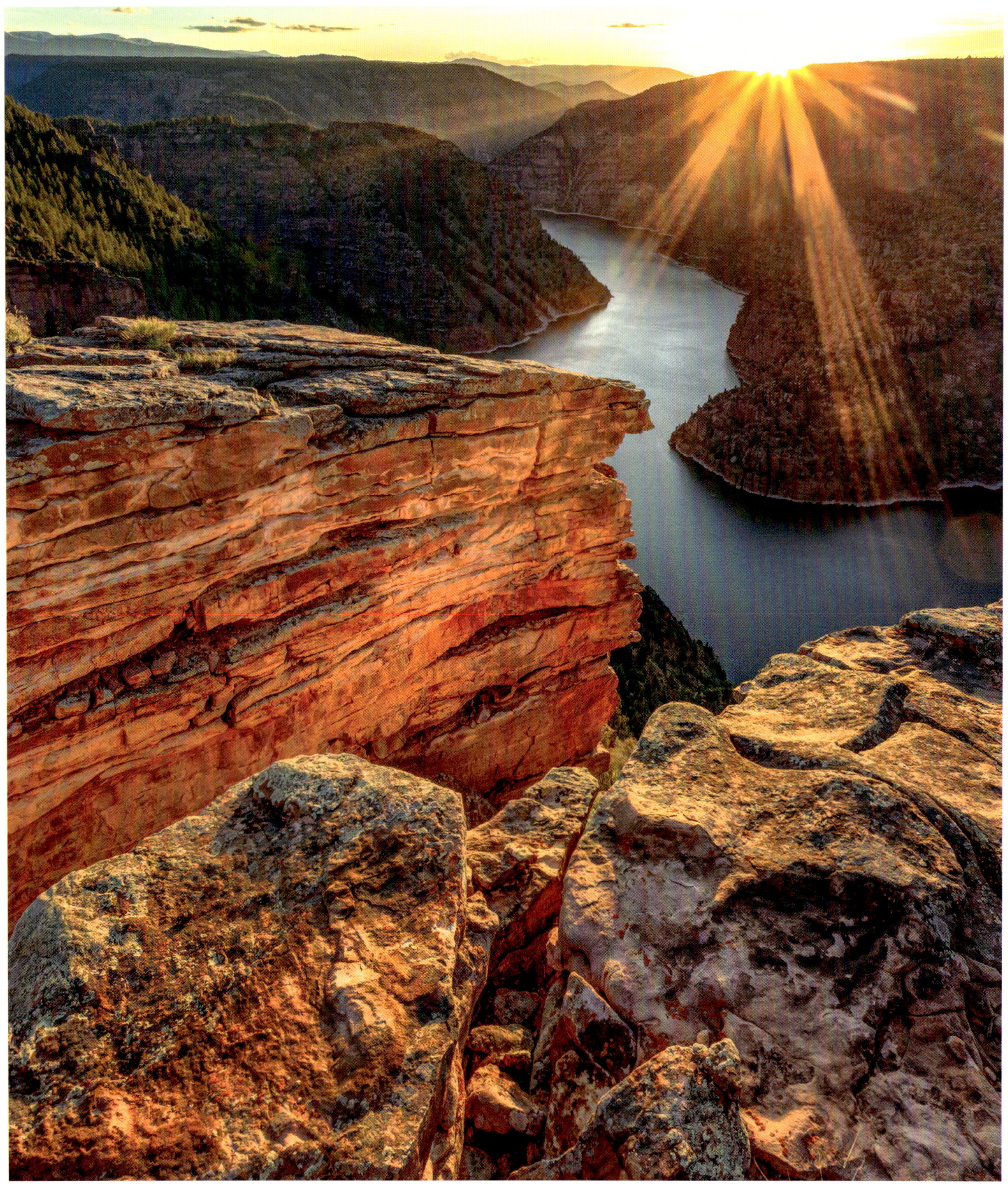

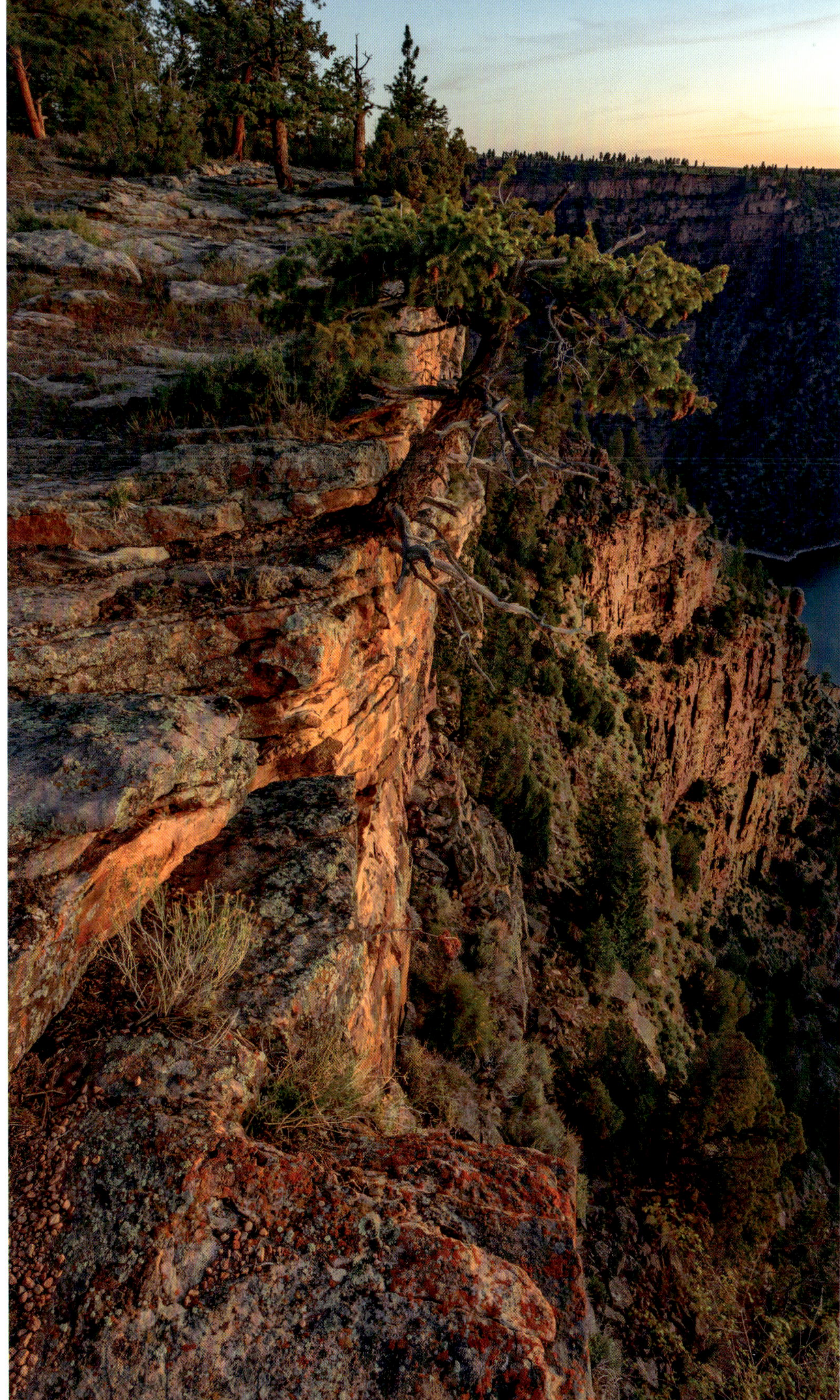

◀

THE GREEN RIVER SLICES THROUGH RED CANYON IN FLAMING GORGE NATIONAL RECREATION AREA.

▶

PINE TREES CLING TO THE STEEP WALLS OF RED CANYON IN FLAMING GORGE NATIONAL RECREATION AREA.

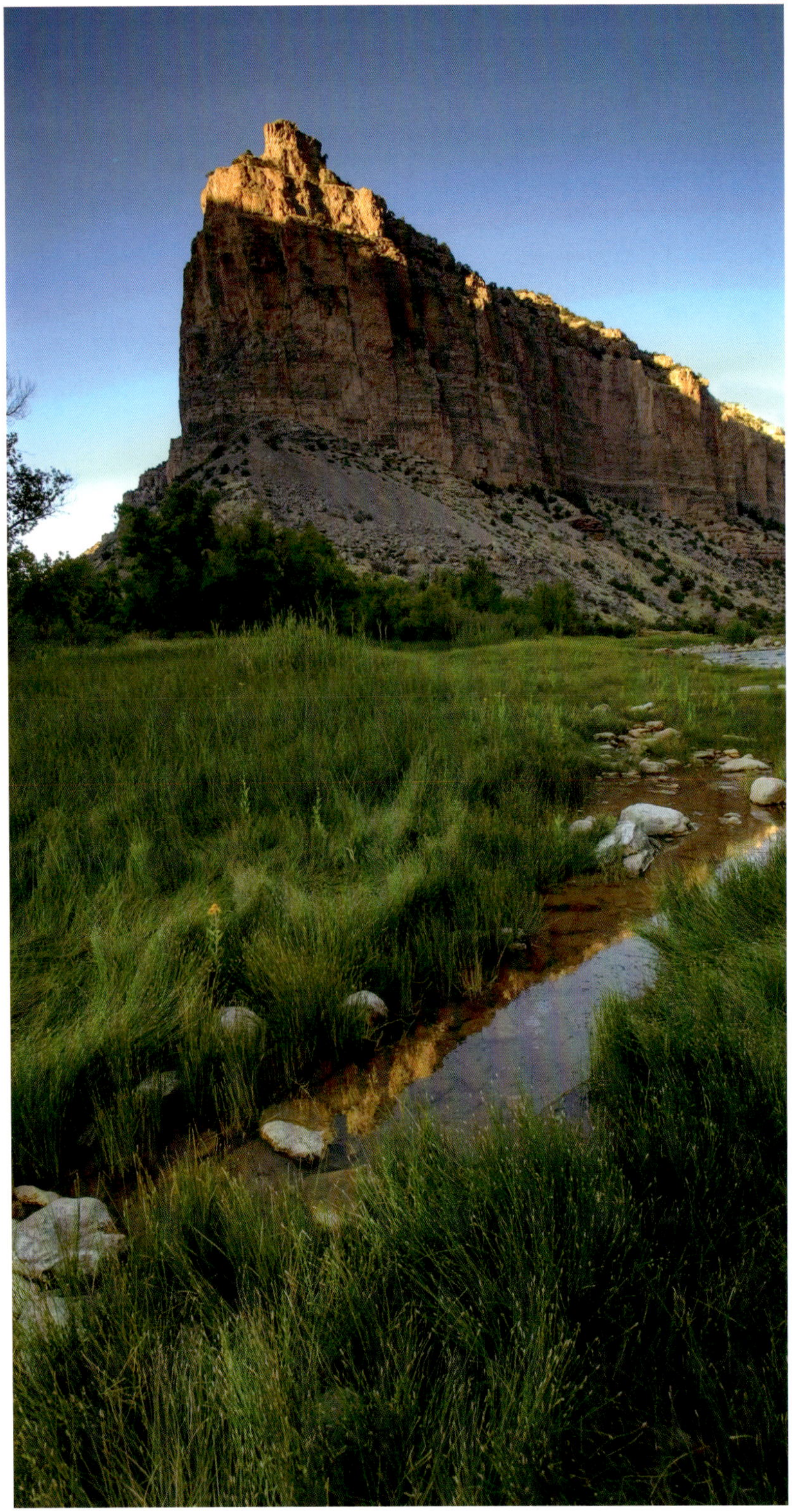

◀

A BREAK IN A CLIFF WALL BORDERING THE GREEN RIVER AT JONES HOLE.

▶

CHRISTMAS MEADOWS ON THE STILLWATER FORK OF THE BEAR RIVER IN UINTA NATIONAL FOREST.

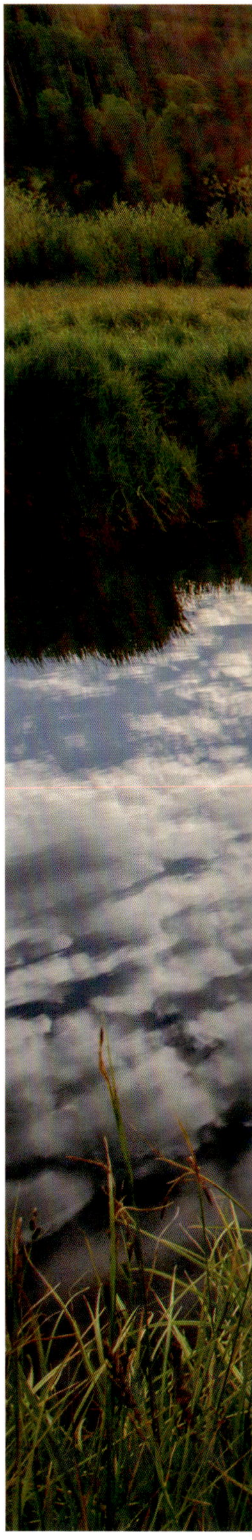

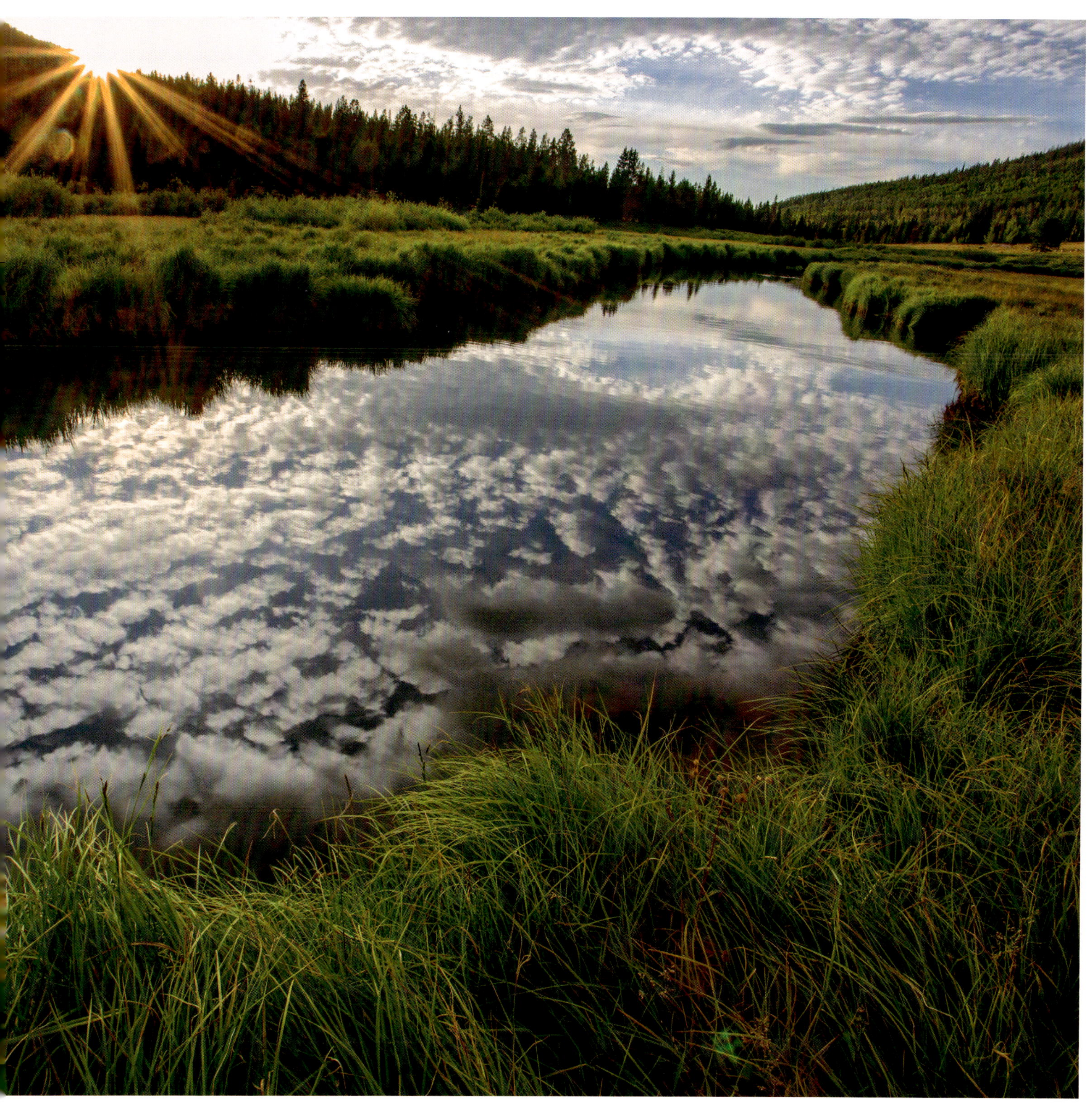

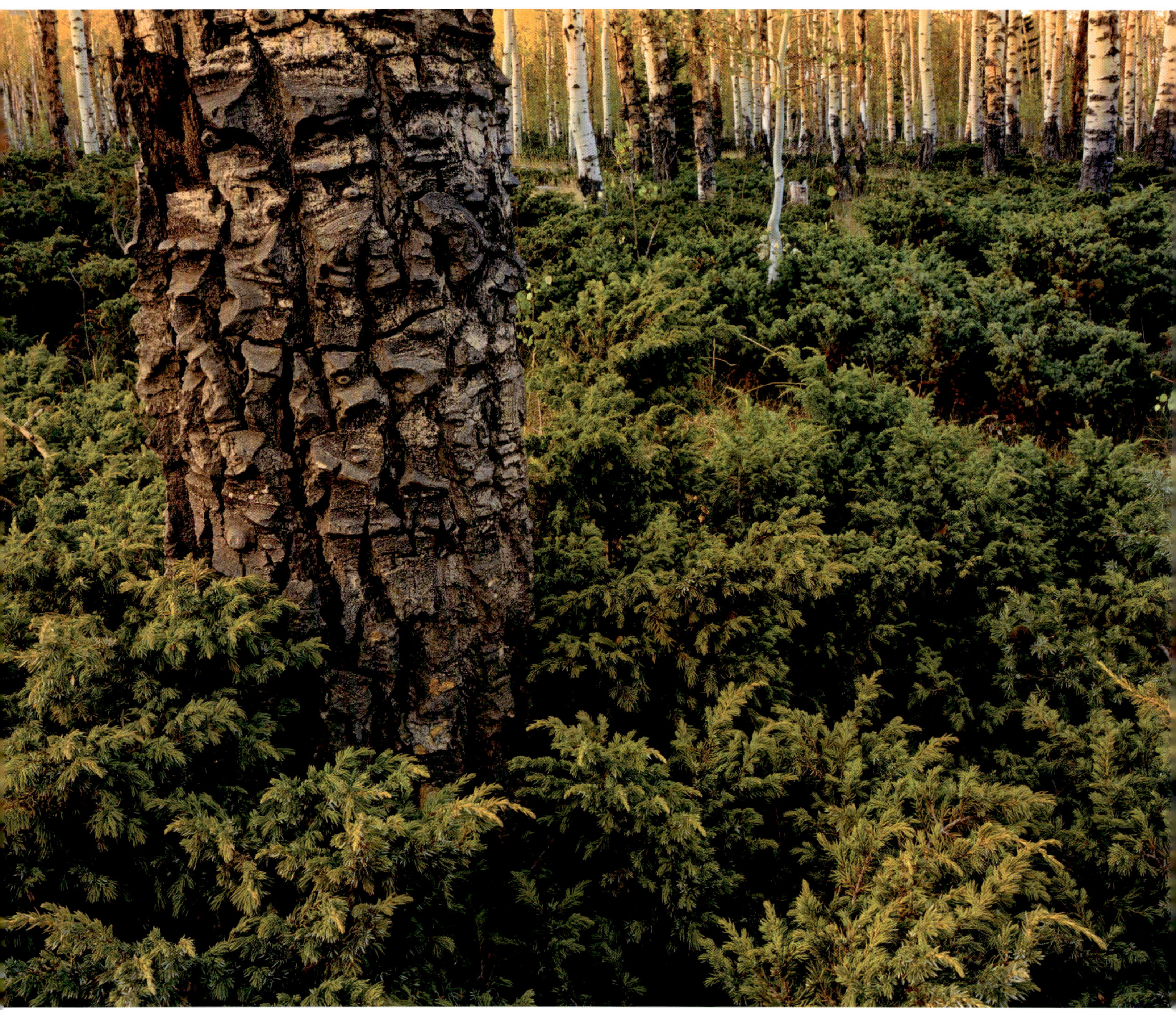

A GNARLED ASPEN TRUNK ALONG THE RED CLOUD LOOP ROAD IN THE ASHLEY NATIONAL FOREST.

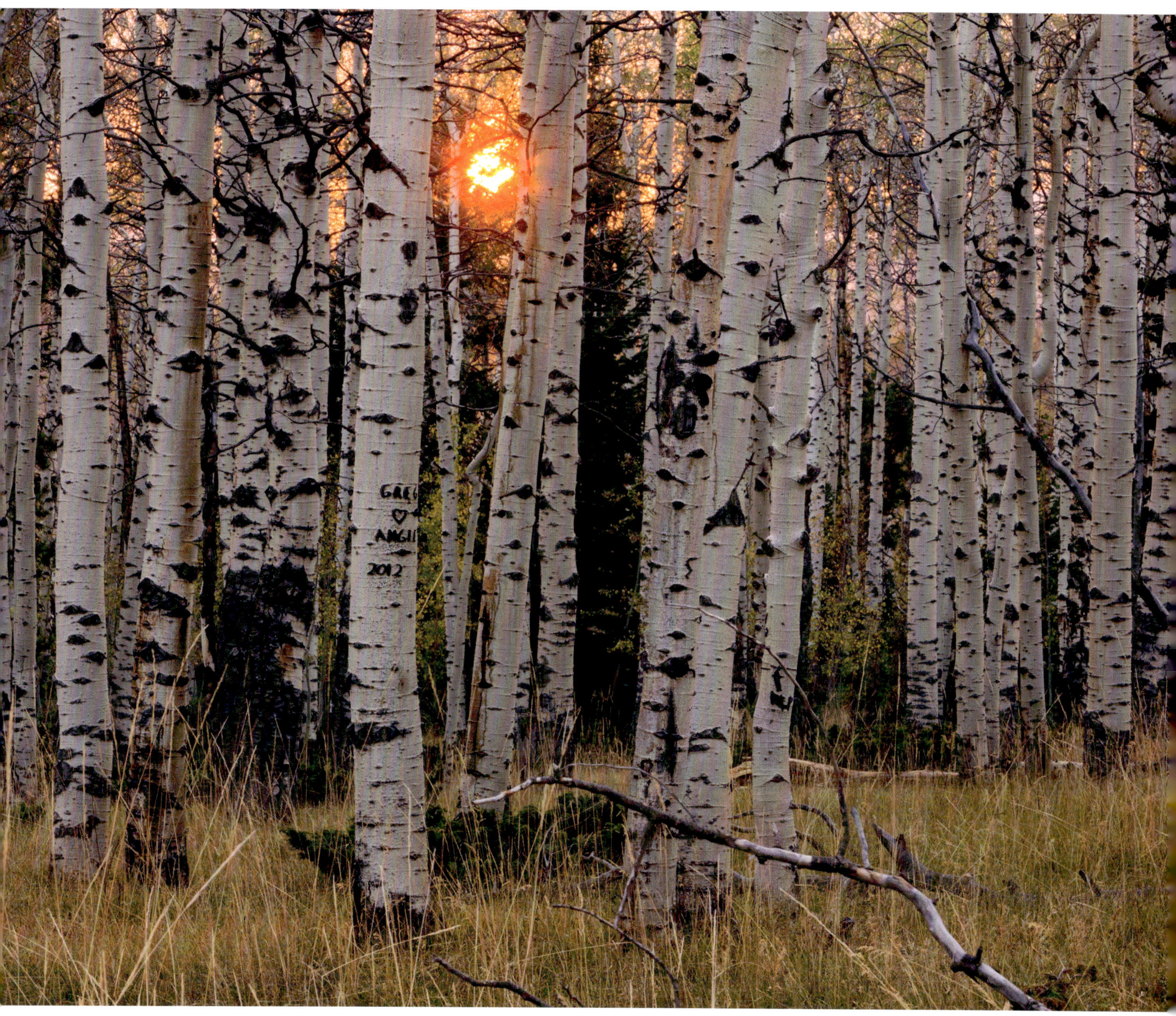

SKIES FILLED WITH WILDFIRE SMOKE CREATE A PINK HAZE IN AN ASPEN GROVE IN THE UINTA RANGE.

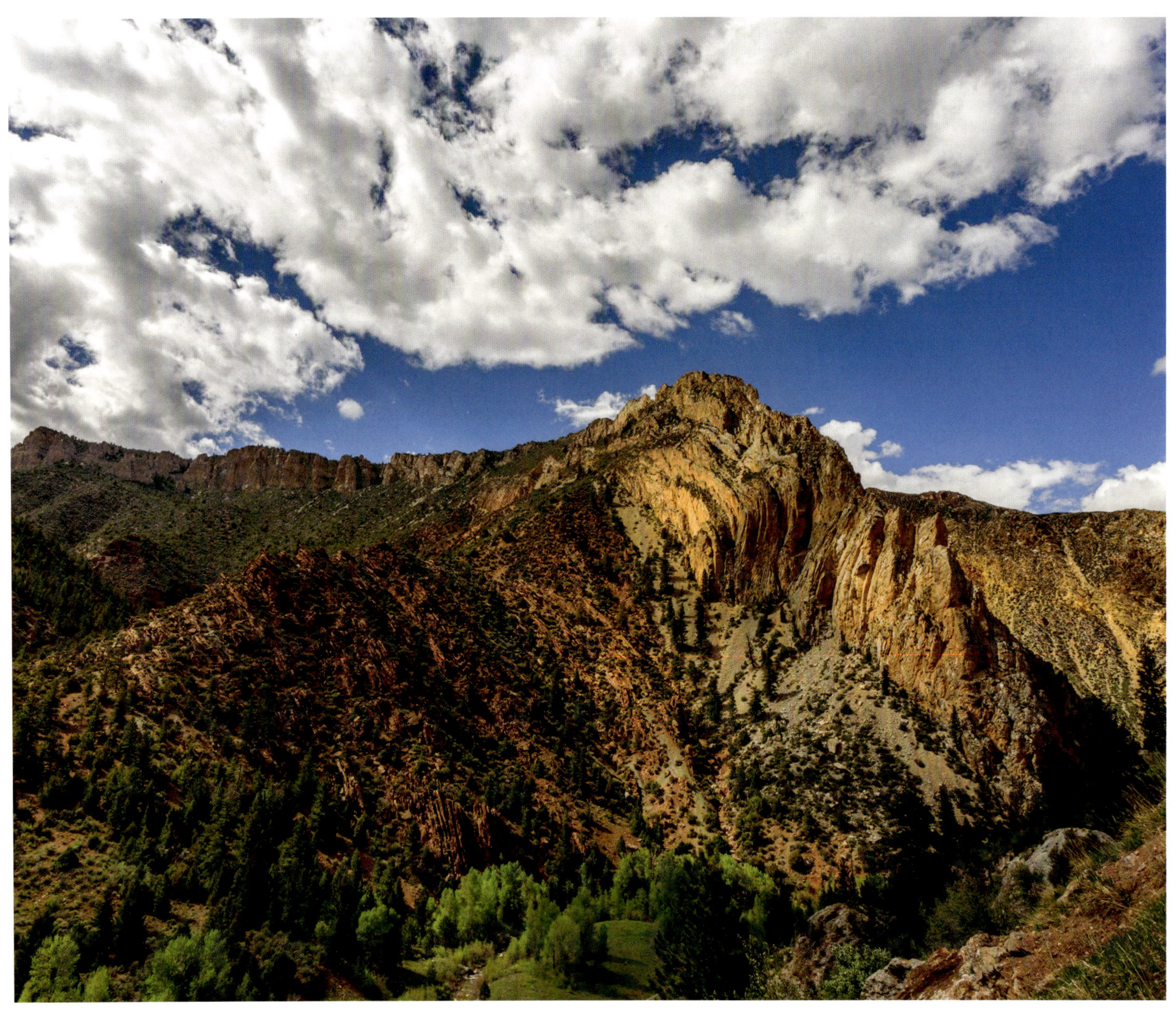

THE UINTA FAULT, SEEN FROM SHEEP CREEK, RUNS FOR MORE THAN 100 MILES ALONG THE NORTH SLOPE OF THE UINTA MOUNTAINS.

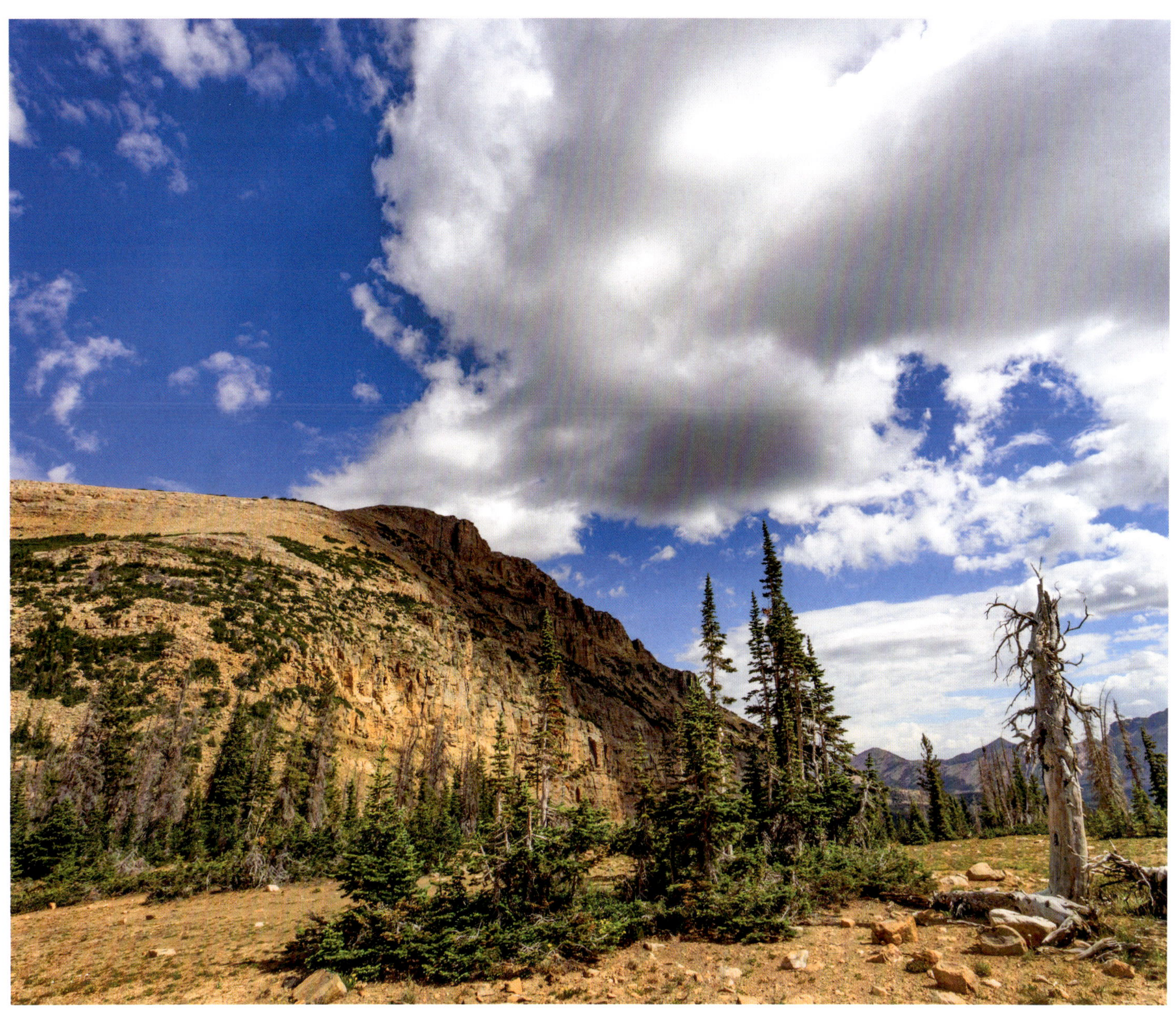

BALD MOUNTAIN AS SEEN FROM THE TRAILHEAD AT 10,693 FEET. THE SUMMIT IS AT 11,949 FEET.

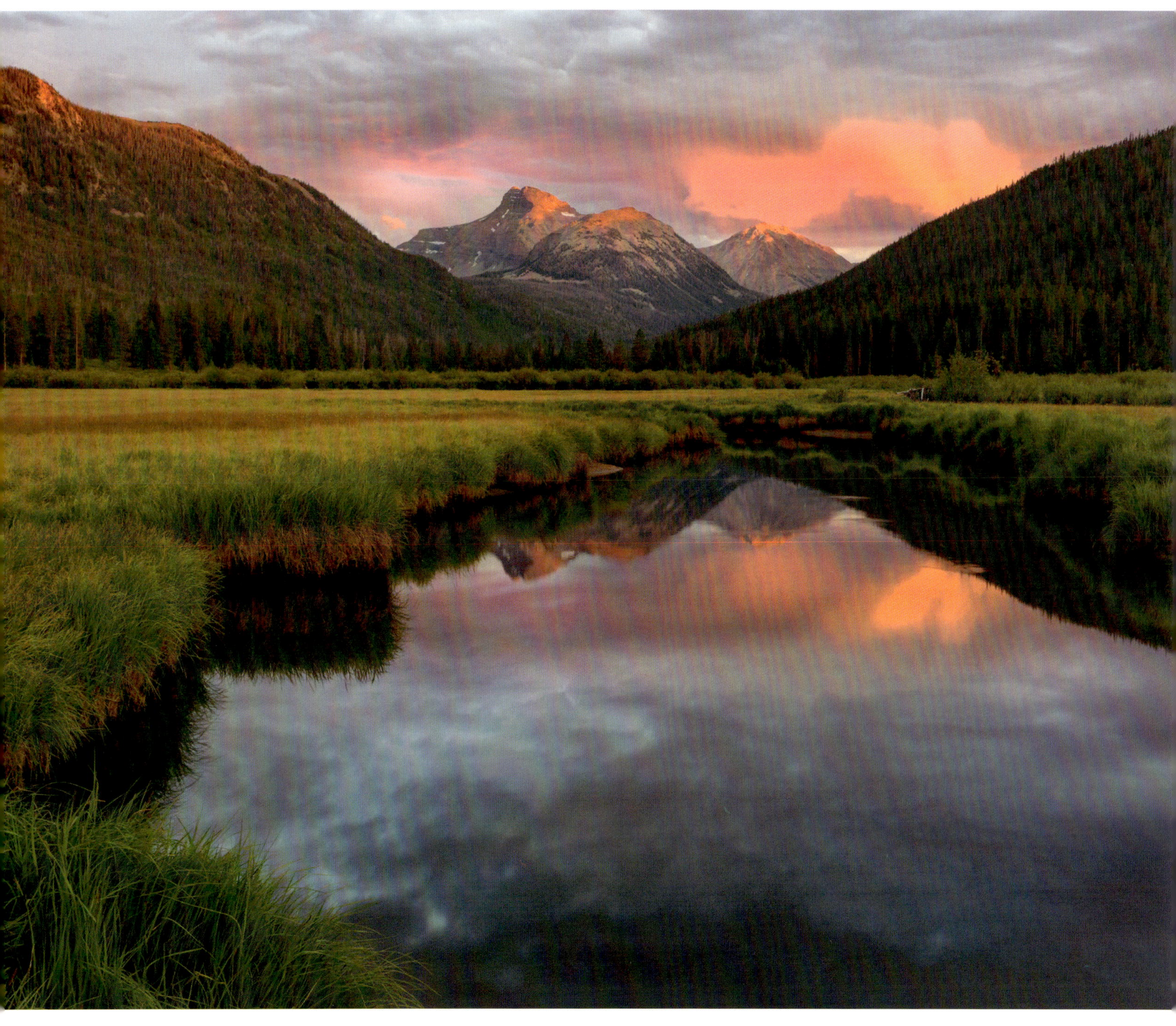

OSTLER PEAK AND SPREAD EAGLE PEAK ARE REFLECTED IN THE STILLWATER FORK OF THE BEAR RIVER.

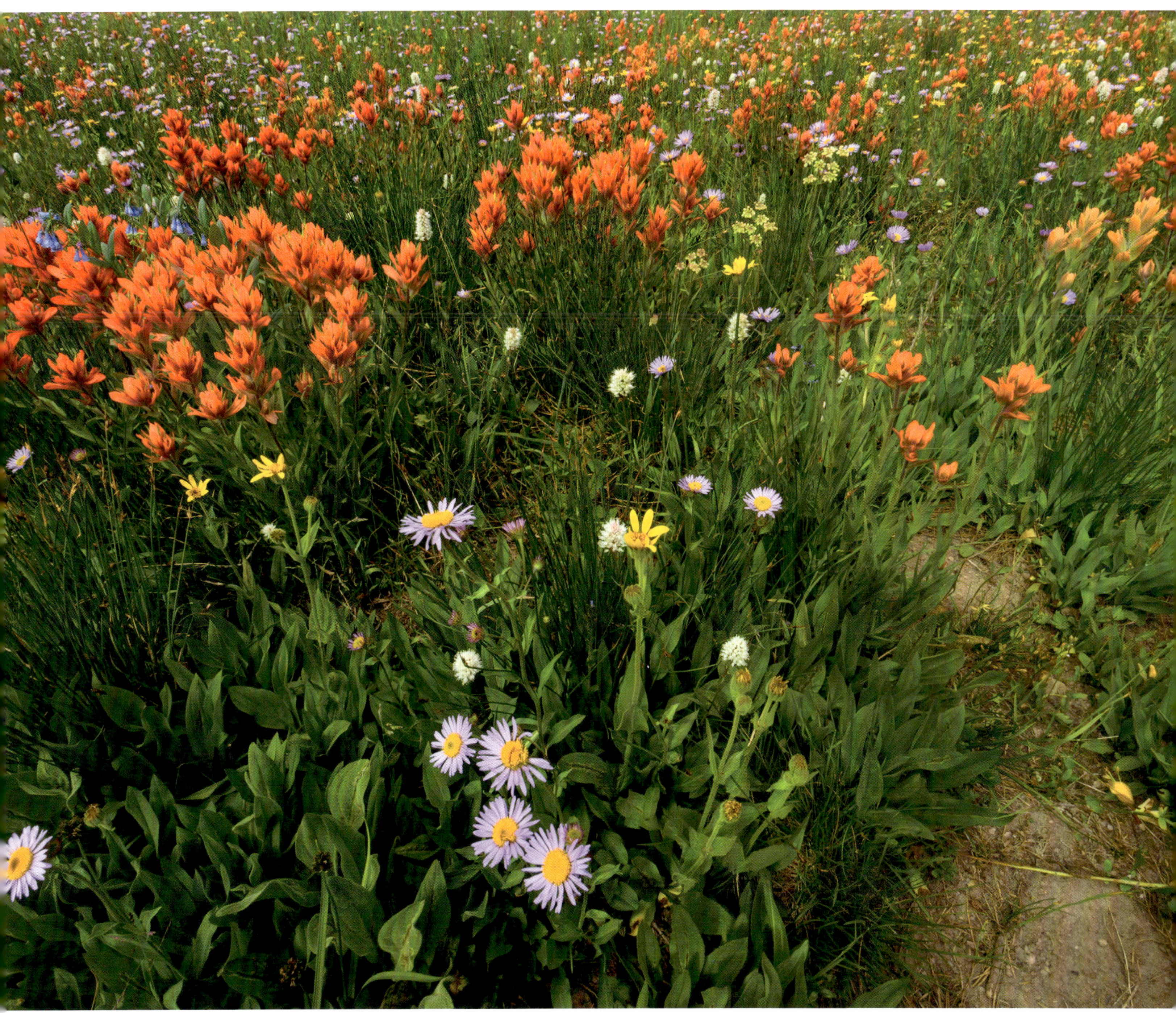

WILDFLOWERS BLOOM IN MIDSUMMER TEMPERATURES IN THE MEADOWS OF THE HIGH UINTAS.

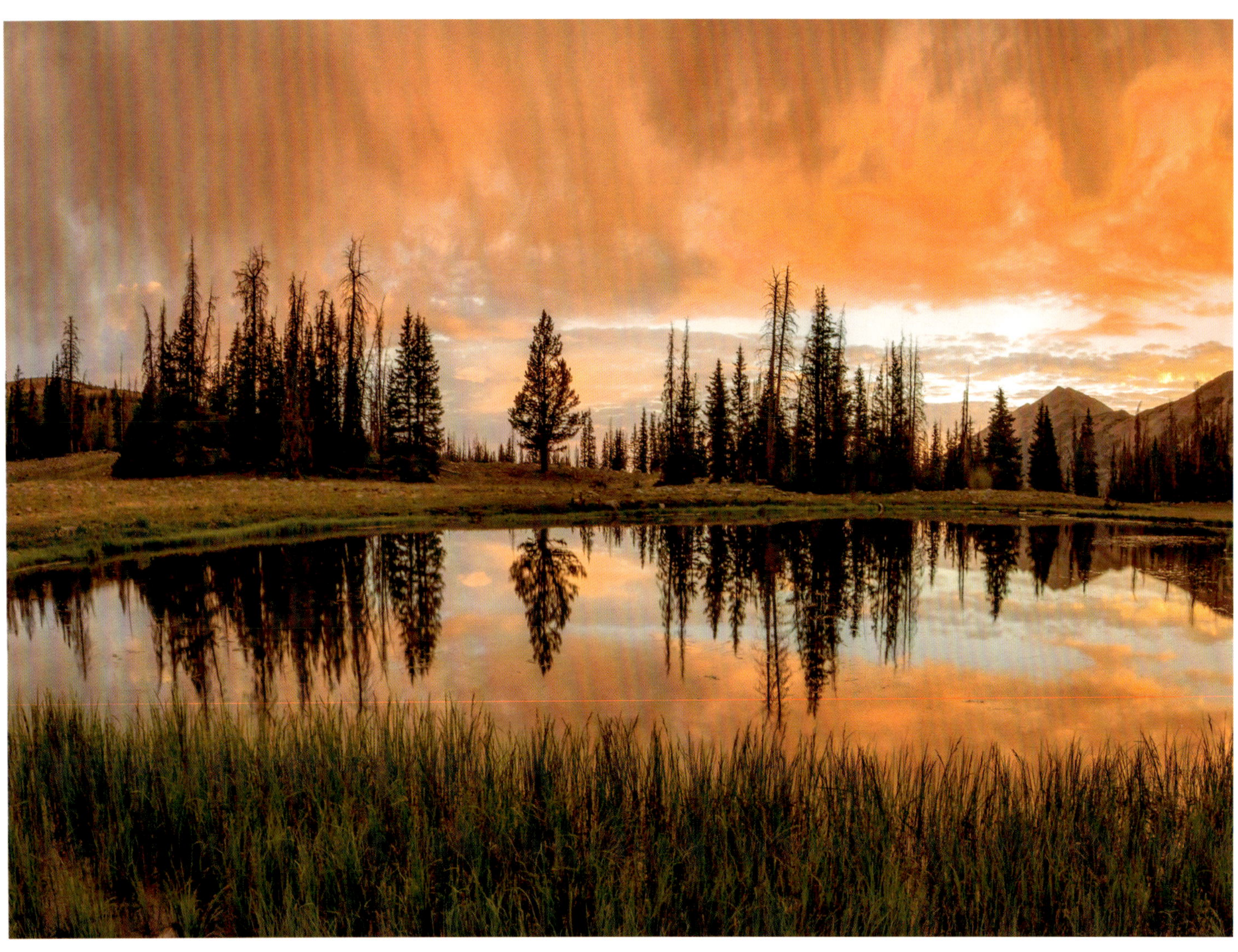

A RAINSTORM LOOMS OVER A SMALL LAKE AT HAYDEN PASS IN THE UINTA RANGE.

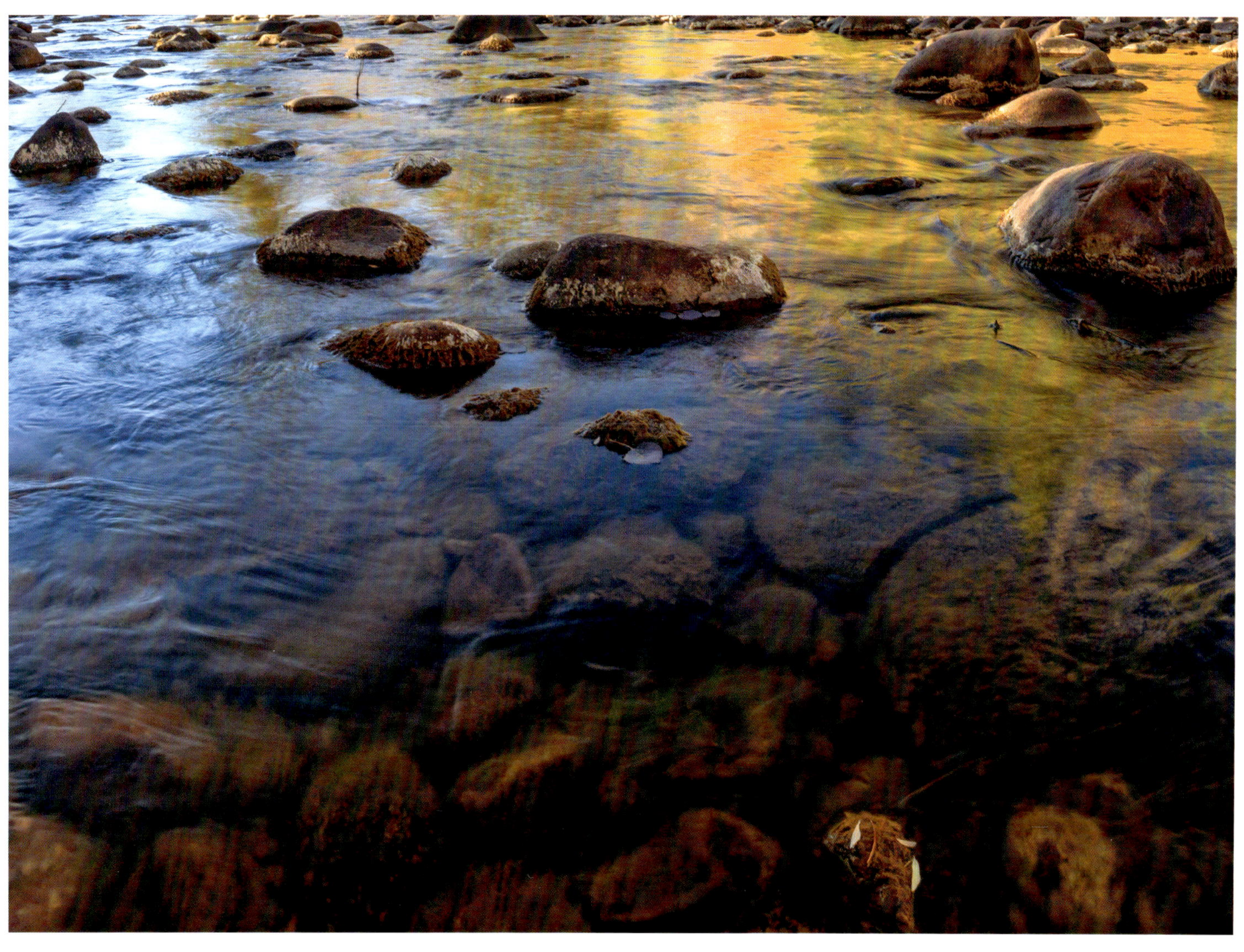

FALL LEAVES AND A BLUEBIRD SKY REFLECT IN THE BEAR RIVER IN THE UINTA RANGE.

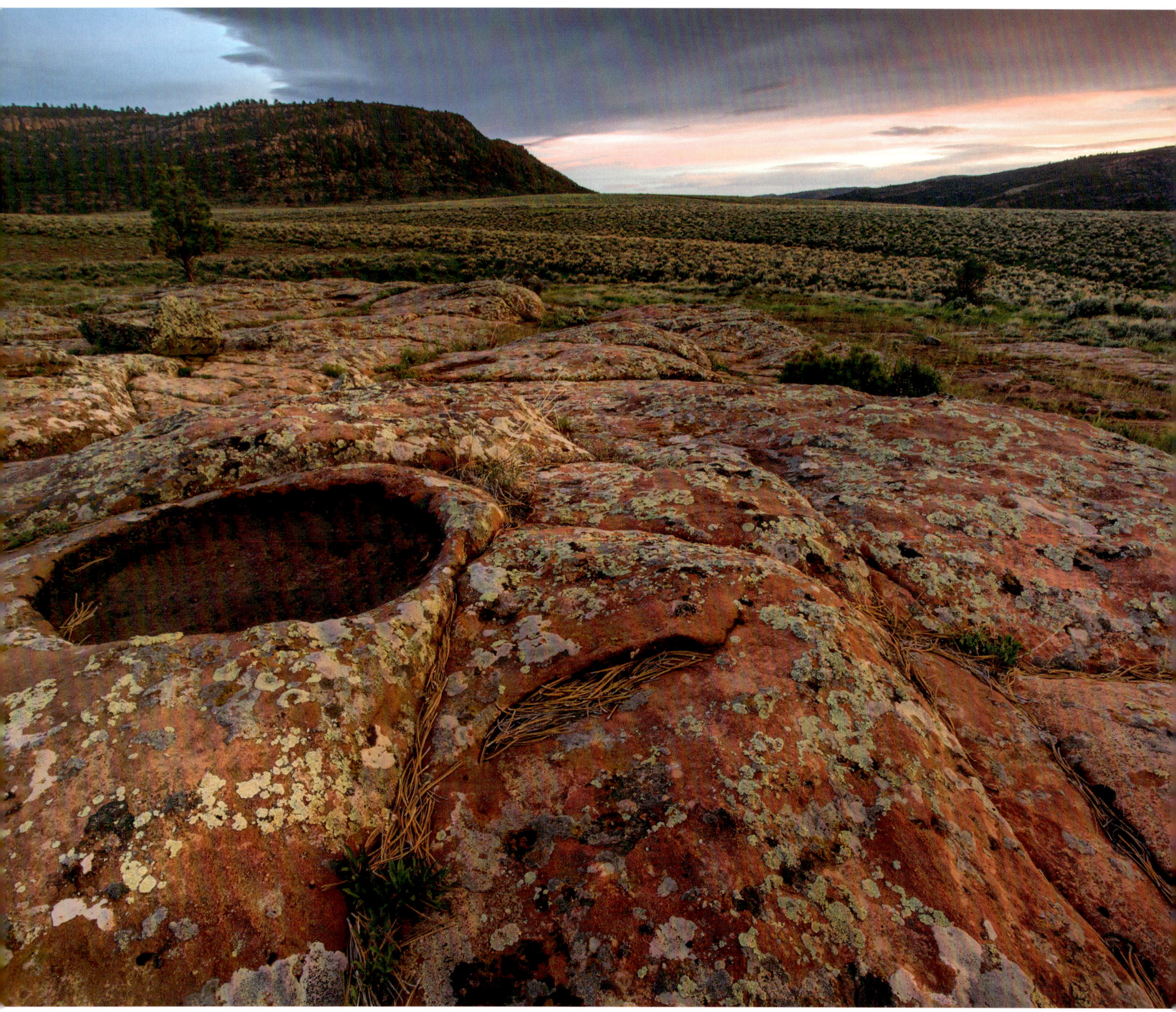

GREEN SPRING GRASSES BLANKET THE DIAMOND MOUNTAIN PLATEAU.

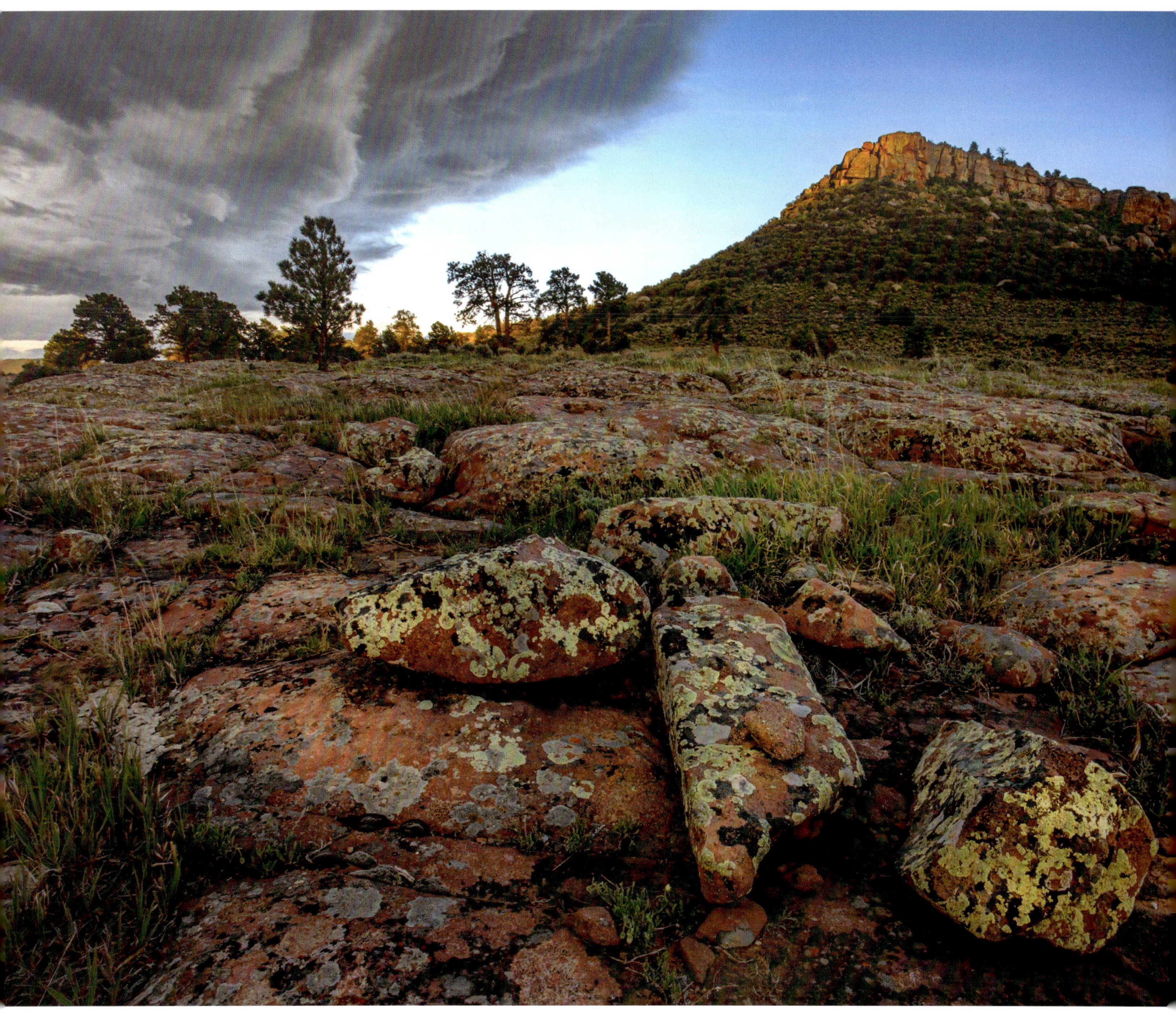

A SUMMER STORM LOOMS OVER RED ROCK CLIFFS NEAR CROUSE RESERVOIR IN THE POT CREEK DRAINAGE.

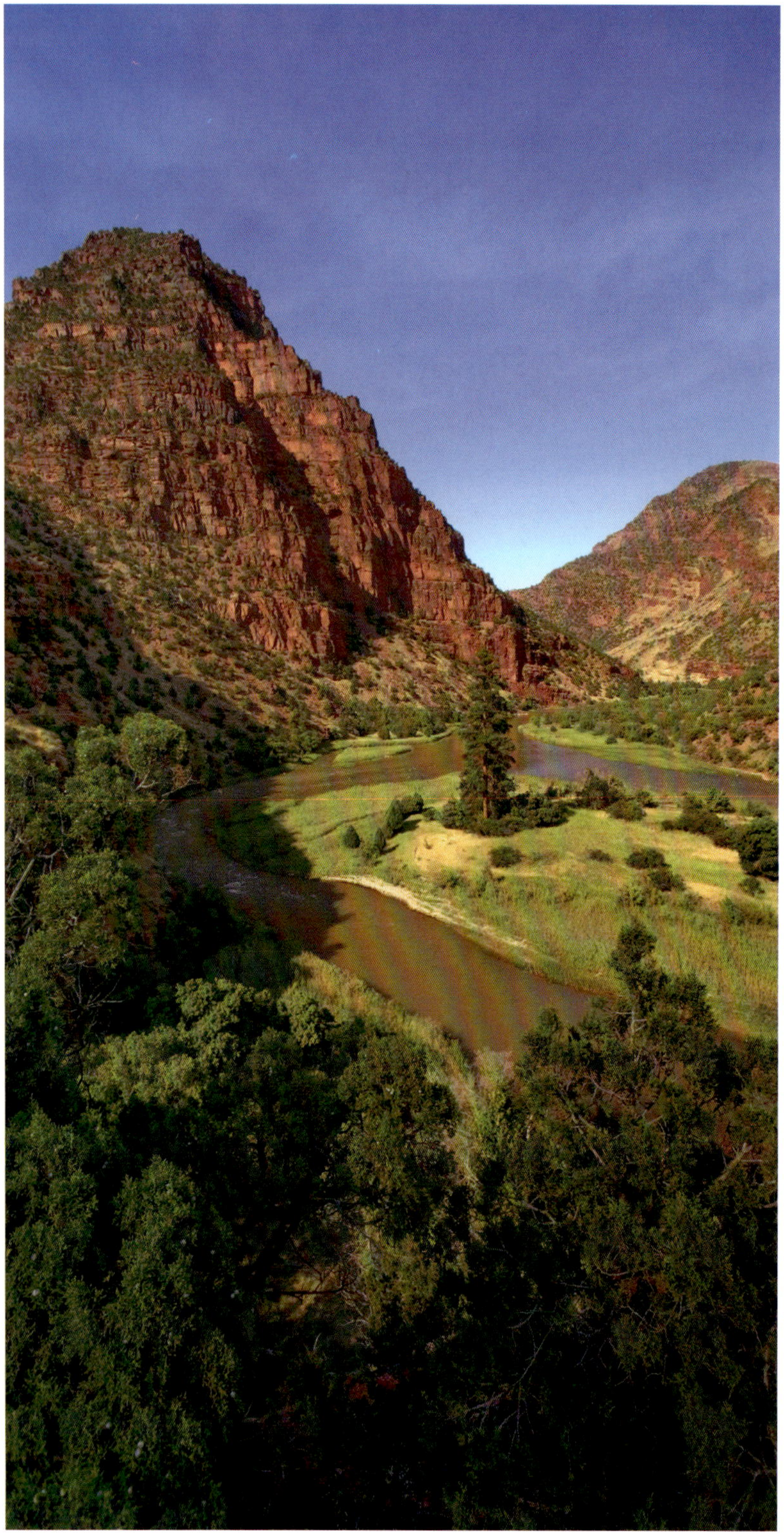

◄

LODORE SANDSTONE FORMATIONS TOWER OVER THE GREEN RIVER NEAR JONES HOLE IN DINOSAUR NATIONAL MONUMENT.

►

THE GREEN RIVER WINDS THROUGH ISLAND PARK IN DINOSAUR NATIONAL MONUMENT.

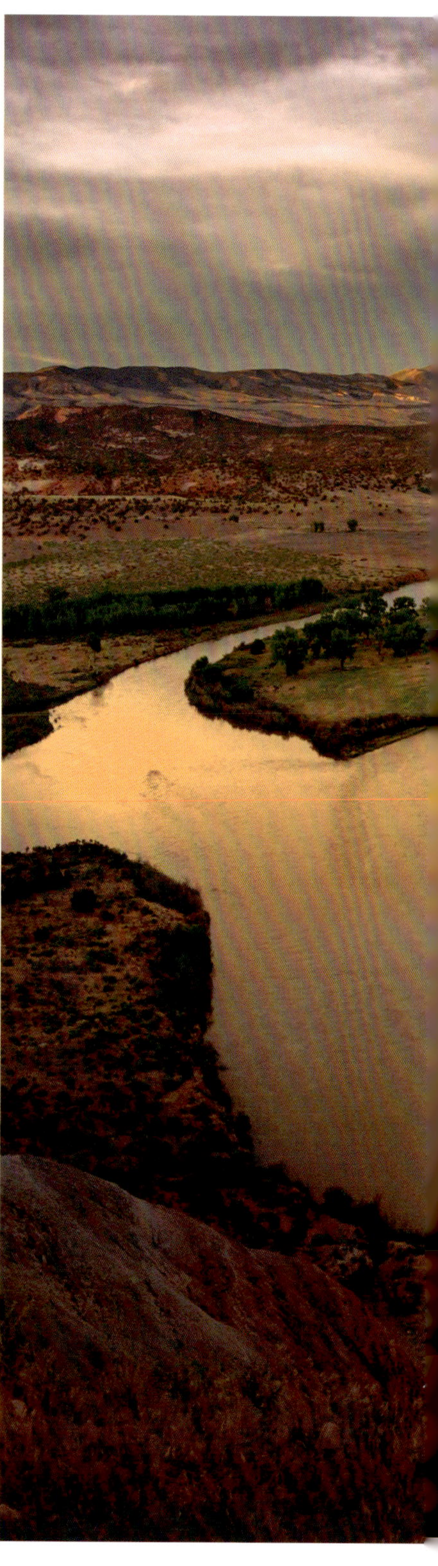

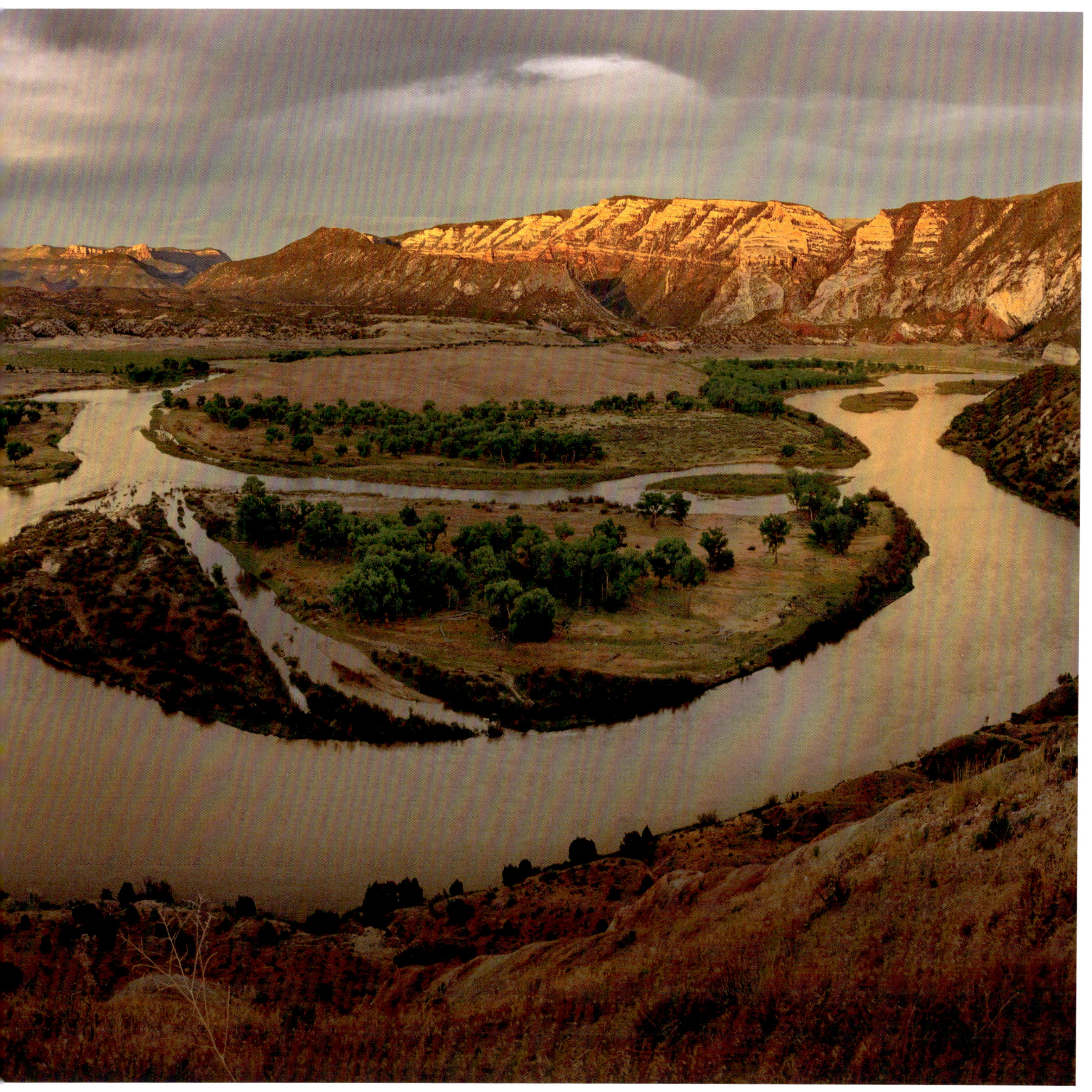

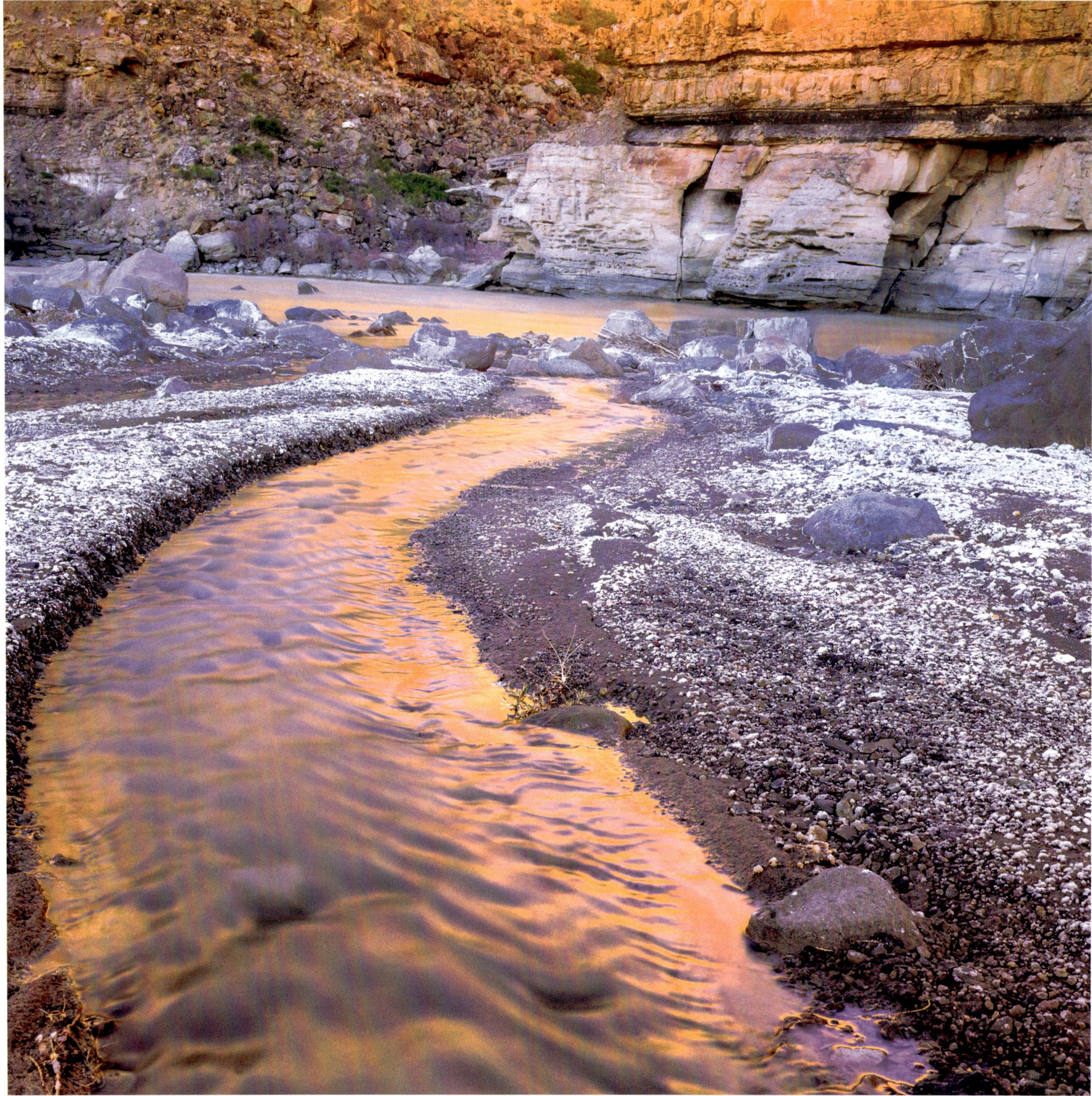

AN ALKALINE-RICH SIDE STREAM JOINS THE GREEN RIVER IN DESOLATION CANYON.

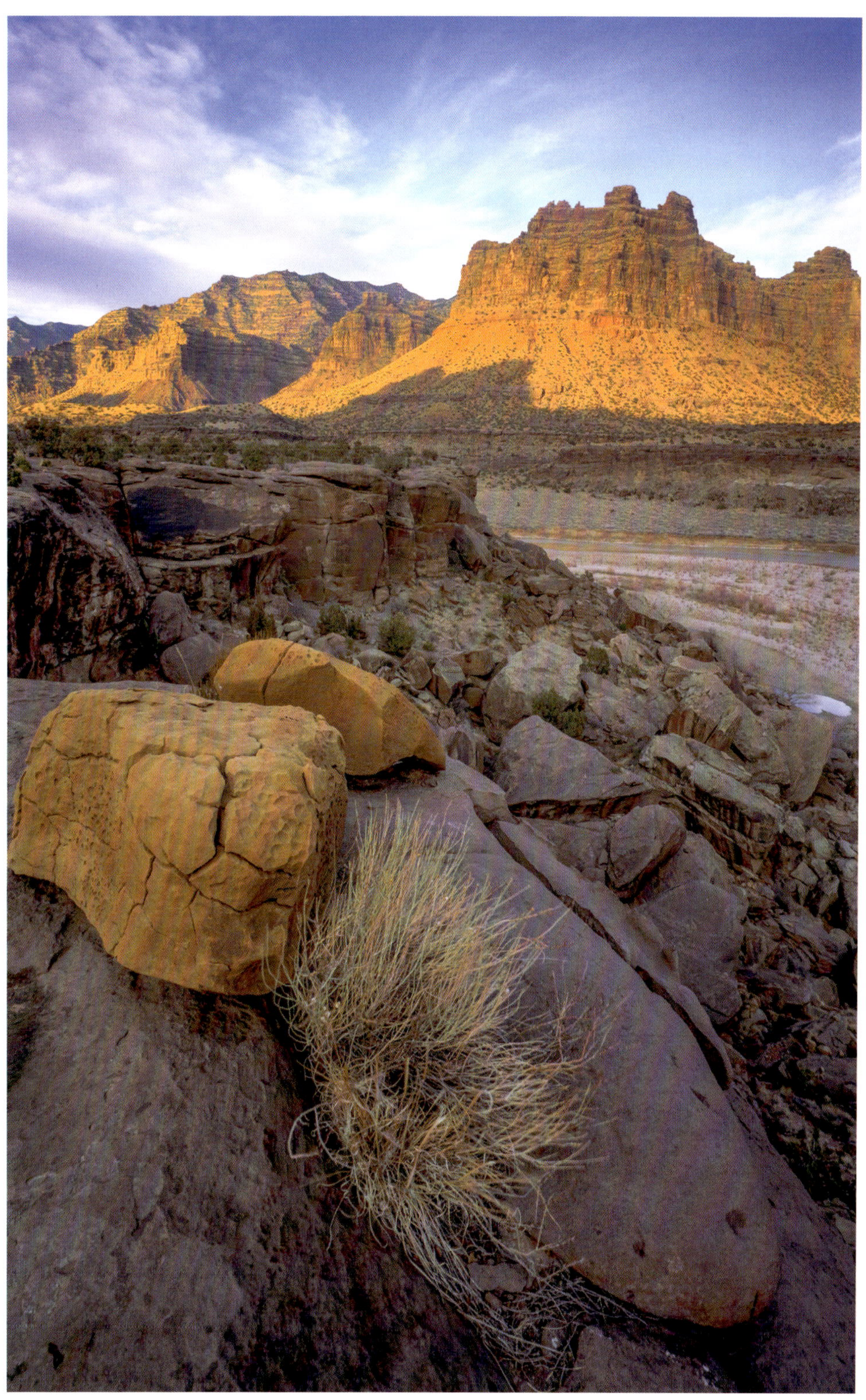

GAZING OVER THE GREEN RIVER FROM A SANDSTONE LEDGE NEAR WIRE FENCE RAPID IN DESOLATION CANYON.

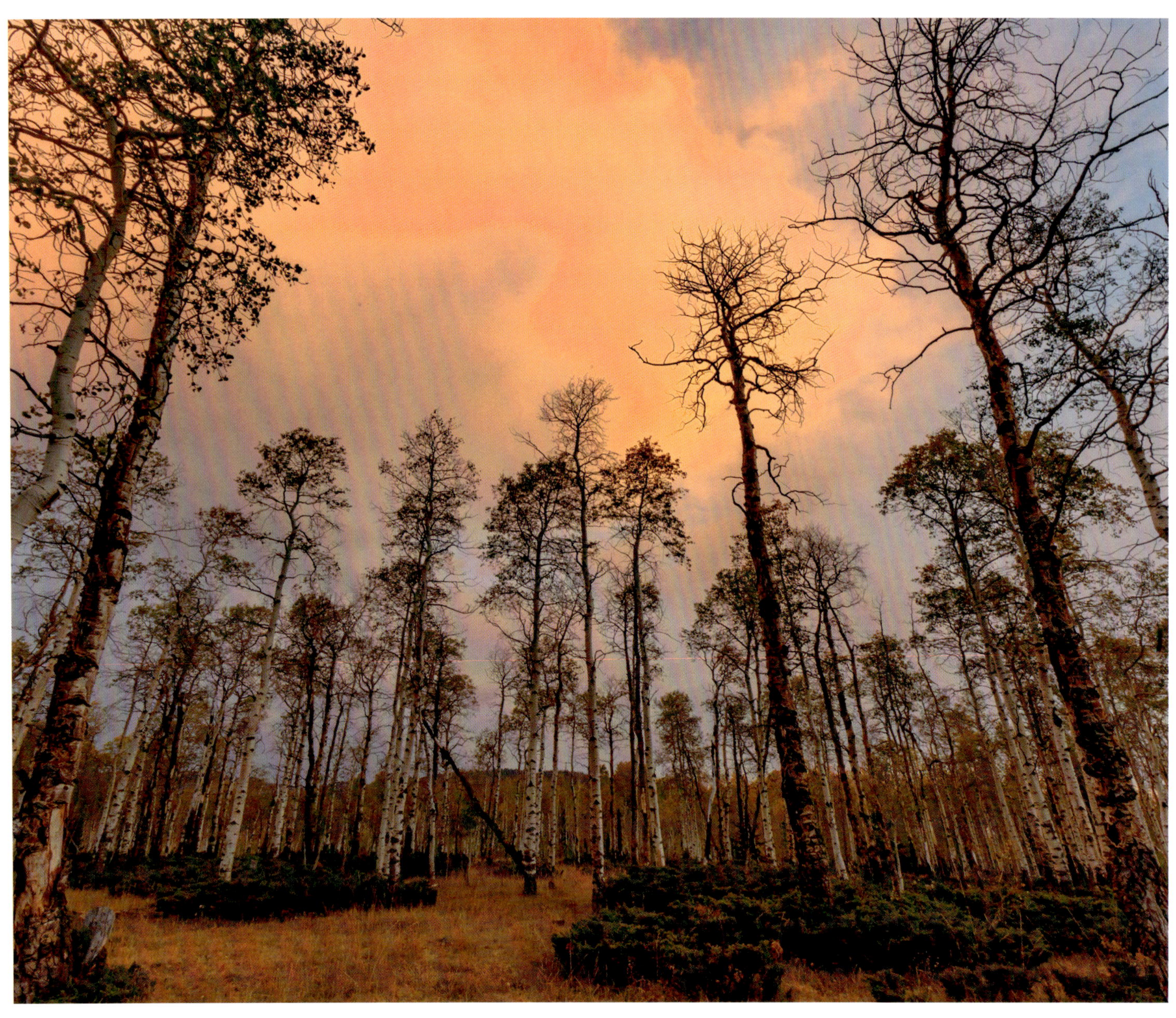

▲

QUAKING ASPENS GREET THE LAST DAYS OF FALL HIGH ON A RIDGE NEAR DUTCH JOHN.

▶

STORM CLOUDS HOVER OVER SANDSTONE FORMATIONS IN RED FLEET STATE PARK.

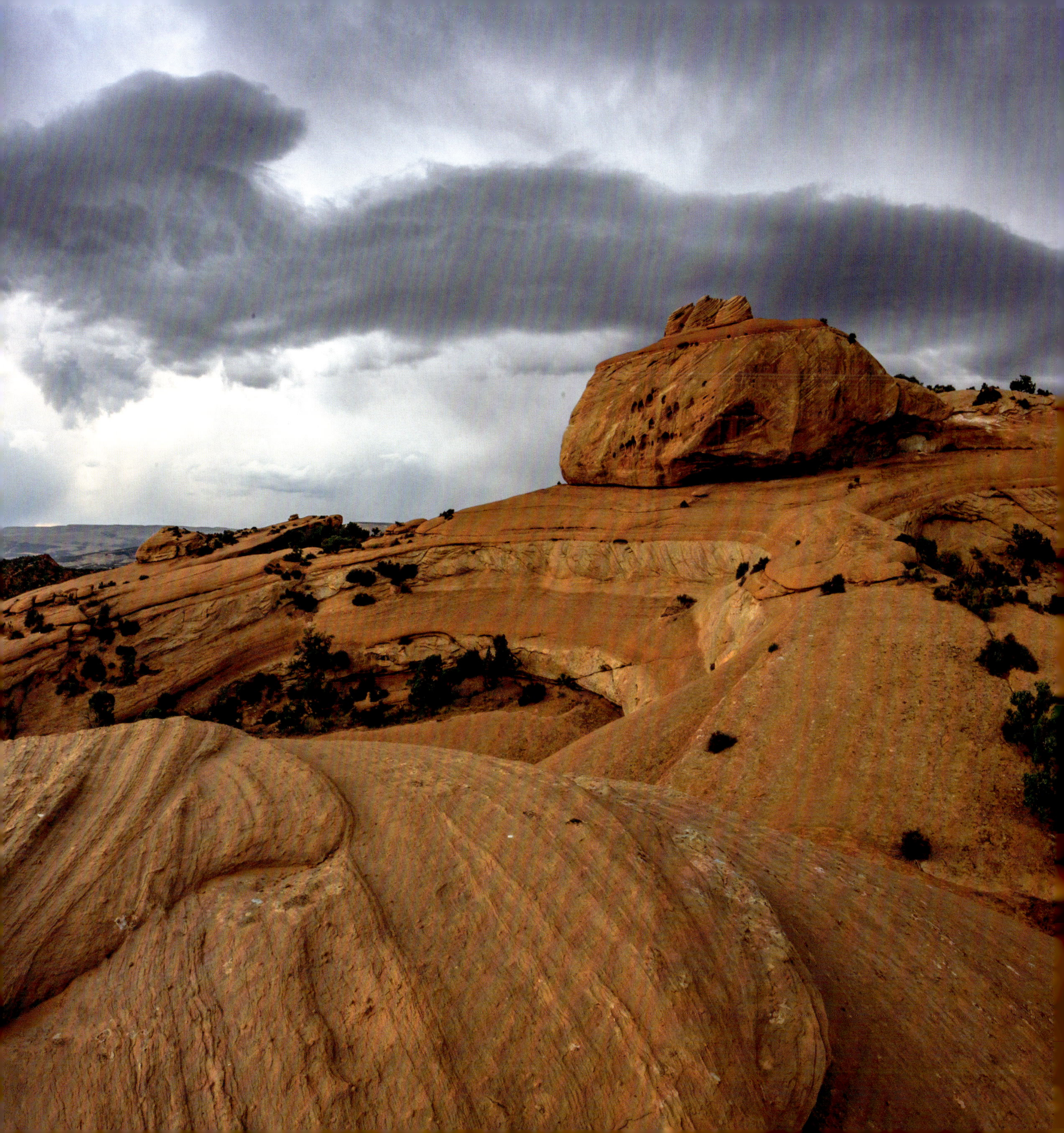

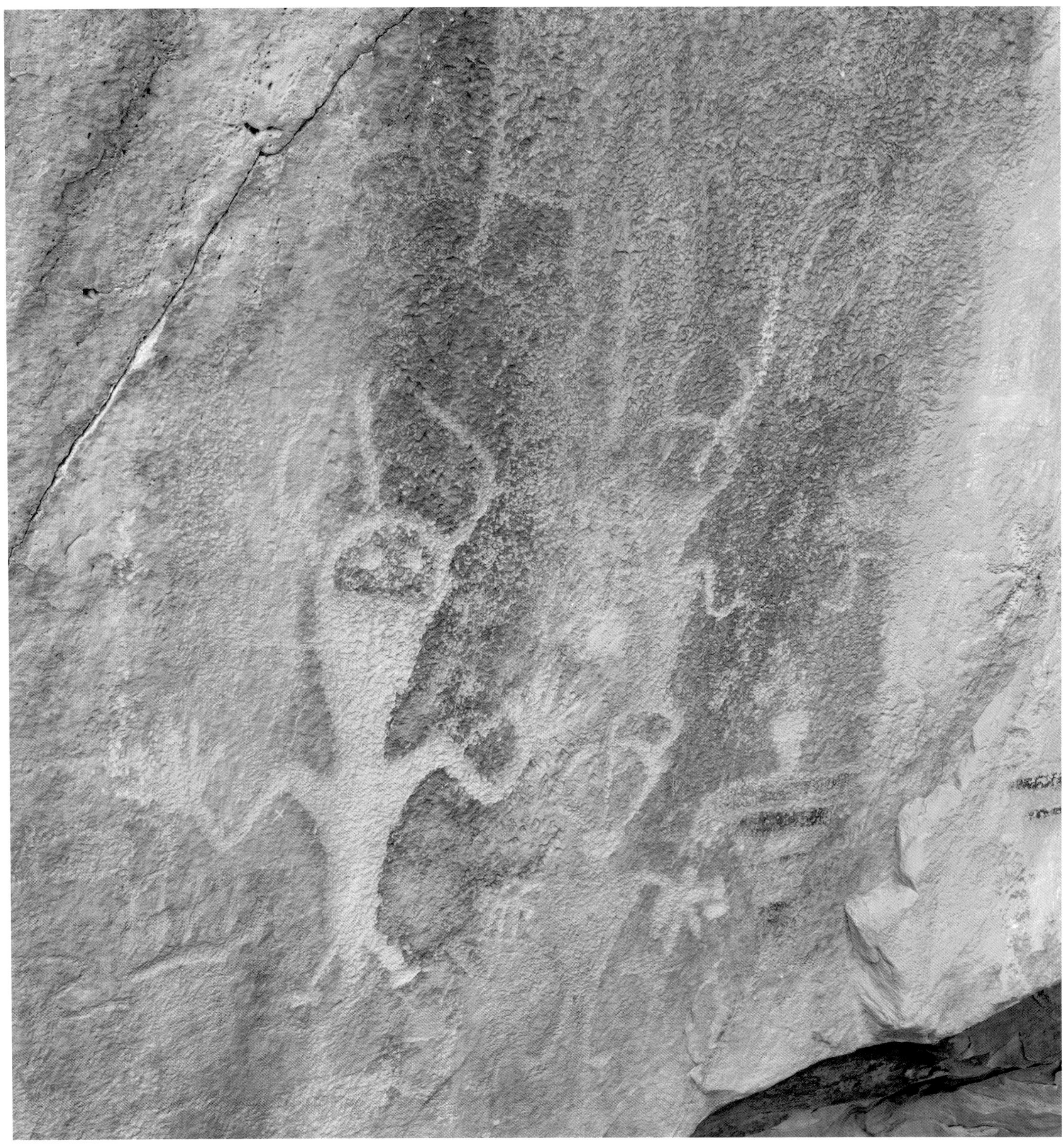

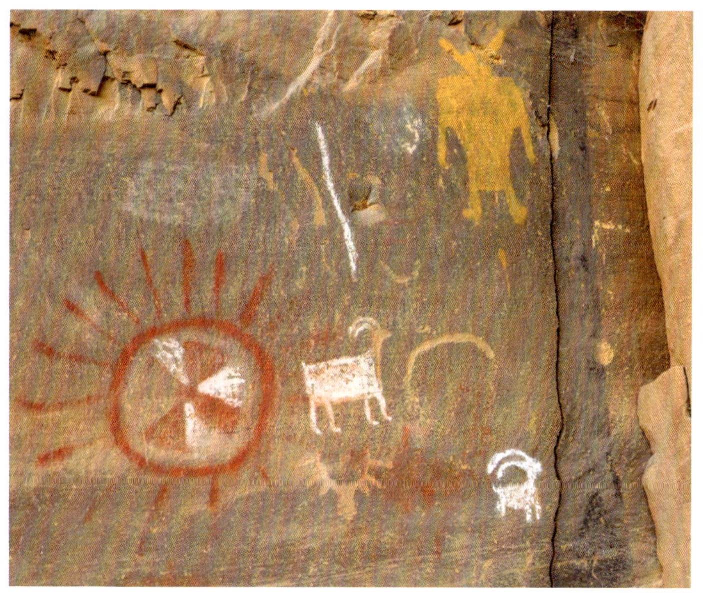

A COLORFUL MIX OF PICTOGRAPHS ALONG THE WALLS OF NINE MILE CANYON.

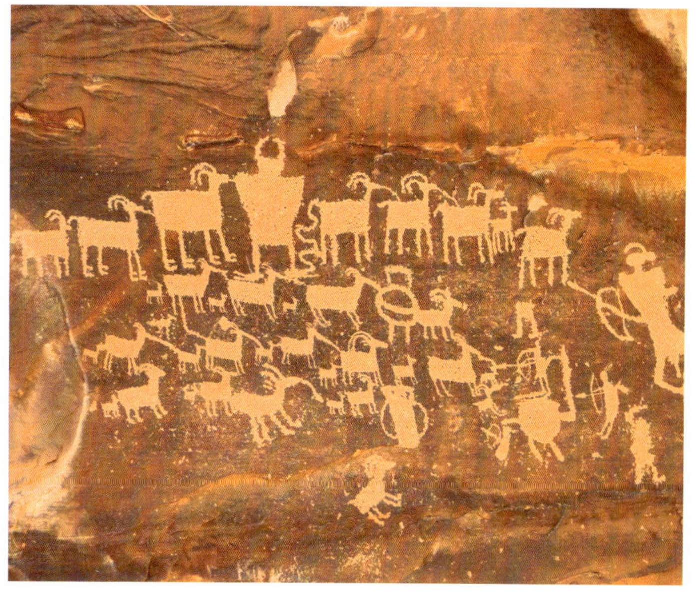

THE GREAT HUNT PANEL OF PICTOGRAPHS IN NINE MILE CANYON.

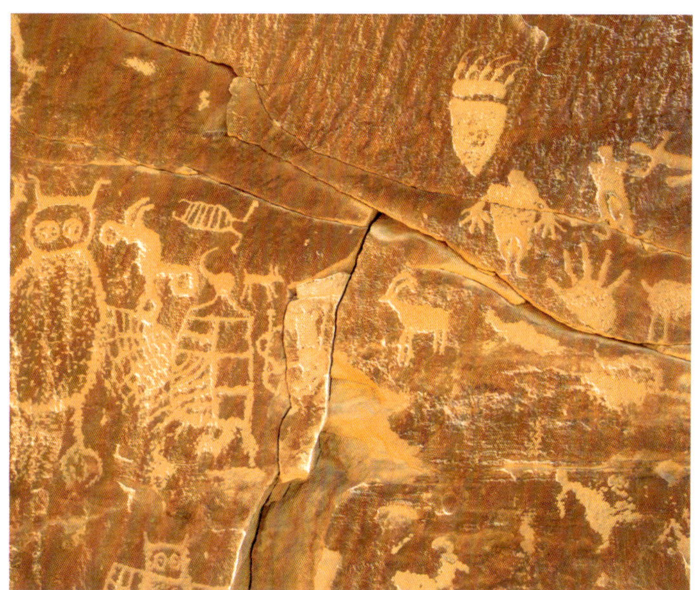

THE OWL PANEL OF PICTOGRAPHS IN NINE MILE CANYON.

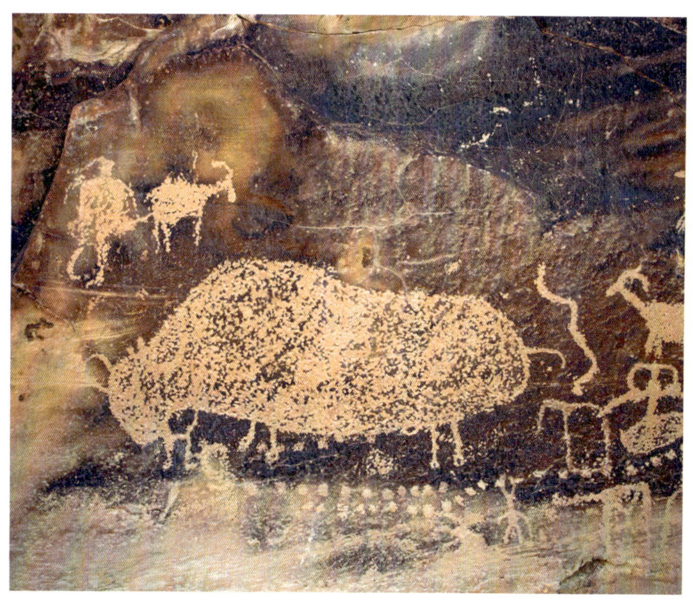

BIG BUFFALO PANEL, THE LARGEST KNOWN BUFFALO PICTOGRAPH IN NINE MILE CANYON.

◀ FREMONT PEOPLE PETROGLYPHS ARE CHARACTERIZED BY TRAPEZOIDAL BODIES, ELABORATE JEWELRY, AND HEADGEAR.

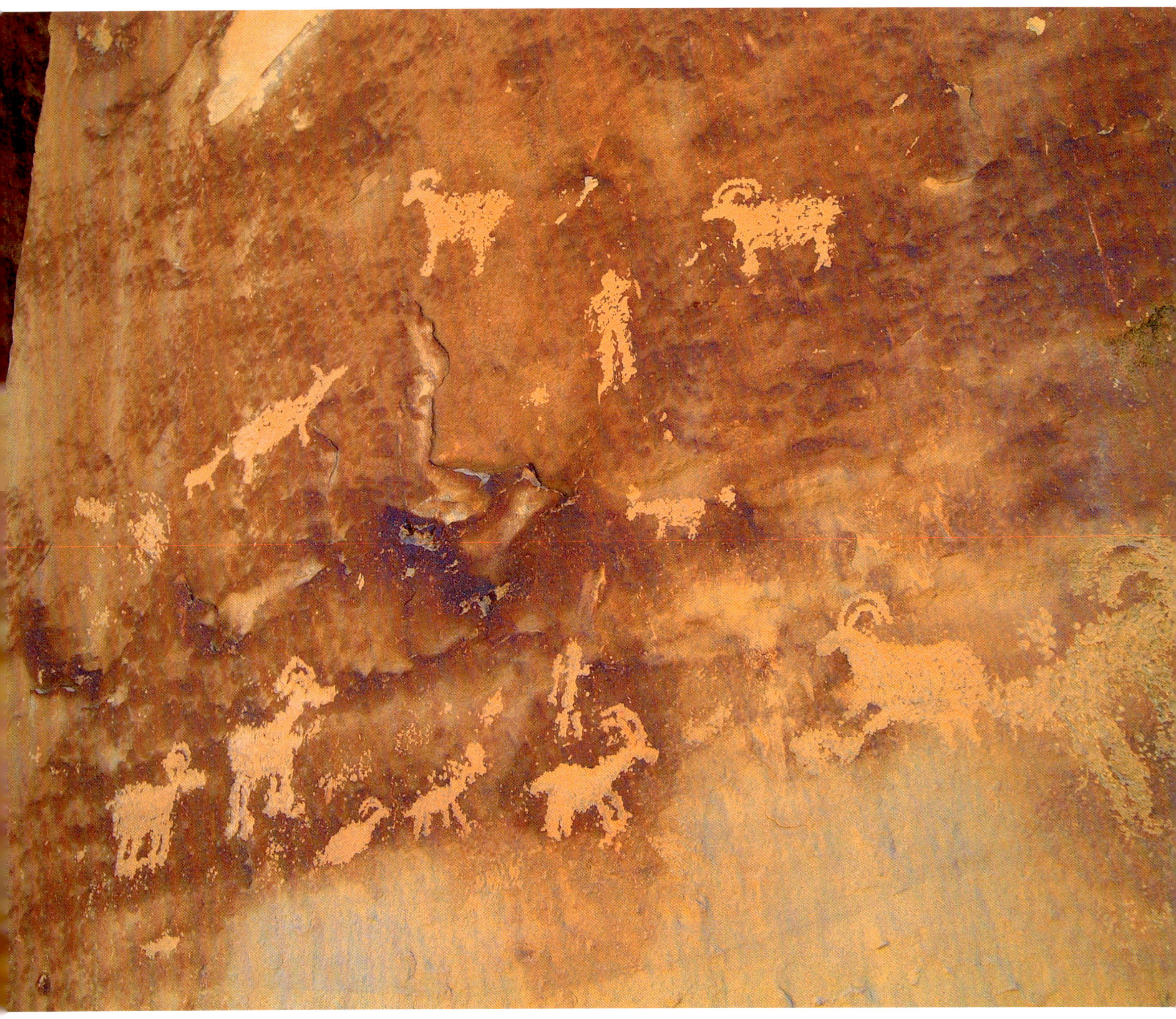

PETROGLYPHS ON A SANDSTONE WALL IN THE DESOLATION CANYON OF THE GREEN RIVER.

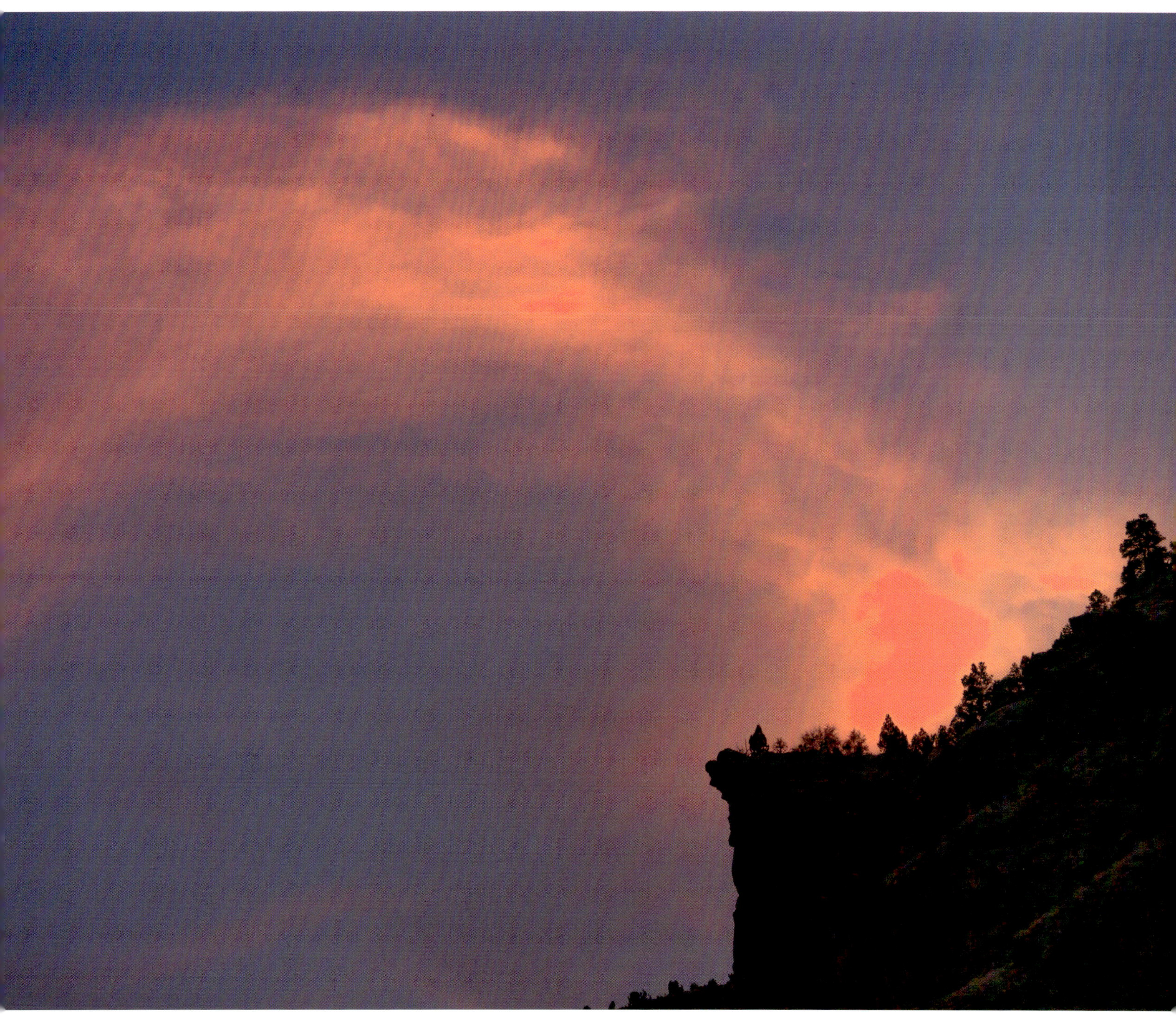

A HAUNTING CLOUD CIRCLES THE ENTRANCE TO NINE MILE CANYON.

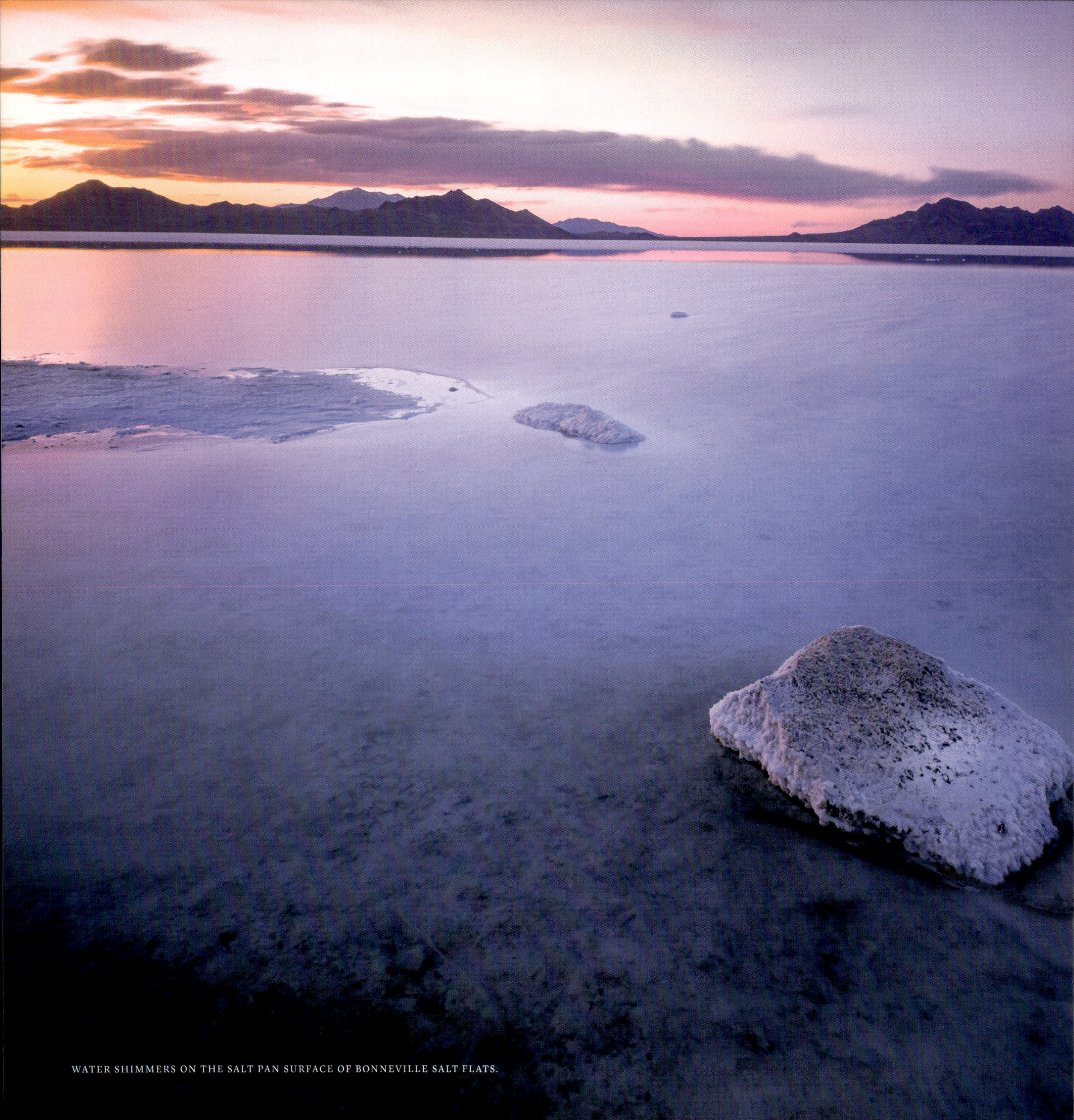

WATER SHIMMERS ON THE SALT PAN SURFACE OF BONNEVILLE SALT FLATS.

WEST DESERT

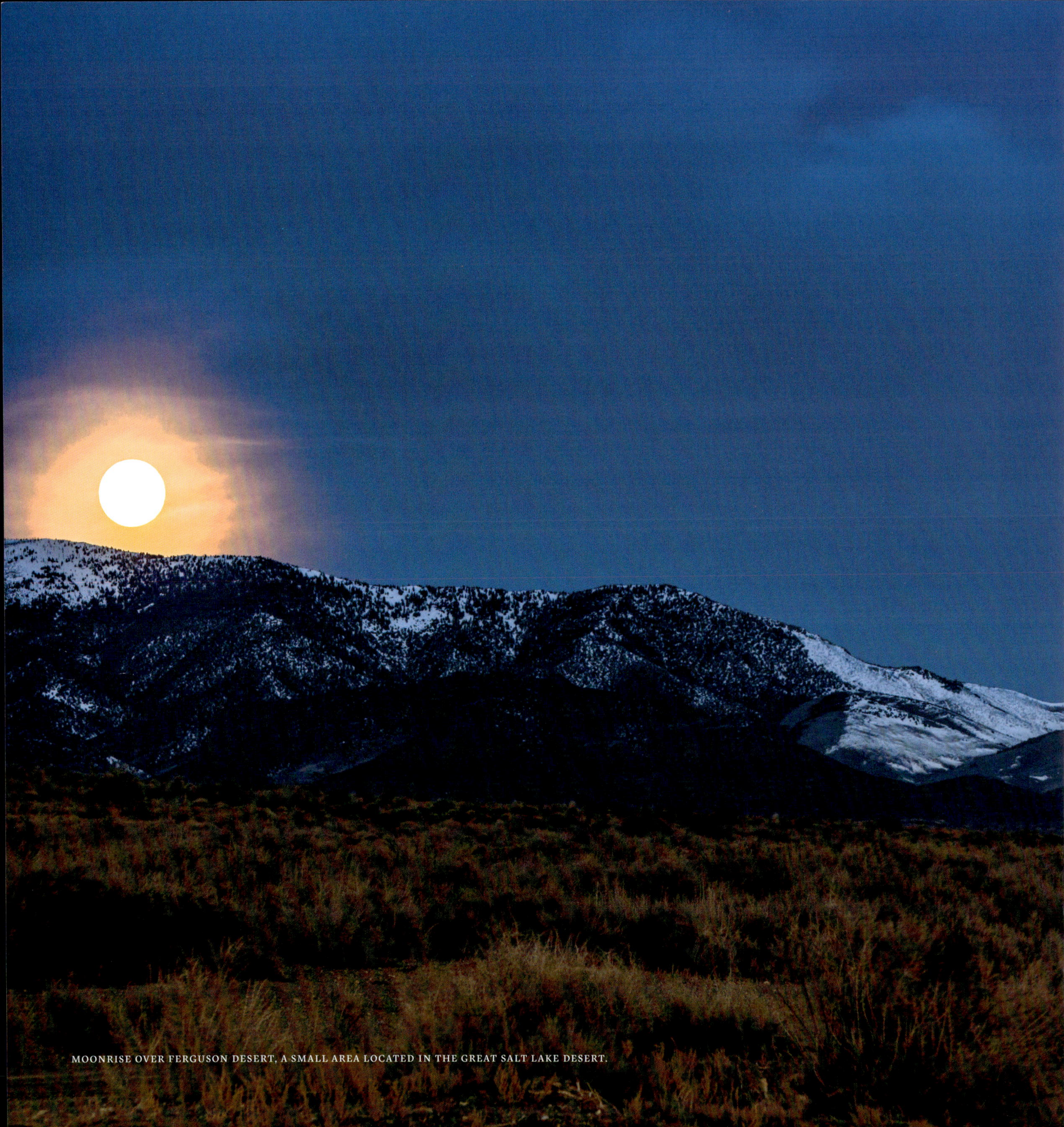

MOONRISE OVER FERGUSON DESERT, A SMALL AREA LOCATED IN THE GREAT SALT LAKE DESERT.

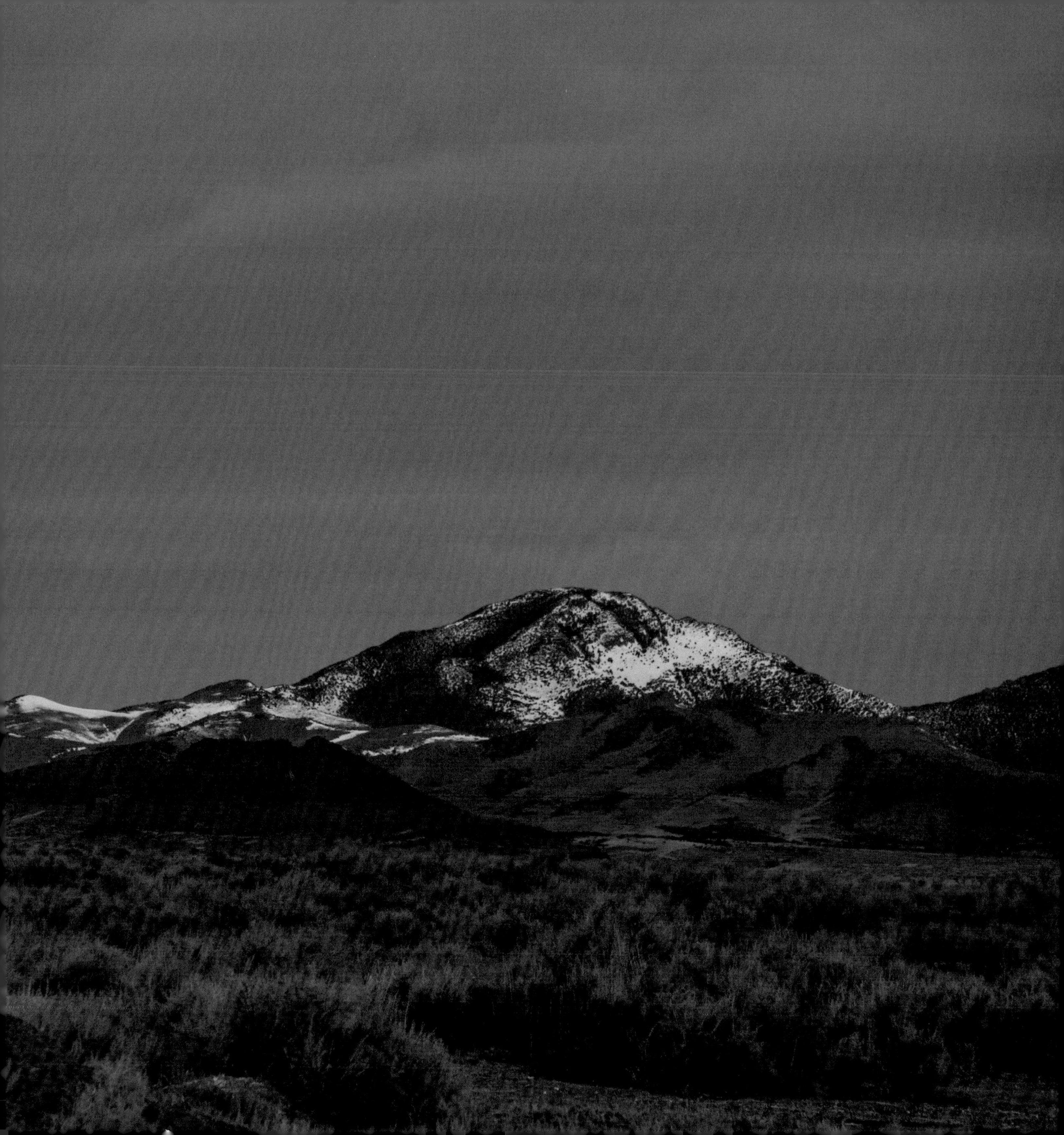

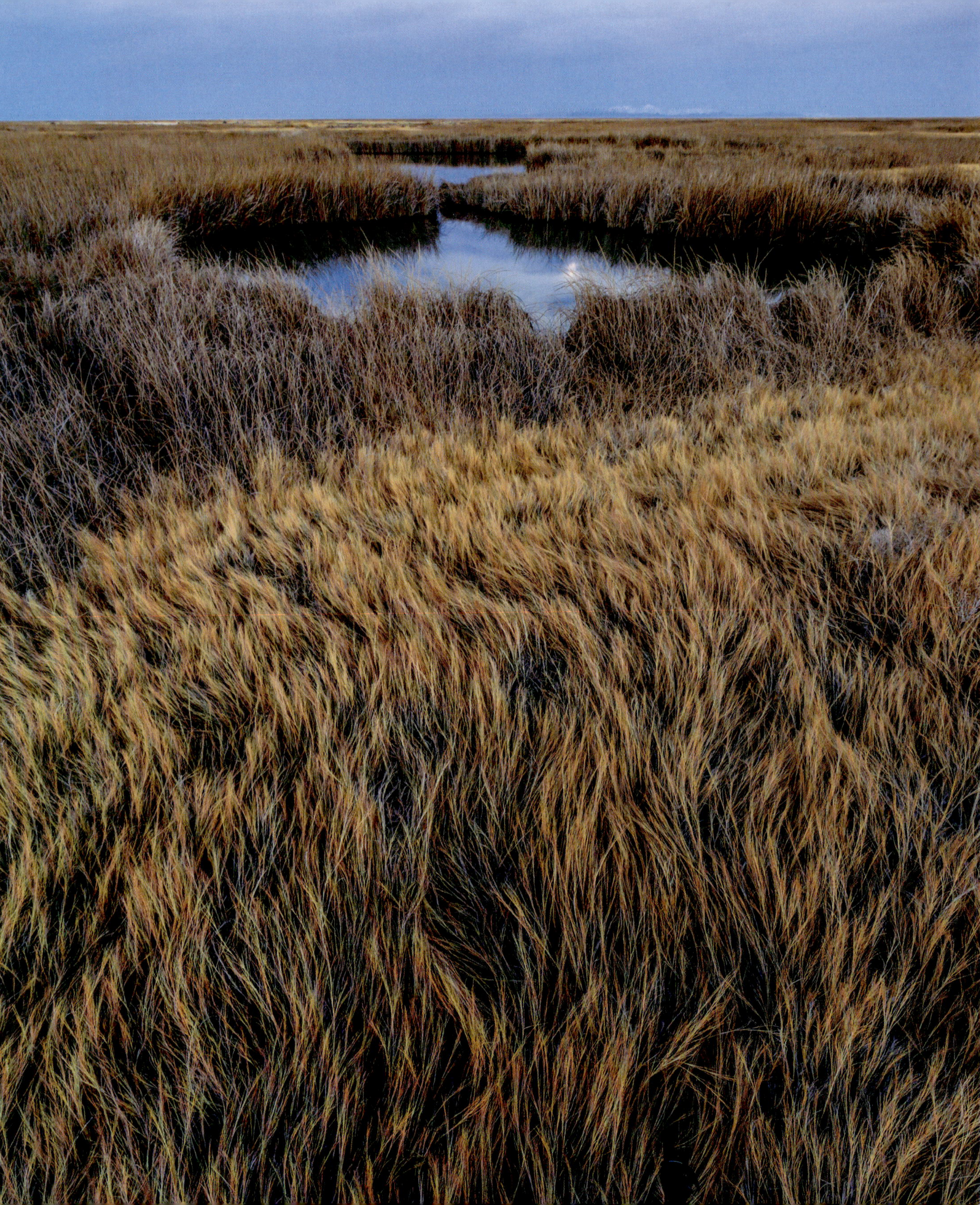

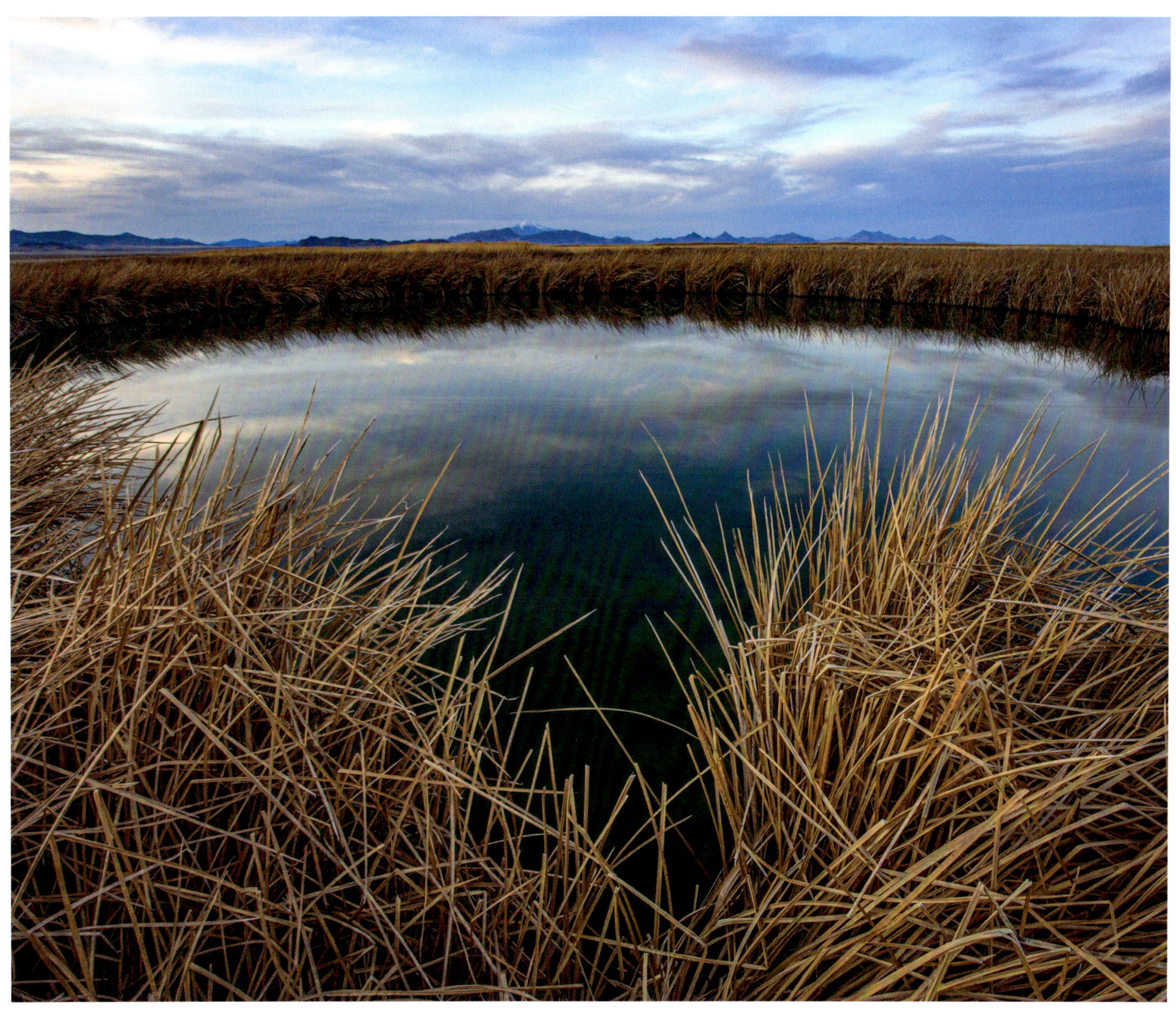

▲
THE BLUE LAKE WILDLIFE MANAGEMENT AREA ON THE UTAH-NEVADA BORDER.

◀
WAVES OF SALTGRASS IN THE BLUE LAKE WILDLIFE MANAGEMENT AREA.

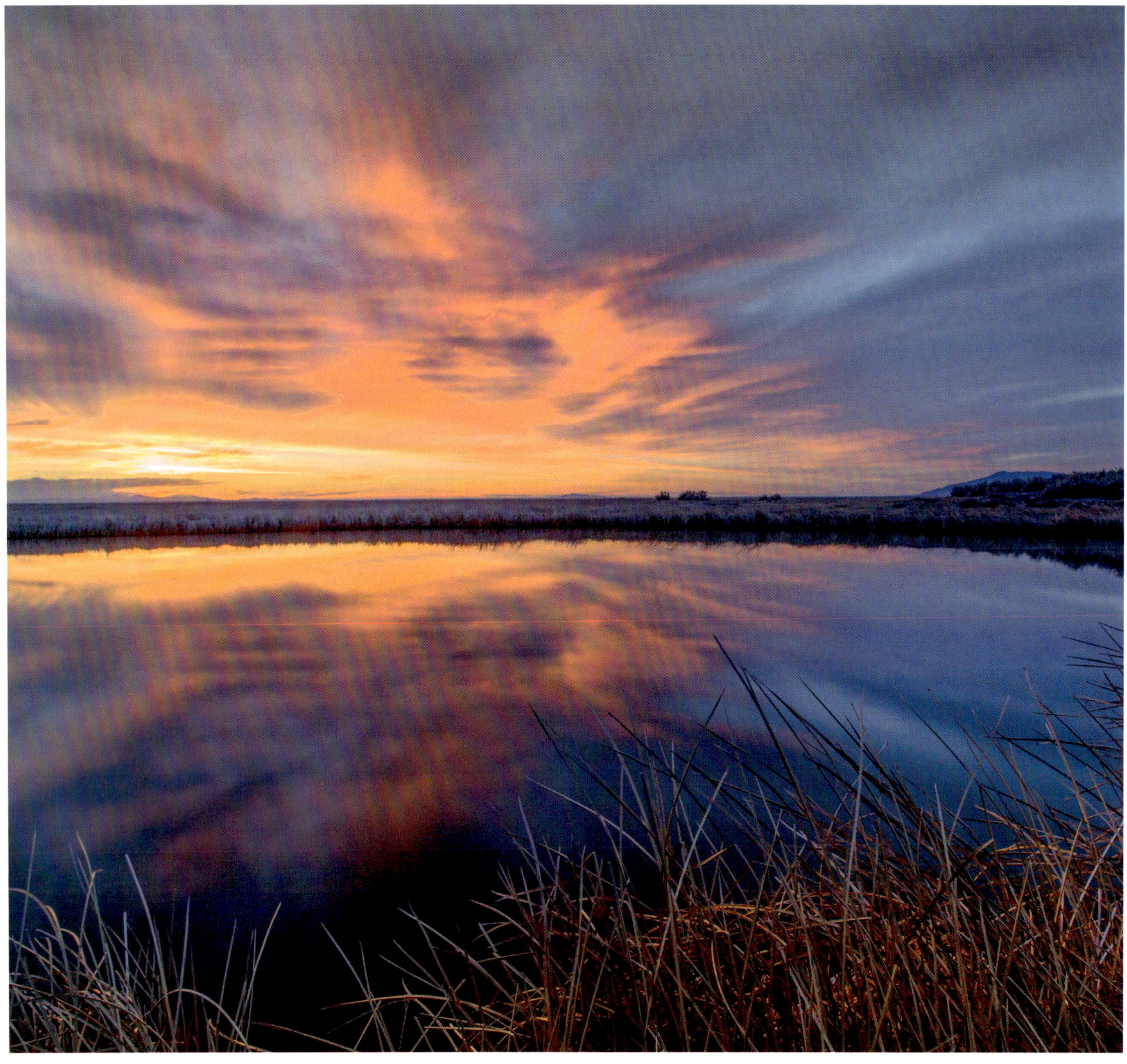

SUNRISE OVER A FRESHWATER SPRING IN THE GREAT SALT LAKE DESERT.

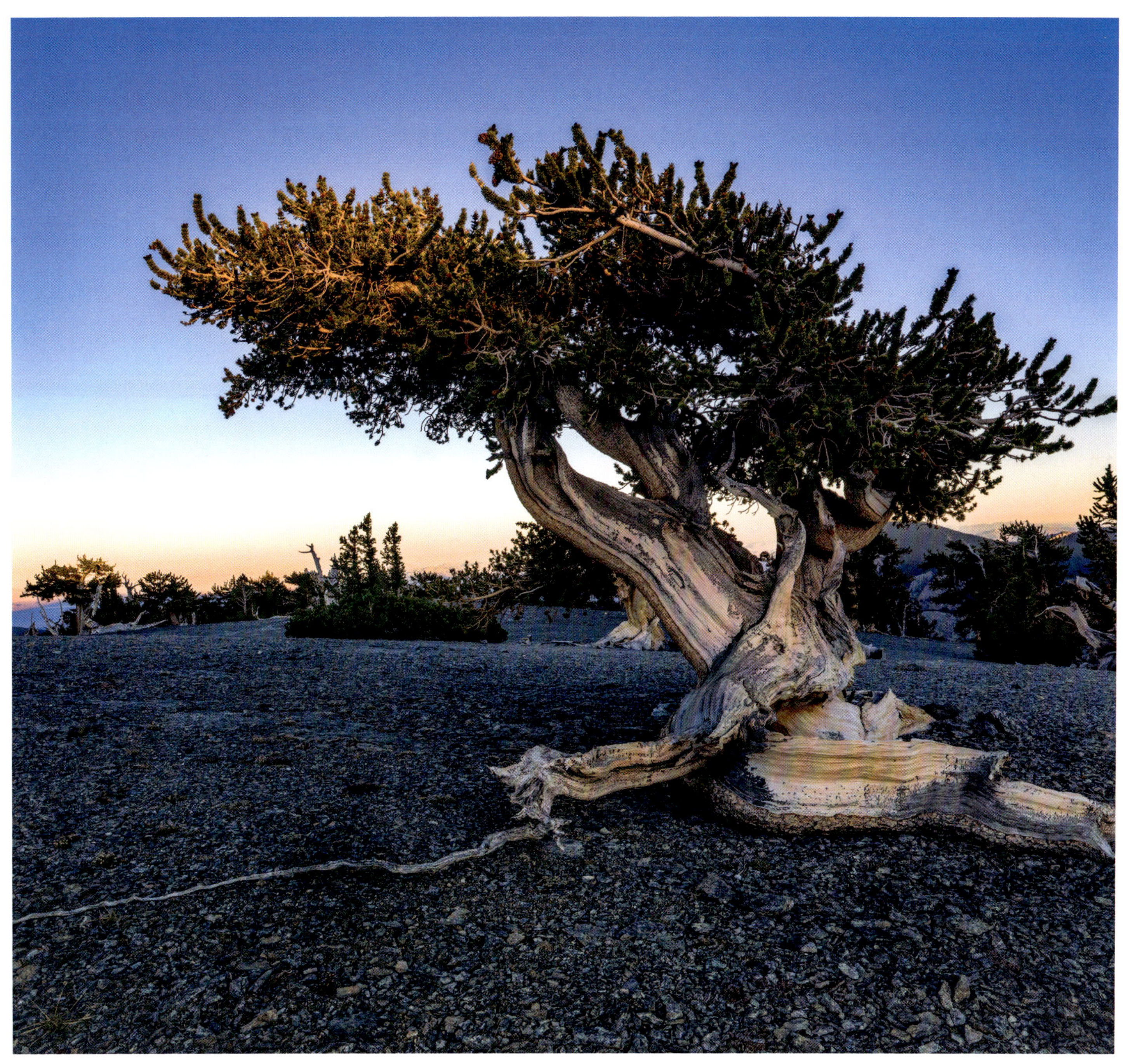

A RESILIENT BRISTLECONE PINE ON THE UTAH-NEVADA BORDER.

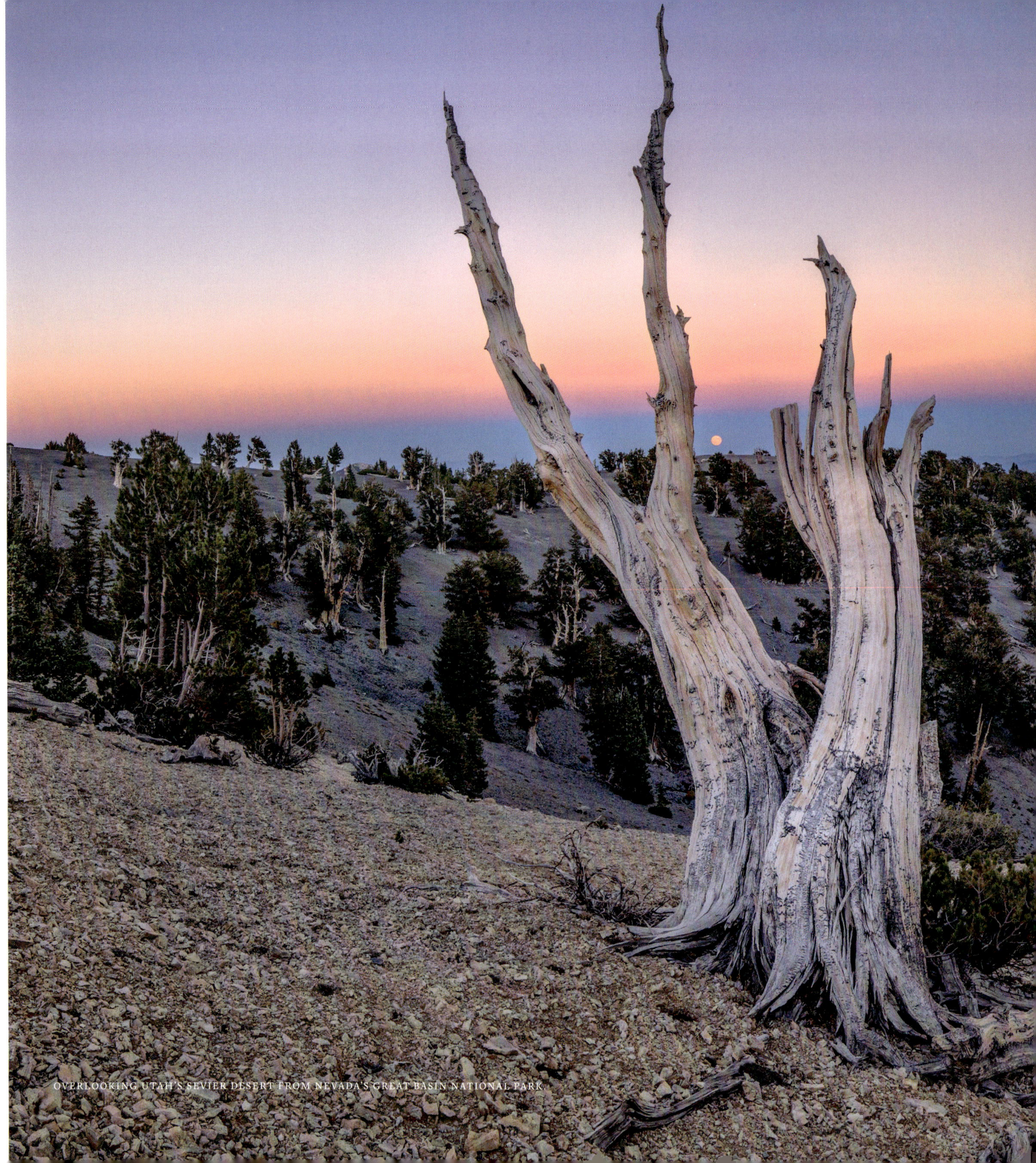

OVERLOOKING UTAH'S SEVIER DESERT FROM NEVADA'S GREAT BASIN NATIONAL PARK

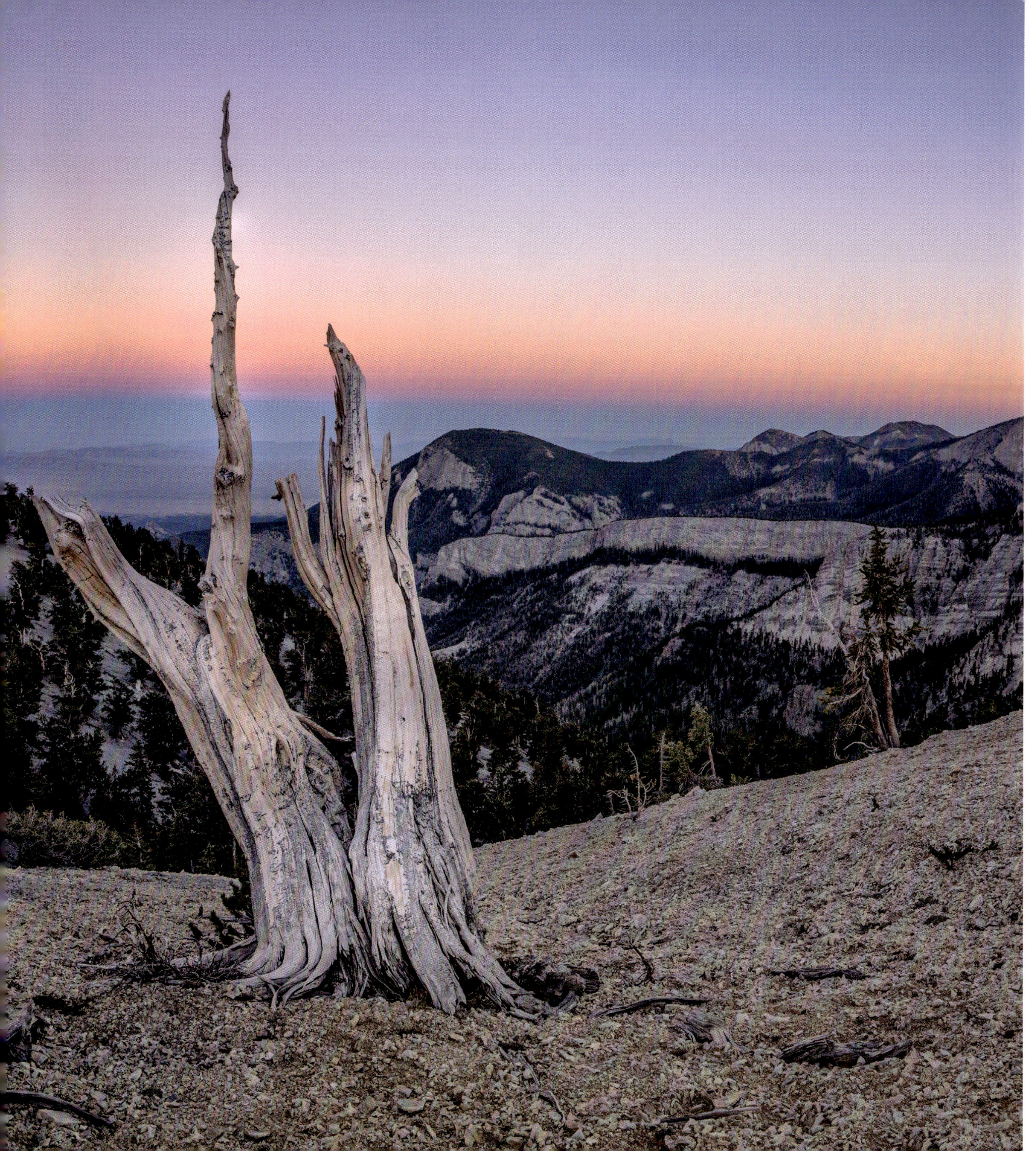

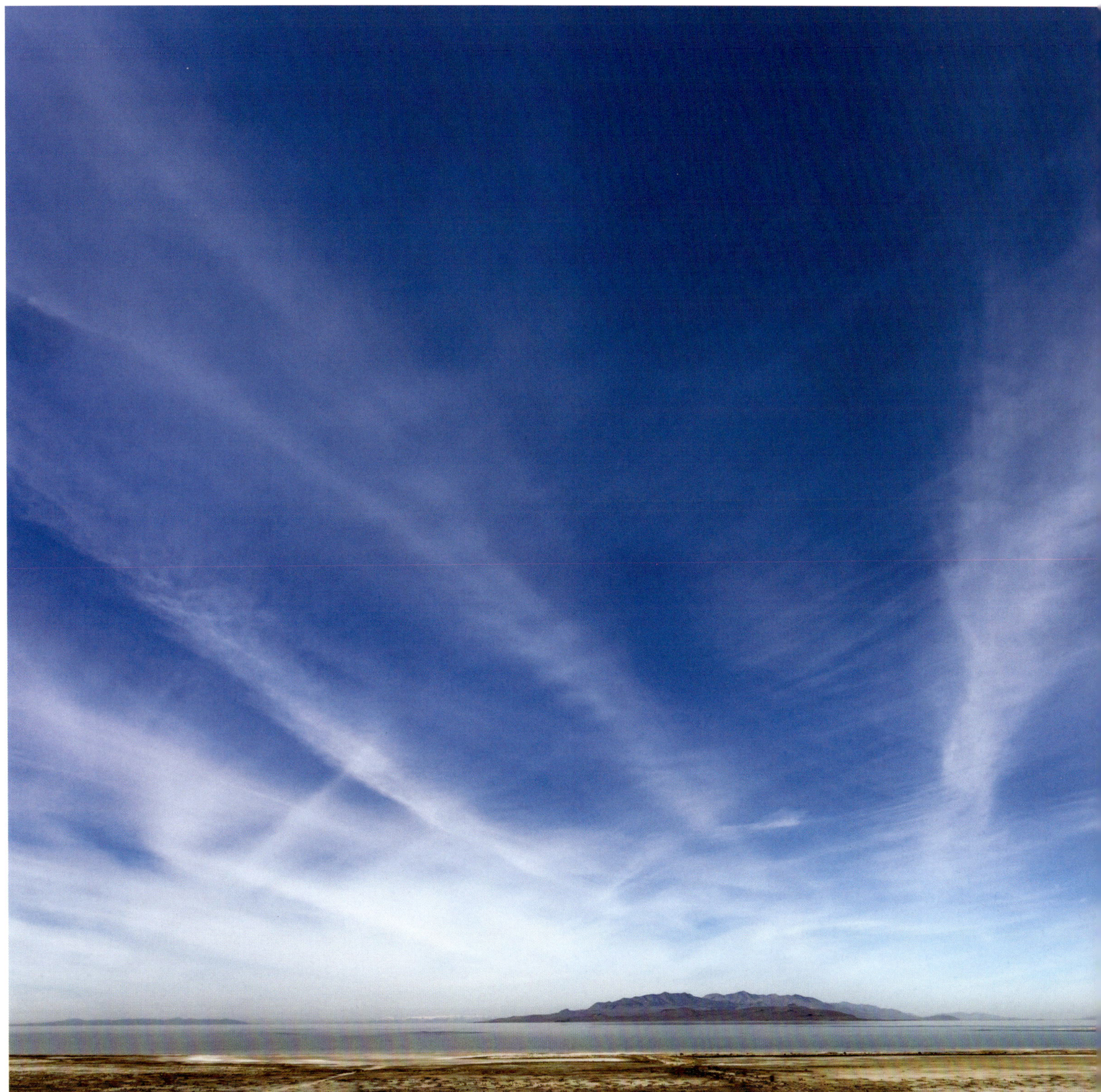

◀

FREMONT ISLAND FLOATING IN THE GREAT SALT LAKE.

▶

FREMONT ISLAND FROM BRIDGER BAY IN ANTELOPE ISLAND STATE PARK.

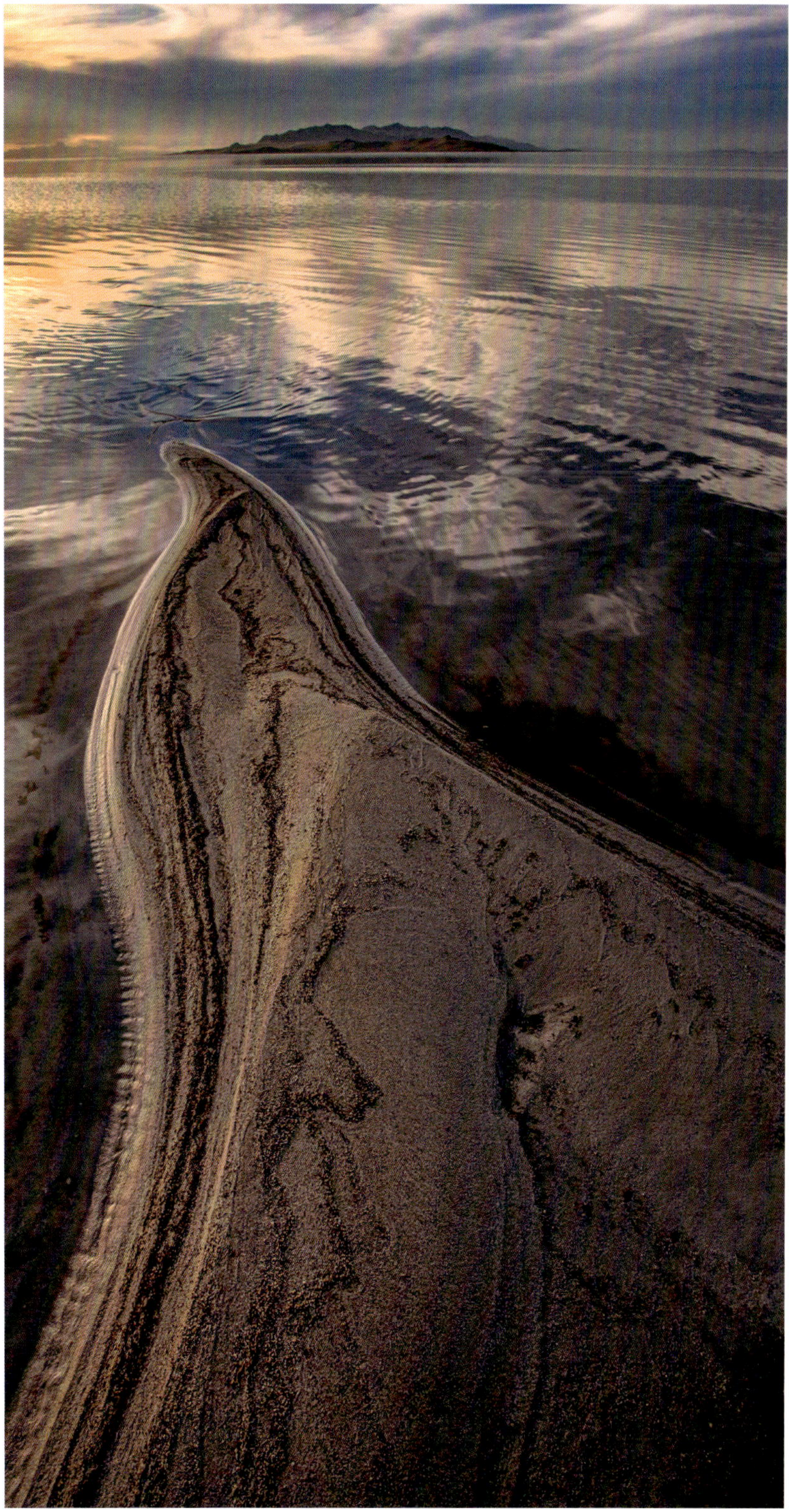

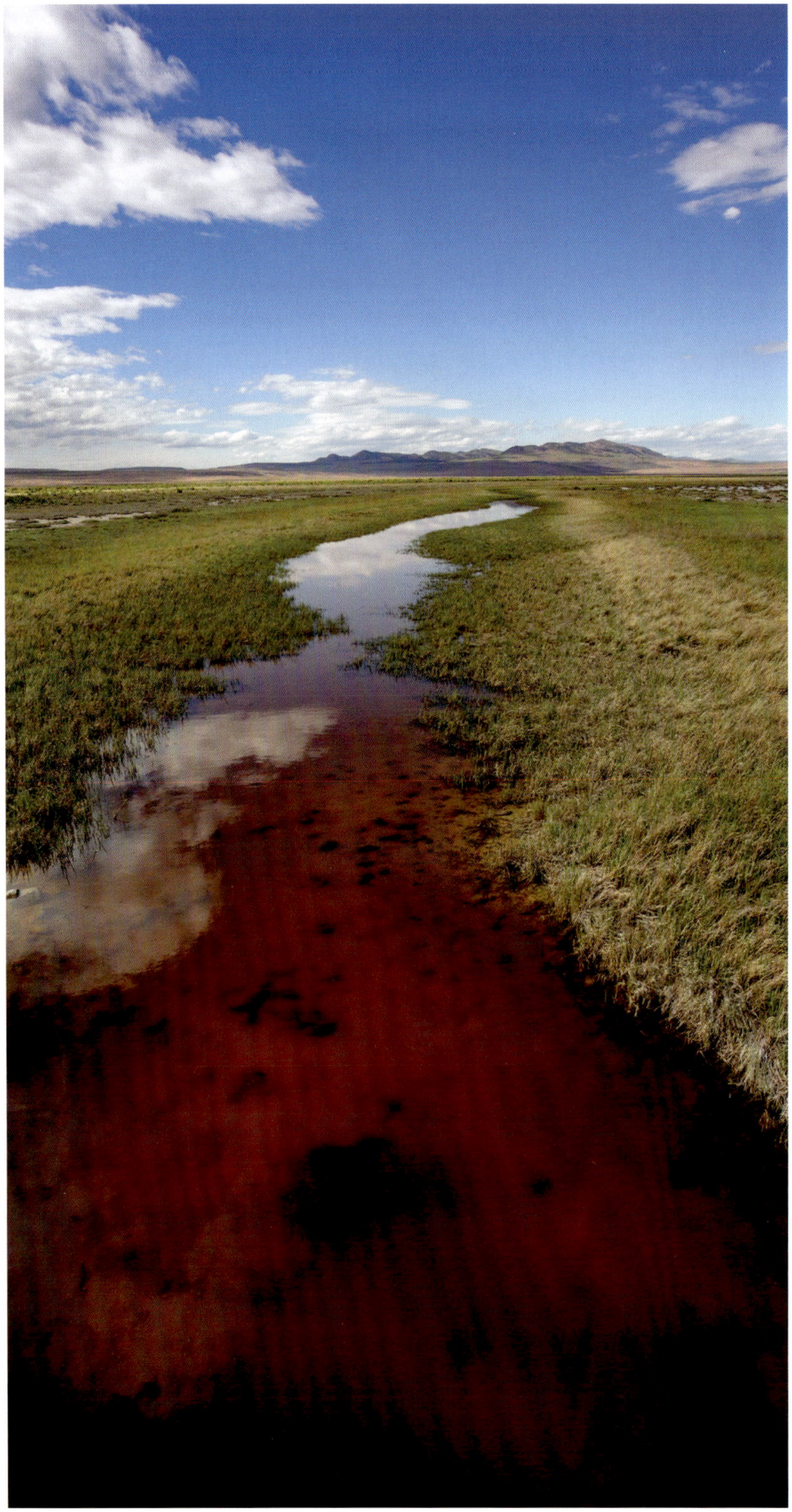

◀

TAINTED WATER SPRINGS FROM THE SALT WELLS FLAT ON THE NORTHERN EDGE OF THE GREAT SALT LAKE.

▶

THE GOOSE CREEK MOUNTAINS REFLECTED IN STANDING WATER ON THE SALT WELLS FLAT.

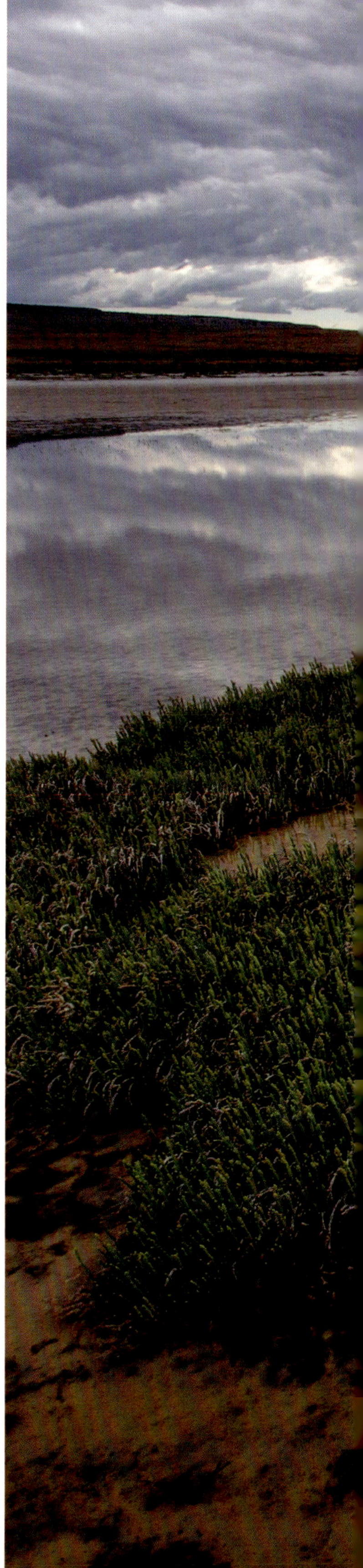

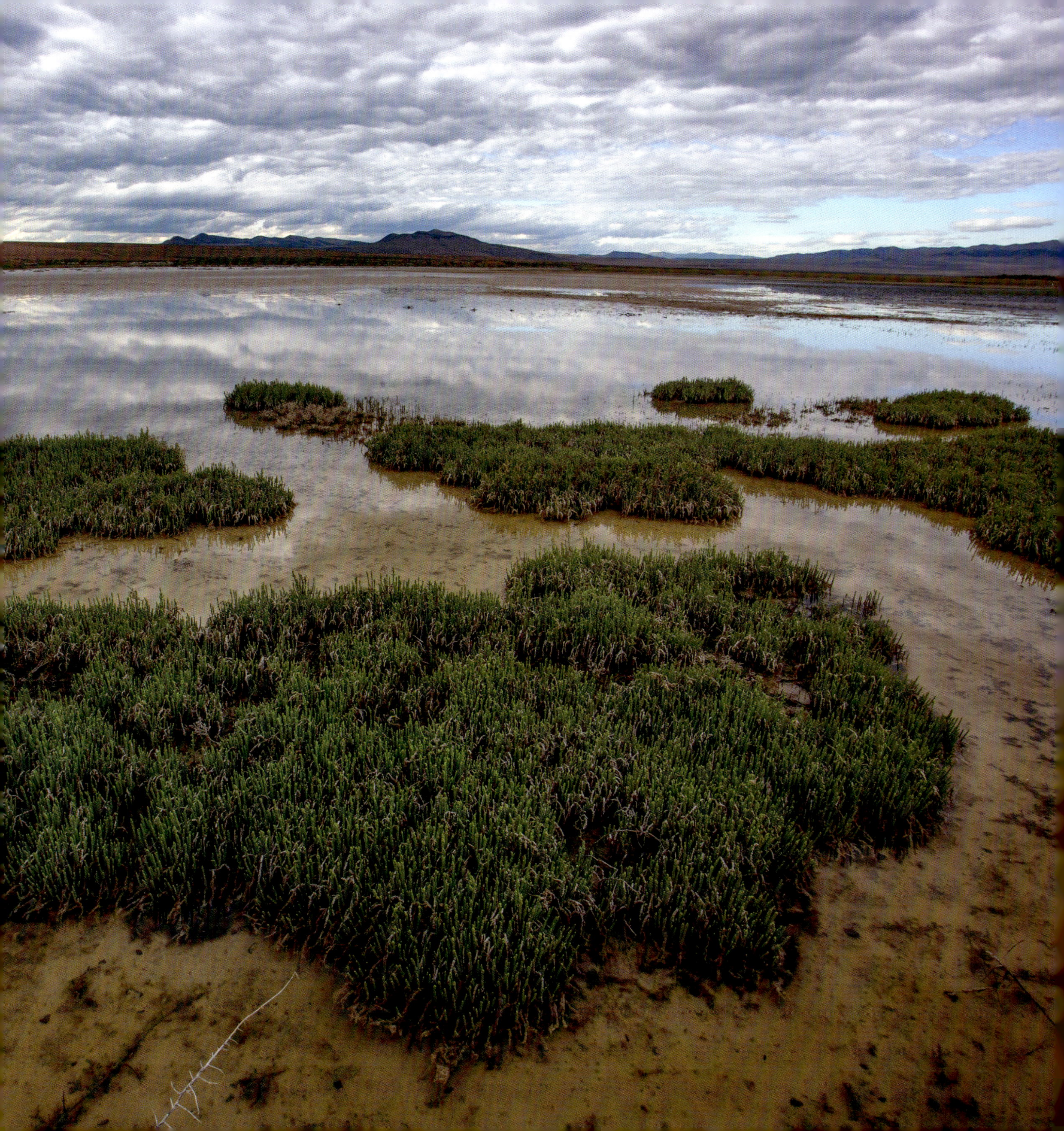

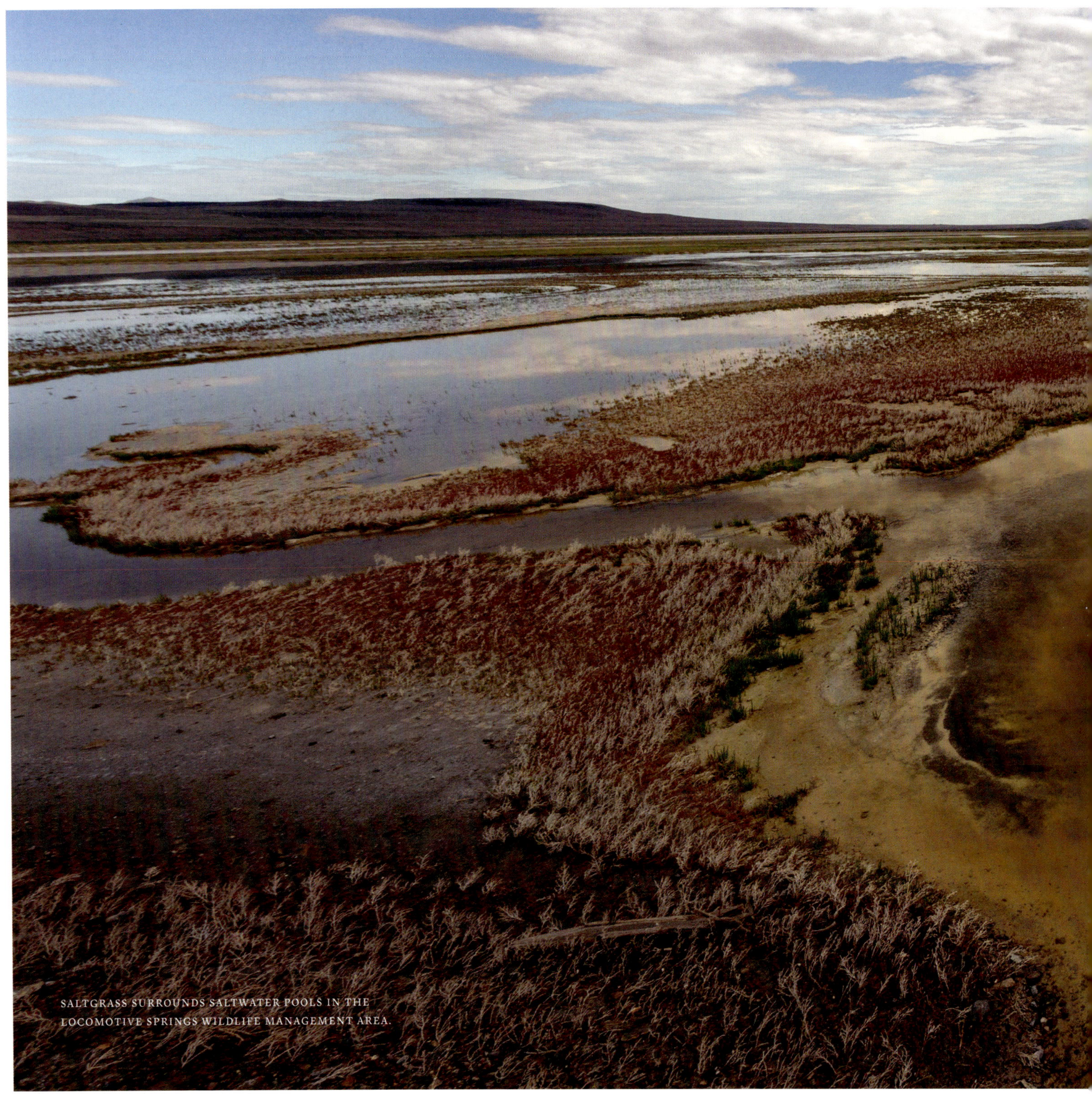

SALTGRASS SURROUNDS SALTWATER POOLS IN THE LOCOMOTIVE SPRINGS WILDLIFE MANAGEMENT AREA.

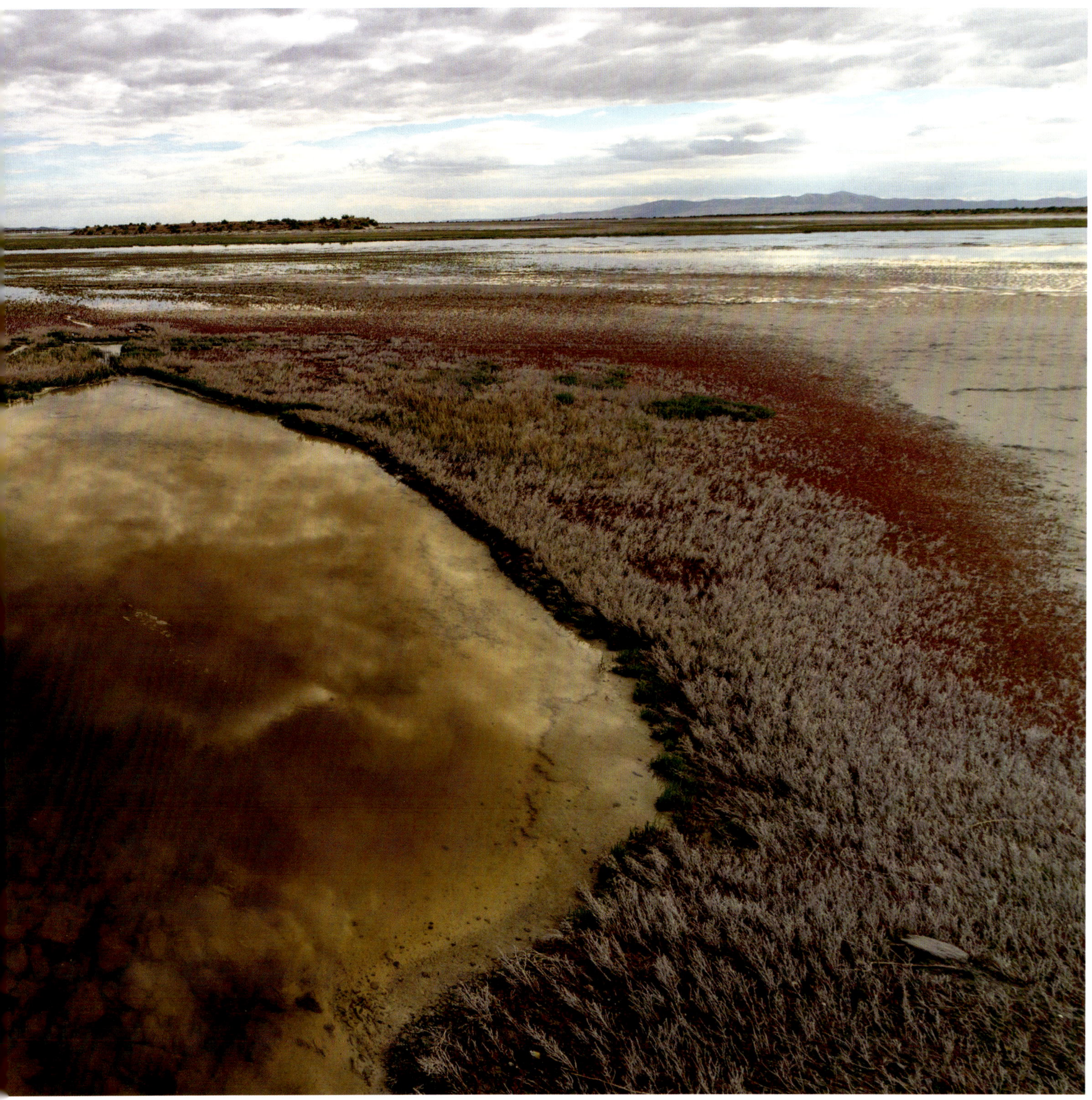

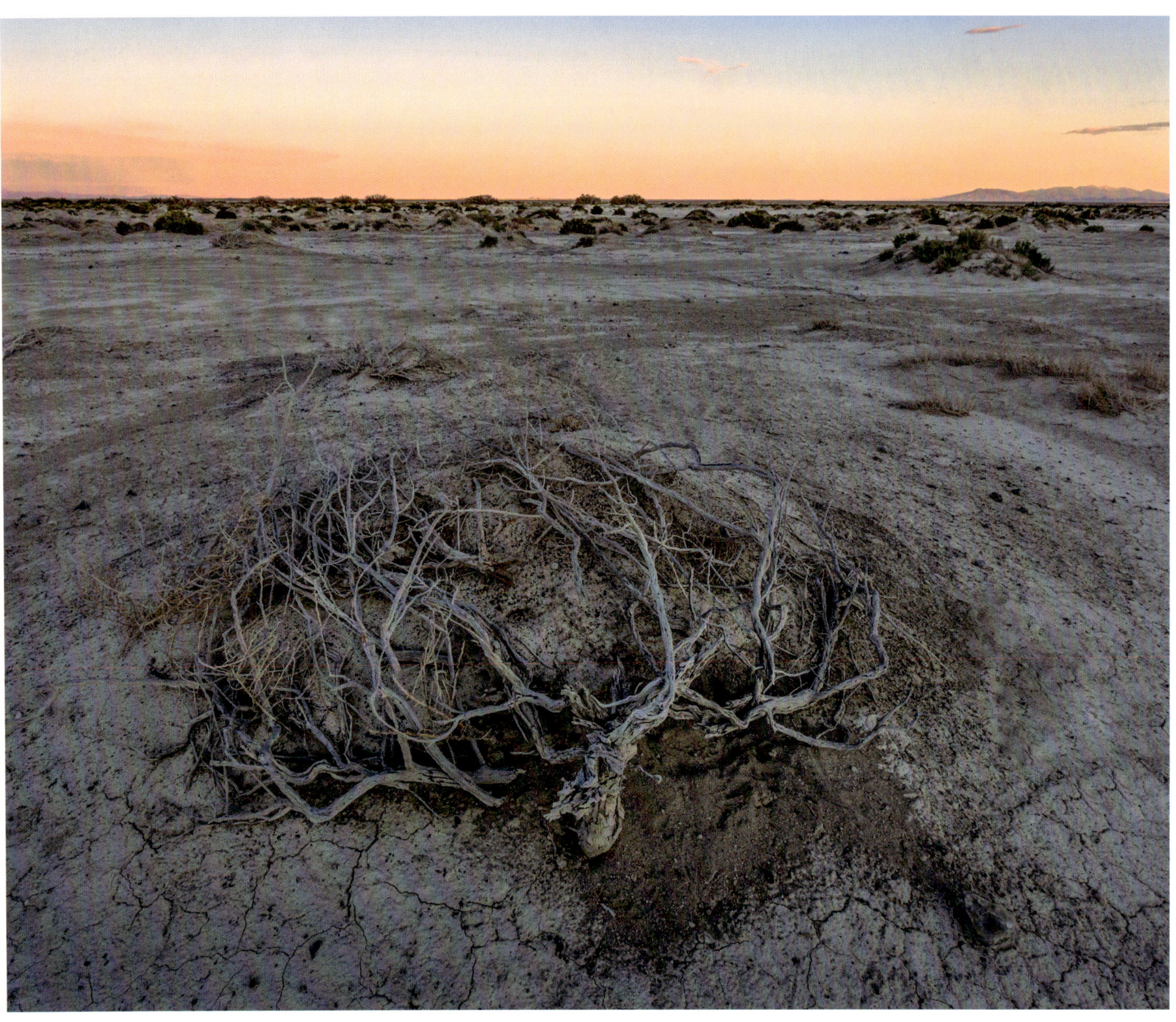

THE HARSH SALT PAN PLAYA STRETCHES FOR MILES ACROSS THE GREAT SALT LAKE DESERT.

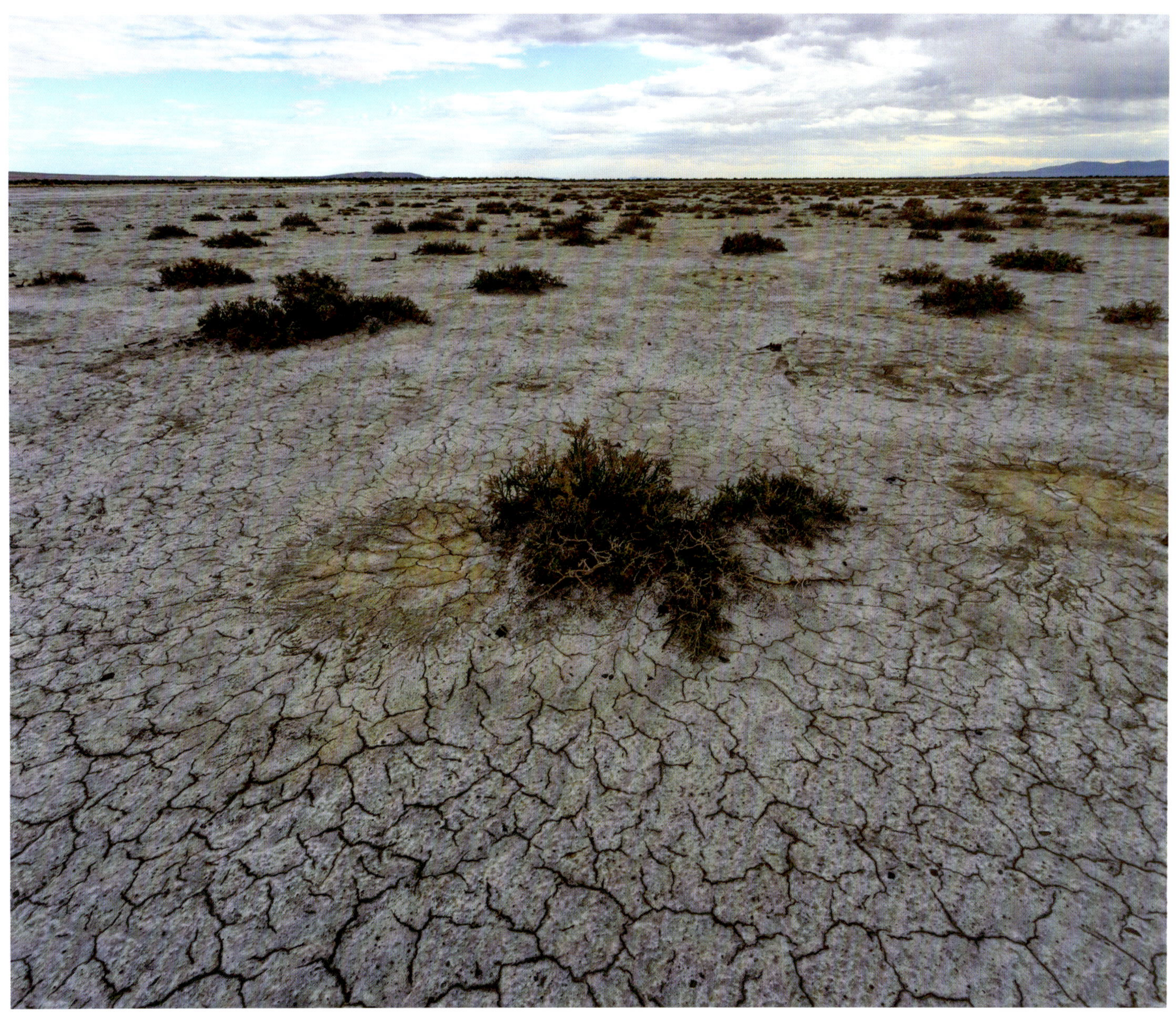

THE BROKEN CRUST OF THE SALT HILLS VALLEY SPREADS ENDLESSLY ACROSS THE WEST DESERT.

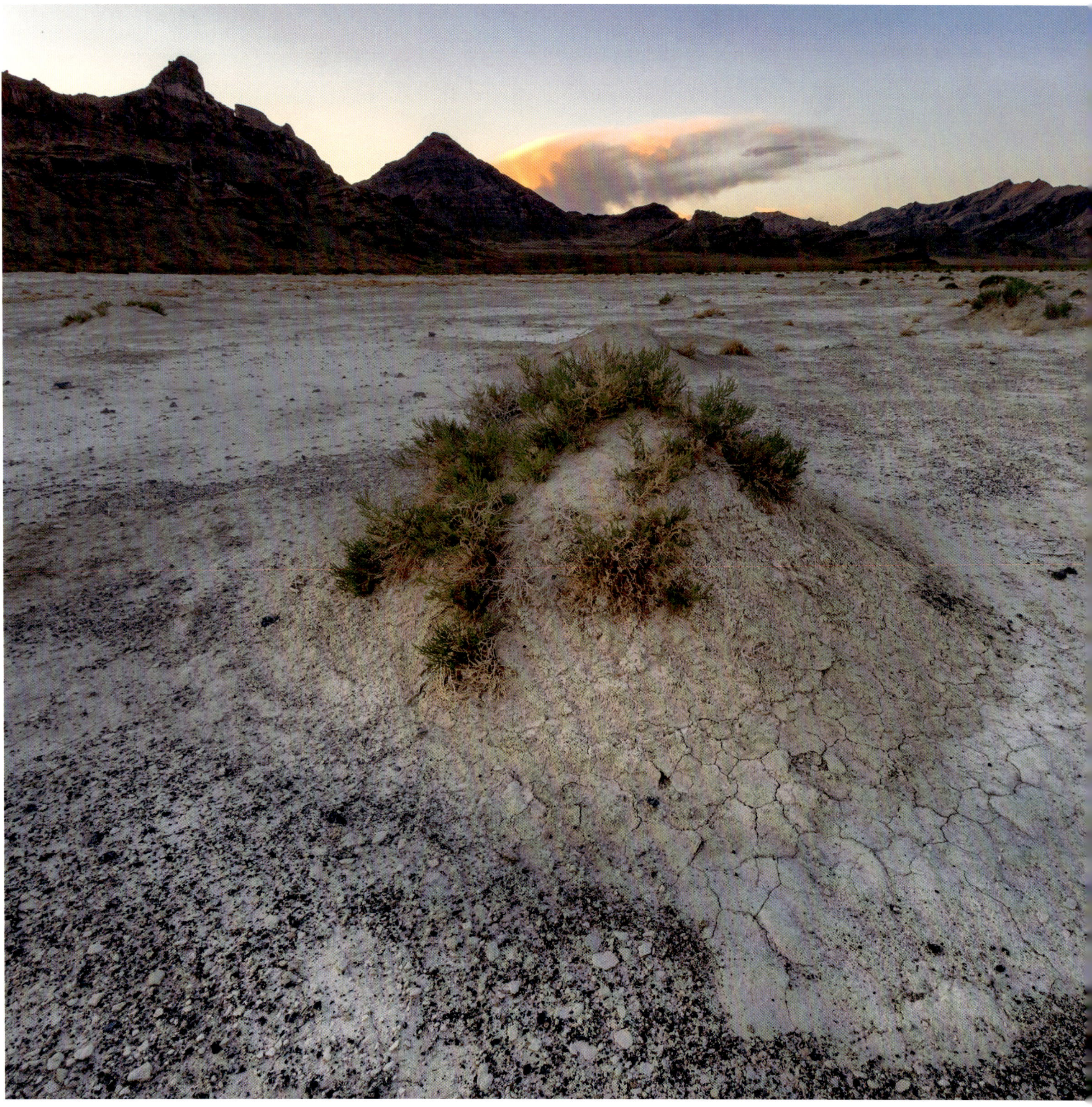

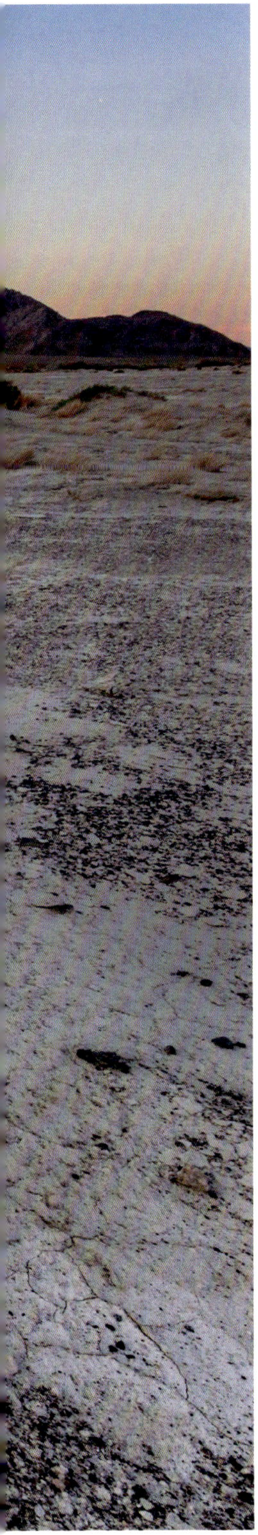

◀

TETZLAFF PEAK IN THE SILVER ISLAND MOUNTAINS BREAKS THE HORIZON OF THE GREAT SALT LAKE DESERT.

▶

THE SILVER ISLAND MOUNTAINS RISE 7,563 FEET ABOVE THE GREAT SALT LAKE DESERT.

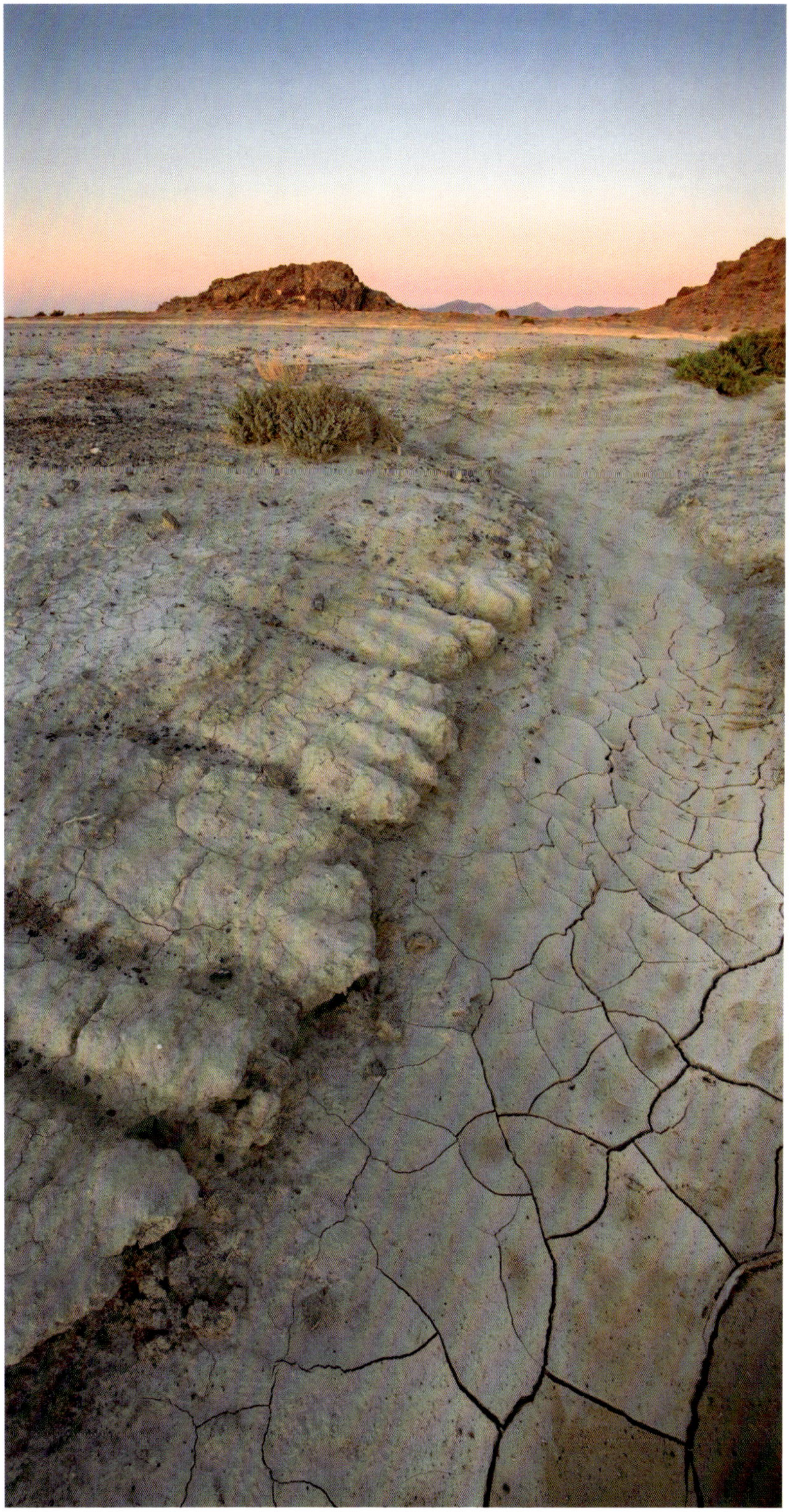

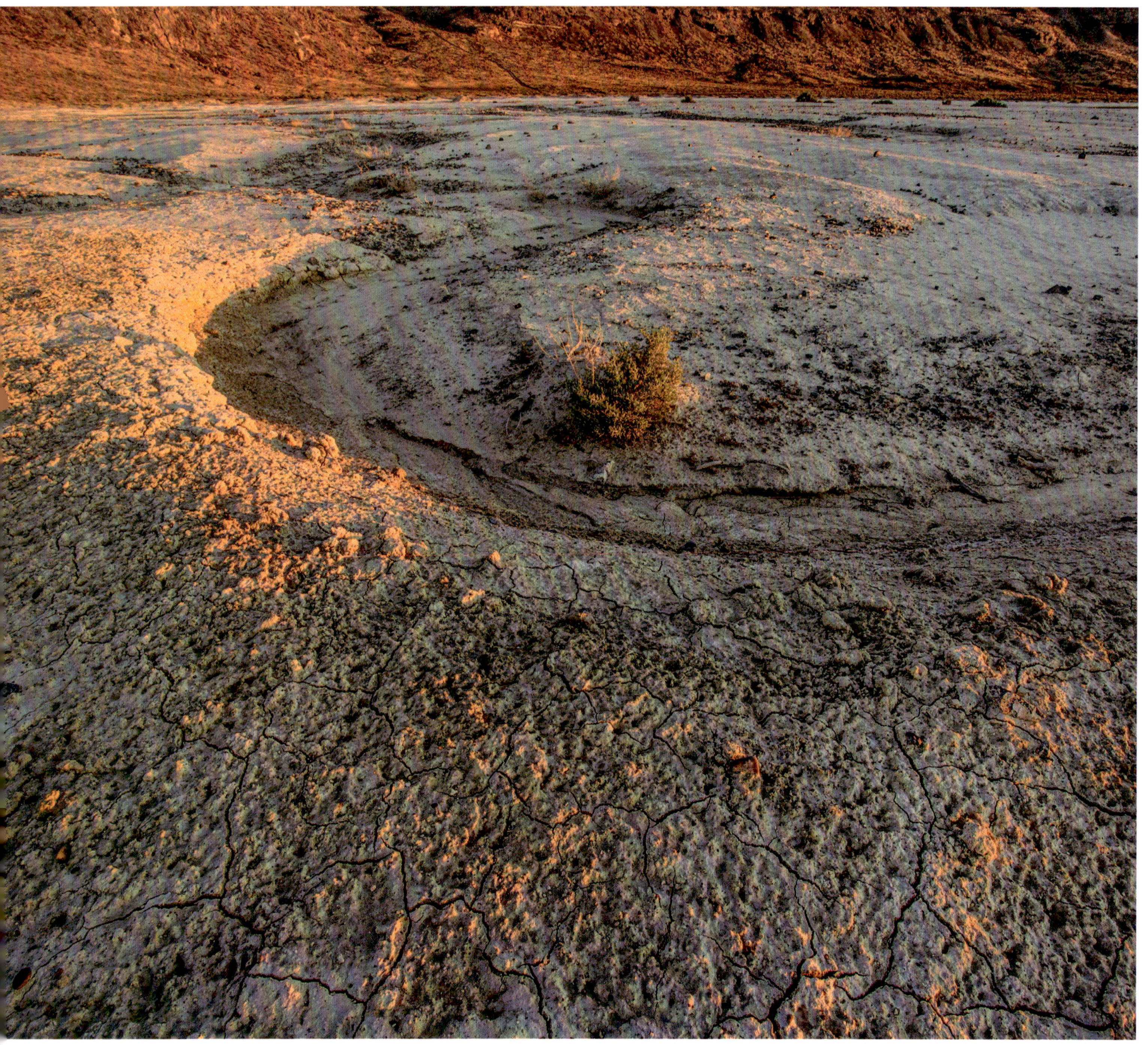

WATER CREATES DEPRESSIONS IN THE FRAGILE SALINE CRUST OF THE WEST DESERT.

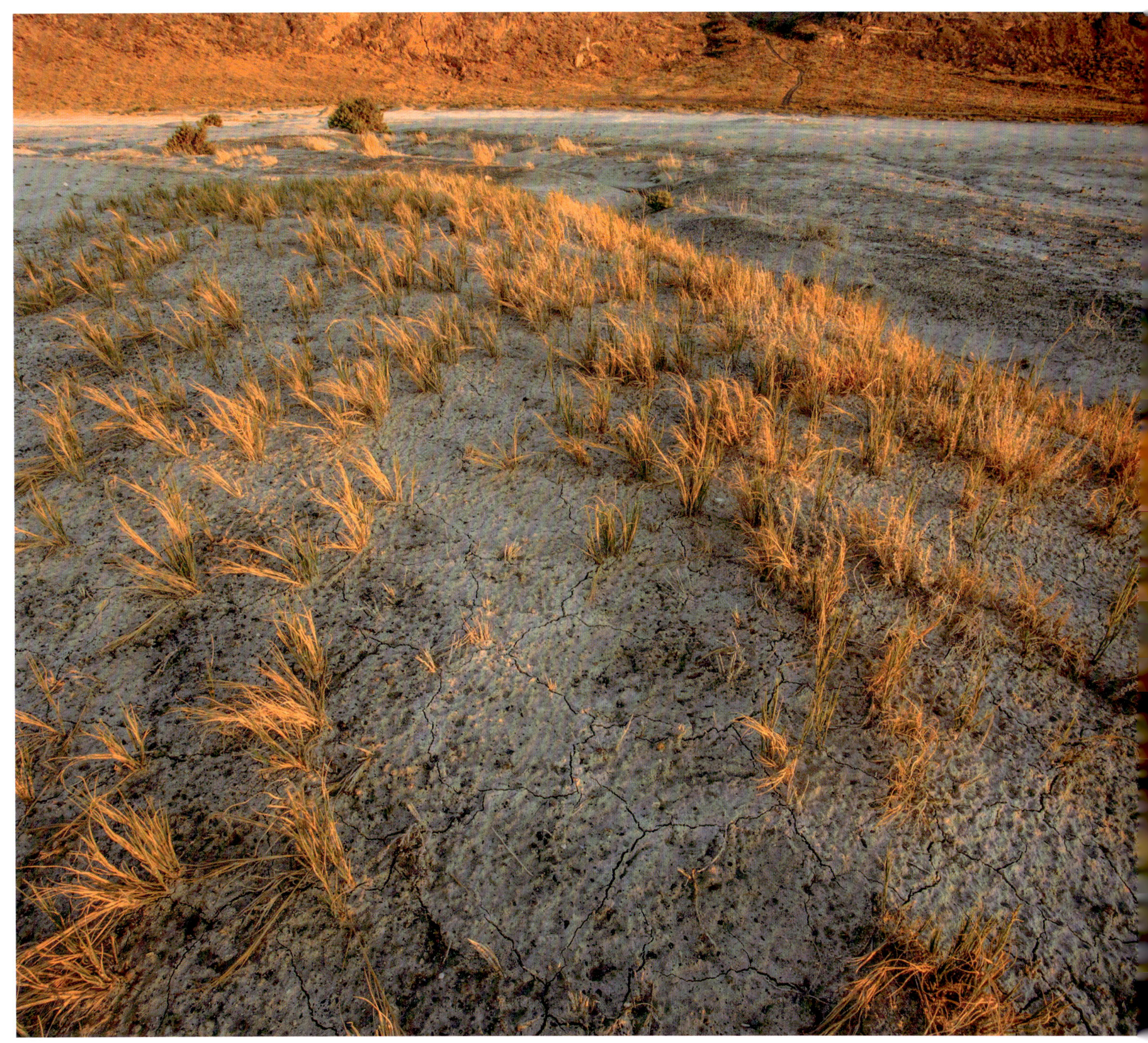

SALTGRASS WARMS IN THE SUMMER SUNRISE OF THE WEST DESERT.

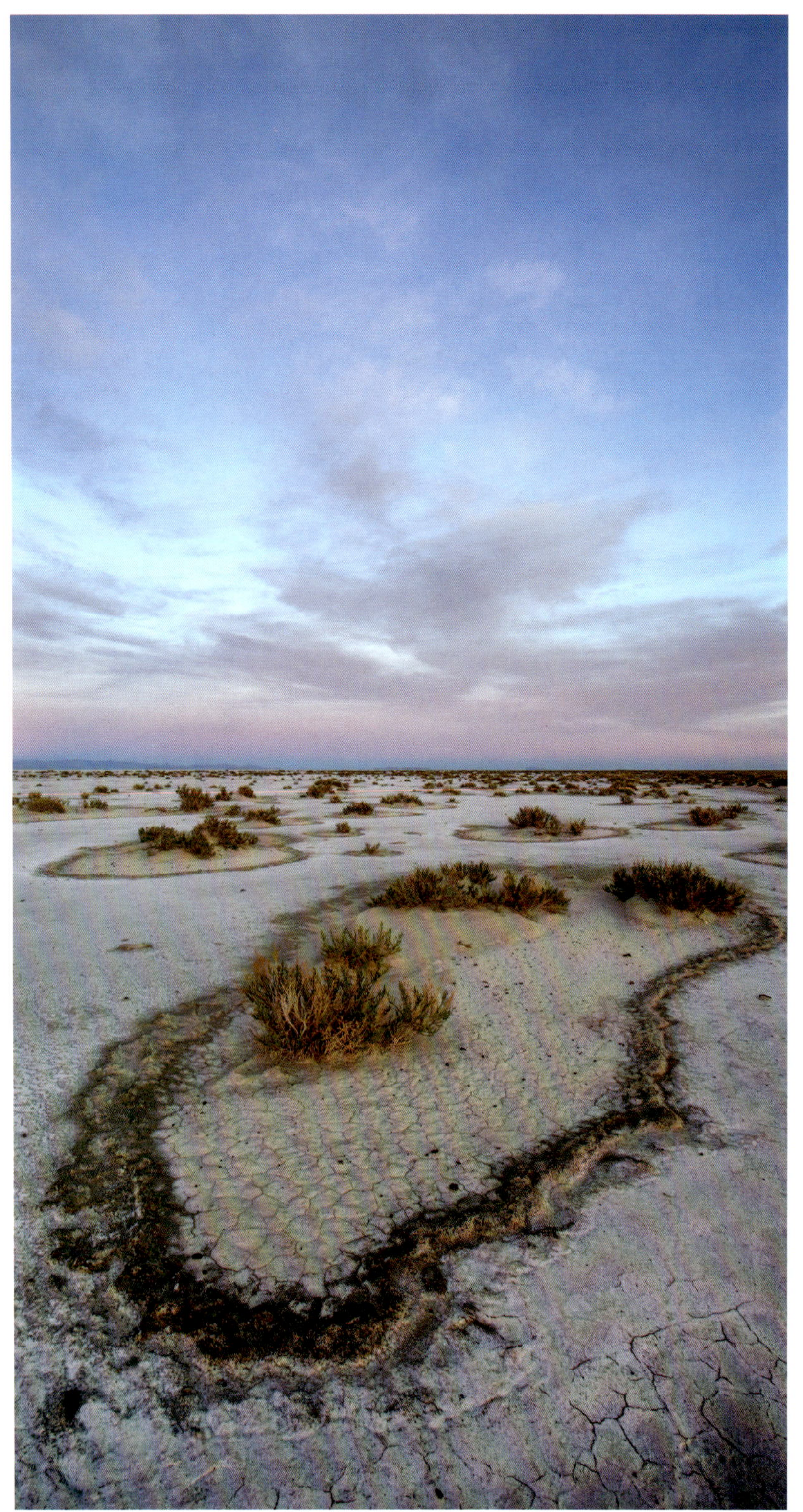

◀

SMALL SAND ISLANDS RISE FROM THE SALT PLAYA IN THE GREAT SALT LAKE DESERT.

▶

THE SILVER ISLAND MOUNTAINS BORDER THE WESTERN EDGE OF THE GREAT SALT LAKE DESERT ON THE UTAH-NEVADA BORDER.

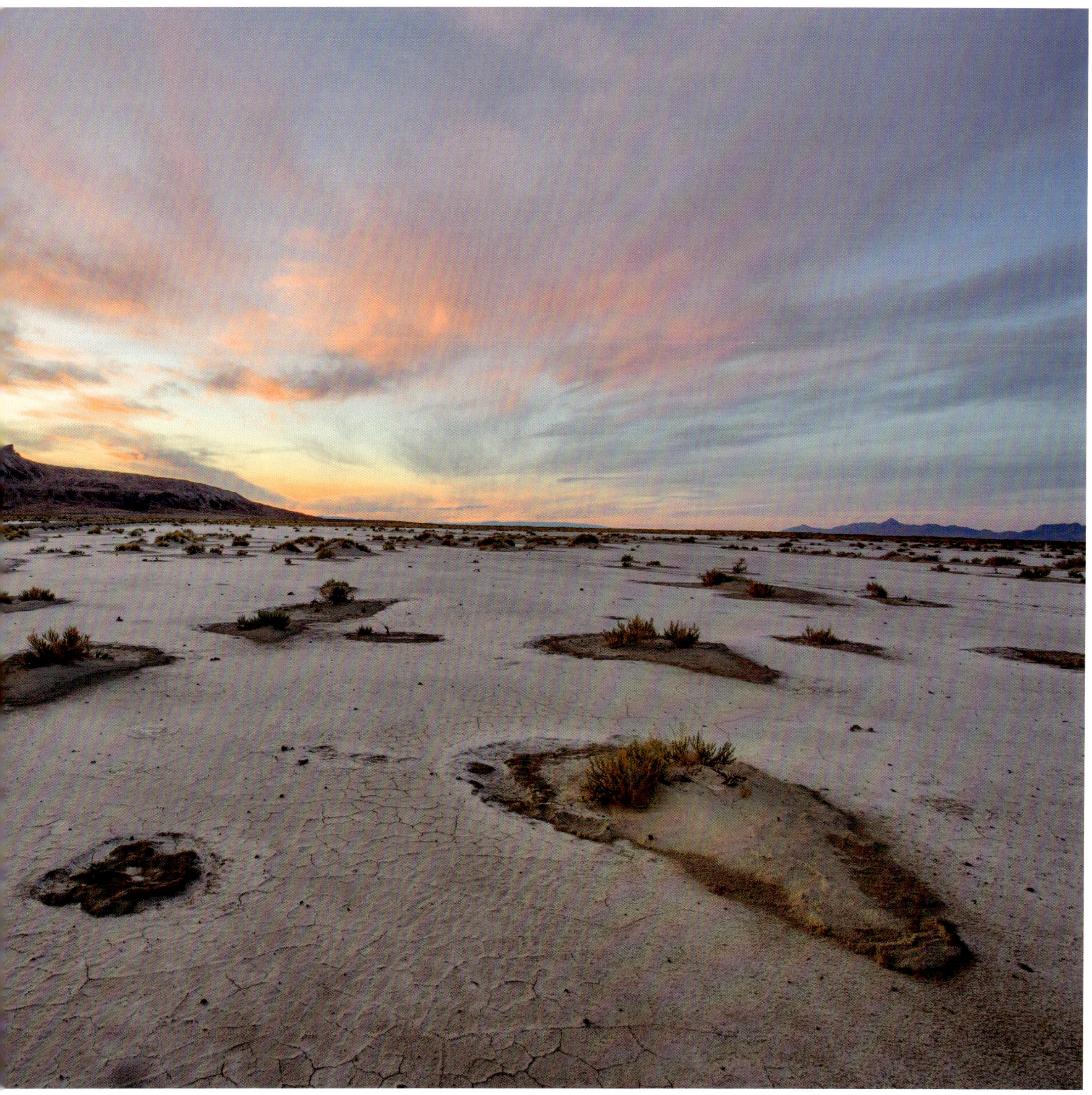

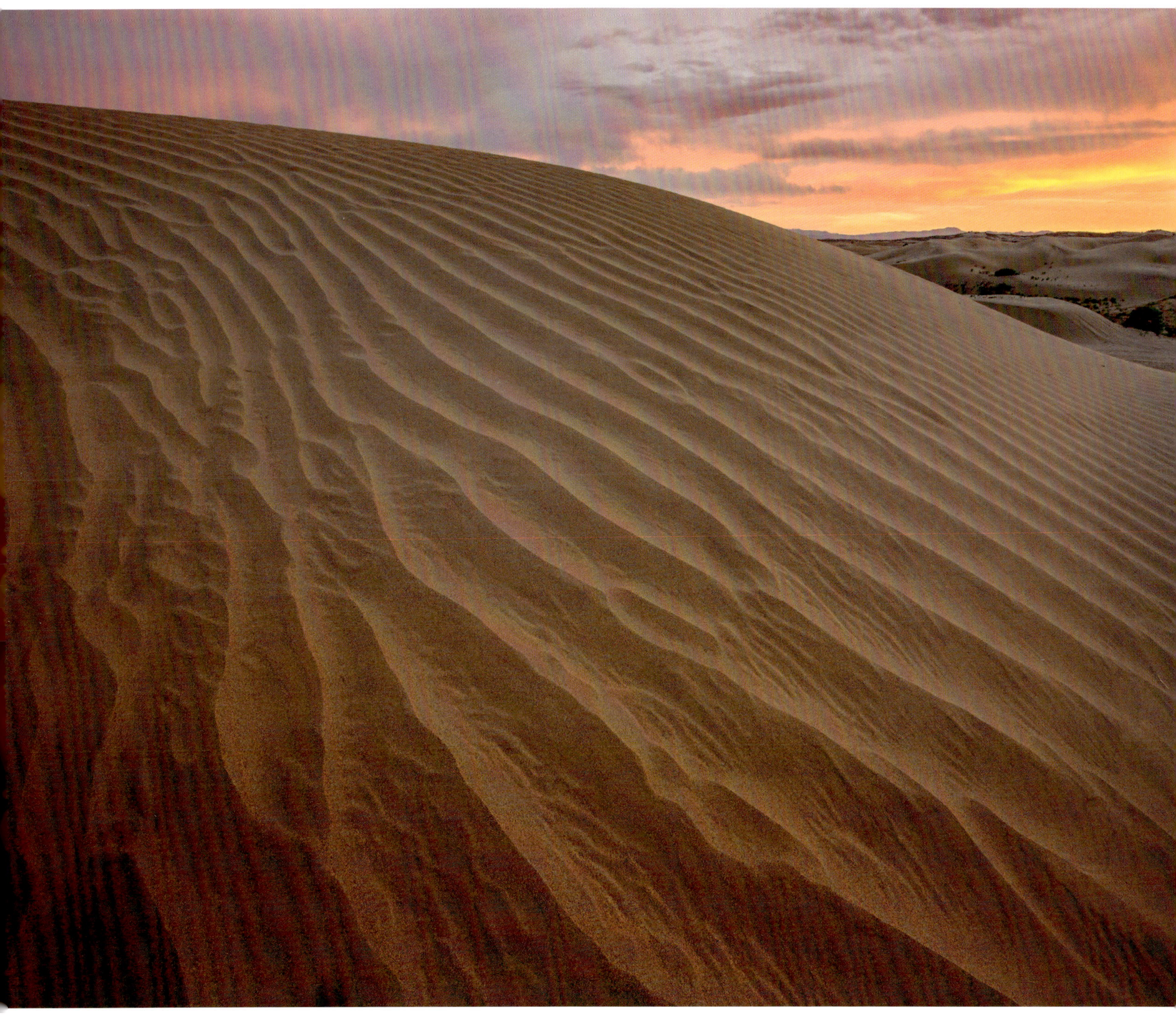

PERFECTLY SCULPTED DUNES IN THE LITTLE SAHARA RECREATION AREA.

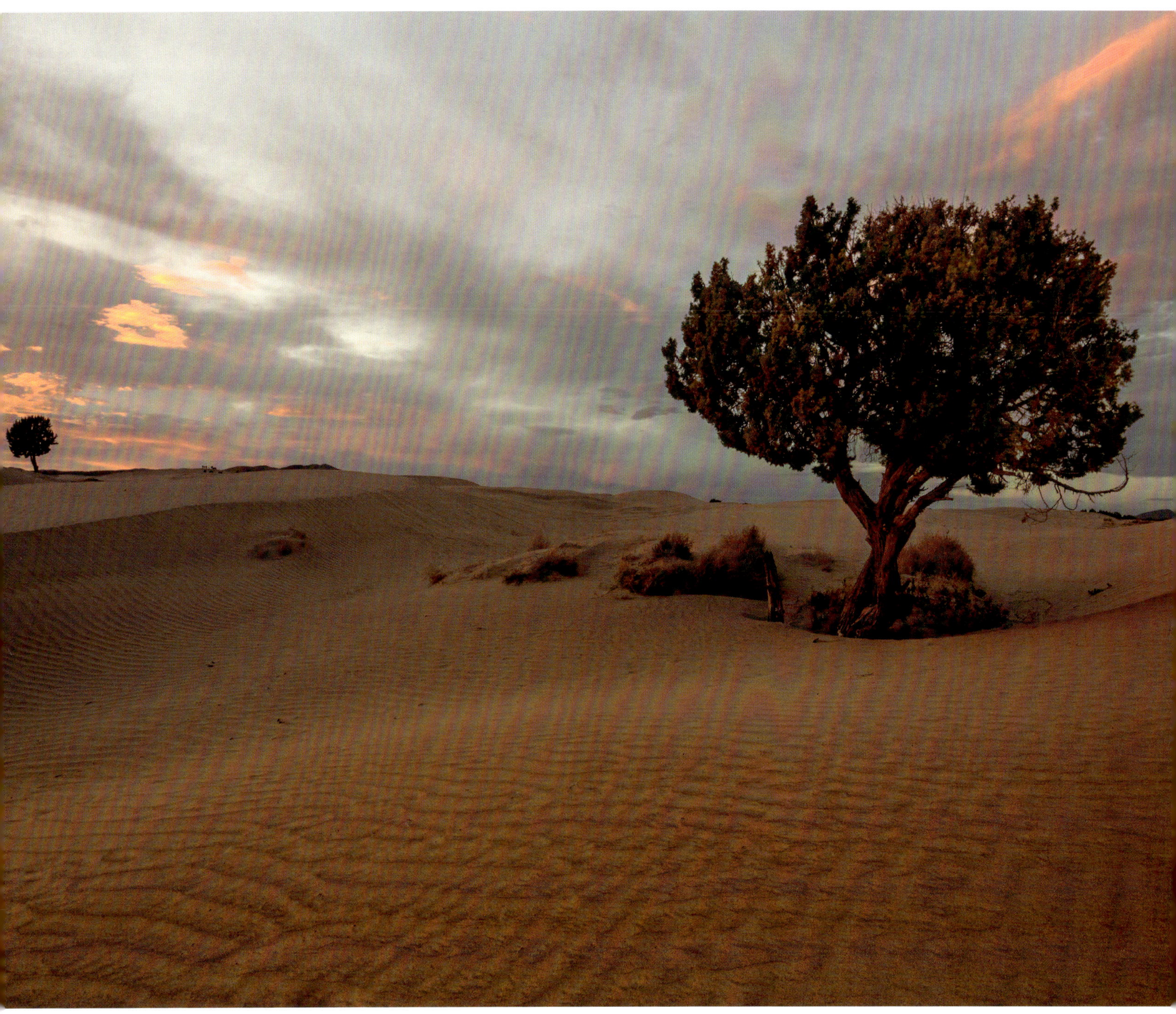

THE LITTLE SAHARA RECREATION AREA OFFERS A HARSH HOME FOR JUNIPER TREES.

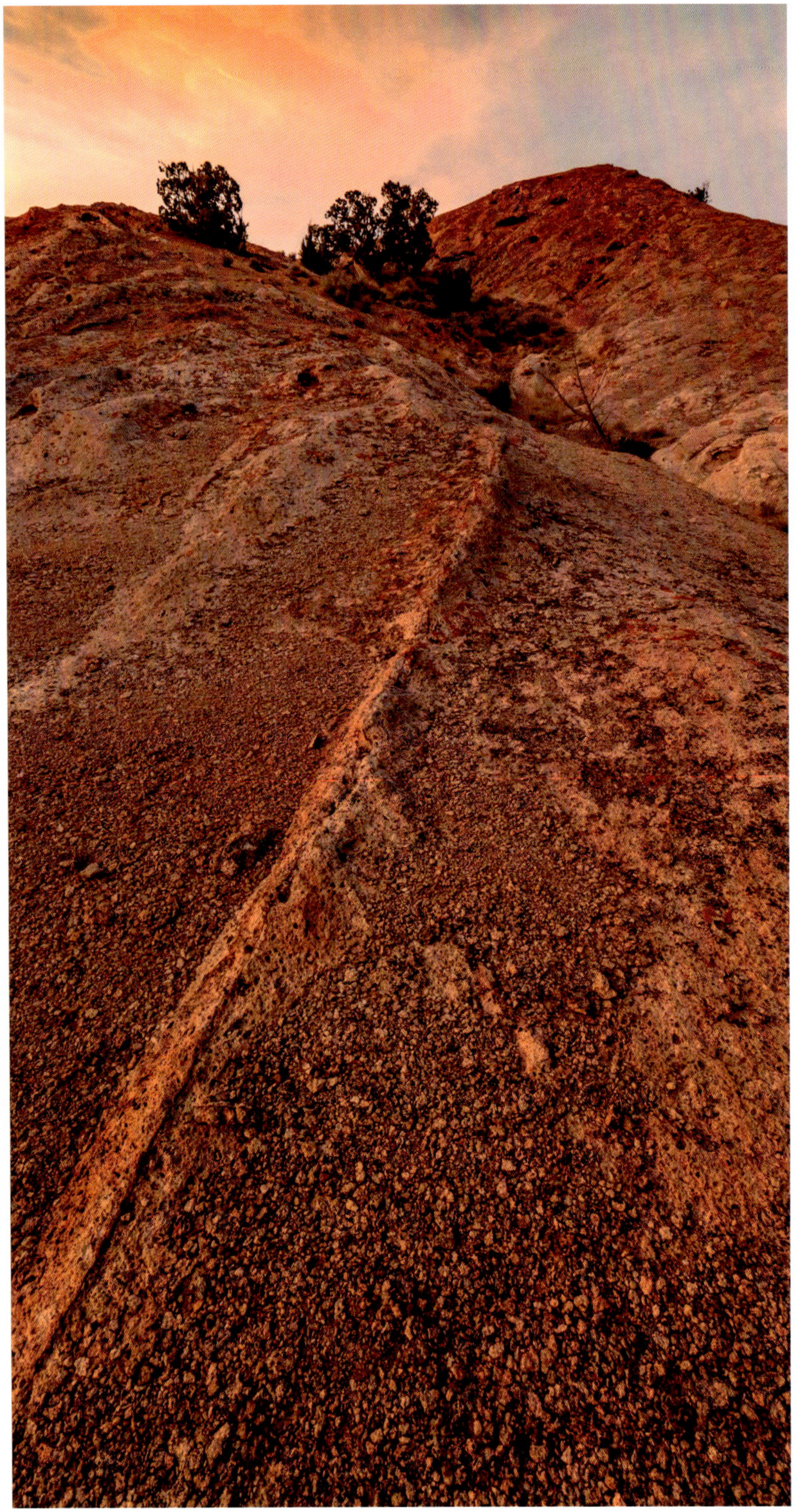

◀

RED ROCK FORMATIONS IN THE DELL, THOMAS RANGE.

▶

THE DELL, IN THE THOMAS RANGE, NEAR TOPAZ MOUNTAIN.

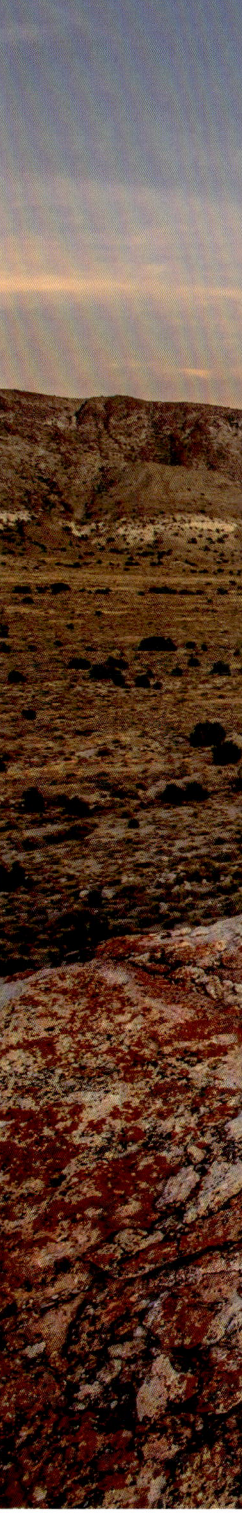

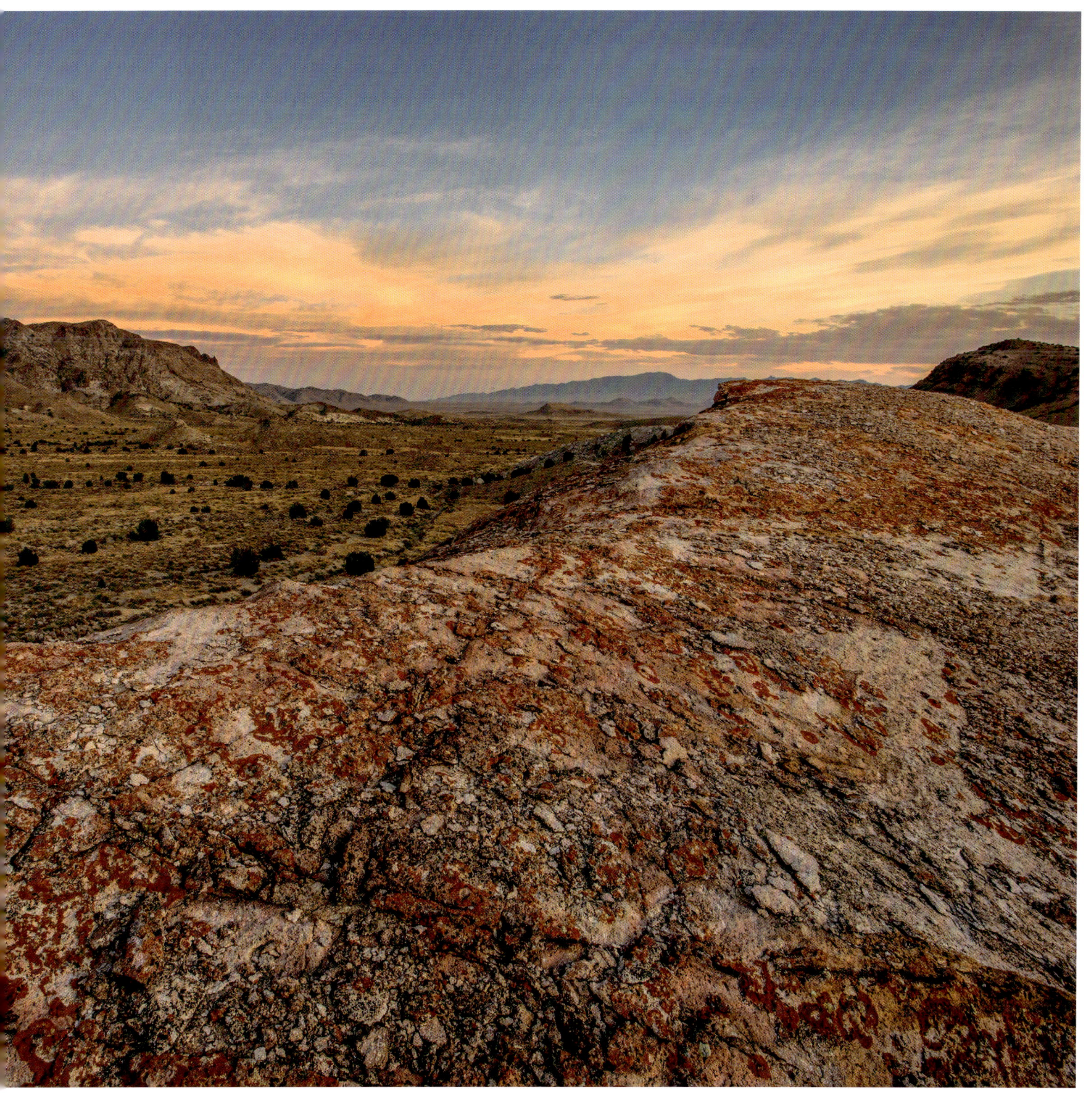

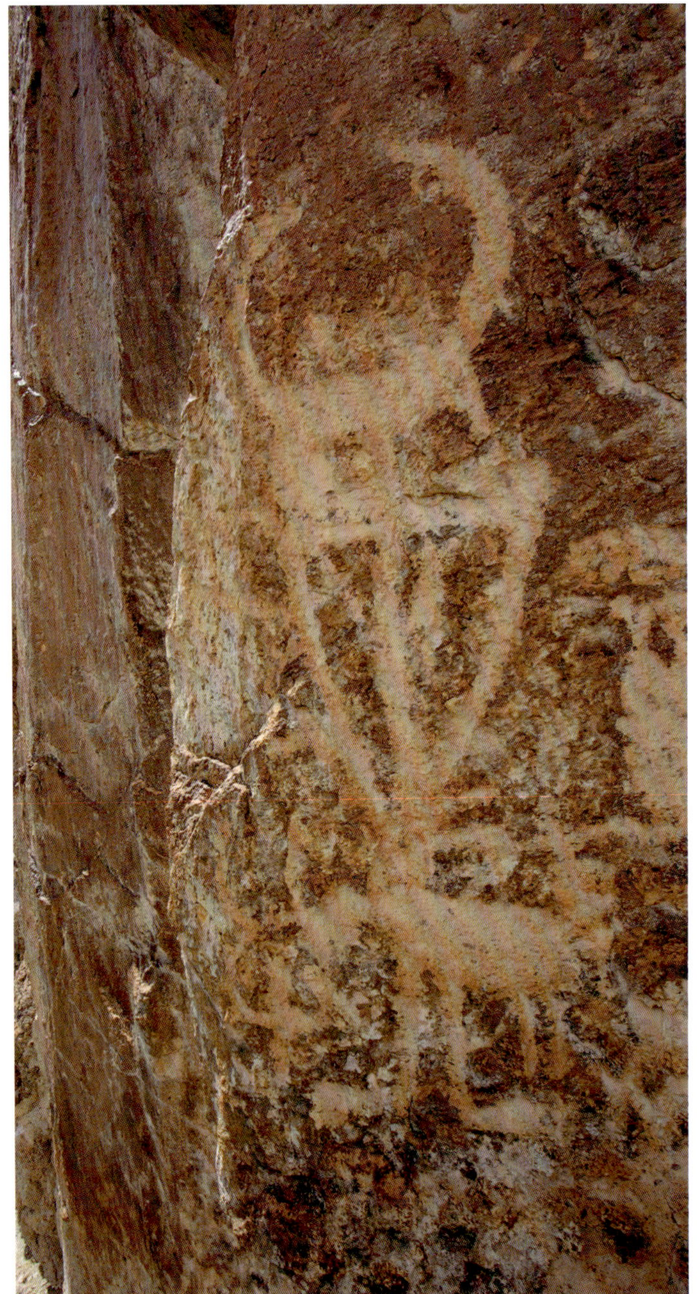

PETROGLYPHS AT FREMONT INDIAN STATE PARK.

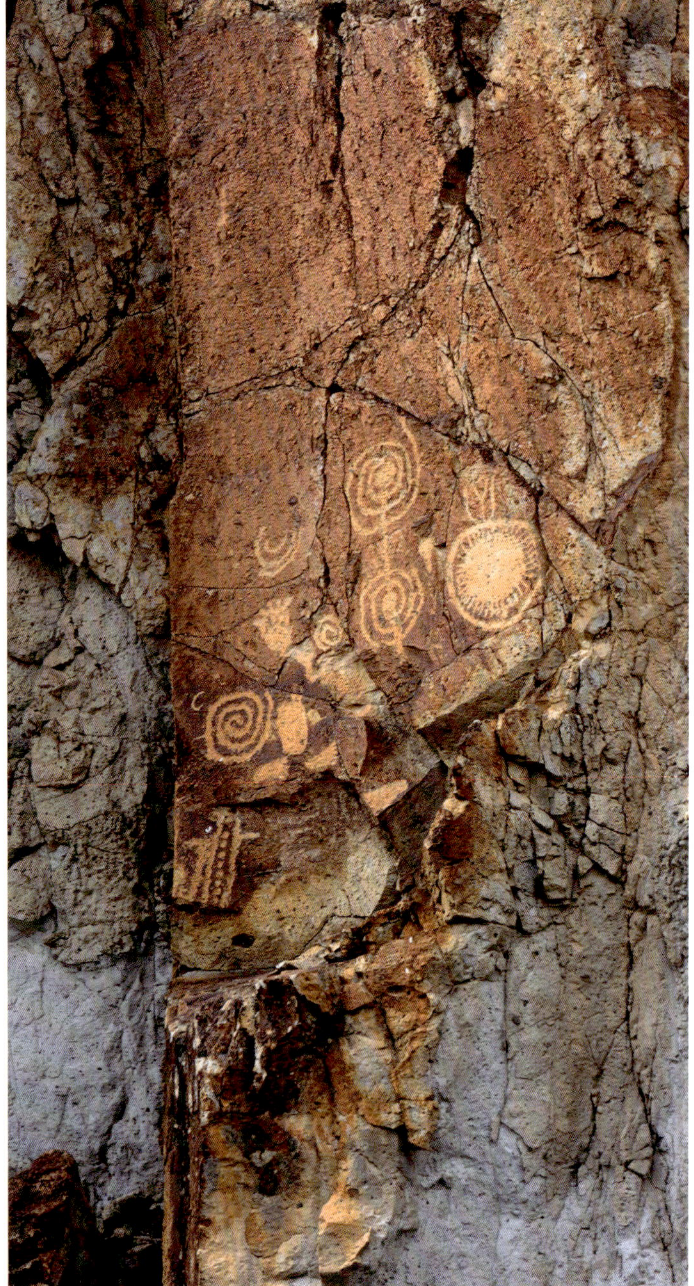

PETROGLYPHS DECORATE THE CLIFF EDGE AT FREMONT INDIAN STATE PARK.

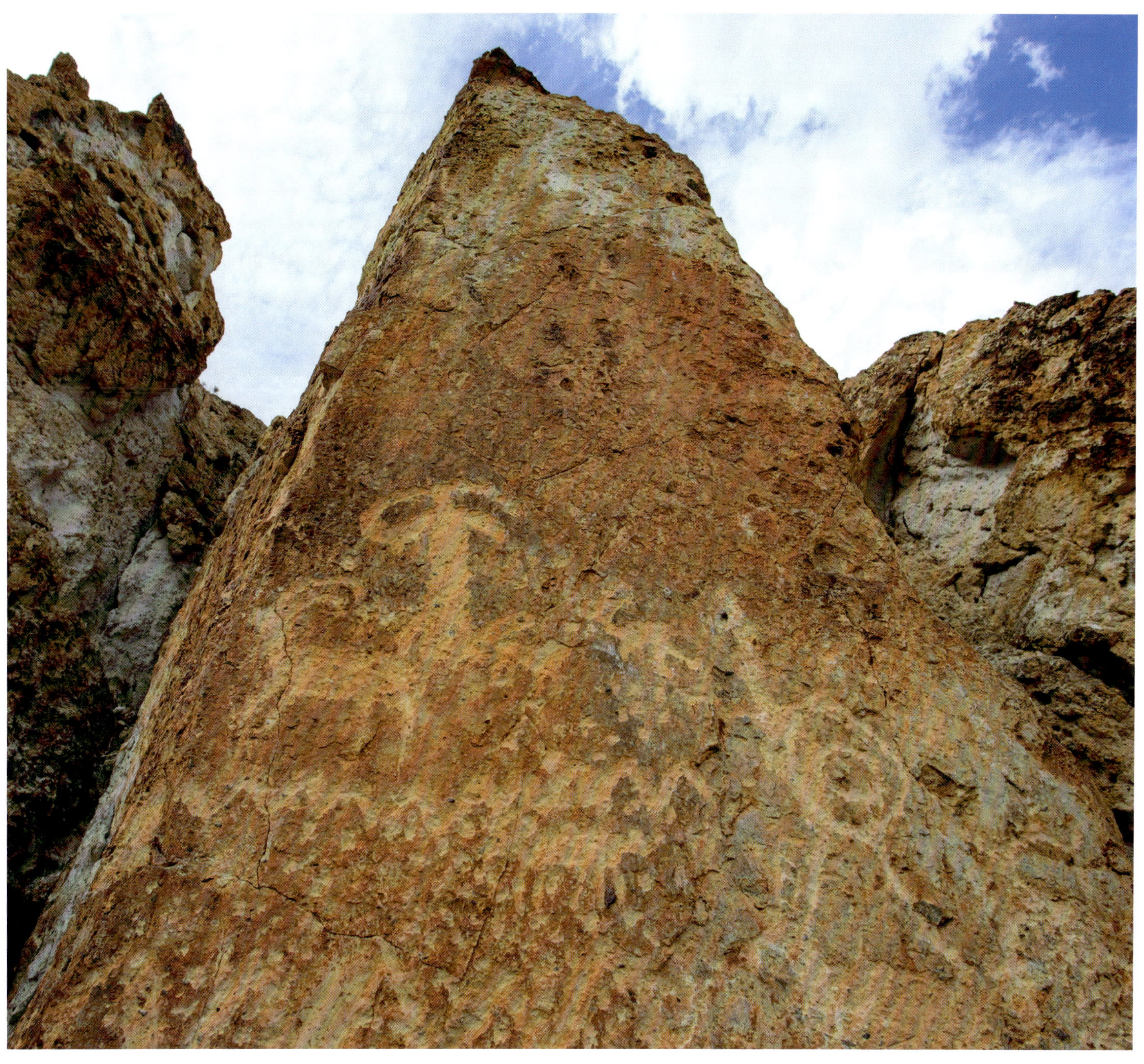

PETROGLYPHS AT FREMONT INDIAN STATE PARK.

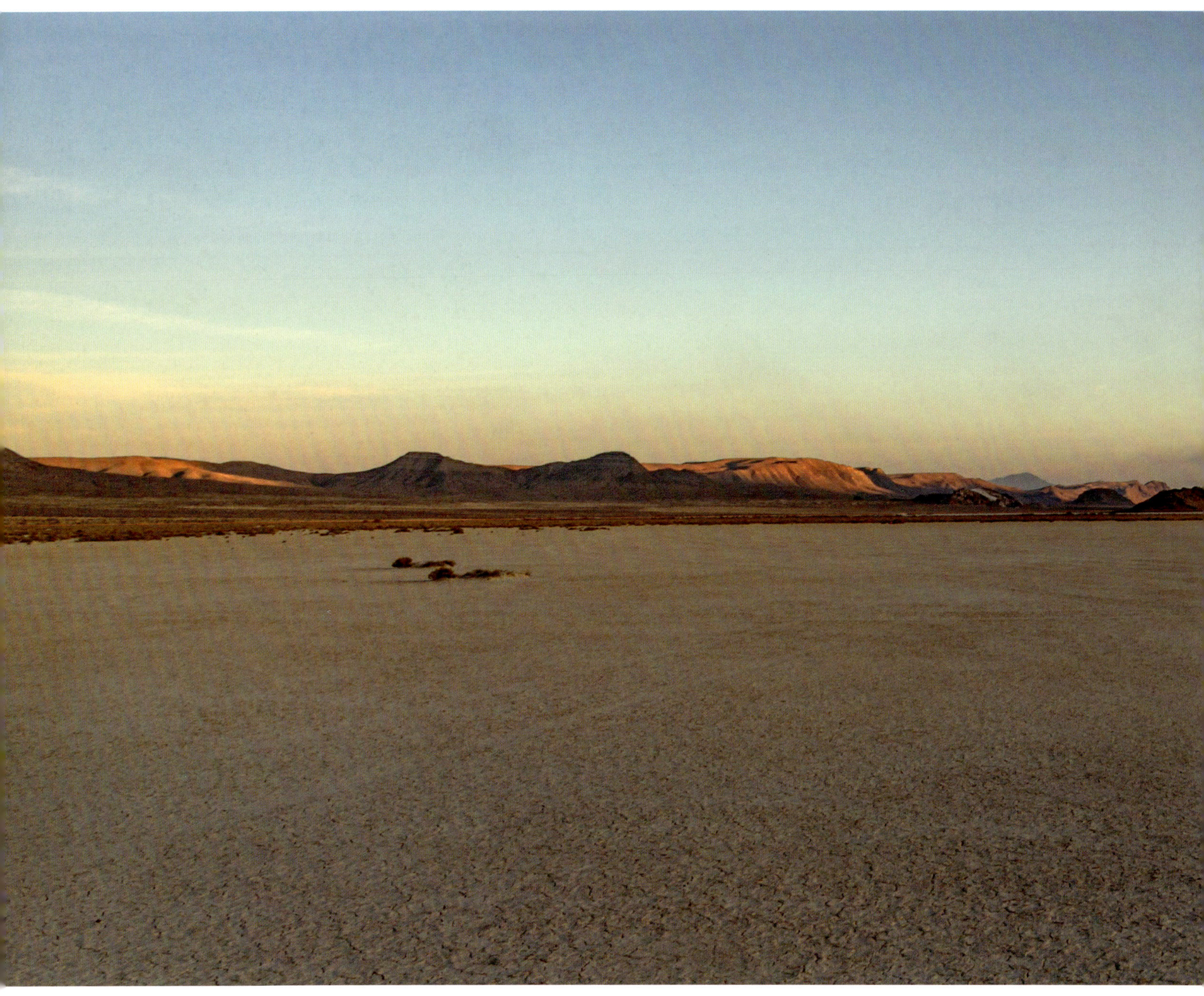

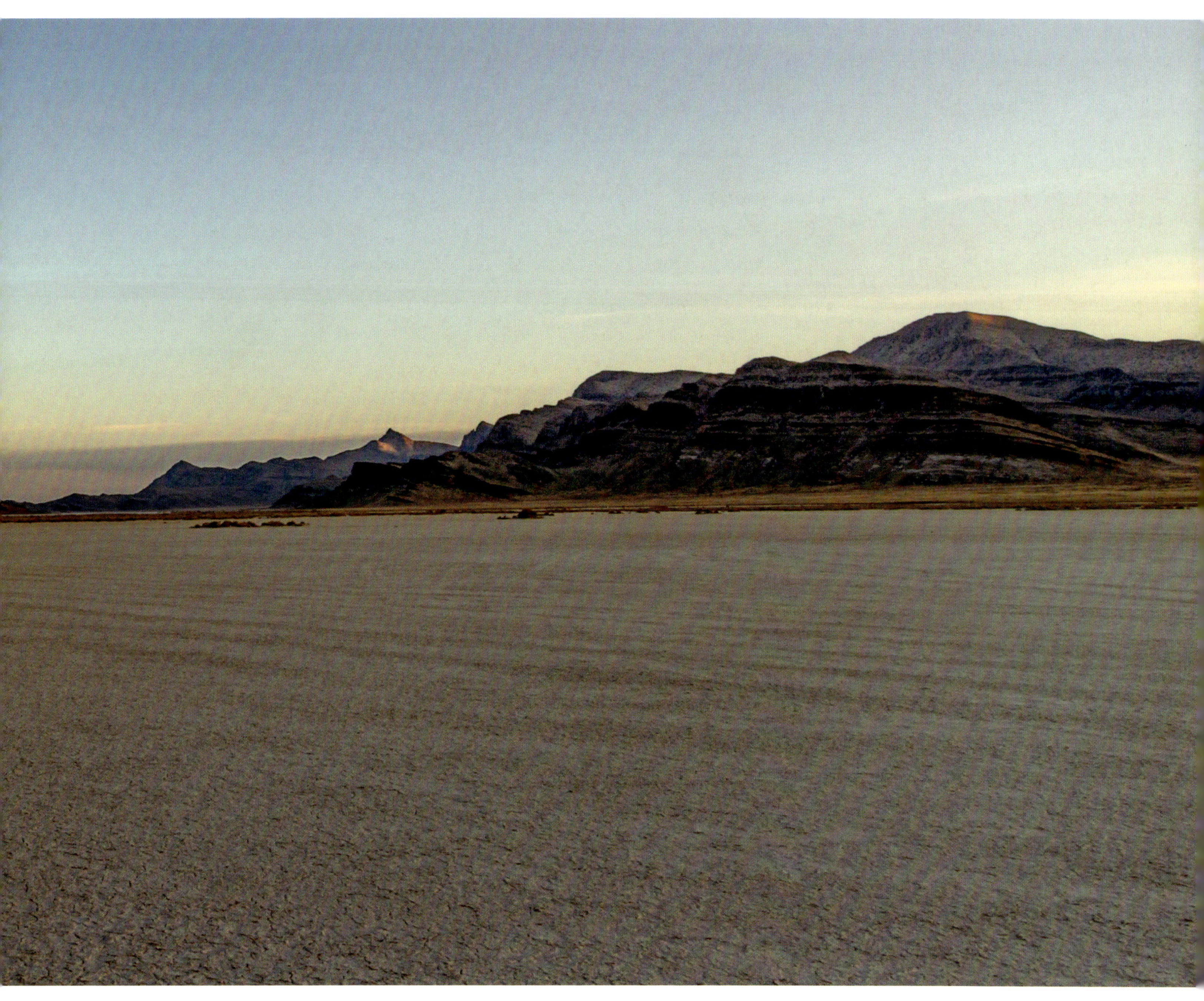

THE TULE VALLEY HARDPAN SEEMS TO FLOW UP TO THE BASE OF THE BURBANK HILLS IN THE FERGUSON DESERT.

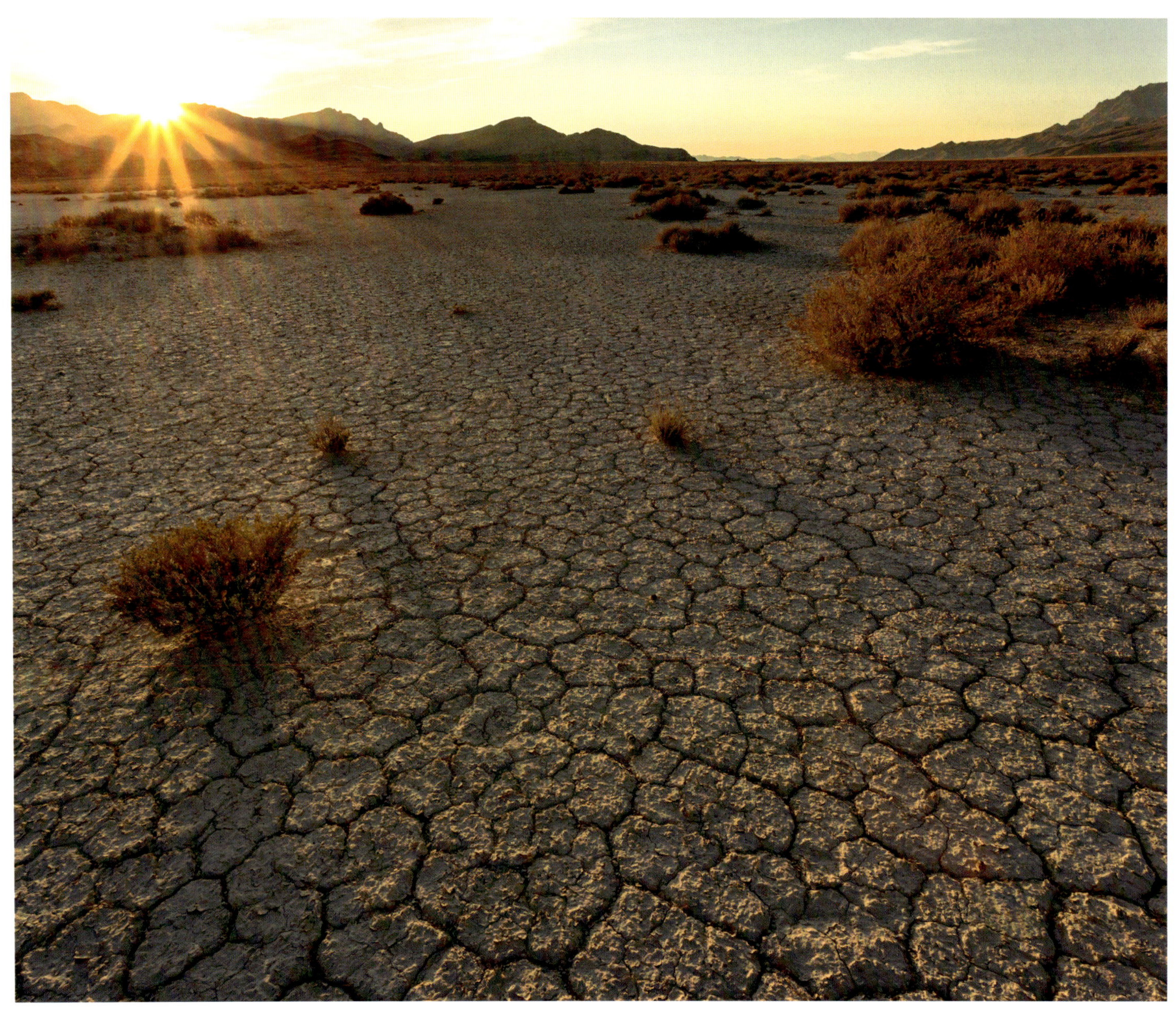

▲
THE SUN DROPS BELOW THE RUGGED RIDGELINES BETWEEN THE NOTCH PEAK AND THE KING TOP WILDERNESS STUDY AREAS.

▶
GRAPHIC PATTERNS IN THE FLAT HARDPAN OF THE TULE VALLEY, CONFUSION RANGE.

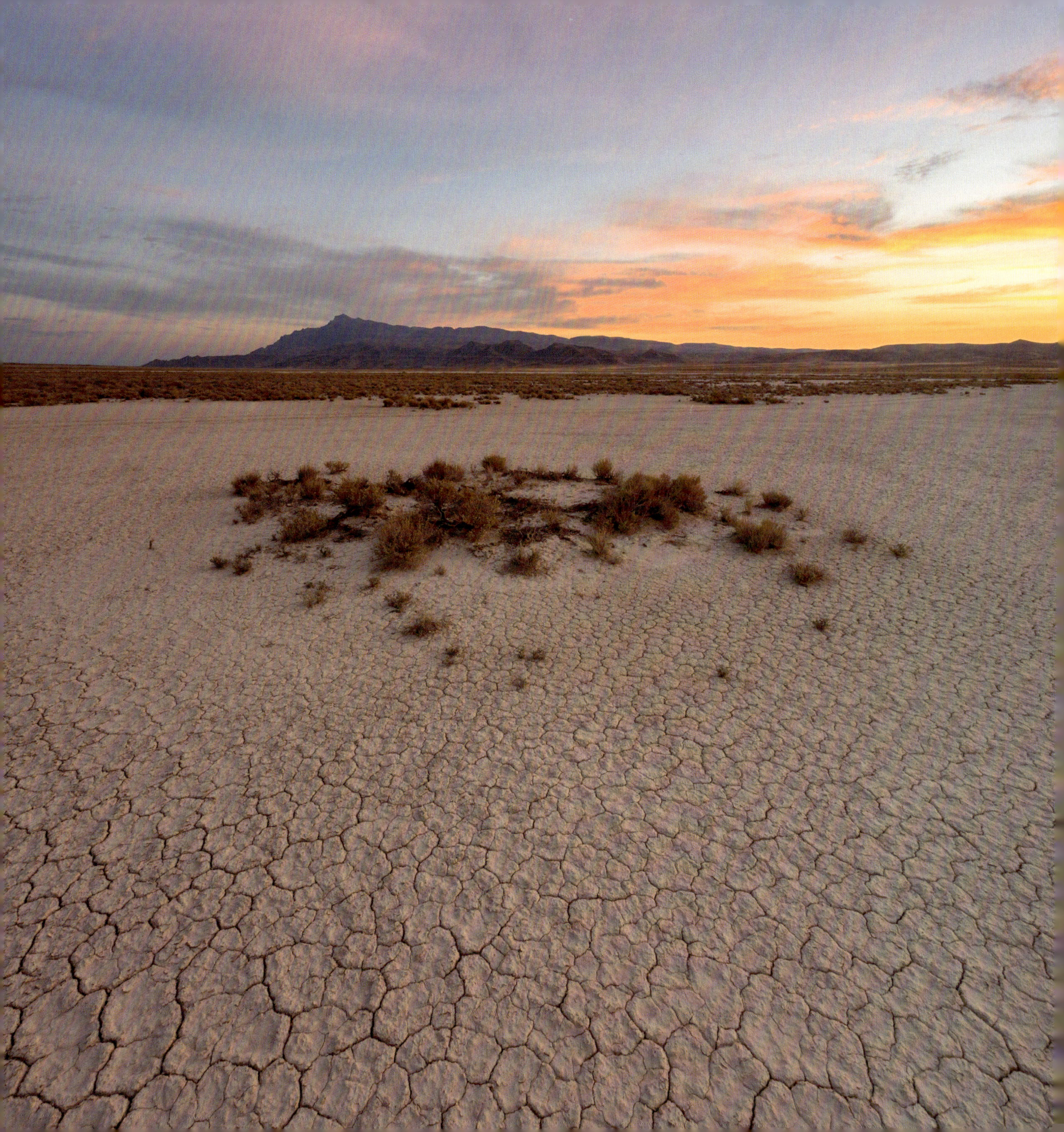

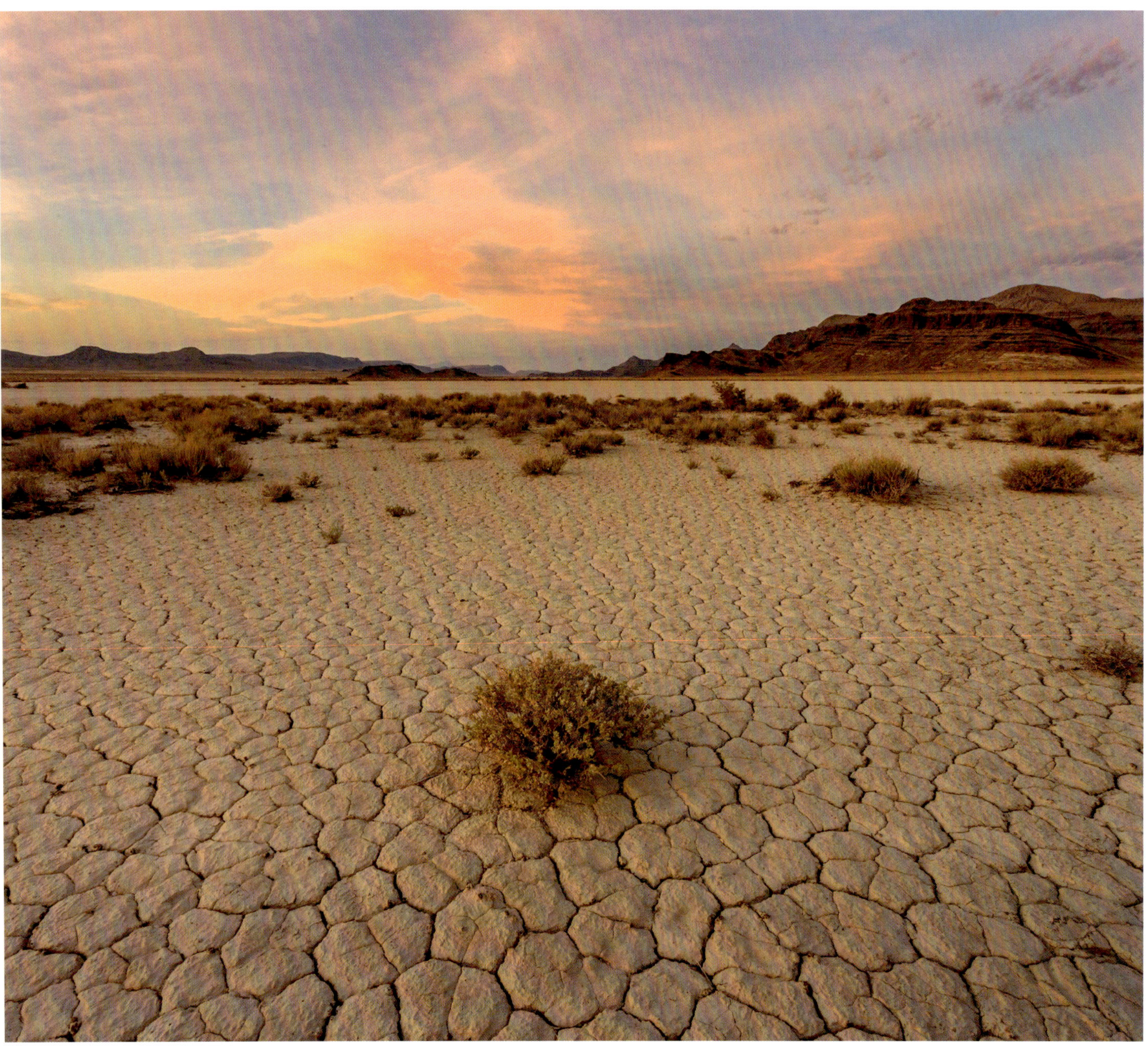

CRACKED EARTH IN THE ARID DESERT BETWEEN THE CONFUSION RANGE AND THE BURBANK HILLS.

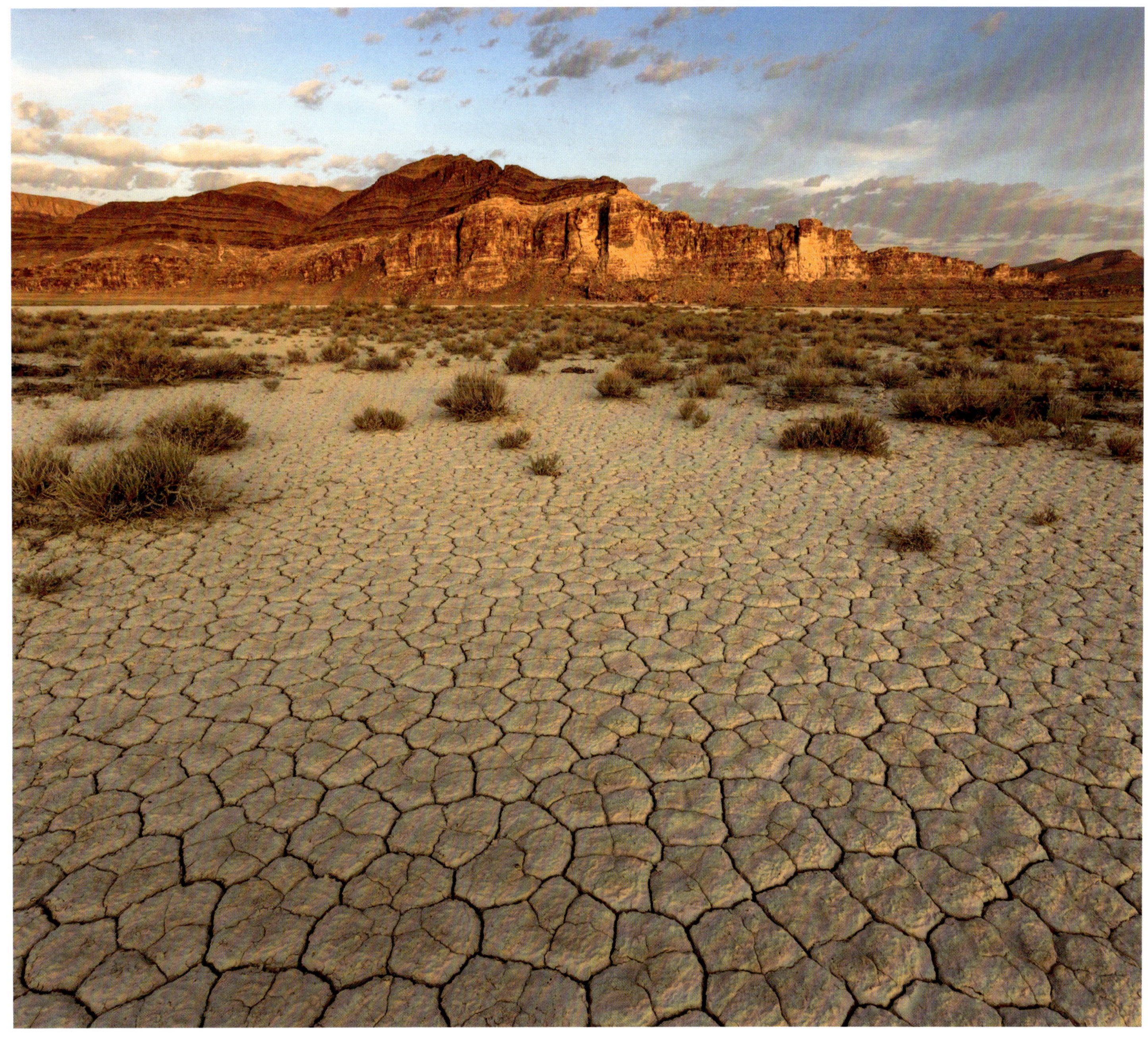

KING TOP WILDERNESS STUDY AREA IN THE SEVIER DESERT.

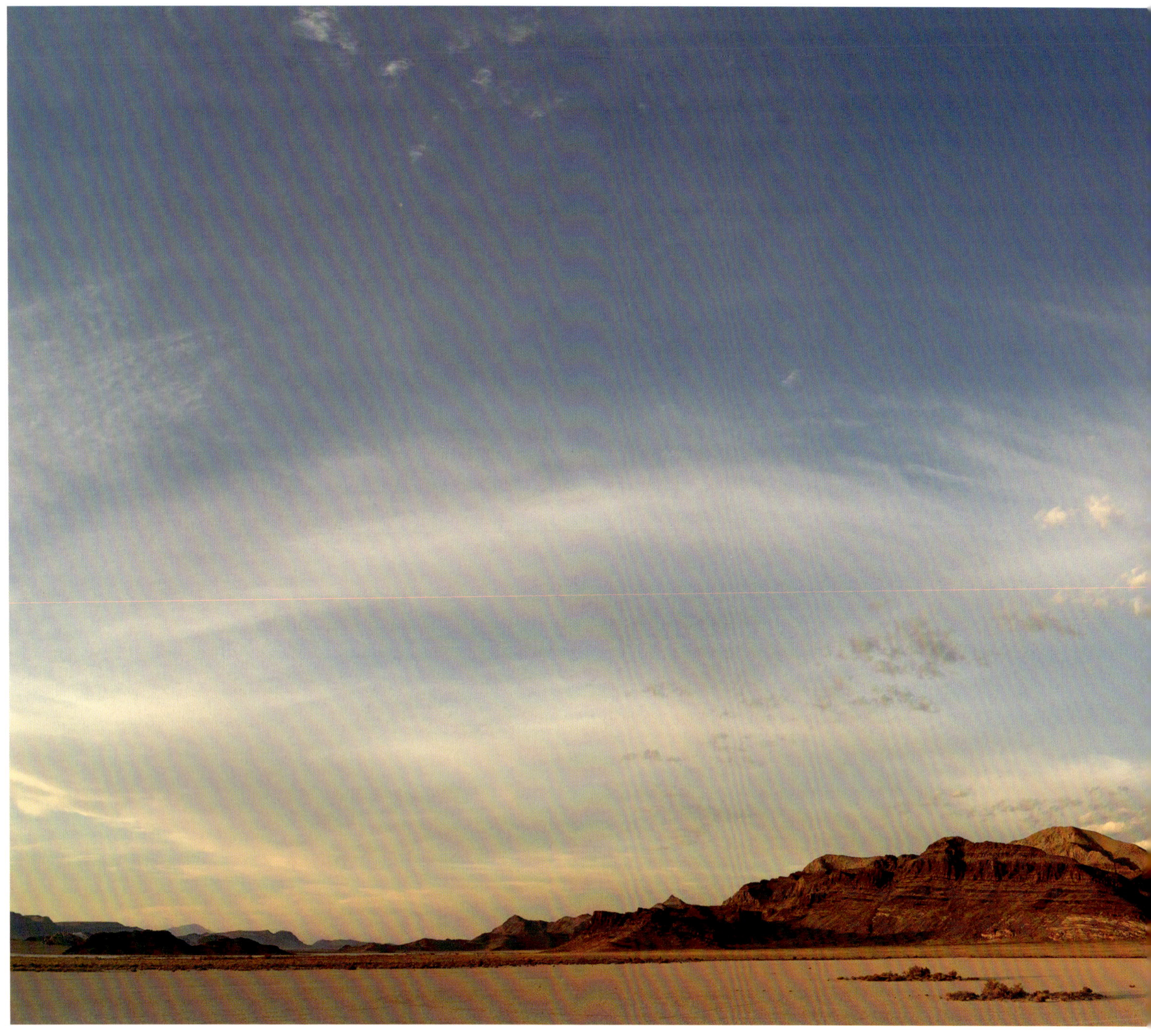

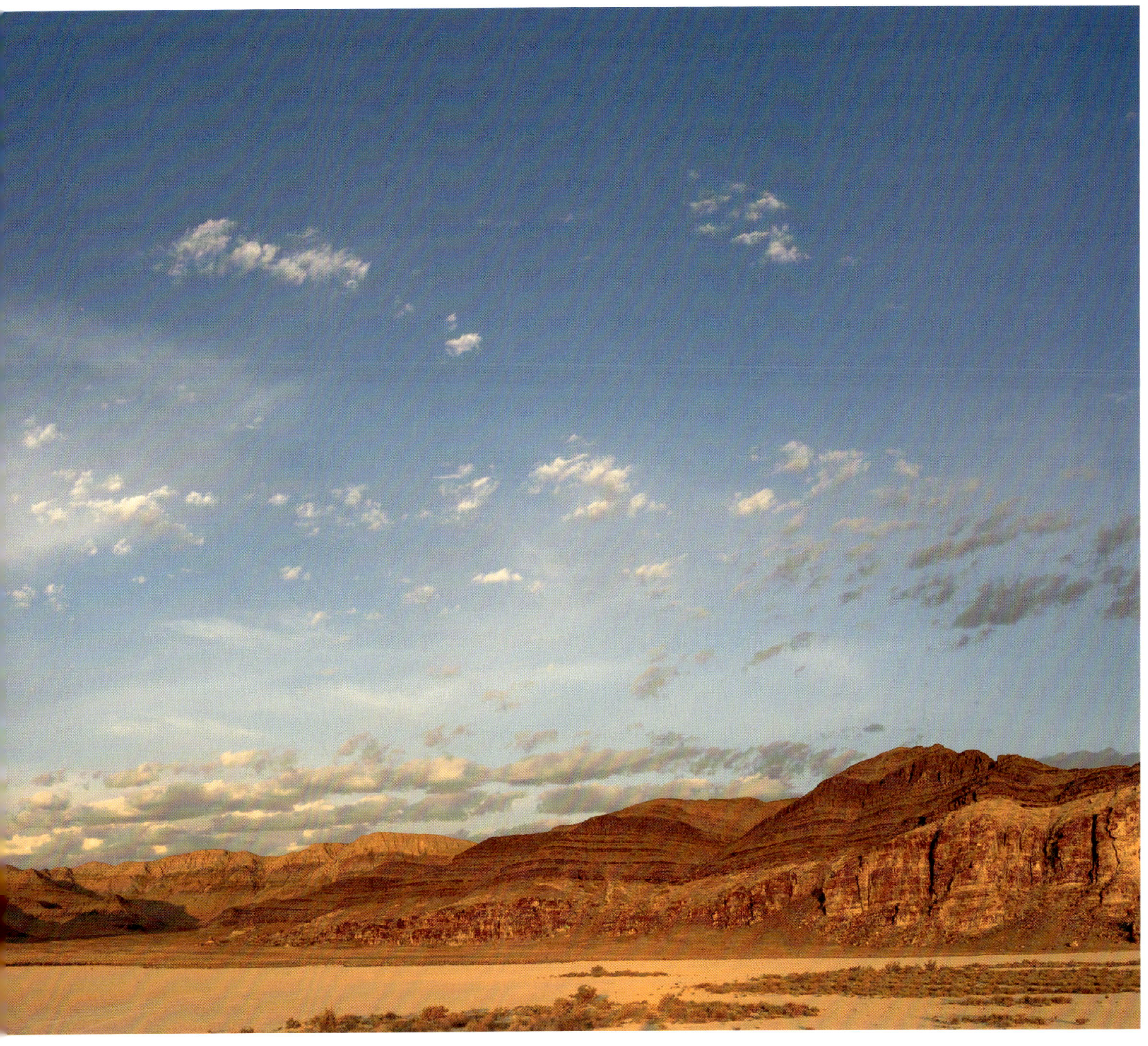

THE BARN HILLS IN THE FERGUSON DESERT, A SUBDESERT OF THE GREAT BASIN.

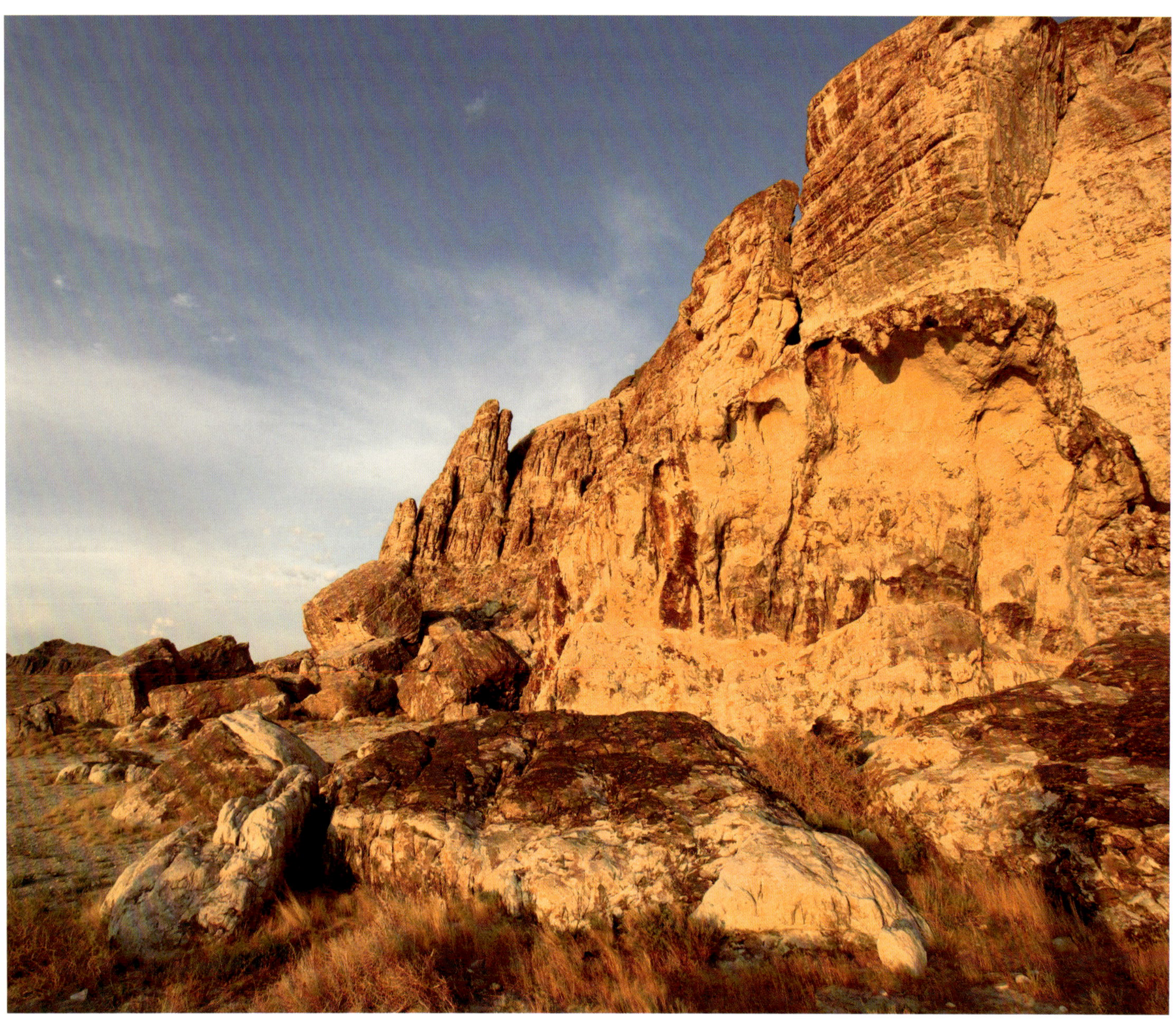

WILD SHAPES IN THE BARN HILLS NEAR THE KING TOP WILDERNESS STUDY AREA.

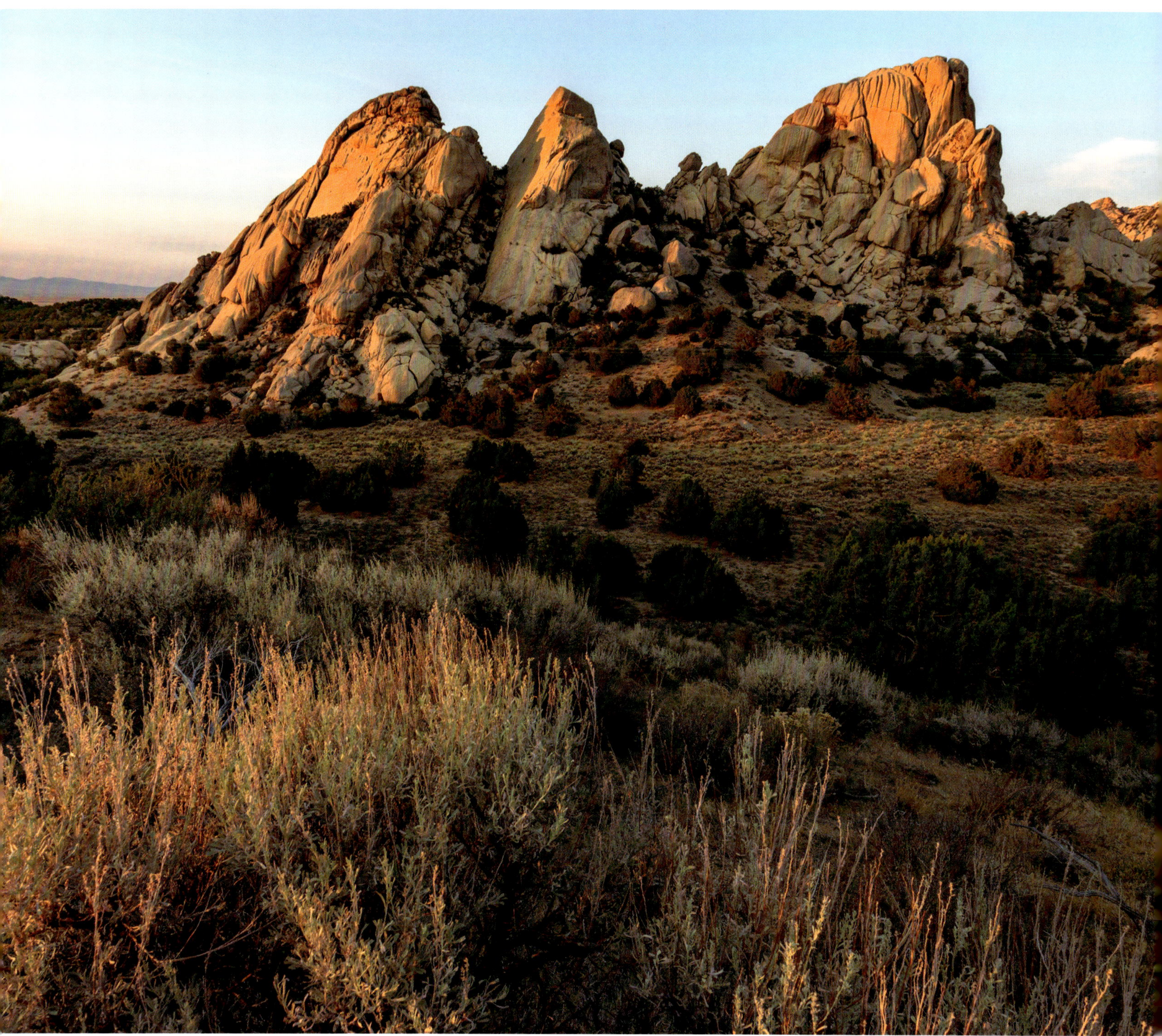

GRANITE FINS RISE FROM THE HIGH DESERT FLOOR OF THE MINERAL MOUNTAINS.

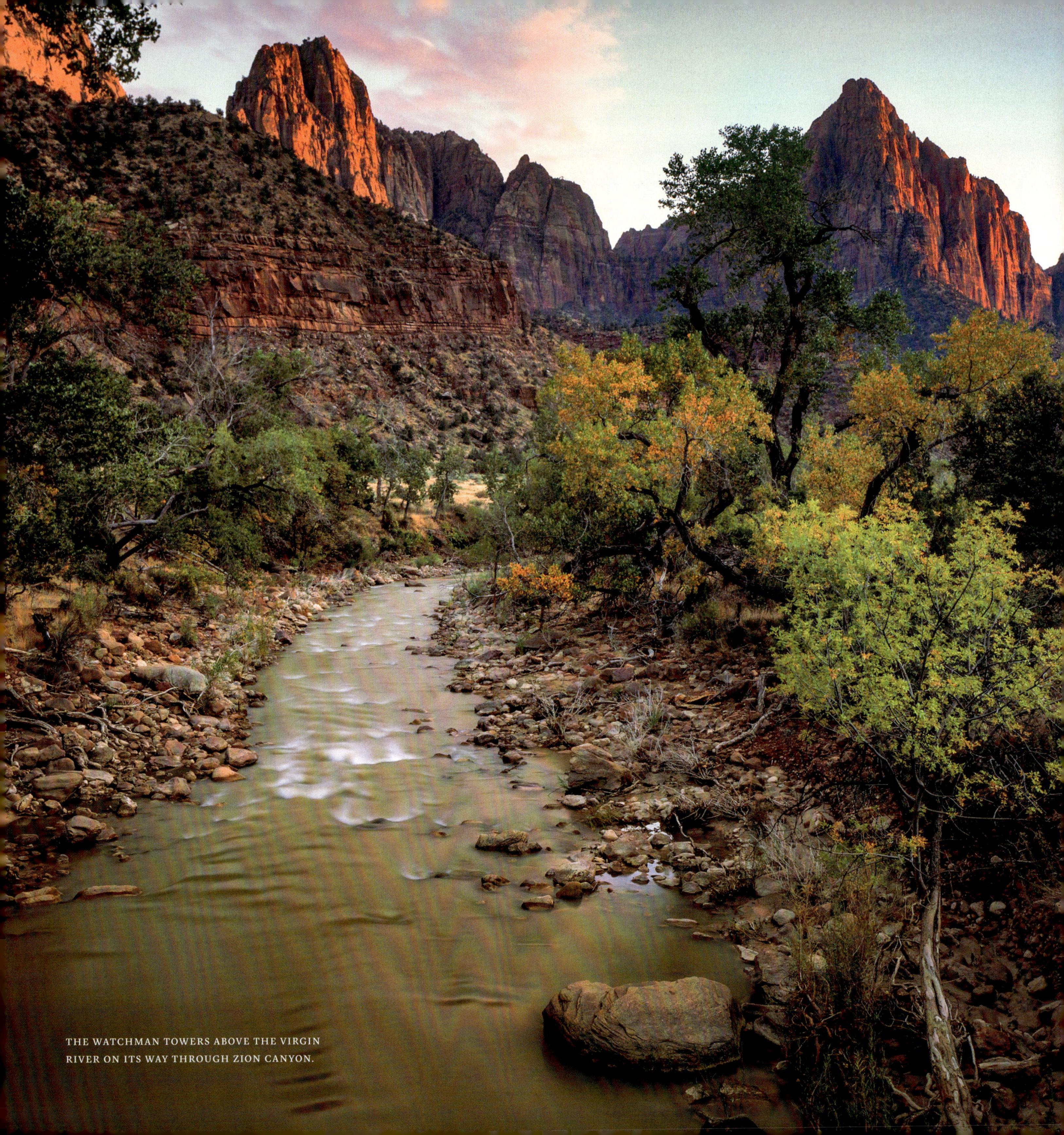

THE WATCHMAN TOWERS ABOVE THE VIRGIN RIVER ON ITS WAY THROUGH ZION CANYON.

SOUTHWEST CANYON COUNTRY

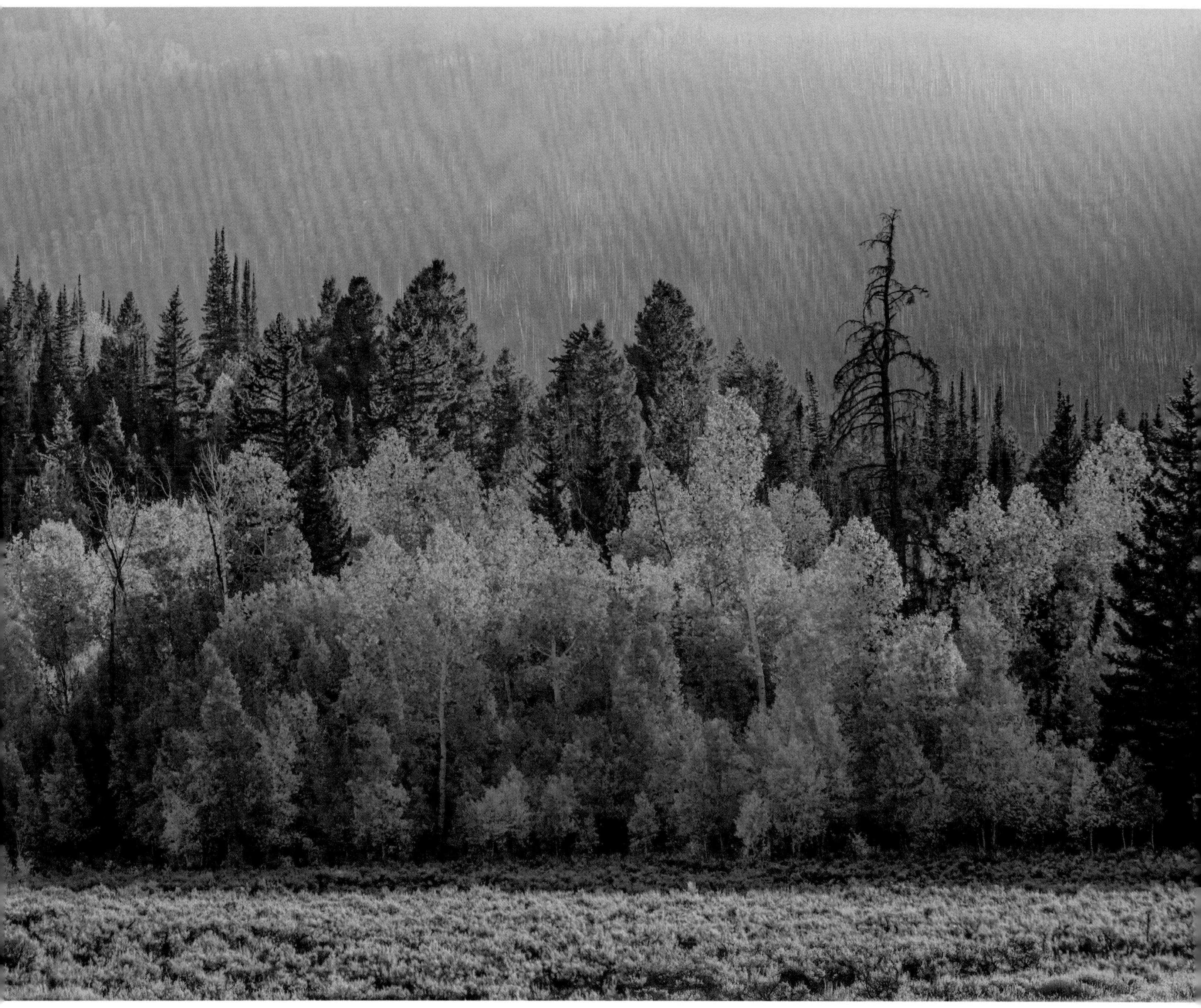

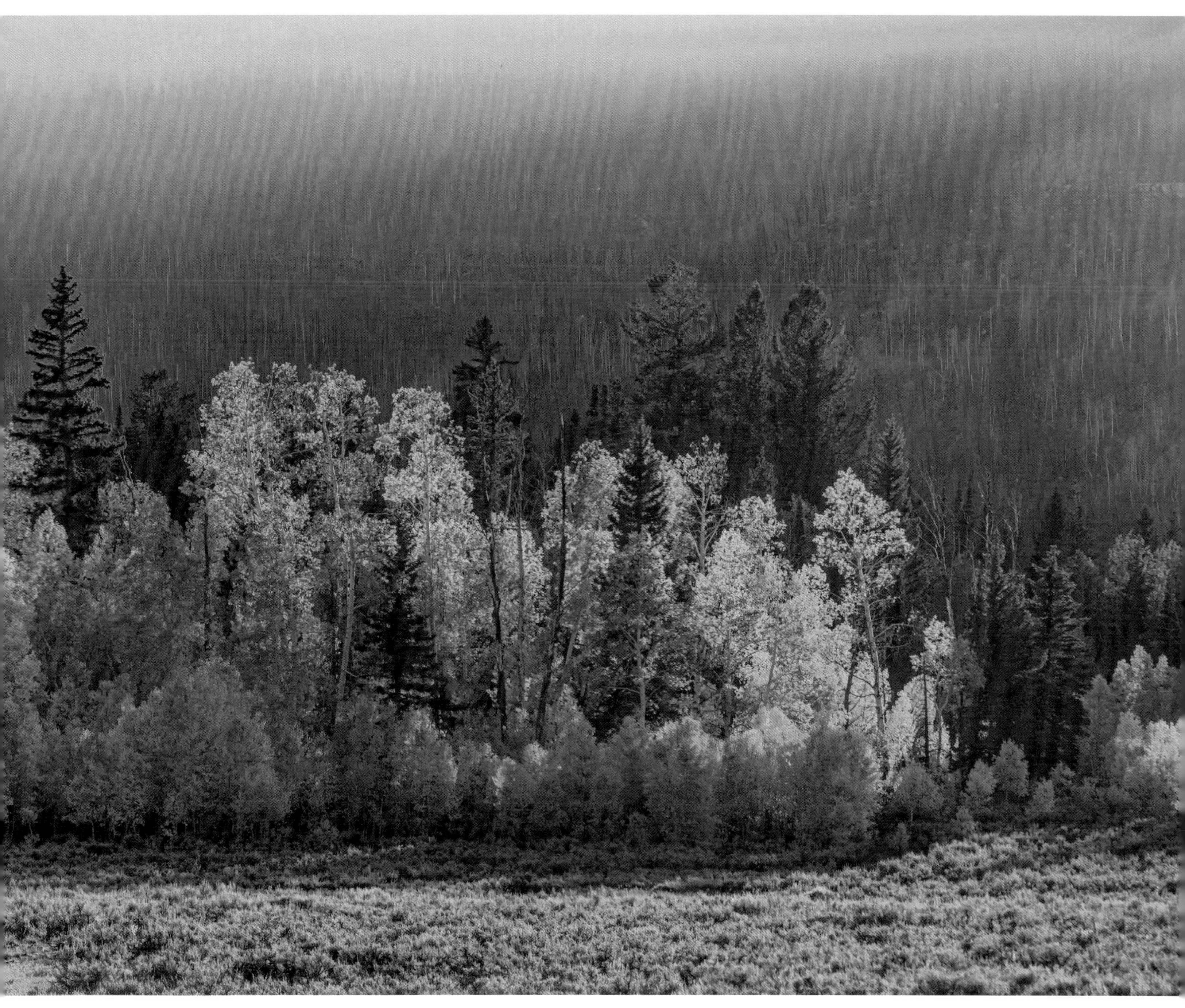

SMOKE-FILLED SKIES ADD TO THE WARMTH OF THE SUNSET ON THE WASATCH PLATEAU.

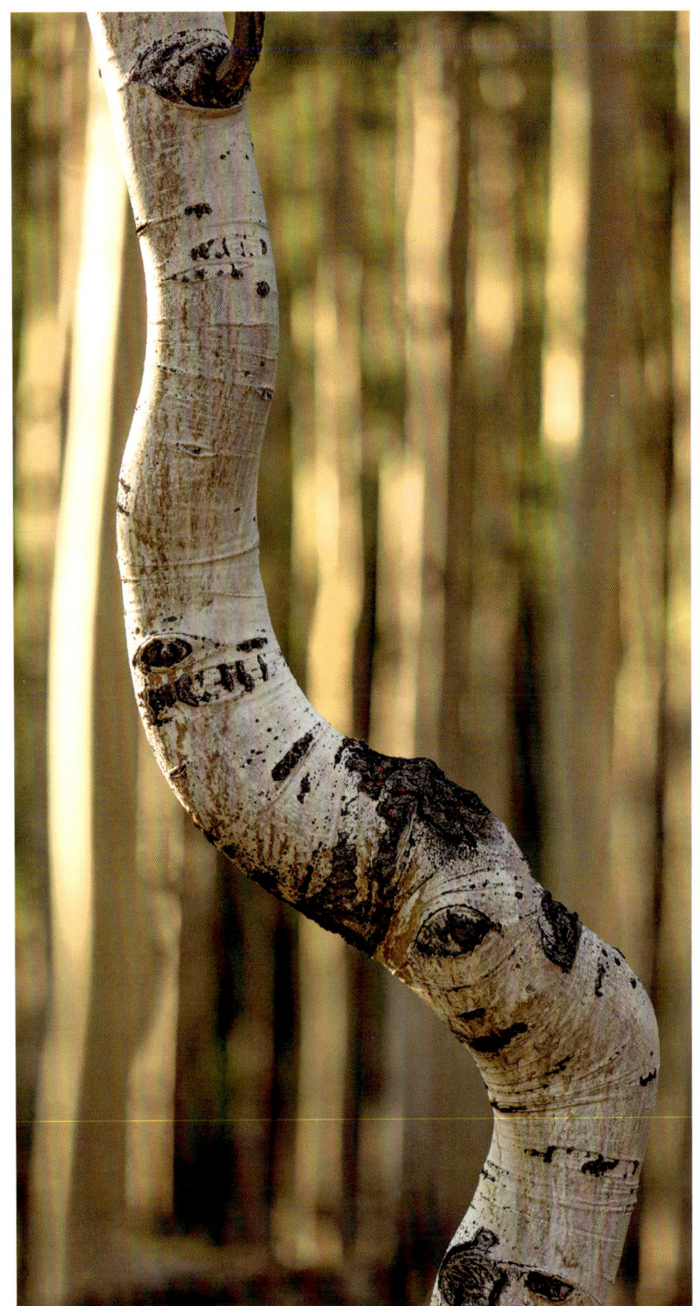

TWISTED ASPEN TRUNKS WARM IN THE SUMMER LIGHT IN THE ASHDOWN GORGE WILDERNESS AREA.

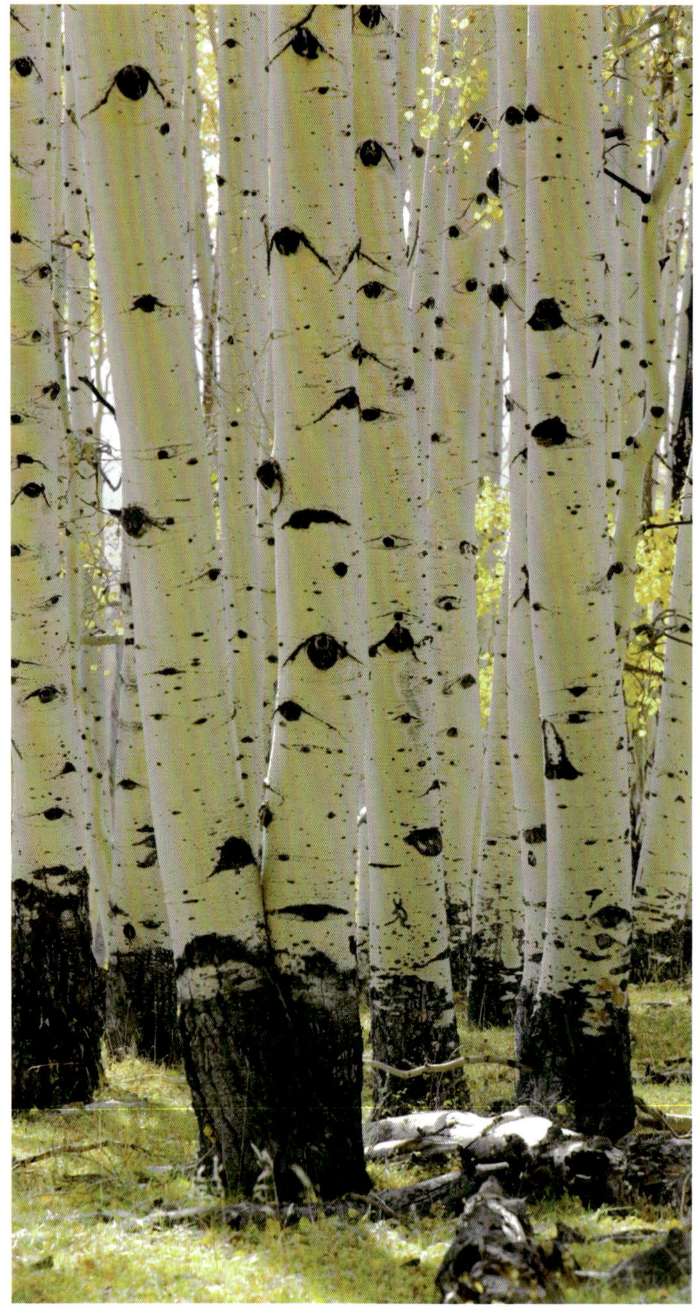

WARM LIGHT AND ASPEN TRUNKS FORM GRAPHIC PATTERNS IN SOUTHERN UTAH'S DIXIE NATIONAL FOREST.

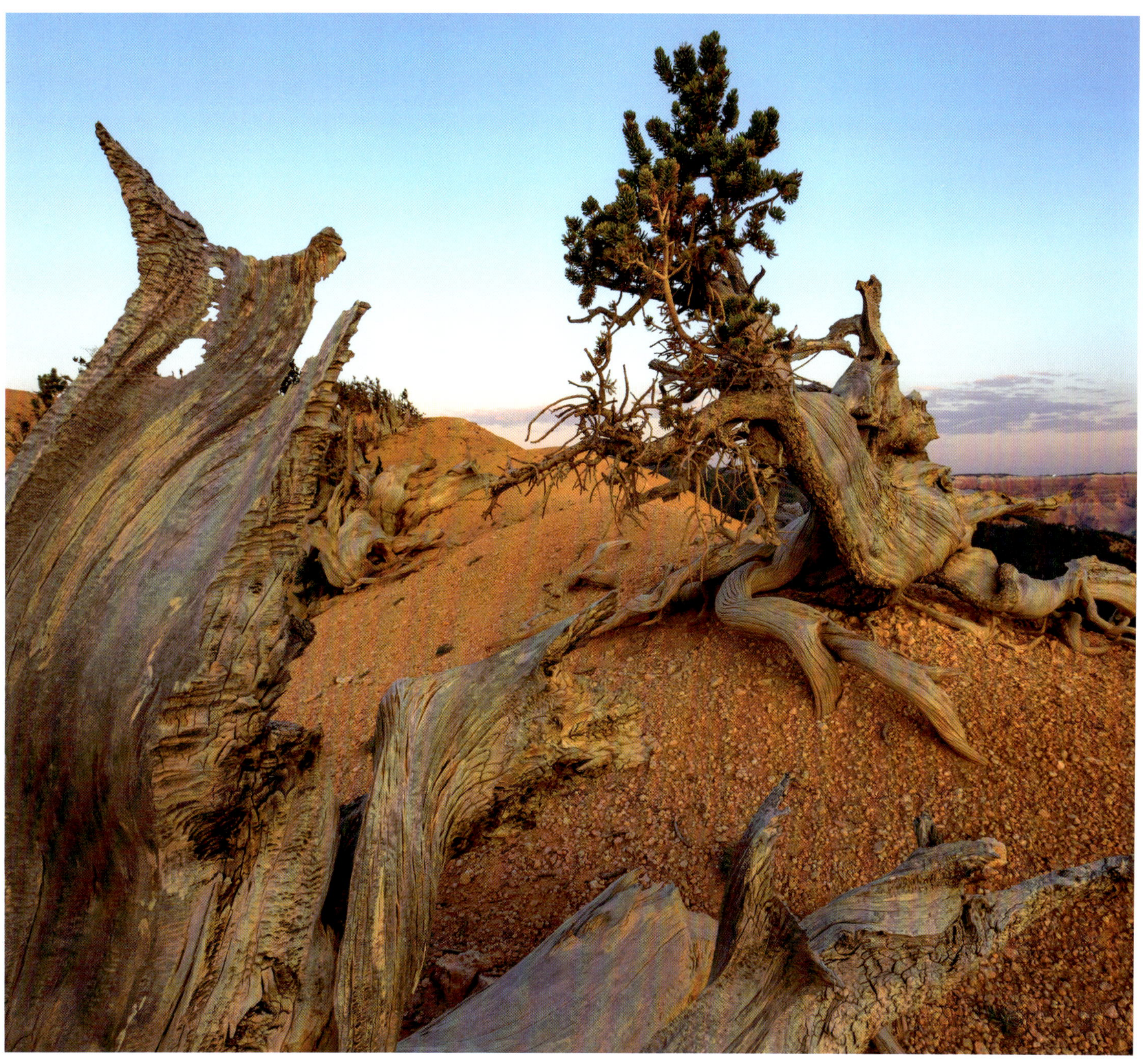

BRISTLECONE PINES GUARD THE VALLEY BETWEEN THE ASHDOWN GORGE WILDERNESS AND THE CEDAR BREAKS NATIONAL MONUMENT.

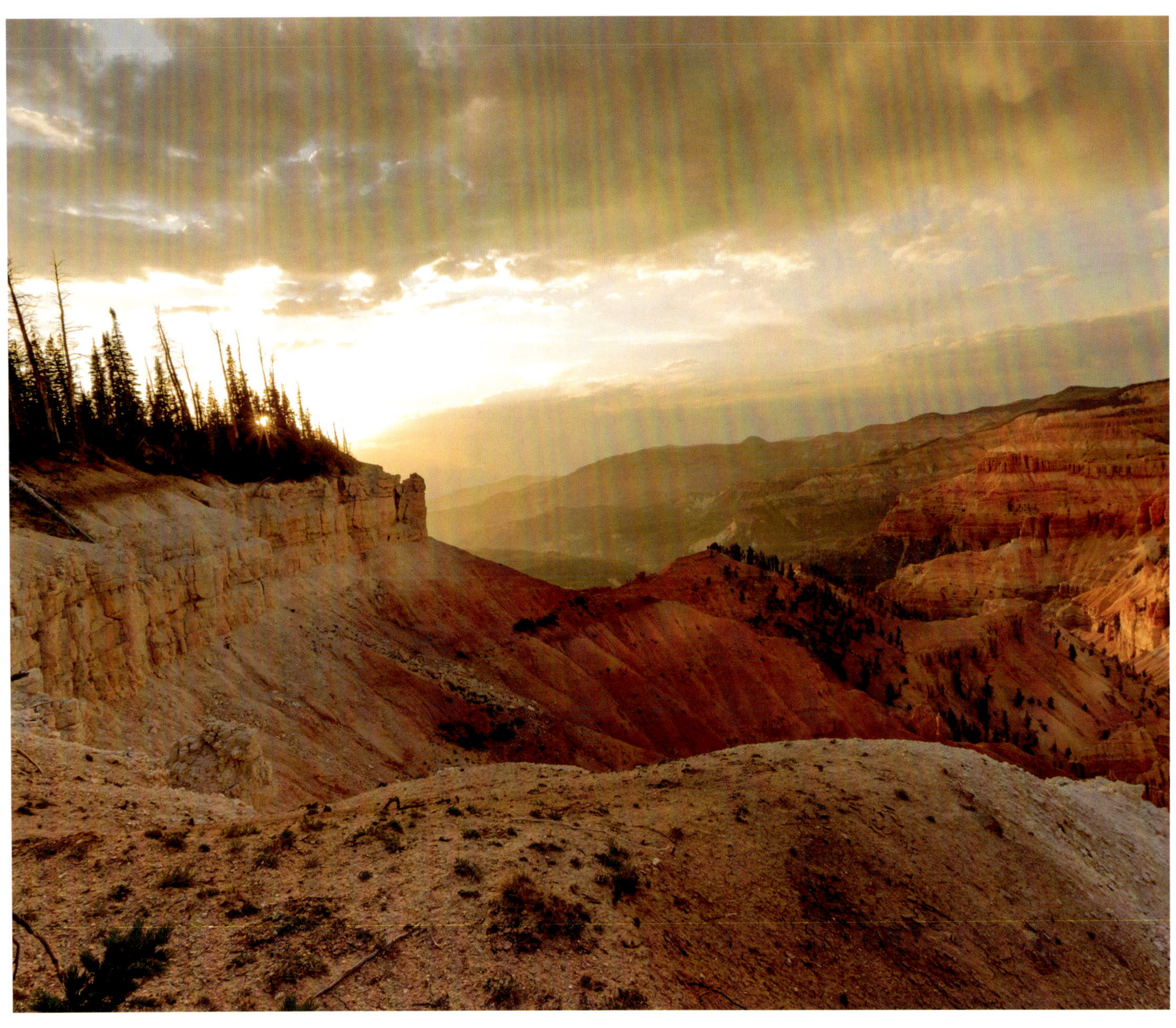

SUNSET DANCES BETWEEN THE CLOUDS AND CLIFFS AT POINT SUPREME IN CEDAR BREAKS NATIONAL MONUMENT.

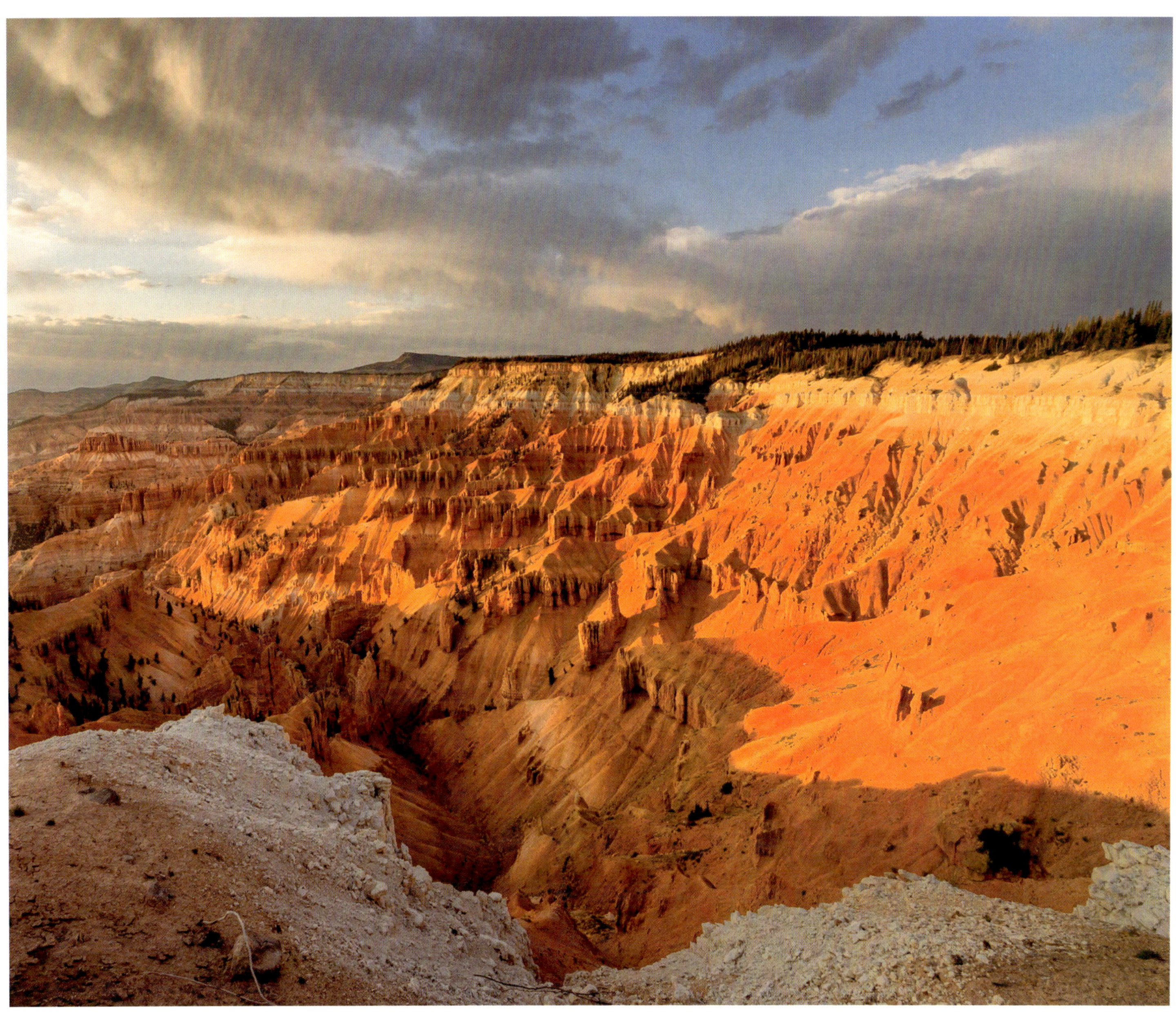

THE SUN BREAKS THROUGH THE CLOUD COVER FOR A SPECTACULAR BURST OF LIGHT IN CEDAR BREAKS NATIONAL MONUMENT.

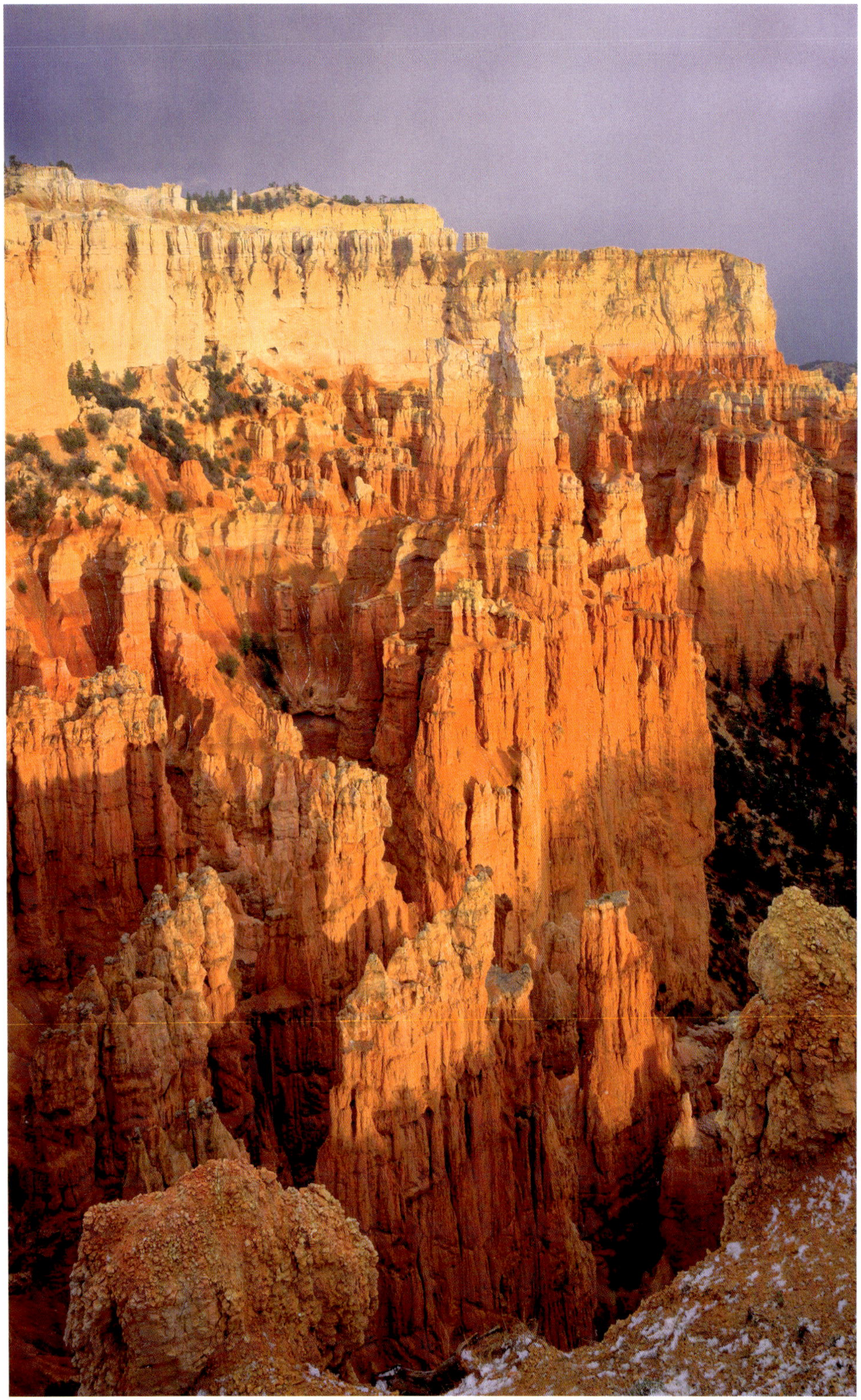

◀

STORM CLOUDS OVER THE UNEARTHLY FORMATIONS OF BRYCE CANYON NATIONAL PARK.

▶

THE SUN BURSTS OVER THE HORIZON AT SUNSET POINT IN BRYCE CANYON NATIONAL PARK.

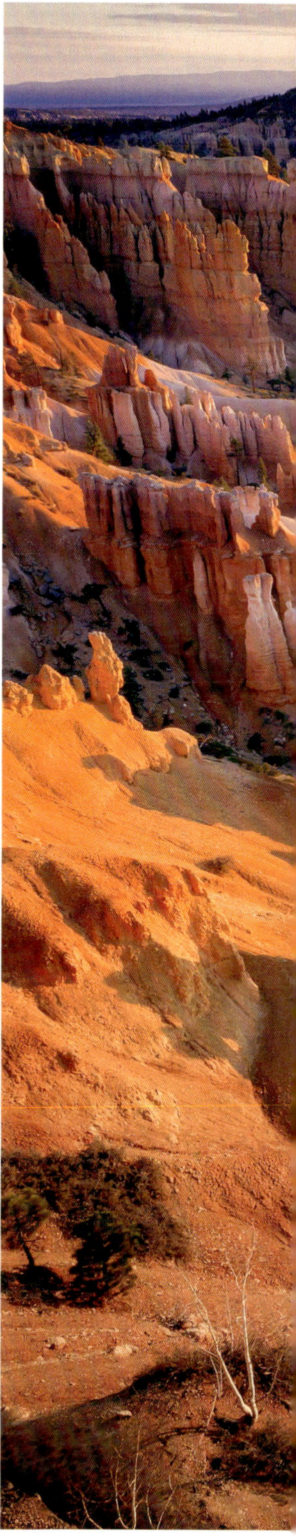

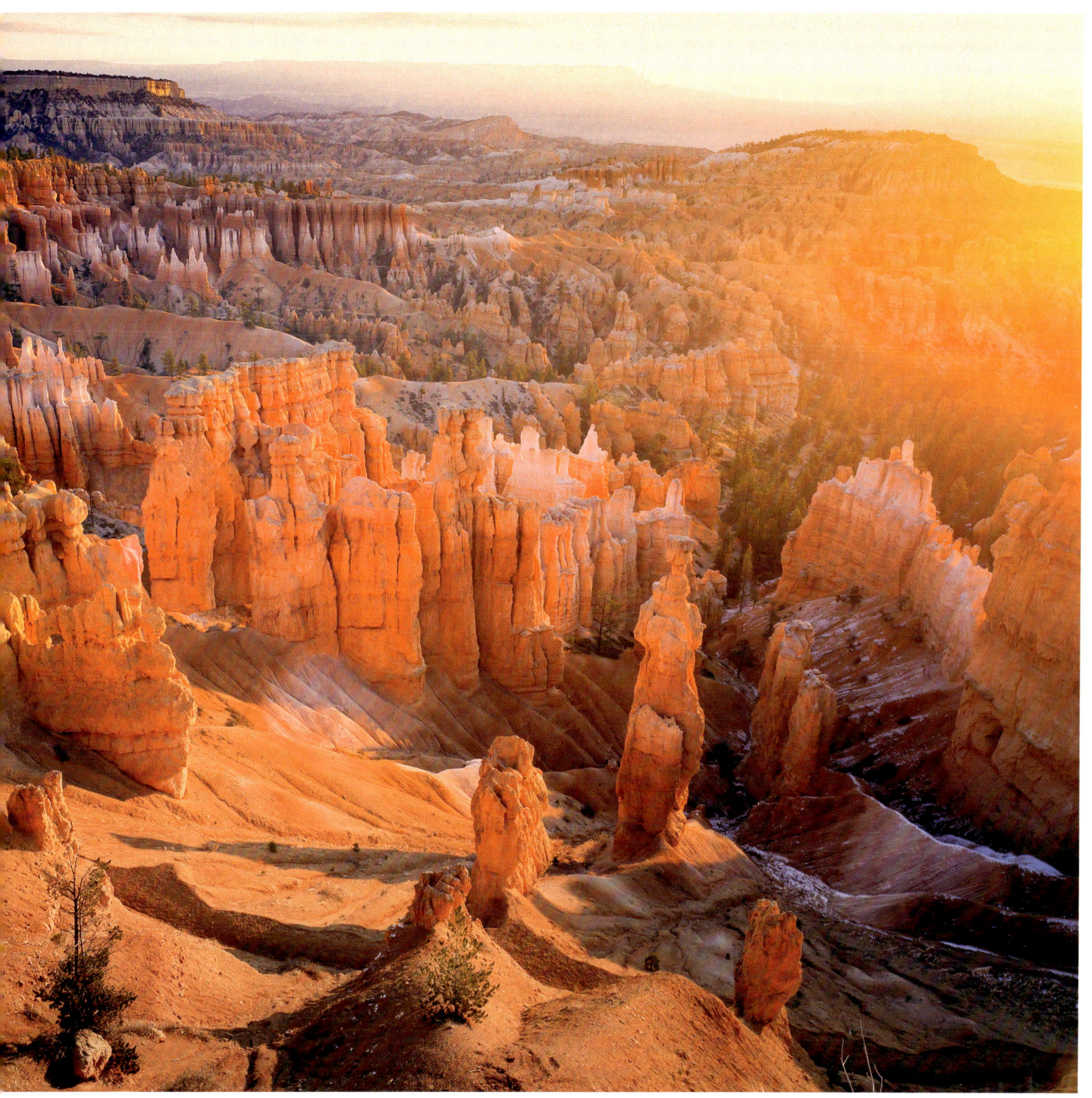

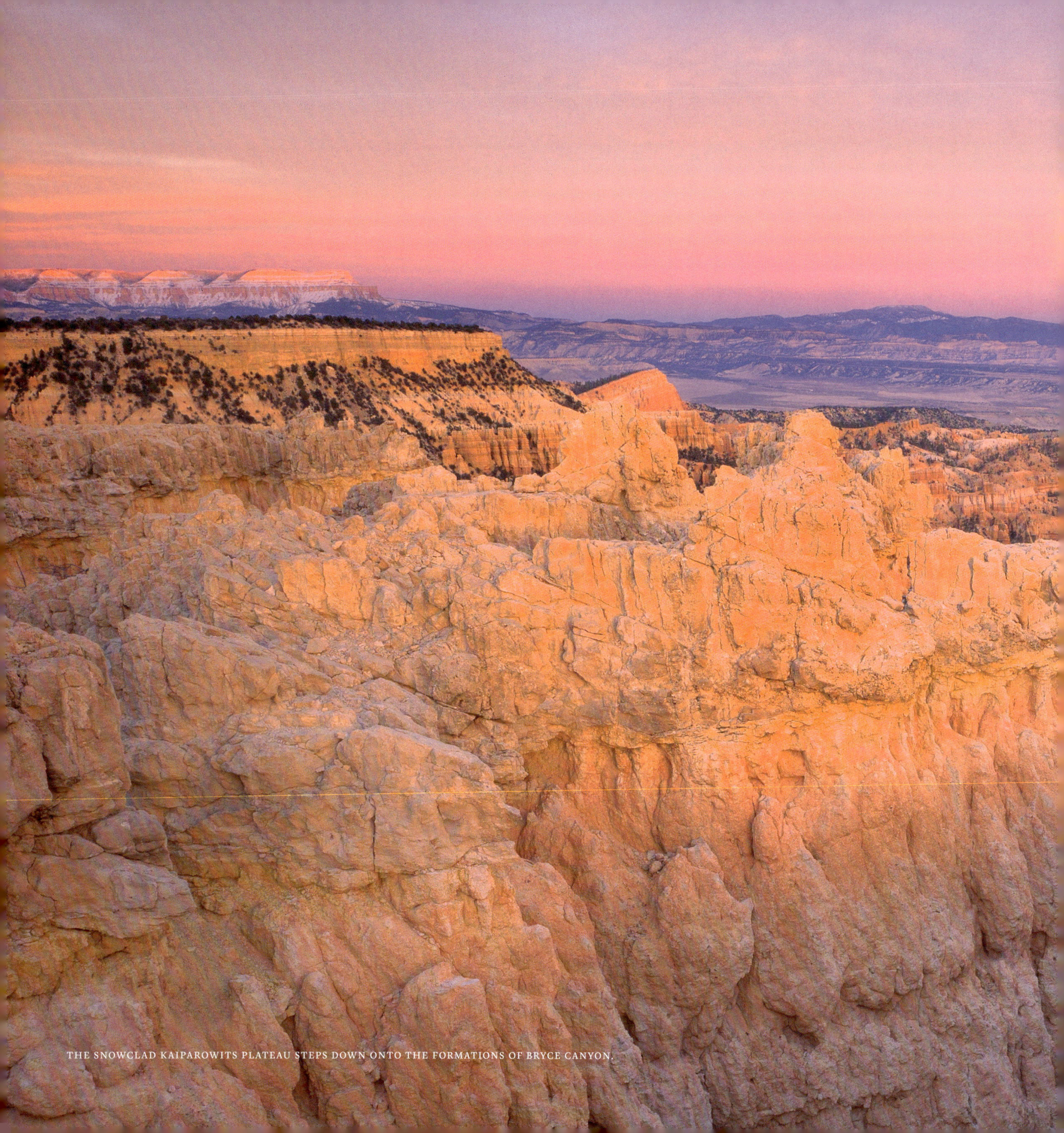

THE SNOWCLAD KAIPAROWITS PLATEAU STEPS DOWN ONTO THE FORMATIONS OF BRYCE CANYON.

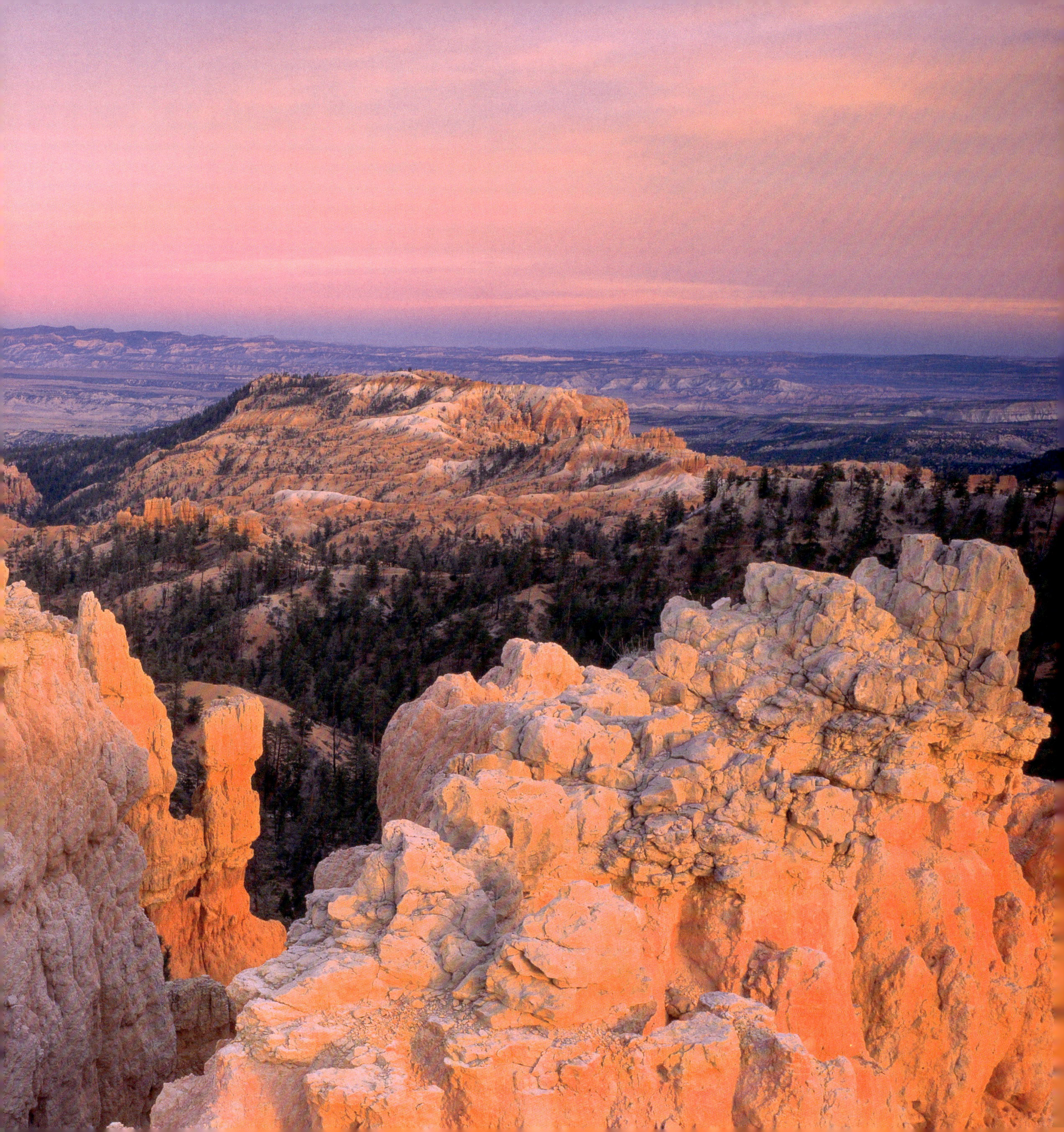

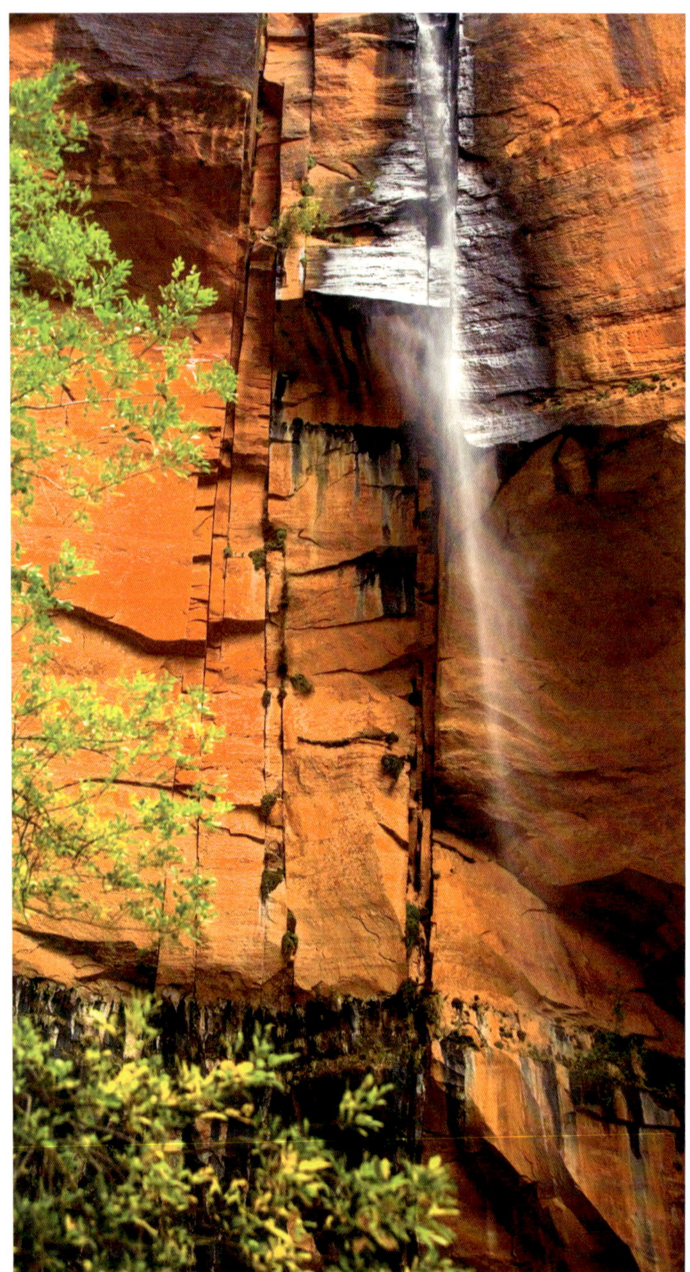

WATER SPILLS OVER THE WALLS OF ZION CANYON AT THE UPPER EMERALD POOLS.

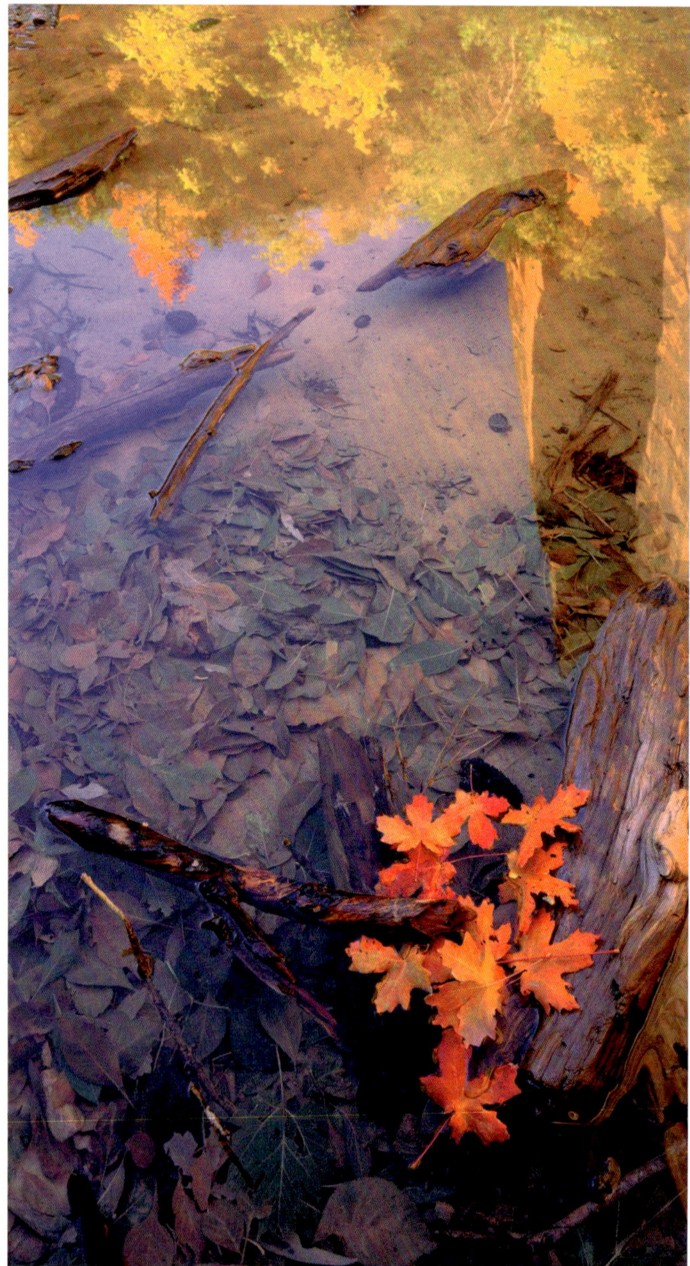

MAPLE LEAVES IN THE UPPER EMERALD POOL, ZION NATIONAL PARK.

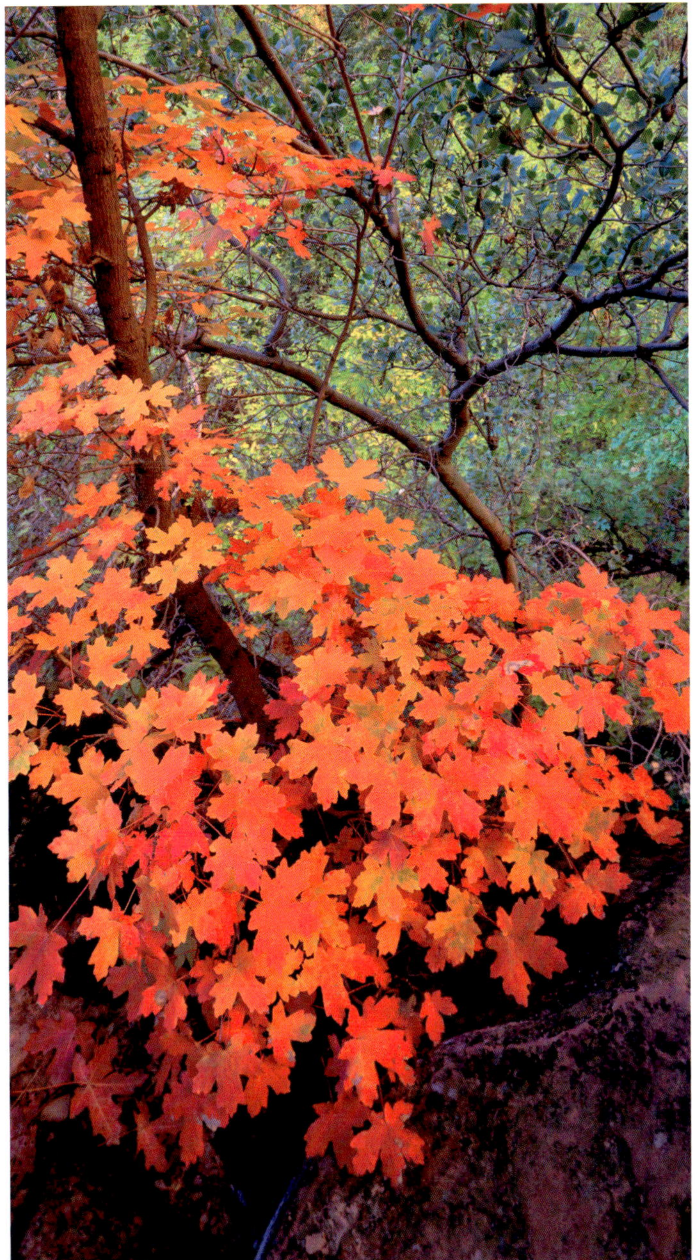

BIGTOOTH MAPLE IN VIBRANT FALL FOLIAGE, ZION NATIONAL PARK.

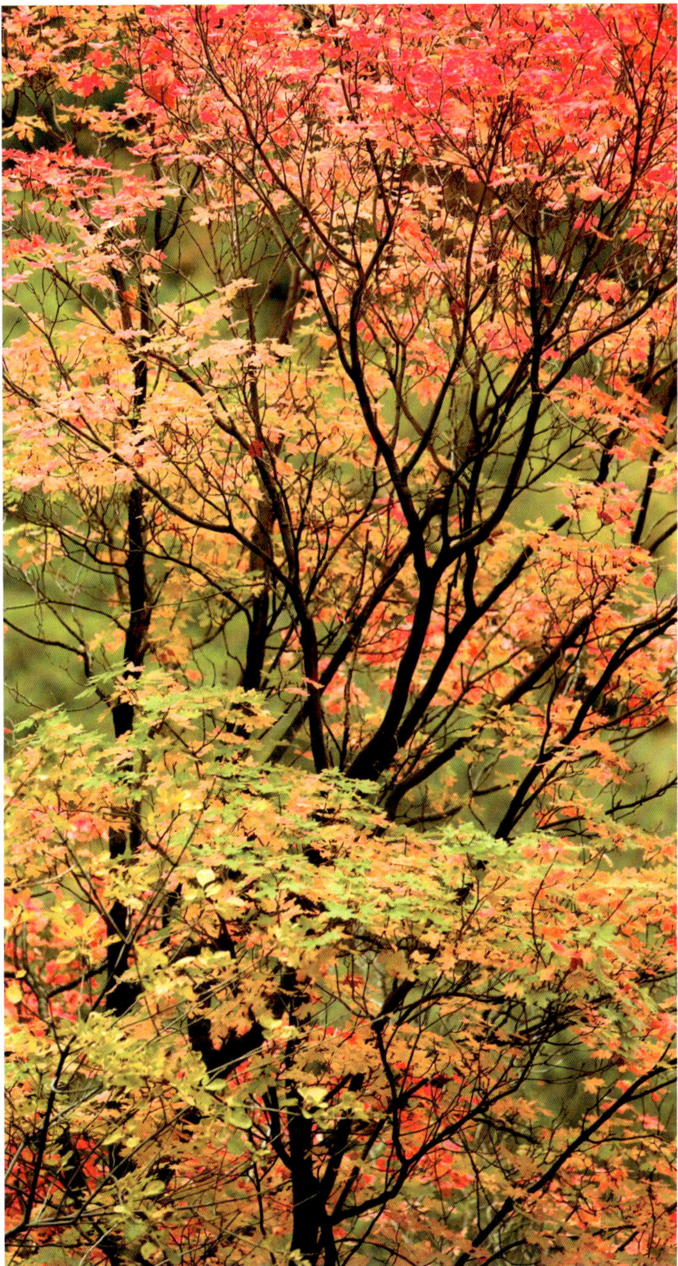

EVERY FALL, BRILLIANT COLOR FILLS ZION CANYON AS COOLER TEMPERATURES PRECEDE WINTER.

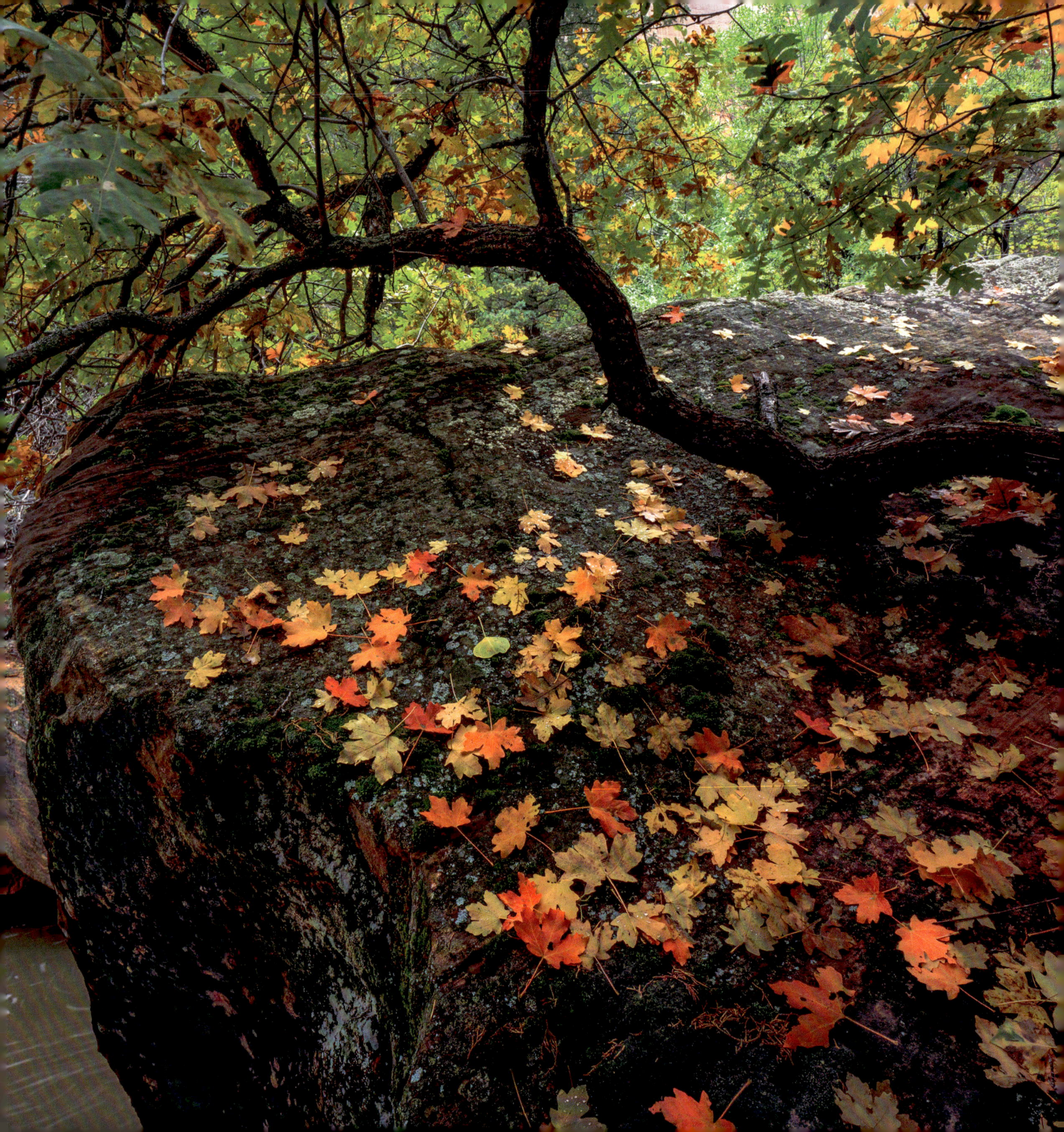

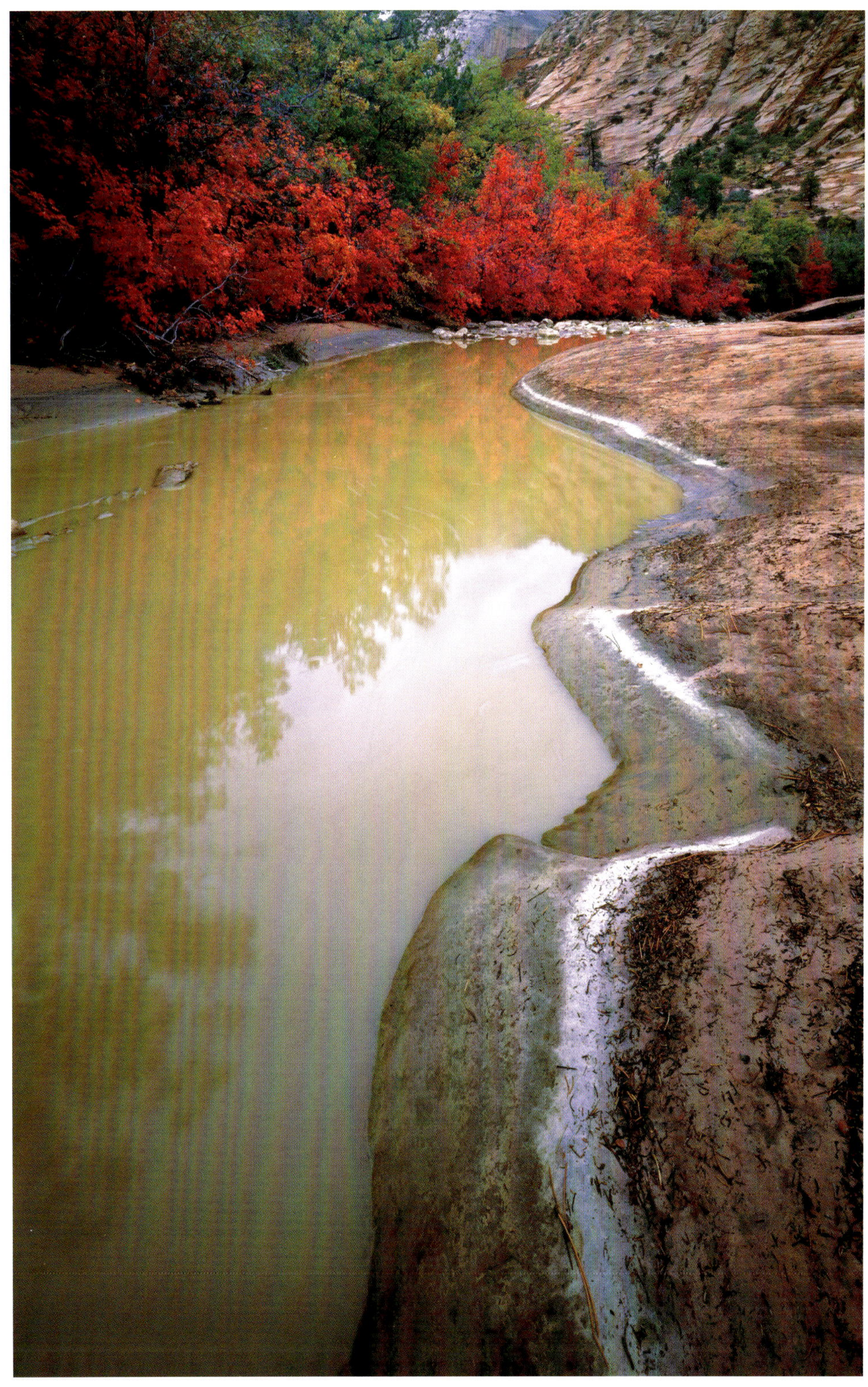

◀

AN OAK TREE TWISTS AROUND A SANDSTONE BOULDER NEAR THE MIDDLE EMERALD POOL IN ZION CANYON.

▶

BIGTOOTH MAPLES LINE A DESERT WASH FILLED WITH FRESH RAINWATER IN ZION NATIONAL PARK.

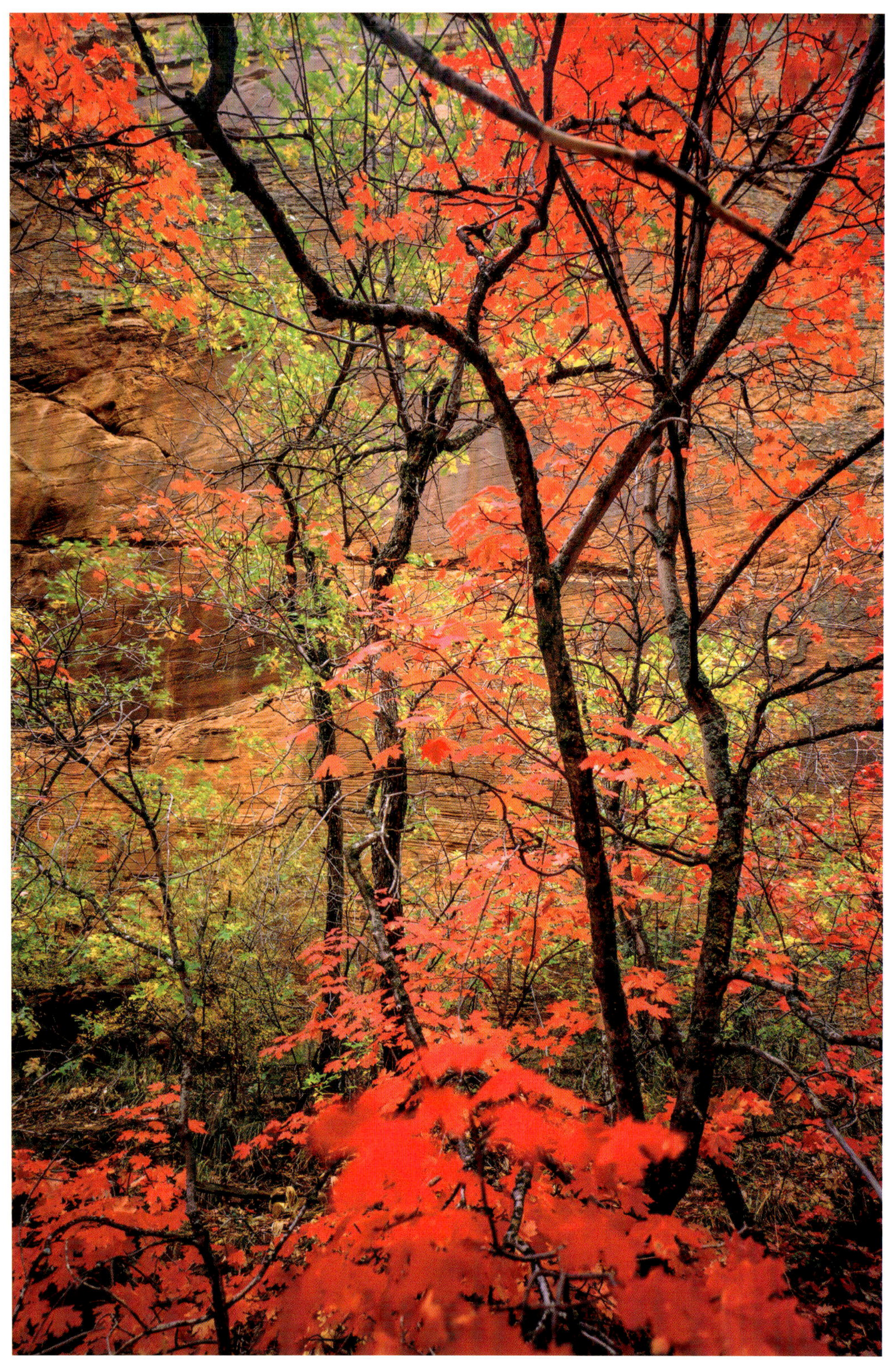

BIGTOOTH MAPLES THRIVE IN THE COOL CANYONS OF ZION NATIONAL PARK.

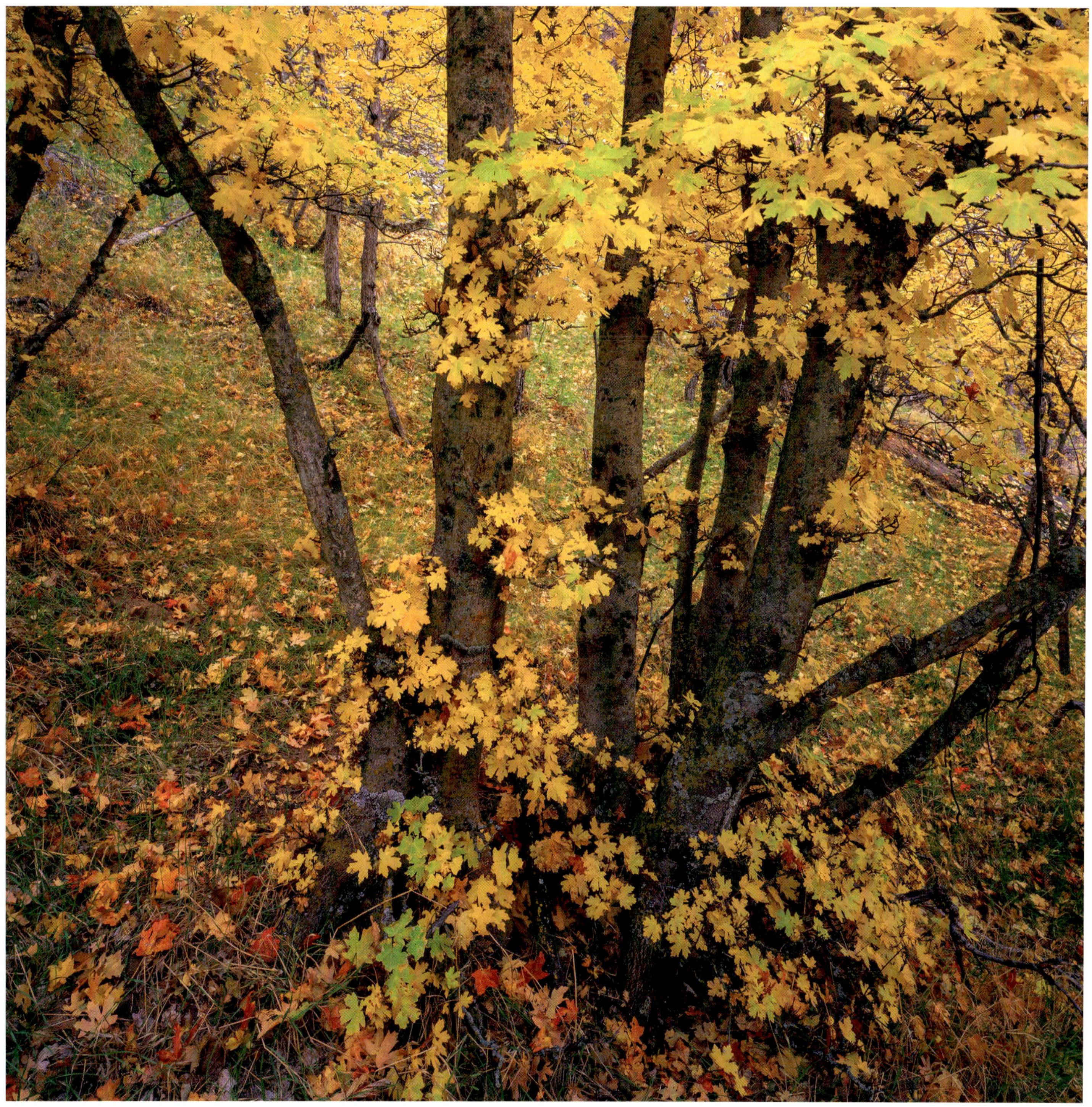

MAPLES IN ZION CANYON DISPLAY THEIR FALL COLORS.

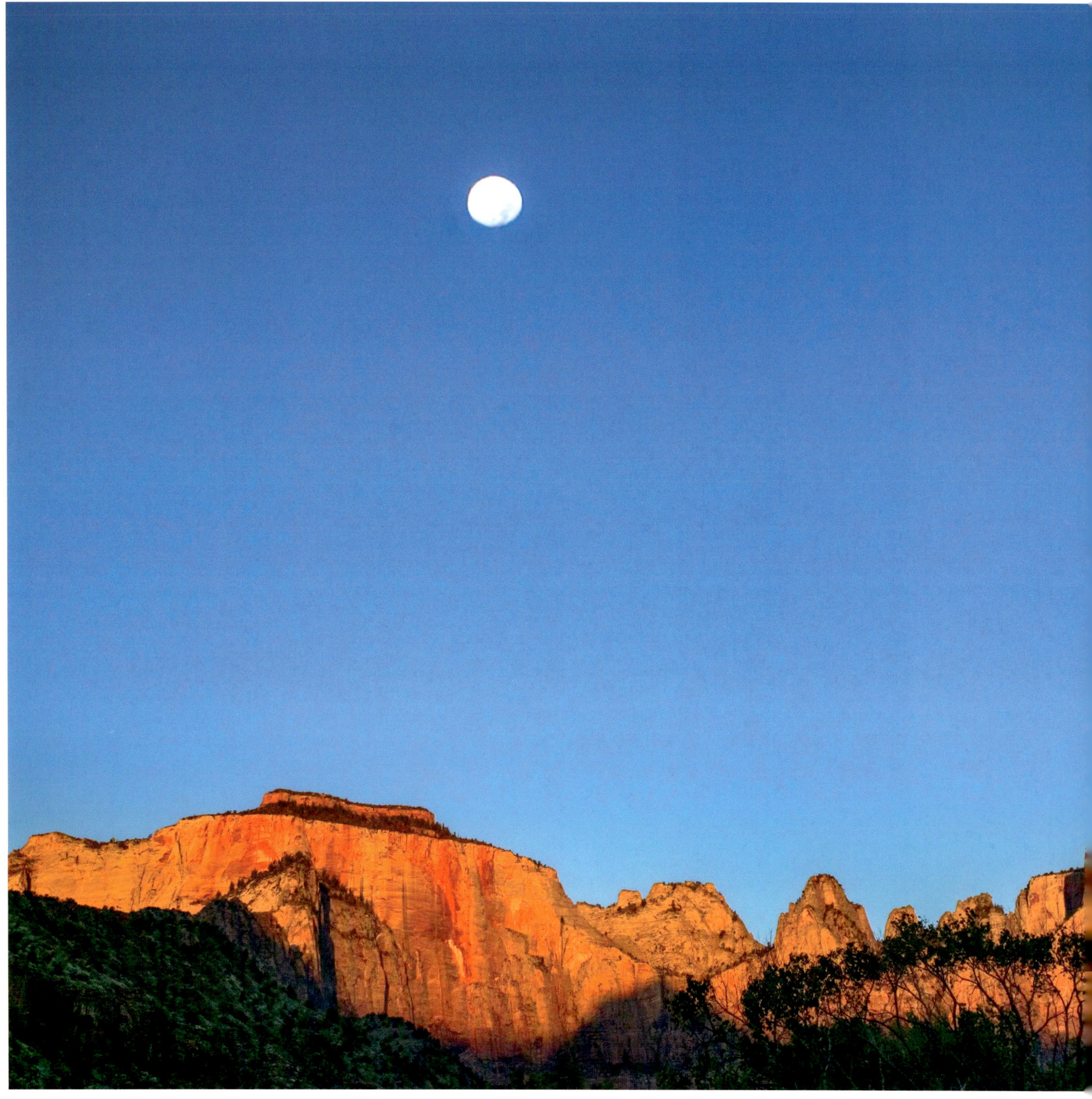

◀

THE MOON SETS
OVER THE WEST TEMPLE
AND THE TOWERS OF
THE VIRGIN, SOME OF
THE HIGHEST PEAKS
IN ZION CANYON.

▶

ICE HANGS FROM THE
EDGE OF A DESERT WASH
IN ZION NATIONAL PARK.

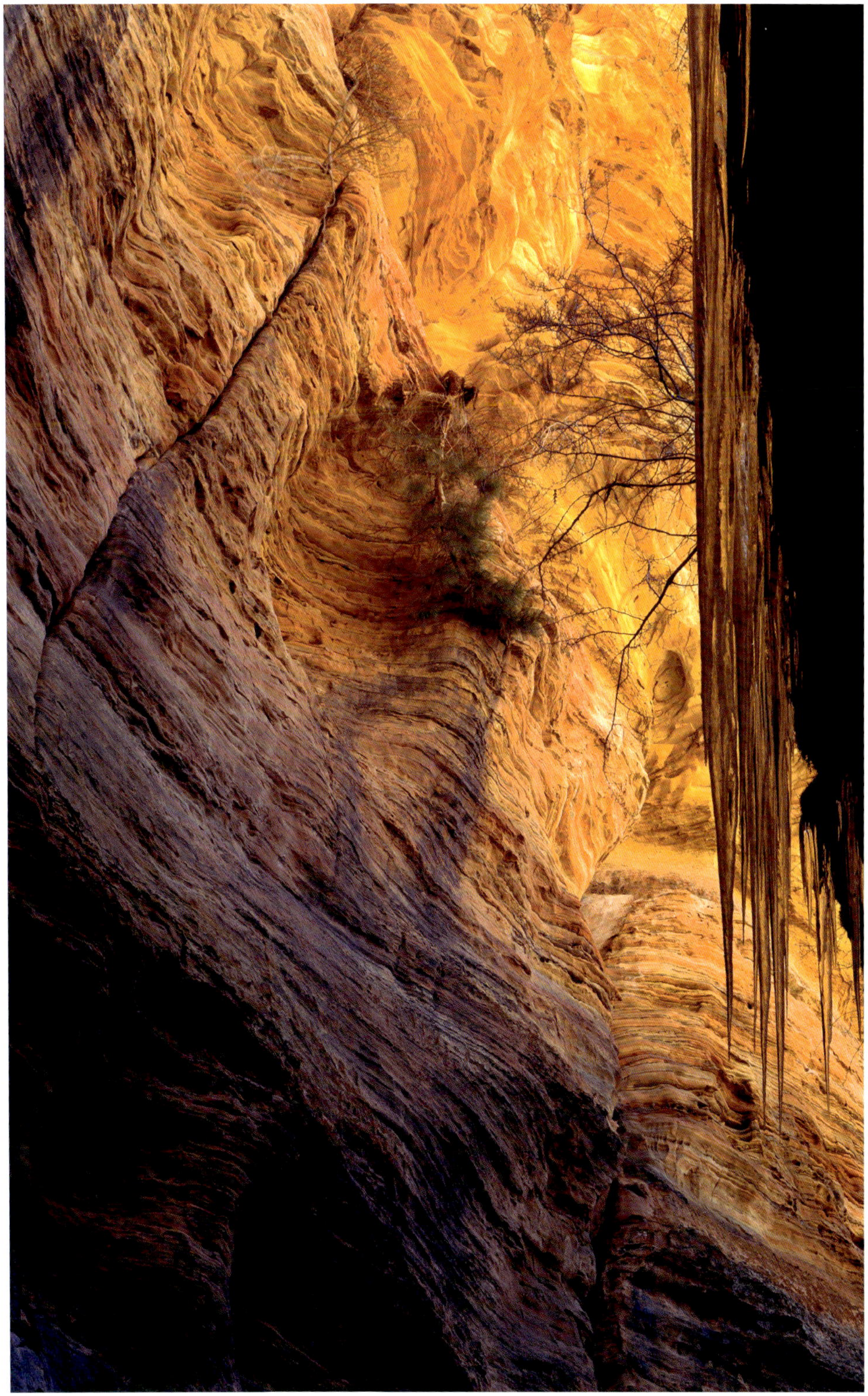

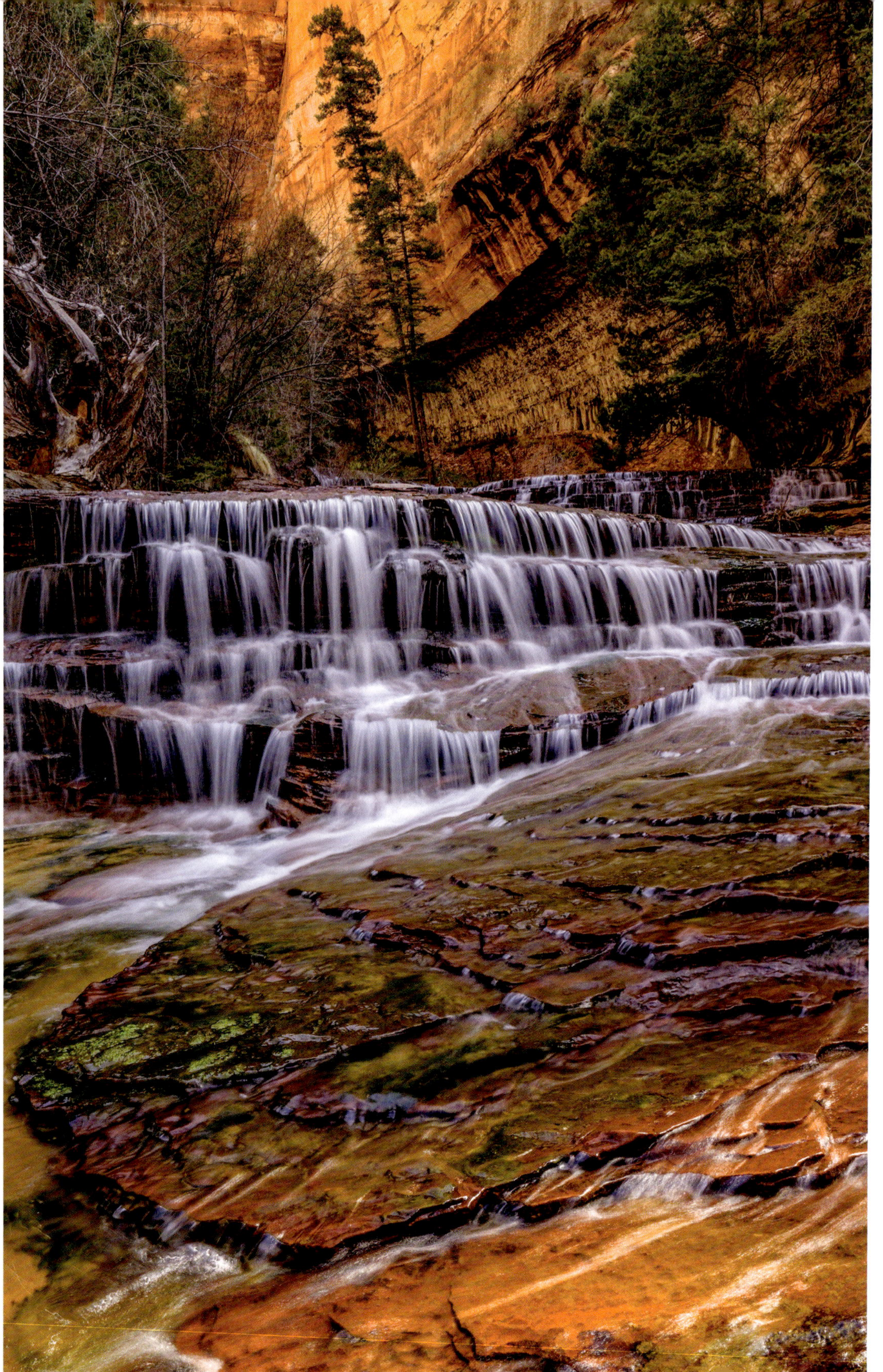

WATERFALLS POUR OVER SANDSTONE TERRACES ON THE LEFT FORK OF NORTH CREEK IN ZION NATIONAL PARK.

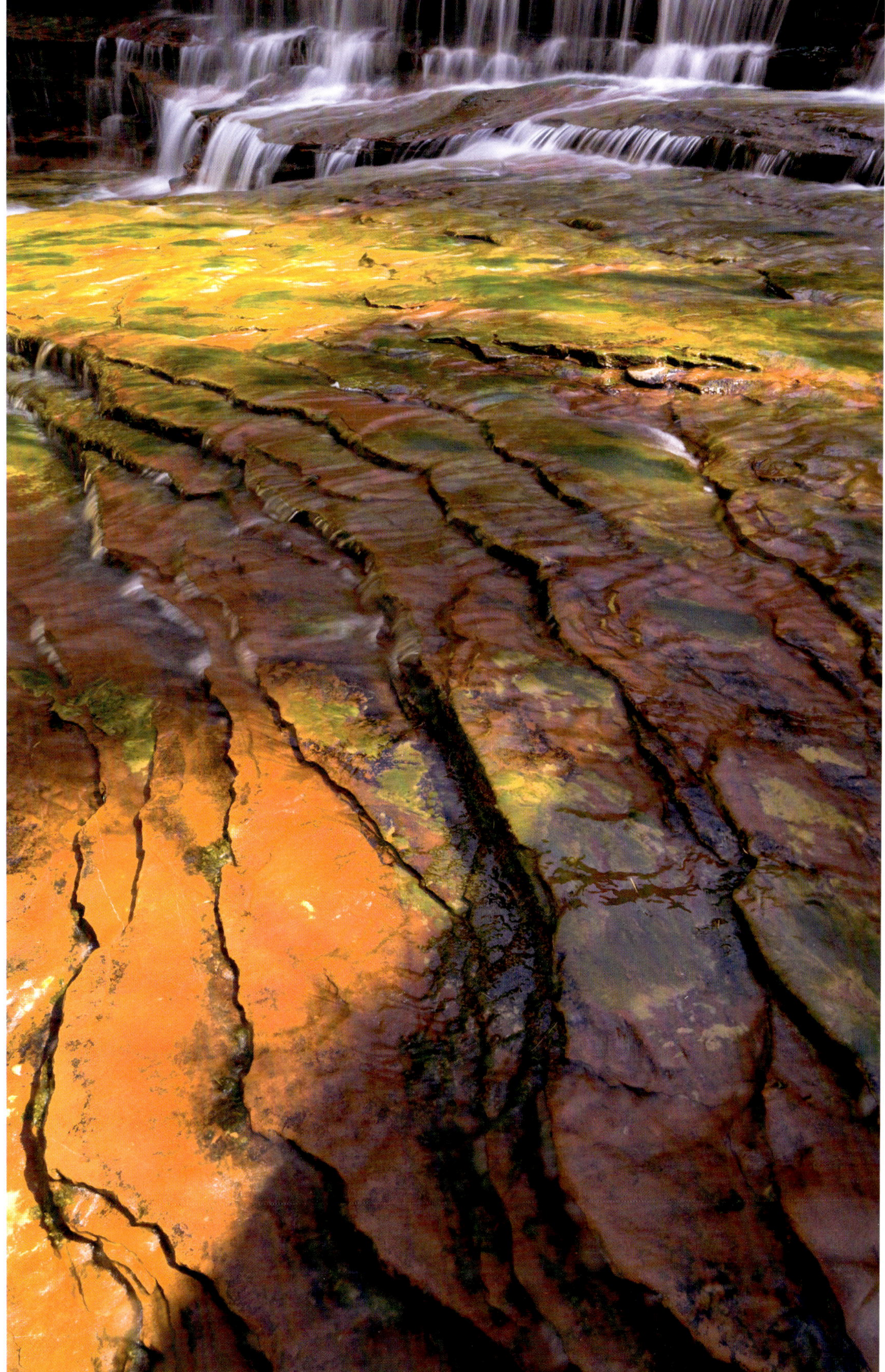

TERRACED STONE LEDGES ON THE LEFT FORK OF NORTH CREEK CREATE TRANQUIL WATERFALLS.

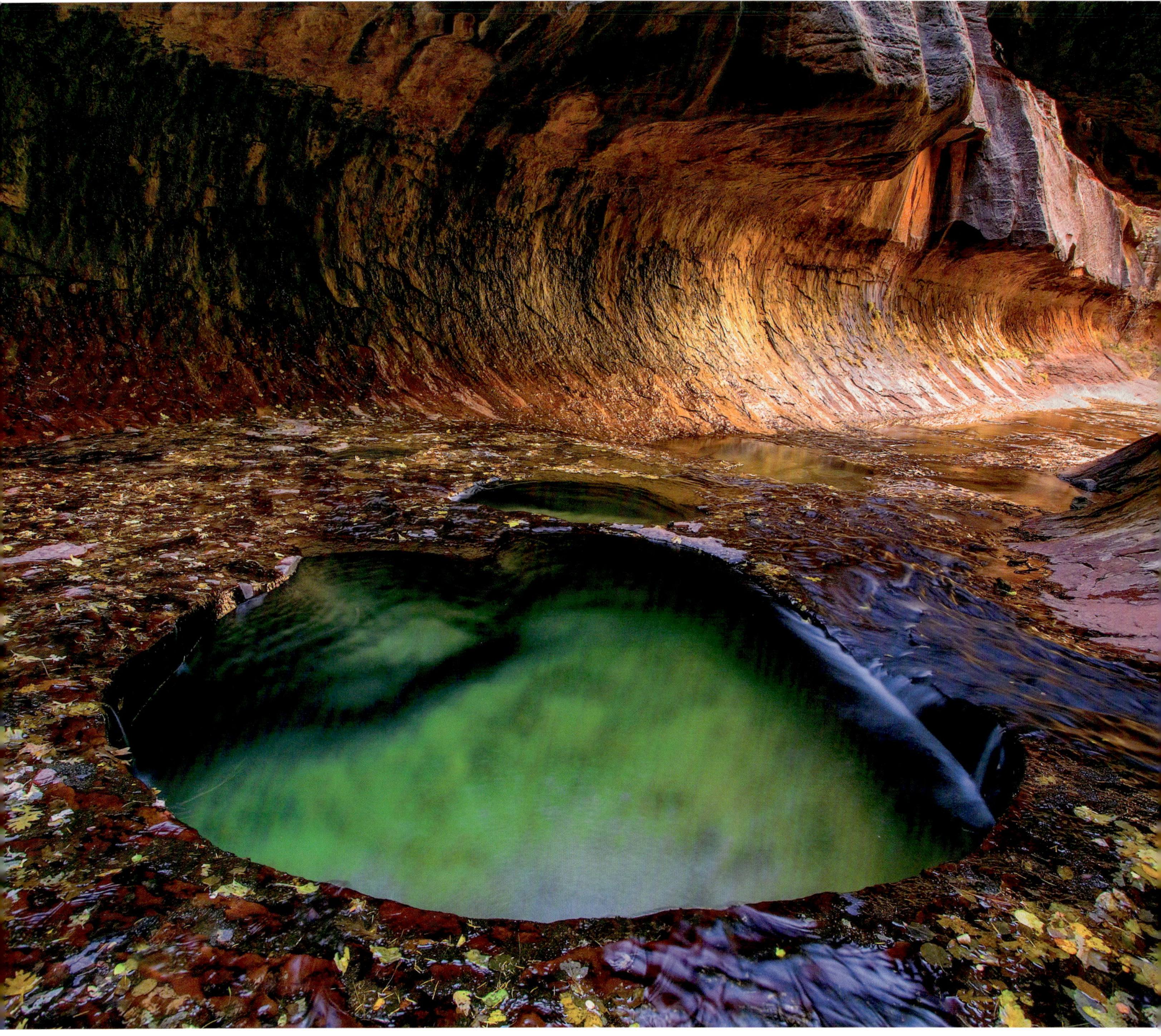

A HEART-SHAPED POOL IN THE LEFT FORK OF NORTH CREEK IN A SECTION KNOWN AS THE SUBWAY.

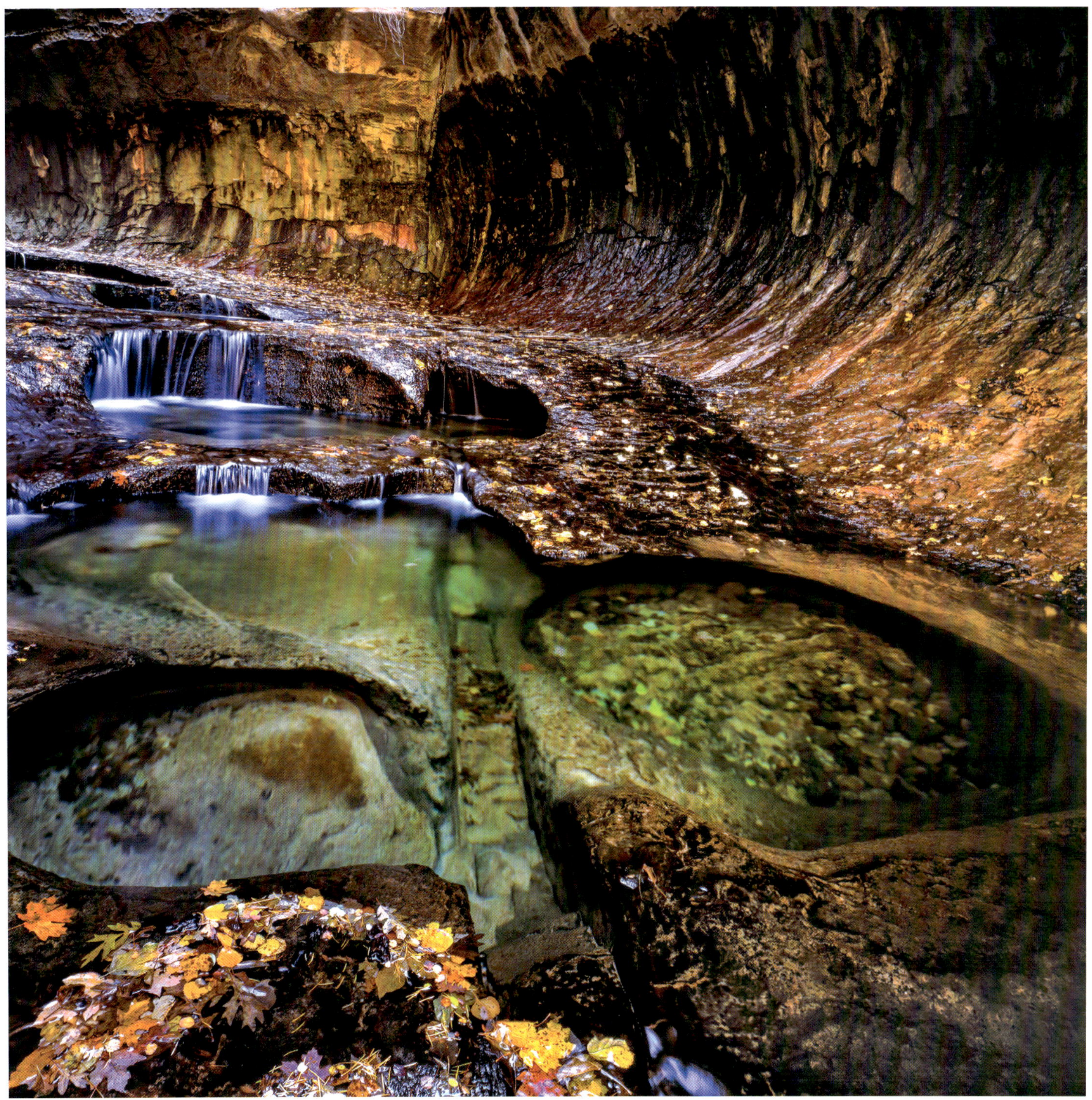

THE TURBULENT WATER OF THE LEFT FORK OF NORTH CREEK CARVES INCREDIBLE FORMATIONS IN THE SUBWAY IN ZION NATIONAL PARK.

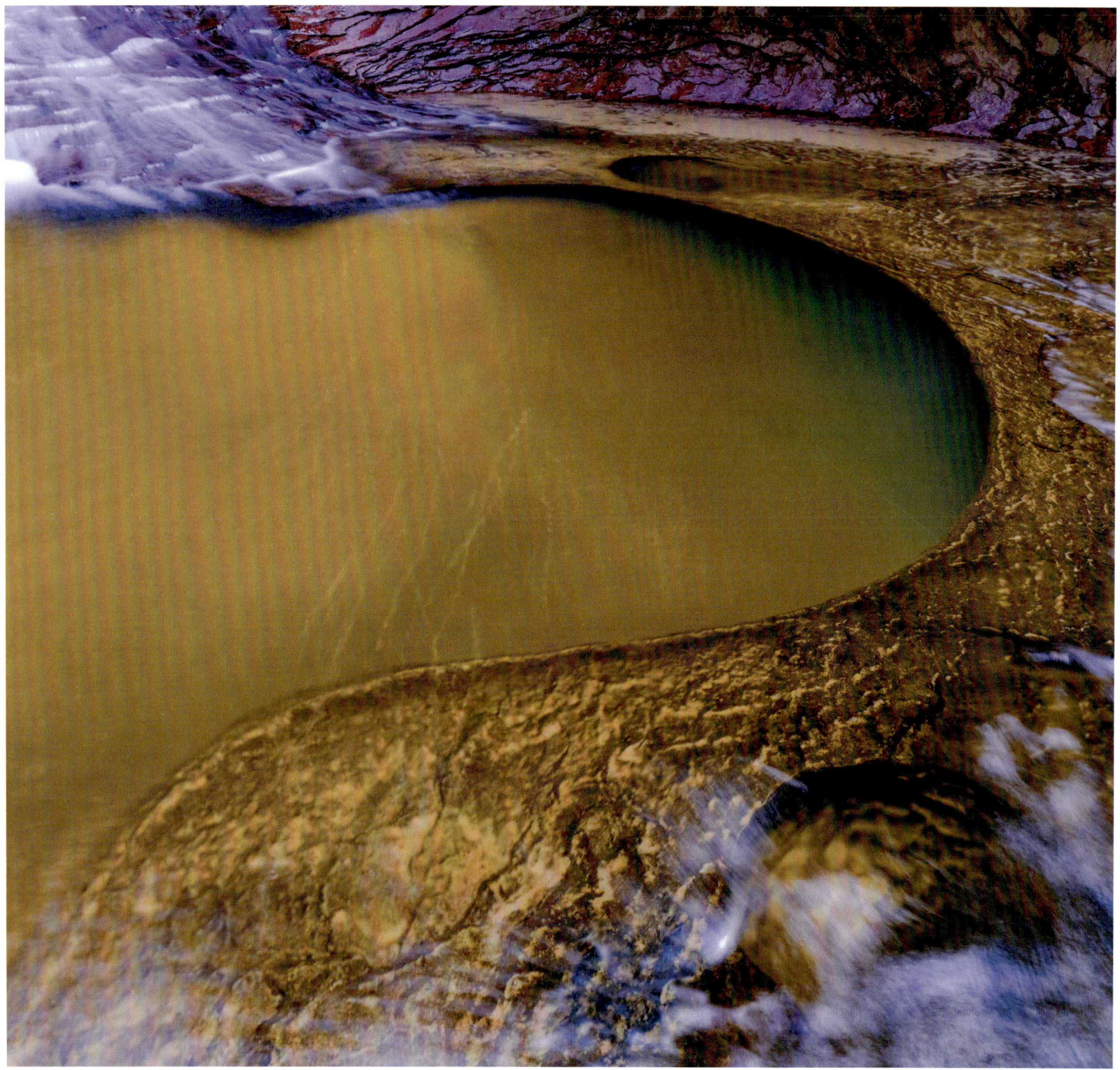

SPRING RUNOFF FROM THE LEFT FORK OF NORTH CREEK CREATES GRAPHIC PATTERNS AND INTENSE COLOR IN THE SUBWAY OF ZION NATIONAL PARK.

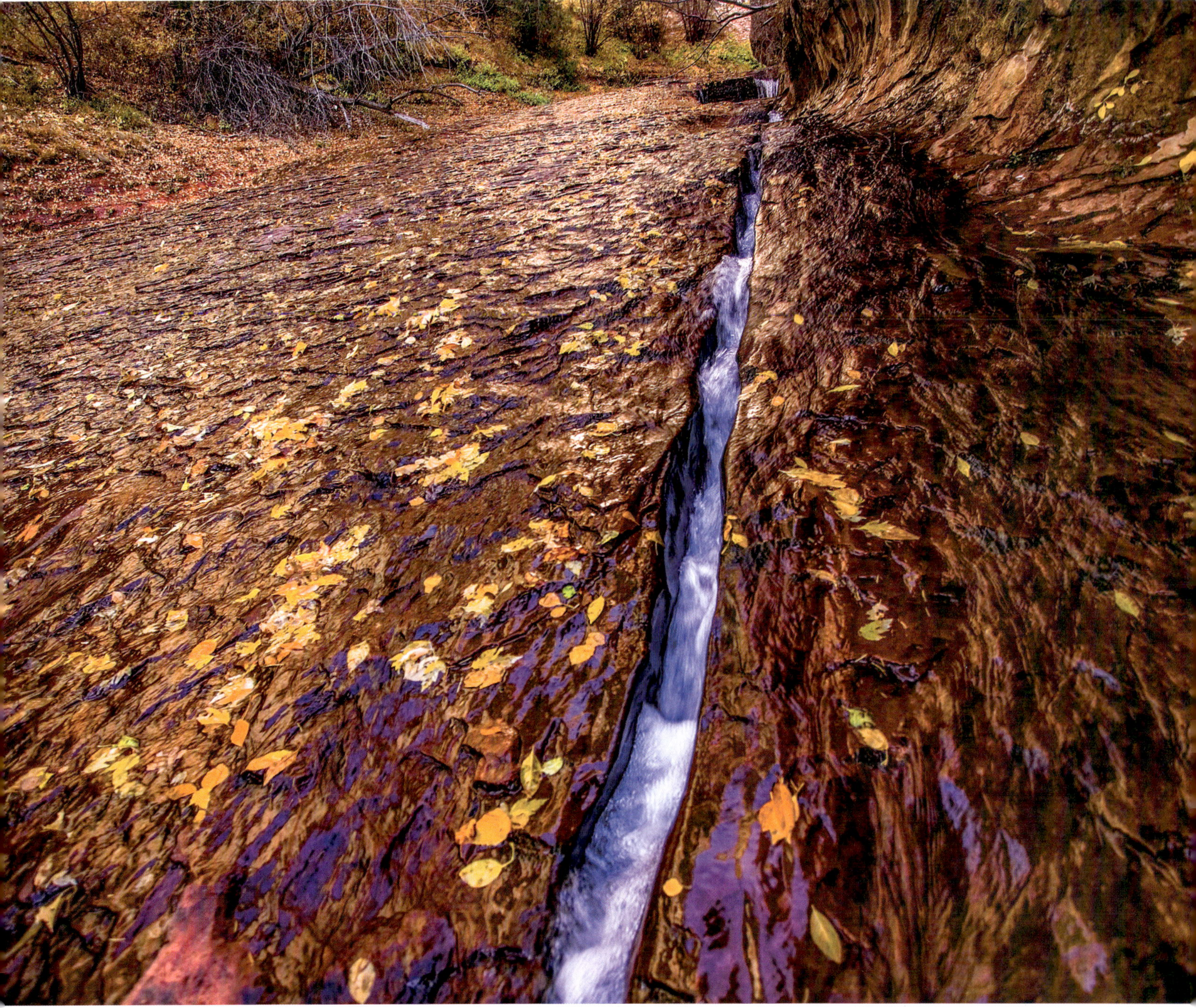

THE LEFT FORK OF NORTH CREEK SLICES THROUGH A RED SANDSTONE SLAB.

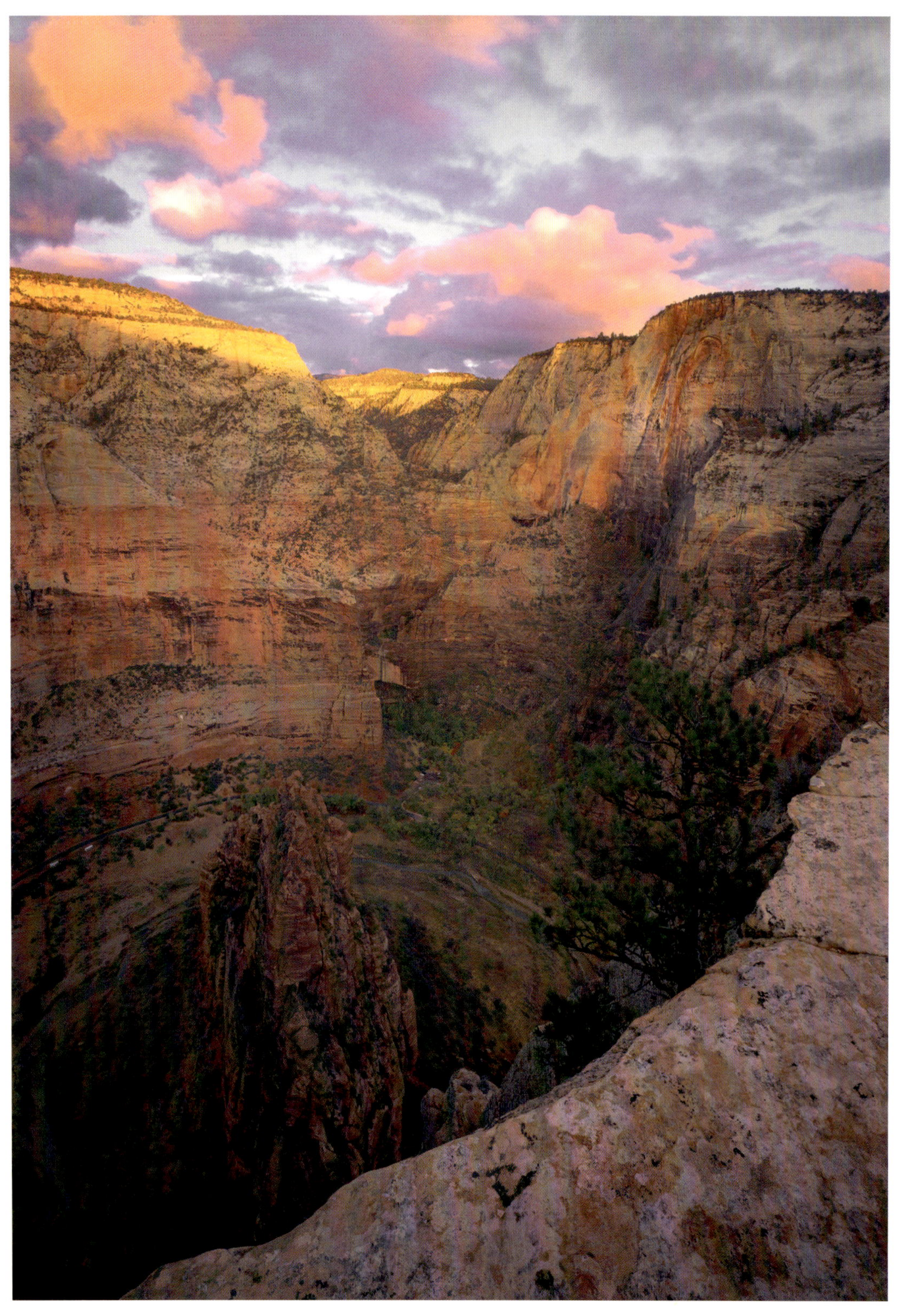

ANGELS LANDING,
OVERLOOKING ZION CANYON.

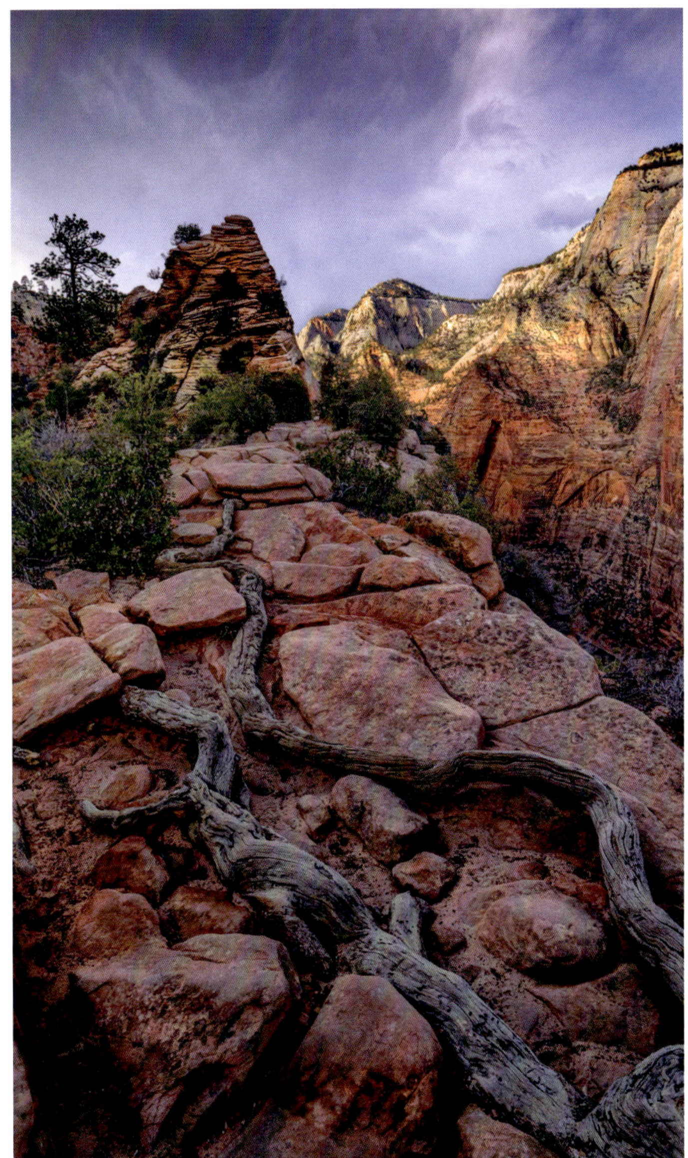

THE ROOTS OF ANCIENT PONDEROSA PINES COVER THE ANGELS LANDING TRAIL HIGH IN ZION NATIONAL PARK.

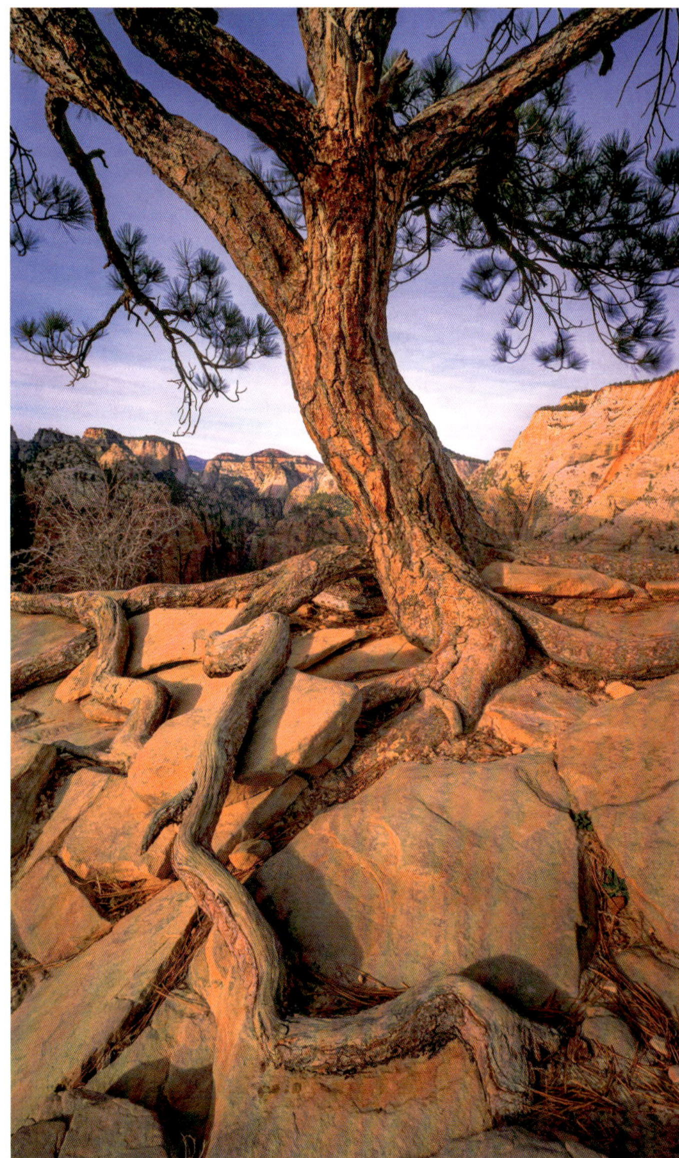

A PONDEROSA PINE STANDS AS A BEACON AT THE SUMMIT OF ZION'S ANGELS LANDING.

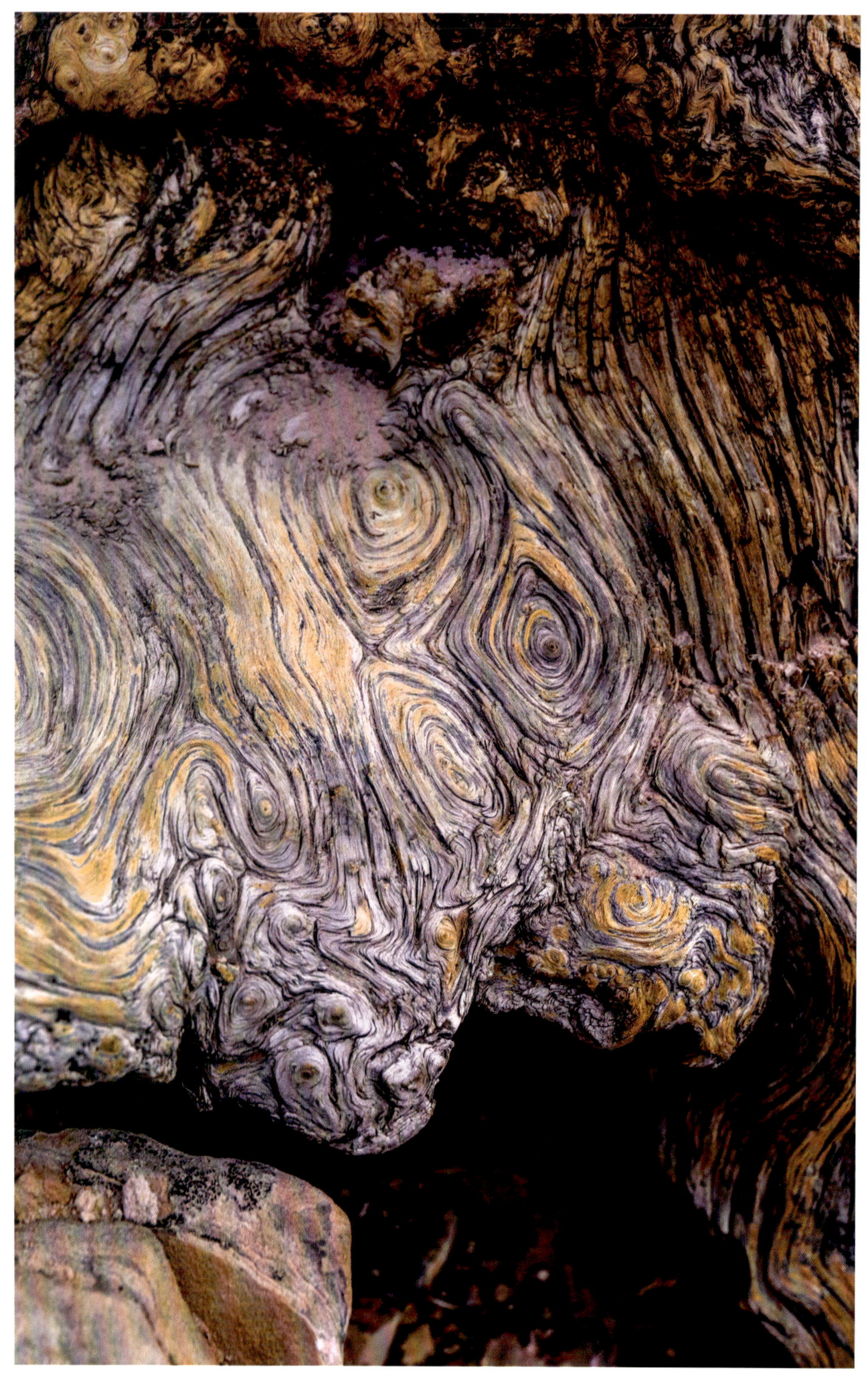

◀

TWISTED BURL WOOD AT THE BASE OF AN ANCIENT PONDEROSA PINE.

▶

THE ANGELS LANDING TRAIL OFFERS A BEAUTIFUL VIEW AT THE SCOUT LOOKOUT ABOVE ZION CANYON'S GIANT SANDSTONE.

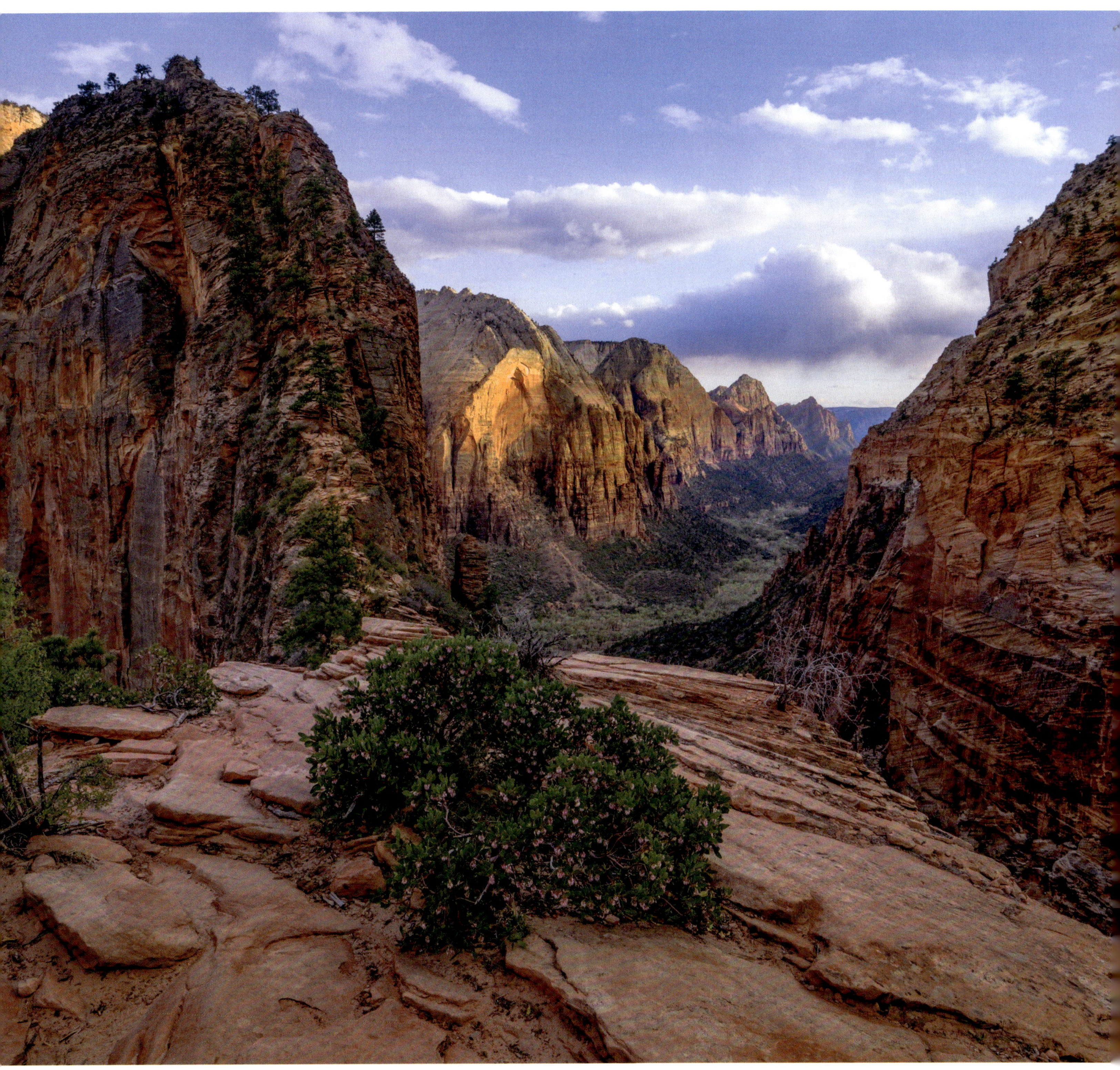

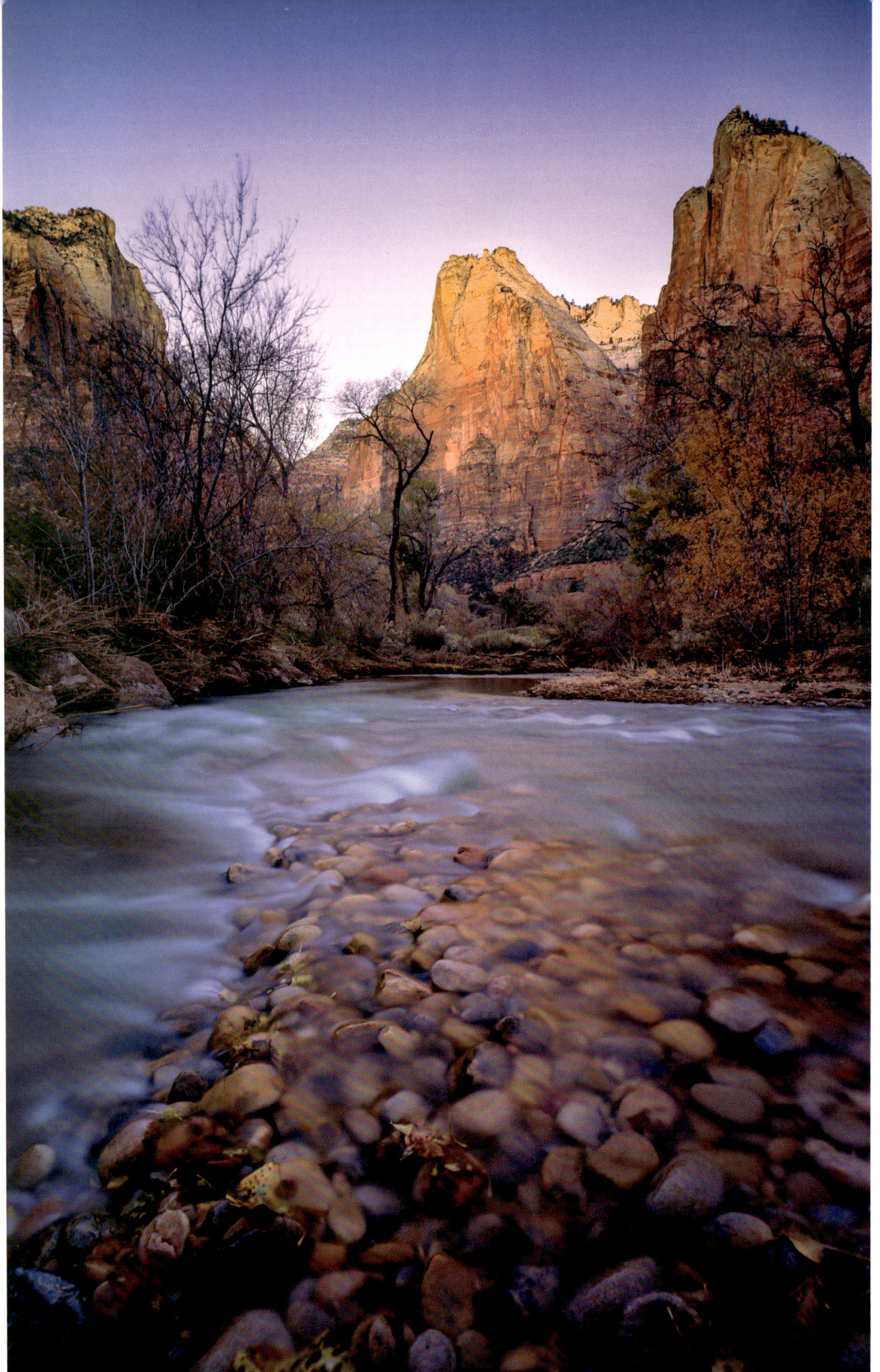

THE VIRGIN RIVER
FLOWS PAST THE COURT
OF THE PATRIARCHS.

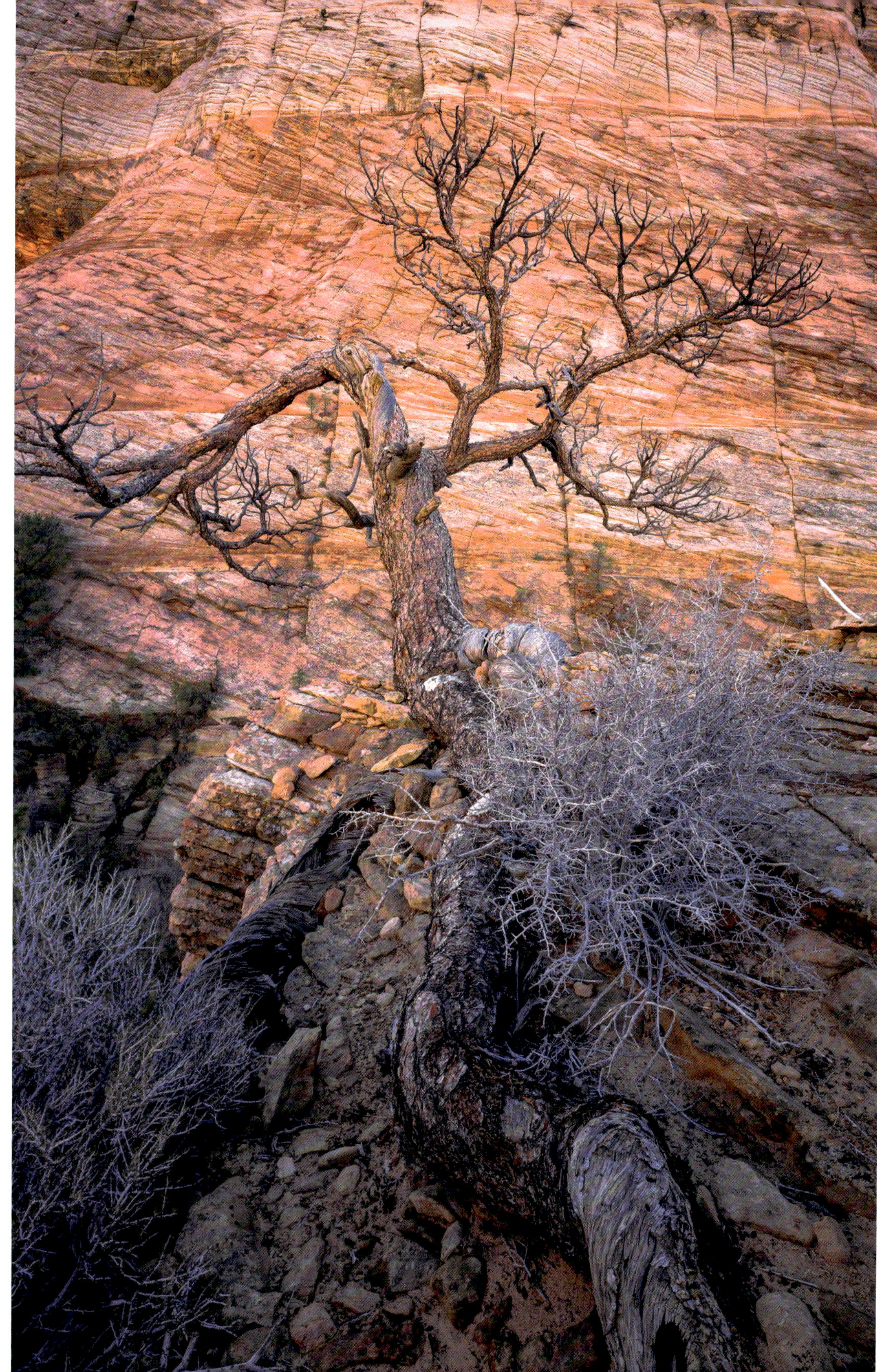

A DEAD PINE HANGS ON THE EXPOSED SANDSTONE OF THE COLORADO PLATEAU NEAR CHECKERBOARD MESA.

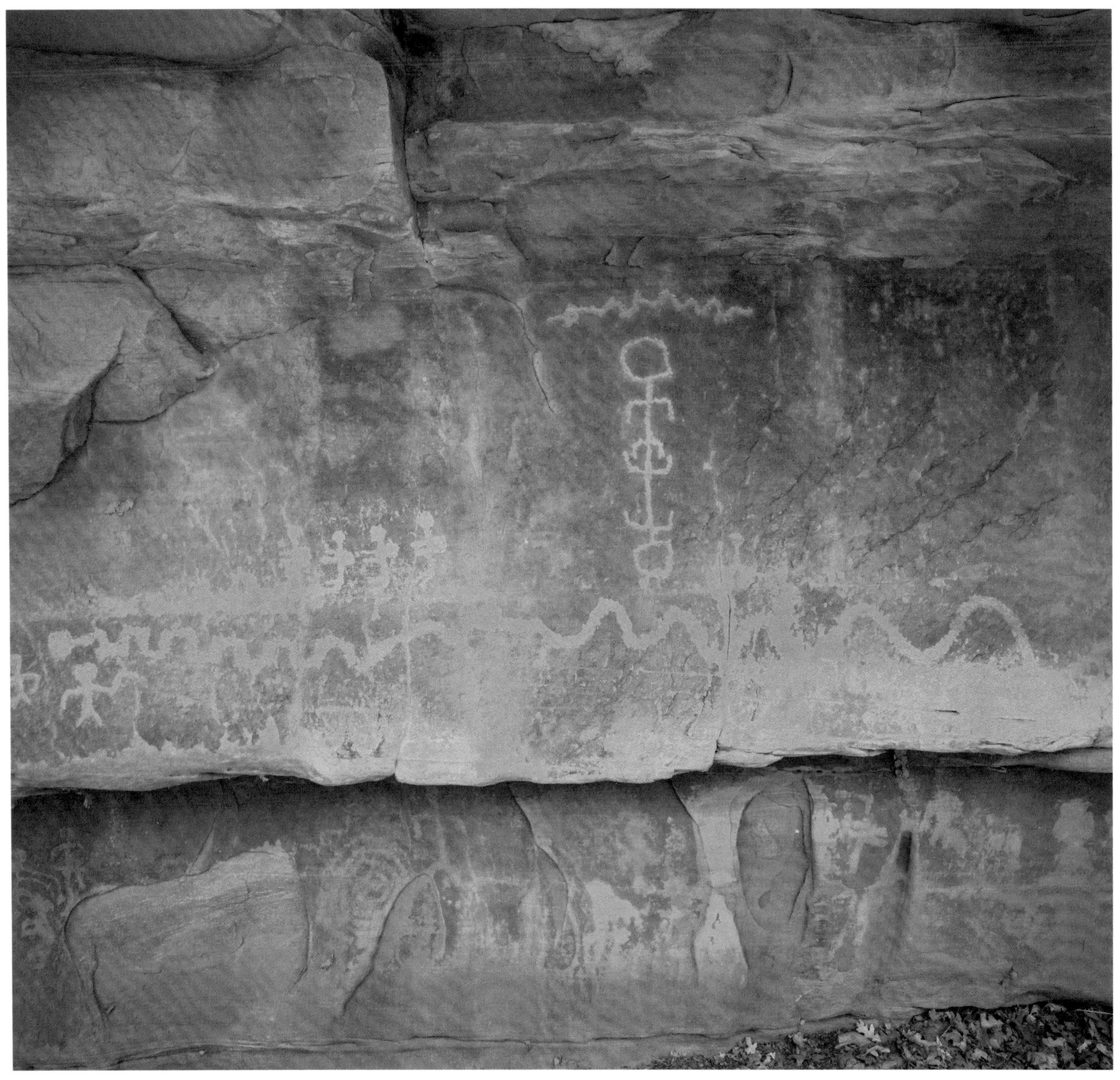

PETROGLYPHS CARVED IN PROTECTED AREAS OF PETROGLYPH CANYON ADORN THE WALL OF ZION NATIONAL PARK.

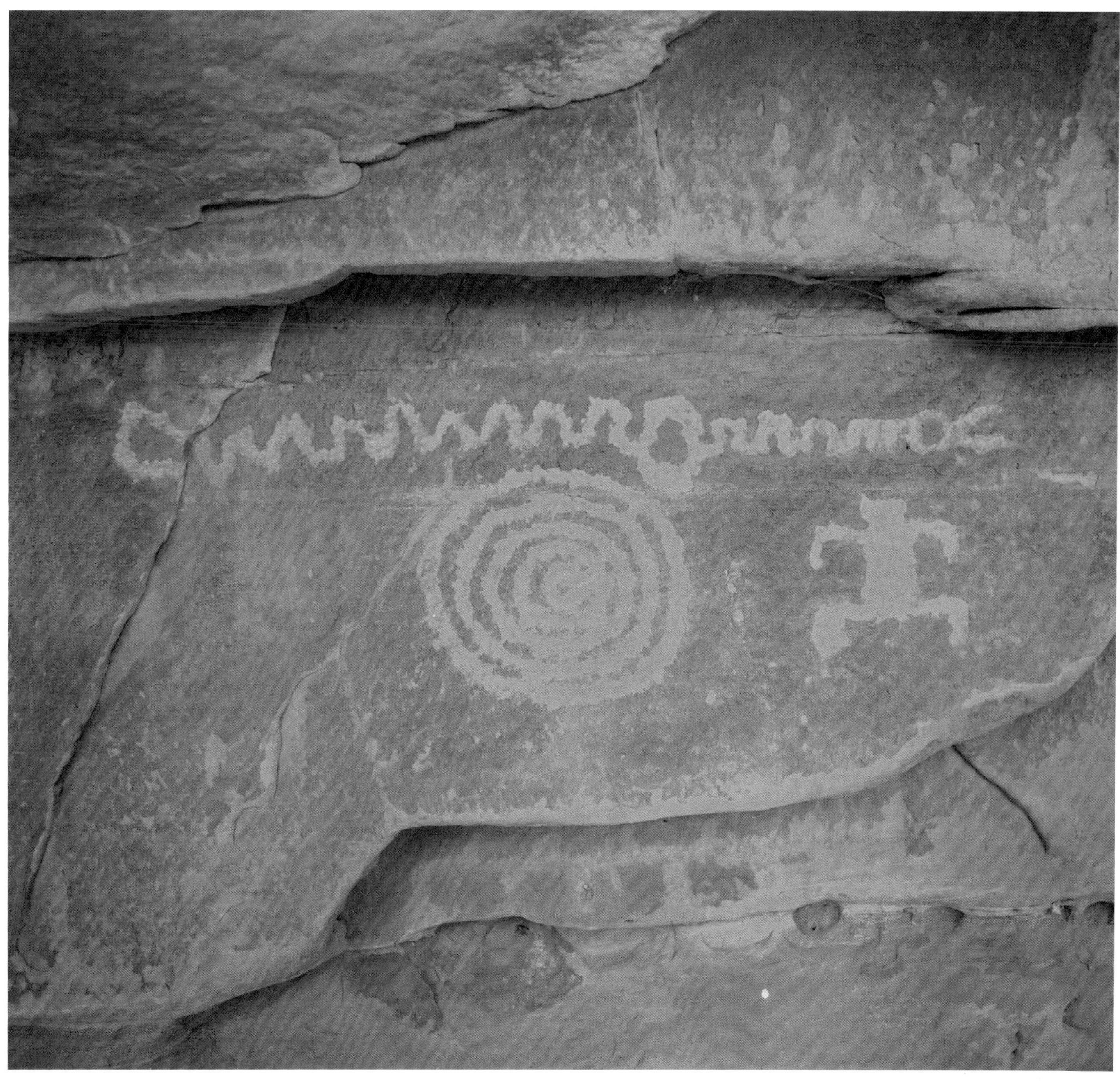

PETROGLYPH DETAILS ENHANCED BY THE WARM LIGHT BOUNCING FROM TIGHT CANYON WALLS.

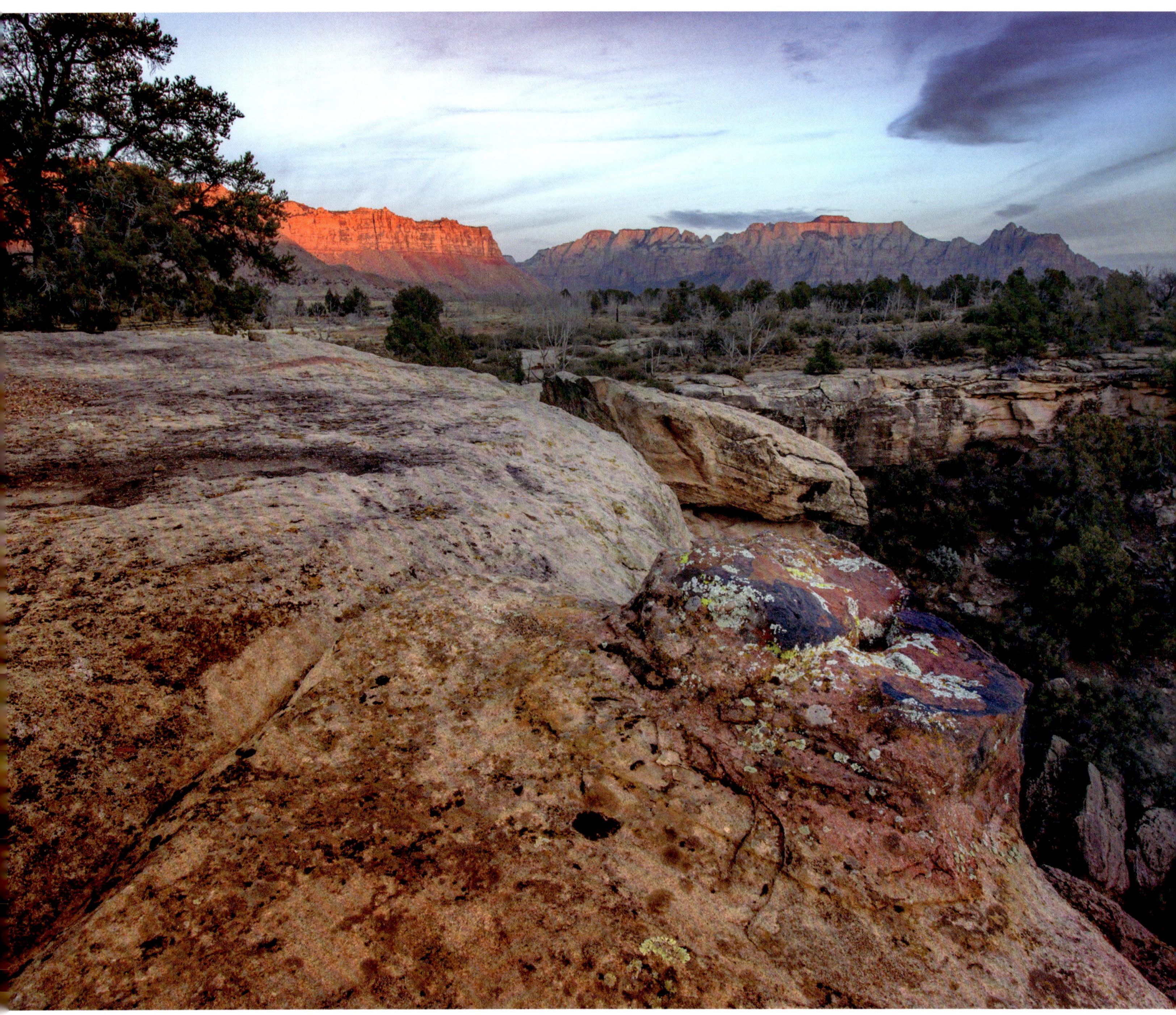

THE BACKSIDE OF ZION'S WEST TEMPLE IS JUST AS SPECTACULAR FROM OUTSIDE THE PARK BOUNDARY.

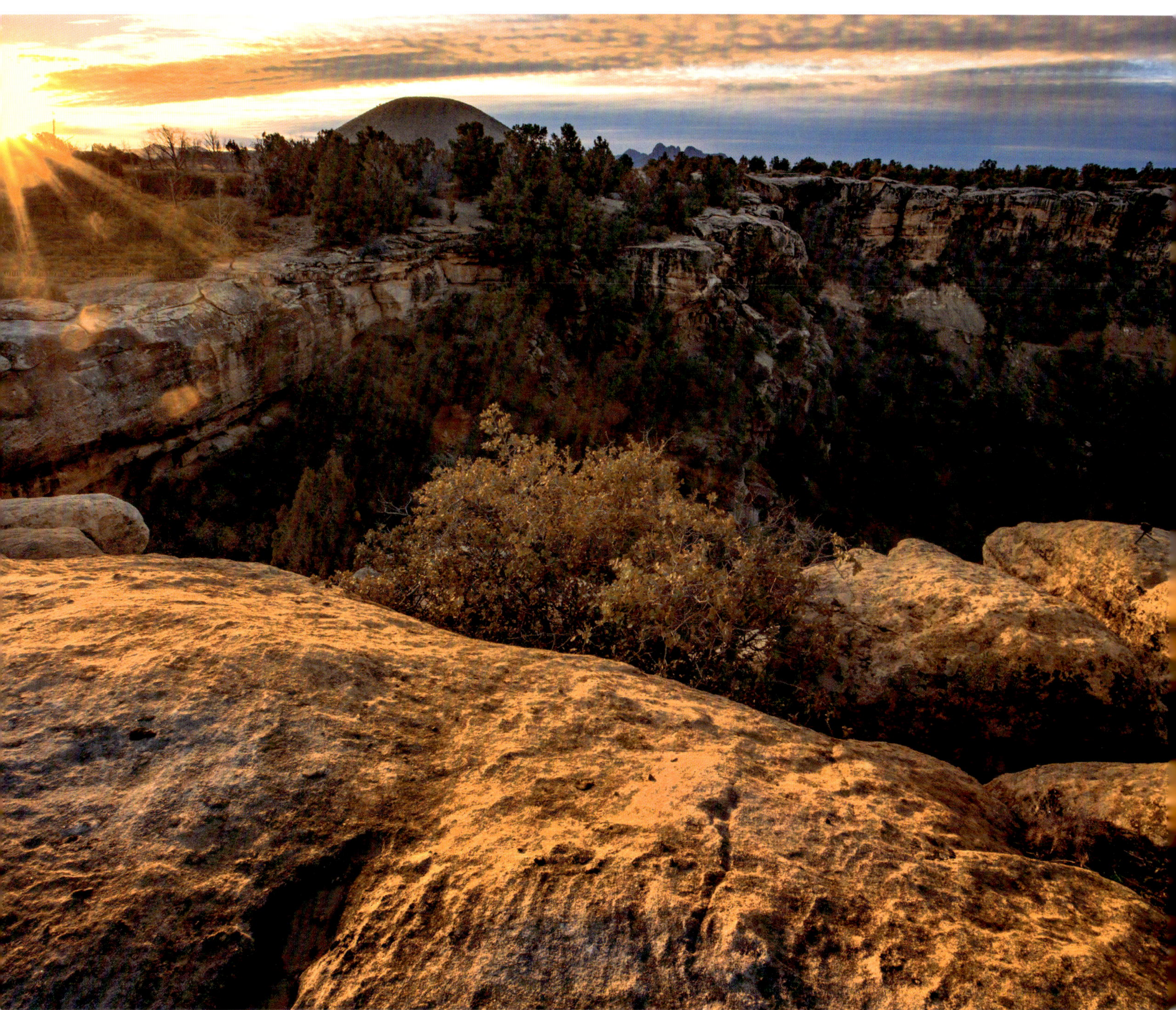

THE BACKSIDE OF ZION BOASTS SPECTACULAR SUNSETS.

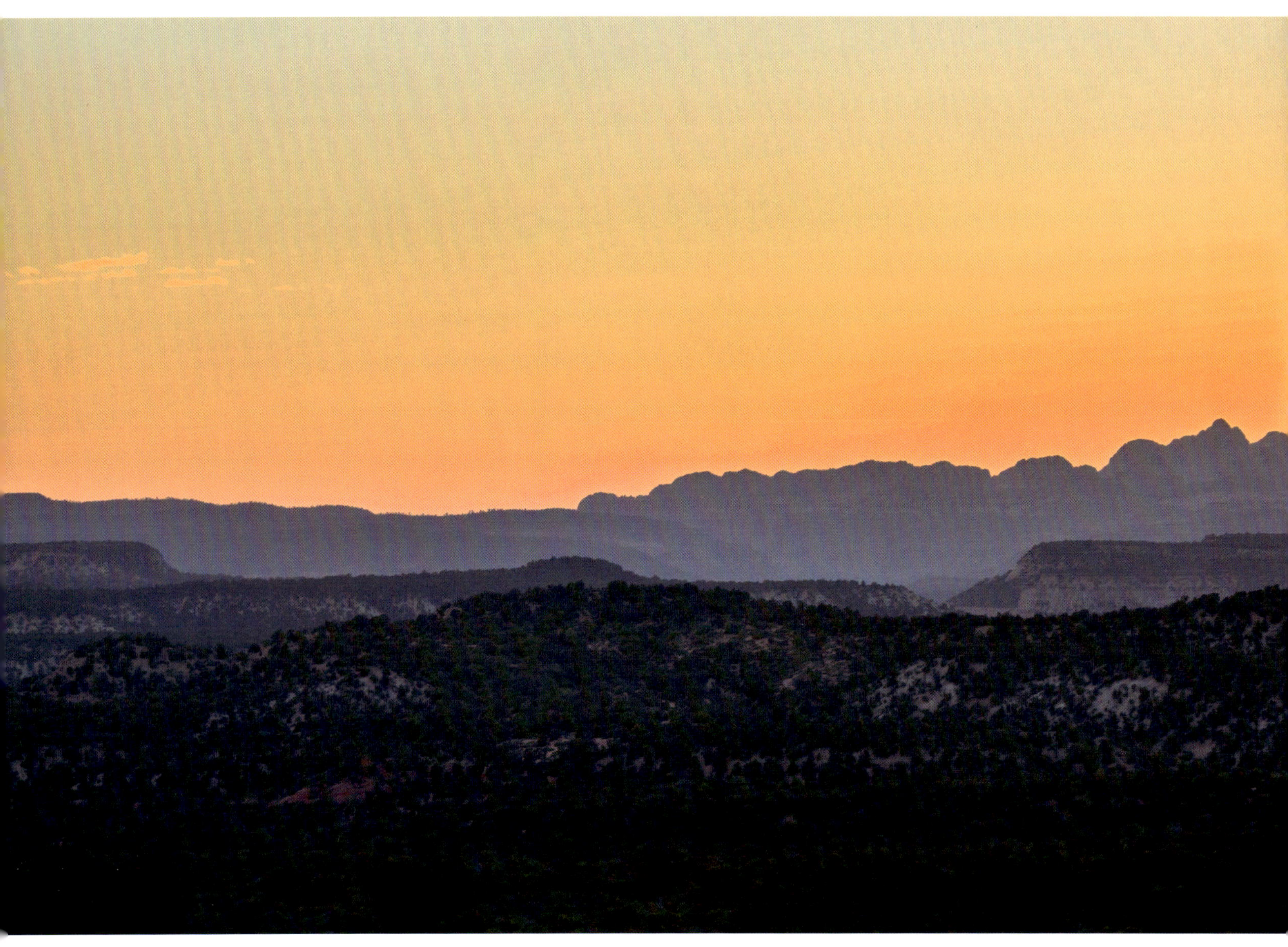

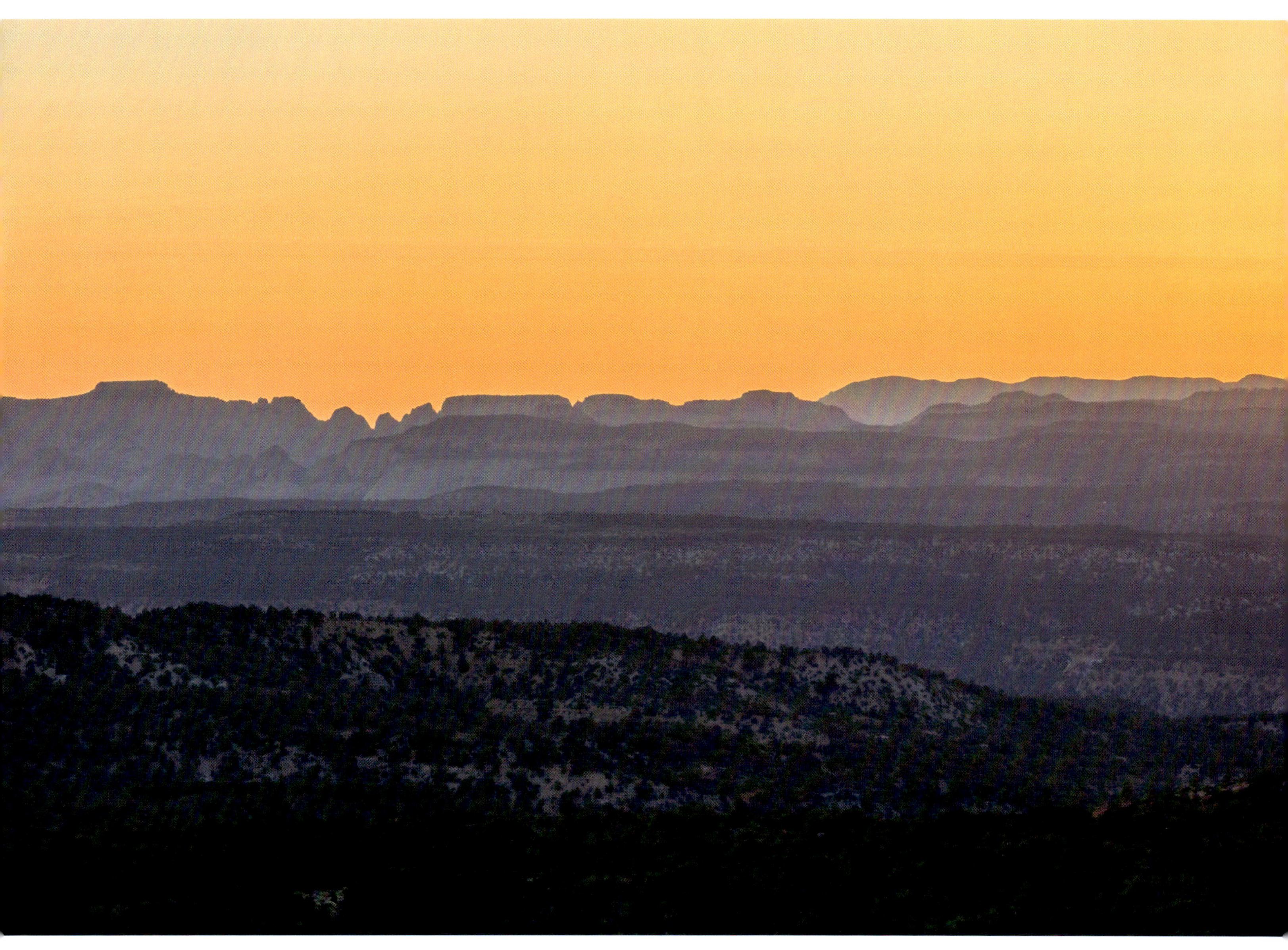

LOOKING ACROSS THE VIRGIN RIVER GORGE TOWARDS ZION FROM THE GLENDALE BENCH.

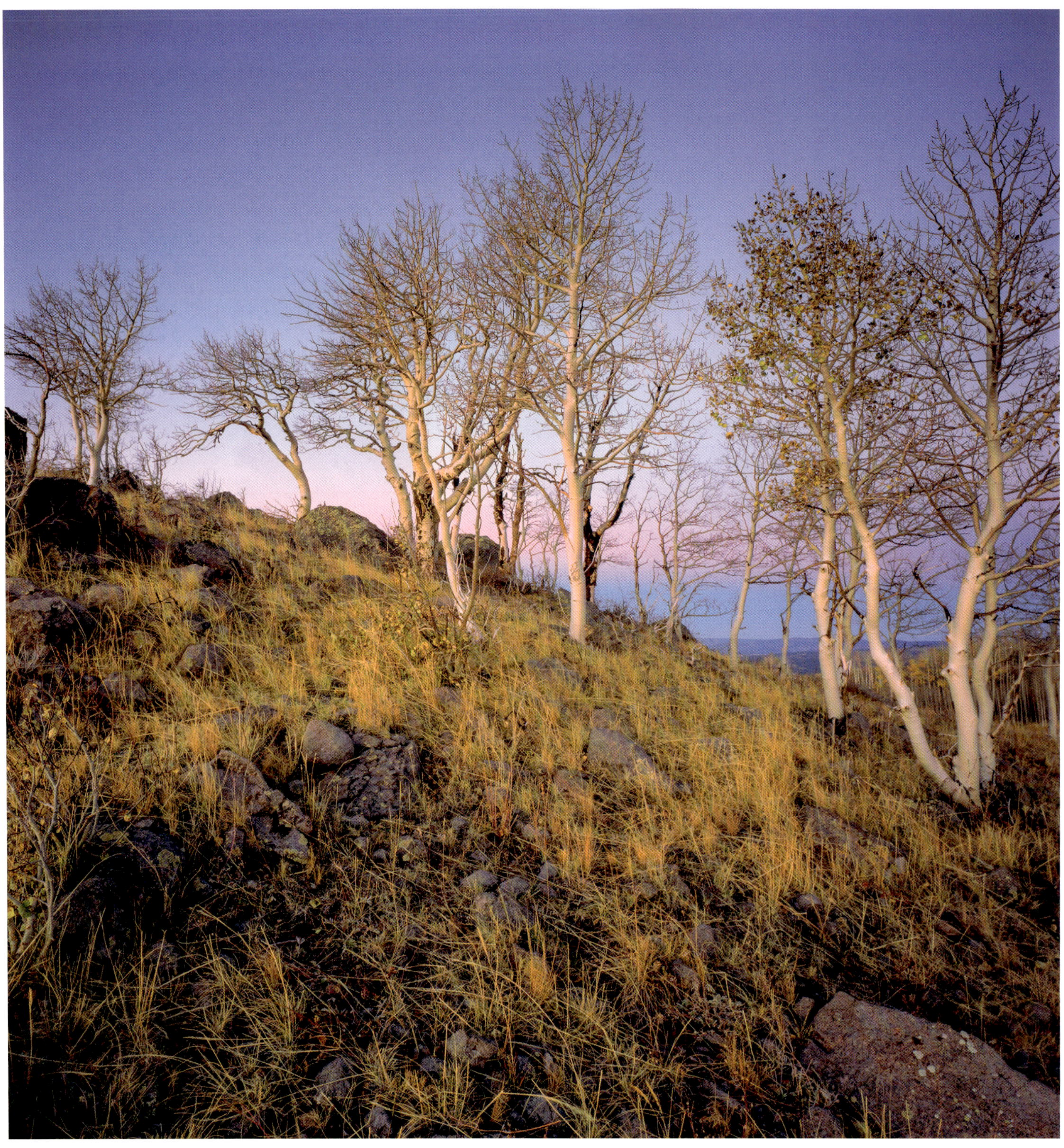

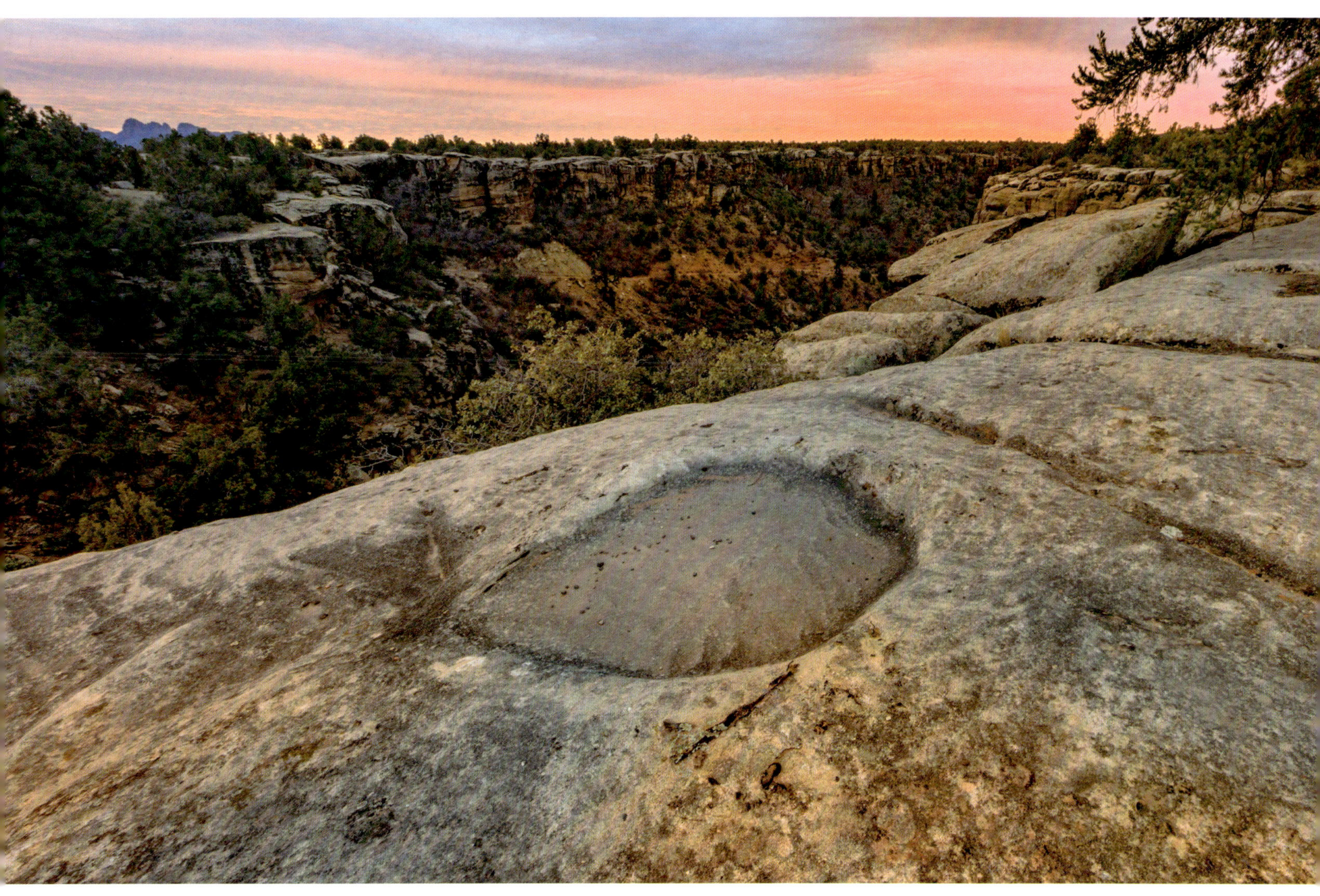

▲
LOOKING DOWNCANYON
AT DALTON WASH, NEAR THE
SMALL TOWN OF VIRGIN.

◀
ASPENS HIGH IN UTAH'S DIXIE
NATIONAL FOREST HAVE DROPPED
THEIR LEAVES IN PREPARATION
FOR THE COMING WINTER.

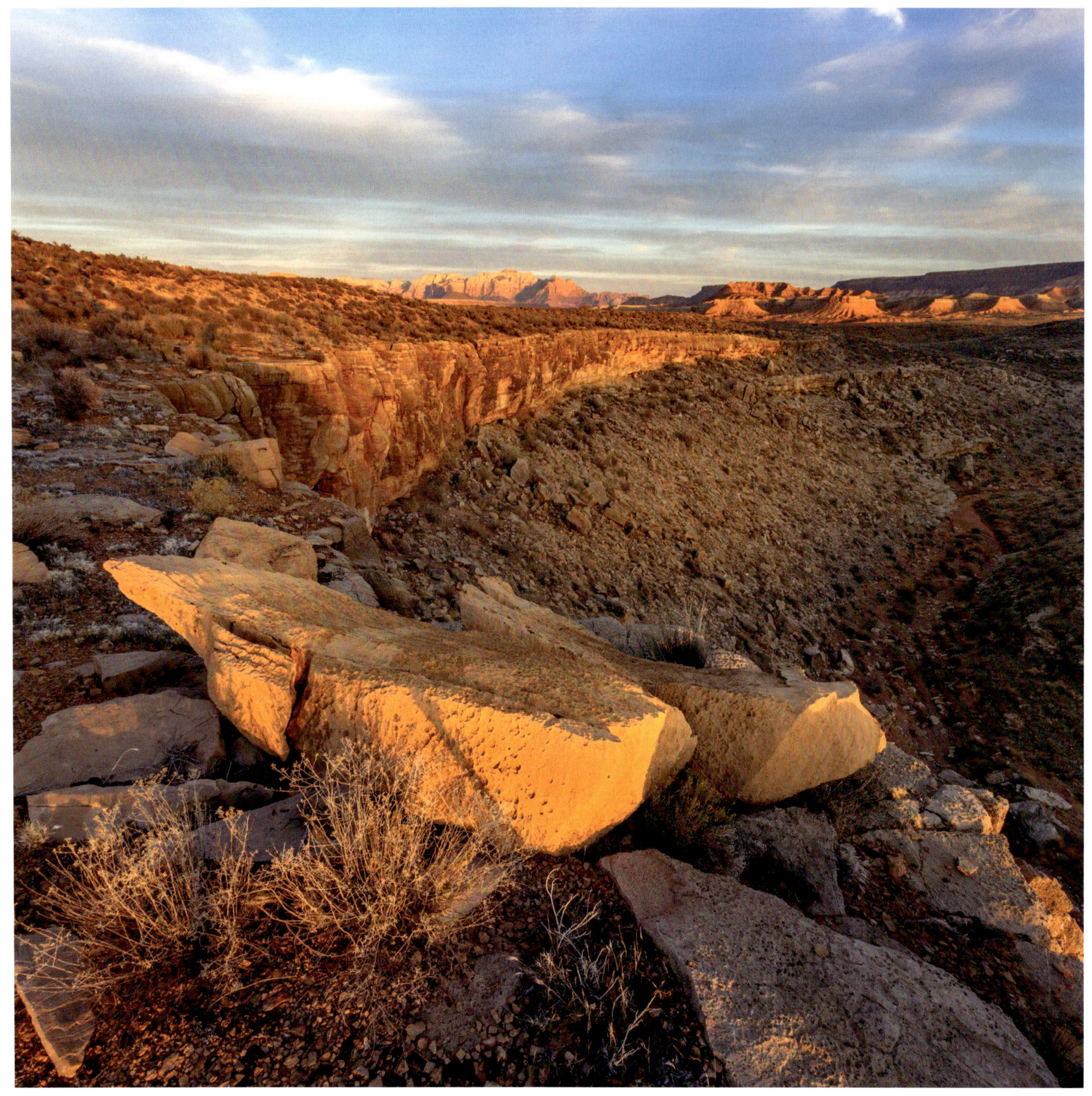

 THE PEAKS OF ZION NATIONAL PARK PEEK OVER THE DESERT EDGE ALONG THE JEM TRAIL NEAR VIRGIN.

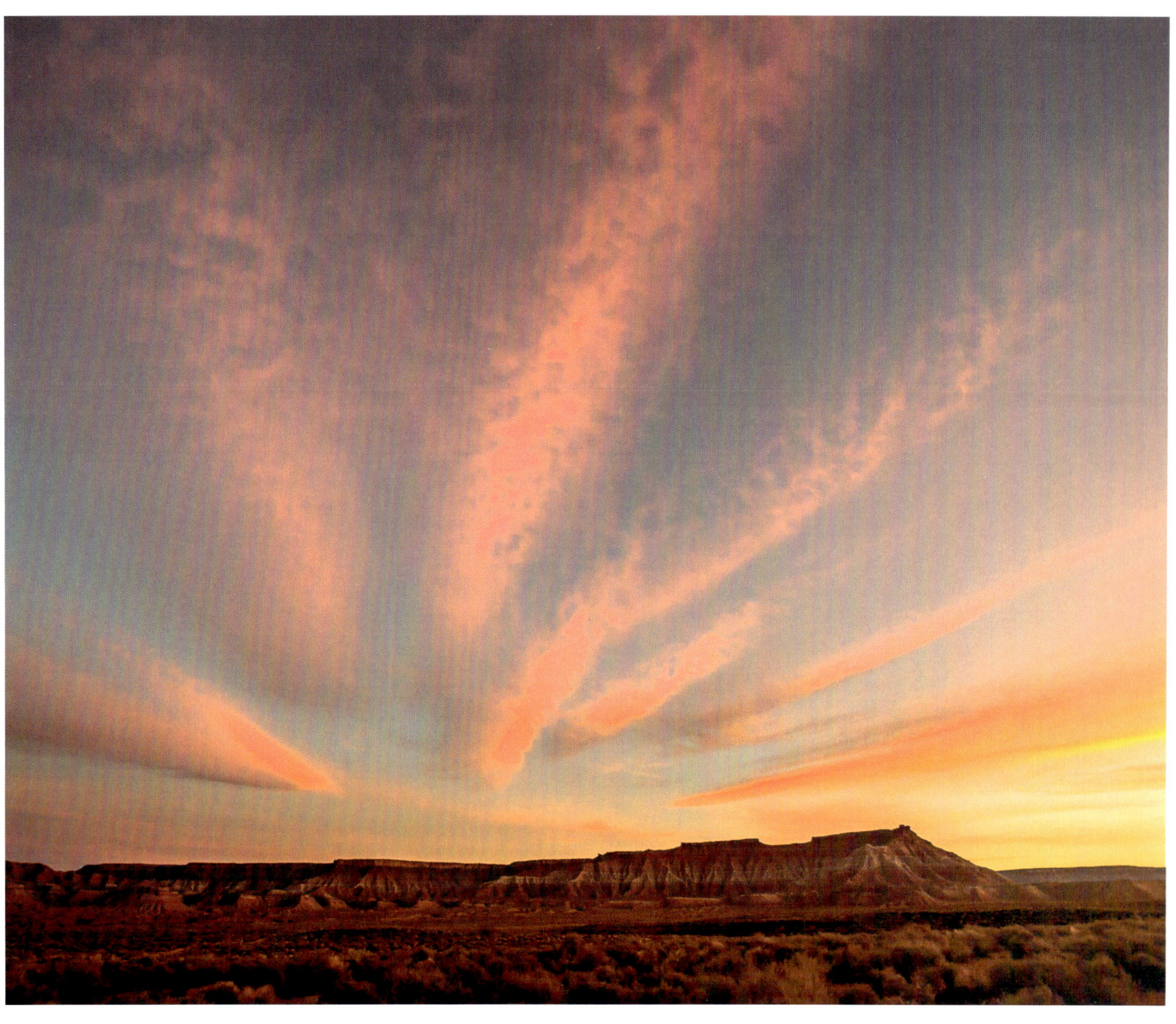

BRILLIANT CLOUDS GUIDE YOU TO THE RIM OF GOOSEBERRY MESA.

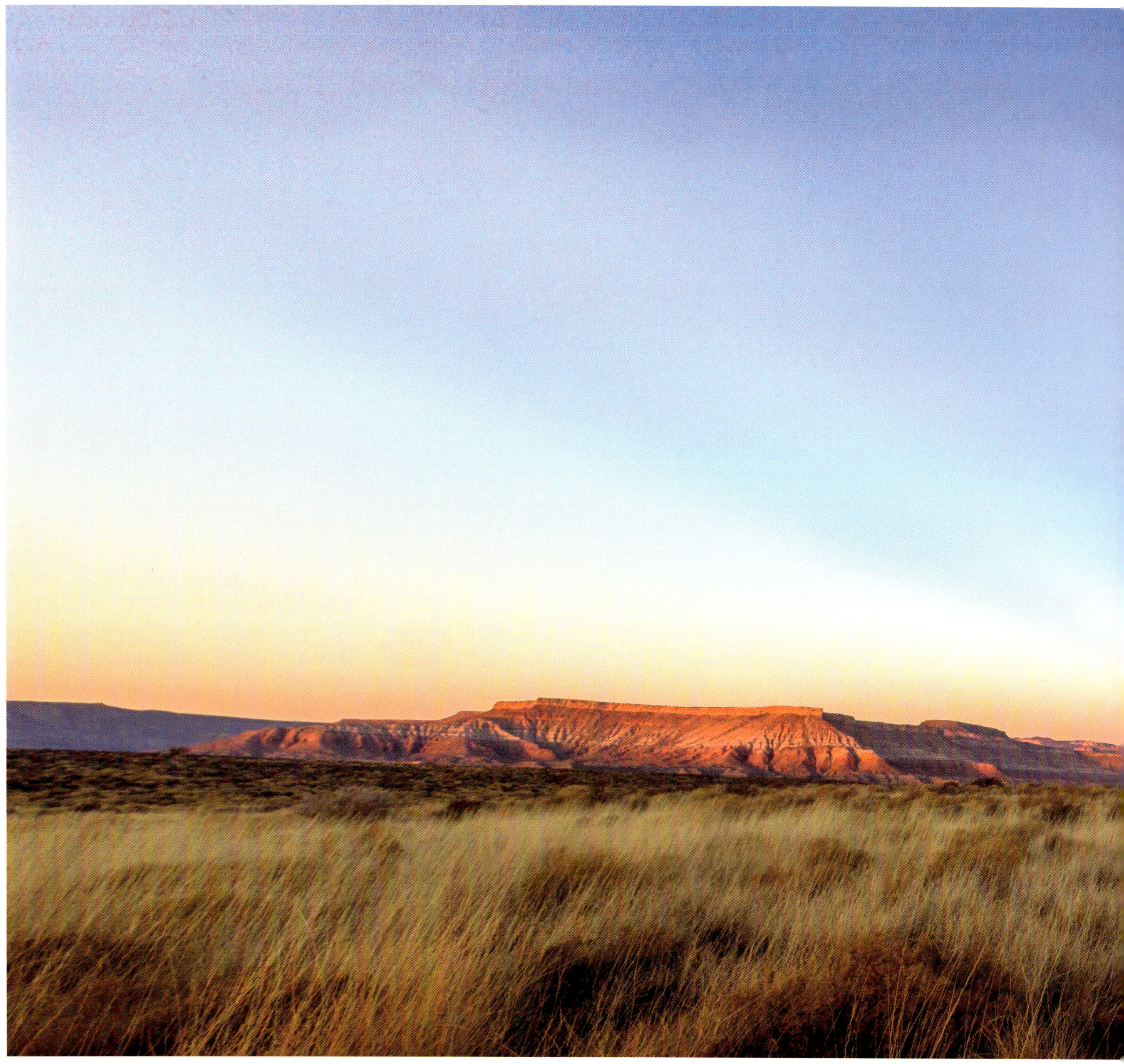

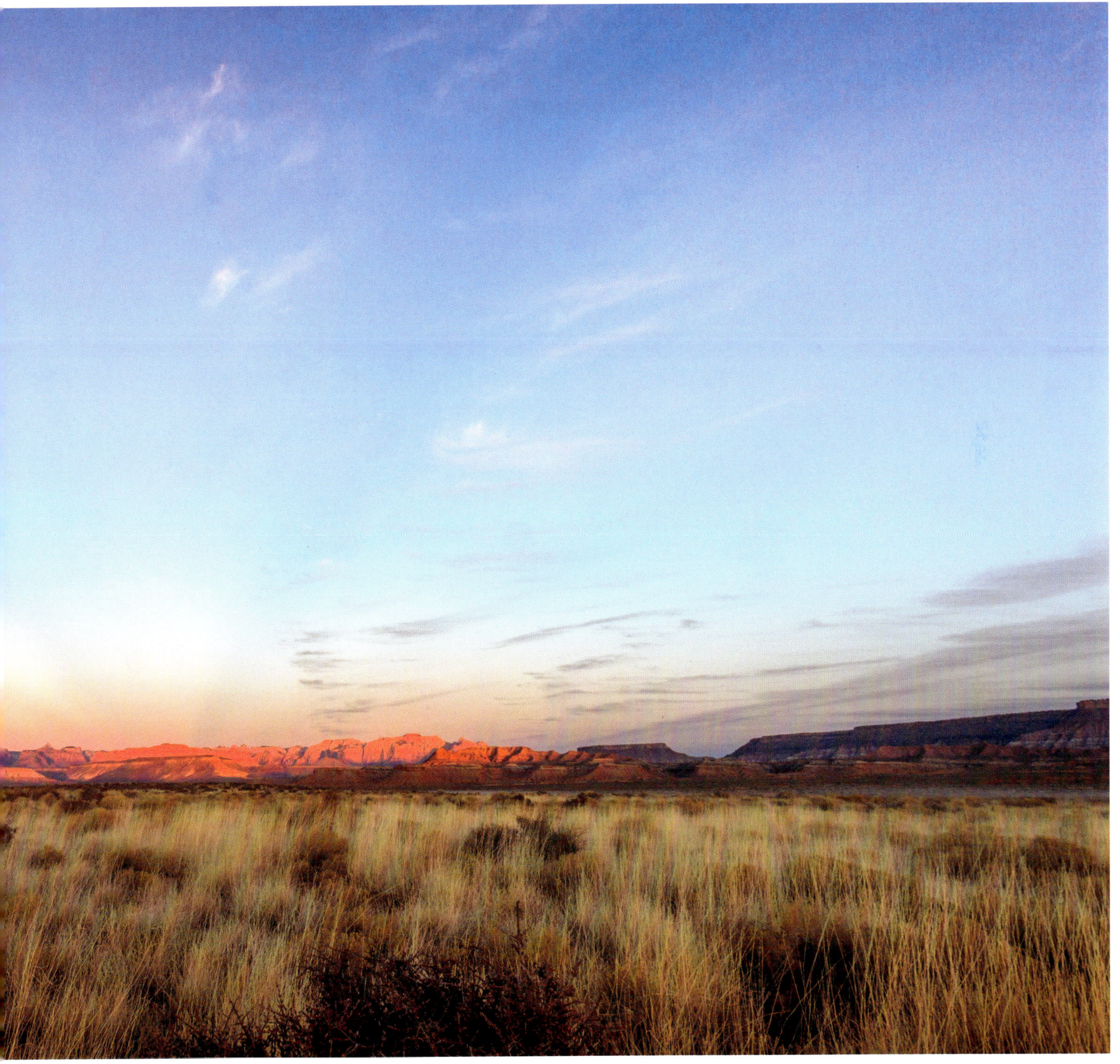

GOLDEN GRASSES COVER THE MESA NEAR LA VERKIN.

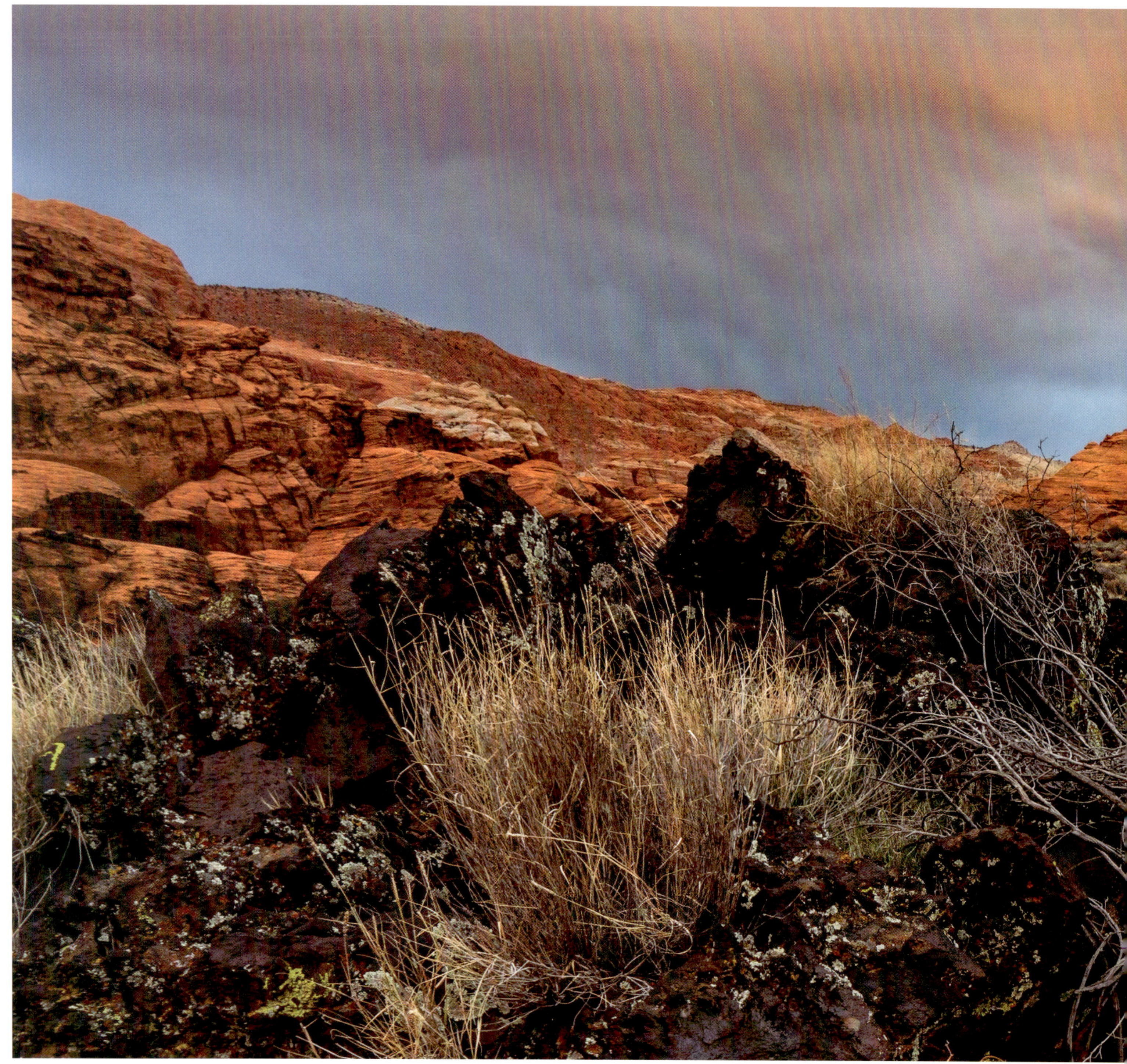

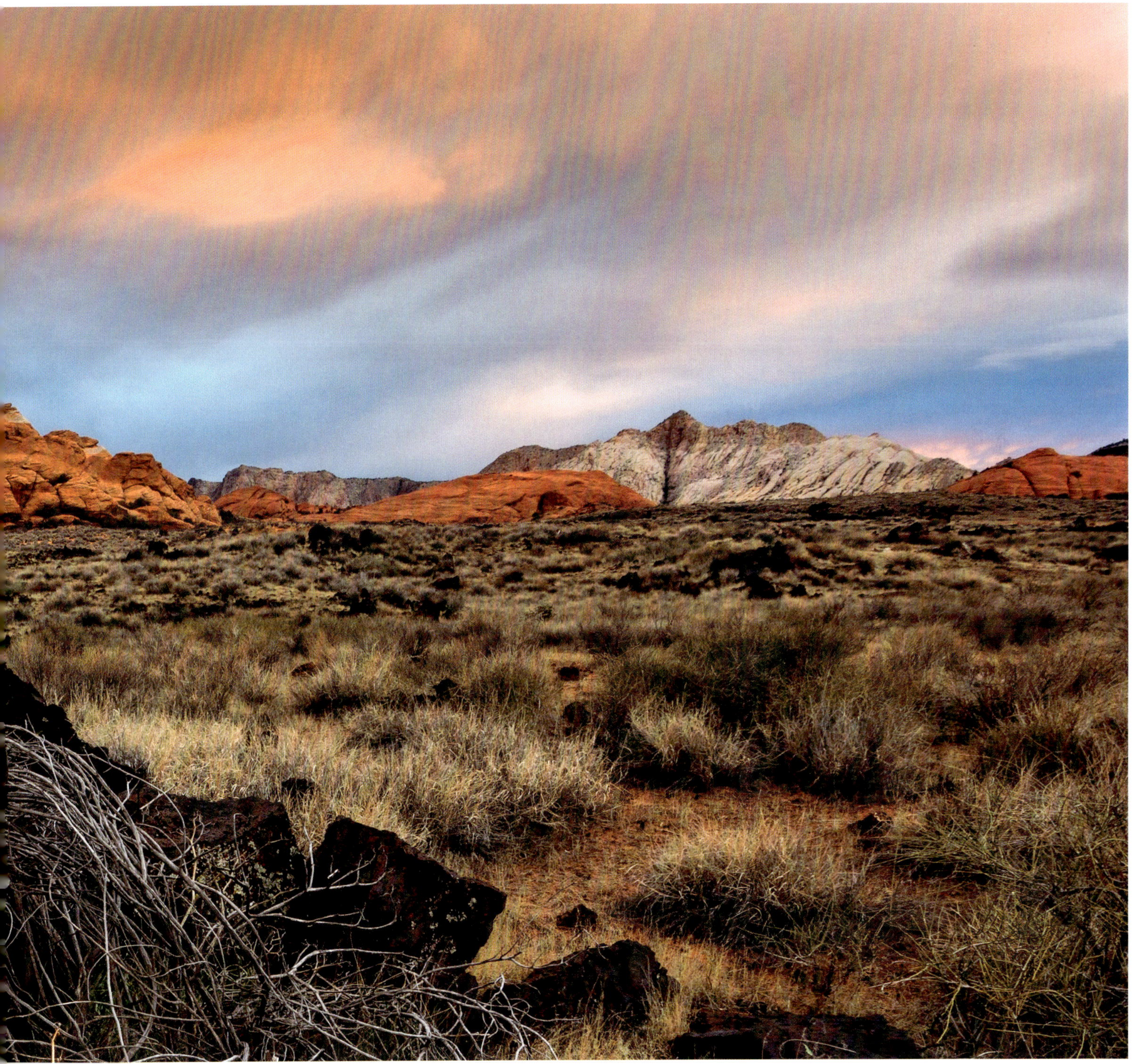

SNOW CANYON BOASTS BEAUTIFUL ROCK FORMATIONS IN A UNIQUE CORNER OF UTAH.

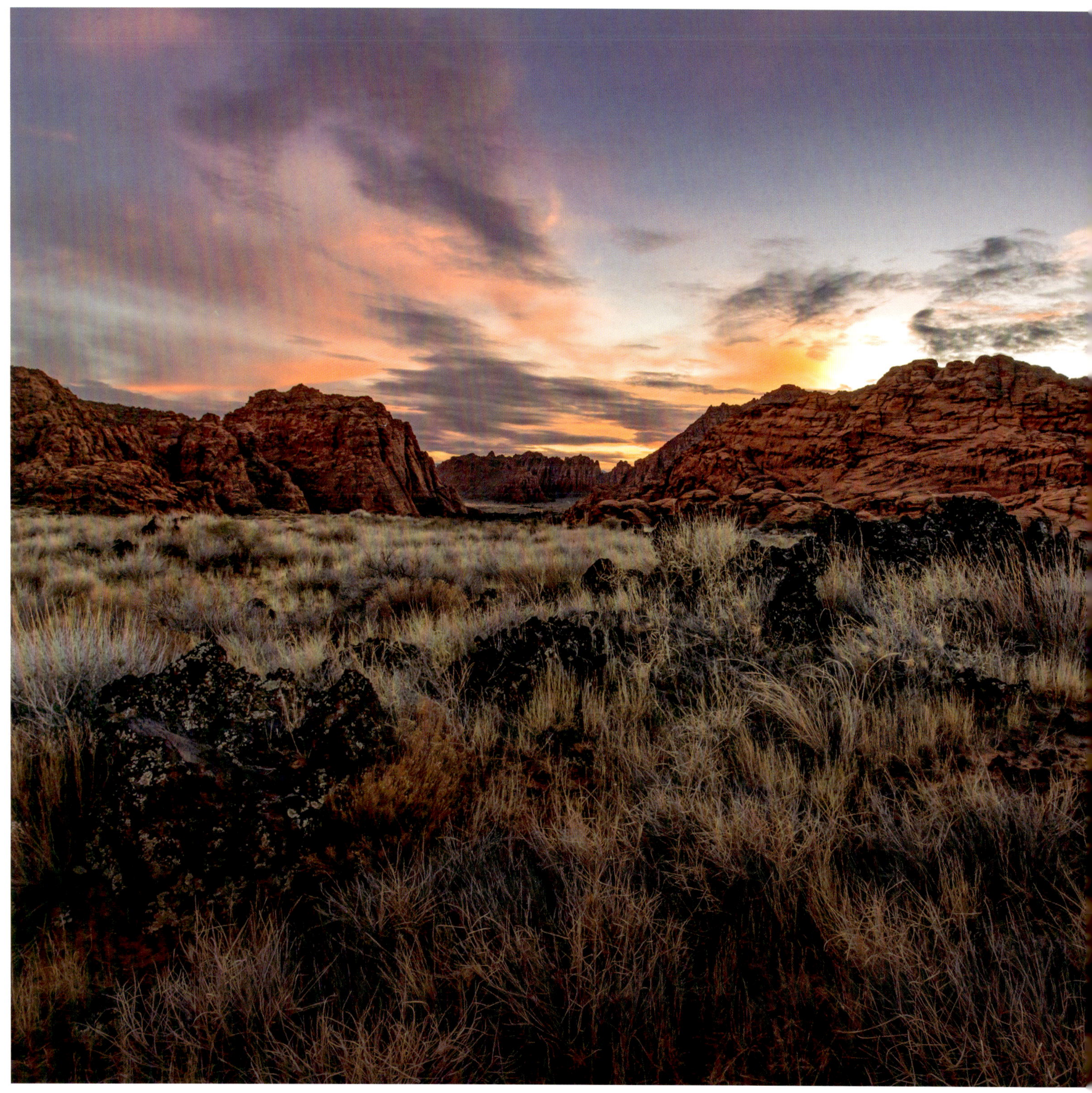

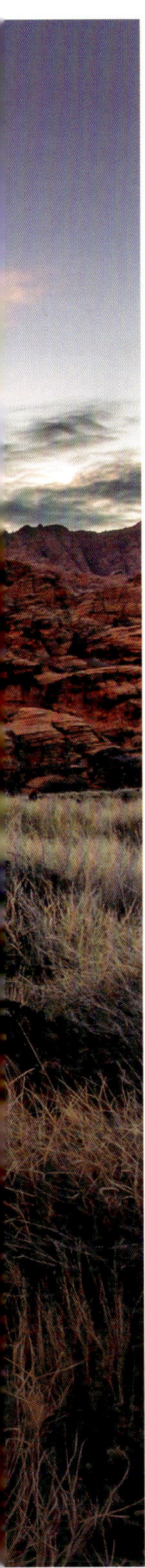

◀

SUNSET IN BEAUTIFUL SNOW CANYON STATE PARK.

▶

DOME-SHAPED SANDSTONE IN THE GRAND STAIRCASE–ESCALANTE NATIONAL MONUMENT.

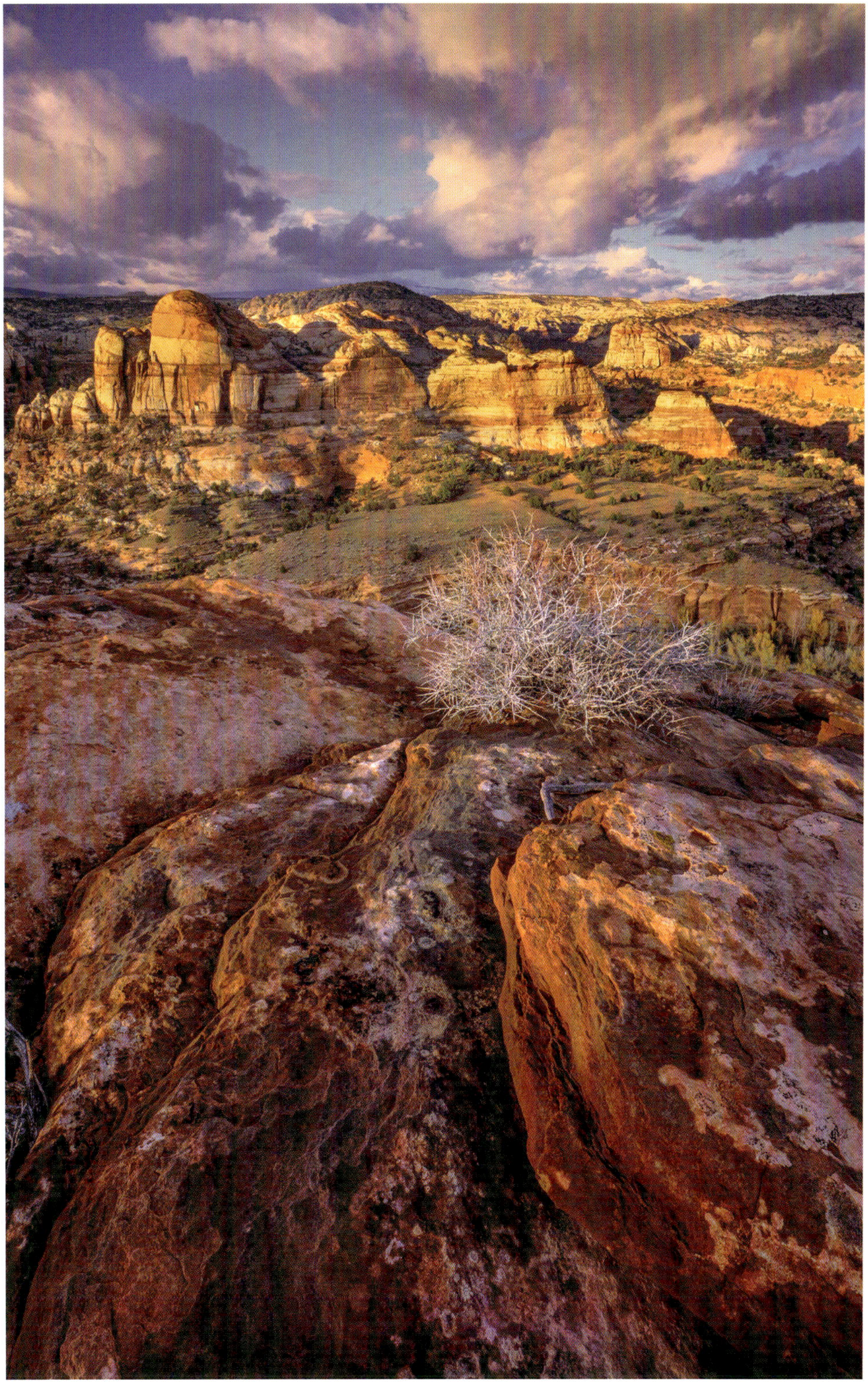

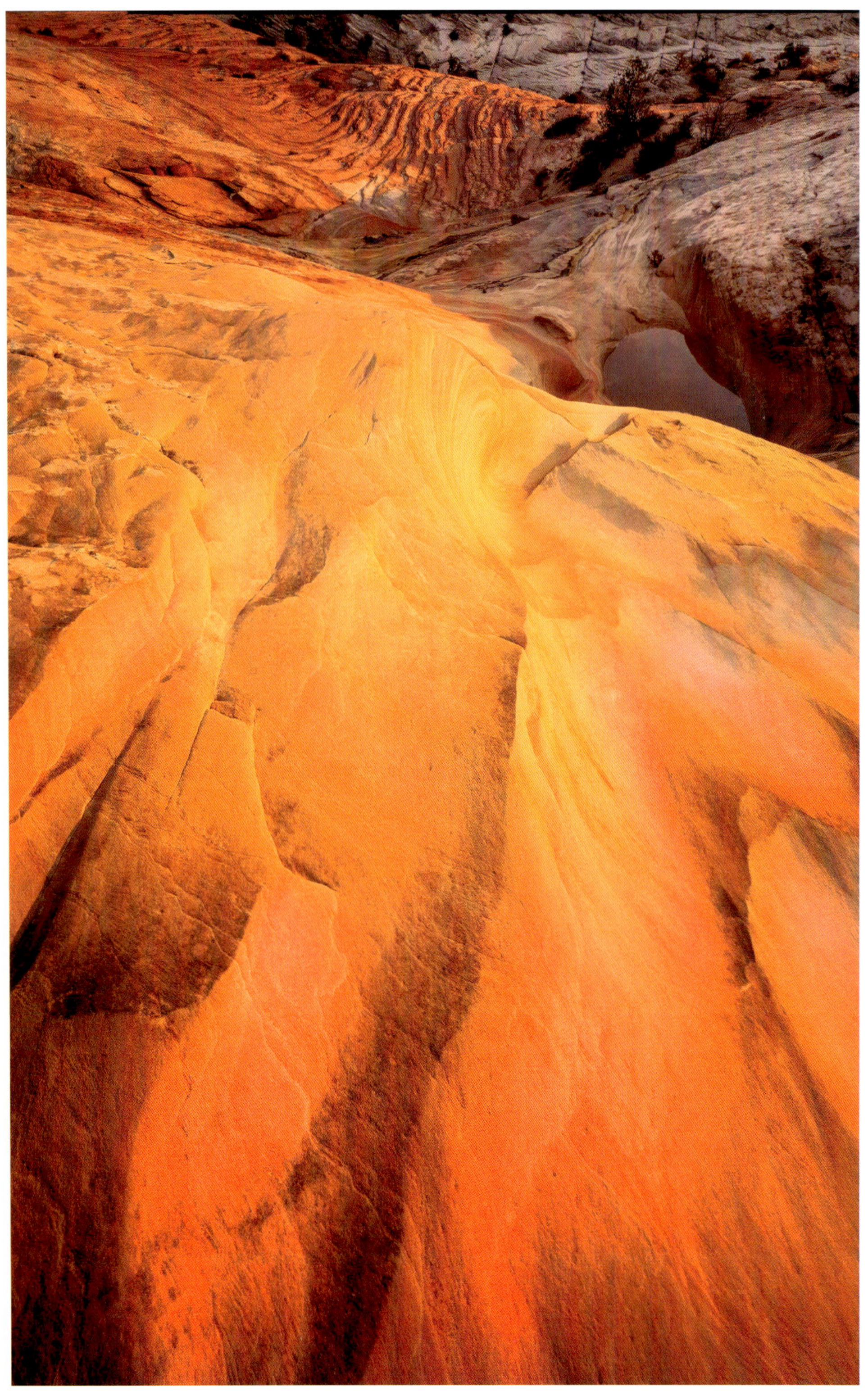

◀
SANDSTONE WAVES IN THE ROLLING ROCK OF THE GRAND STAIRCASE–ESCALANTE NATIONAL MONUMENT.

▶
STRONG VERTICAL LINES CARVED INTO THE PINK-RED CLIFFS OF THE GULCH, IN THE HEART OF THE GRAND STAIRCASE–ESCALANTE NATIONAL MONUMENT.

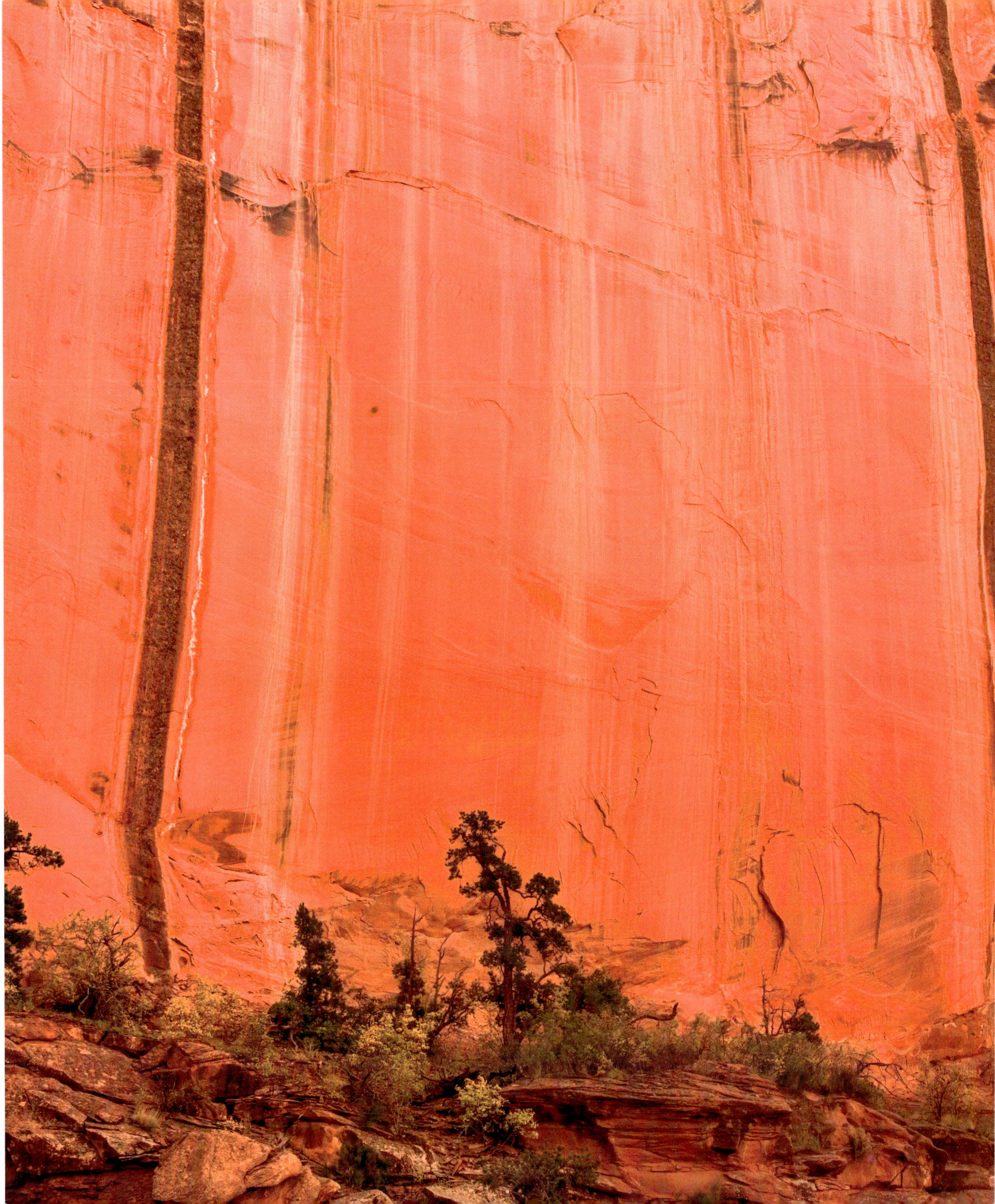

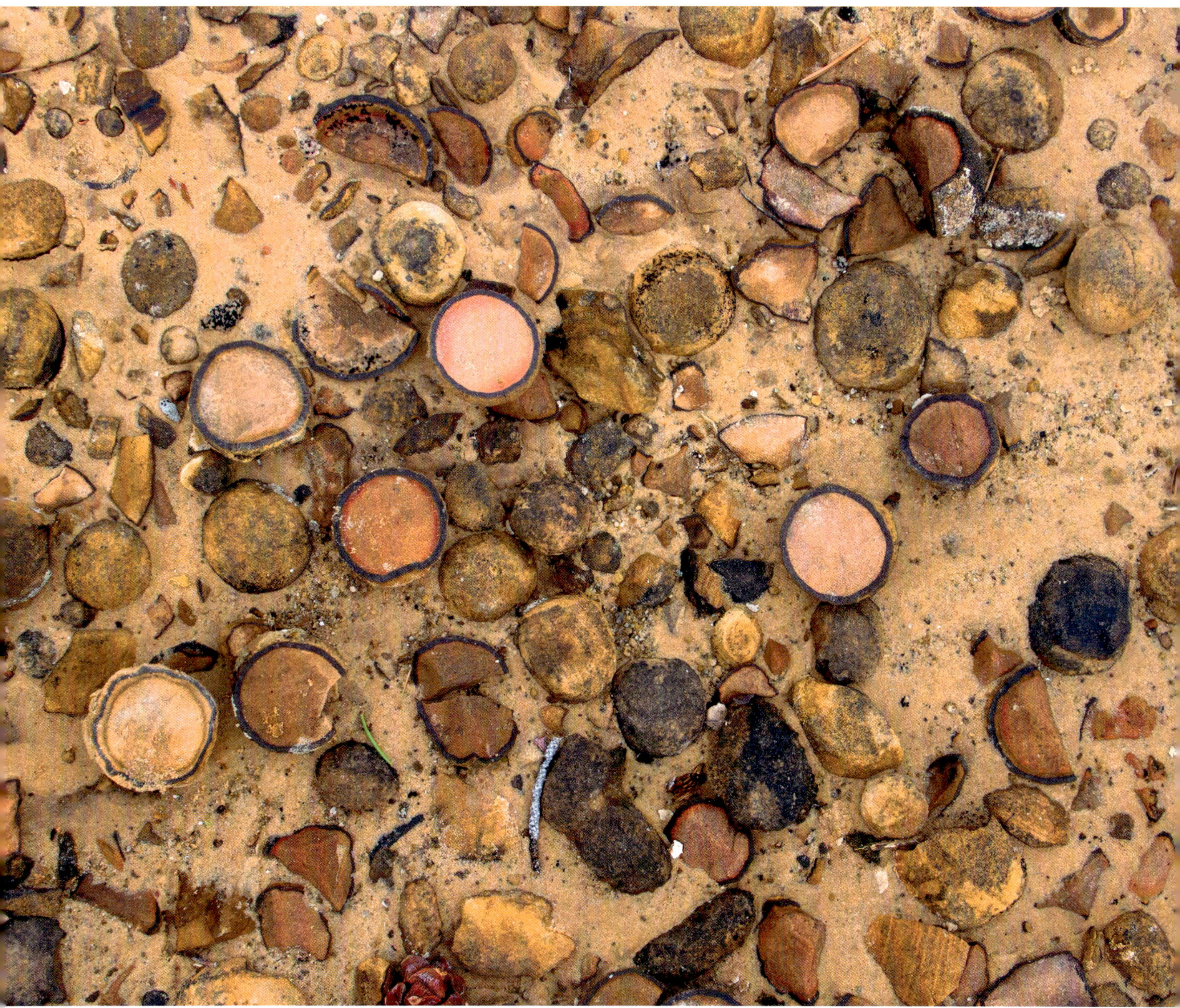

MOQUI MARBLES BURIED IN THE SAND IN THE GRAND STAIRCASE–ESCALANTE NATIONAL MONUMENT.

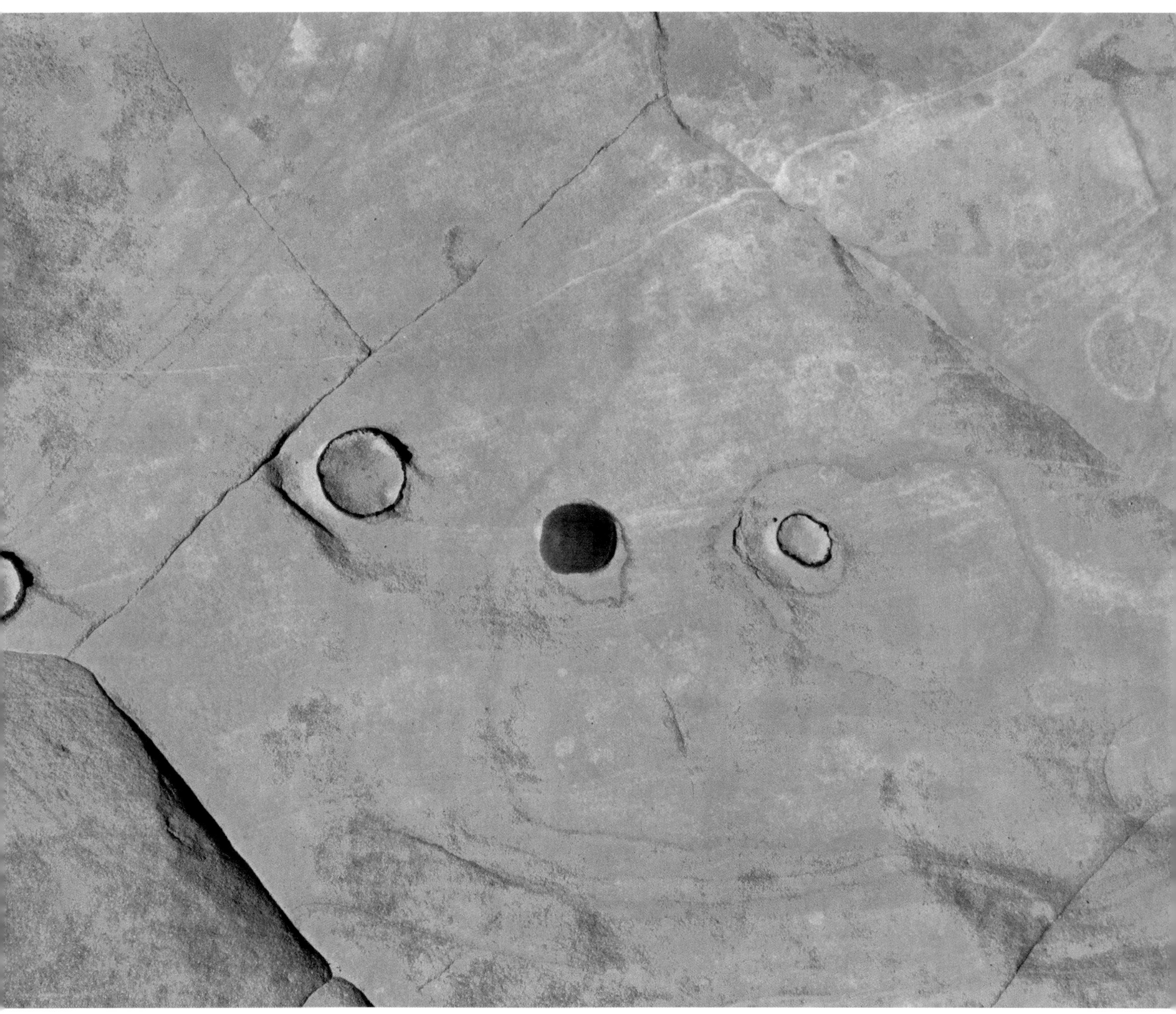

BEAUTIFUL PATTERNS ON SPENCER FLAT, HIGH IN THE ESCALANTE.

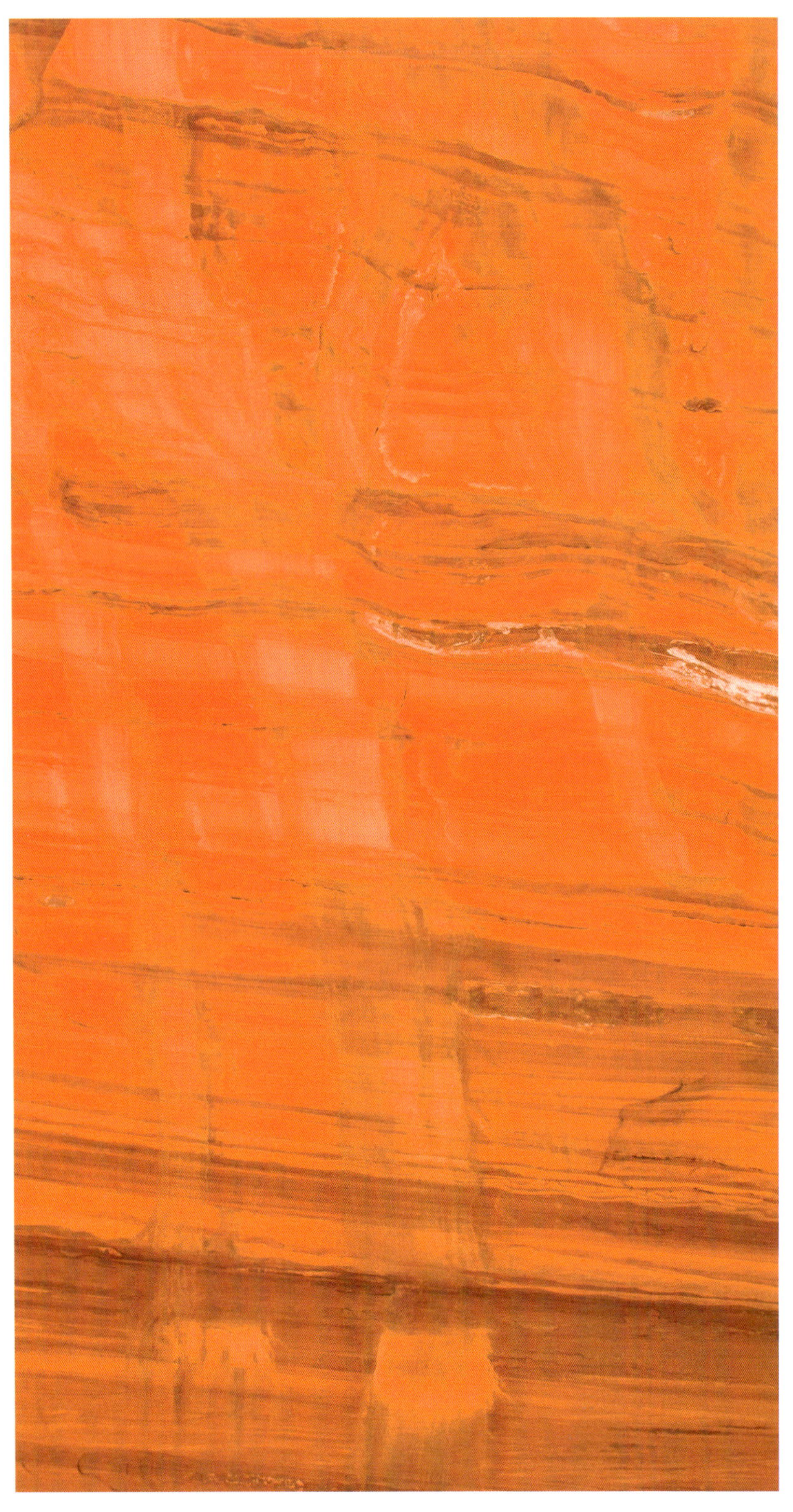

◂

GRAPHIC PATTERNS EMERGE IN THE SANDSTONE LAYERS OF THE GRAND STAIRCASE–ESCALANTE NATIONAL MONUMENT.

▸

SANDSTONE FINS HOVER OVER PHIPPS WASH IN THE GRAND STAIRCASE–ESCALANTE NATIONAL MONUMENT.

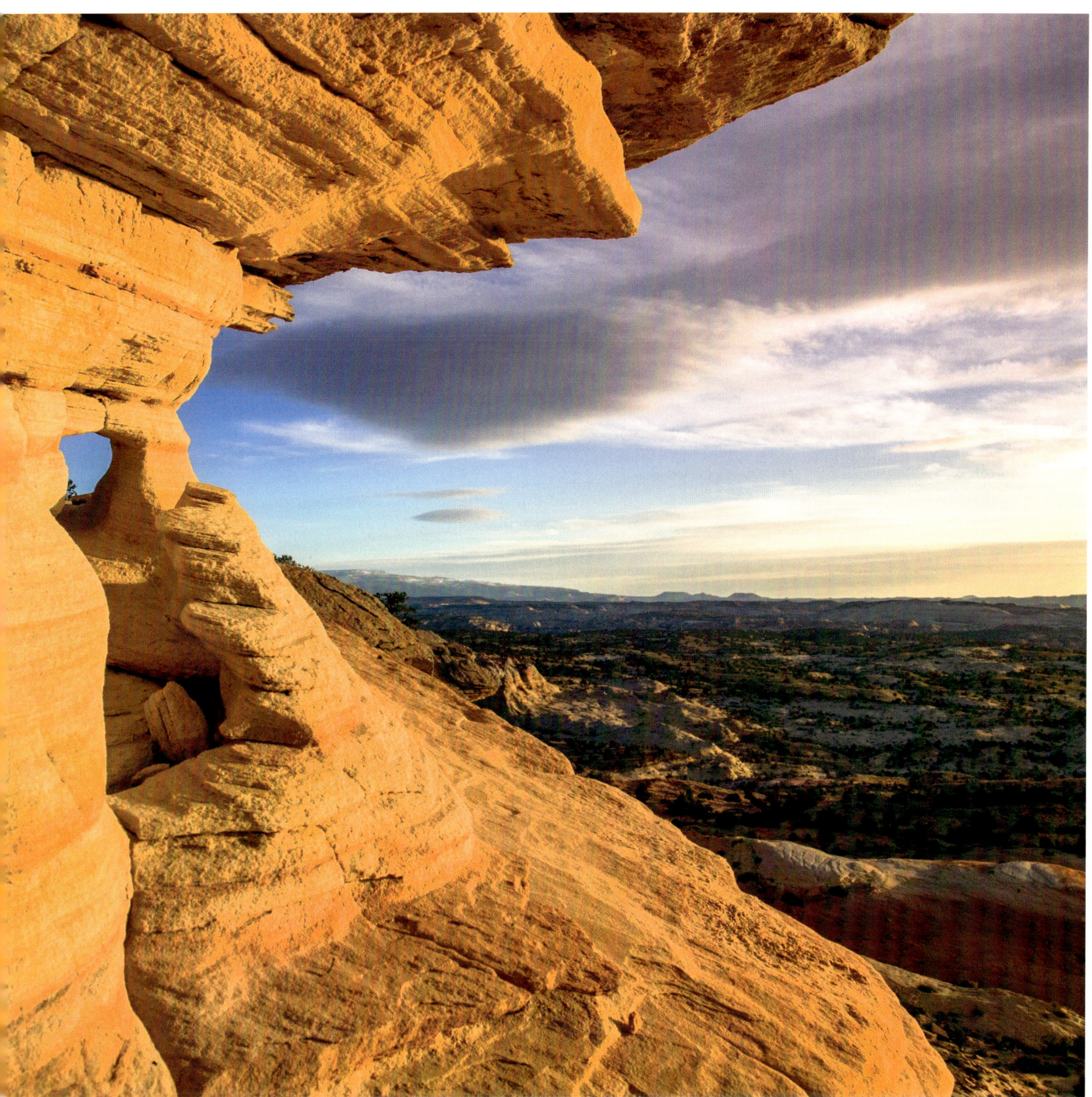

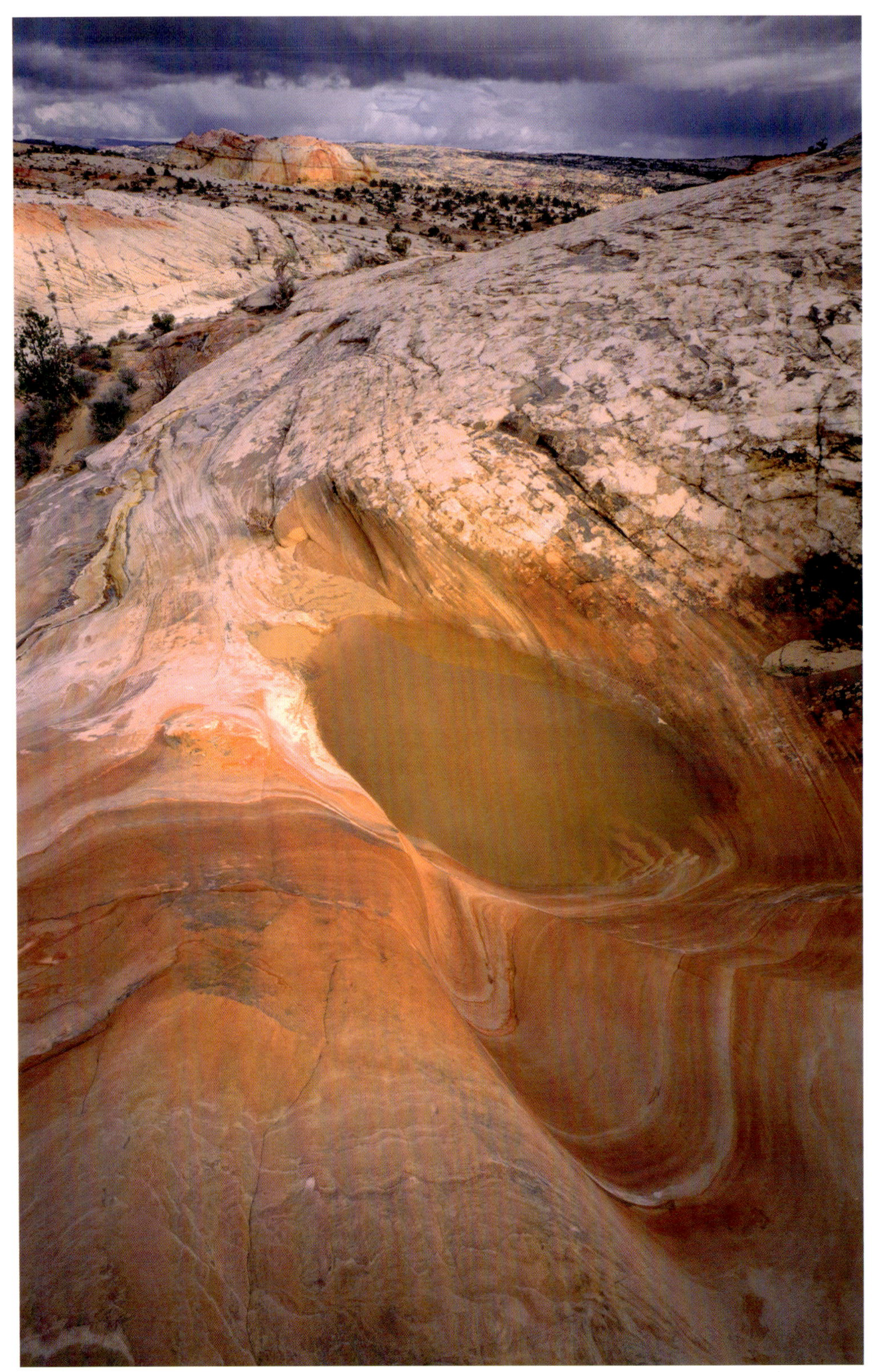

RAINWATER FILLS SMALL POCKETS IN THE ROCK OF THE GRAND STAIRCASE–ESCALANTE.

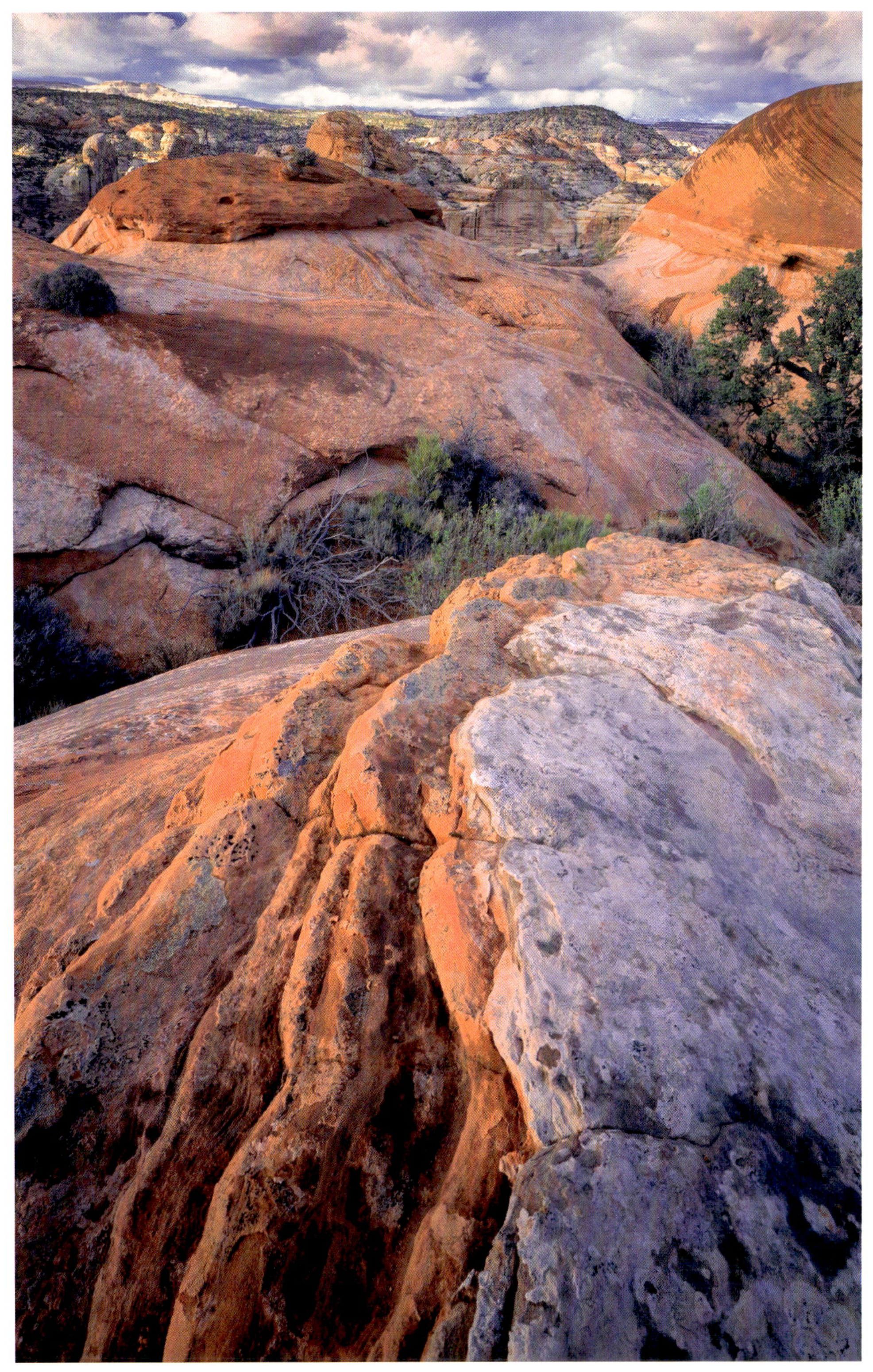

SEEMINGLY ENDLESS SANDSTONE FORMATIONS COVER THE INACCESSIBLE LANDSCAPE OF THE GRAND STAIRCASE OF THE ESCALANTE.

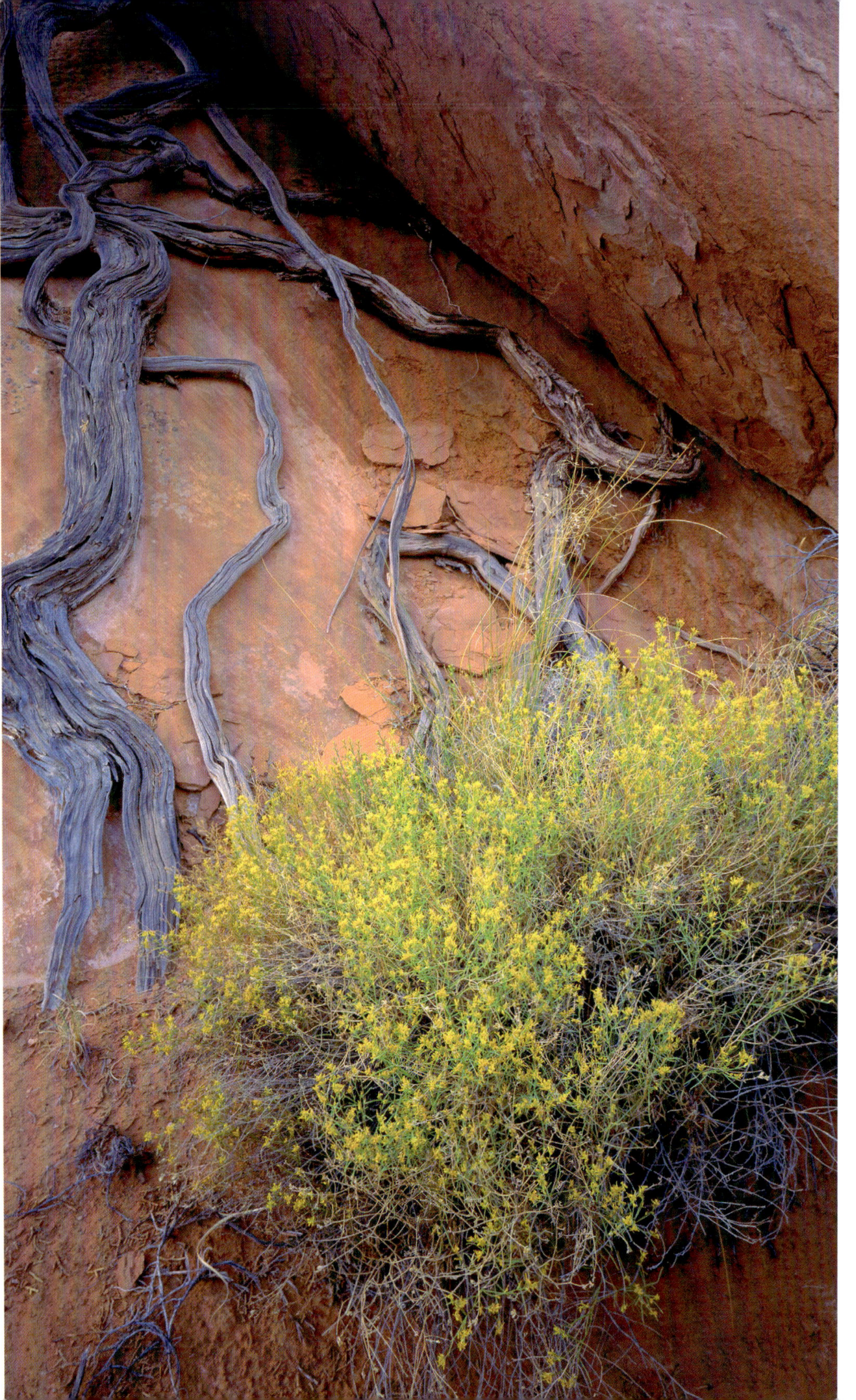

RABBITBRUSH BLOOMS IN THE RED ROCK COUNTRY OF THE GRAND STAIRCASE–ESCALANTE NATIONAL MONUMENT.

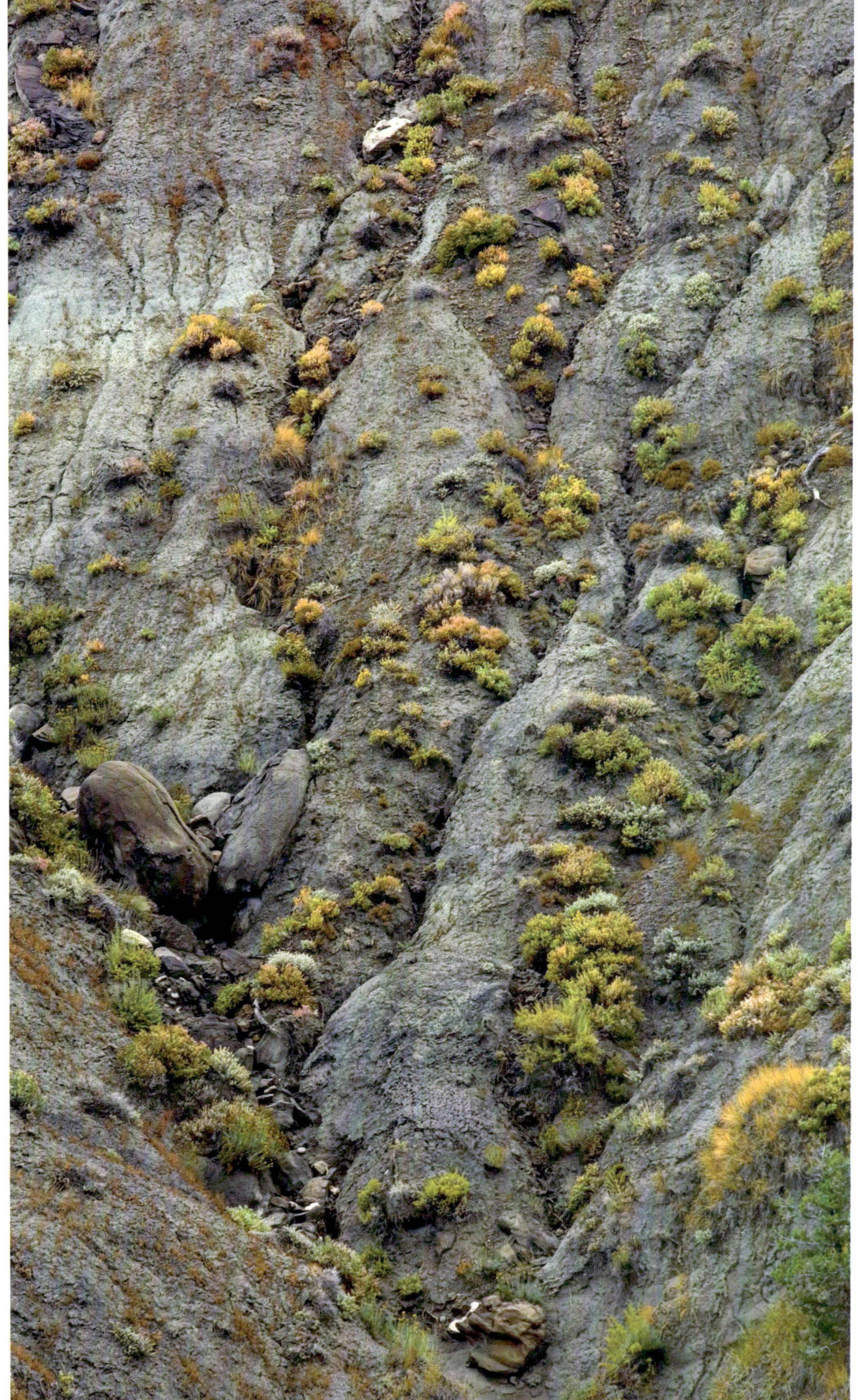

FALL COLORS HIGHLIGHTED BY GRAY SOIL ALONG THE NORTHERN EDGE OF THE GRAND STAIRCASE–ESCALANTE NATIONAL MONUMENT.

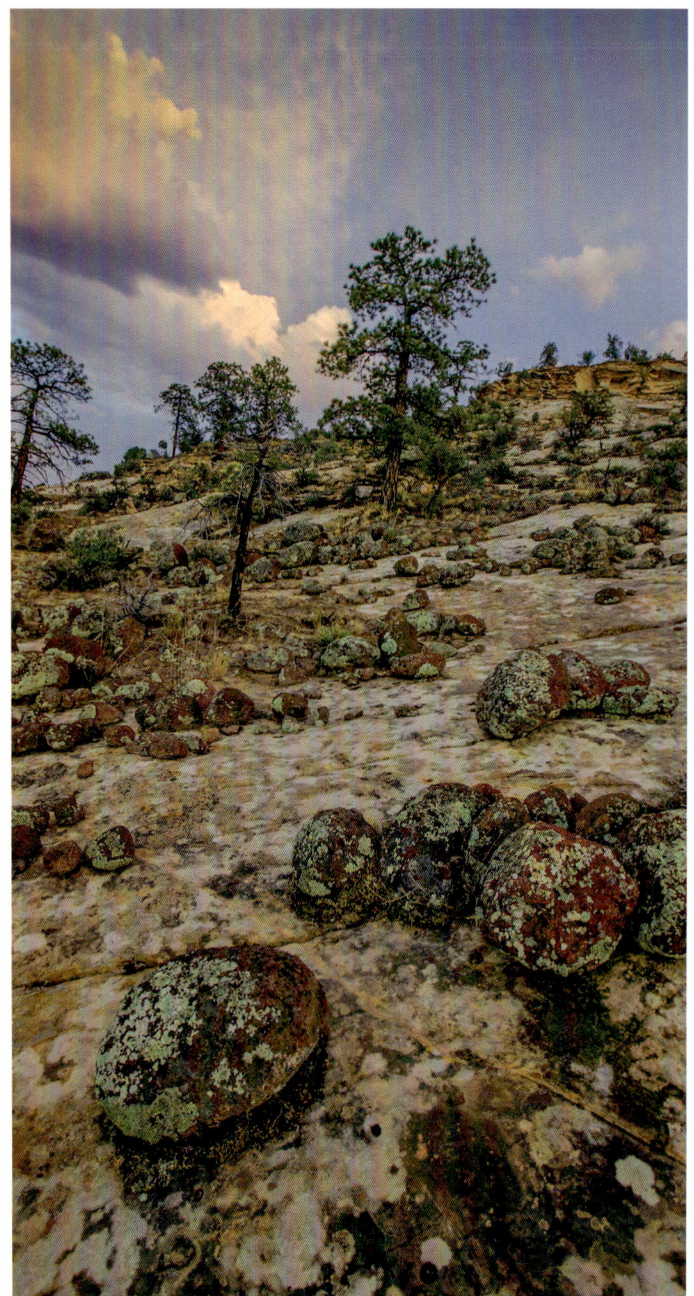

ROUND LICHEN-COVERED BOULDERS REST ON THE WHITE SANDSTONE OF BLACK BOULDER MESA NEAR BOULDER, UTAH.

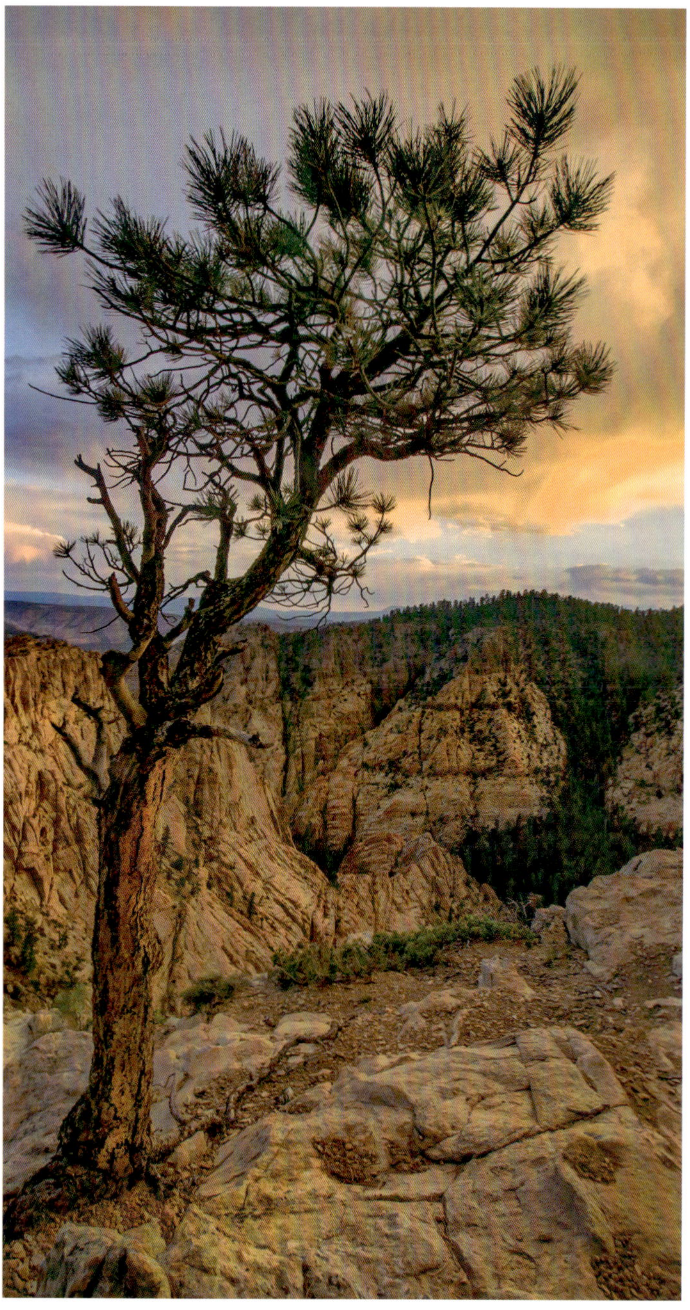

PINE TREES GRIP A SANDSTONE OUTCROPPING ON THE EDGE OF HELLS BACKBONE IN GRAND STAIRCASE–ESCALANTE NATIONAL MONUMENT.

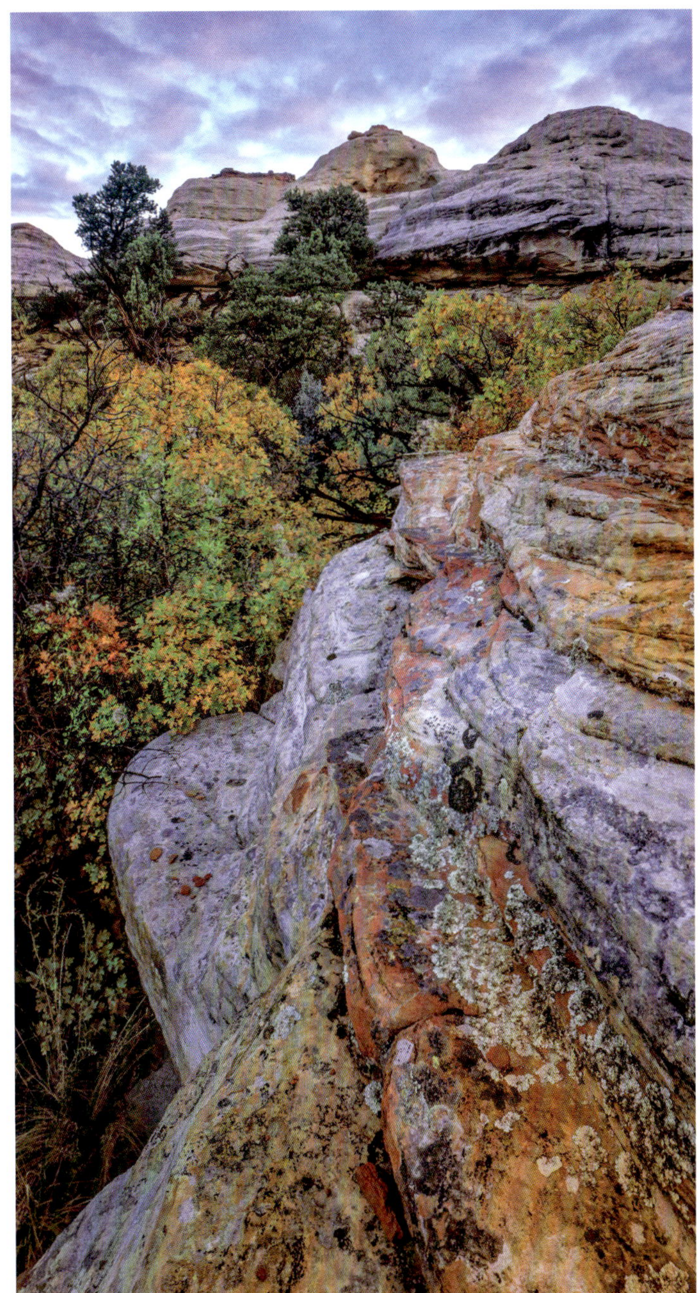

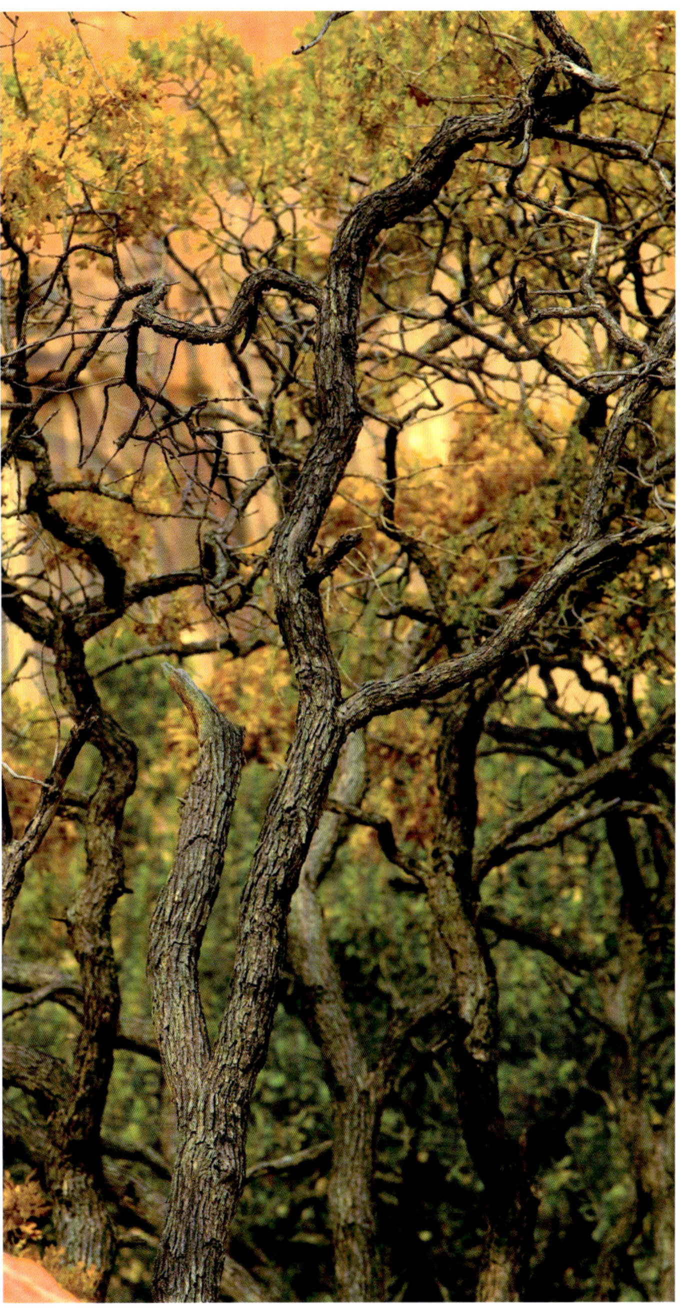

SCRUB OAKS LINE THE BOTTOM OF DESERT WASHES NEAR WOLVERINE CANYON IN THE GRAND STAIRCASE–ESCALANTE NATIONAL MONUMENT.

TWISTED OAK TREES IN FALL FOLIAGE LINE THE CREEK BOTTOM ALONG THE CALF CREEK FALLS TRAIL IN THE GRAND STAIRCASE–ESCALANTE NATIONAL MONUMENT.

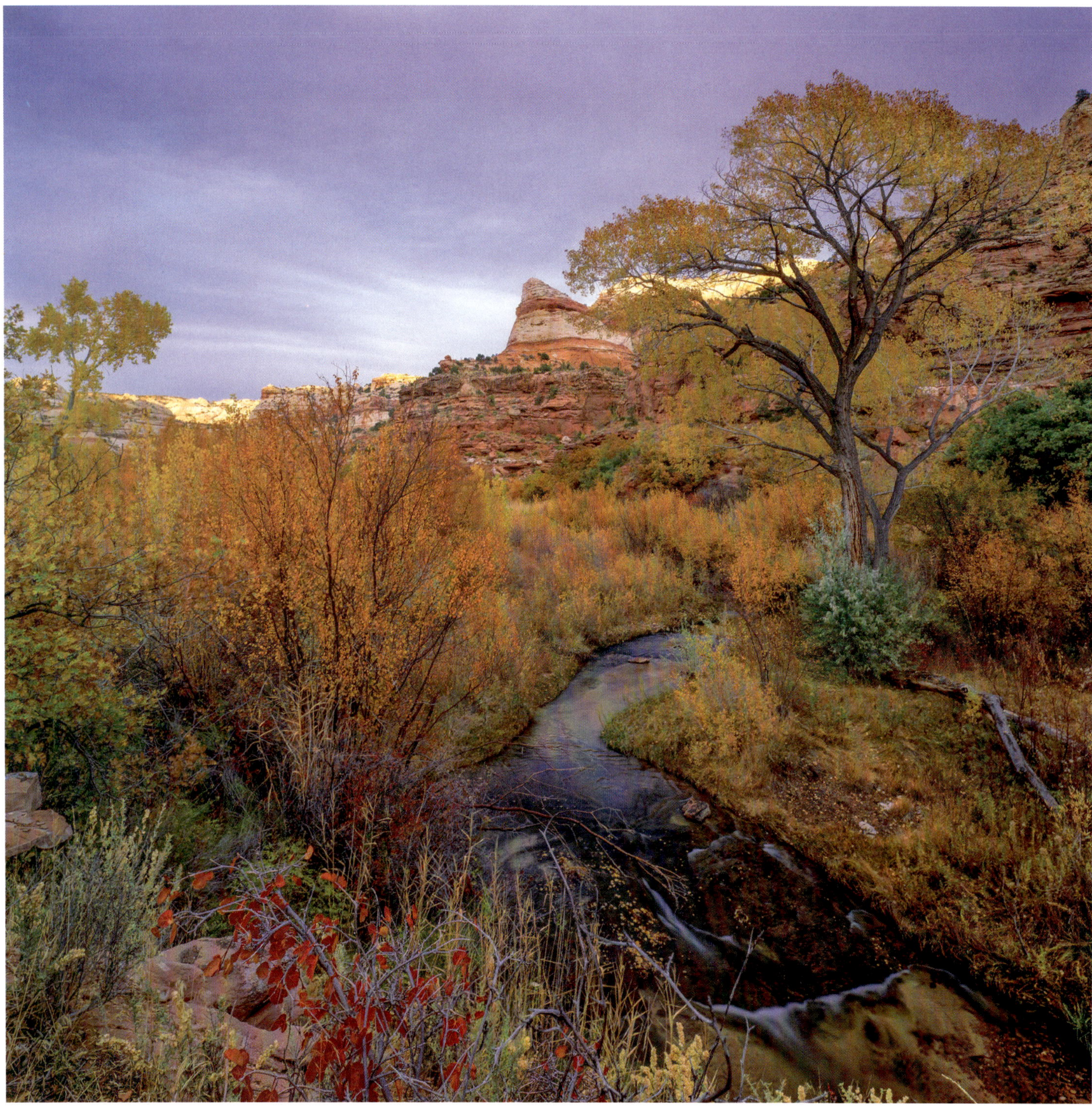

CALF CREEK MAKES ITS WAY THROUGH SANDSTONE OUTCROPPINGS IN THE GRAND STAIRCASE–ESCALANTE NATIONAL MONUMENT.

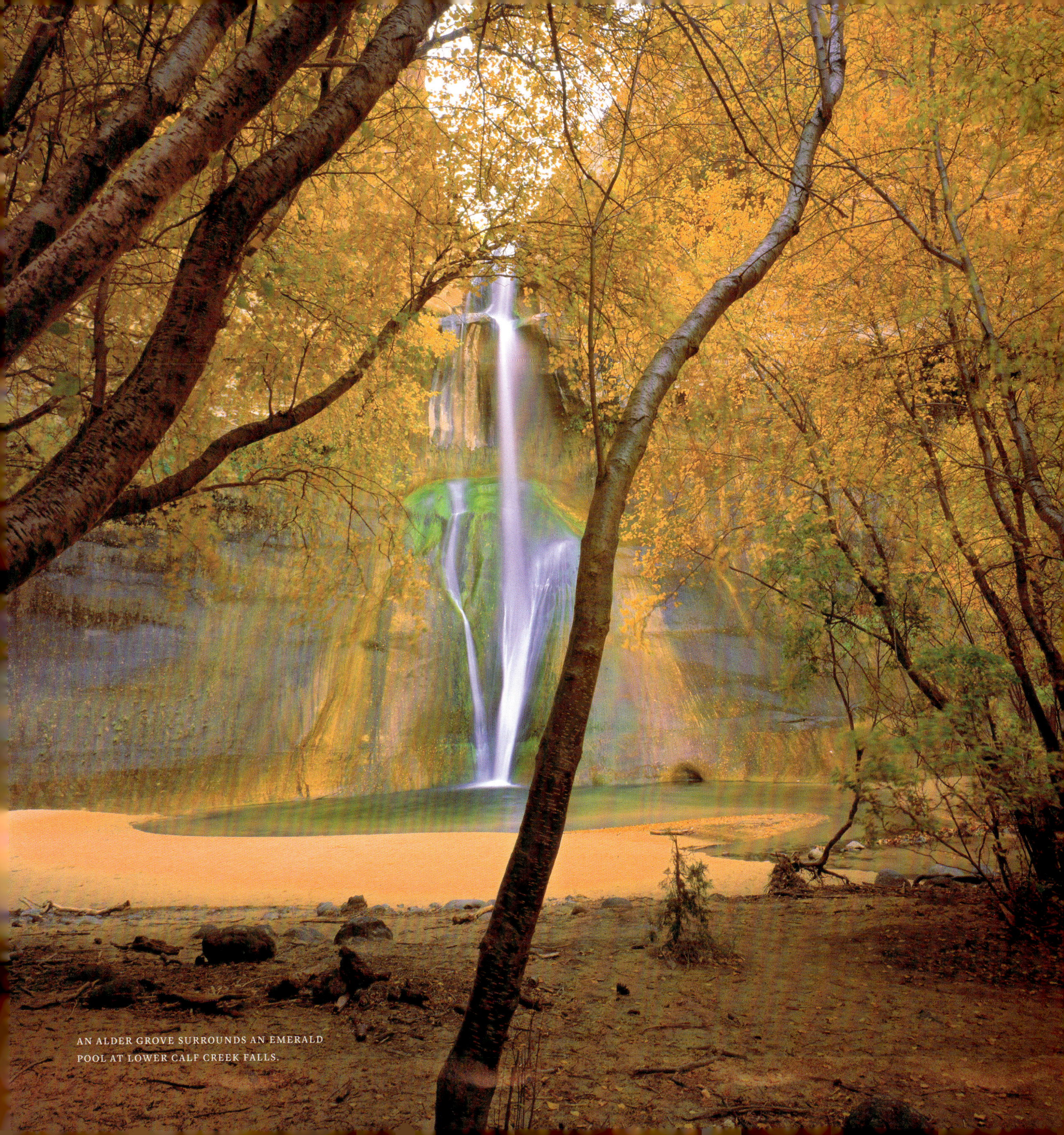

AN ALDER GROVE SURROUNDS AN EMERALD POOL AT LOWER CALF CREEK FALLS.

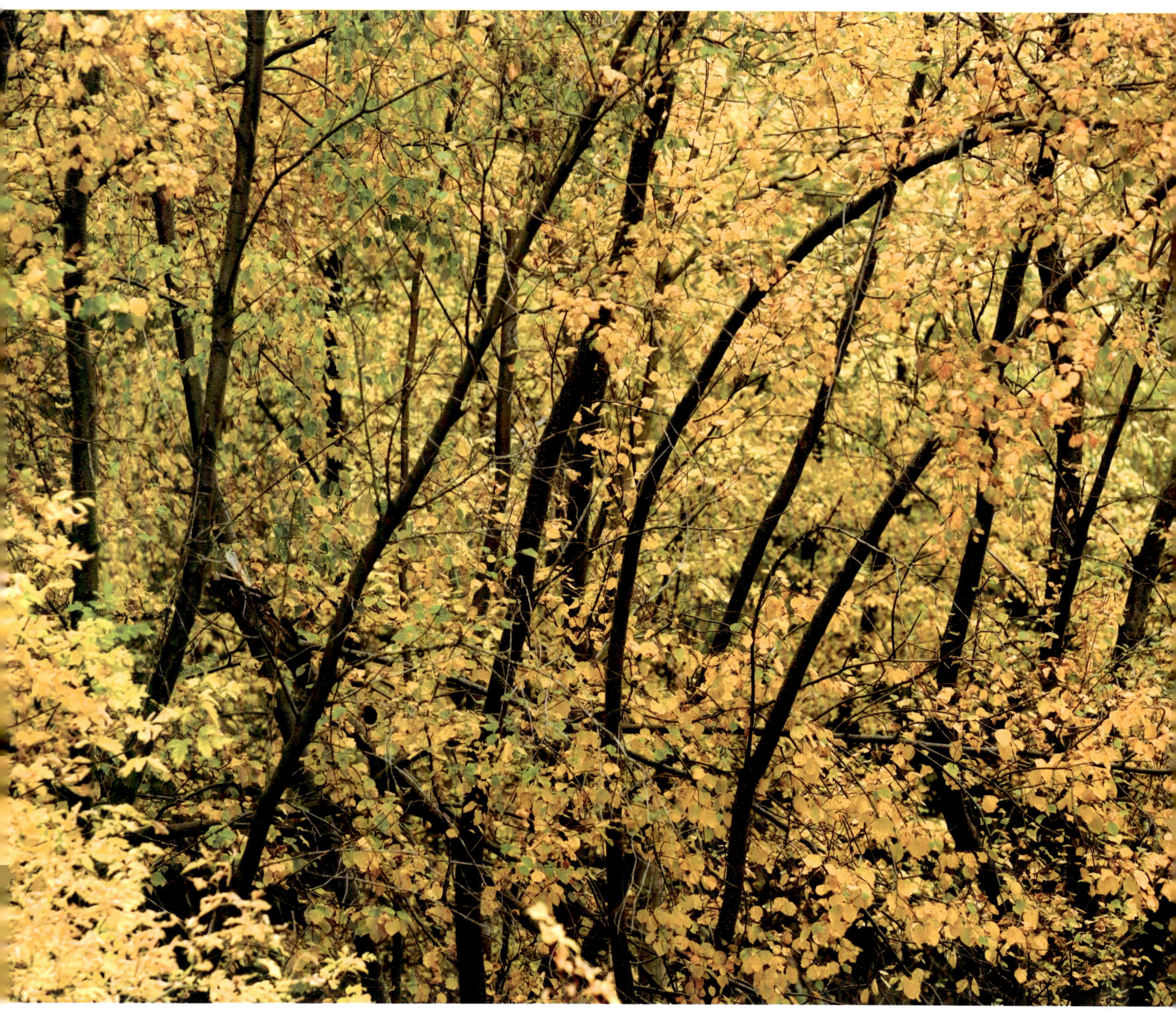

ALDERS IN THEIR FALL FOLIAGE CREATE A GRAPHIC BACKGROUND ALONG THE CALF CREEK FALLS TRAIL IN THE GRAND STAIRCASE–ESCALANTE NATIONAL MONUMENT.

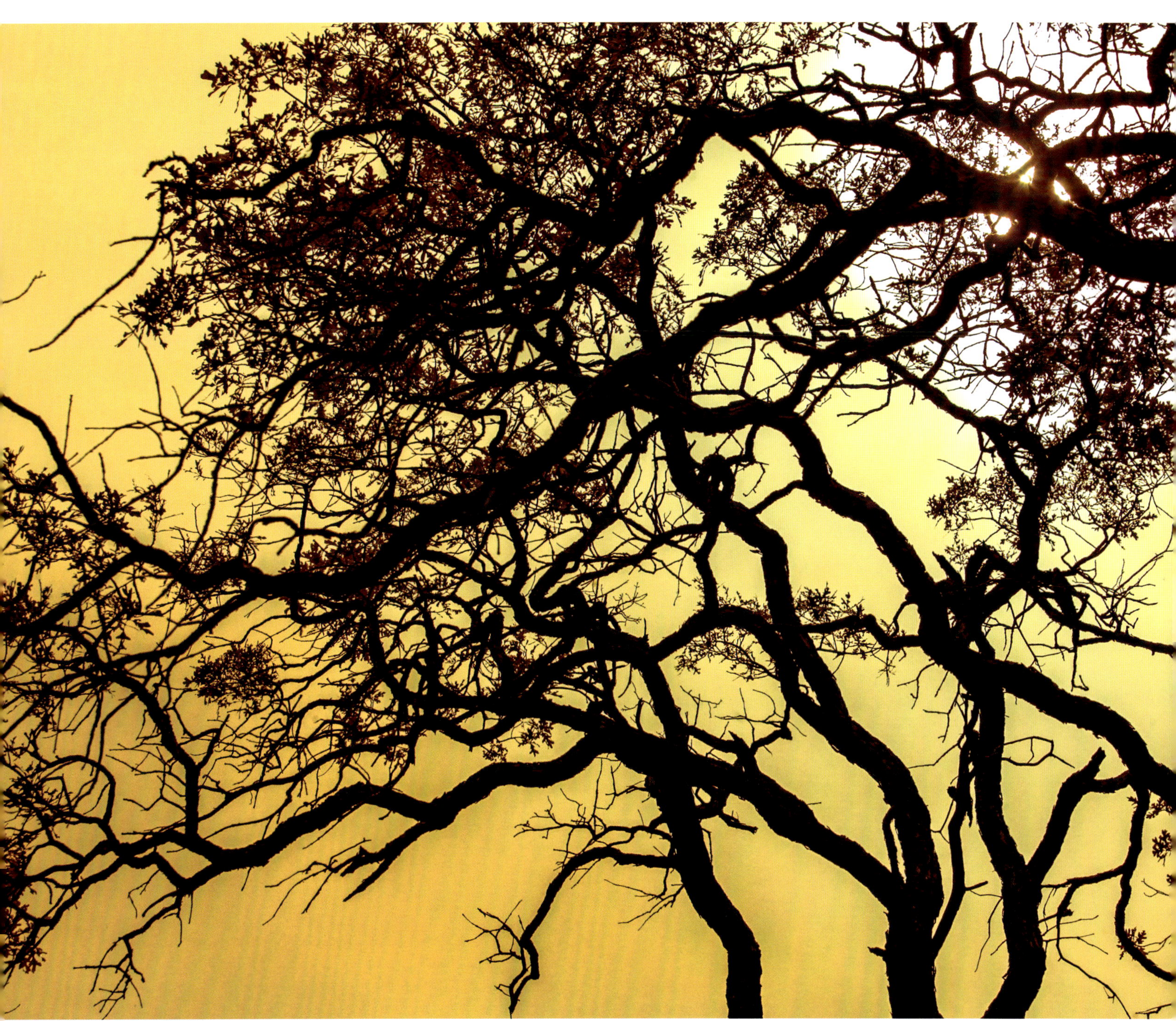

TWISTED OAK TREES IN FALL FOLIAGE LINE THE CREEK BOTTOM ALONG THE CALF CREEK FALLS TRAIL IN THE GRAND STAIRCASE–ESCALANTE NATIONAL MONUMENT.

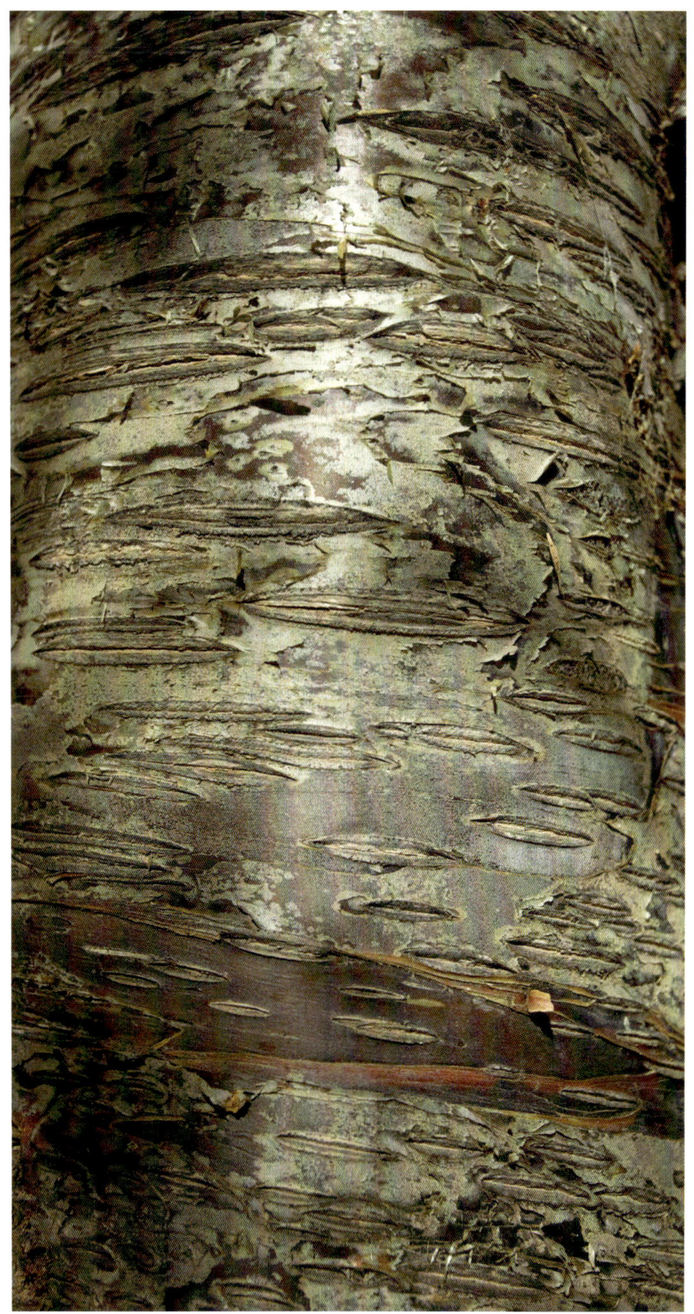

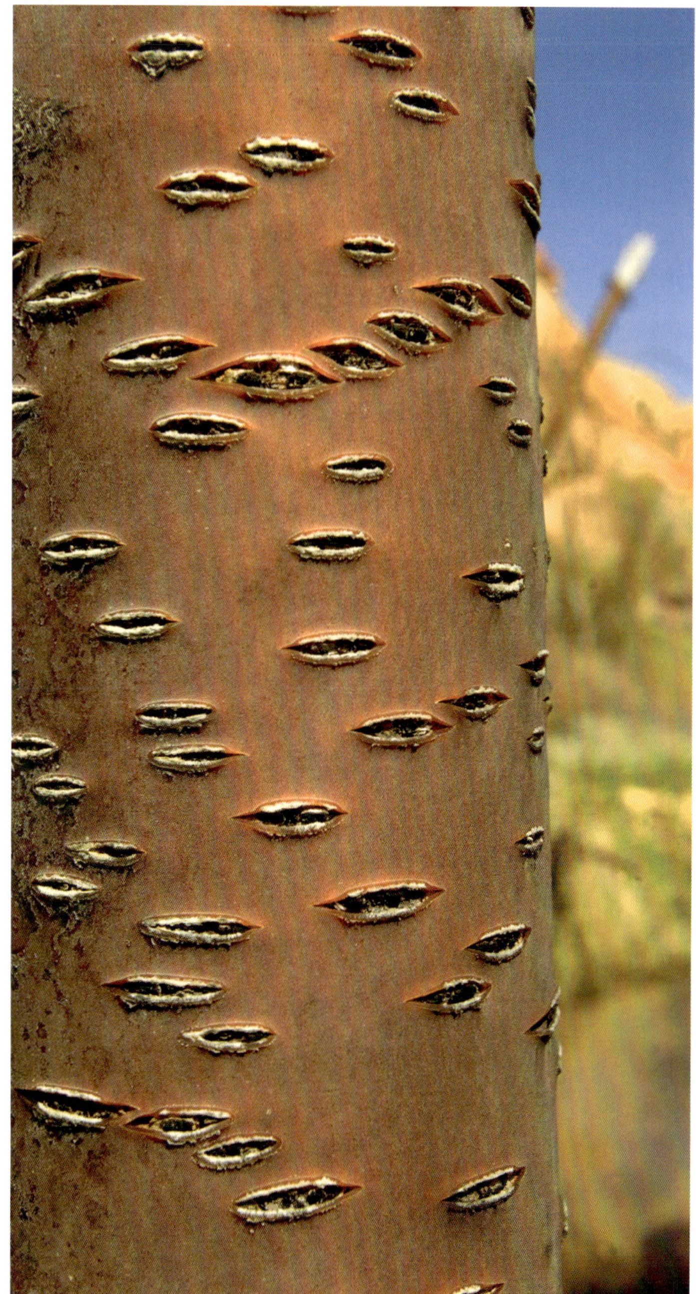

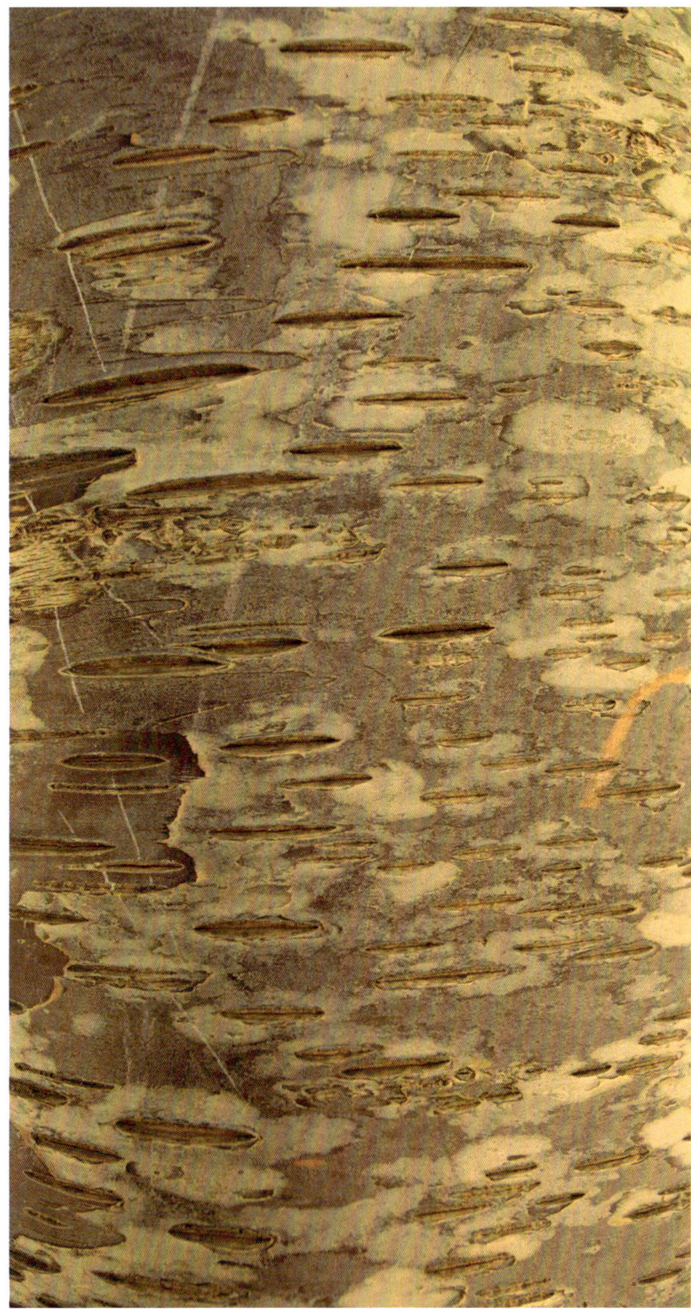

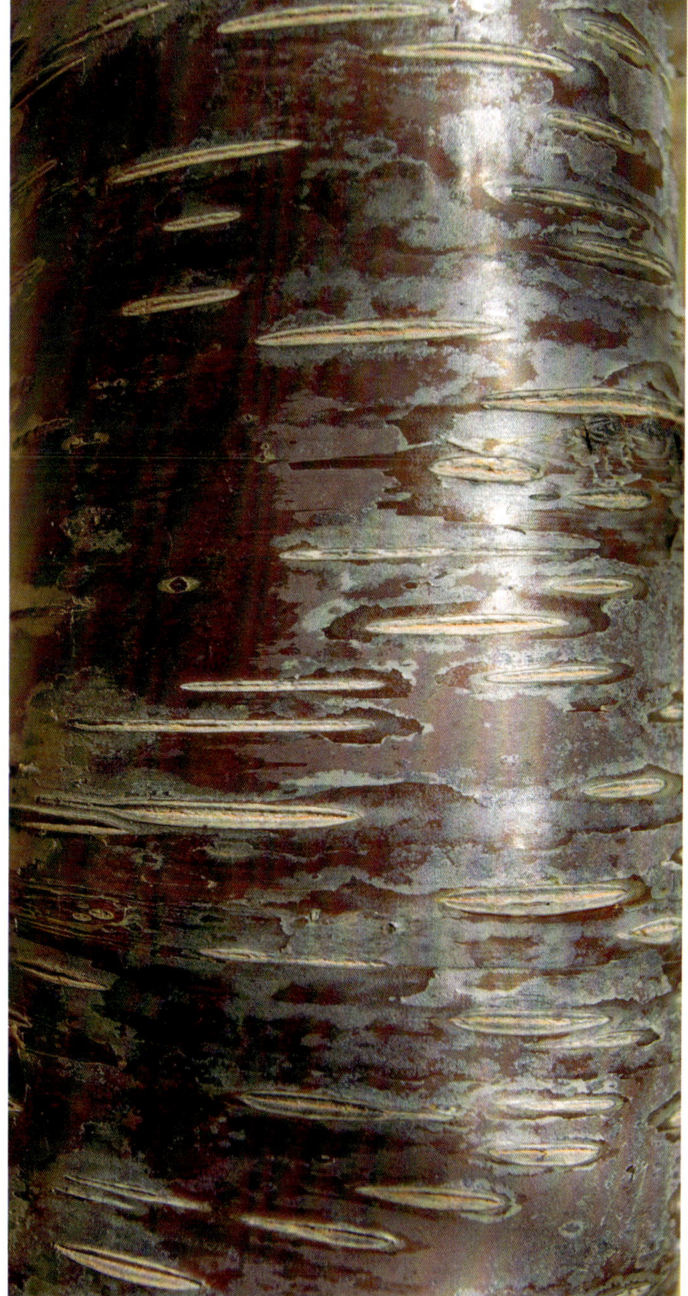

GRAPHIC PATTERNS TYPICAL OF ALDERS THAT LINE THE BOTTOM OF CALF CREEK IN THE GRAND STAIRCASE–ESCALANTE NATIONAL MONUMENT.

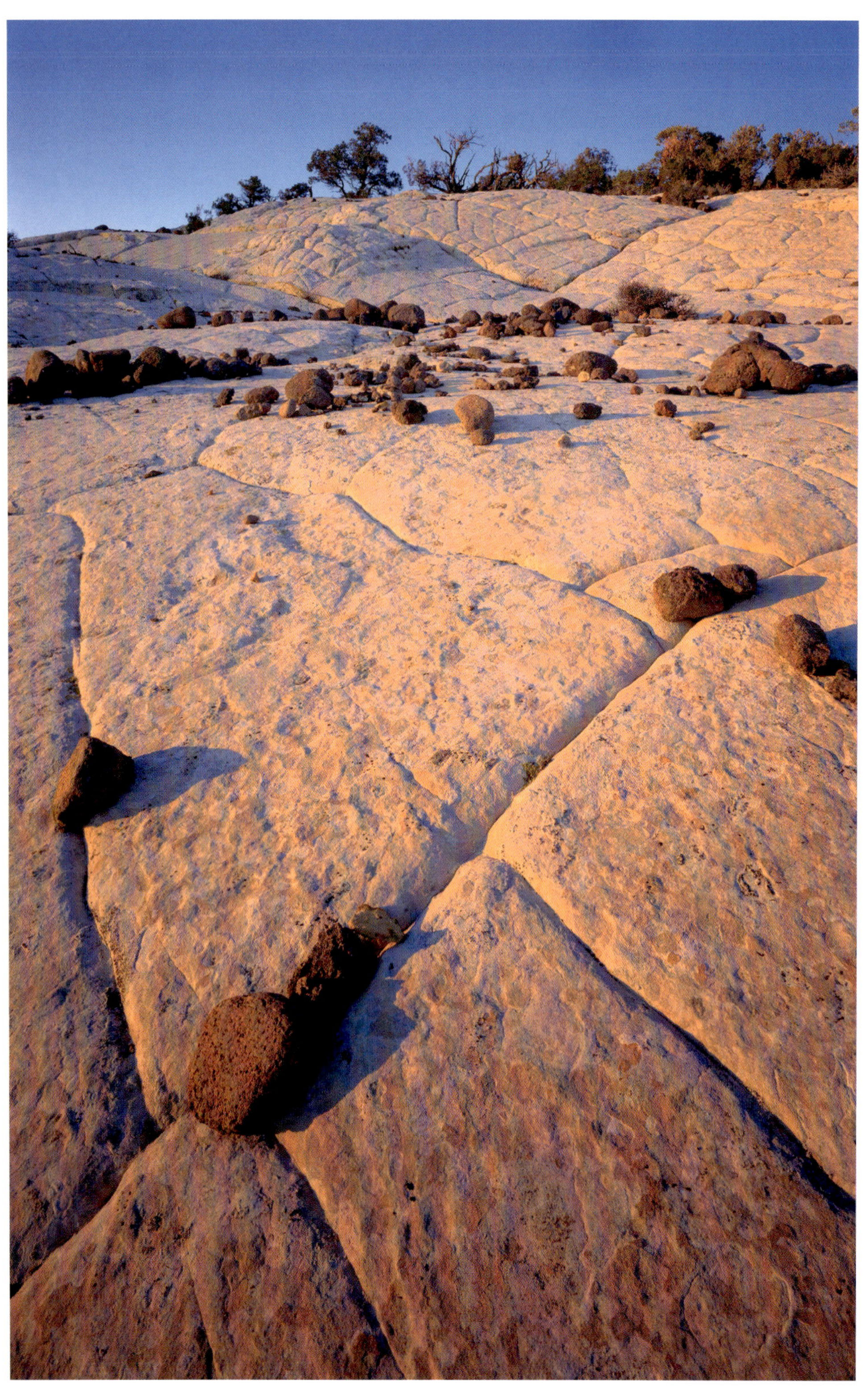

CHECKERBOARD PATTERNS
IN THE SANDSTONE OF THE
GRAND STAIRCASE–ESCALANTE
NATIONAL MONUMENT.

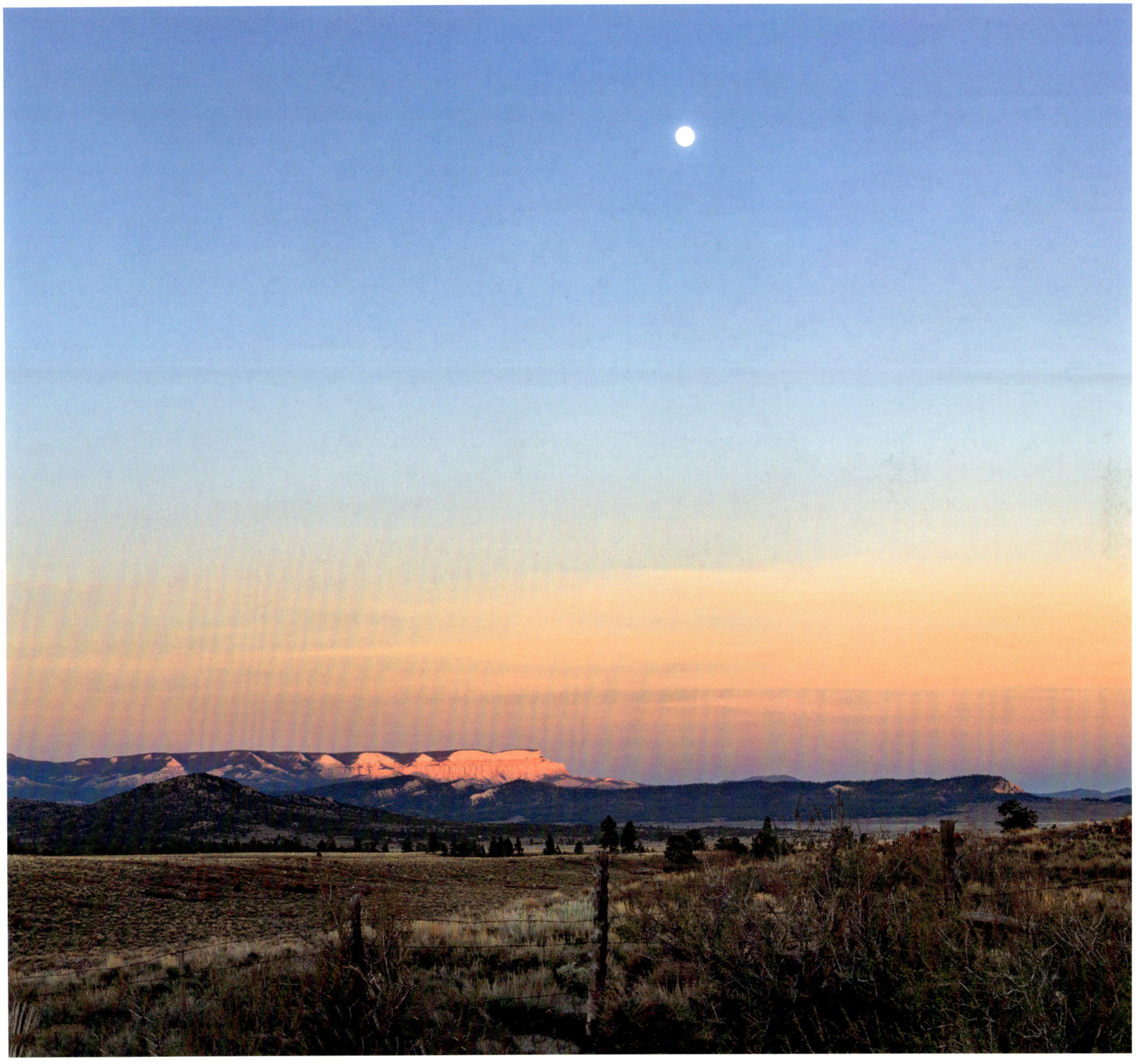

MOONRISE OVER PAUNSAUGUNT PLATEAU AT THE TOP OF THE GRAND STAIRCASE–ESCALANTE NATIONAL MONUMENT.

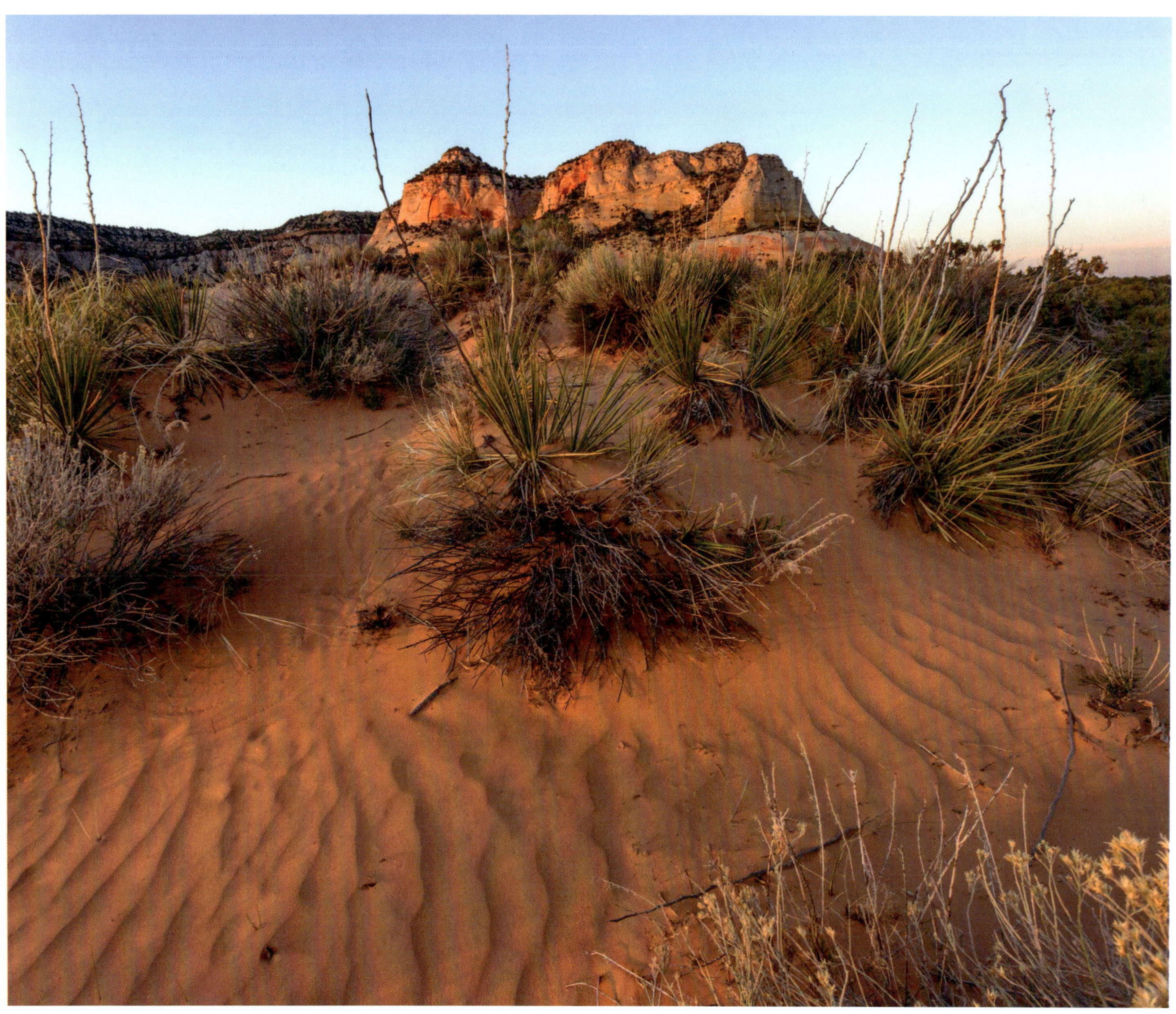

PINK SAND AND THE ELKHEART CLIFFS GLOW IN A CLASSIC DESERT SUNSET.

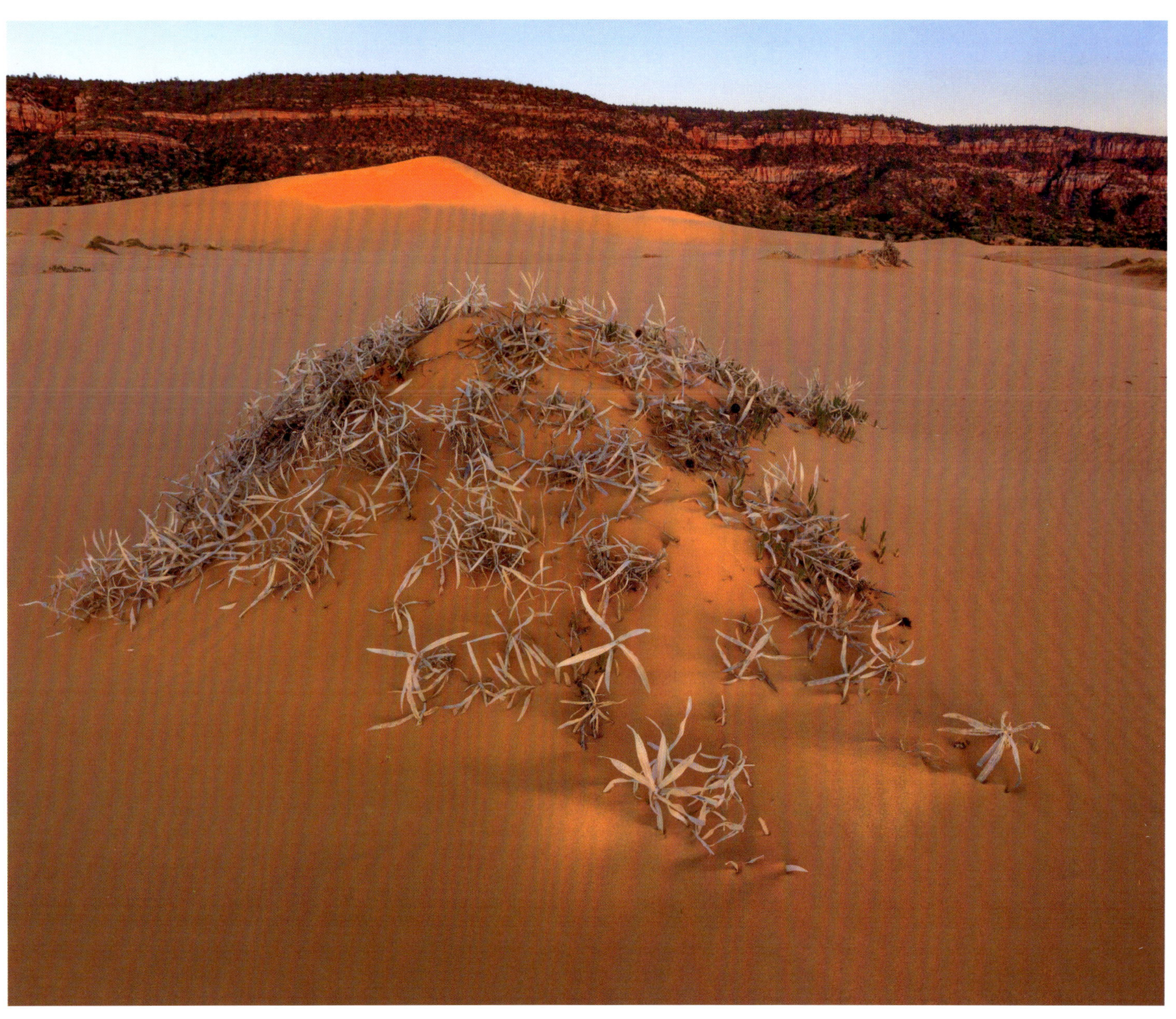

THE VERMILION CLIFFS RISE BEHIND THE SAND AT THE CORAL PINK SAND DUNES STATE PARK.

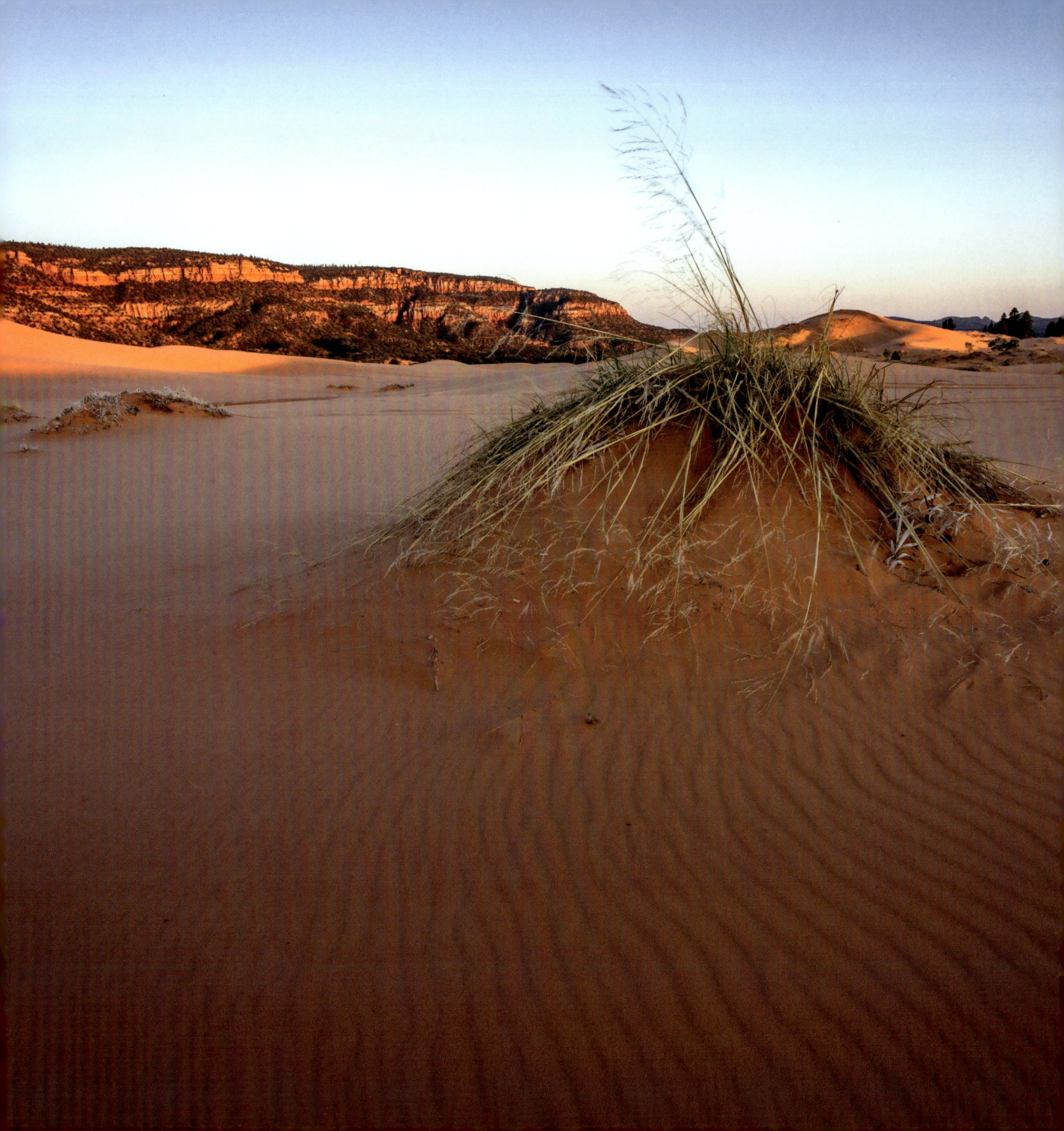

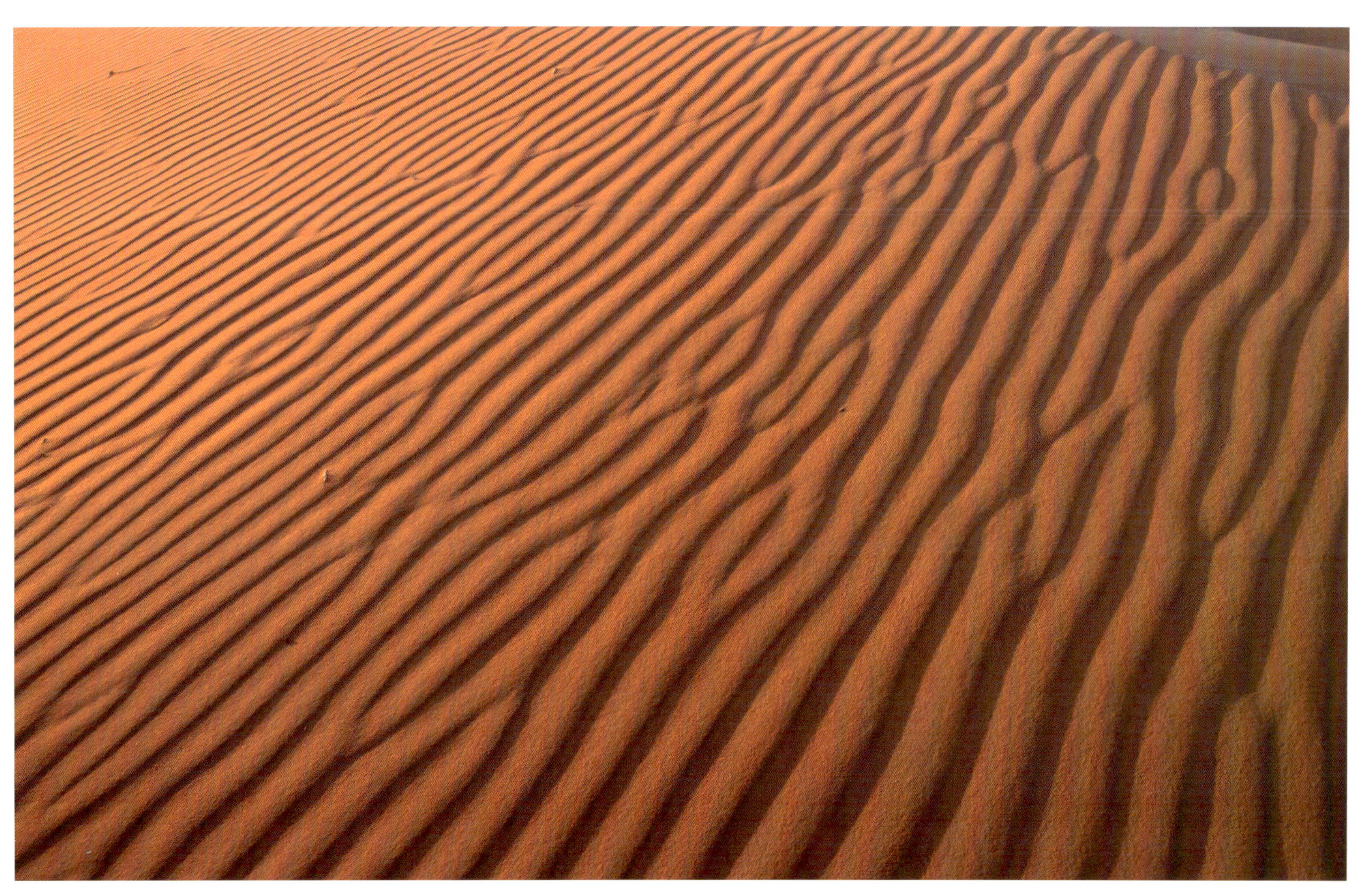

▲
DETAIL OF THE SILKY PATTERNS
IN CORAL PINK SAND DUNES.

◀
LONG GRASS GROWS FROM A VEGETATION
CLUMP IN THE CORAL PINK SAND DUNES.

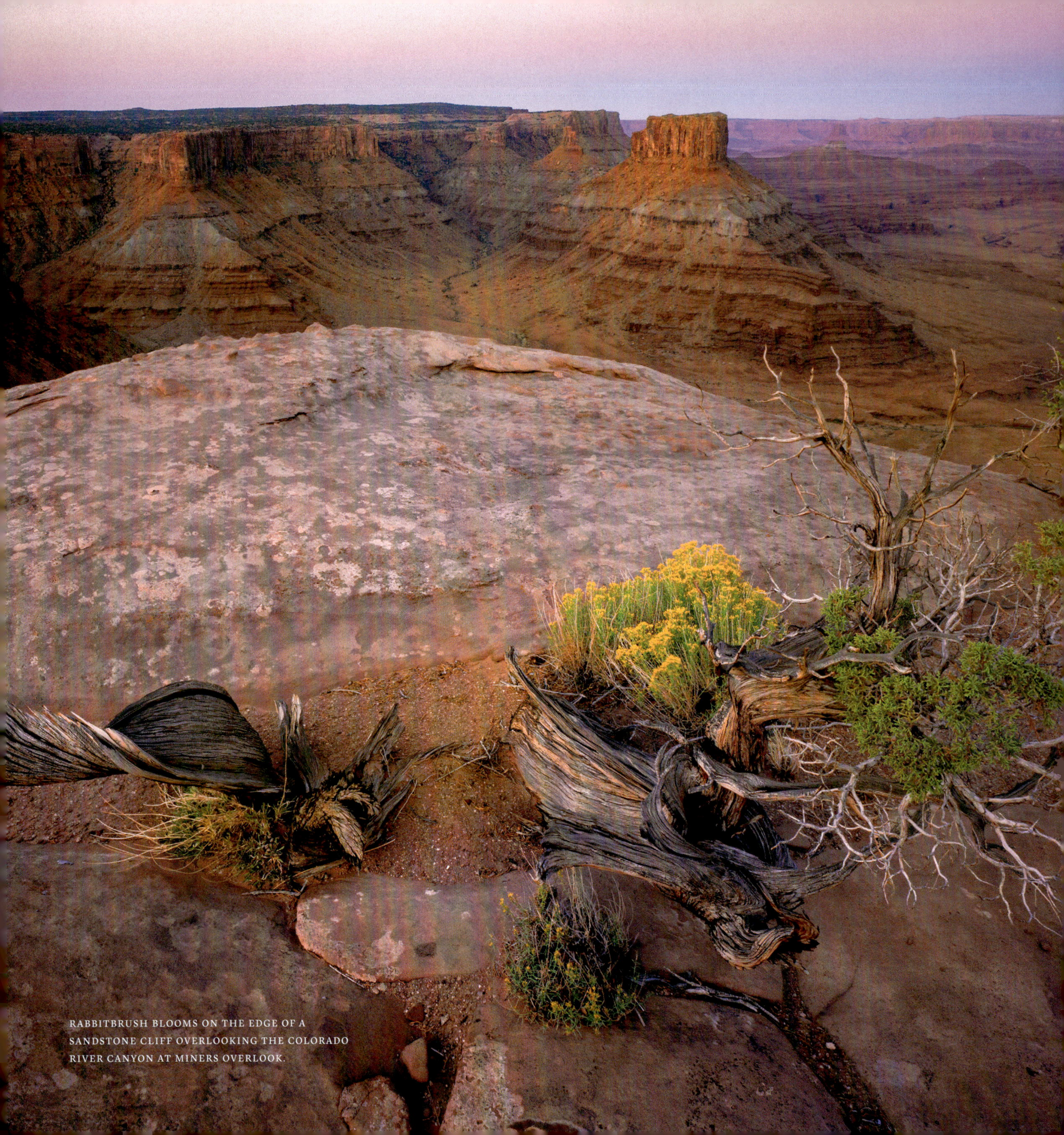

RABBITBRUSH BLOOMS ON THE EDGE OF A SANDSTONE CLIFF OVERLOOKING THE COLORADO RIVER CANYON AT MINERS OVERLOOK.

SOUTHEAST CANYON COUNTRY

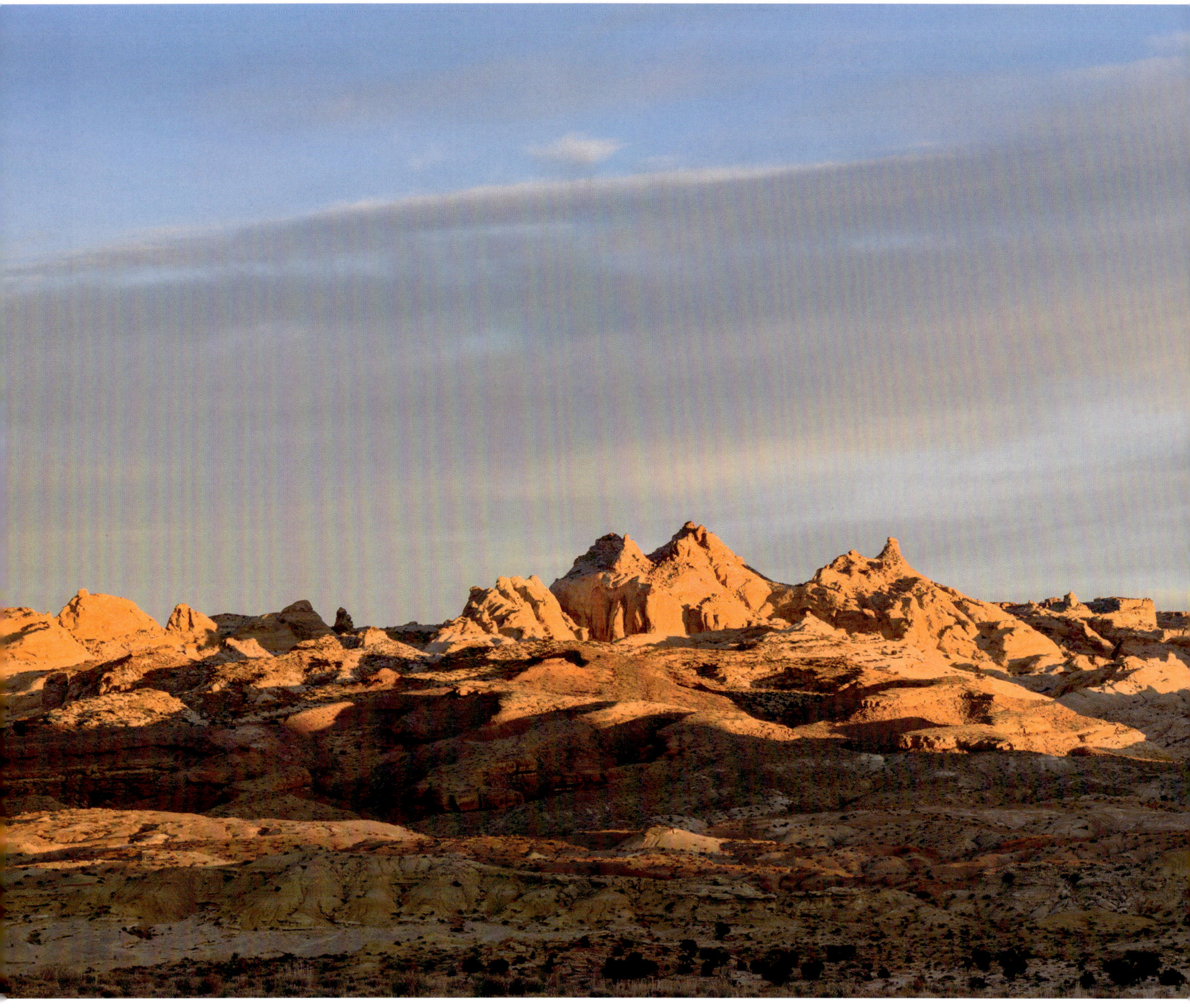

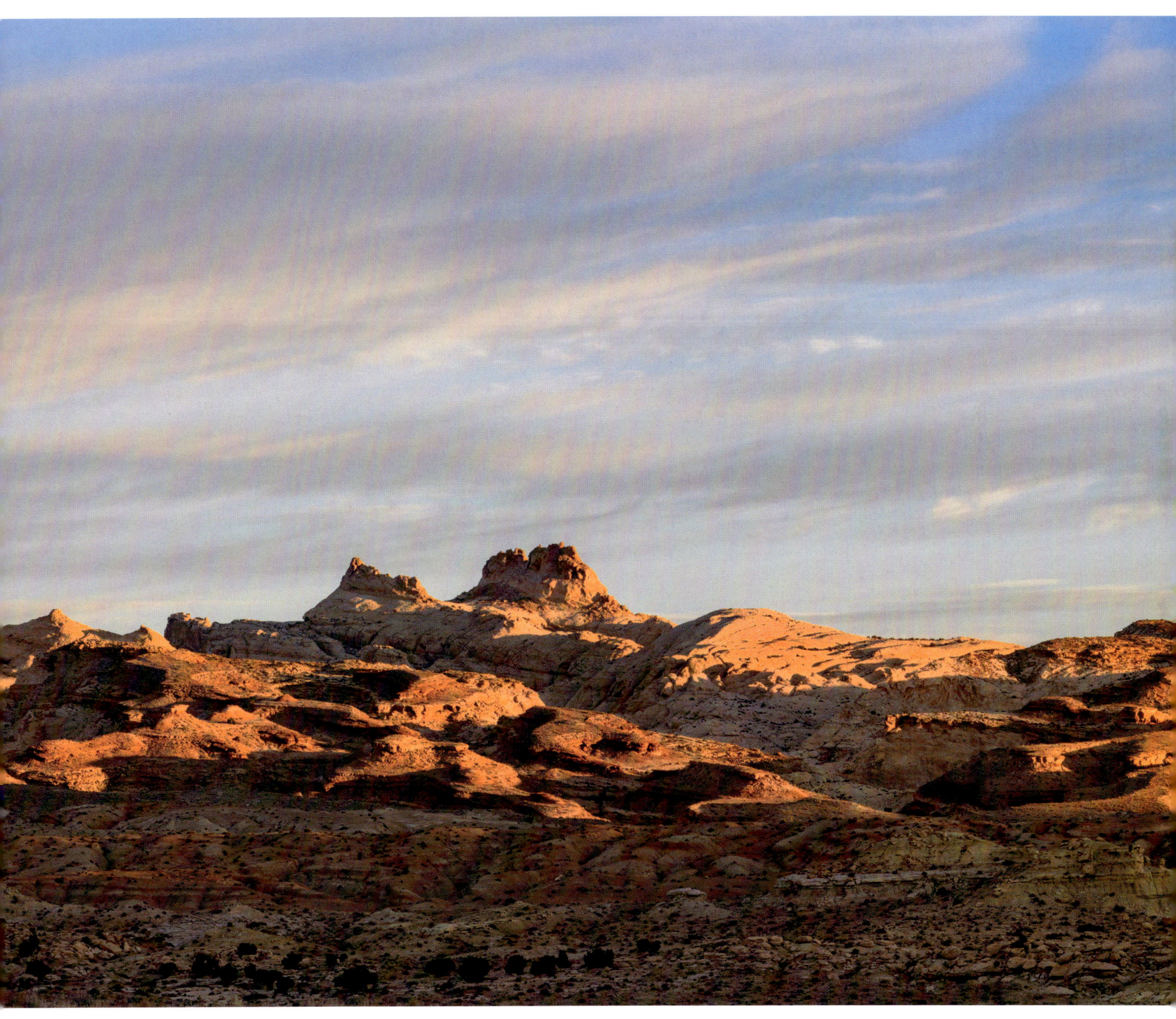

SUNRISE GLOWS ON THE SAN RAFAEL REEF.

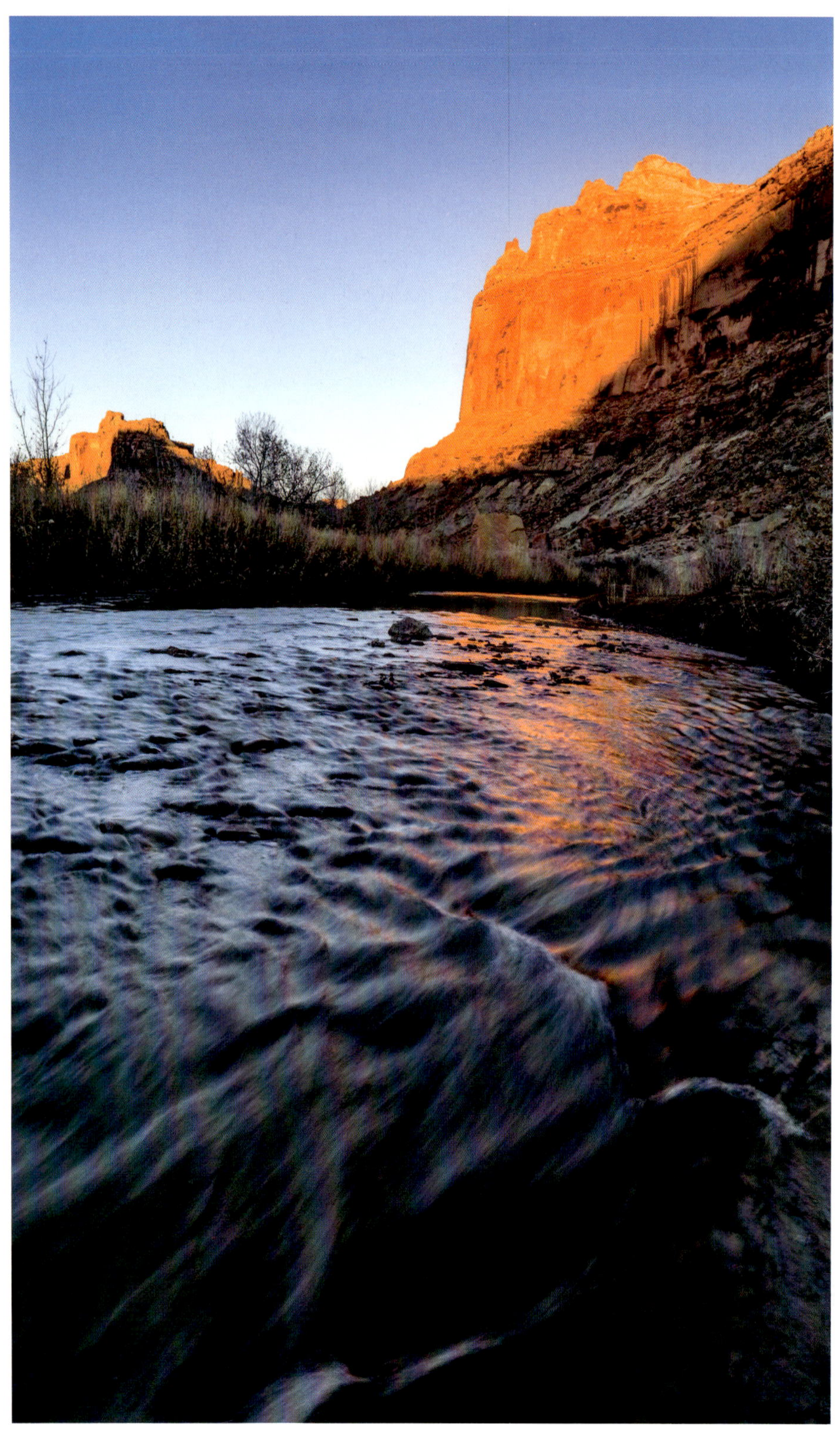

THE SAN RAFAEL RIVER FROM THE
SWINGING BRIDGE IN THE BUCKHORN WASH.

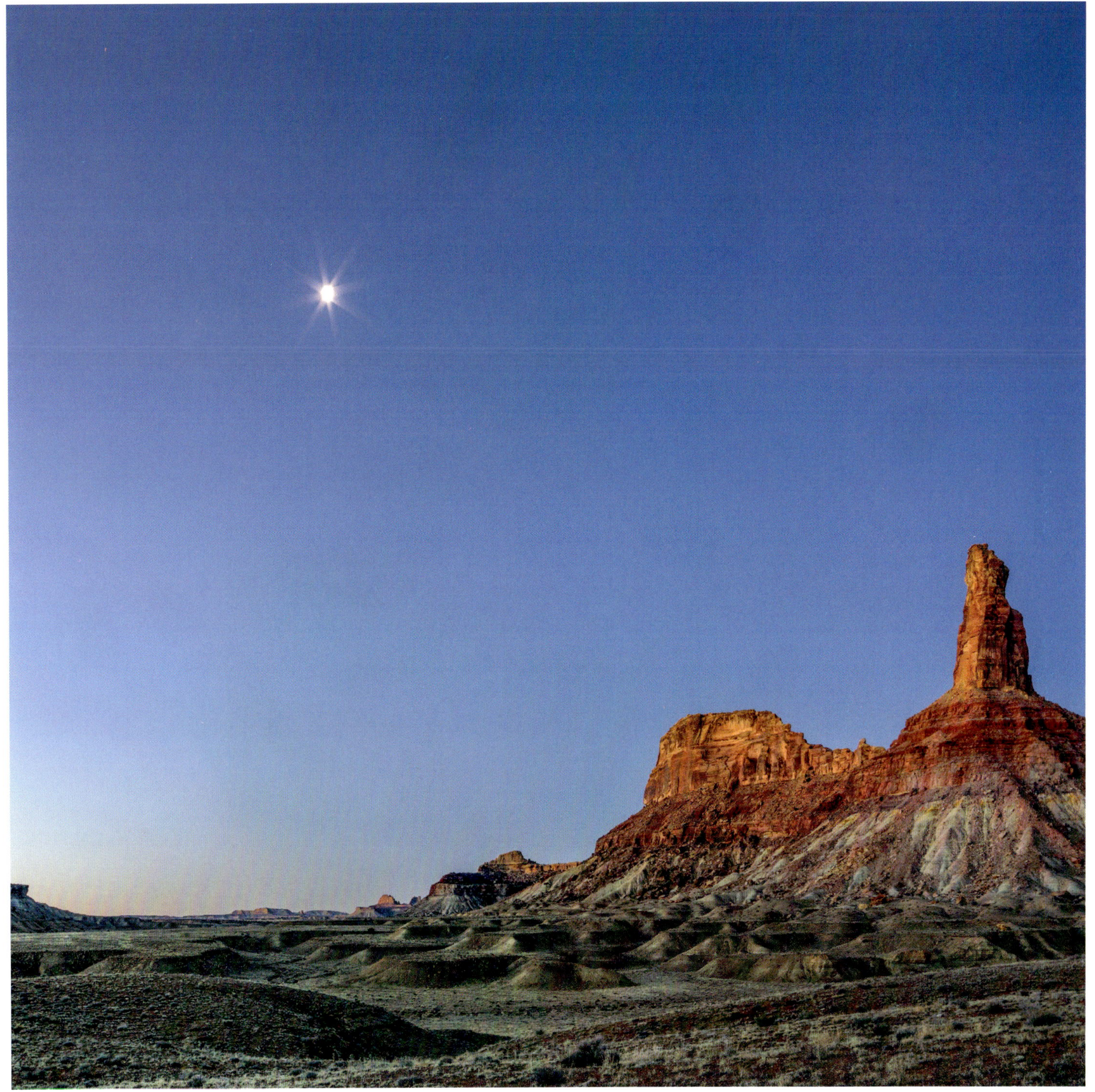

BOTTLENECK PEAK RISES ABOVE THE DESERT FLOOR OF THE SAN RAFAEL SWELL.

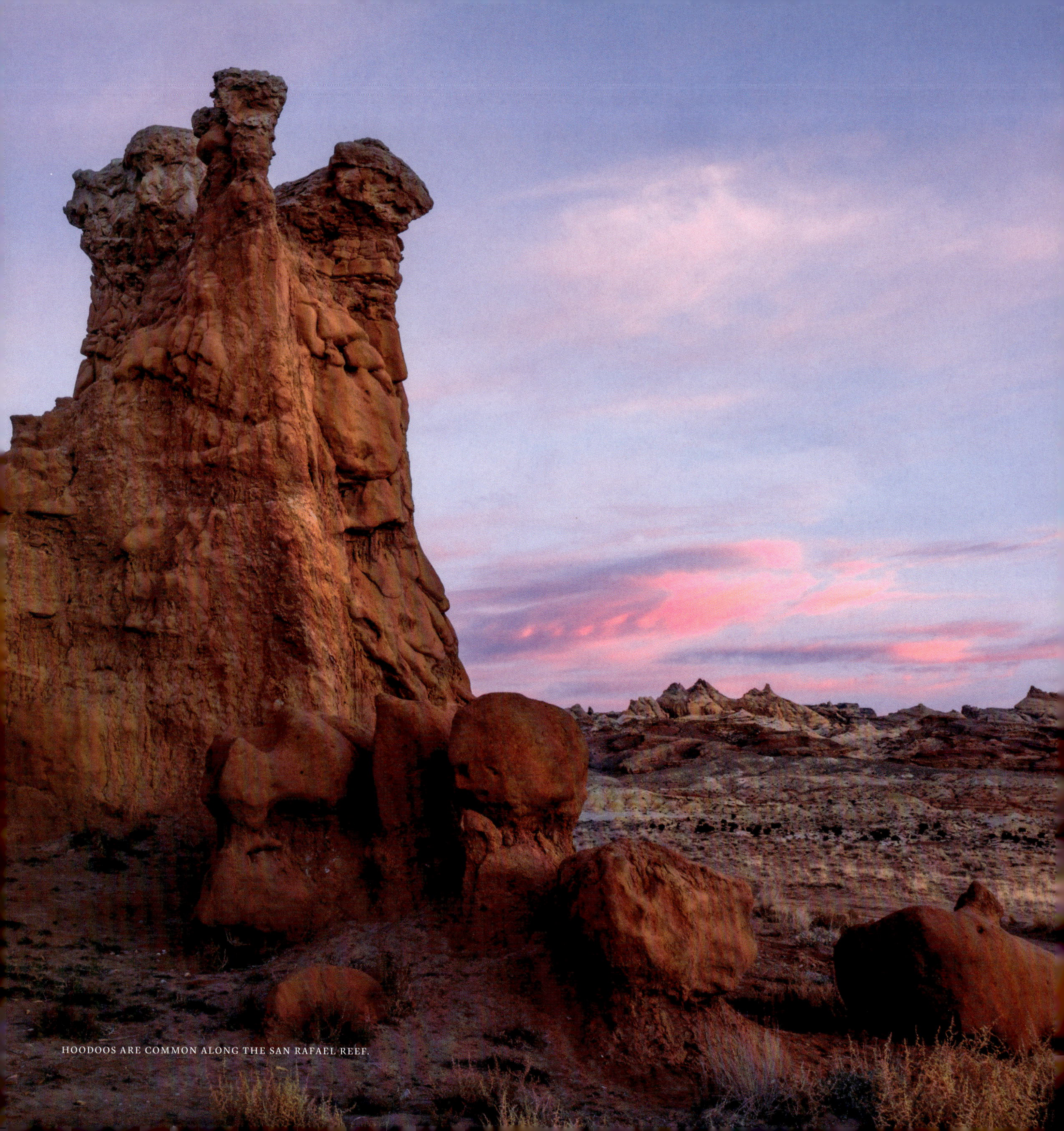

HOODOOS ARE COMMON ALONG THE SAN RAFAEL REEF.

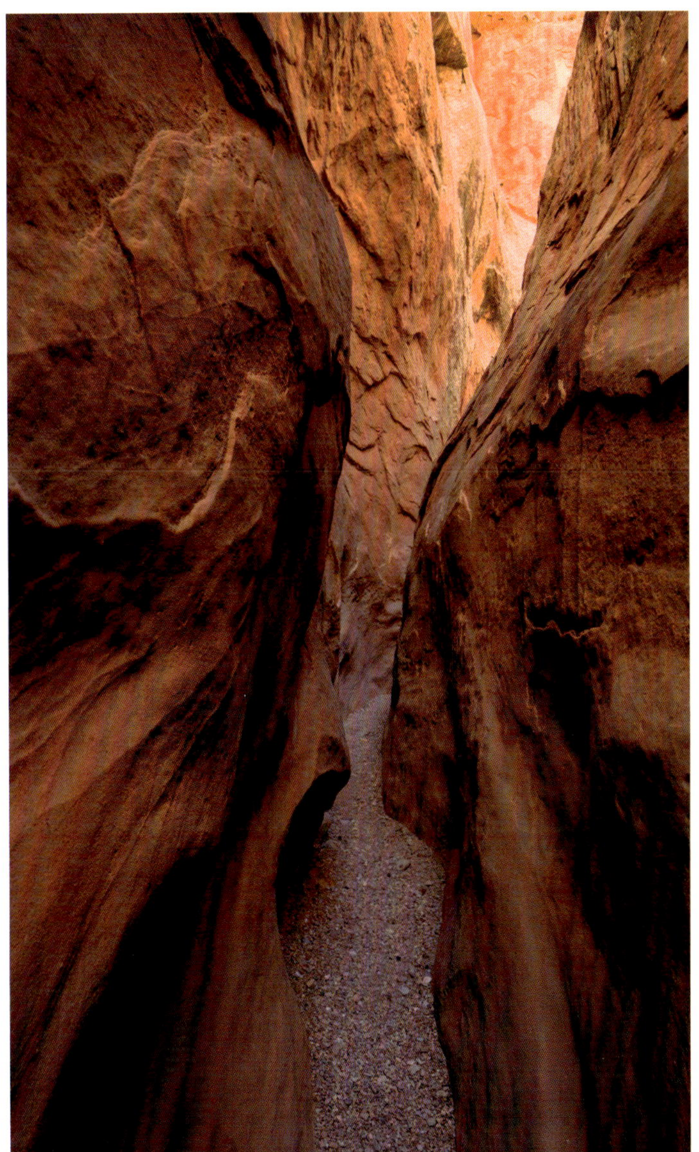

LITTLE WILD HORSE
CANYON, A SLOT CANYON IN
THE SAN RAFAEL SWELL.

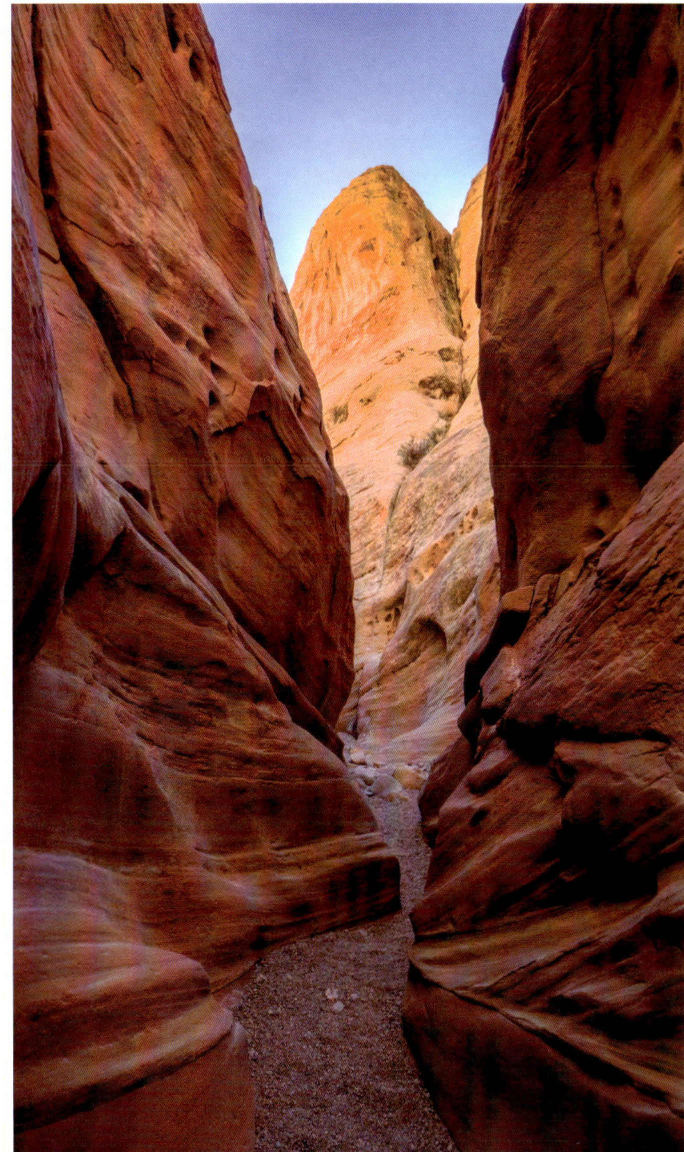

WARM MORNING LIGHT SPILLS
INTO THE LITTLE WILD HORSE SLOT
CANYON, SAN RAFAEL SWELL.

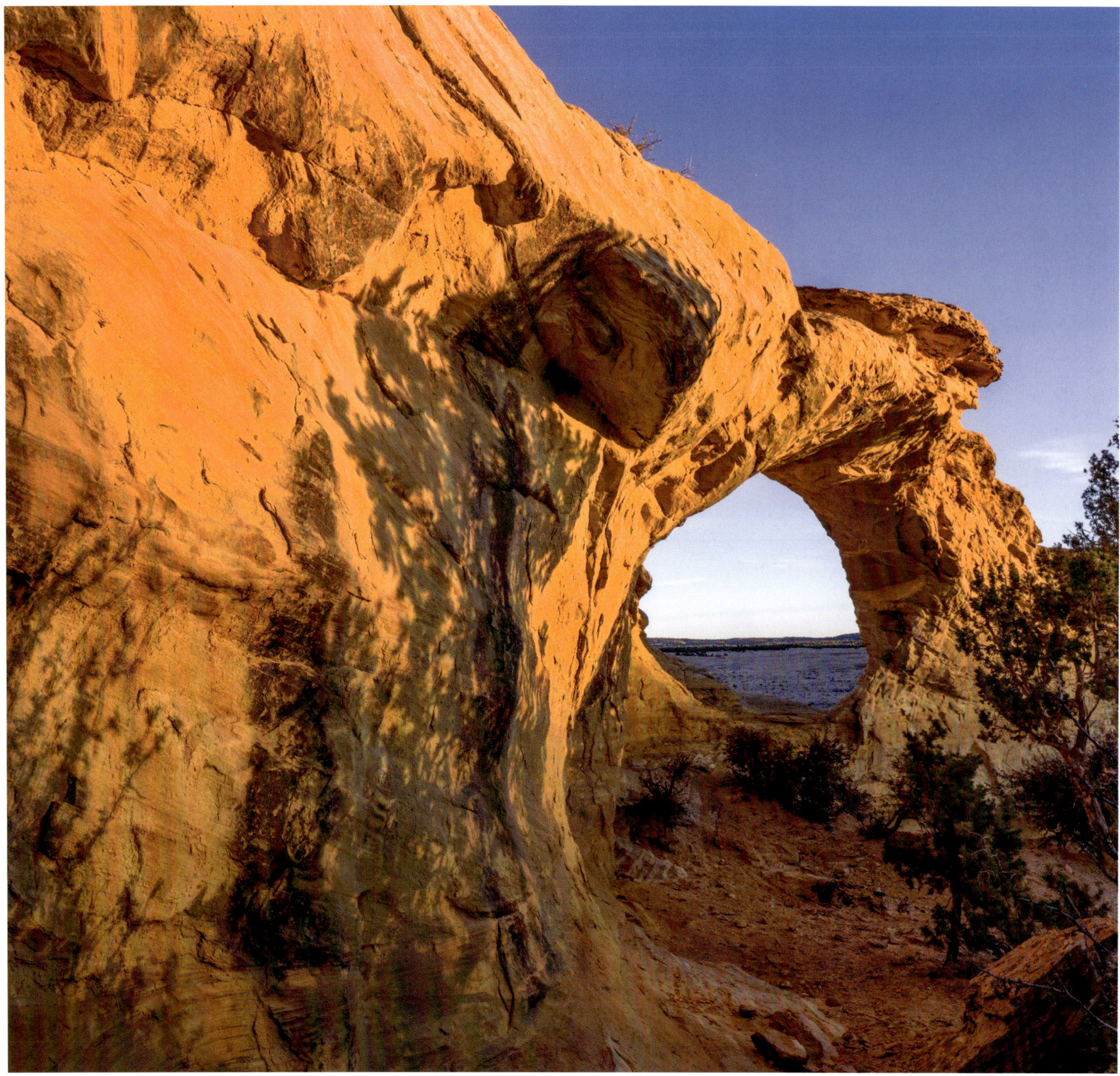

DUTCHMAN ARCH IN THE HEAD OF SINBAD COUNTRY, SAN RAFAEL SWELL.

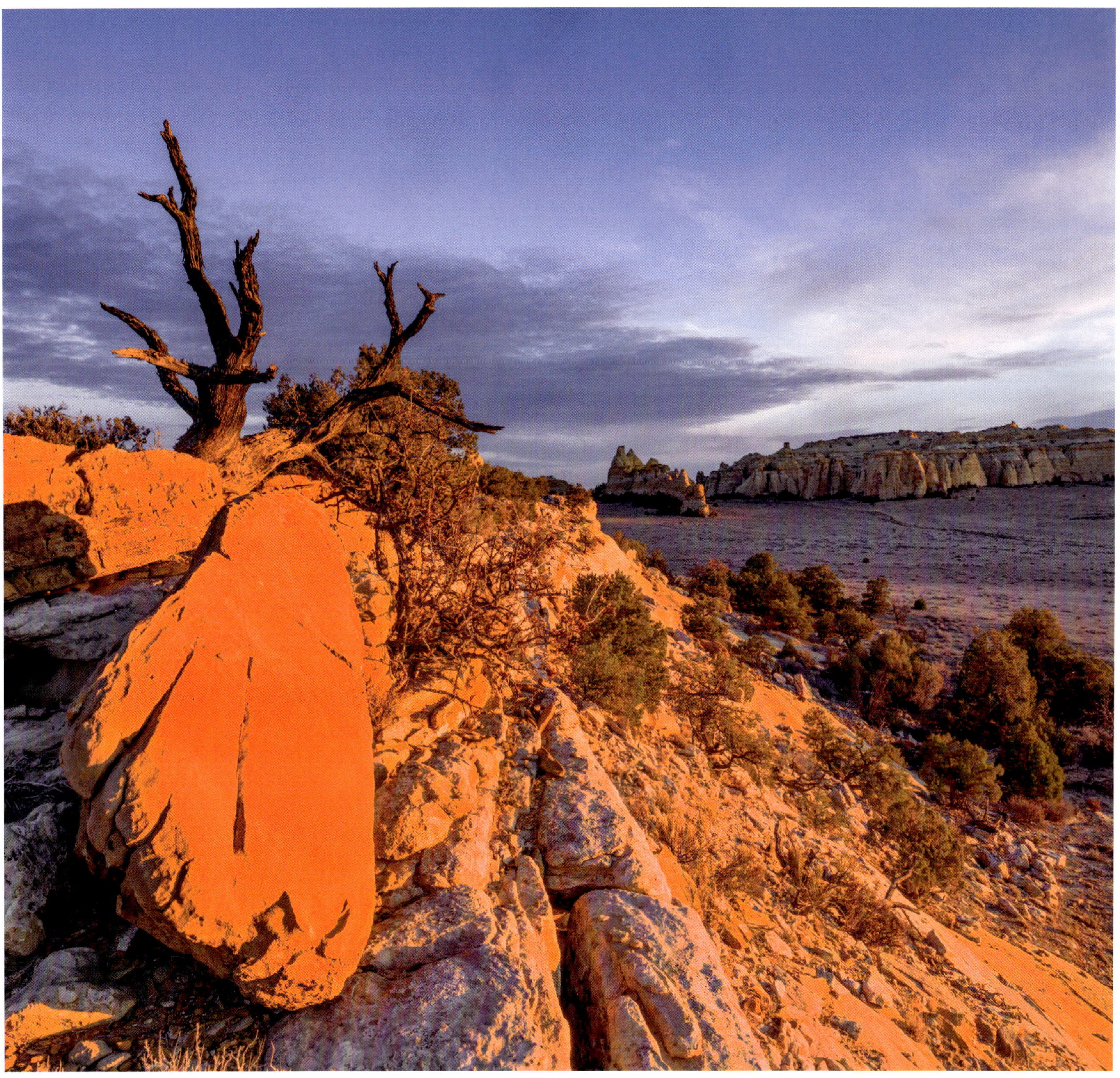

LOCOMOTIVE POINT IN THE HEAD OF SINBAD COUNTRY, SAN RAFAEL SWELL.

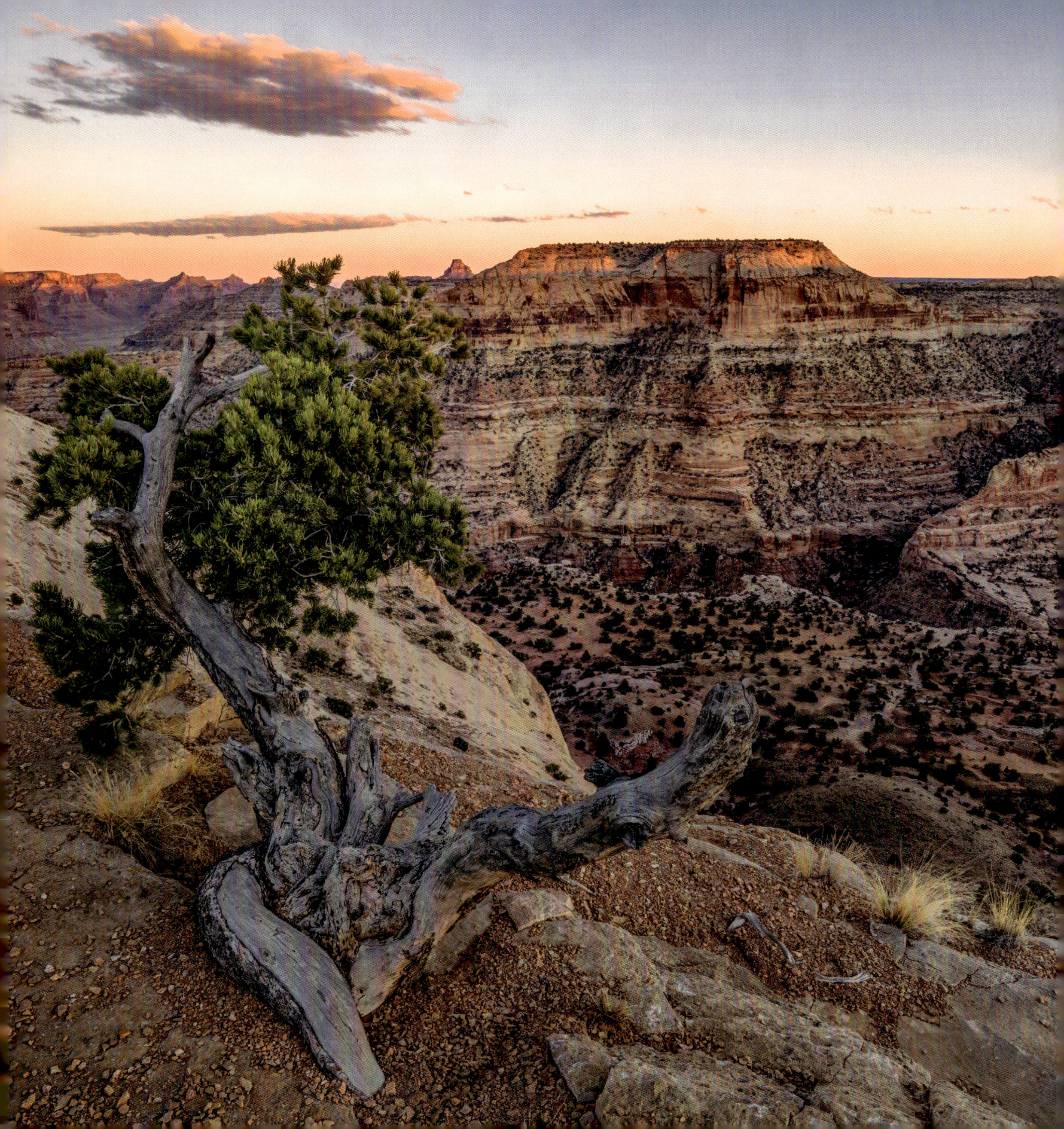

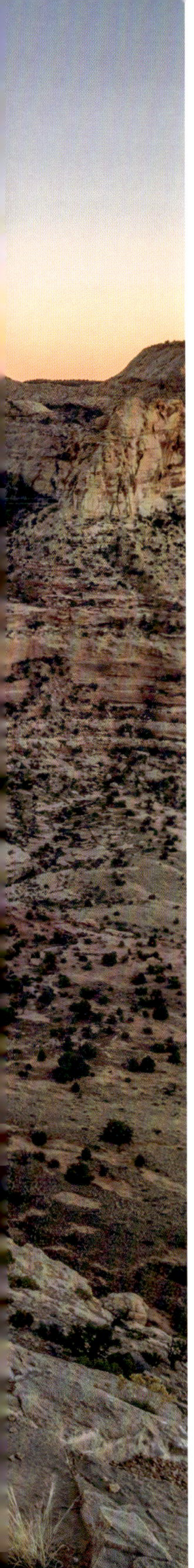

◀

SANDSTONE PEAKS RISE ABOVE THE SAN RAFAEL RIVER CANYON AT THE WEDGE OVERLOOK.

▶

TWIN BRIDGES, KNOWN AS THE EYES OF SINBAD, IN THE SANDSTONE REEF OF THE SAN RAFAEL SWELL.

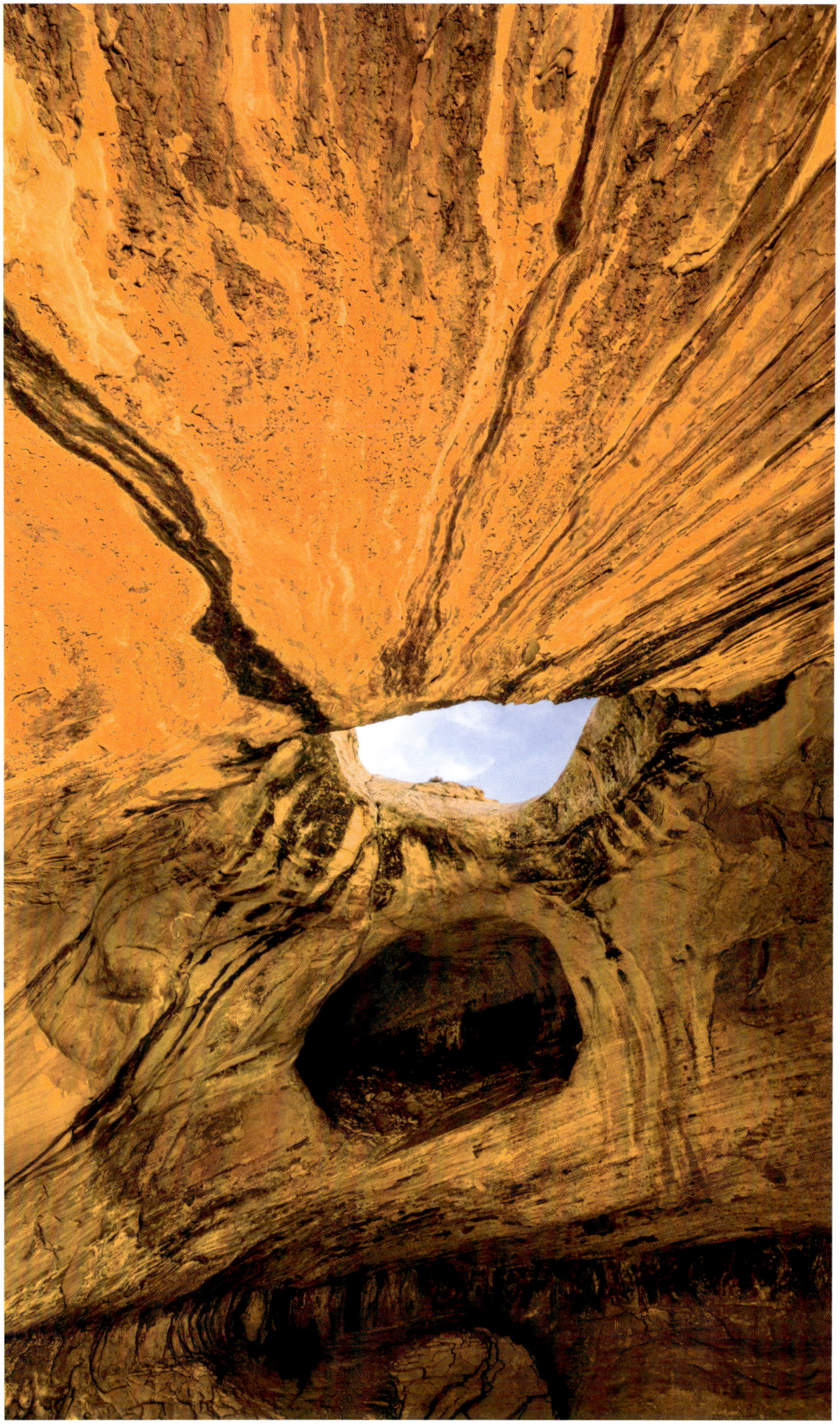

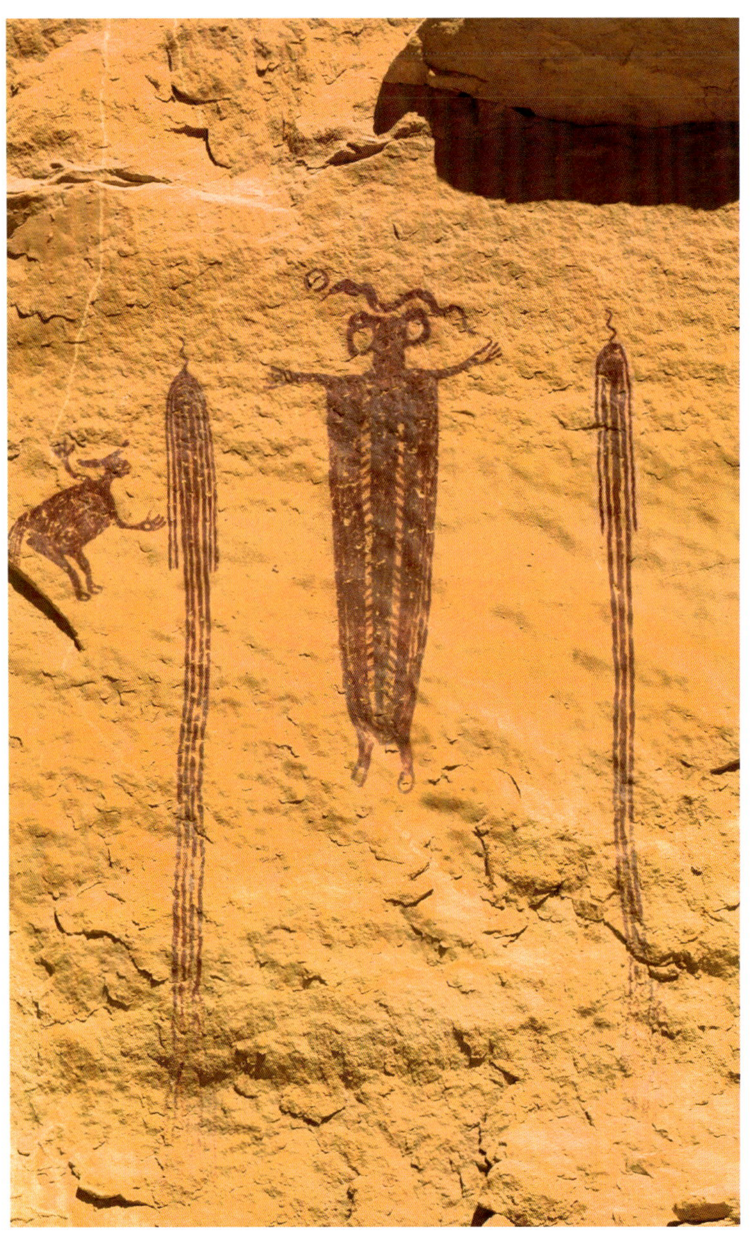

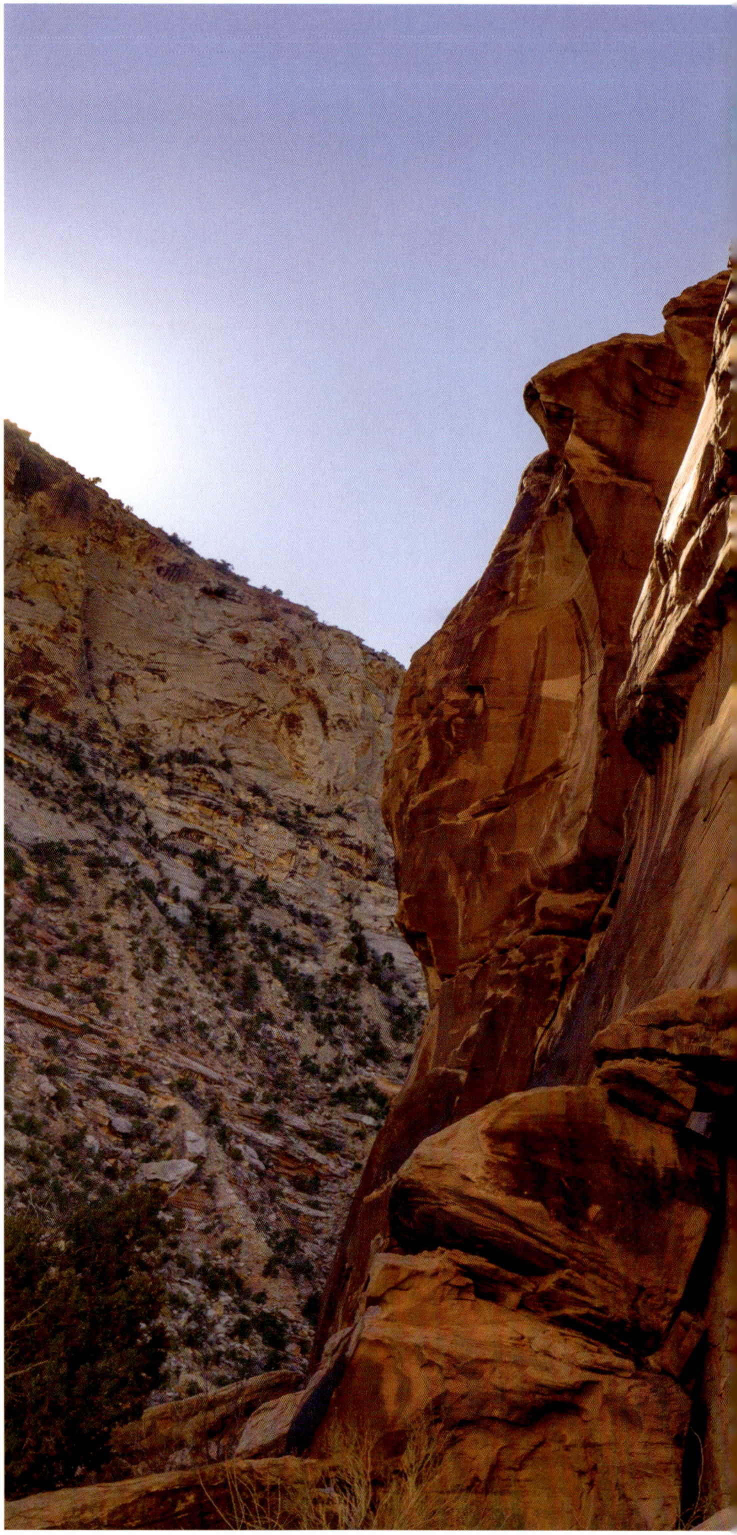

▲

HEAD OF SINBAD PICTOGRAPHS NEAR LOCOMOTIVE POINT, SAN RAFAEL SWELL.

▶

THE BUCKHORN WASH PICTOGRAPH PANEL, SAN RAFAEL SWELL.

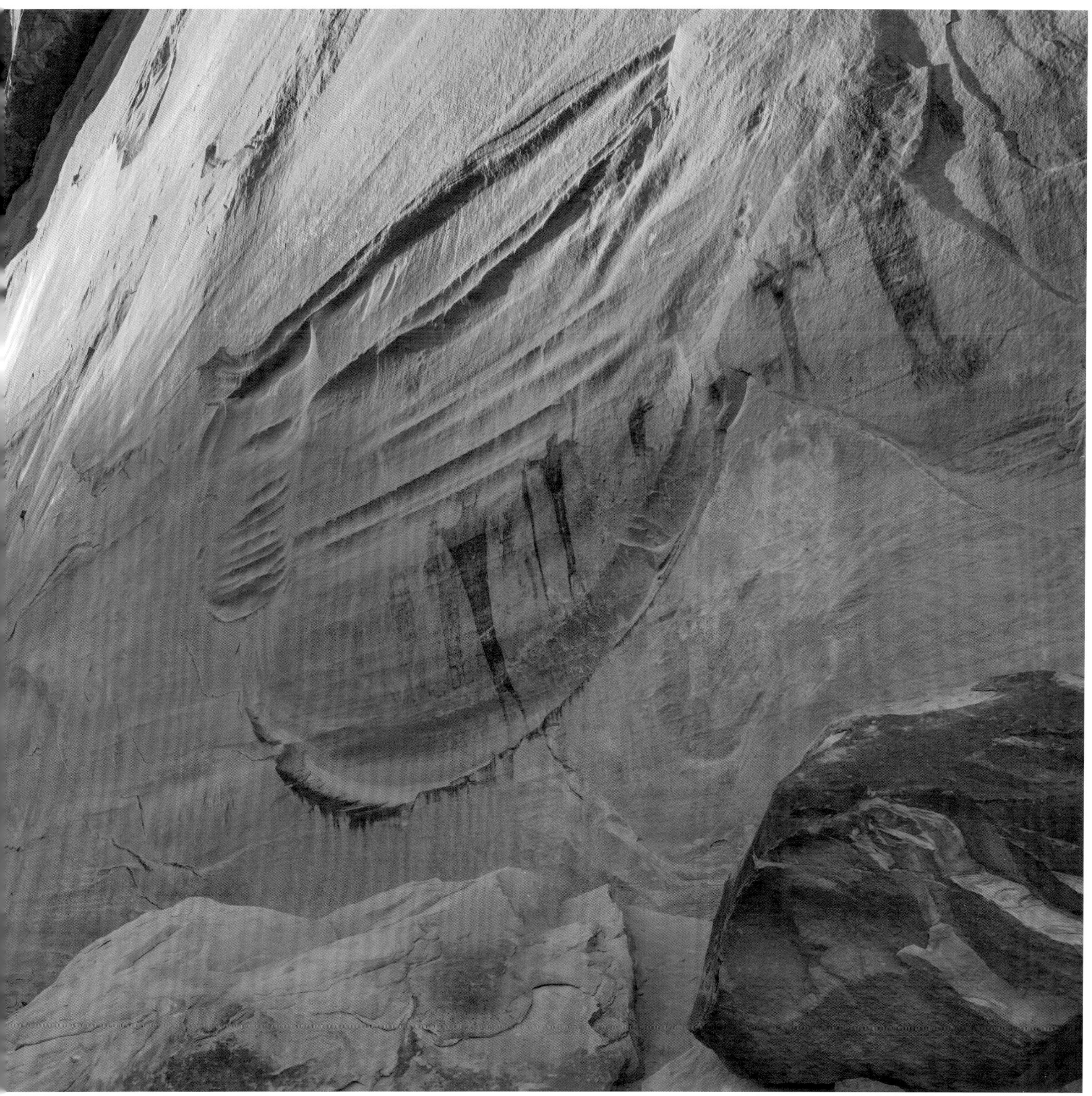

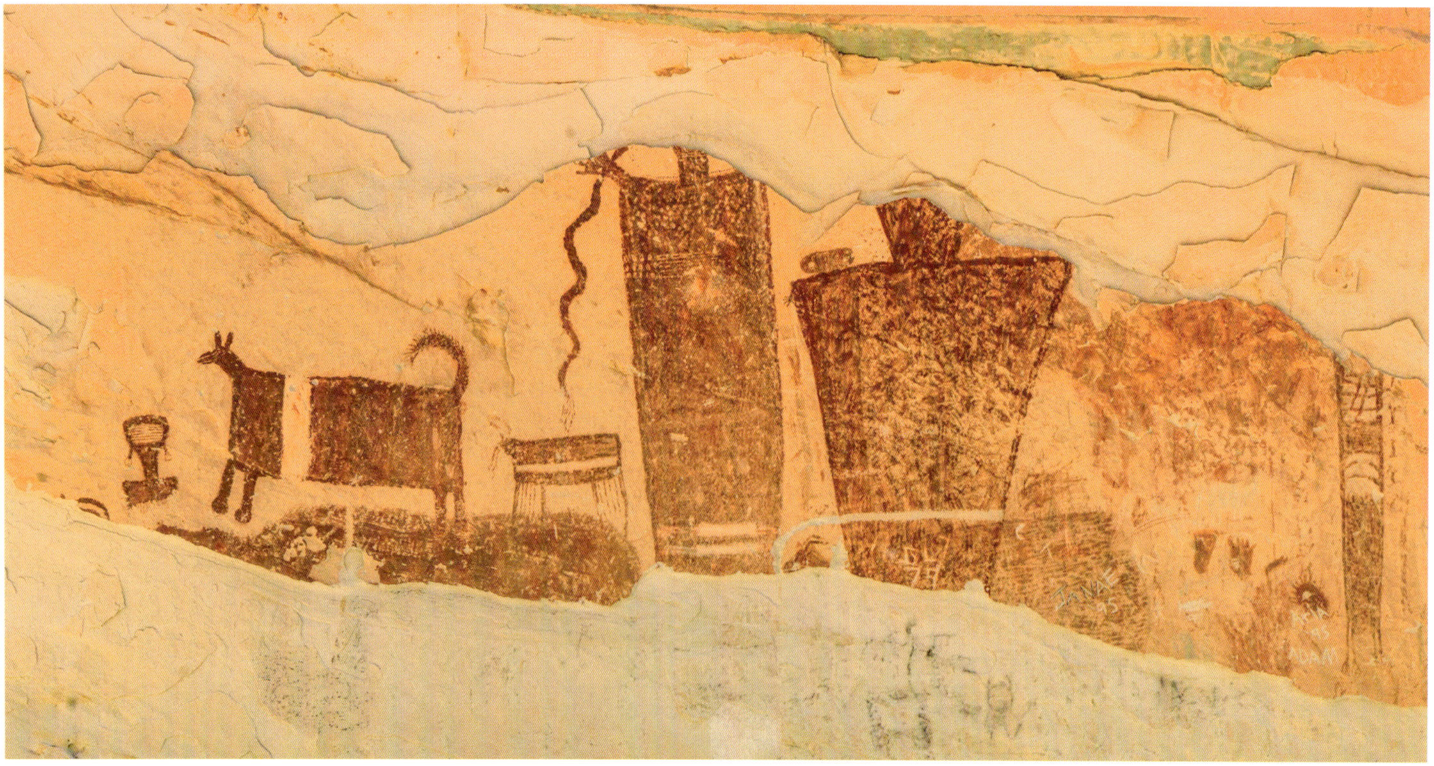

▲ TEMPLE MOUNTAIN PICTOGRAPH PANEL, SAN RAFAEL SWELL.

ANGEL FIGURES IN THE BUCKHORN WASH PICTOGRAPH PANEL, SAN RAFAEL SWELL. ▼

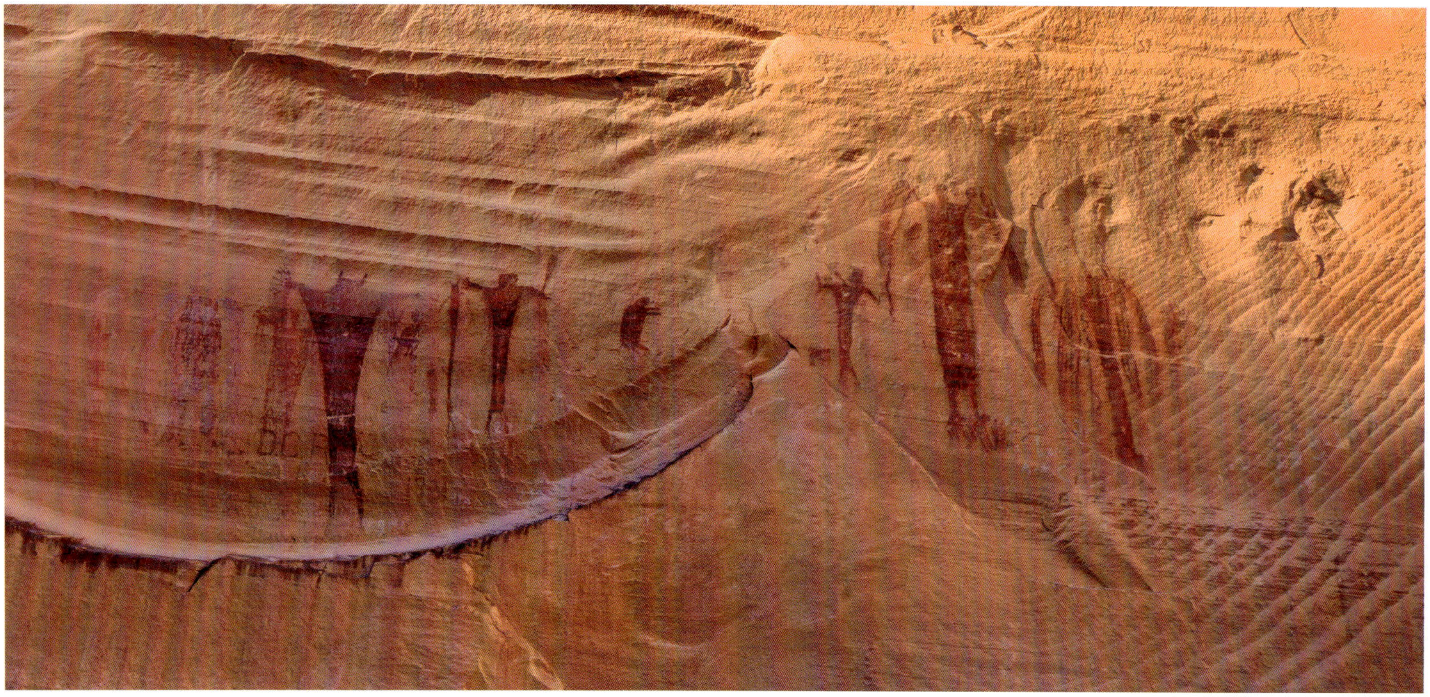

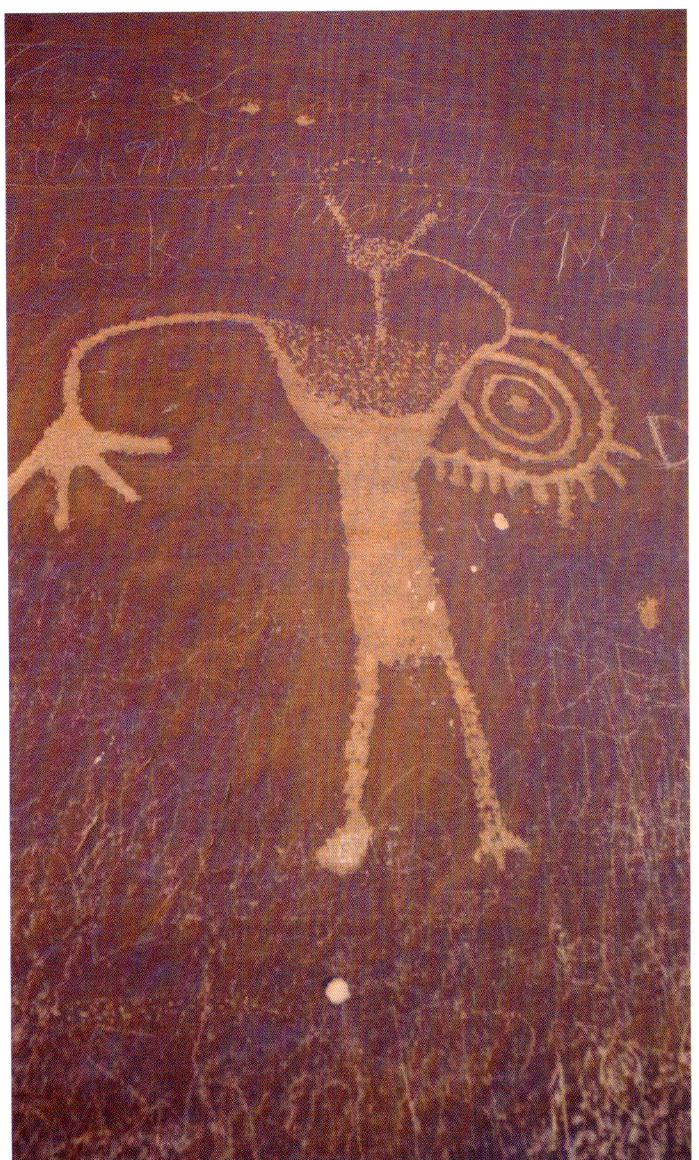

A FREMONT PICTOGRAPH IN BUCKHORN WASH IN THE SAN RAFAEL SWELL.

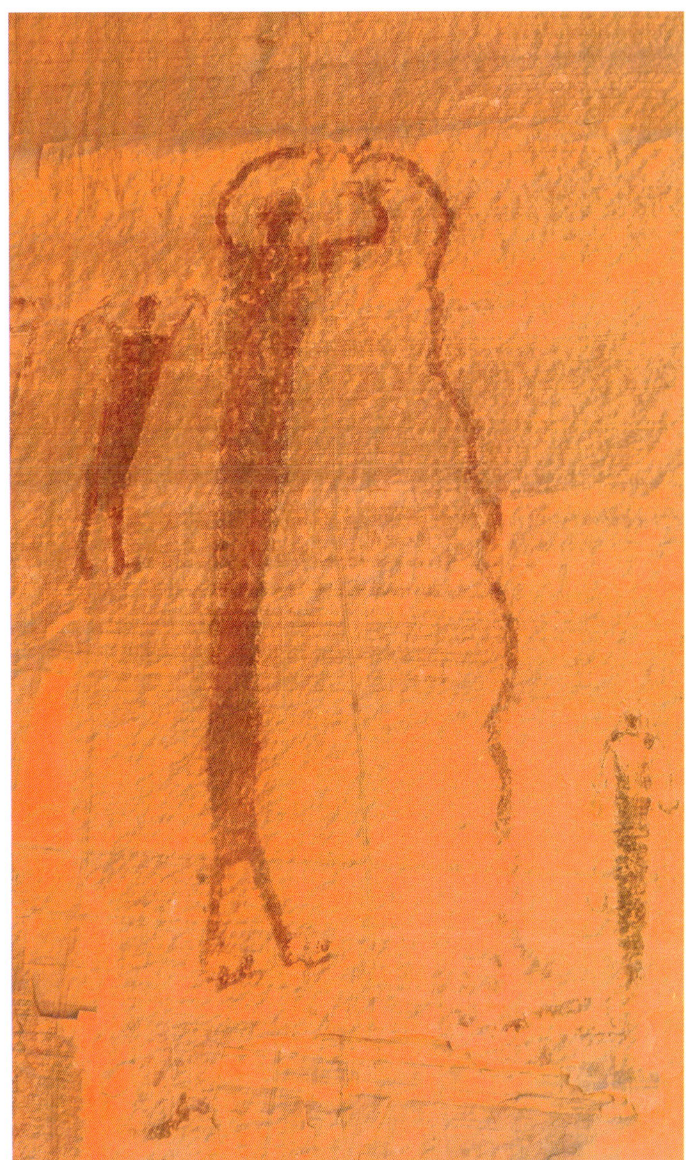

A FREMONT PICTOGRAPH IN BUCKHORN WASH IN THE SAN RAFAEL SWELL.

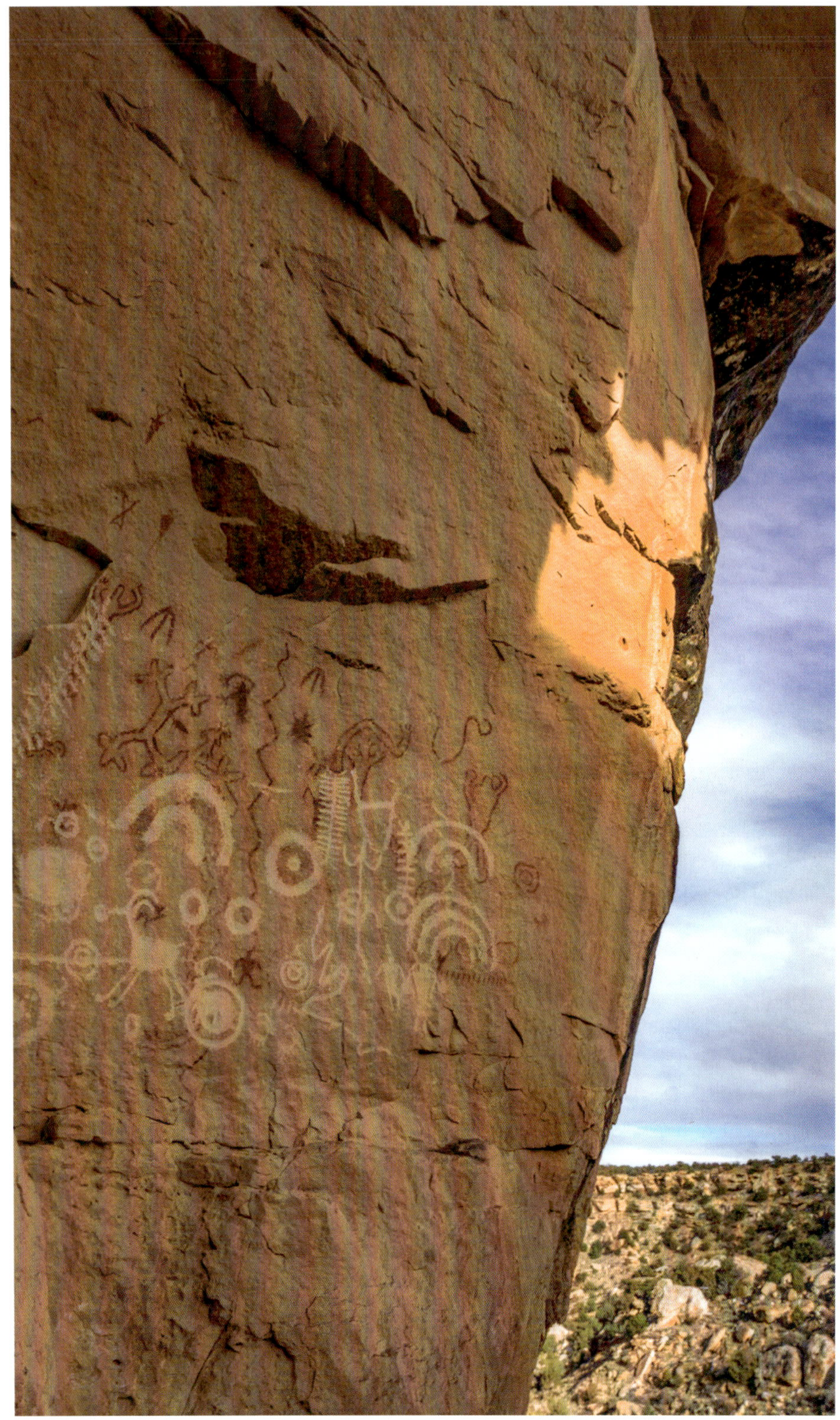

SHORT CANYON PICTOGRAPHS, SAN RAFAEL SWELL.

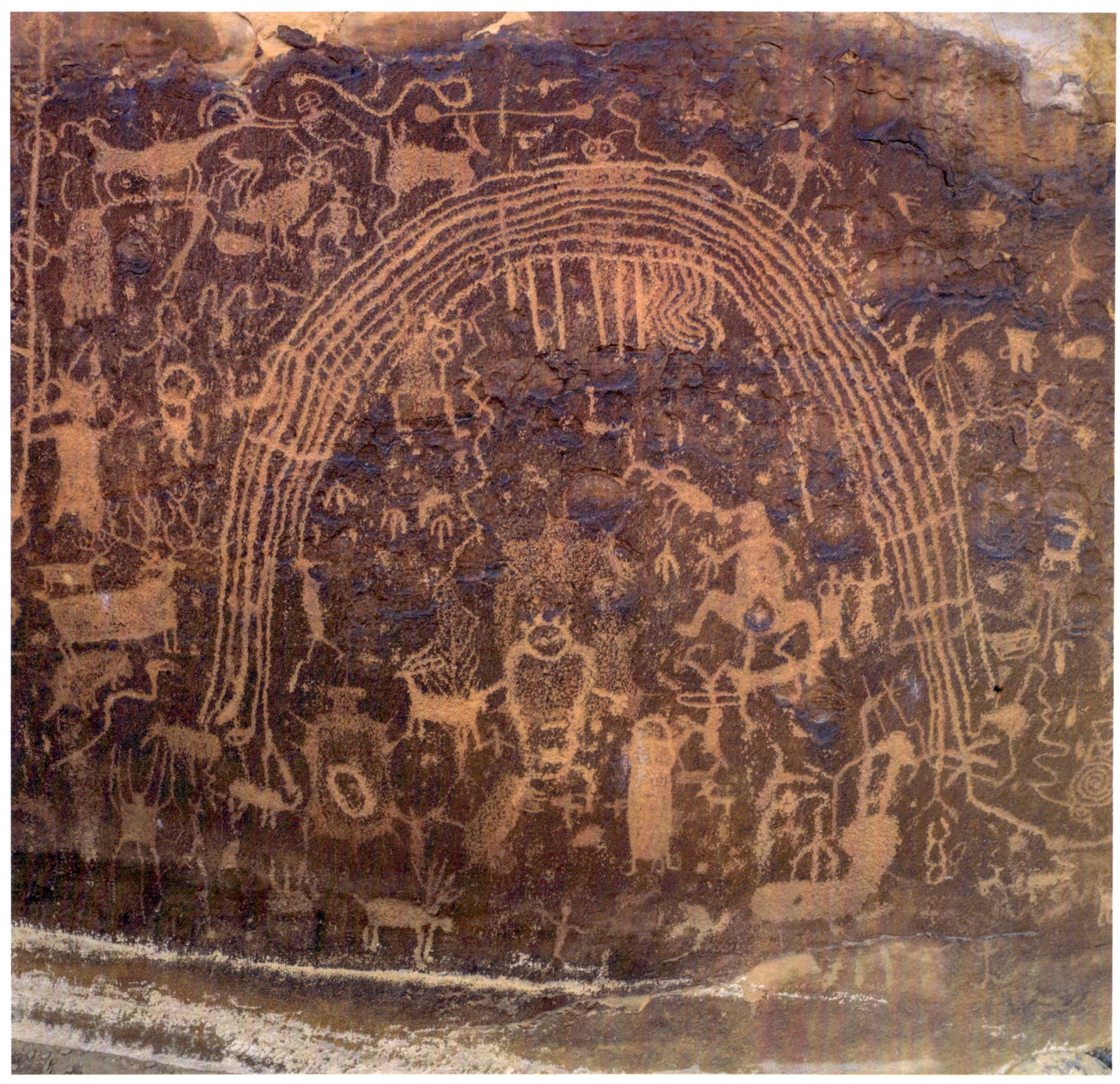

THE ROCHESTER ROCK ART PANEL IN THE MOLEN REEF, SAN RAFAEL SWELL.

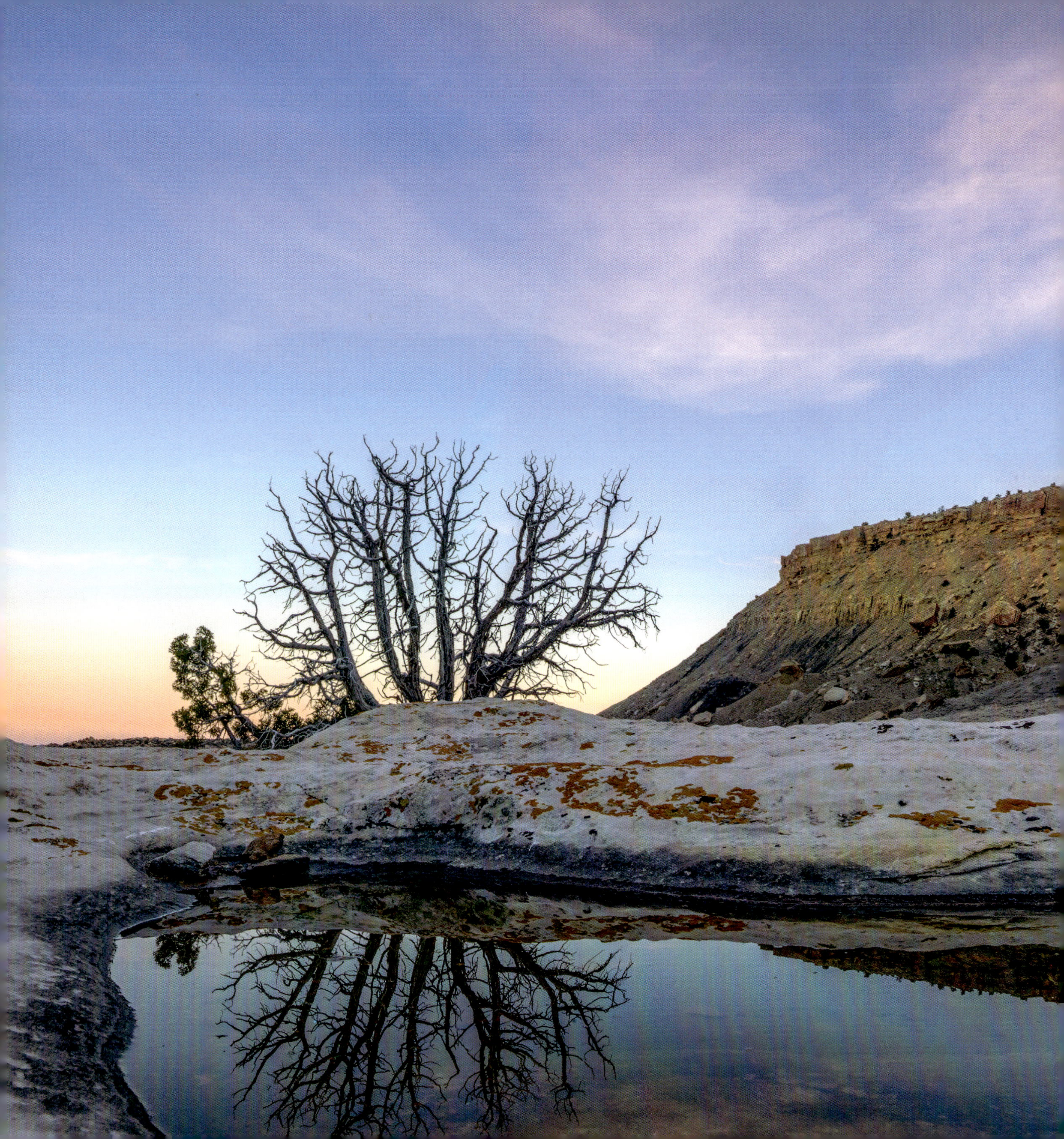

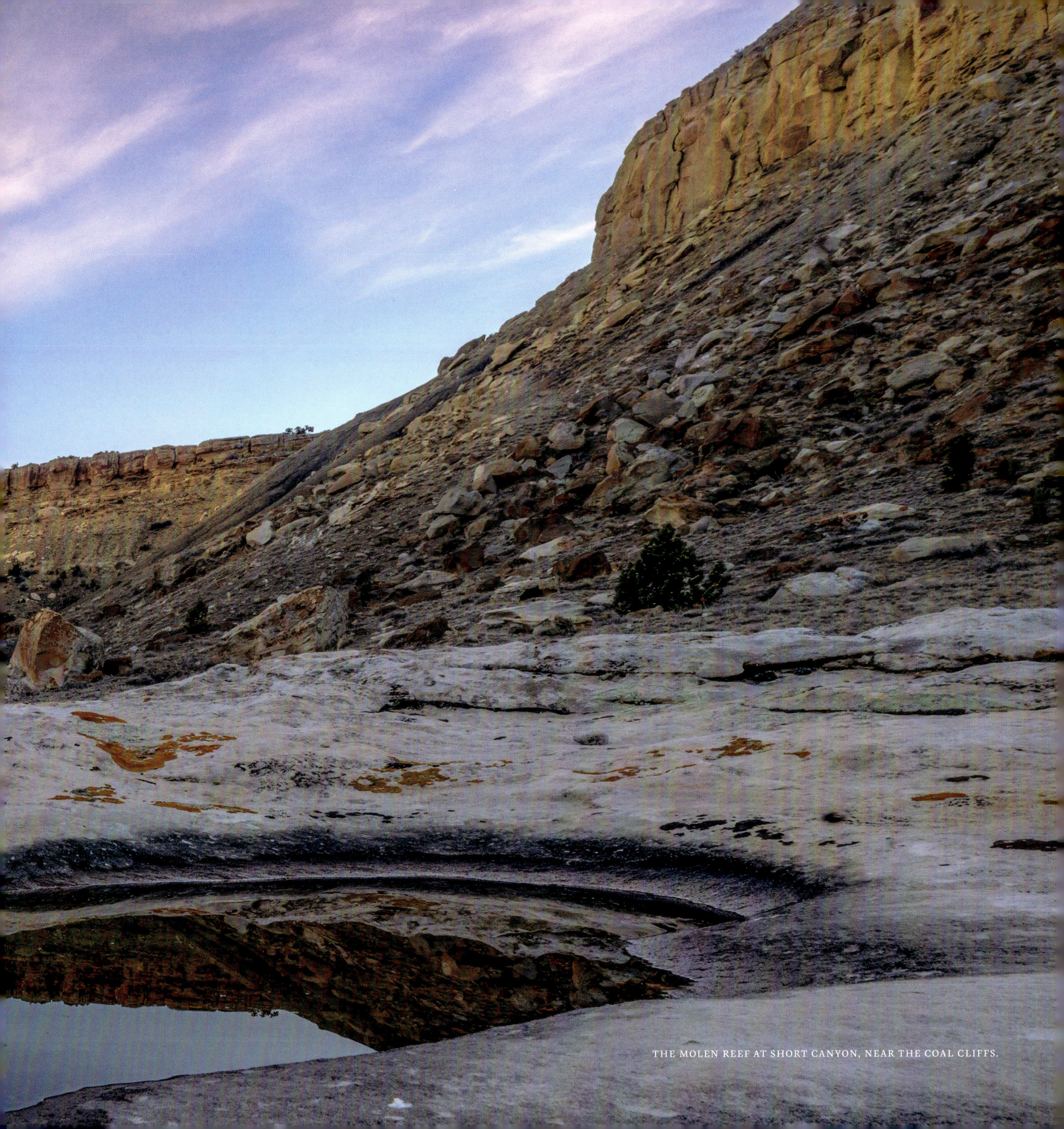

THE MOLEN REEF AT SHORT CANYON, NEAR THE COAL CLIFFS.

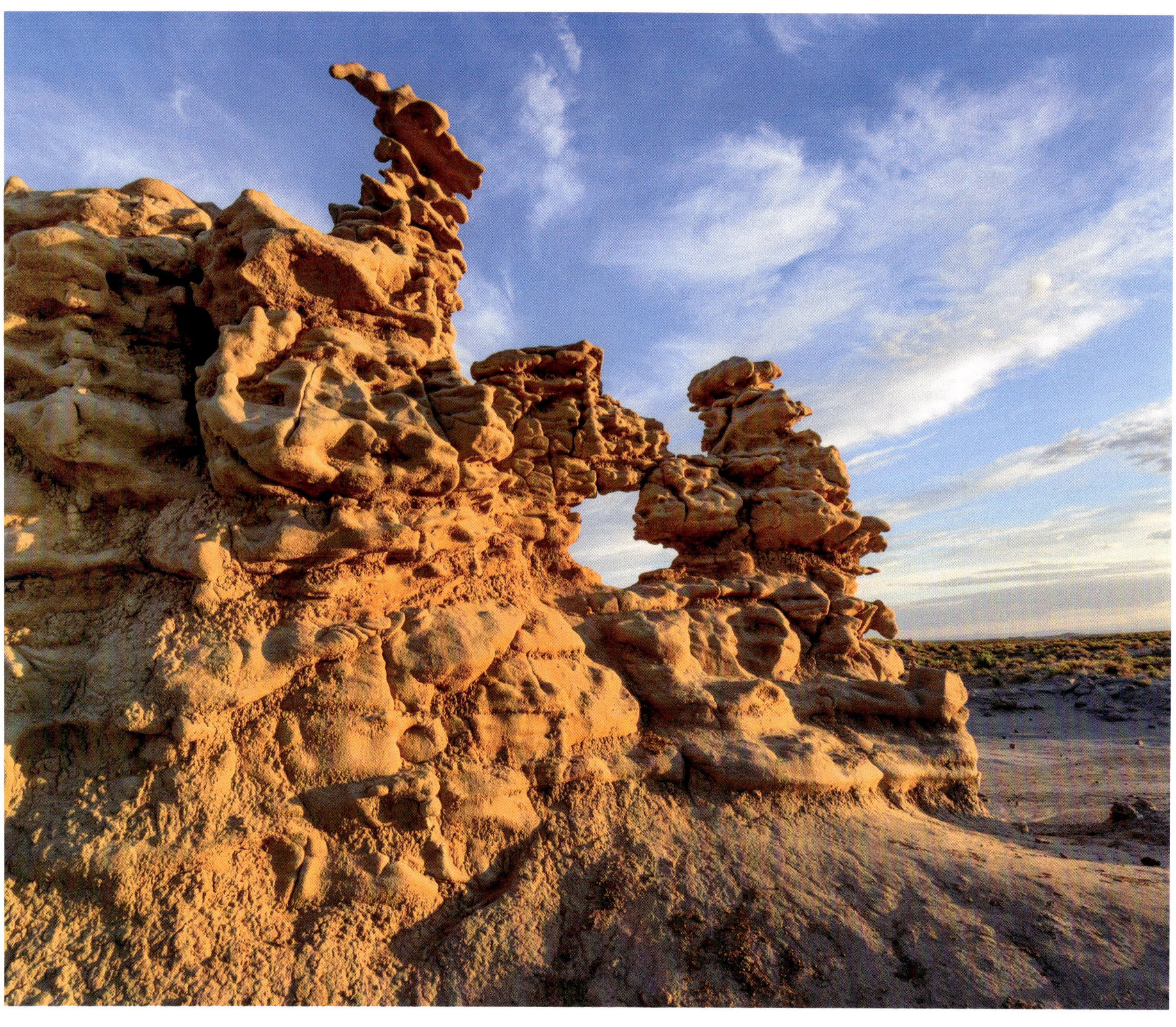

THE MYSTICAL SCULPTED SHAPES OF FANTASY CANYON.

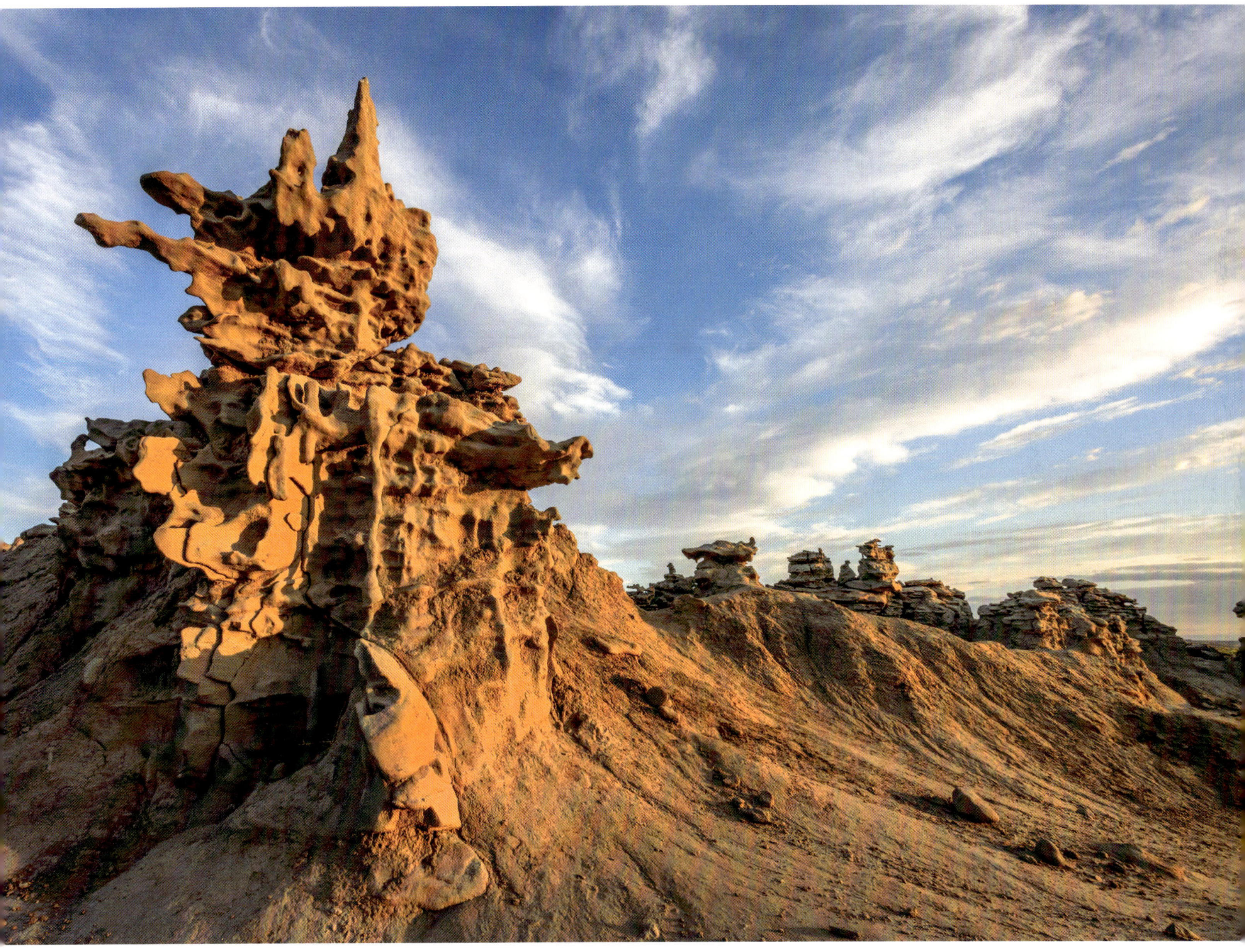

THE WITCH, ONE OF THE WELL-KNOWN FORMATIONS IN FANTASY CANYON.

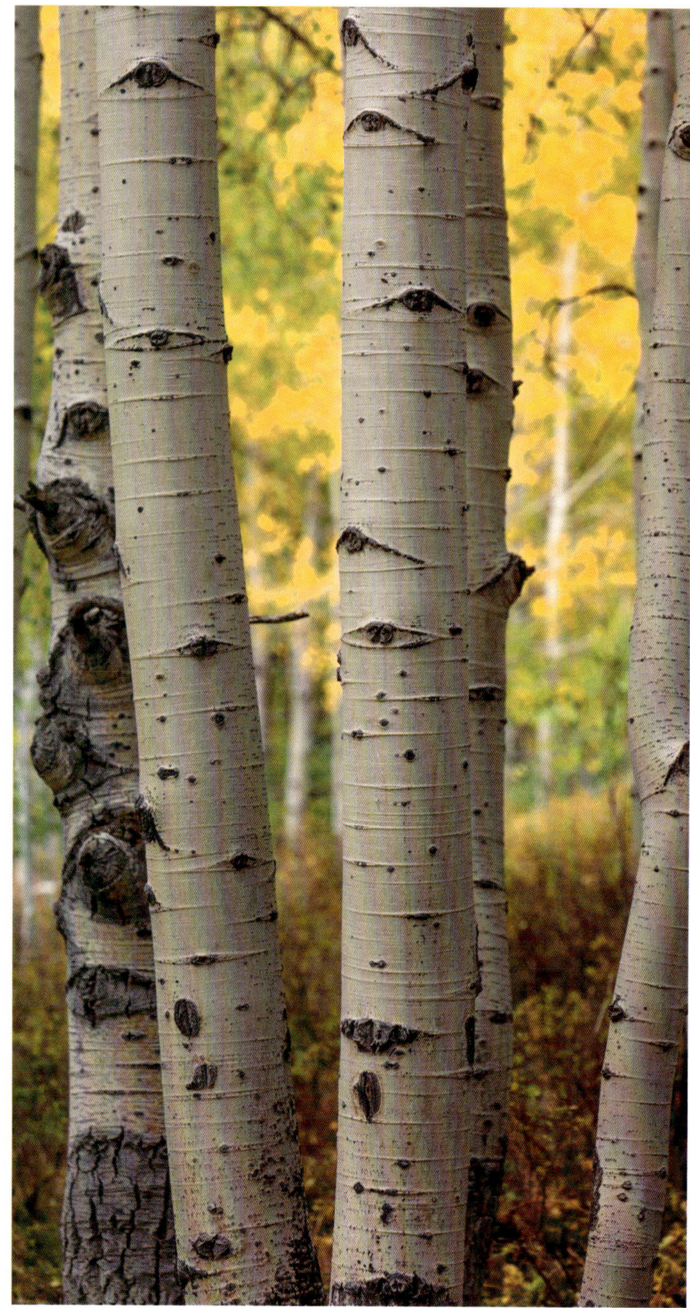

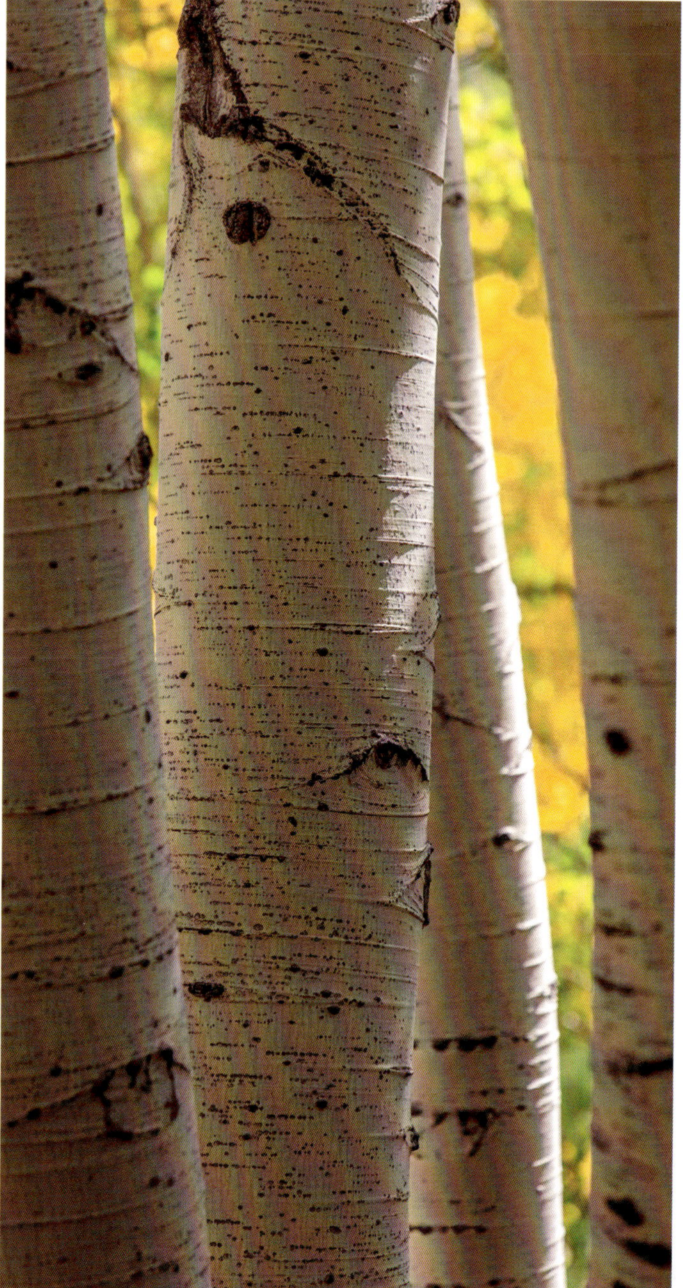

DETAILS OF ASPEN TREES IN THE MANTI-LA SAL NATIONAL FOREST.

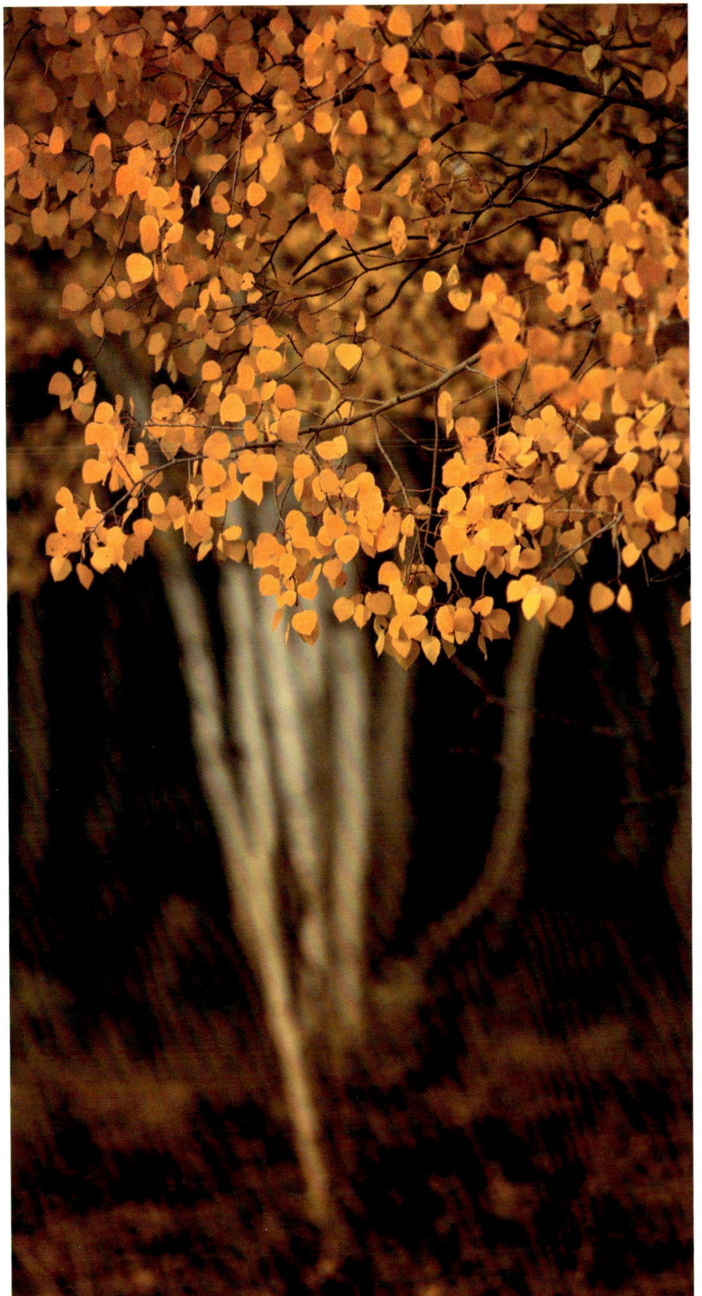

DANCING GHOST ASPENS IN FALL FOLIAGE HIGH IN THE MANTI-LA SAL NATIONAL FOREST.

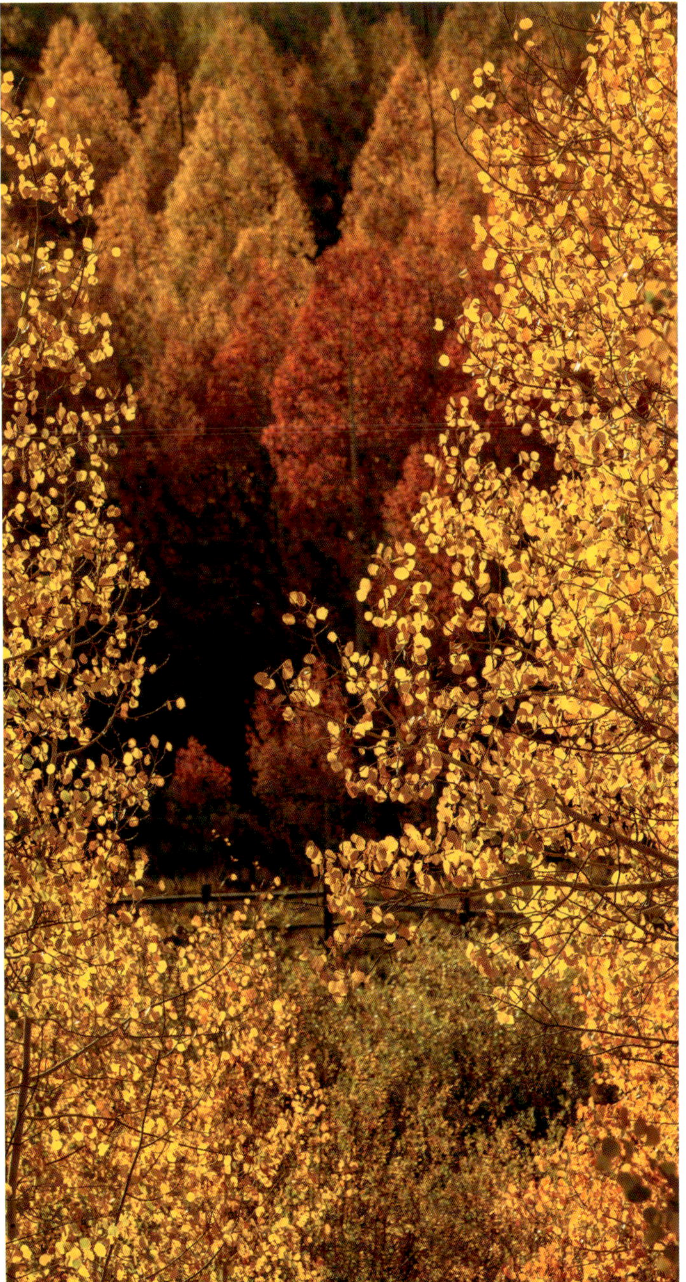

RED AND YELLOW LEAVES COLOR THE MANTI-LA SAL NATIONAL FOREST IN JOES VALLEY.

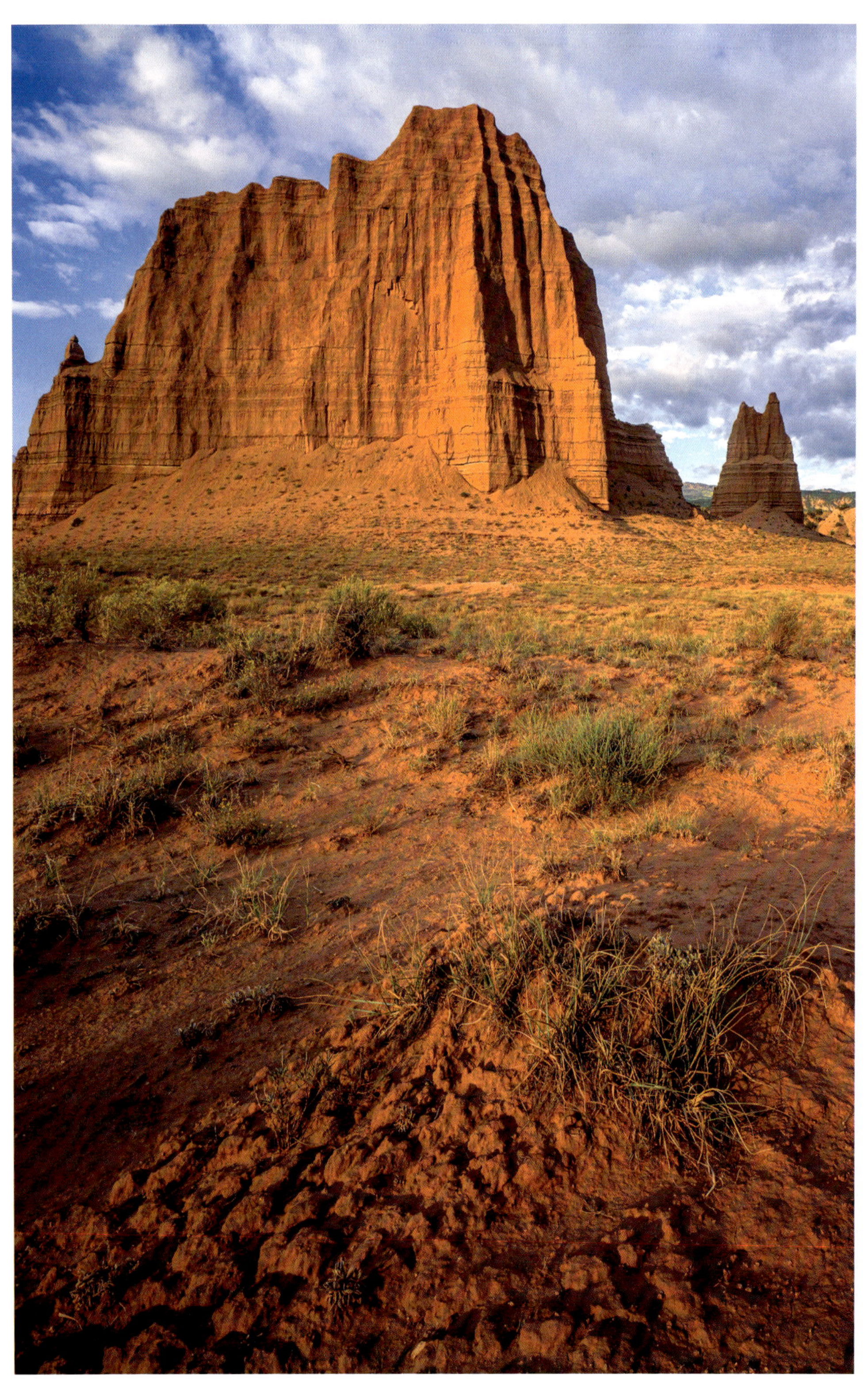

DAWN'S RAYS STRIKE THE TEMPLE OF THE SUN IN THE CATHEDRAL VALLEY DISTRICT OF CAPITOL REEF NATIONAL PARK.

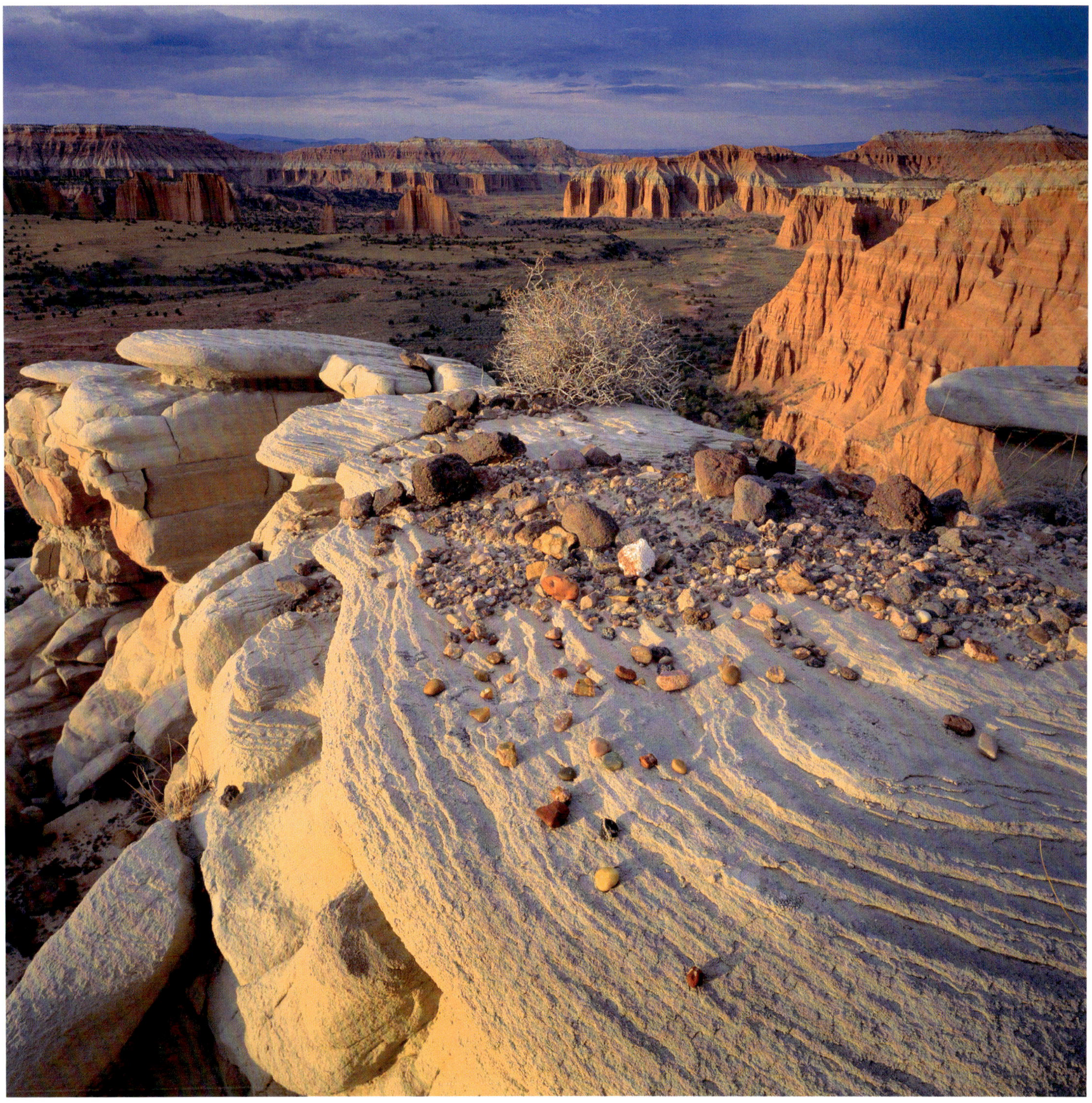

OVERLOOKING CATHEDRAL VALLEY IN CAPITOL REEF NATIONAL PARK.

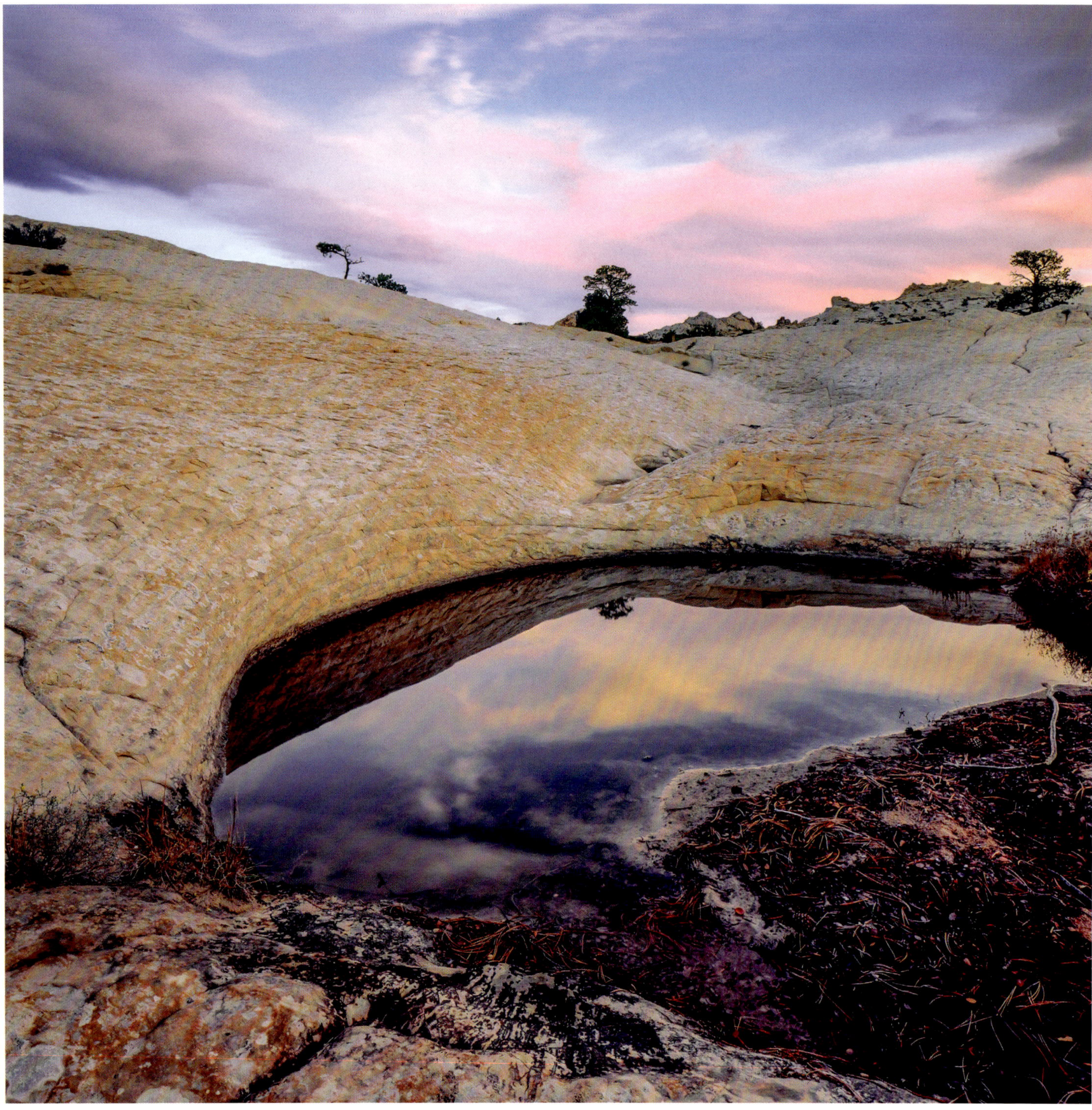

A TINAJA (WATER POCKET) NEAR OAK CREEK IN CAPITOL REEF NATIONAL PARK.

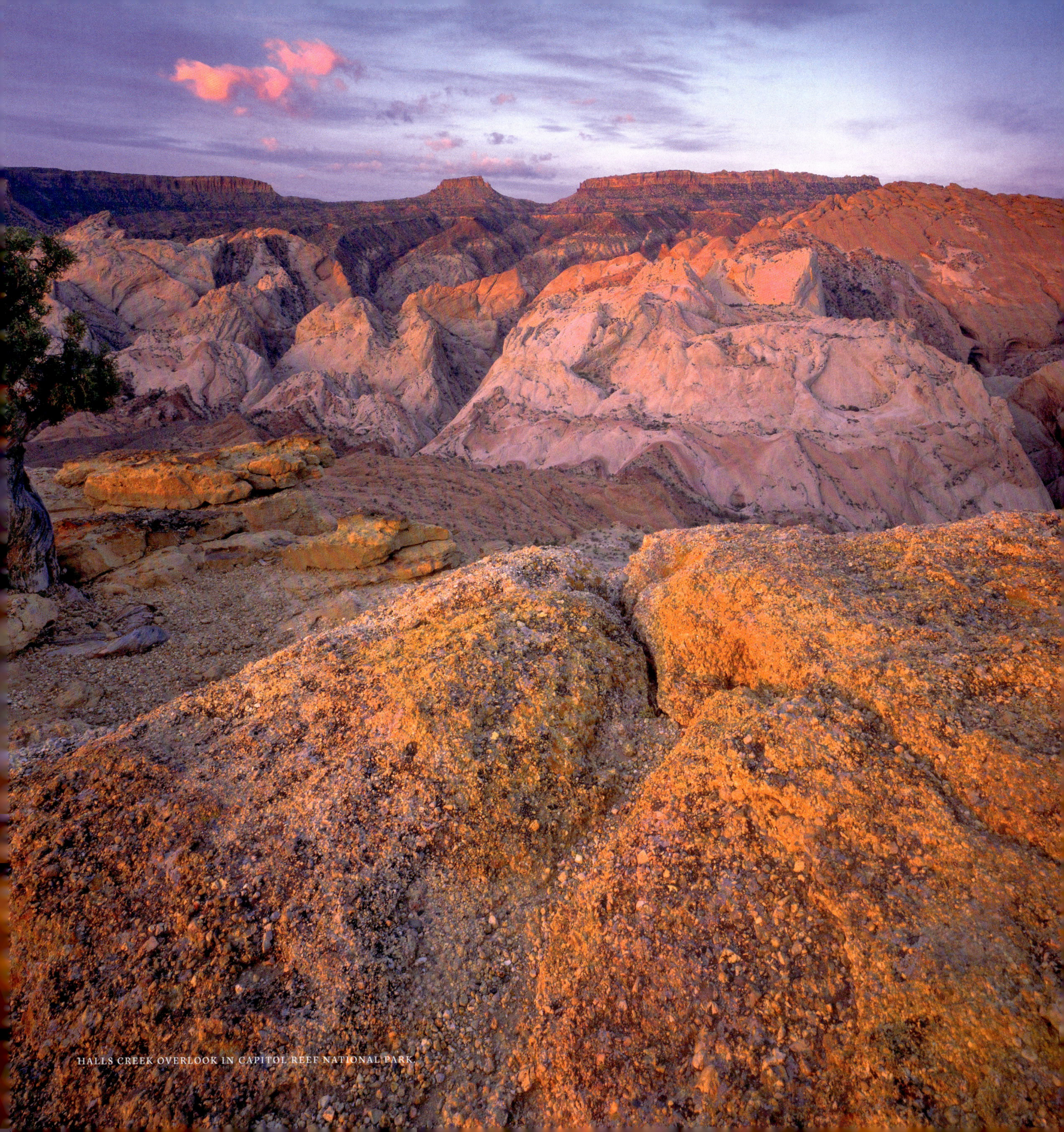

HALLS CREEK OVERLOOK IN CAPITOL REEF NATIONAL PARK.

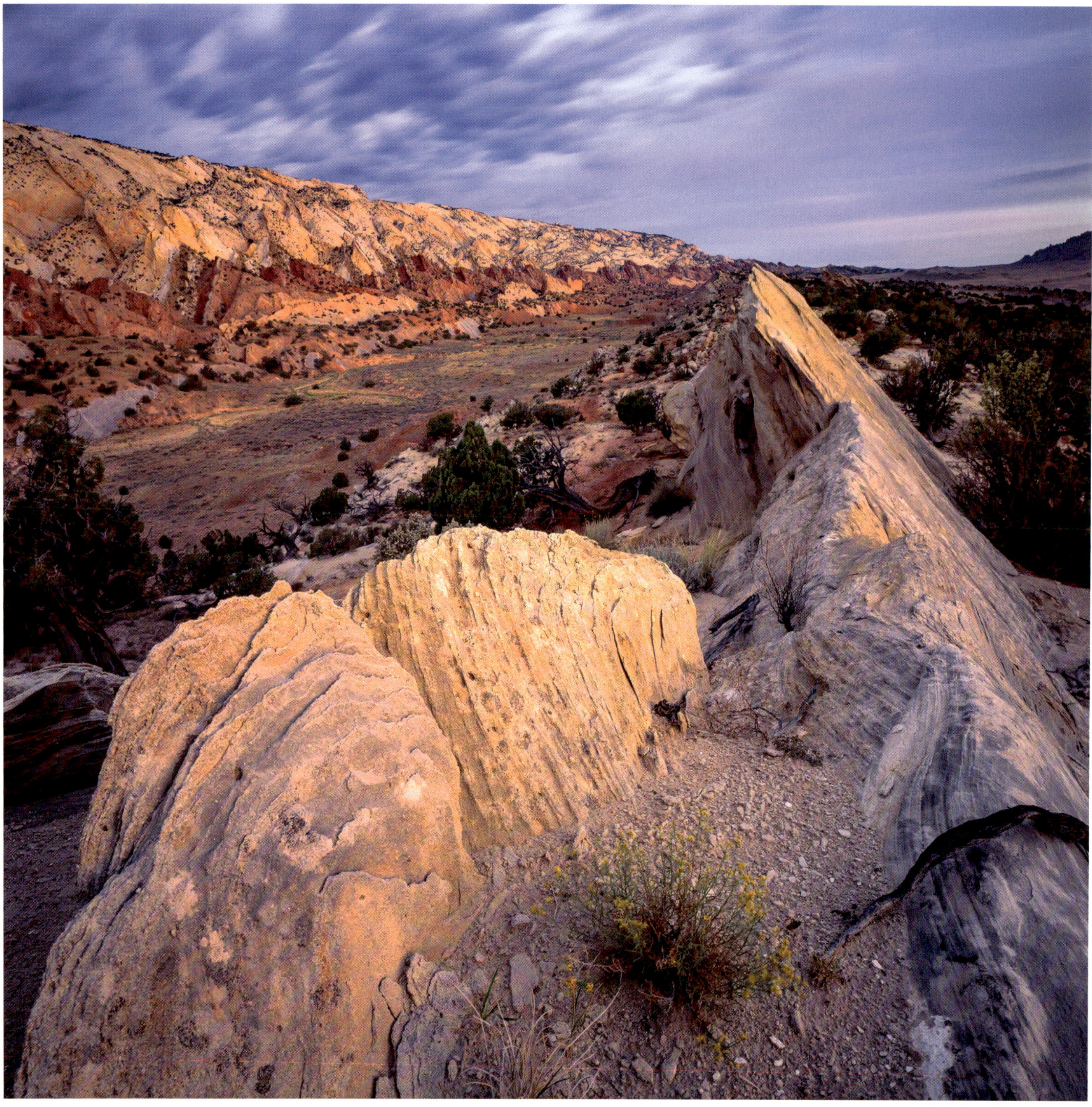

THE DESERT DROPS AWAY ALONG THE SHARP FAULT LINE OF THE WATERPOCKET FOLD.

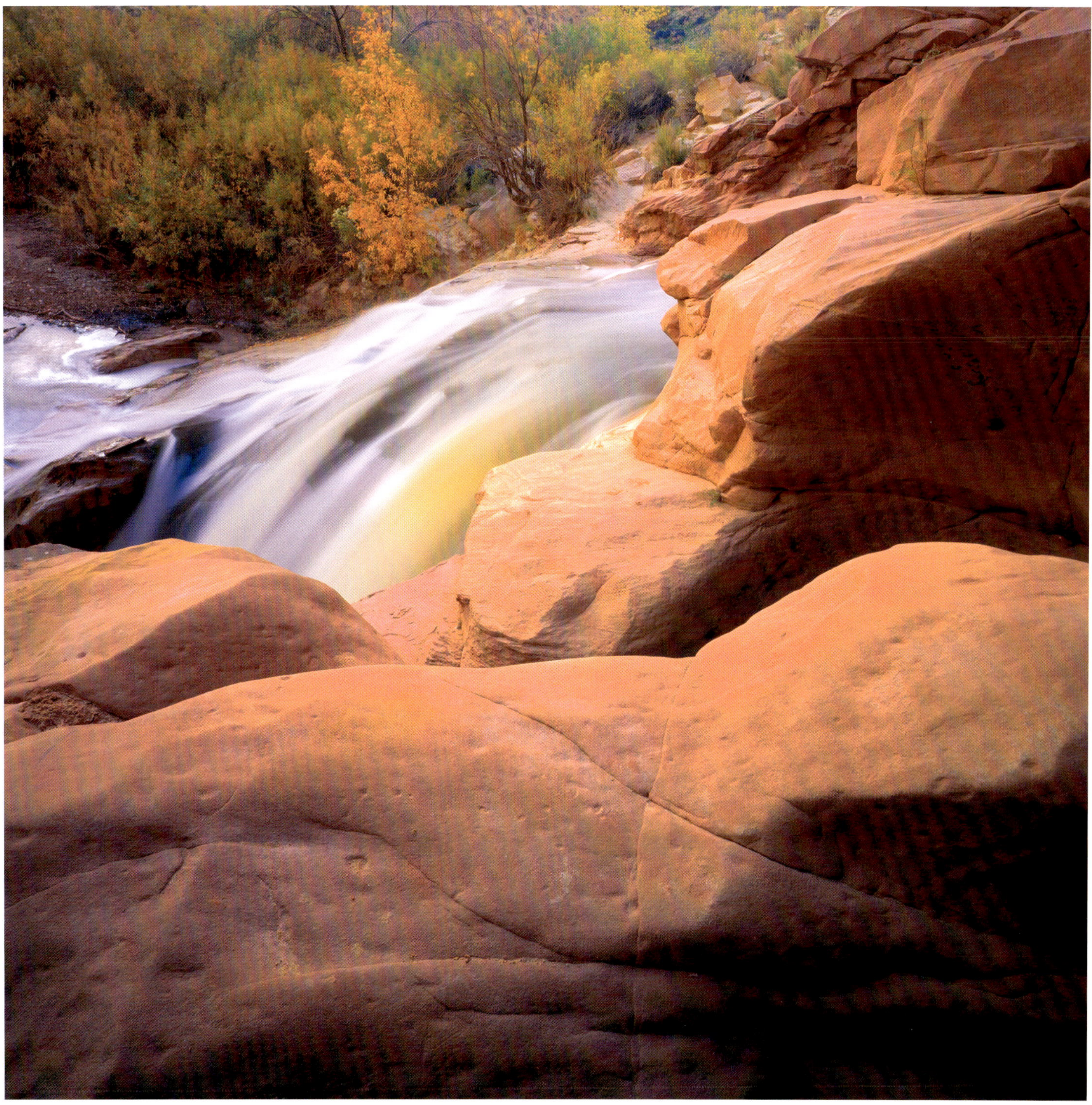

THE FREMONT RIVER CUTS THROUGH SANDSTONE IN CAPITOL REEF NATIONAL PARK.

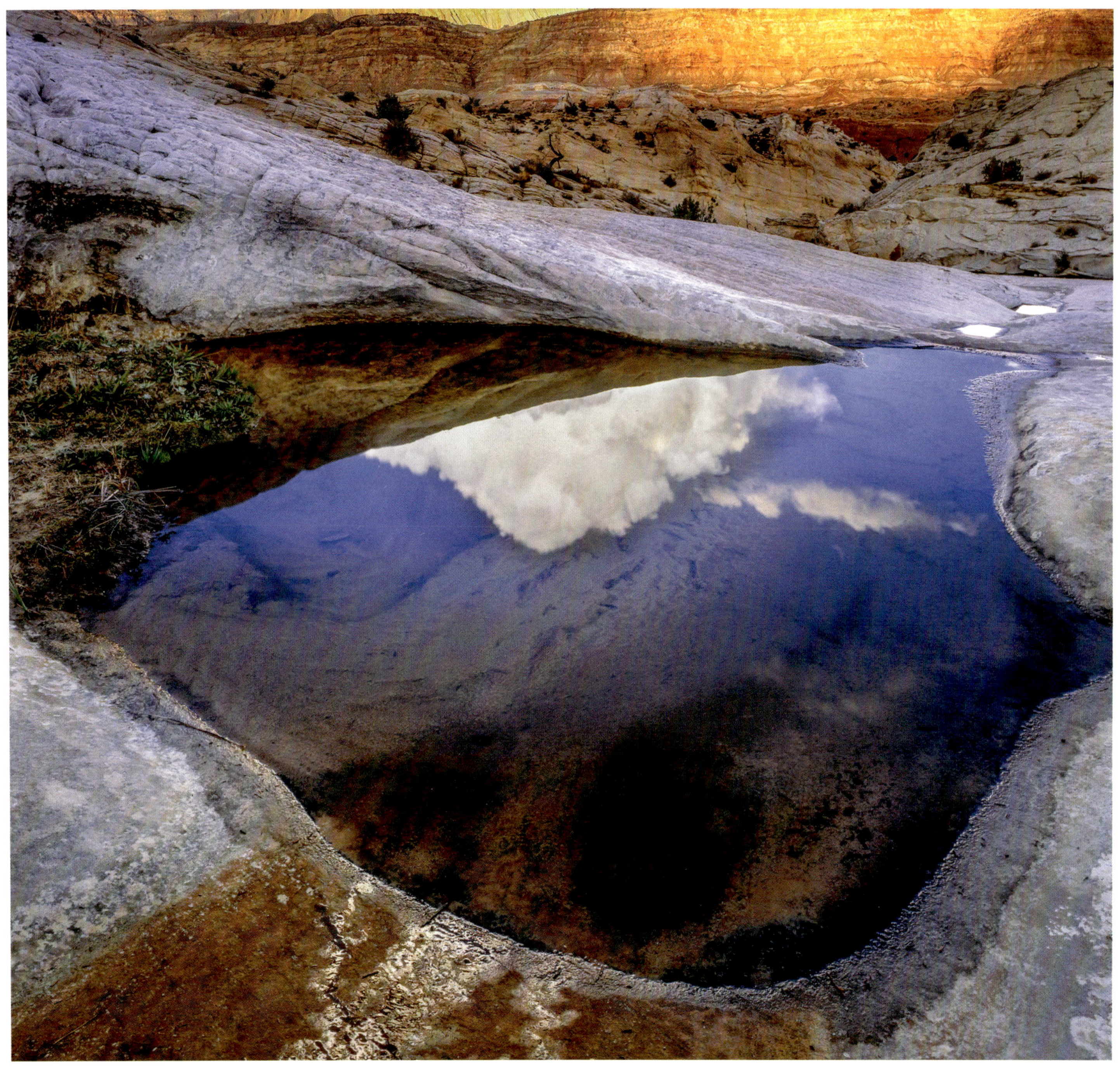

A THUNDERSTORM REFLECTS IN A CLEAR BLUE POOL, WILLOW TANKS.

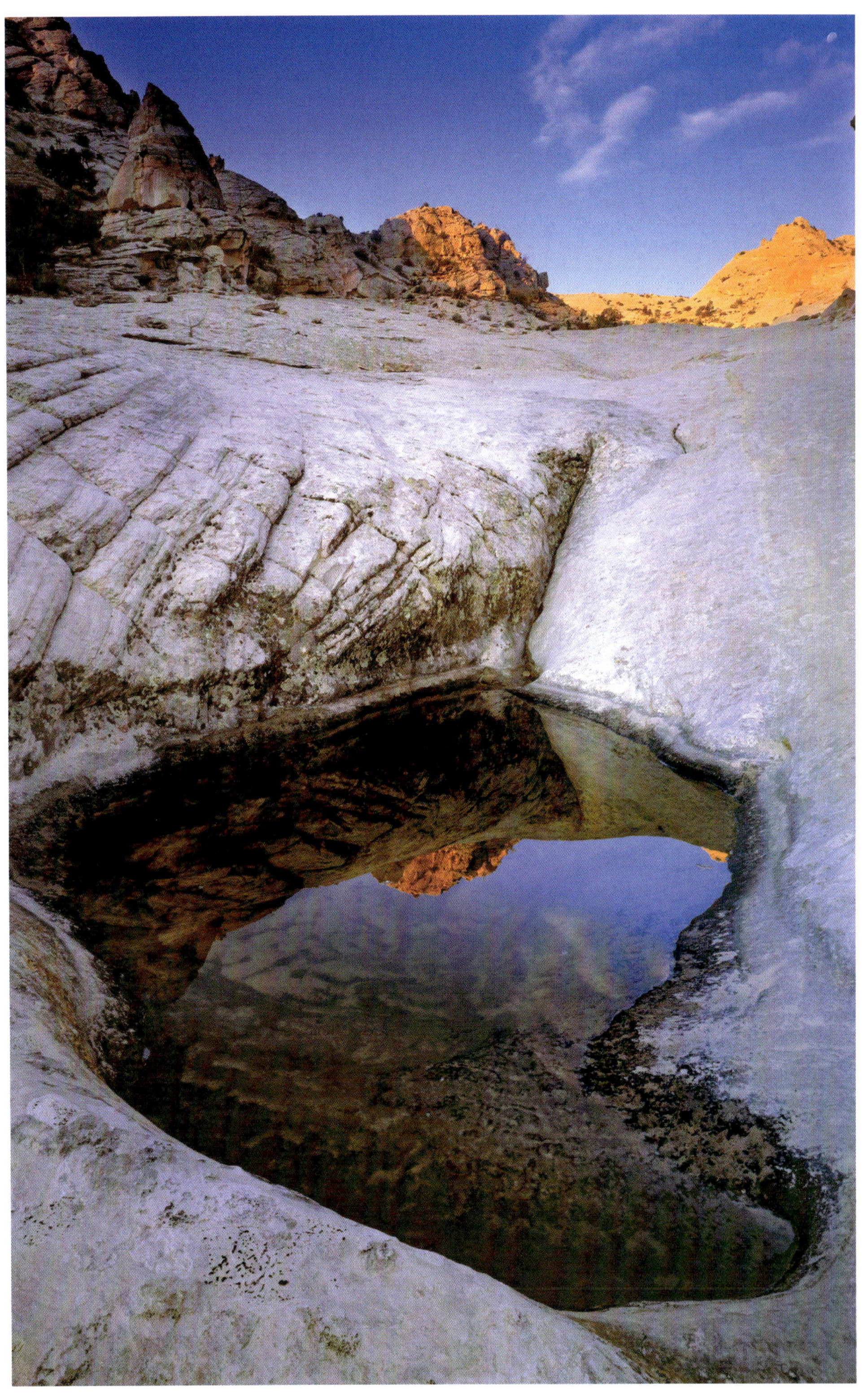

COOL CLEAR RUNOFF FILLS THE
WILLOW TANKS ON THE SOUTHERN EDGE
OF CAPITOL REEF NATIONAL PARK.

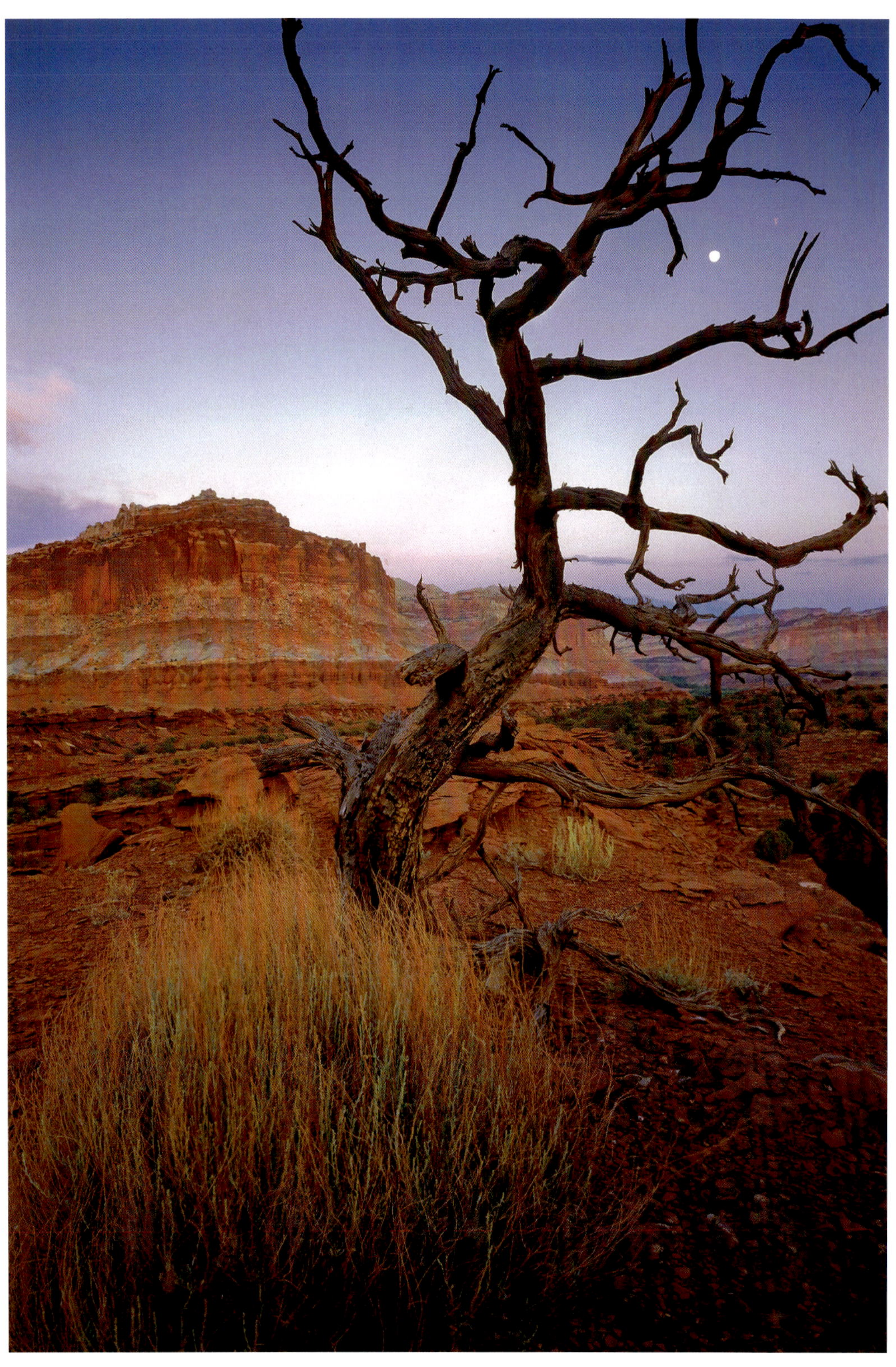

MOONRISE ON THE WESTERN EDGE
OF CAPITOL REEF, NEAR TORREY.

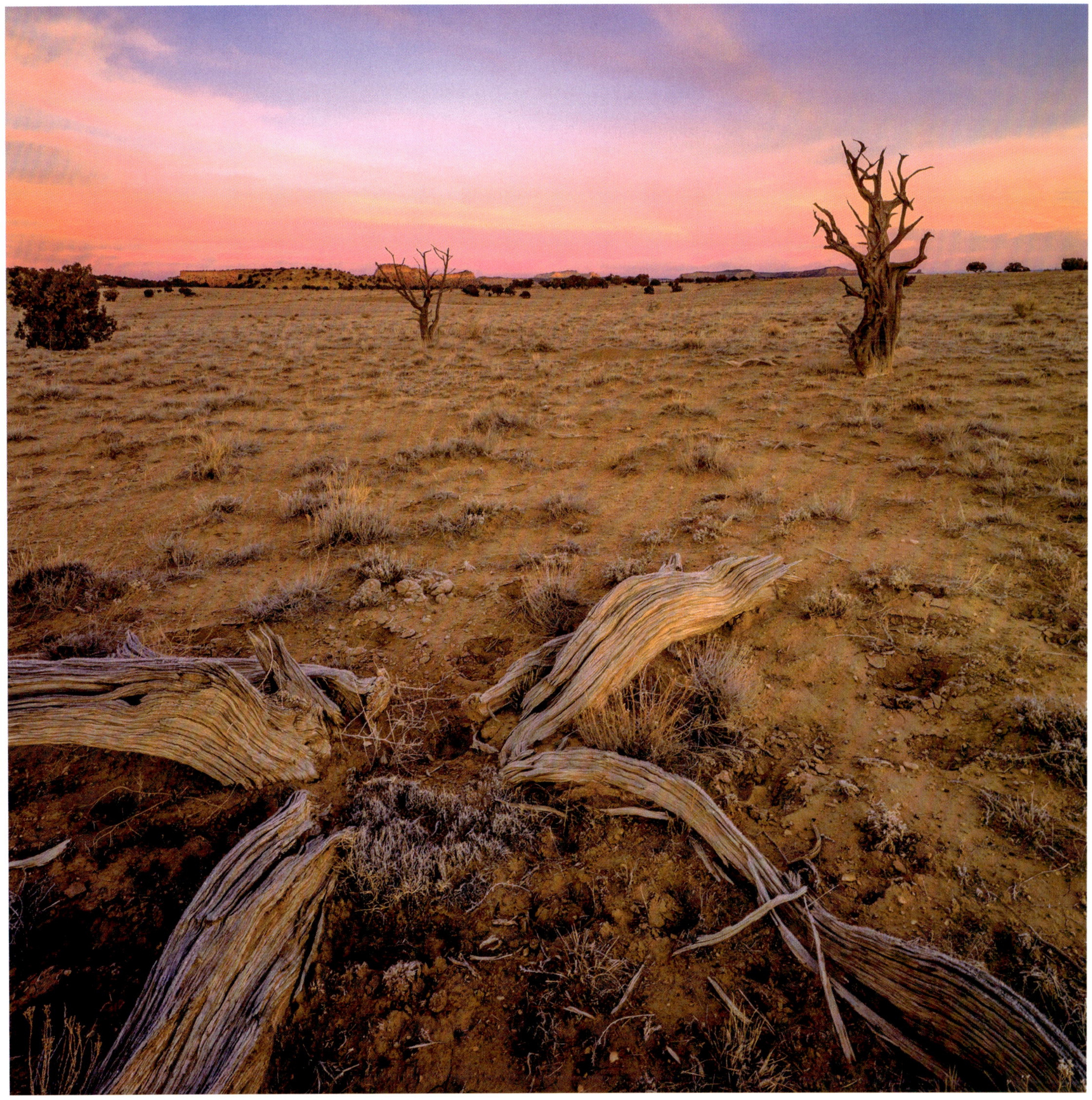

JUNIPER SKELETONS IN THE ARID HIGH DESERT NEAR TEMPLE MOUNTAIN.

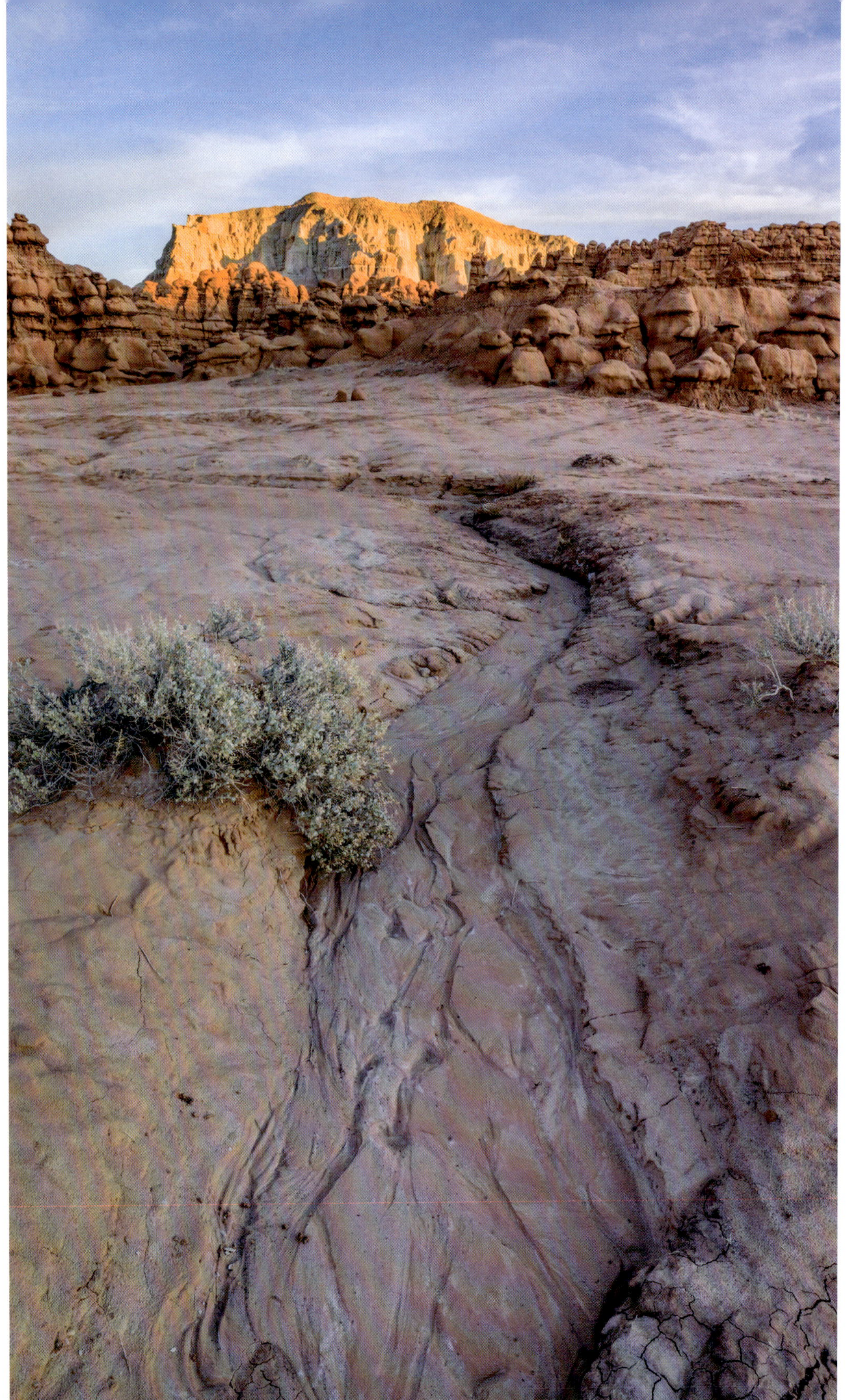

MOLLY'S CASTLE ILLUMINATED
BY MORNING LIGHT,
GOBLIN VALLEY STATE PARK.

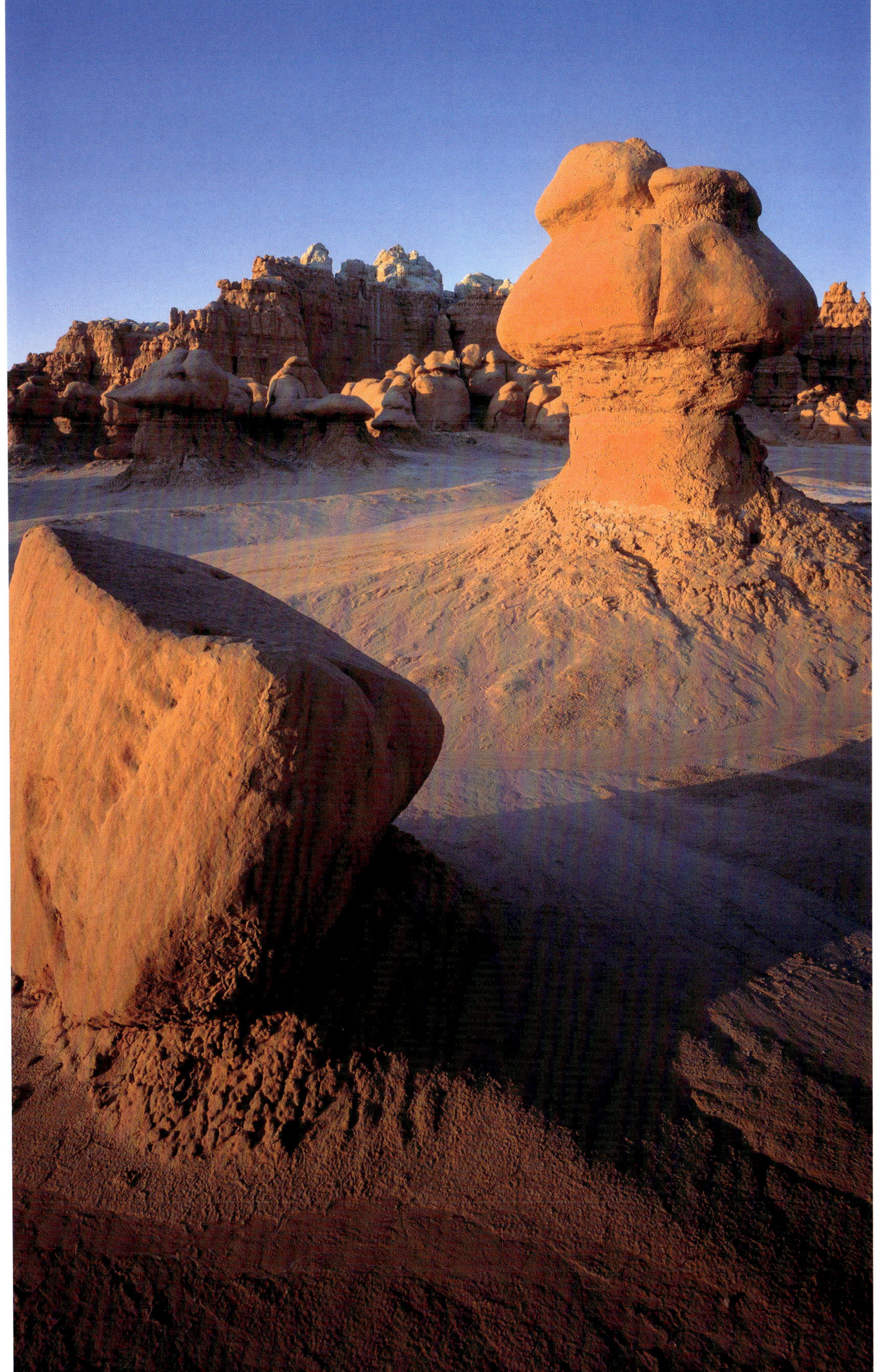

ABSTRACT SHAPES DOT THE HORIZON IN GOBLIN VALLEY STATE PARK.

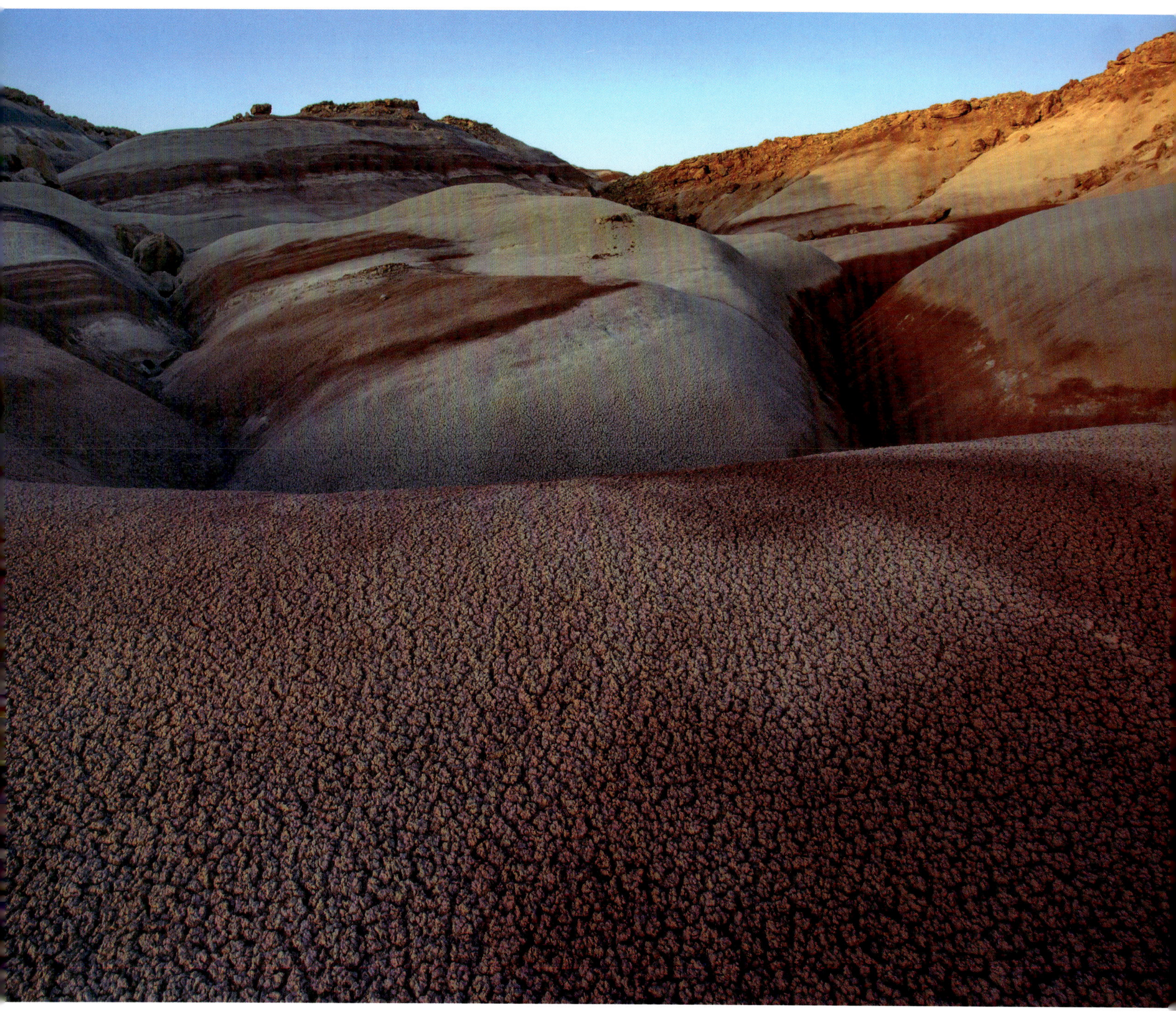

COLORFUL FRAGILE BENTONITE CLIFFS IN THE CAINEVILLE WASH.

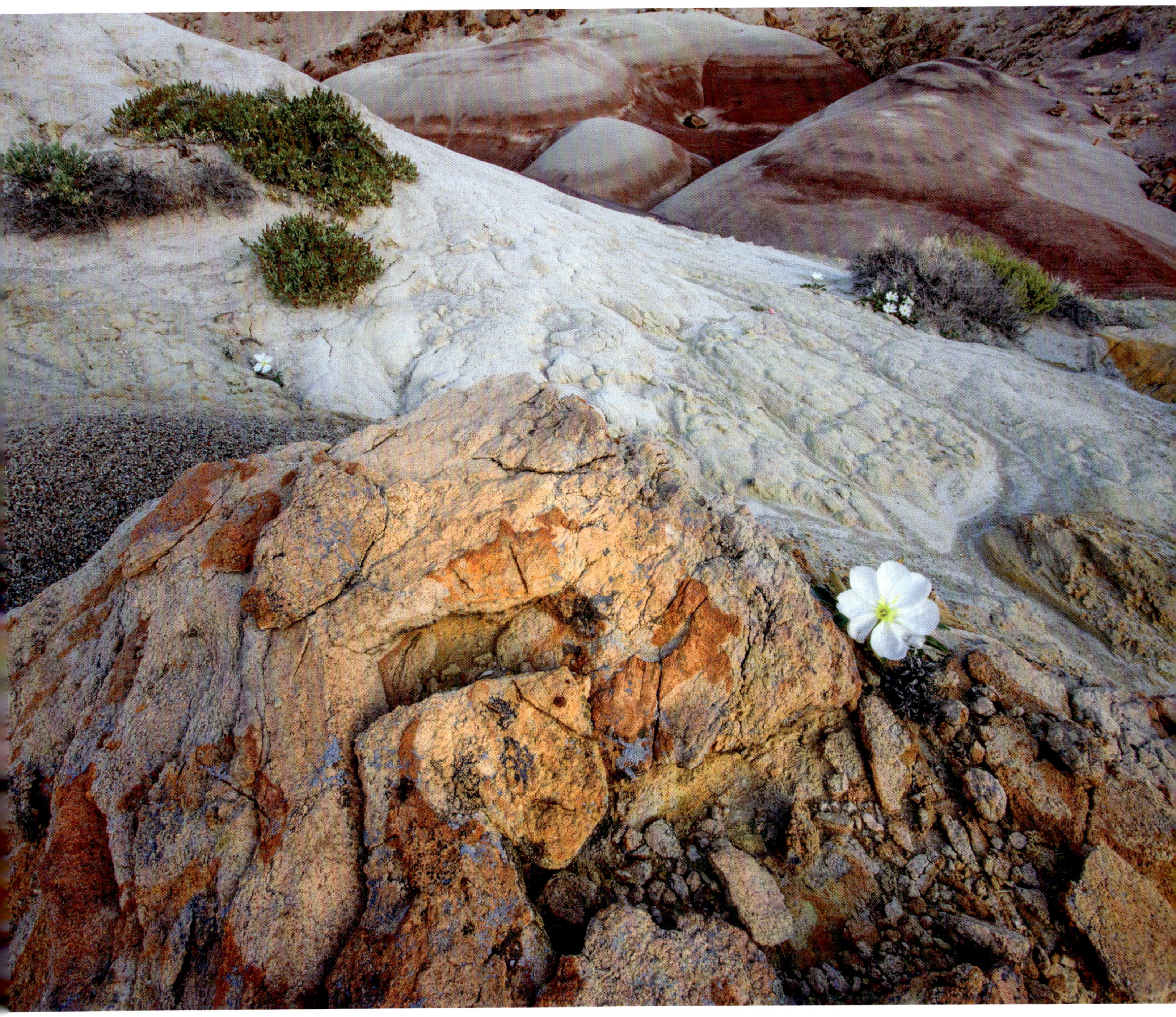

DESERT PRIMROSE BLOOMS IN THE BENTONITE CLIFFS OF THE CAINEVILLE WASH.

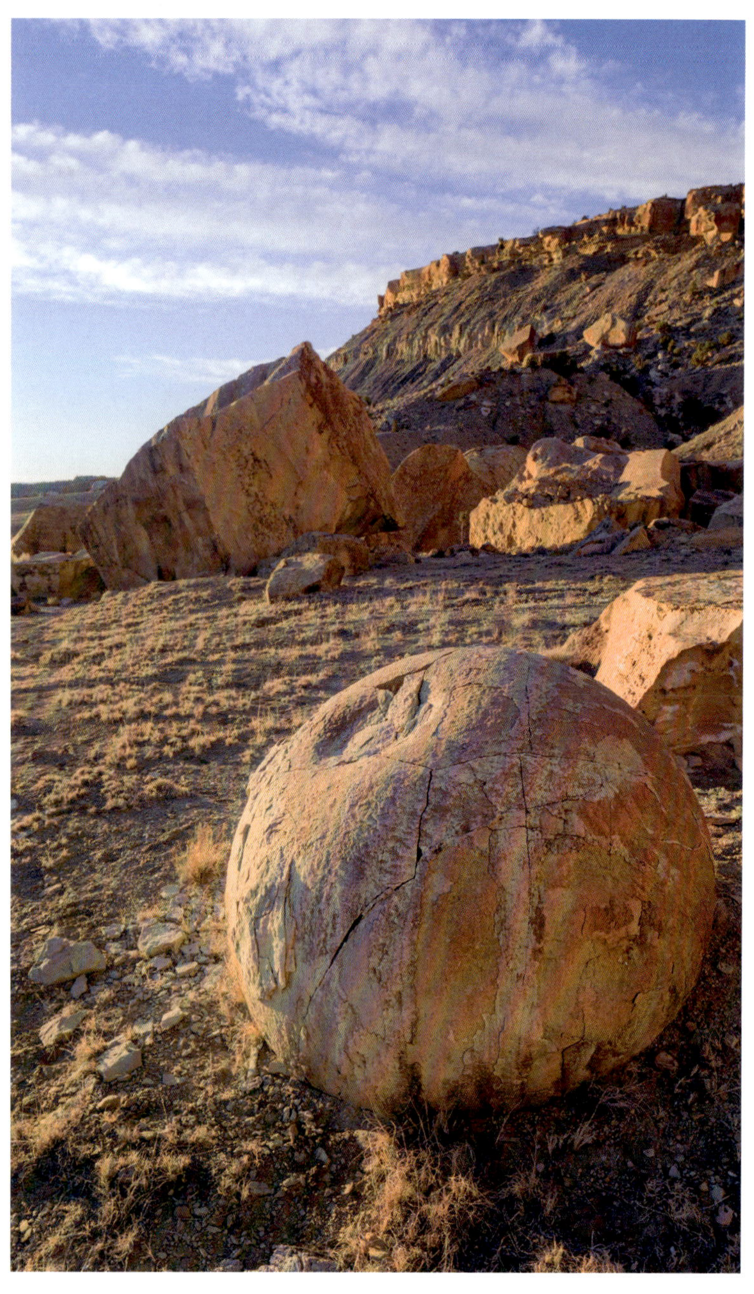

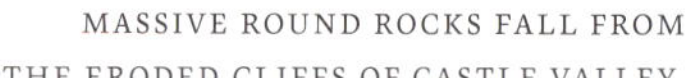

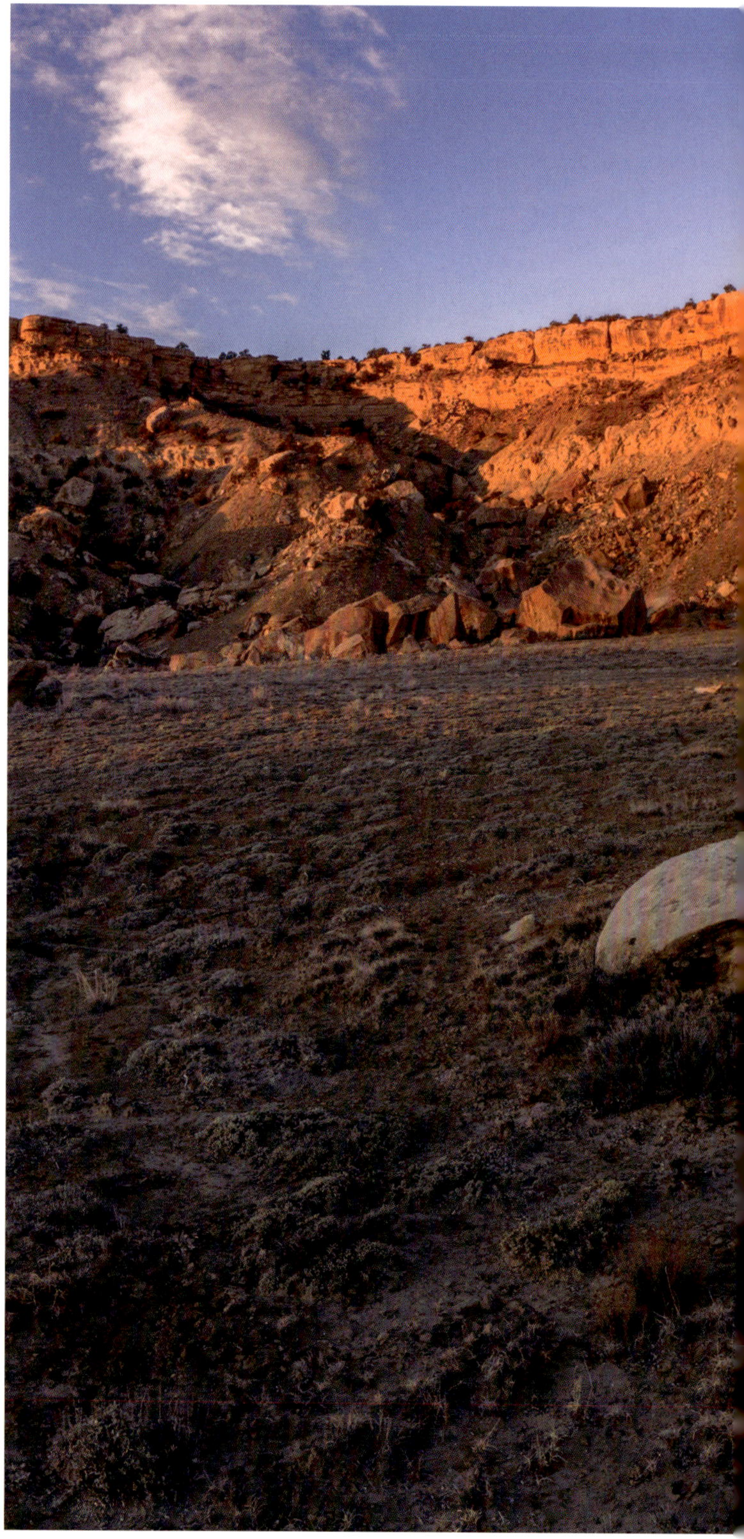

▲ MASSIVE ROUND ROCKS FALL FROM THE ERODED CLIFFS OF CASTLE VALLEY.

▶ THE RED LEDGES, MOLEN REEF AT SHORT CANYON, CASTLE VALLEY.

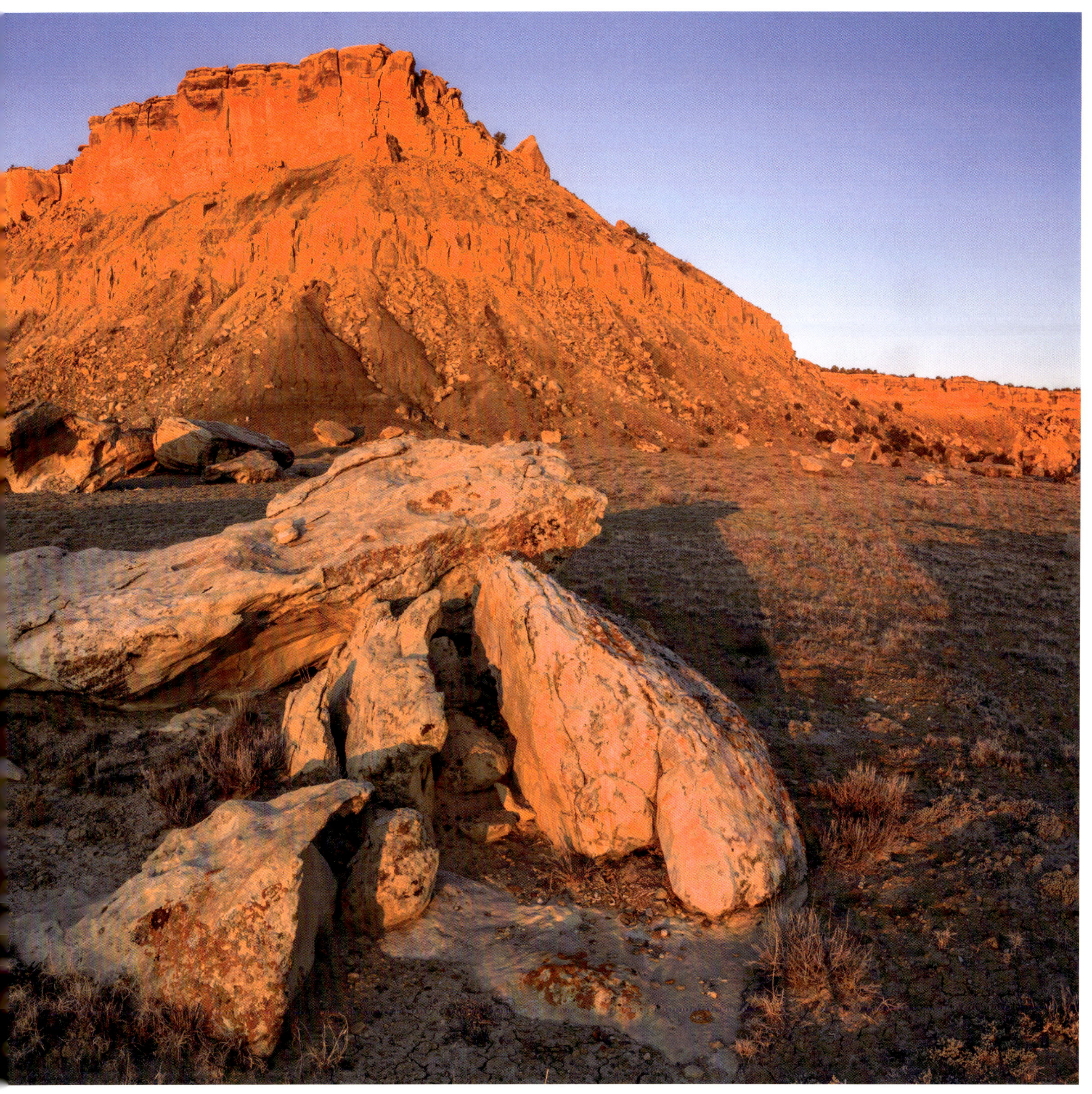

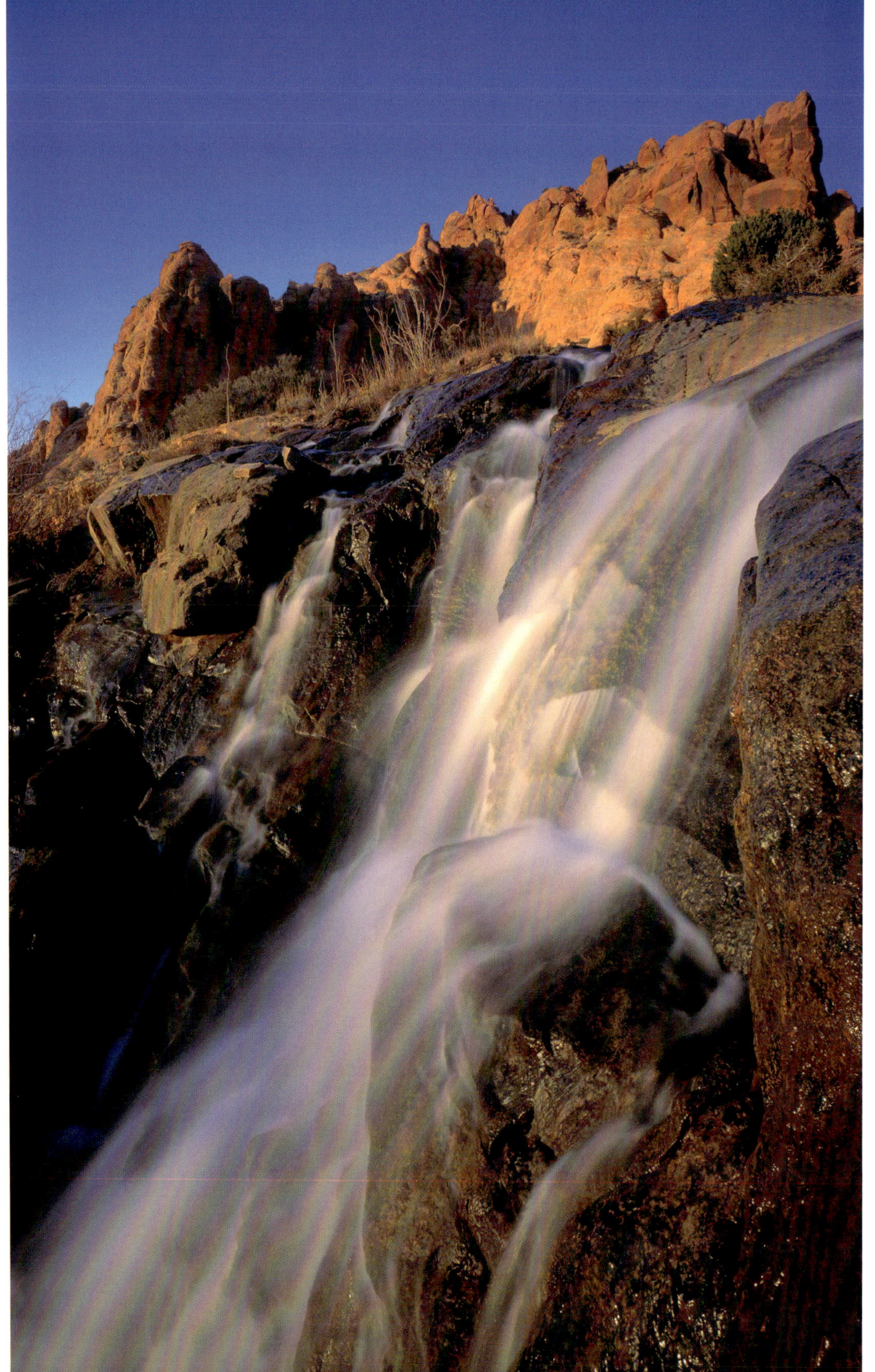

MILL CREEK WATERFALL FLOWS INTO KEN'S LAKE NEAR MOAB.

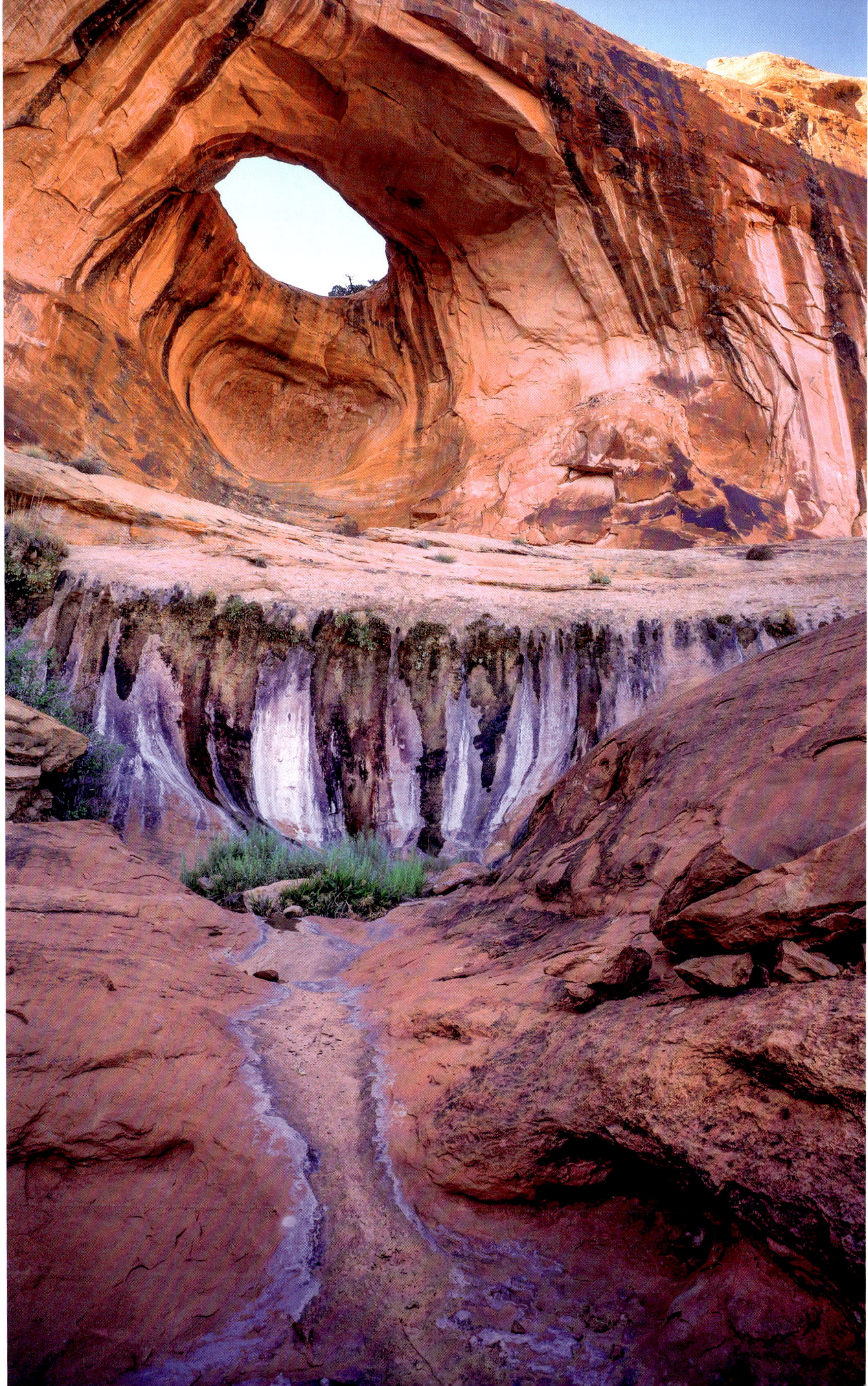

CORONA ARCH IN THE
COLORADO PLATEAU NEAR MOAB.

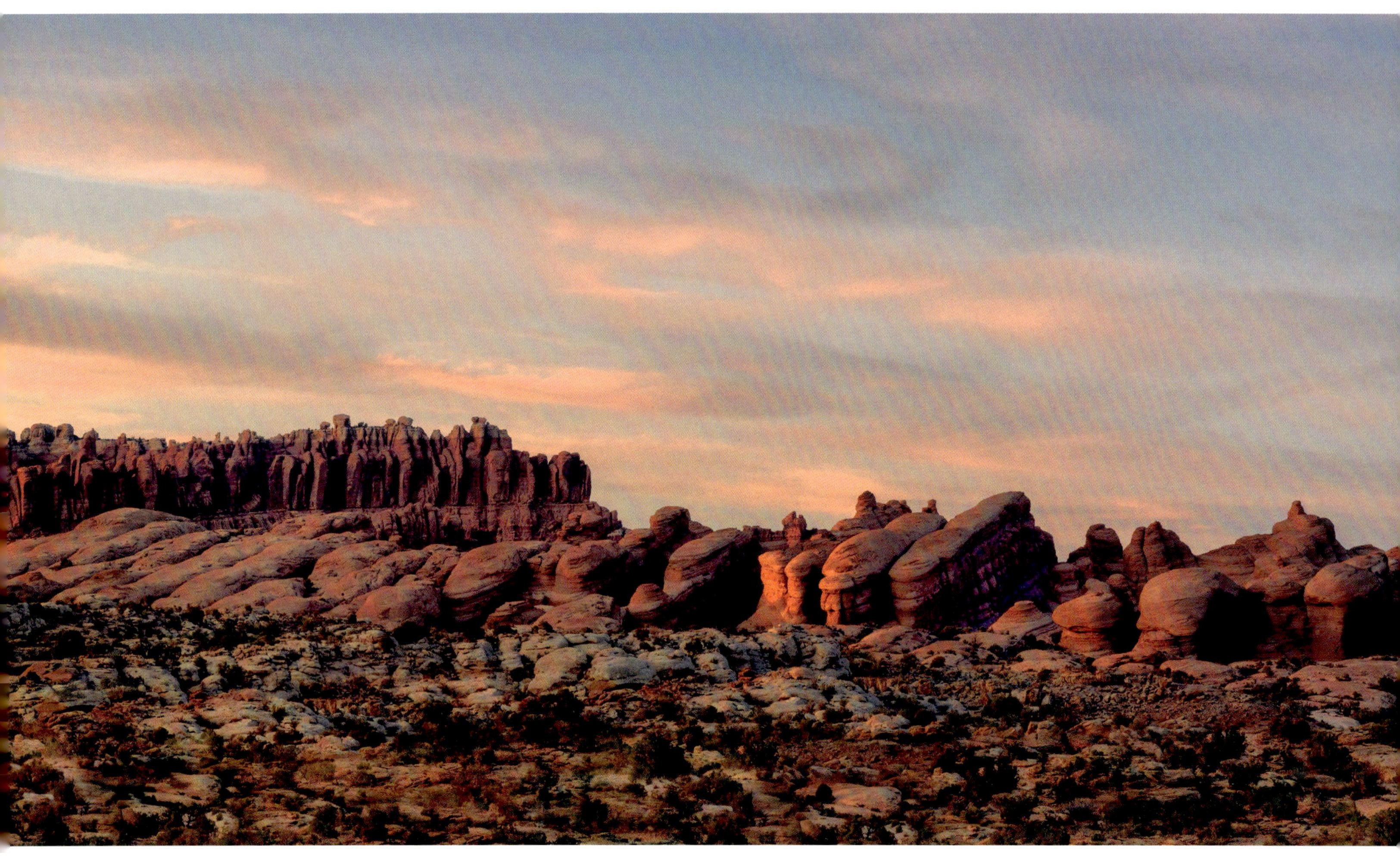

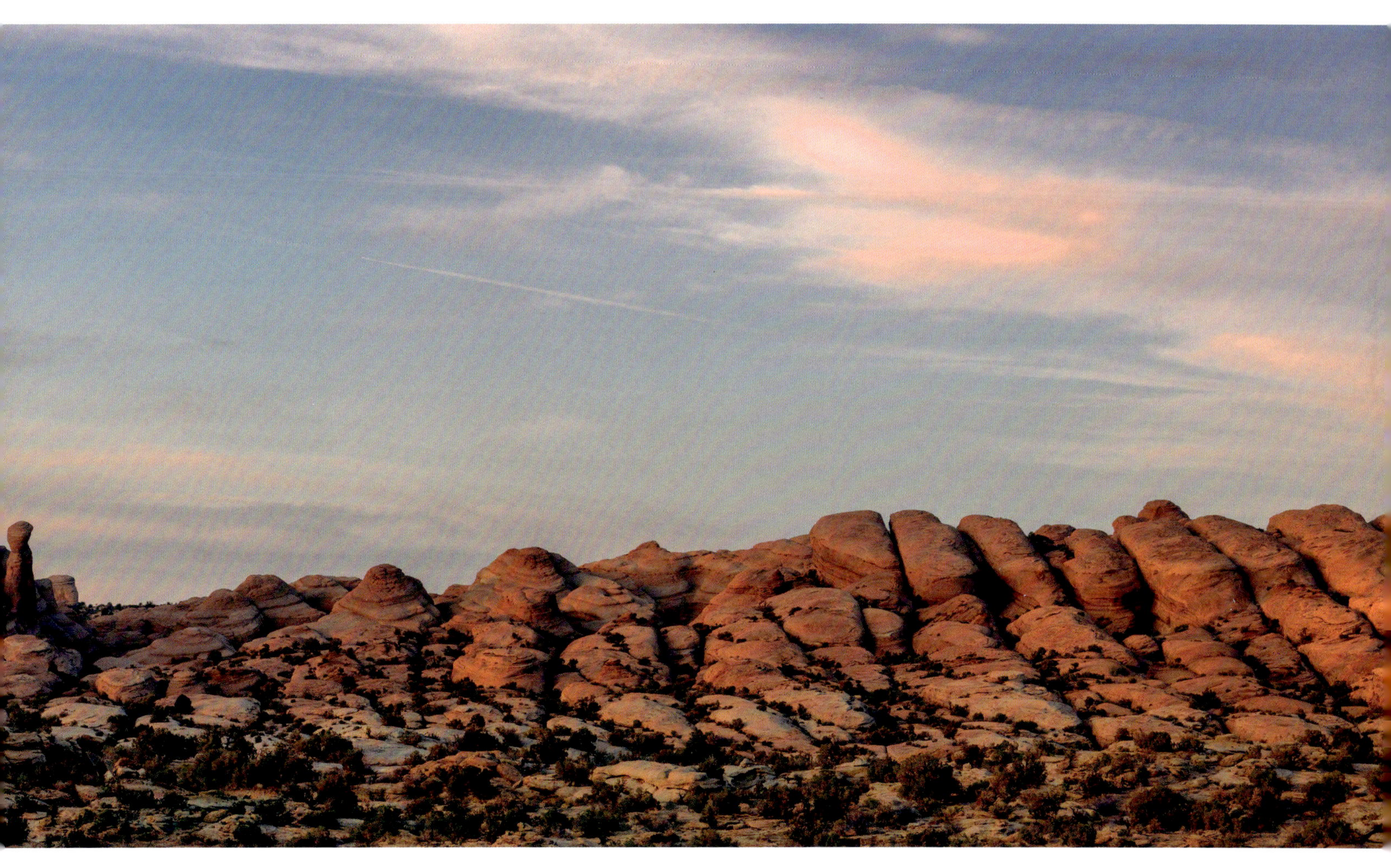

DIFFUSE LIGHT FALLS ON THE KLONDIKE BLUFF HOODOOS IN ARCHES NATIONAL PARK.

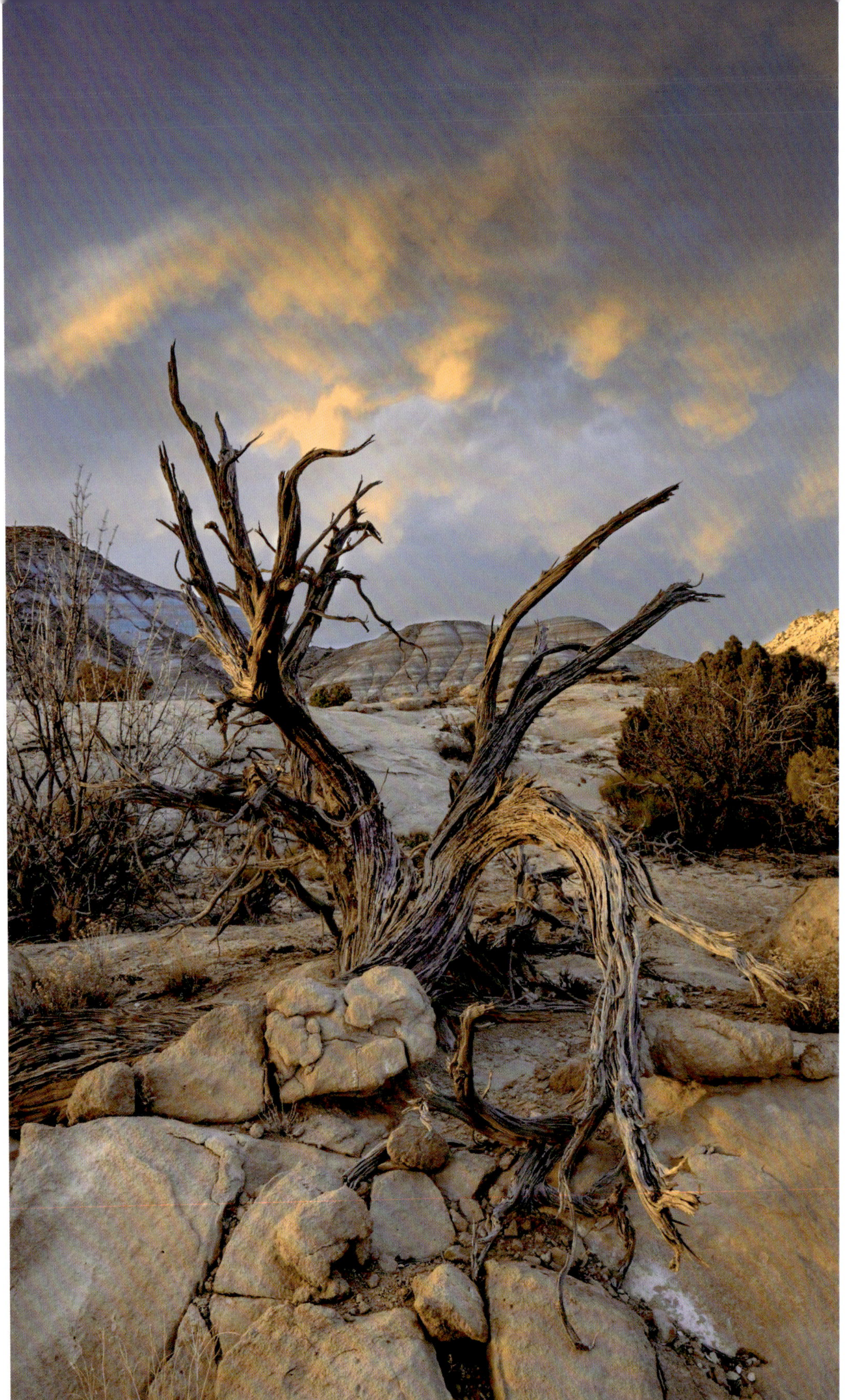

THE SKELETON OF A CEDAR TREE
PERCHES ON A ROCKY OUTCROP ALONG
THE DALTON WELLS ROAD IN MOAB.

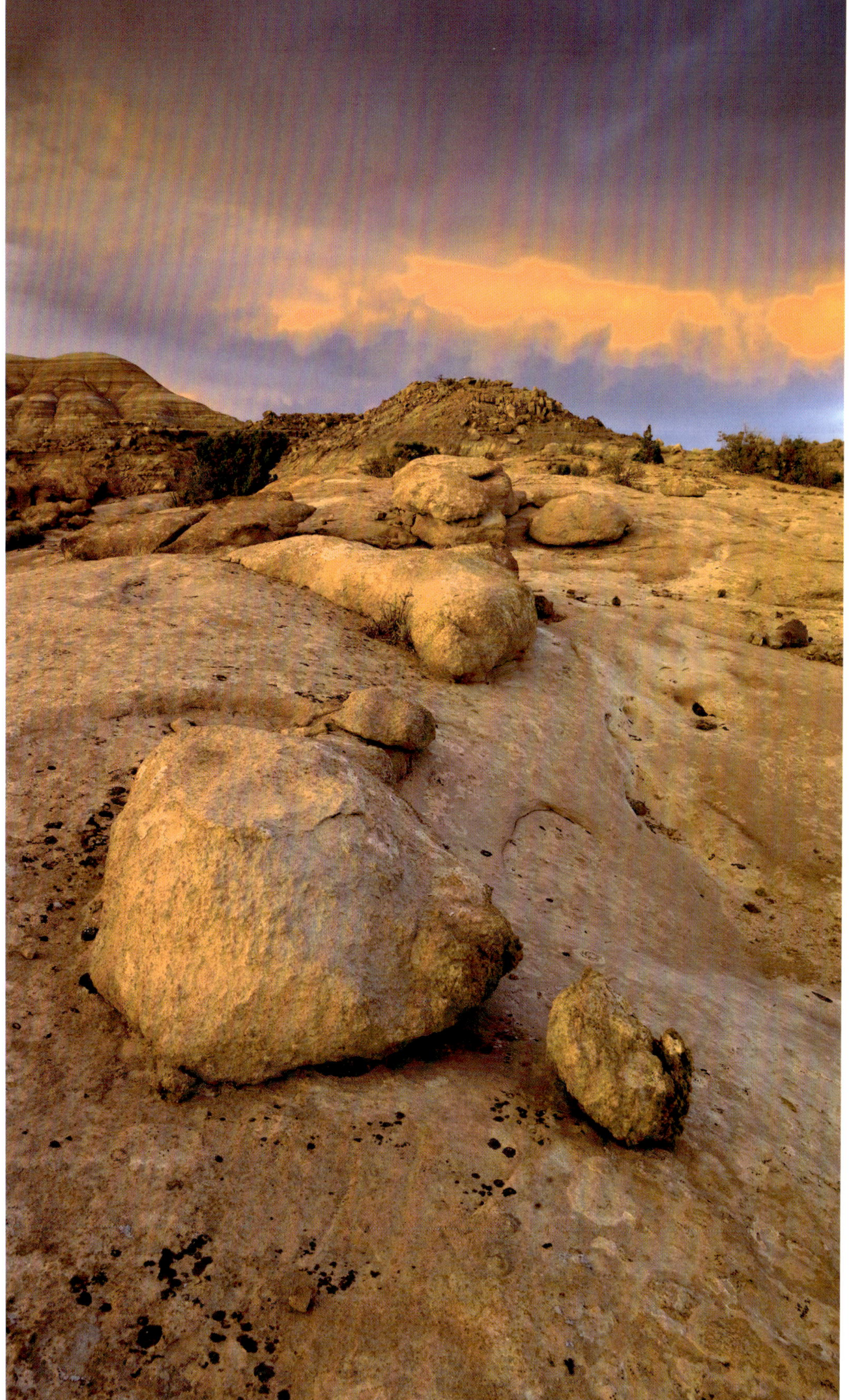

STORM CLOUDS HANG OVER ERODED ROCK FORMATIONS IN THE DRY SALT VALLEY OF ARCHES NATIONAL PARK.

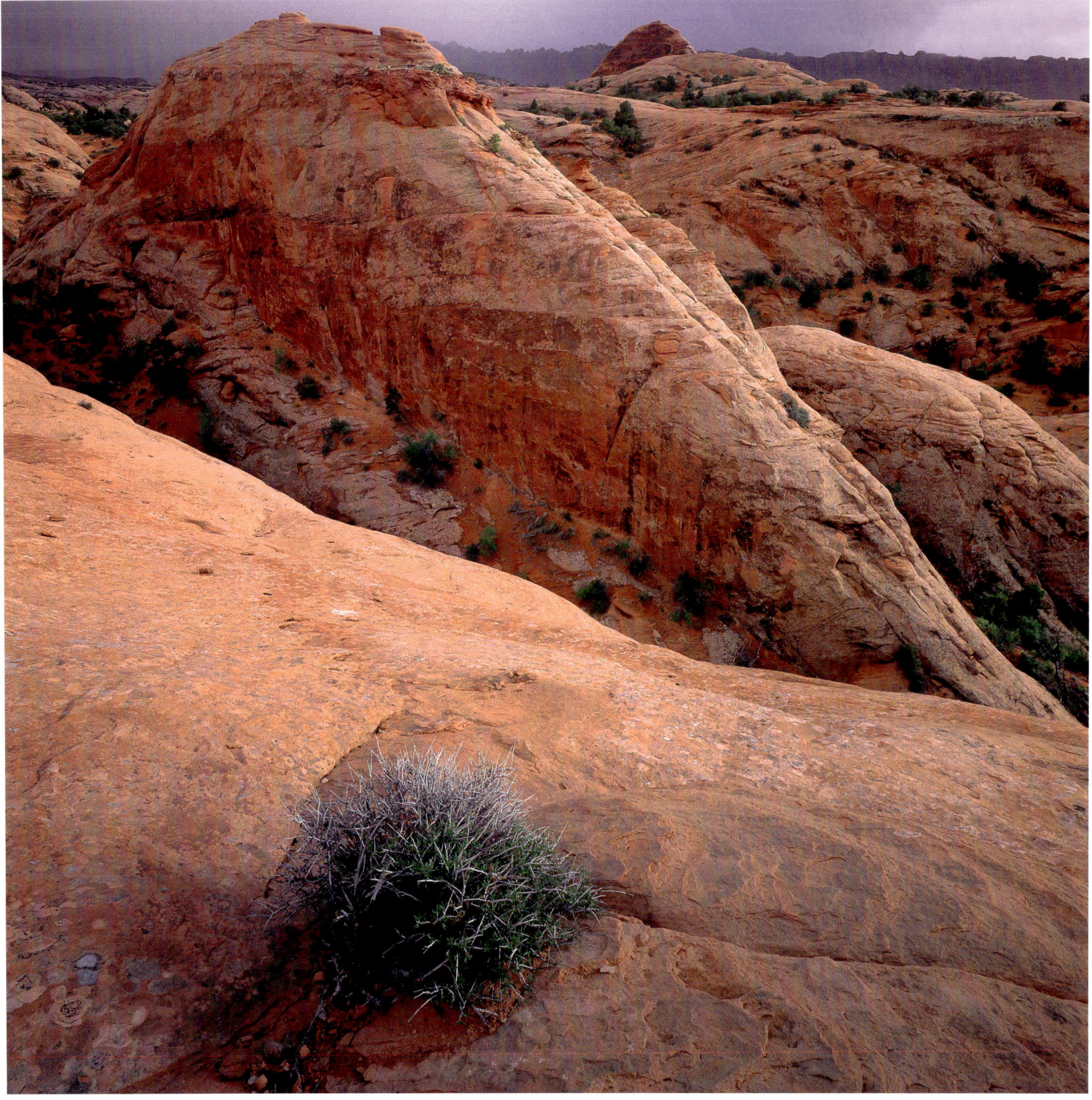

STORM CLOUDS THREATEN THE DRAMATIC SLICKROCK DUNES ON THE MOAB RIM.

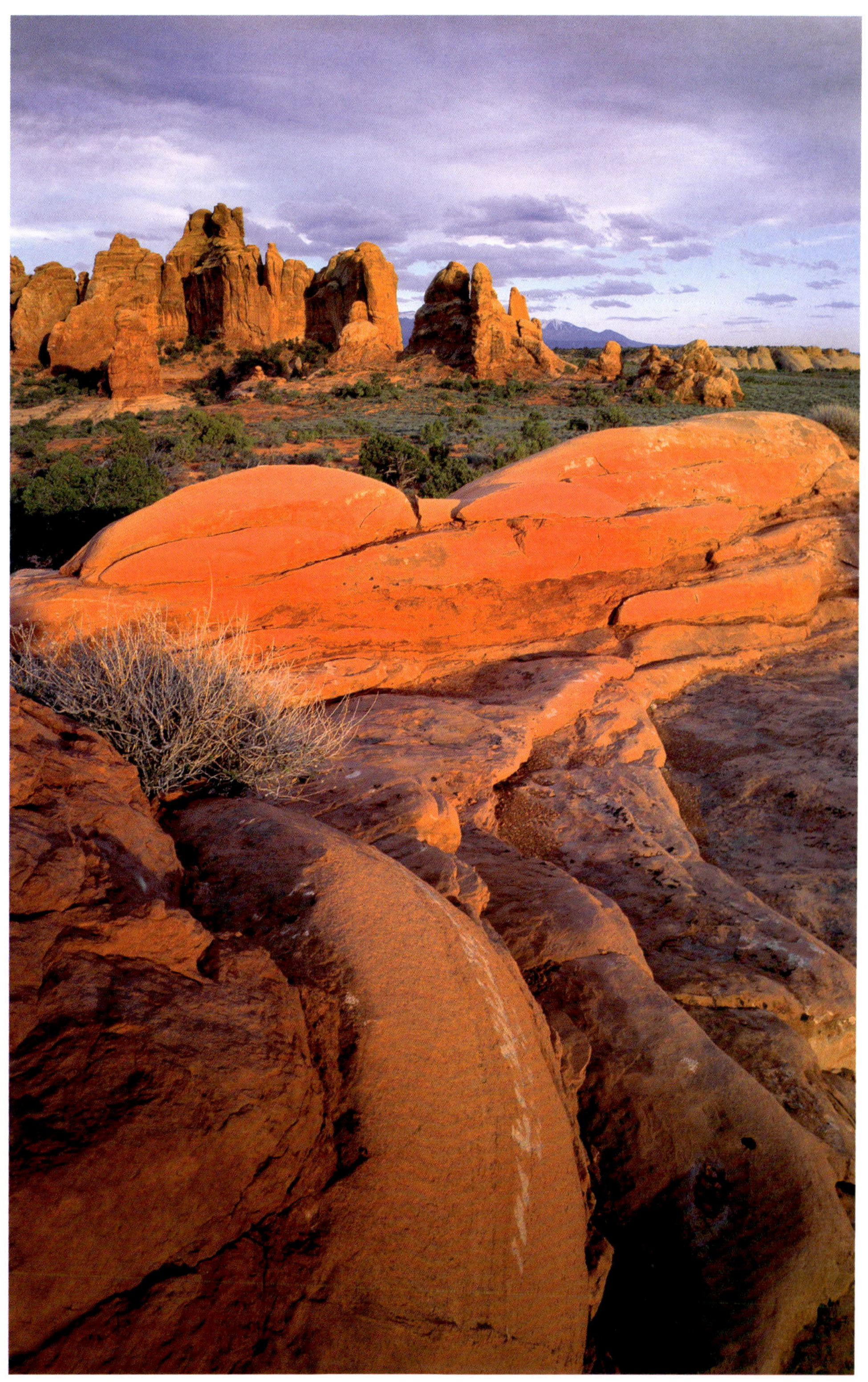

SANDSTONE FINS RISE FROM THE DESERT FLOOR IN RED ROCK COUNTRY, ARCHES NATIONAL PARK.

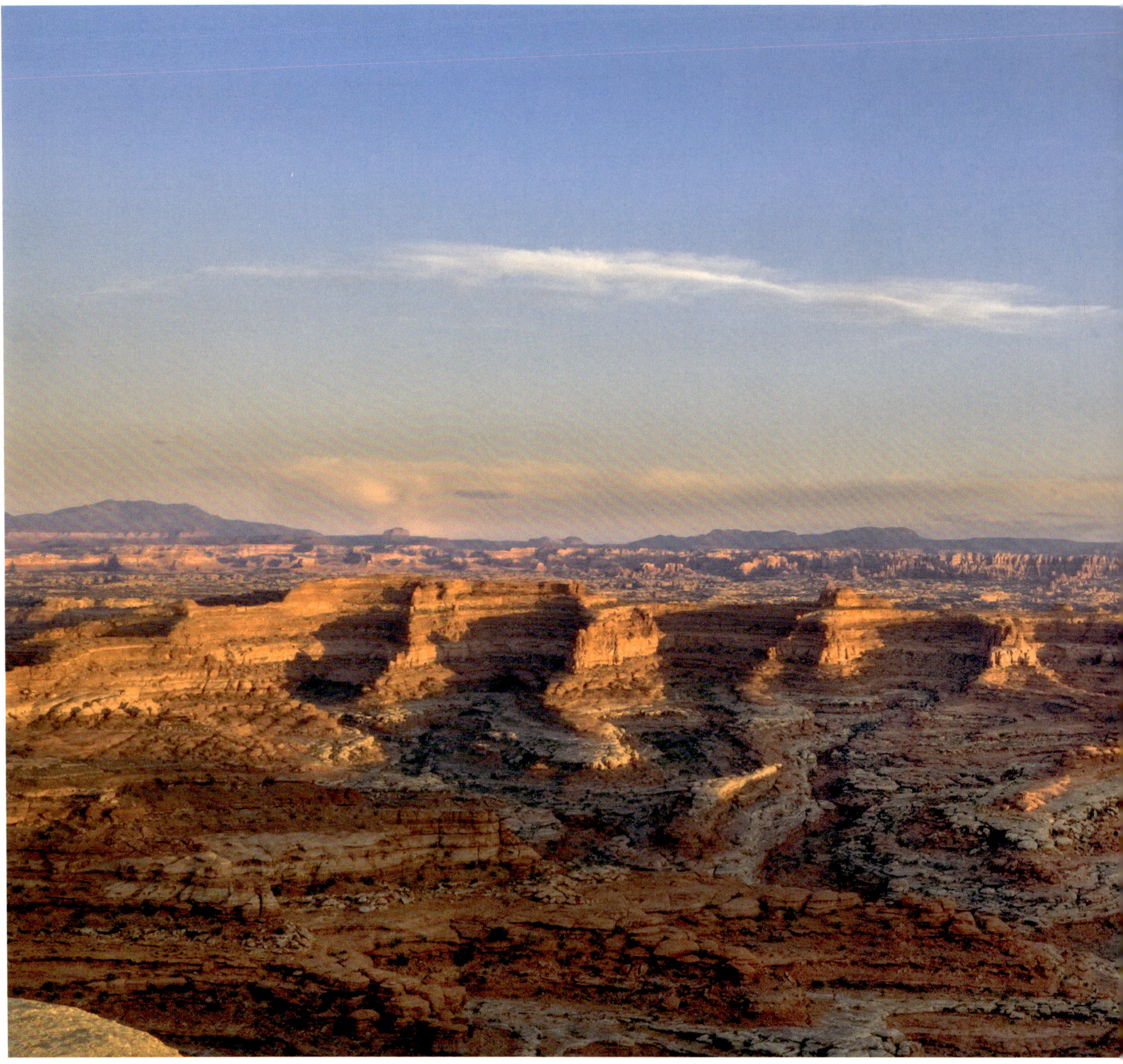

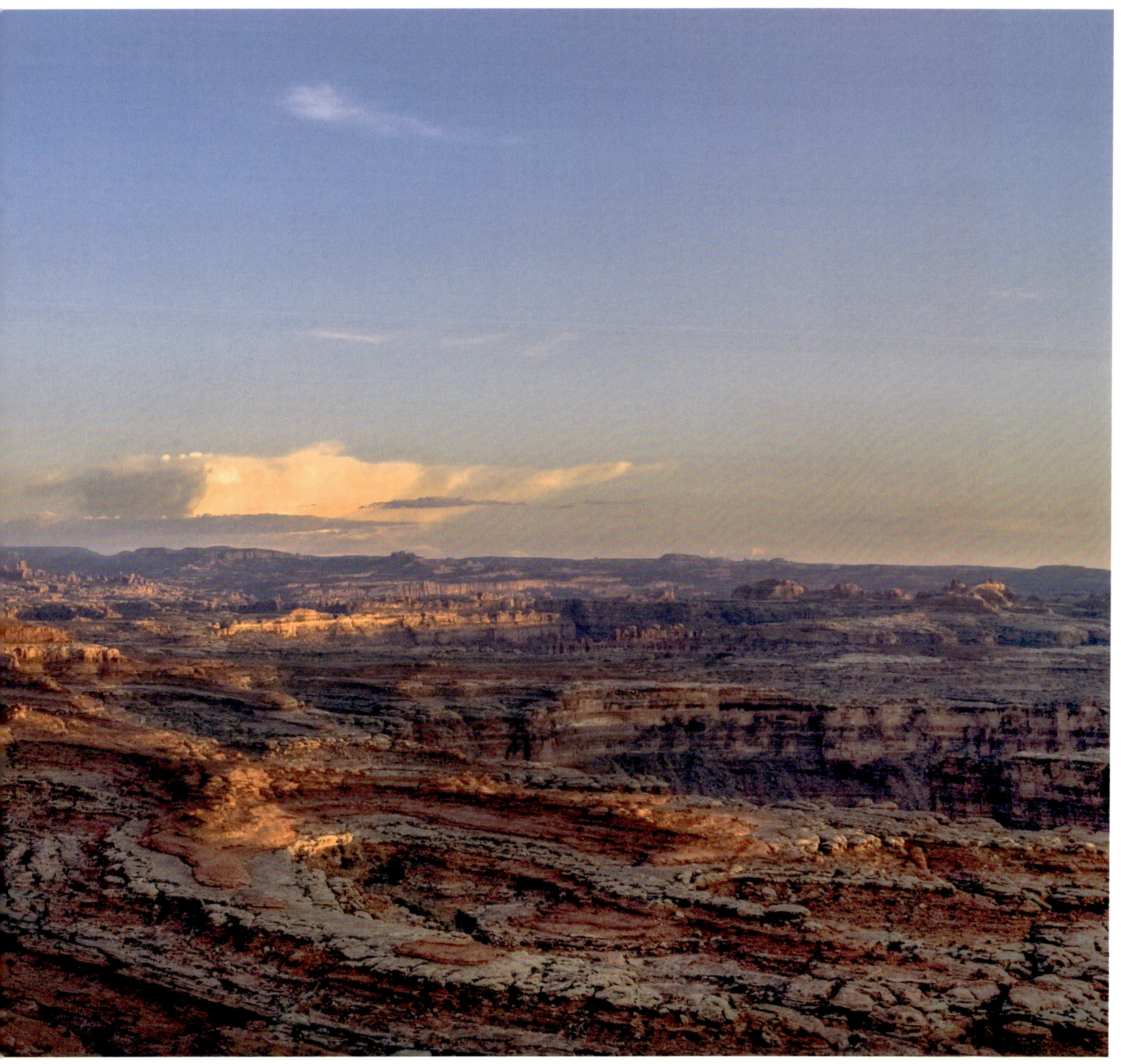

THE NEEDLES AND MAZE DISTRICTS OF CANYONLANDS NATIONAL PARK FROM THE WHITE CRACK CAMP OVERLOOK.

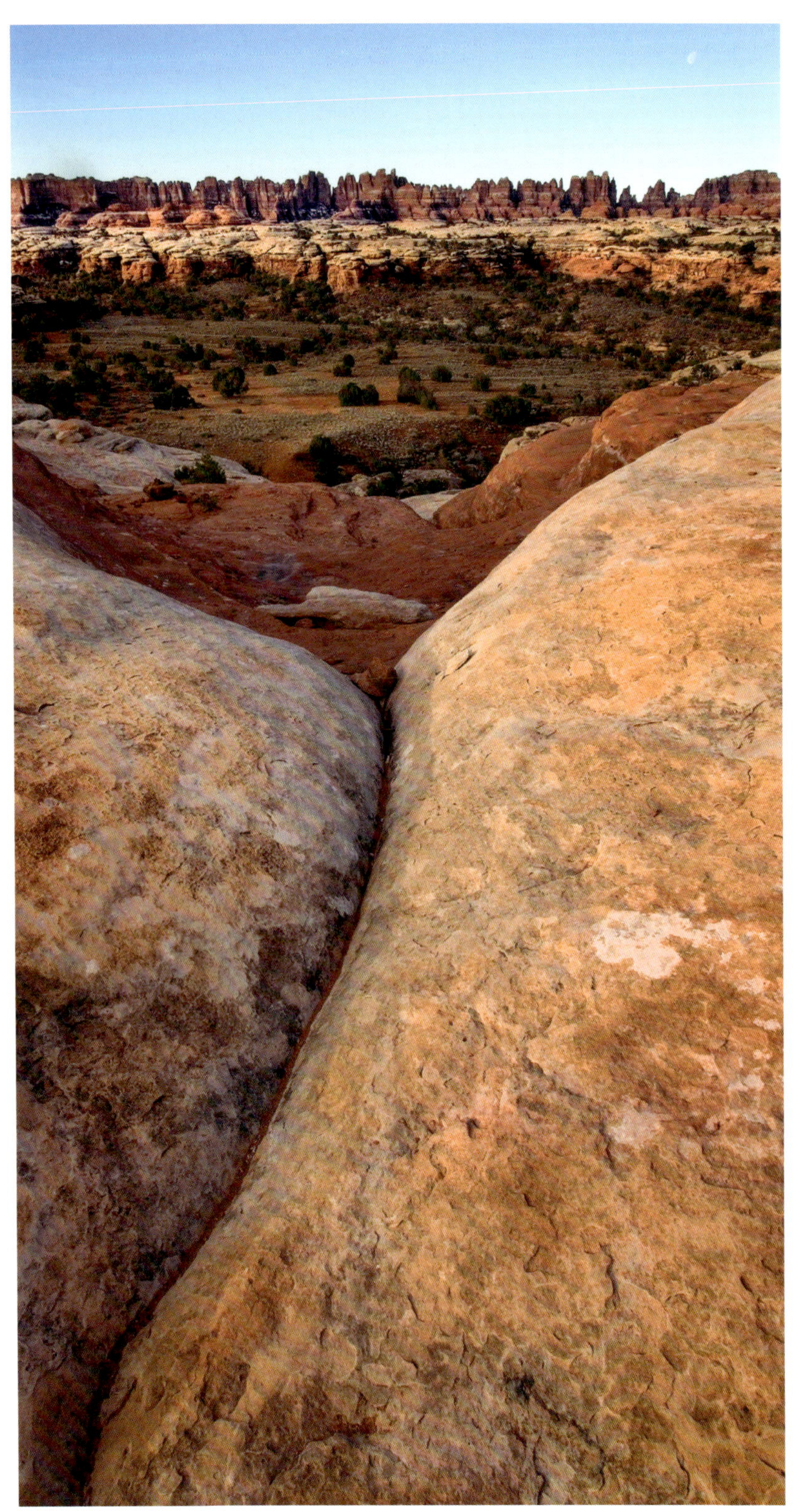

◀ SANDSTONE FORMATIONS CREATE SENSUOUS SHAPES IN THE NEEDLES DISTRICT OF CANYONLANDS NATIONAL PARK.

▶ THE WHITE RIM FROM THE GREEN RIVER OVERLOOK IN CANYONLANDS NATIONAL PARK.

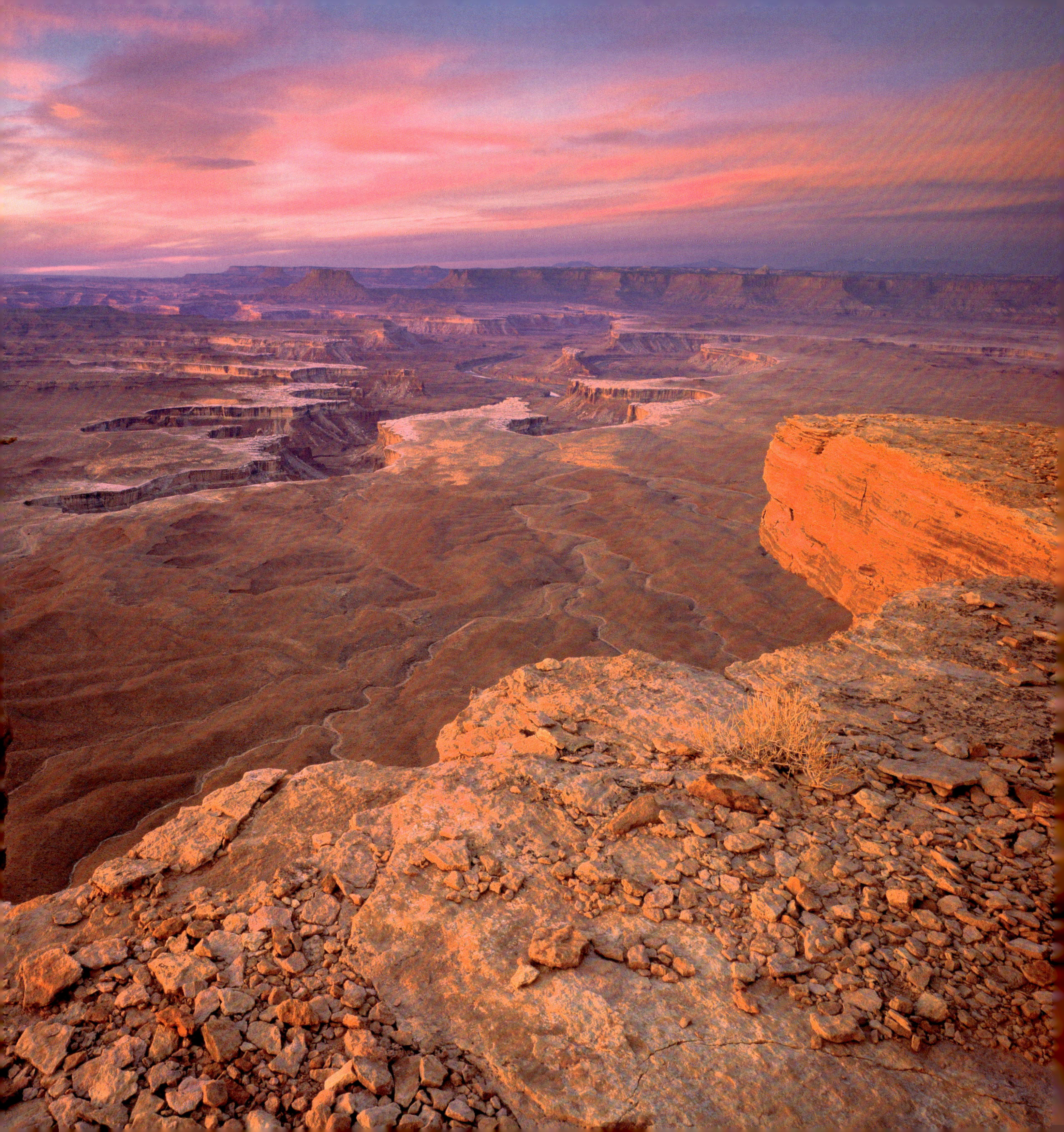

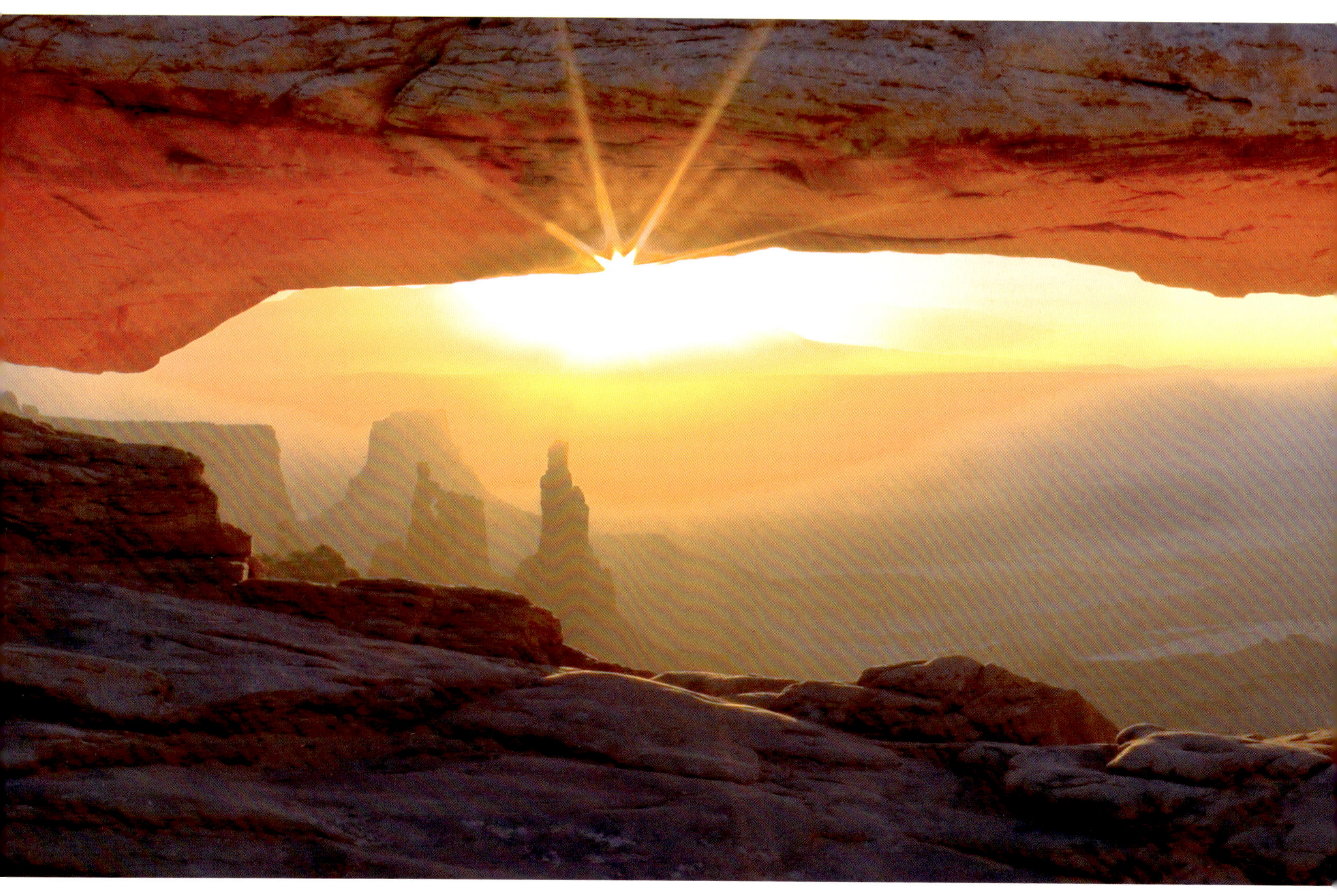

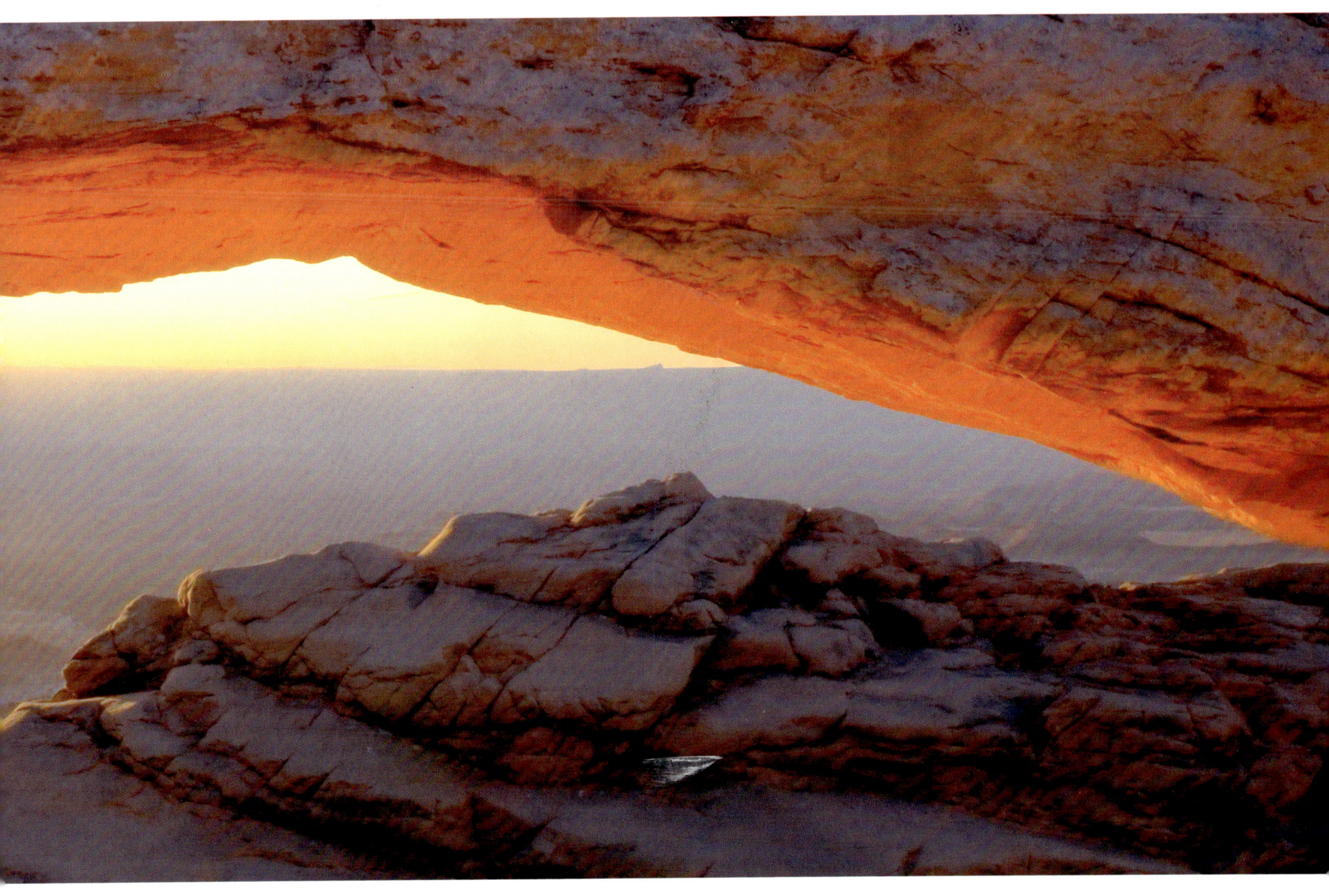

MESA ARCH SPANS THE HORIZON ABOVE THE WHITE RIM TRAIL IN CANYONLANDS NATIONAL PARK.

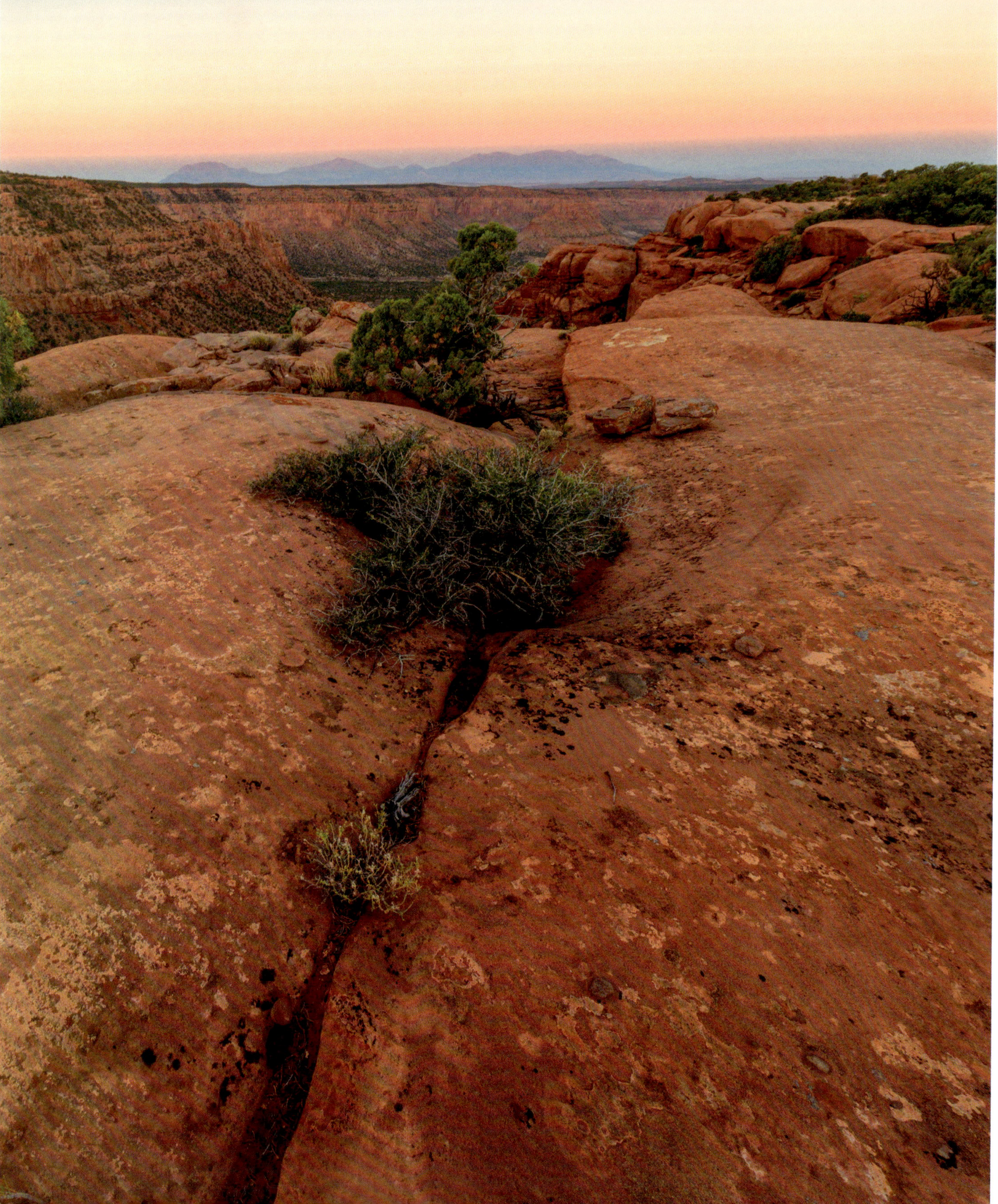

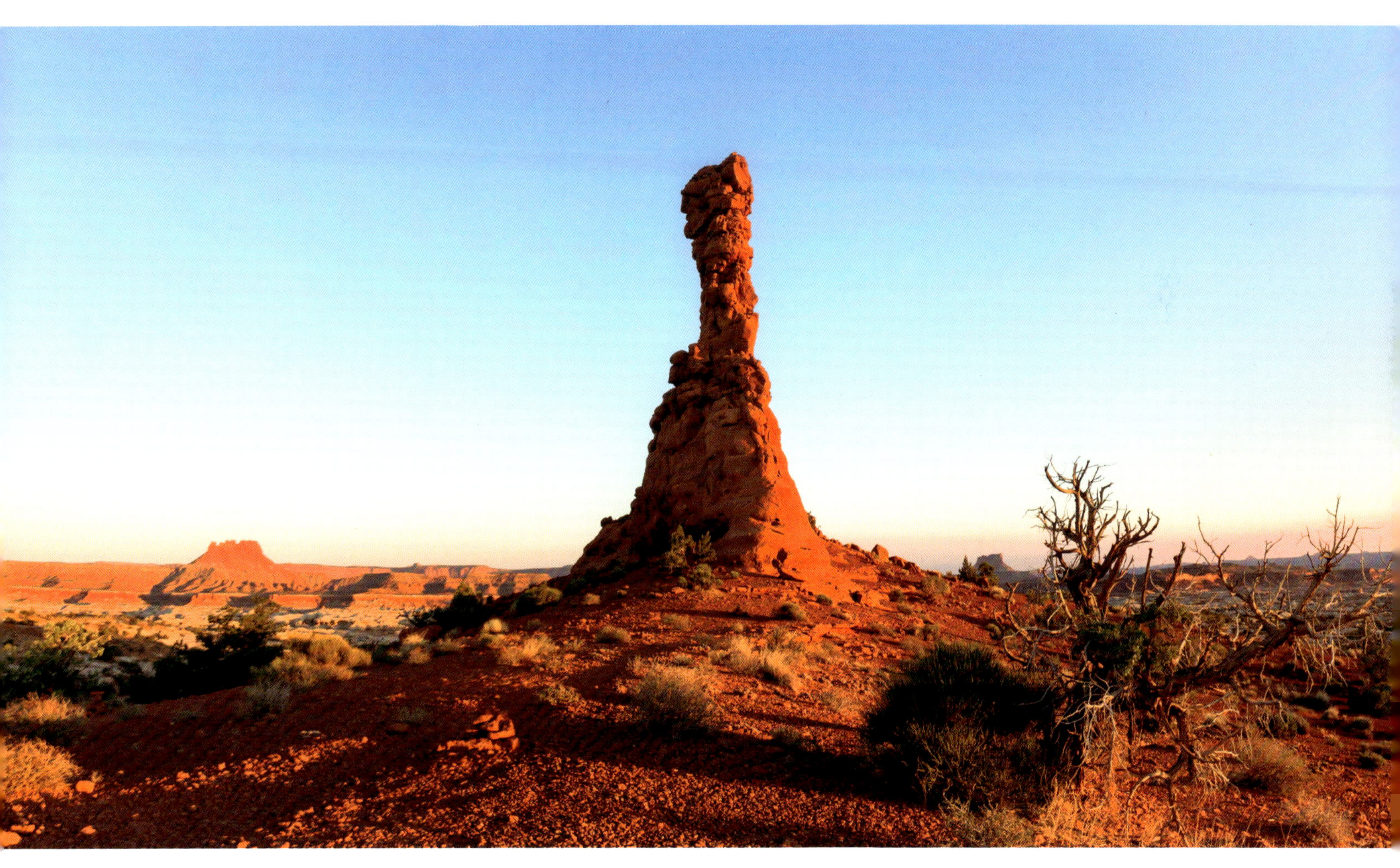

▲
CHIMNEY ROCK RISES FROM THE ARID DESERT IN CANYONLANDS NATIONAL PARK.

◀
SMOKE-FILLED SKIES CAST AN EERIE GLOW OVER THE HENRY MOUNTAINS.

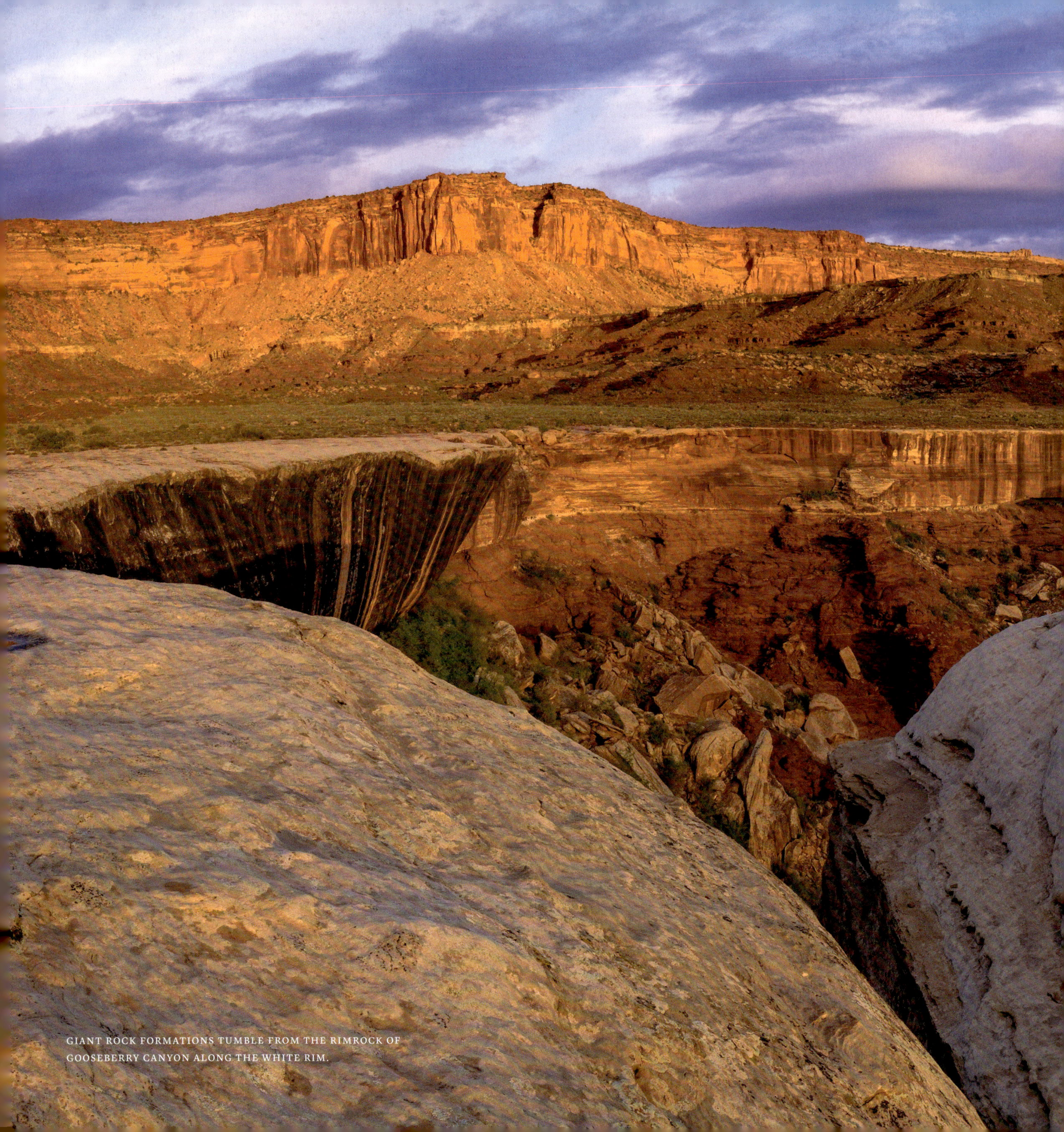

GIANT ROCK FORMATIONS TUMBLE FROM THE RIMROCK OF GOOSEBERRY CANYON ALONG THE WHITE RIM.

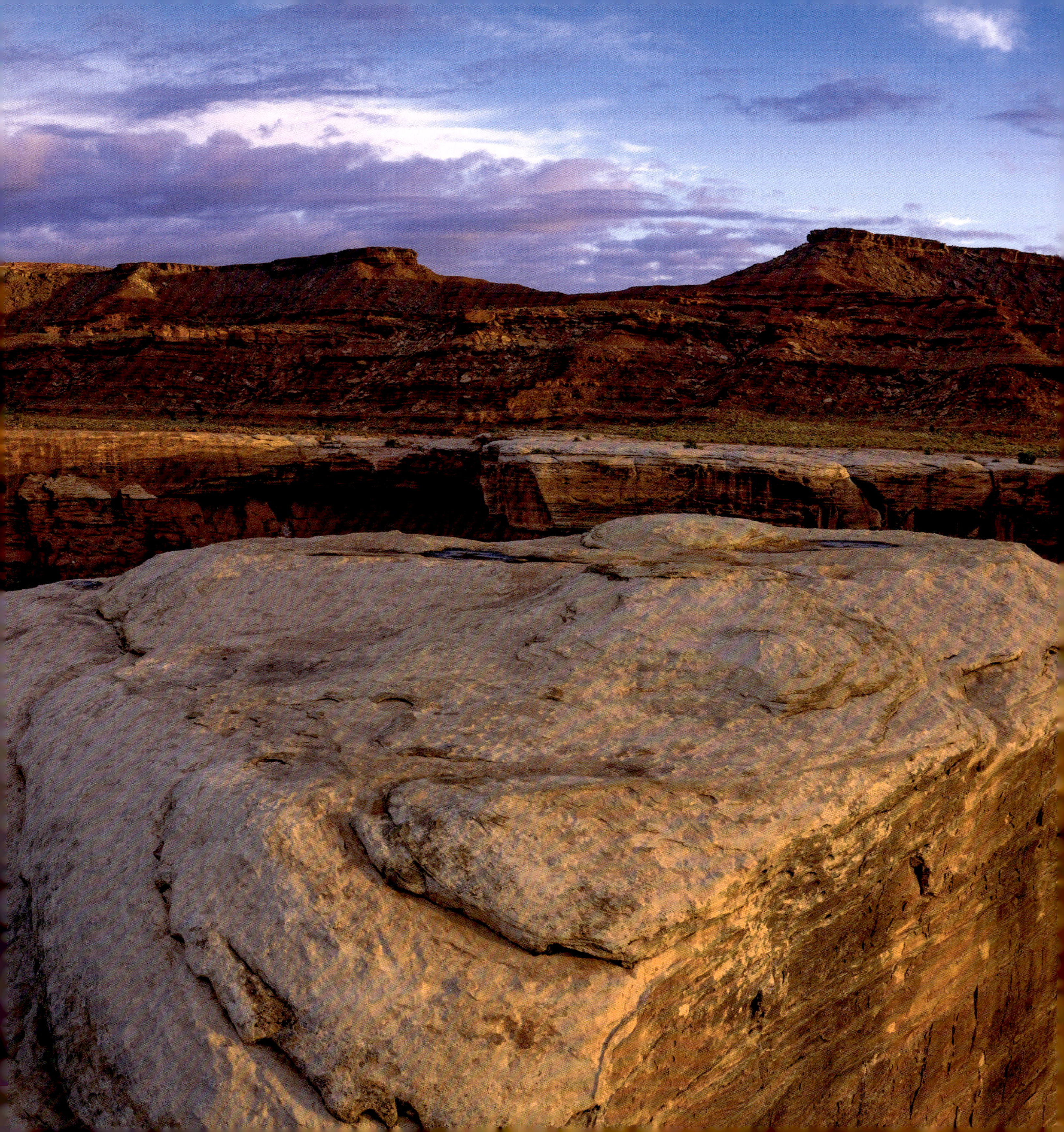

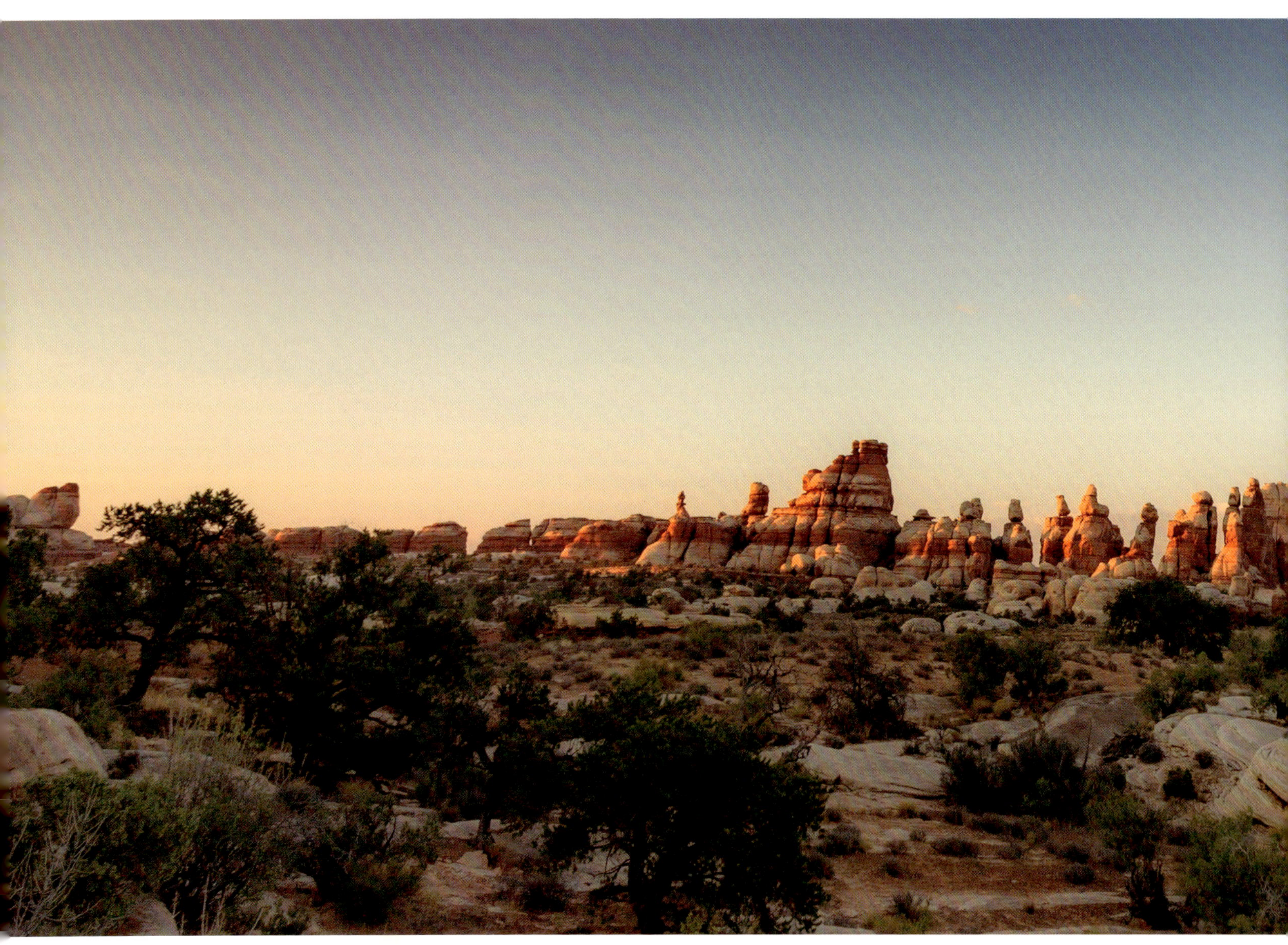

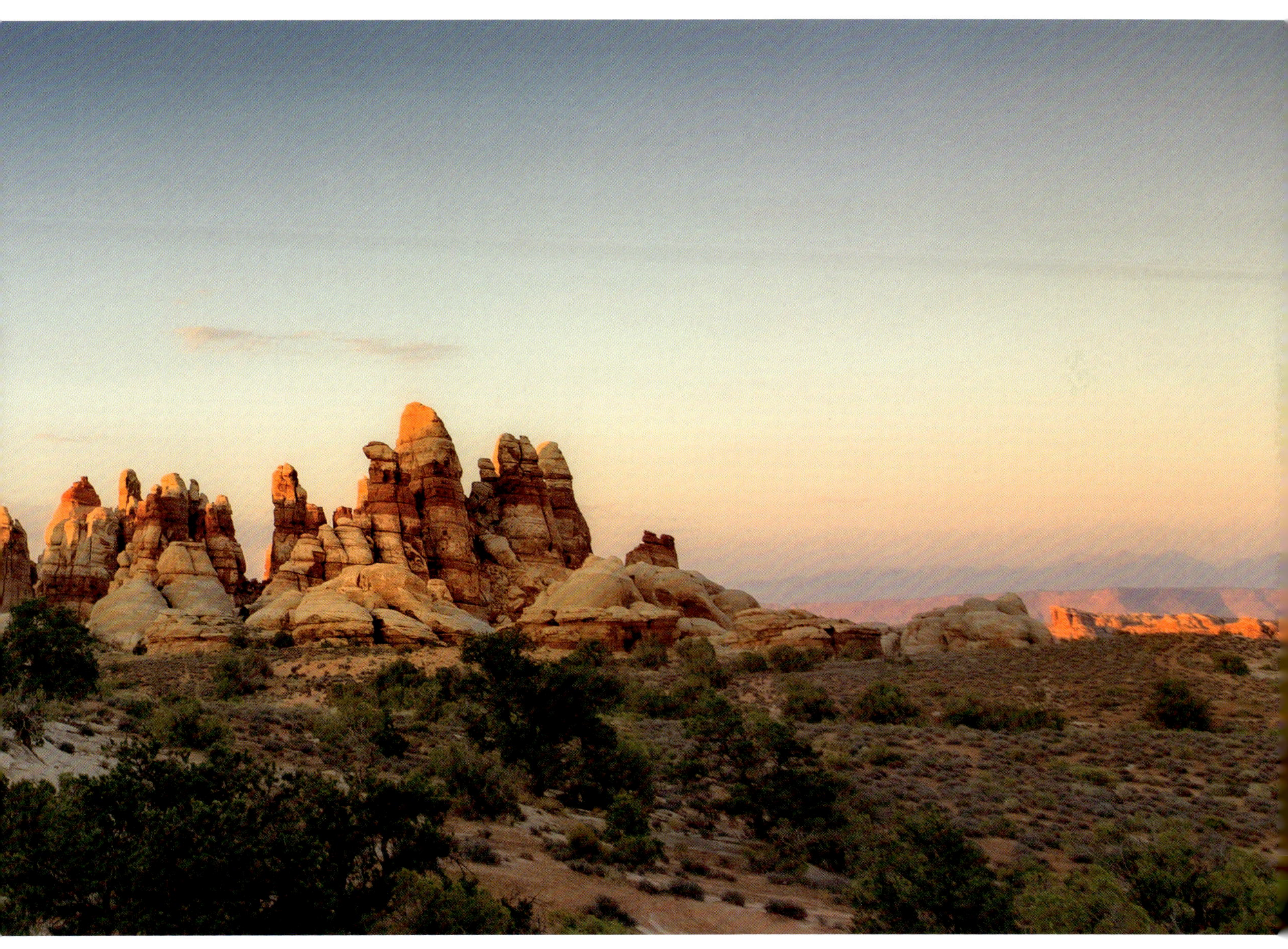

CLASSIC ROCK FORMATIONS AT THE DOLL HOUSE IN THE MAZE DISTRICT OF CANYONLANDS NATIONAL PARK.

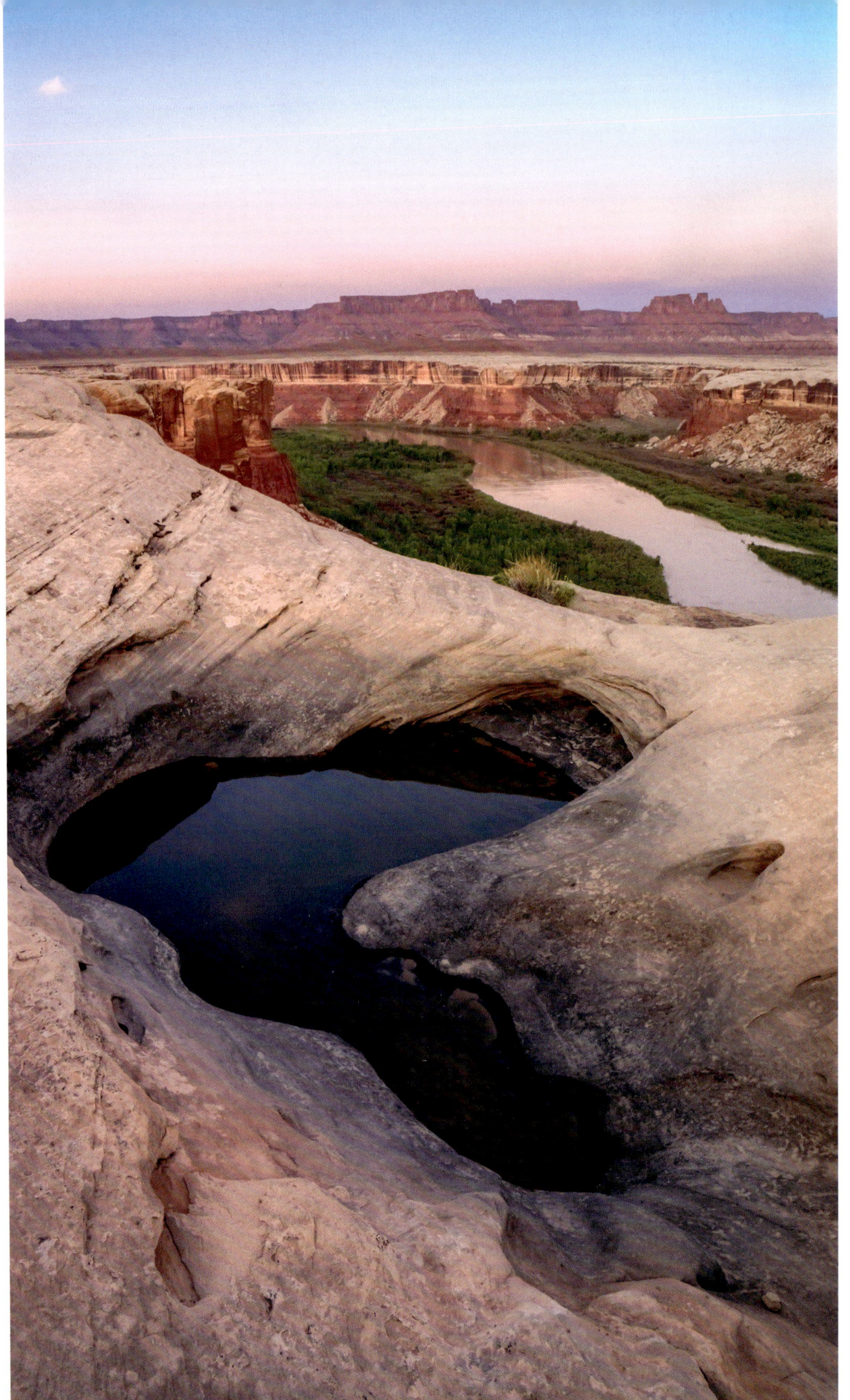

WATER HOLES FILLED WITH RAIN BRING LIFE TO THE HARSH DESERT ENVIRONMENT OF CANYONLANDS NATIONAL PARK.

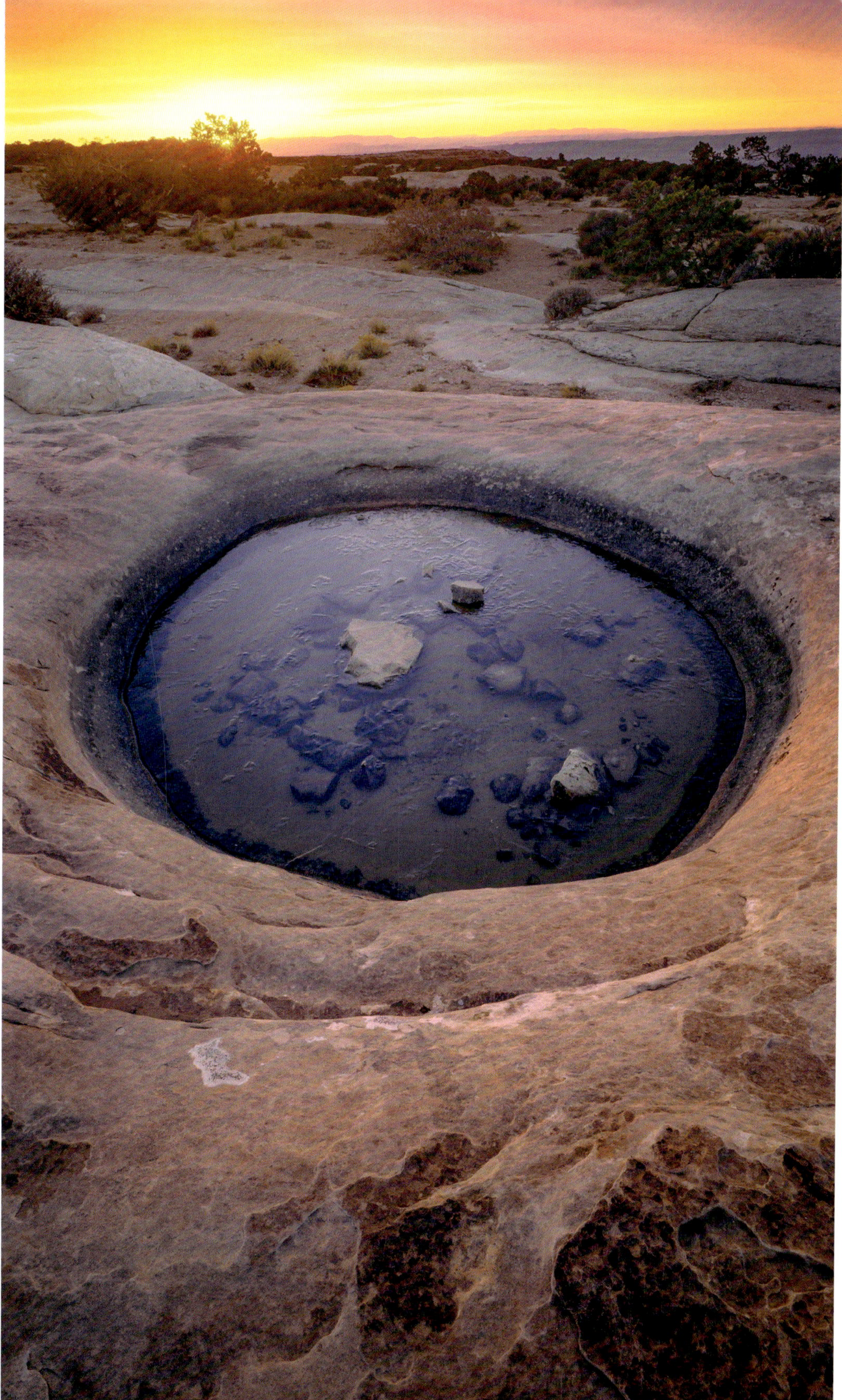

A SMALL WATER HOLE FREEZES
IN THE CHILLY MORNING
TEMPERATURES AT MULEY POINT
NEAR THE VALLEY OF THE GODS.

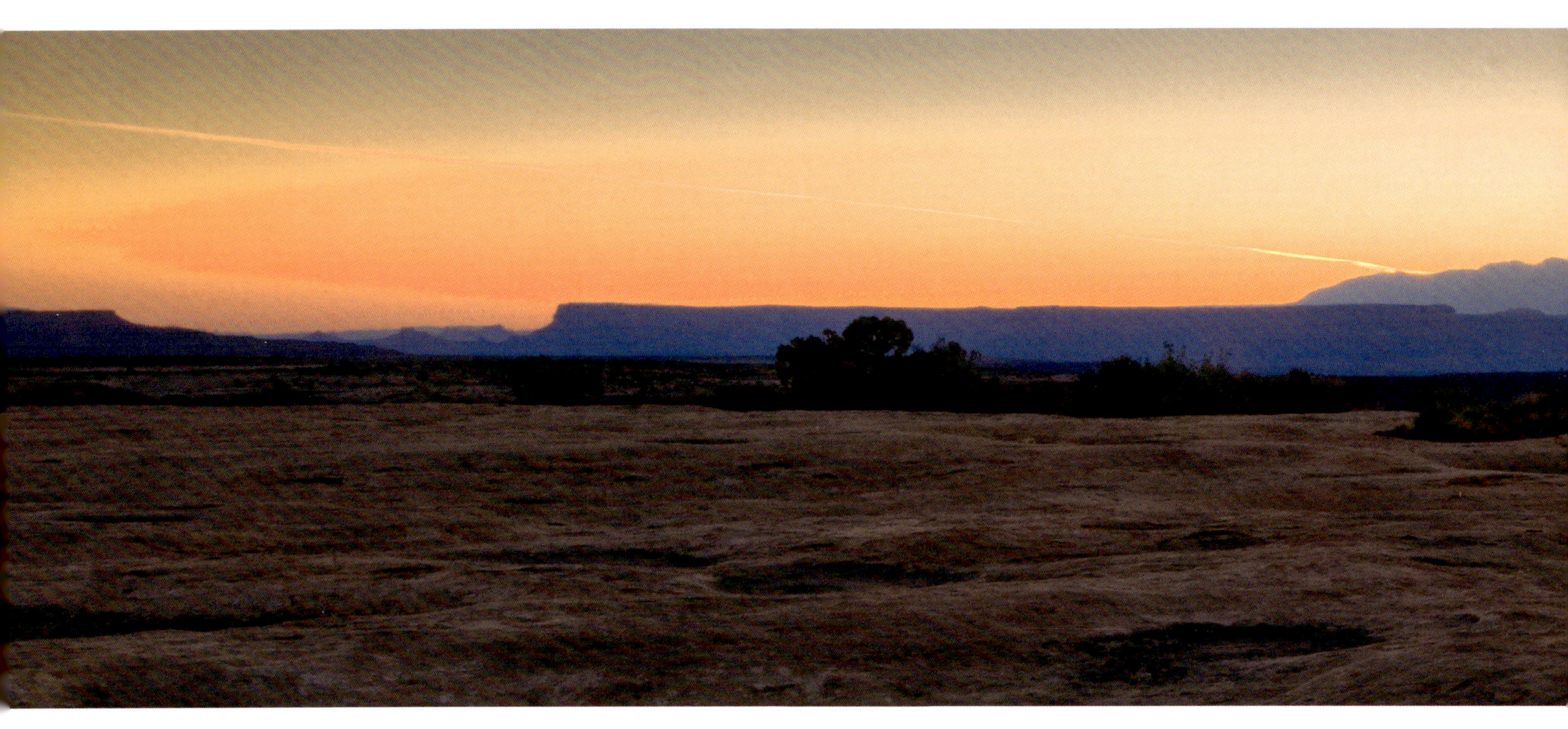

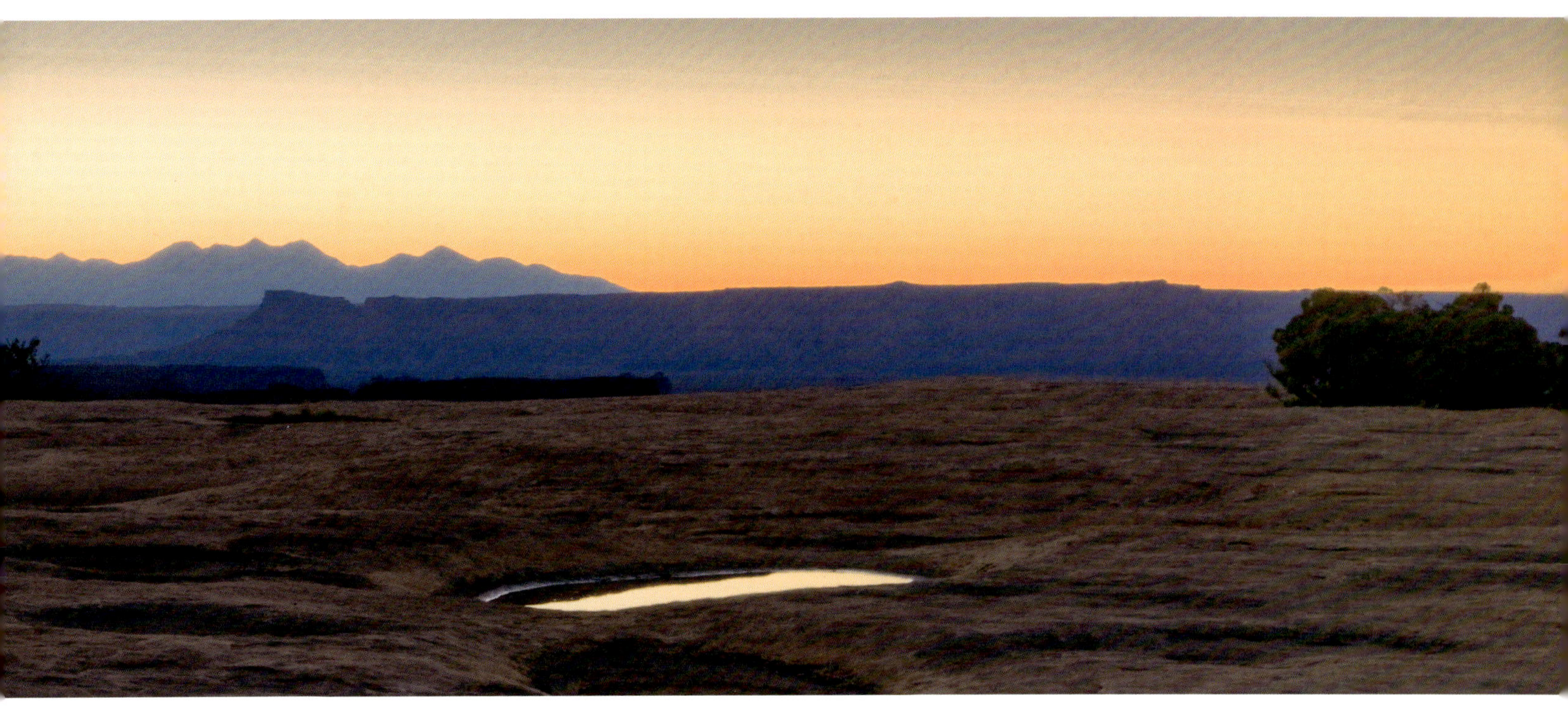

THE LA SAL RANGE RISES ABOVE SANDSTONE SLABS ON THE WHITE RIM.

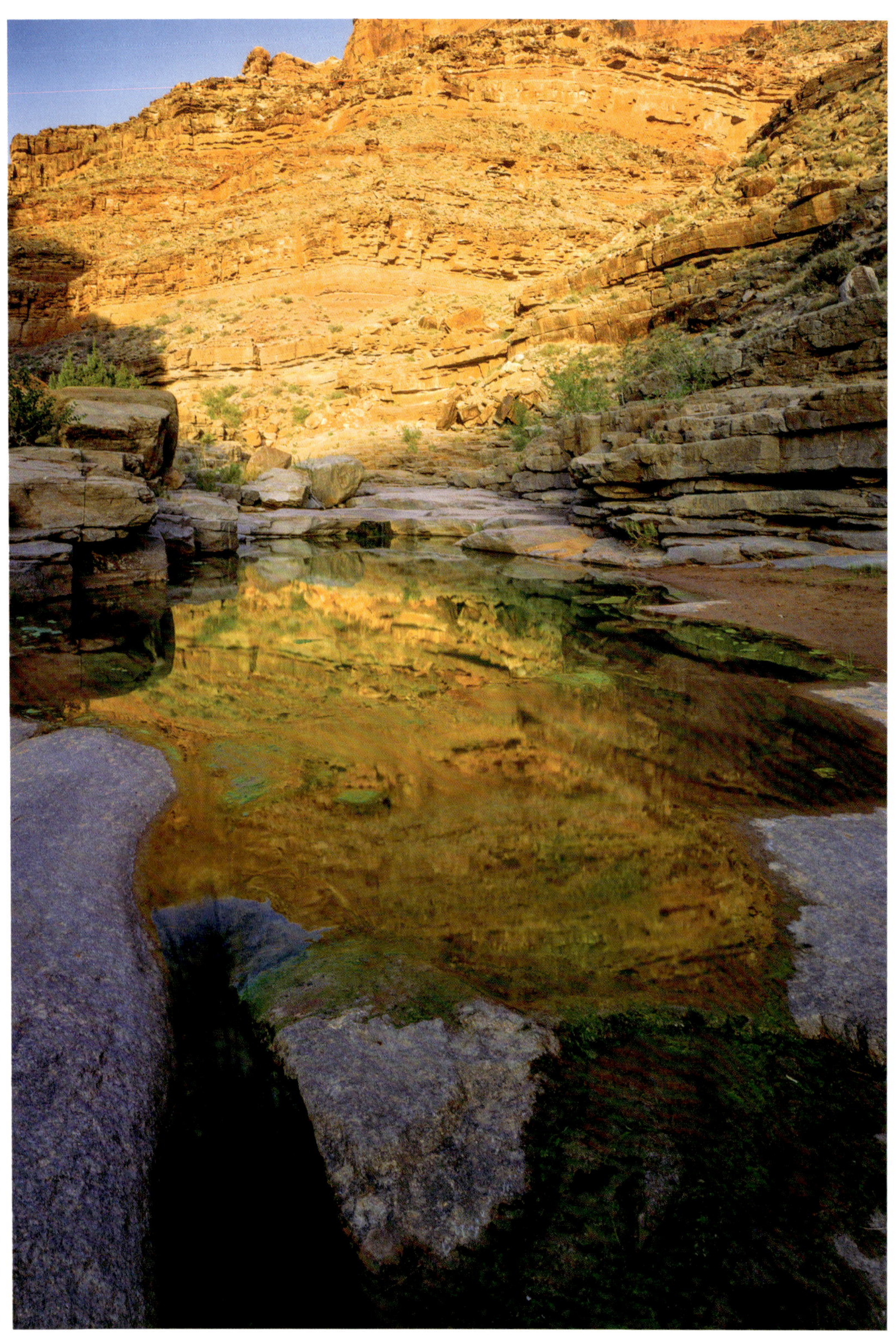

WATER CASCADES OVER SANDSTONE LEDGES IN SLICKHORN CANYON ON ITS WAY TO THE SAN JUAN RIVER.

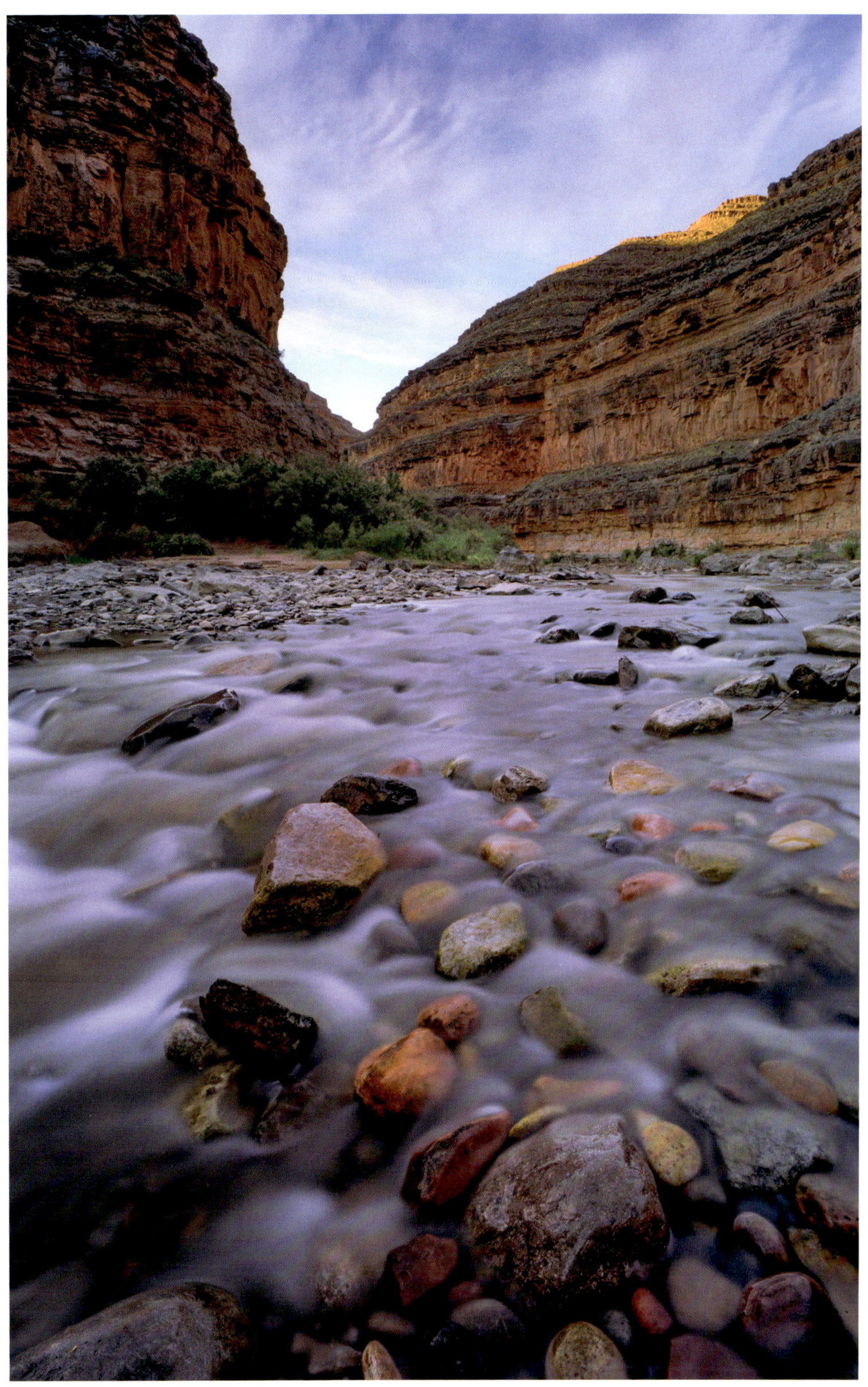

THE SAN JUAN RIVER CASCADES OVER COLORFUL ROCKS LINING THE RIVER BOTTOM NEAR JOHNS CANYON.

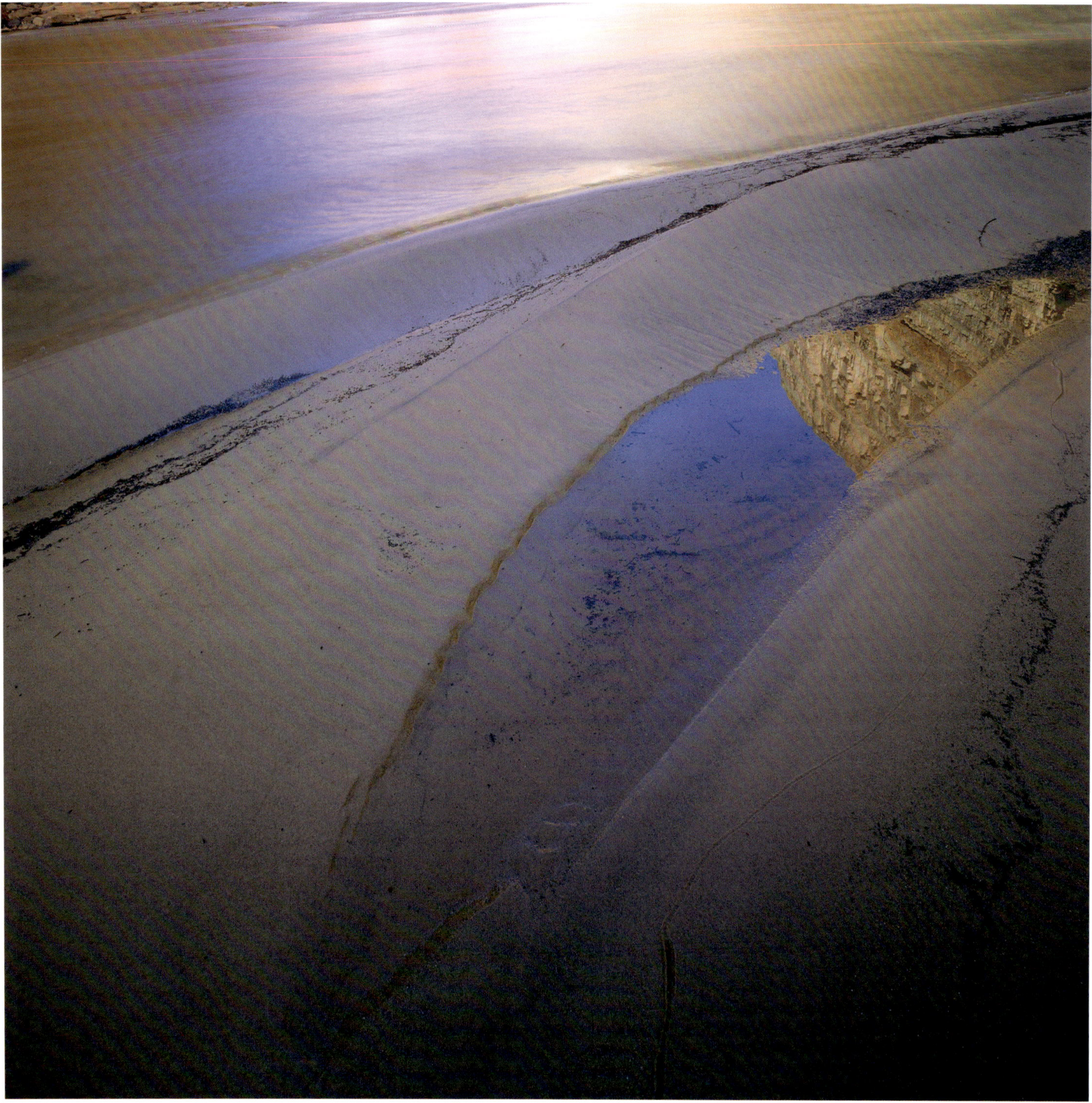

GRAPHIC PATTERNS IN THE SAND ALONG THE SAN JUAN RIVER NEAR MEXICAN HAT.

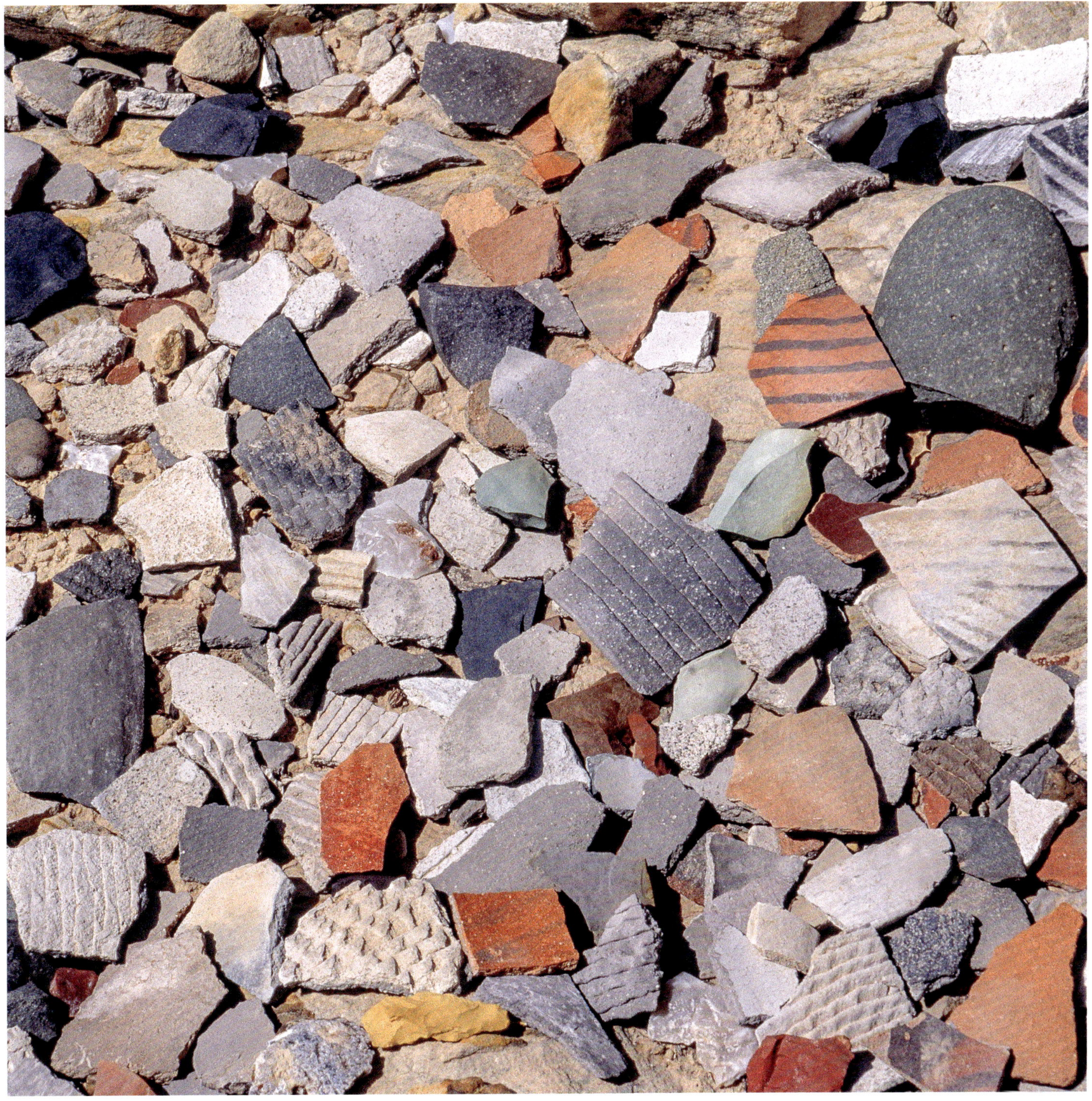

POTTERY SHARDS FOUND ALONG THE SAN JUAN RIVER INDICATE A ONCE-ROBUST NATIVE AMERICAN POPULATION.

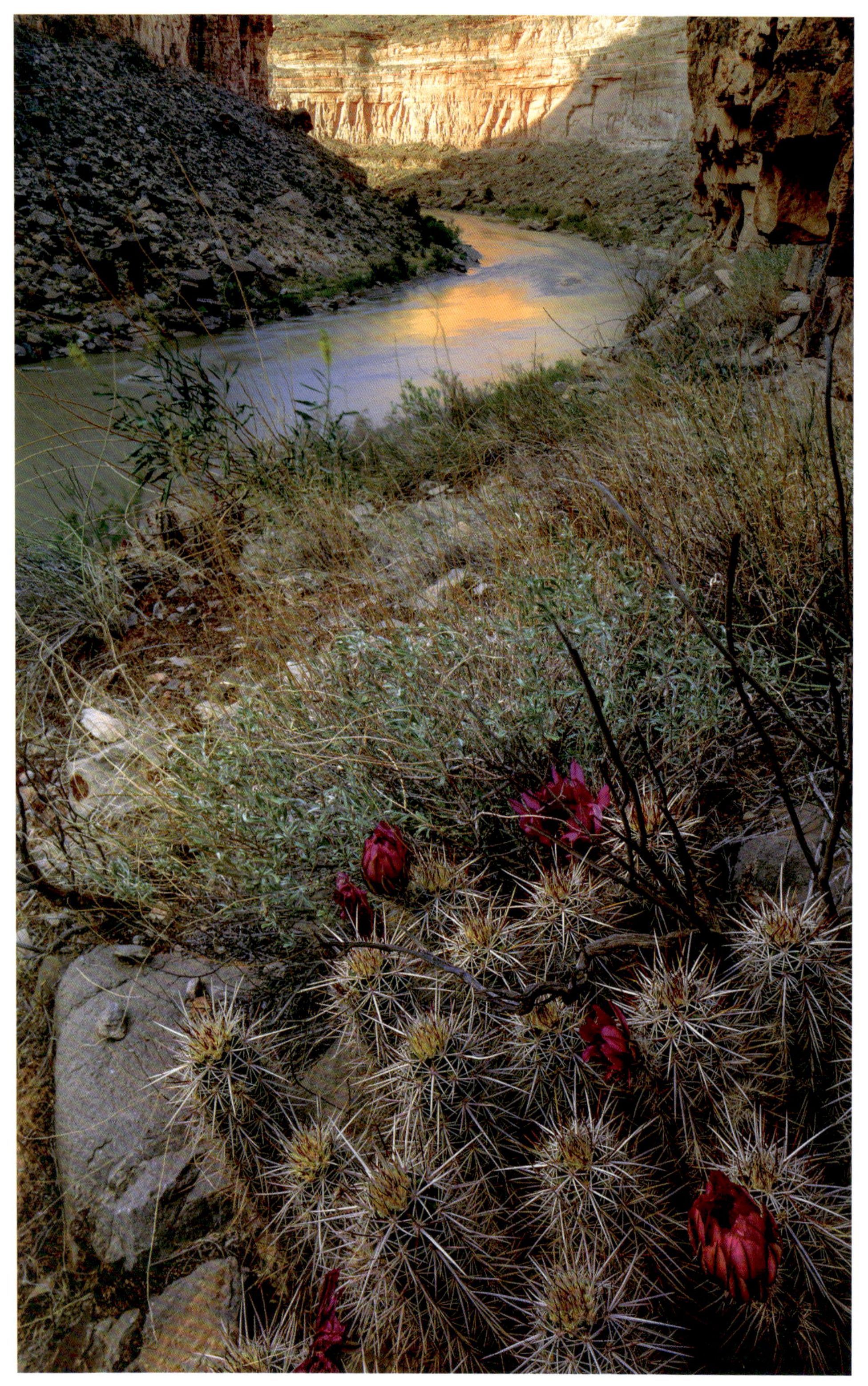

◀

BARREL CACTUS BLOOMS ALONG THE SHORE IN THE GOOSENECKS OF THE SAN JUAN RIVER.

▶

PATTERNS IN THE SLOW-MOVING SAN JUAN RIVER NEAR JOHNS CANYON.

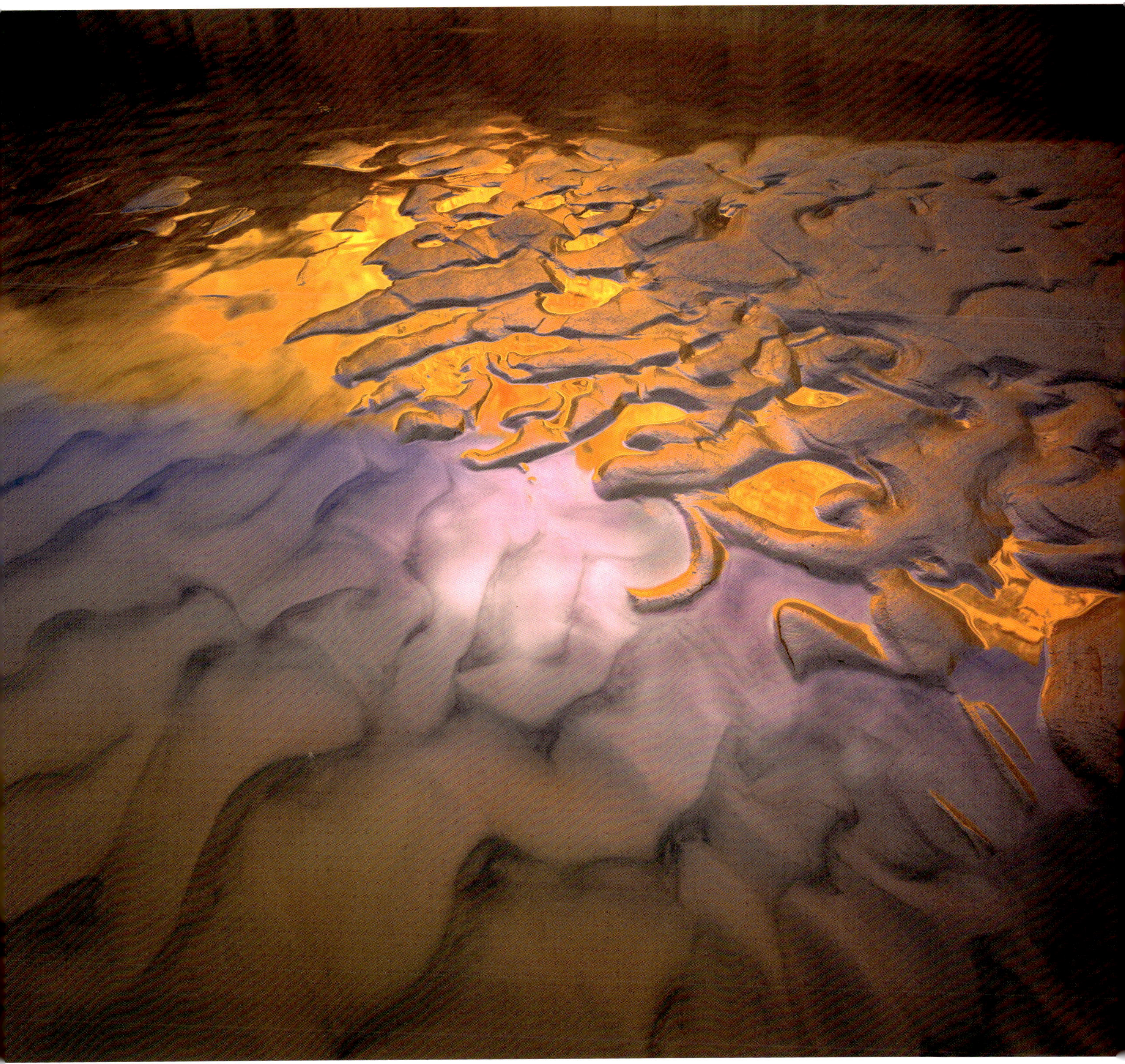

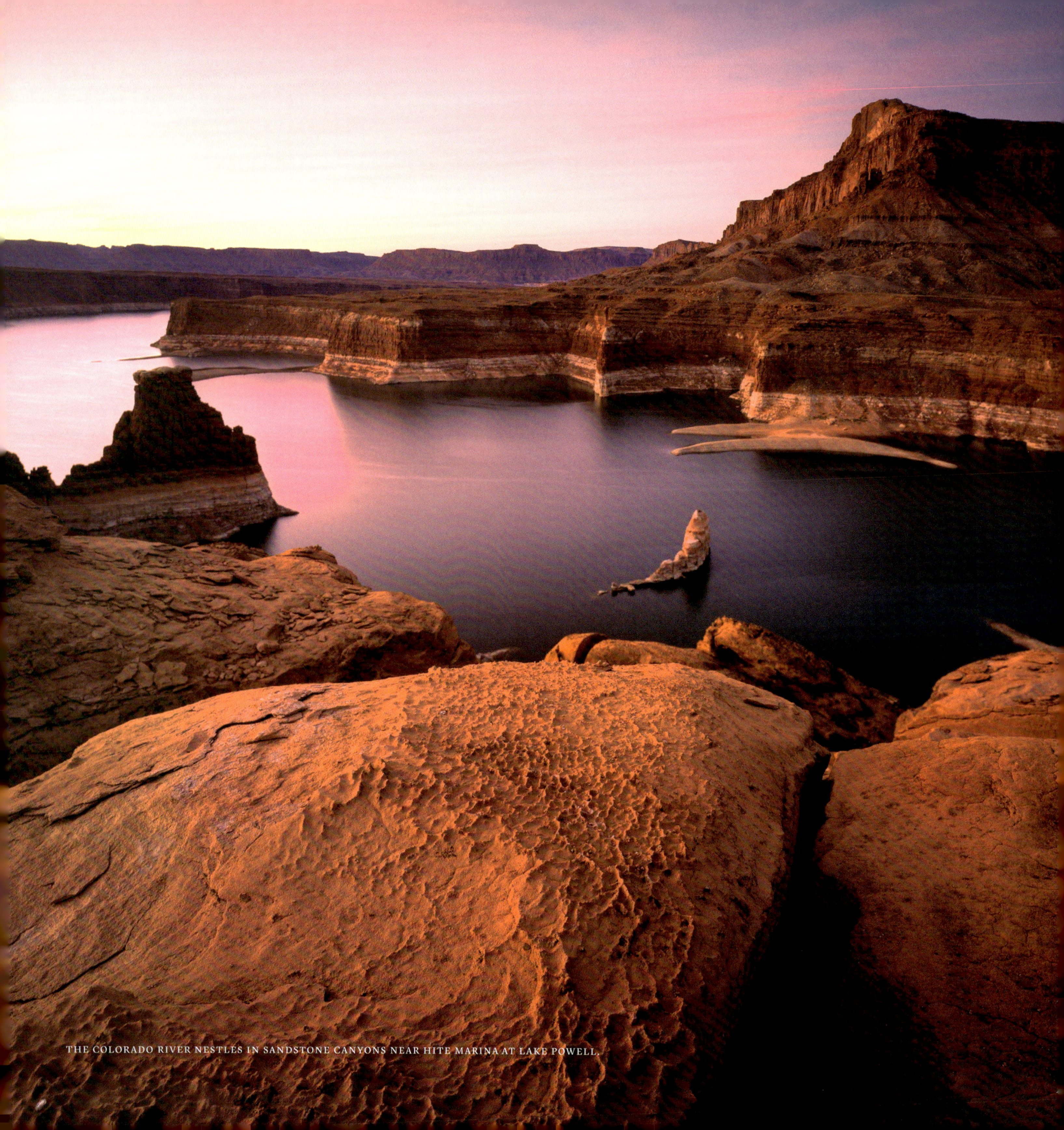

THE COLORADO RIVER NESTLES IN SANDSTONE CANYONS NEAR HITE MARINA AT LAKE POWELL.

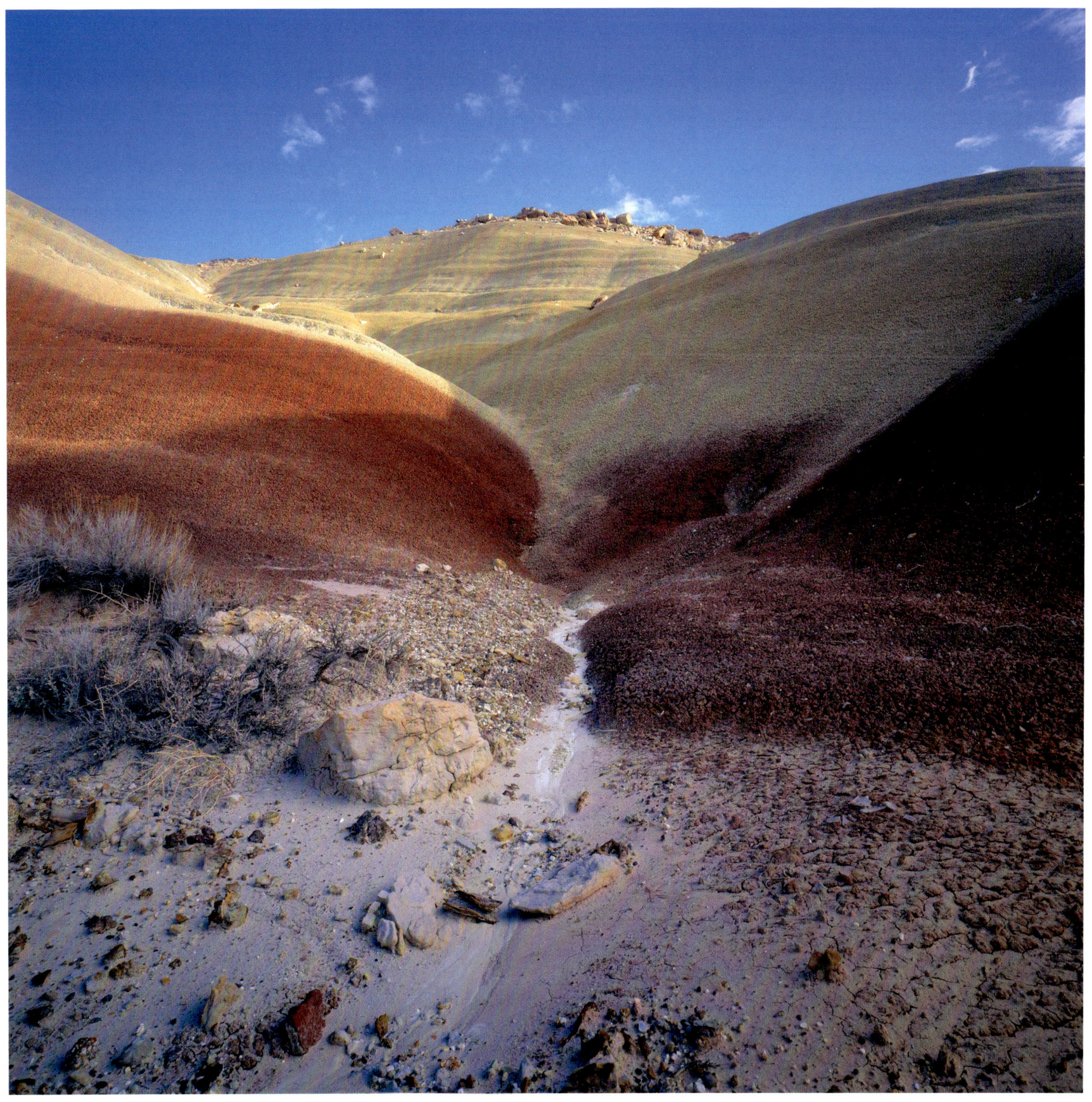

MINERALS IN BENTONITE CLAY DECORATE THE PARCHED DESERT LANDSCAPE NEAR HALLS CROSSING.

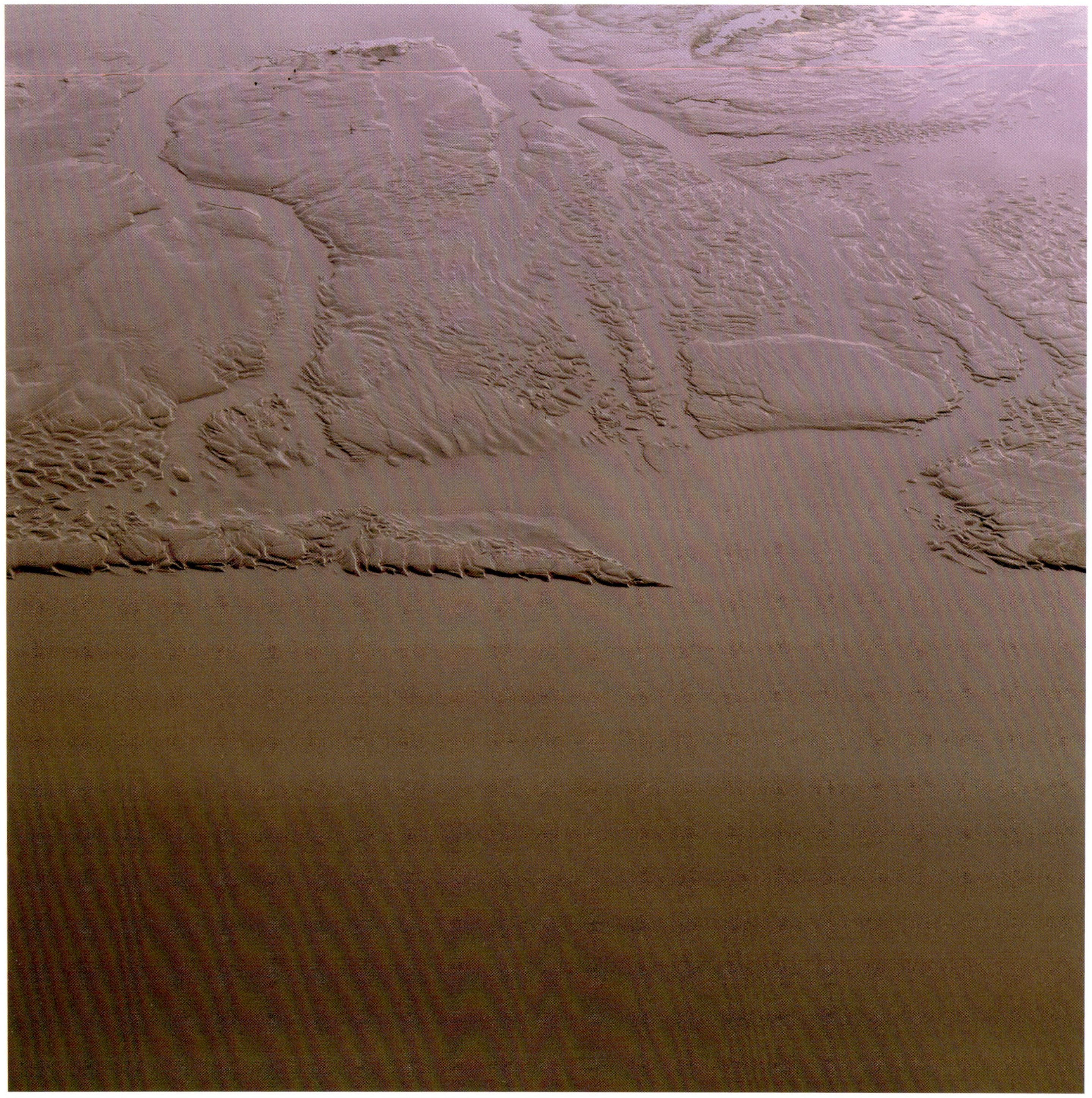

THE MUDDY CONFLUENCE OF THE COLORADO RIVER AND THE DIRTY DEVIL NEAR HITE MARINA.

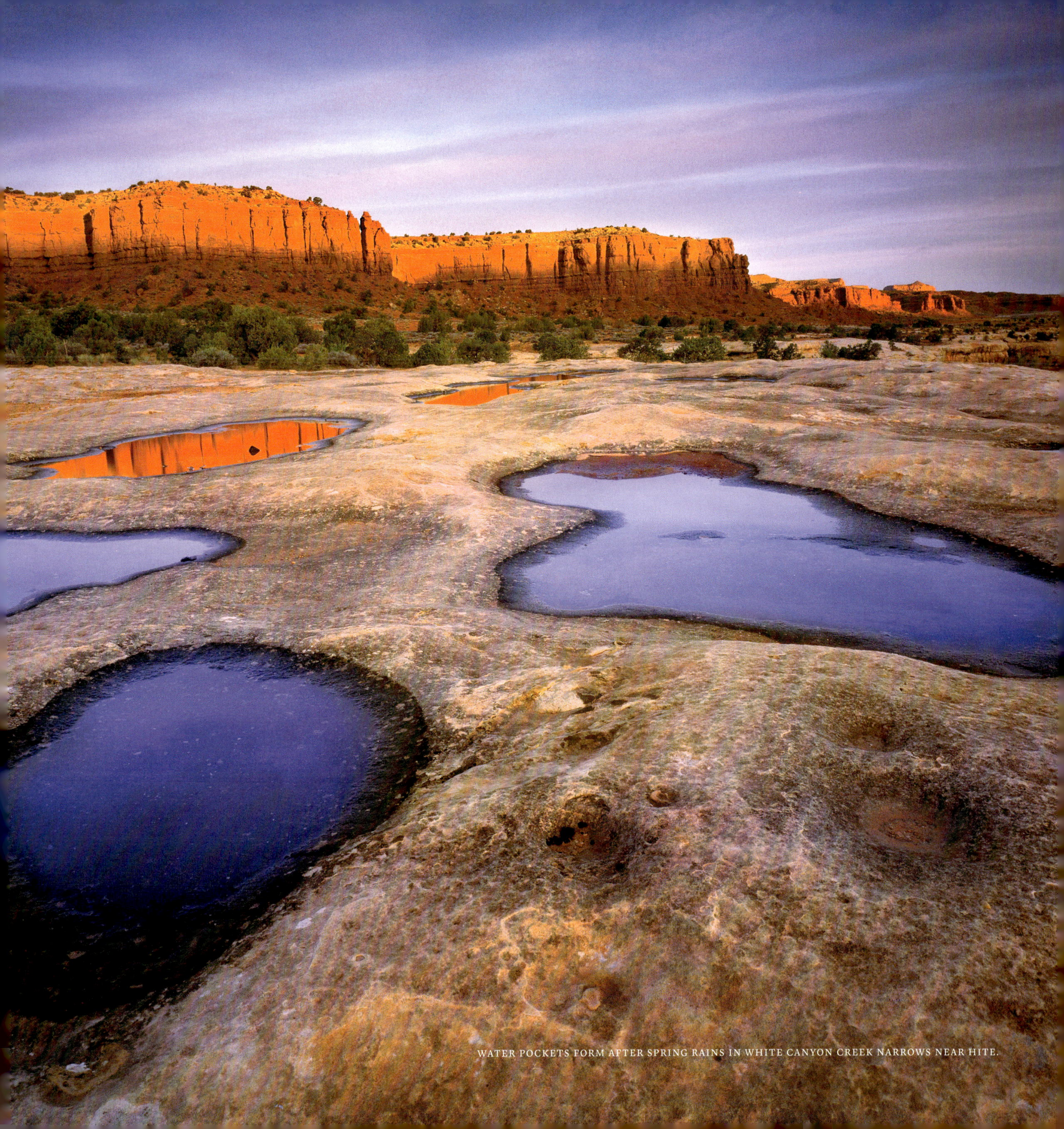

WATER POCKETS FORM AFTER SPRING RAINS IN WHITE CANYON CREEK NARROWS NEAR HITE.

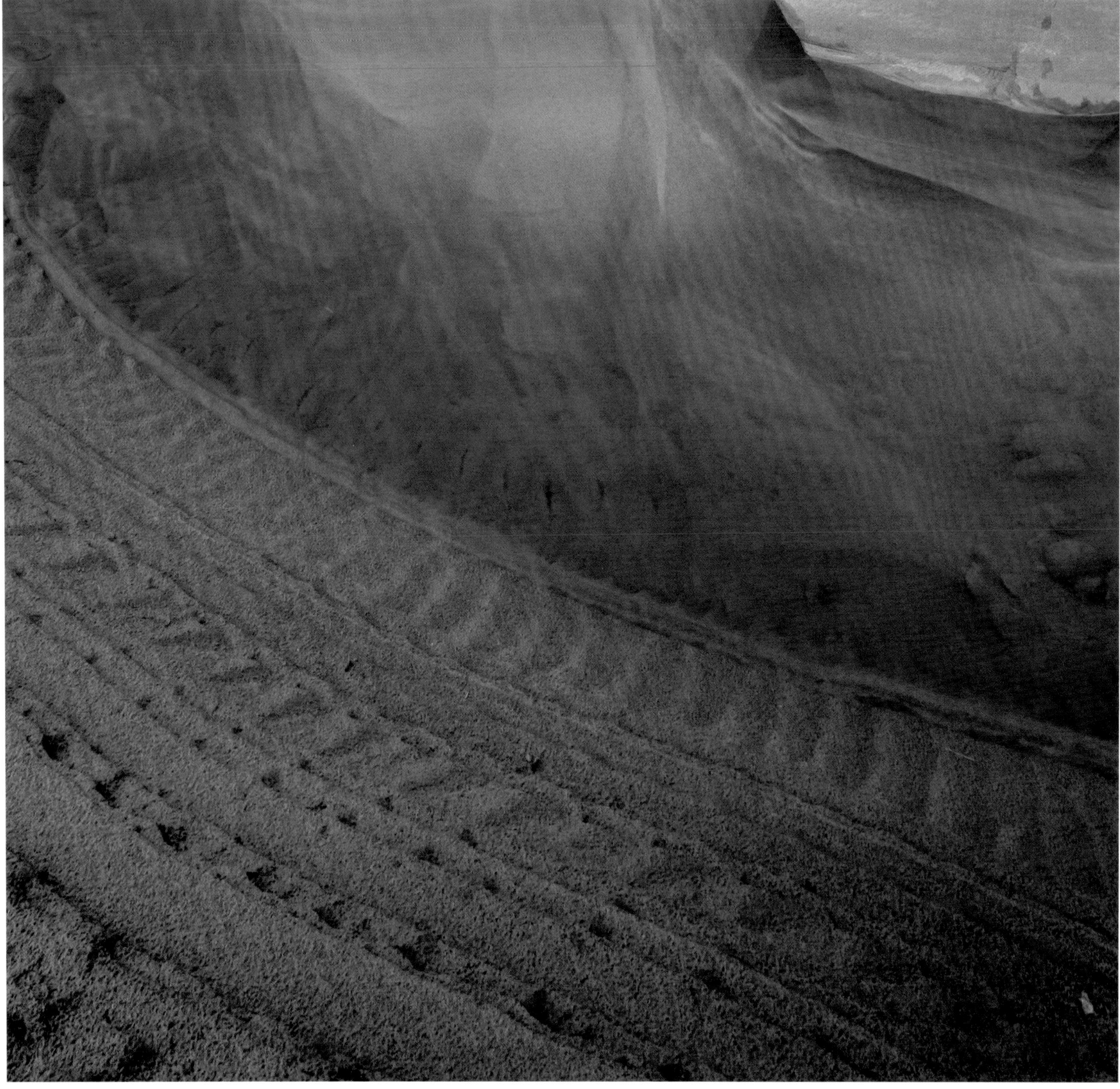

 PATTERNS FORMED BY WATER FLUCTUATIONS IN NATURAL BRIDGES NATIONAL MONUMENT.

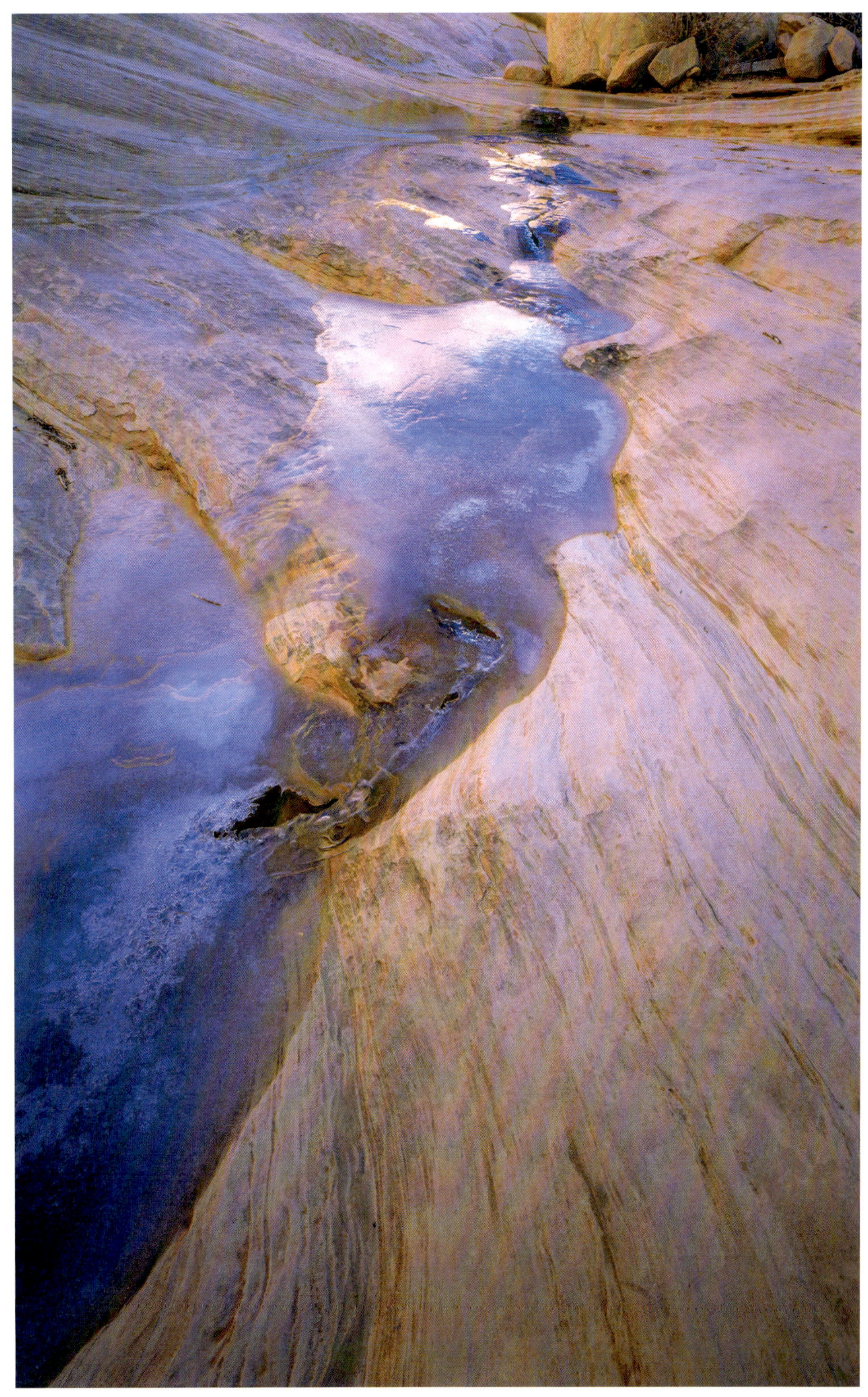

ICE FORMS IN THE SHADED AREA OF A DESERT WASH, NATURAL BRIDGES NATIONAL MONUMENT.

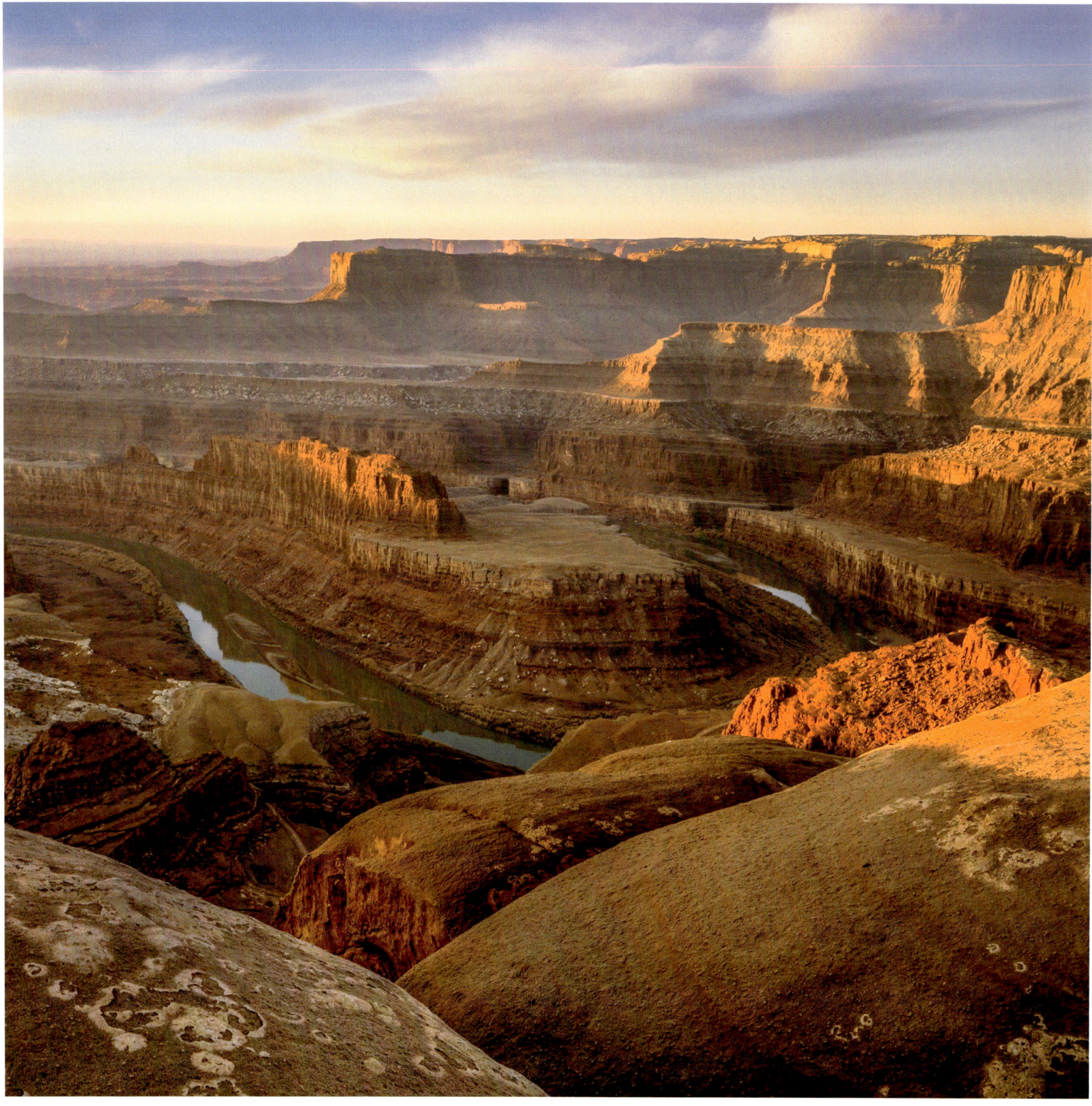

THE GOOSENECK OF THE COLORADO, IN DEAD HORSE POINT STATE PARK.

ABOUT THE AUTHOR

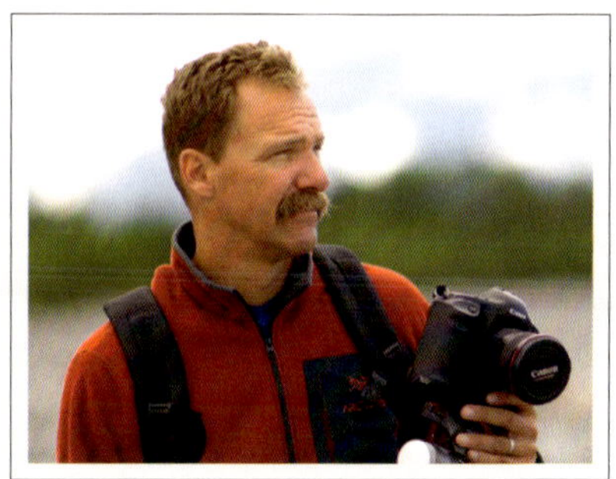

Mark Lisk has long roamed the deserts, mountains, and river canyons of the American West by foot. A graduate of the Brooks Institute of Photography, Mark climbs from the sea to high ridges and plains, gathering within his camera worlds of color and expanse that few ever see or capture in any form. From dry curls of patterned lake bottom to the tiniest brilliant lichen set before a vast line of granite peaks, Mark's foregrounds set him apart. His work fits whole universes of wilderness into single frames under glass. Mark's photographs stand alone in ten other books: *Idaho Impressions* (1997), *Salmon River Country* (2004), *Desert Water* (2005), *Idaho: Portrait of a State* (2007), *Owyhee Canyon Lands* (2008), *The Owyhee Canyonlands: An Outdoor Adventure Guide* (2013), *Void* (2013), *Sawtooth-White Cloud* (2016), *Idaho: Discover the Gem State* (2019), and *Arizona: Discover the Grand Canyon State* (2020).

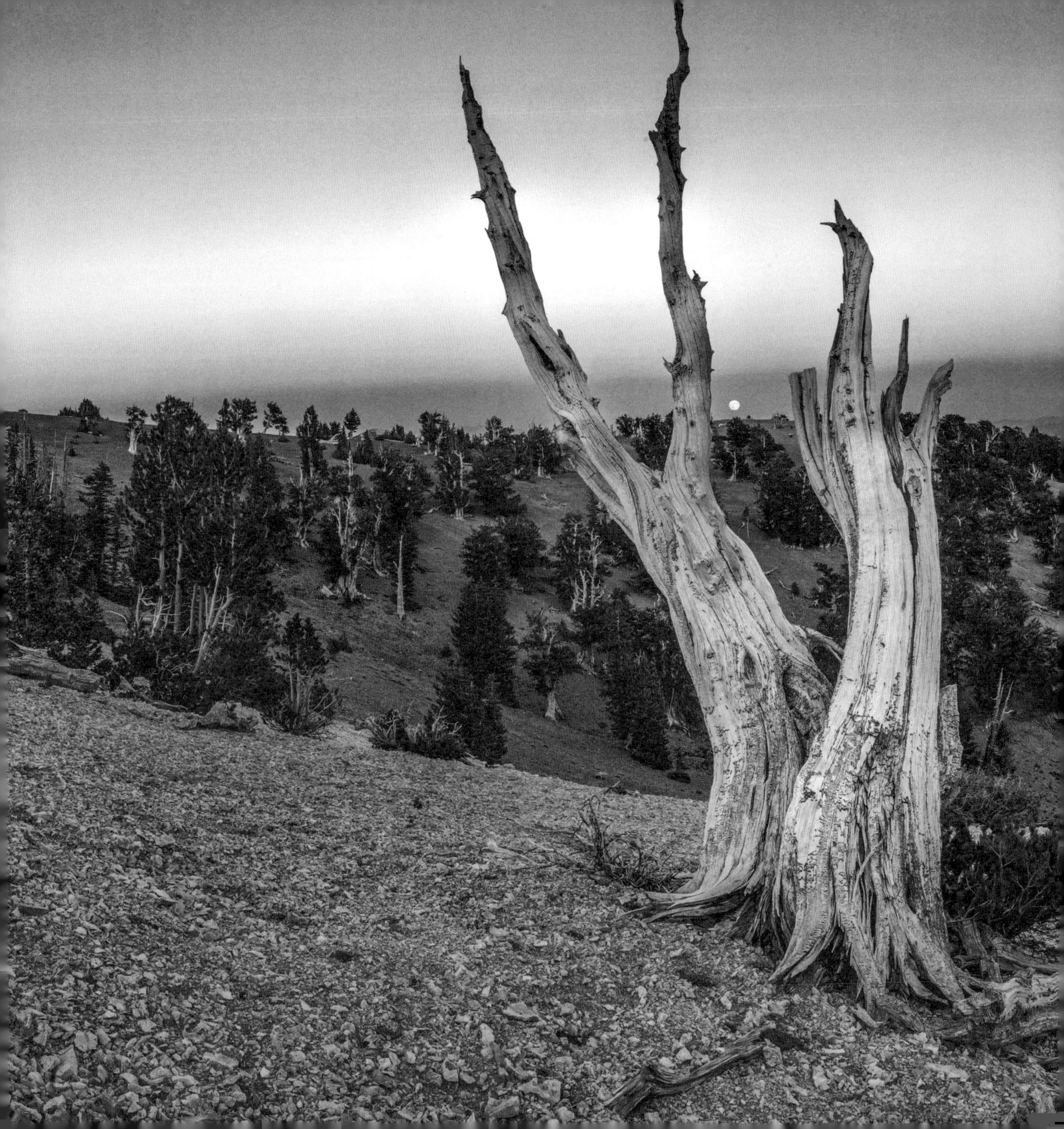